S0-AVP-490

Fisherman's Bible

2nd Edition

The World's Most Comprehensive Angling Reference

Edited by Jay Cassell

SKYHORSE PUBLISHING

Copyright © 2015 by Skyhorse Publishing, Inc.

All rights reserved. No part of this book may be reproduced in any manner without the express written consent of the publisher, except in the case of brief excerpts in critical reviews or articles. All inquiries should be addressed to Skyhorse Publishing, 307 West 36th Street, 11th Floor, New York, NY 10018.

Skyhorse Publishing books may be purchased in bulk at special discounts for sales promotion, corporate gifts, fund-raising, or educational purposes. Special editions can also be created to specifications. For details, contact the Special Sales Department, Skyhorse Publishing, 307 West 36th Street, 11th Floor, New York, NY 10018 or info@skyhorsepublishing.com.

Skyhorse® and Skyhorse Publishing® are registered trademarks of Skyhorse Publishing, Inc.®, a Delaware corporation.

Visit our website at www.skyhorsepublishing.com.

Library of Congress Cataloging-in-Publication Data is available on file.

10 9 8 7 6 5 4 3 2 1

Cover design by Owen Corrigan

ISBN: 978-1-63220-702-9
Ebook ISBN: 978-1-63450-037-1

Printed in Canada

Note: Every effort has been made to record specifications and descriptions of rods, reels, lures, and lines accurately, but the Publisher can take no responsibility for errors or omissions. The prices shown for rods, reels, lures, and lines are manufacturers' suggested retail prices and are furnished for information only. These were in effect at press time and are subject to change without notice. Purchasers of the book have complete freedom of choice in pricing for resale.

CONTENTS

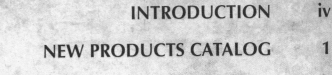

INTRODUCTION

You have just purchased the second edition of the wildly popular *Fisherman's Bible*. It was first published in 2014 as an adjunct to our annual *Shooter's Bible,* a book that more than 7 million people have bought since that book's inception in the 1920s. It was our feeling that if shooters and hunters wanted a book such as the *Shooter's Bible,* and a new and revised one every year at that, then wouldn't fishermen want a similar book as well? After all, anglers are every bit as passionate about their sport, and their gear, as hunters are. So last year we spent a great deal of time and effort assembling as much gear and related text as possible for the first edition of the *Fisherman's Bible,* and came out with a book that we were quite proud of, one with thousands of new and currently produced rods, reels, lures, and lines. Also last year, I stated that it was our intention to publish a new and updated edition of this compendium every year, and, with this second edition, that is exactly what we are doing. As you'll see, we have even more gear, more *stuff,* than last year. We know you'll enjoy it.

To give some background, Skyhorse Publishing publishes many fishing, hunting, shooting, and outdoor books. One of our most popular books, one of our bestsellers, is indeed the *Shooter's Bible.* The *Shooter's Bible* was first published in 1925 and has been published annually, and in some cases bi-annually, ever since. As stated, more than seven million copies have been sold in that time, and it continues to be the ultimate reference book for millions of people who want information on new guns, ammunition, optics, and accessories, as well as up-to-date prices and specs for thousands of firearms.

According to recent statistics, there are almost sixteen million hunters in the United States. That pales in comparison to the number of anglers in the United States. A 2011 survey conducted by the U.S. Fish and Wildlife Service found that there are more than 35 million fresh- and salt-water anglers in the US. It is, as Kirk Deeter of Trout Unlimited's *Trout* magazine notes, a $48 billion industry—bigger than golf!

This second edition of the *Fisherman's Bible* is the result of our editorial team gathering information on all fresh- and salt-water rods, reels, lines,

and lures that are currently in production. Just as the *Shooter's Bible* provides up-to-date information on in-production firearms, ammunition, optics, and reloading equipment, the *Fisherman's Bible* does the same on the fishing side. In this tome, you will find specs and figures for everything fishing. The New Products section, in the front of the book, highlights everything new, every rod, reel, line, and lure that has been introduced in the past twelve months. Photos of every piece of gear are included, with the New Product section featuring color photographs.

As we do with the *Shooter's Bible,* next year we will take all of the new products that appear in this second edition and incorporate them into the main section of the book. All rods, reels, lines, and lures that are no longer in production will be removed. All prices will then be double-checked and updated. There will be a new New Products

EDITOR JAY CASSELL INSPECTS AN ORVIS RECON FLY ROD AT THE 2015 FLY FISHING SHOW IN SOMERSET, NEW JERSEY.

NEW DAY, BIG FISH, AND LOTS OF GREAT NEW TACKLE TO HANDLE THEM—AS ALWAYS, THE NEW GEAR FOR THIS SEASON IS STRONGER, LIGHTER, AND MORE TECHNICALLY ADVANCED THAN EVER BEFORE.
PHOTO CREDIT: FRANK SARGEANT.

section next year, featuring everything that has been introduced by the tackle companies from the date this edition was published to the date the third edition comes out.

Our research team has made every effort to get all specs and prices correct. We have scoured all of the websites, we have attended ICAST, the trade show of the American Sportfishing Association held annually in either Orlando or Las Vegas, plus we have gone to as many regional angling-related shows as possible. As I write this column, I'm still unpacking luggage and brochures after returning home from the 23rd annual Fly Fishing Show held in Somerset, New Jersey. It was there, for example, where I had the opportunity to examine the new Recon fly rods just now being introduced by the Orvis Company. Competitively priced, they should become instantly popular. I also had my eye on that company's Helios 2 fly rod. Something tells me I'll be trout fishing with one of those, probably a 5-weight, sometime this spring.

And speaking of this spring, don't miss Frank Sargeant's feature on new new rods and reels for 2015. Frank, who has been in the fishing business for many years and who really knows what he's talking about, has done a solid job researching all things new—for bass fishing, salt water, panfish, walleyes, you name it. If you're a bass angler, you just know you're going to drool at G.Loomis's new IMX lineup of technique-specific rods. Featuring "Jig & Worm" casting and spinning rods, "Mag Bass" casting rods, Carolina rig, Flip/Punch technique, swimbait, umbrella rig, spinnerbait, topwater, and jerkbait casting rods, plus spinning models for DropShot and ShakyHead use, the IMX bass rods "provide a new level in weight reduction, sensitivity, and strength," according to company spokesman Bruce Holt. I've never used anything made by 13 Fishing, probably because they're a young company, but I bet one of their Concept Series baitcasters on top of an IMX jerkbait casting rod would be a pretty sweet combination.

As for the salt, I can't help but take a look at Shimano's new Stella SW reels. There are twelve new models and picking just the right one might be tough. I might have to get two, one for stripers and bluefish in Long Island Sound, then something heavier for some offshore work out of Montauk. But maybe I should get a Saragosa model for offshore. And then I have to figure out what rod to use with it! A pleasant dilemma, to say the least.

As you thumb through the pages of this second edition of the *Fisherman's Bible*, please understand that we have made every effort to include gear from every tackle company on earth. If anything is missing, we want to know about it. Please contact us at skyhorsepublishing.com, and we'll make sure to include any missing information in next year's edition.

Good fishing!

Jay Cassell
Editorial Director
Skyhorse Publishing
New York, New York
February 2, 2015

NEW PRODUCTS 2014–2015

1 Rods   **35 Reels**   **70 Lures**

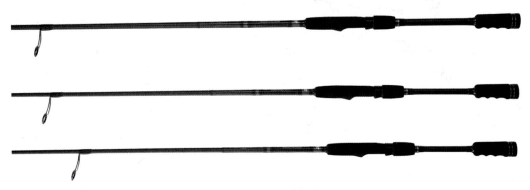

ABU GARCIA FANTASISTA REGISTA

Model: FNRS610-4, FNRS70-5, FNRS76-5
Length: 6'10"; 7'; 7'3"
Power: ML; M; M
Action: F; F; F
Pieces: 1; 1; 1
Line Weight: 4-10 lbs; 6-12 lbs; 8-14 lbs

Guide Count: 9; 9; 9
Lure Weight: 1/8-1/2 oz; 1/4-3/4 oz; 1/4-3/4 oz
Features: Tetra axial carbon construction provides an increase in strength and durability; Fuji titanium frame guides with alconite inserts; high density EVA gives greater sensitivity and durability; micro guide system.
Price: **$499.95**

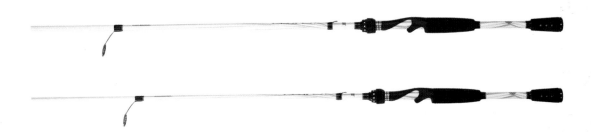

ABU GARCIA VERITAS 2.0

Model: VRTS66-5, VRTS66-6, VRTS69-4, VRTS70-5, VRTS70-6, VRTS662-5, VRTS662-6, VRTS702-5
Length: 6'6"; 6'6"; 6'9"; 7'; 7'; 6'6"; 6'6"; 7'
Power: M; MH; ML; M; MH; M; MH; M
Action: F, MF; F; F; F; F; MF; F
Pieces: 1; 1; 1; 1; 1; 2; 2; 2
Line Weight: 6-12 lbs; 8-14 lbs; 6-10 lbs; 6/12 lbs; 8-14 lbs; 6-12 lbs; 8-14 lbs; 6-12 lbs
Guide Count: 7

Lure Weight: 1/8-1/2 oz; 1/4-3/4 oz; 1/8-1/2 oz; 3/16-5/8 oz; 1/4-3/4 oz; 1/8-1/2 oz; 1/4-3/4 oz; 3/16-5/8 oz
Features: Thirty-ton graphite for a lightweight balanced design; spiral carbon core construction provides an increase in break strength of the rod; titanium alloy guides with SiC inserts allow for a lightweight balanced rod; Abu-designed extreme exposure reel seat for increased blank contact and sensitivity; micro click reel seat hood design allows for improved reel fit; high density EVA gives greater sensitivity and durability; Texas rigged hook keeper for all bait applications.
Price: **$99.95**

BASS PRO BIONIC BLADE XPS SLIM GRIP

Model: BNB66MSS, BNB66MHSS, BNB70MSS, BNB70MHSS-2
Length: 6'6"; 6'6"; 7'; 7'
Power: M; MH; M; MH
Action: F; F; F; F
Pieces: 1; 1; 1; 2
Line Weight: 4-12 lbs; 6-17 lbs; 4-12 lbs; 6-17 lbs

Guide Count: N/A
Lure Weight: 1/8-1/2 oz; 1/4-5/8 oz; 1/8-1/2 oz; 1/4-5/8 oz
Features: Slim profile grip; minimalist cork fore grip; classic full cork butt; full-contact reel seat with Soft Touch finish; IM8 blank with ArmorCore Technology; Pacific Bay Hialoy guides; multi-purpose hook keeper.
Price: **$79.99**

BASS PRO JOHNNY MORRIS CARBONLITE SLIM GRIP
Model: N/A
Length: 6′6″; 6′6″; 7′; 7′
Power: M; MH; M; MH
Action: F; F; F; F
Pieces: 1; 1; 1; 1

Line Weight: 4-12 lbs; 6-17 lbs; 4-12 lbs; 6-17 lbs
Guide Count: N/A
Lure Weight: 1/8-1/2 oz; 1/4-5/8 oz; 1/8-1/2 oz; 1/4-5/8 oz
Features: Slim profile grip; P-Tec polyfoam split grip; Carbon Coil Technology; RT4 graphite blank; line ID system built into the rod butt; Durable Pac Bay titanium guides; 2-piece minimalist reel seat with Soft Touch coatings.
Price: . . . .$99.99–$109.99

BASS PRO JOHNNY MORRIS SIGNATURE SERIES
Model: JMR68MS, JMR68MHS, JMR72MS, JMR72MHS
Length: 6′8″; 6′8″; 7′2″; 7′2″
Power: M; MH; M; MH
Action: XF; XF; F; F
Pieces: 1; 1; 1; 1
Line Weight: 4-12 lbs; 6-17 lbs; 4-12 lbs; 6-17 lbs
Guide Count: N/A
Lure Weight: 1/8-1/2 oz; 1/4-5/8 oz; 1/8-1/2 oz; 1/4-5/8 oz

Features: RT5 graphite rod blanks with Carbon Coil Technology to maximize rod strength and weight reduction while minimizing rod blank diameter for an ultra sensitive, super strong fishing rod; skeletonized reel seats transfer the lightest strikes directly to angler's hand by maximizing blank exposure while reducing weight; Fuji KR Concept guides minimize friction for smooth, long casts; cork grips reduce fatigue; provides strength for hauling bass as well as finesse to feel light-biting walleye and trout.
Price: $149.99

BERKLEY CHERRYWOOD HD ICE
Model: CWICE24UL, CWICE26ML, CWICE27L, CWICE30M
Length: 24″; 26″; 27″; 30″
Power: UL; ML; L; M
Action: N/A
Pieces: 1
Line Weight: N/A

Guide Count: N/A
Lure Weight: N/A
Features: 100 percent fiberglass blanks; durable rod finish; full cork handles; graphite sliding ring reel seat; stainless steel guides and inserts.
Price: $9.99

BERKLEY E-MOTION PERFORMANCE SERIES
Model: BCEMO641M-MF, BCEMO671MH-F, BCEMO691M-M, BCEMO691M-MF, BCEMO691M-F, BCEMO6101H-XF, BCEMO701MH-F, BCEMO721MH-MF, BCEMO761MH-F, BCEMO761XH-F, BCEMO791MH-M, BSEMO661ML-MF, BSEMO691M-M, BSEMO691M-F, BSEMO701MH-XF
Length: 6′4″; 6′7″; 6′9″; 6′9″; 6′9″; 6′10″; 7′; 7′2″; 7′3″; 7′3″; 7′9″; 6′6″; 6′9″; 6′9″; 7′
Power: M; MH; M; M; M; H; MH; MH; MH; XH; MH; ML; M; M; MH
Action: MF; F; M; MF; F; XF; F; MF; F; F; M; MF; M; F; XF

Pieces: 1
Line Weight: 8-17 lbs; 12-20 lbs; 8-17 lbs; 8-17 lbs; 8-17 lbs; 12-25 lbs; 12-20 lbs; 12-20 lbs; 12-20 lbs; 15-30 lbs; 12-20 lbs; 4-10 lbs; 6-12 lbs; 6-12 lbs; 8-14 lbs
Guide Count: 10; 10; 10; 10; 10; 10; 10; 10; 11; 11; 13; 9; 9; 9; 9
Lure Weight: 1/4-3/4 oz; 1/8-3/4 oz; 1/4-3/4 oz; 1/4-3/4 oz; 1/4-3/4 oz; 3/8-1 1/2 oz; 1/4-1 oz; 1/4-1 oz; 1/4-1 oz; 1/2-3 oz; 1/4-1 oz; 1/16-3/8 oz; 1/8-1/2 oz; 1/8-1/2 oz; 1/4-3/4 oz
Features: A unique blend of 30- and 24-ton graphite; hybrid design guide system; H.E.T. (High Energy Transfer) reel seat with soft coat texture; ergonomically shaped high density EVA split-grip handles.
Price: $79.95

BERKLEY HERITAGE

Model: BSH561L-MF, BSH601ML-F, BSH602ML-F, BSH661M-F, BSH662M-F, BSH661MH-XF, BSH662MH-XF, BSH691ML-F, BSH692ML-F, BSH691M-F, BSH701ML-F, BSH702M-F
Length: 5'6"; 6'; 6'; 6'6"; 6'6"; 6'6"; 6'6"; 6'9"; 6'9"; 6'9"; 7'; 7
Power: L; ML; ML; M; M; MH; MH; ML; ML; M ML; M
Action: MF; F; F; F; F; XF; XF; F; F; F; F; F
Pieces: 1; 1; 2; 1; 2; 1; 2; 1; 2; 1; 1; 2

Line Weight: 1-6 lbs; 4-10 lbs; 4-10 lbs; 6-12 lbs; 6-12 lbs; 10-17 lbs; 10-17 lbs; 4-10 lbs; 4-10 lbs; 6-12 lbs; 4-10 lbs; 6-12 lbs
Guide Count: 6; 7; 7; 8; 8; 8; 8; 8; 8; 8; 9; 9
Lure Weight: 1/32-1/4 oz; 1/16-5/8 oz; 1/16-5/8 oz; 1/8-3/4 oz; 1/8-3/4 oz; 1/4-3/4 oz; 1/4-3/4 oz; 1/16-5/8 oz; 1/16-5/8 oz; 1/8-3/4 oz; 1/16-5/8 oz; 1/8-3/4 oz
Features: 100 percent carbon fiber blank construction; stainless steel guides and inserts; traditional full cork handle for durability and comfort.
Price: **$59.95**

CABELA'S FISH EAGLE 50 TRAVEL

Model: FE50S704-4-B, FE50S702-4-B, FE50S664-4-B, FE50S663-4-B, FE50S603-4-B
Length: 7'; 7'; 6'6"; 6'6"; 6'
Power: M; L; M; ML; ML
Action: F
Pieces: 4
Line Weight: 8-12 lbs; 2-8 lbs; 6-12 lbs; 4-10 lbs; 4-10 lbs
Guide Count: N/A
Lure Weight: 1/4-3/4 oz; 1/16-3/8 oz; 1/4-5/8 oz; 1/8-5/8 oz; 1/8-5/8 oz

Features: Made with high-quality HM50 graphite, 50 million-PSI modulus blanks equipped with Pac Bay stainless steel guide frames with Hialoy ceramic inserts, making it durable and resistant to wear, and reducing line friction for consistently longer casts and smoother retrieves; feature down-locking fore grips for flawless security, eliminating exposed reel-seat threads; outfitted with cork grips with rubberized accents for a better grasp; pearl gray-green color with matte finish; breaks down into four pieces and fits in the included rod case for easy portability.
Price: **$119.99**

CABELA'S PREDATOR MUSKY

Model: PMUS796-F, PMUS796-F-2
Length: 7'9"
Power: H
Action: F
Pieces: 1; 2
Line Weight: 15-30 lbs
Guide Count: N/A

Lure Weight: 3/4-3 oz
Features: Boasts IM8 blanks for a combination of heavy-duty strength and castability; stainless steel frames, double foot Fuji guides with aluminum oxide, and Pac Bay tip top with carbide deliver longer, smoother casting performance; graphite Fuji reel seat locks; Winn grips with EVA trim offer a strong grip and all-day comfort.
Price: **$149.99**

CABELA'S TOURNEY TRAIL SALMON/ STEELHEAD

Model: TTSS906-2-B, TTSS1006-2-B, TTSS864-2-B, TTSS904-2-B
Length: 9'; 10'; 8'6"; 9'
Power: H; H; M; M
Action: MF
Pieces: 2
Line Weight: 10-20 lbs; 10-20 lbs; 8-12 lbs; 8-12 lbs

Guide Count: N/A
Lure Weight: 1/2-1 1/2 oz; 1/2-2 oz; 3/8-3/4 oz; 3/8-3/4 oz
Features: Made with IM8 graphite blanks; black stainless steel guide frames resist bending and titanium-oxide guiding-ring material facilitates excellent line flow; downlocking graphite palm-swell reel seat eliminates exposed threads and uses soft-touch paint to deliver all-day comfort; cork grips withstand the wear and tear of fishing for seasons of use.
Price: **$79.99**

CABELA'S XML

Model: XMLS601-2, XMLS602-1, XMLS604-1, XMLS663-1, XMLS663-2, XMLS664-1, XMLS664XF-1, XMLS664-2, XMLS665-1, XMLS702-2, XMLS703-1, XML703-2, XMLS704-1, XMLS704-2, XMLS705-1, XMLS705-2
Length: 6'; 6'; 6'; 6'; 6'6"; 6'6"; 6'6"; 6'6"; 6'6"; 6'6"; 7'; 7'; 7'; 7'; 7'; 7'
Power: UL; ML; M; ML; ML; M; M; M; MH; L; ML; ML; M; M; MH; MH
Action: F; F; F; F; F; F; XF; F; F; F; F; F; F; F; F; F
Pieces: 2; 1; 1; 1; 2; 1; 1; 2; 1; 2; 1; 2; 1; 2; 1; 2
Line Weight: 2-6 lbs; 4-8 lbs; 6-12 lbs; 4-8 lbs; 4-8 lbs; 6-12 lbs; 6-12 lbs; 6-12 lbs; 8-20 lbs; 2-8 lbs; 4-8 lbs; 4-8 lbs; 6-12 lbs; 6-12 lbs; 8-20 lbs; 8-20 lbs
Guide Count: N/A

Lure Weight: 1/16-3/8 oz; 1/8-3/8 oz; 1/4-5/8 oz; 1/8-3/8 oz; 1/8-3/8 oz; 1/4-5/8 oz; 1/4-5/8 oz; 1/4-5/8 oz; 3/8-1 oz; 1/16-3/8 oz; 1/8-3/8 oz; 1/8-3/8 oz; 1/4-5/8 oz; 1/4-5/8 oz; 3/8-1 oz; 3/8-1 oz
Features: Built on the legendary XML 64 million-modulus, spiral-core-technology graphite blanks; feature lightweight, super-durable SS316 stainless steel Alps guides, double-coated with black chrome for maximum corrosion resistance; precise guide spacing compacts the distance between guides from the middle to the tip of the rod, increasing sensitivity and decreasing line drag; has a palm-swell reel seat; grips made of premium cork with thread-covering downlocking fore grips; butts are compatible with Cabela's Weight-Balancing System.
Price: **$149.99**

CABELA'S XML TRAVEL

Model: XMLS603-4, XMLS664XF-4, XMLS703-4, XMLS704-4
Length: 6'; 6'6"; 7'; 7'
Power: ML; M; ML; M
Action: F; XF; F; F
Pieces: 4
Line Weight: 4-8 lbs; 6-12 lbs; 4-8 lbs; 6-12 lbs
Guide Count: N/A
Lure Weight: 1/8-3/8 oz; 1/4-5/8 oz; 1/8-3/8 oz; 1/4-5/8 oz

Features: Built on the legendary XML 64 million-modulus, spiral-core-technology graphite blanks; features lightweight, super-durable stainless steel Alps guides, double-coated with black chrome for maximum corrosion resistance; Concept spacing increases sensitivity while decreasing line drag; palm-swell Aero reels seats; premium cork grips and thread-covering downlocking fore grips; butts are compatible with the XML Weight-Balance System; Cordura nylon case and nylon storage sleeve included.
Price: **$159.99**

CASTAWAY INVICTA

Model: INV-DSM7
Length: 7'
Power: M
Action: MF
Pieces: N/A
Line Weight: 8-14 lbs
Guide Count: N/A

Lure Weight: 1/4-5/8 oz
Features: 40-ton, 12-toe carbon fiber, carbon intruded resins, ALPS bronze SS316 stainless guides/bronze zirconium rings; custom Winn non-slip floating split grips; ALPS TexTouch triple exposed reel seat; double locking hood; CastAway Static Zoned Guide Spacing.
Price: **$249.99**

CASTAWAY SKELETON

Model: SKX-DSM7
Length: 7'
Power: M
Action: MF
Pieces: N/A
Line Weight: 8-14 lbs
Guide Count: N/A
Lure Weight: 1/4-5/8 oz

Features: Multi-modulus blended carbon fiber for the ultimate balance of weight and sensitivity; balance induced resins provide superior strength and consistent actions; ALPS SS316 stainless black/black aluminum oxide rings stand up to all of the newest "Super Braids" with strong and corrosion-resistant frames; PY Grade-A custom cork/composite ring split grips; proprietary CastAway Double Exposed Blank-Thru Reel Seat; CastAway Static Zoned Guide Spacing for maximum casting distance and stress distribution.
Price: **$169.99**

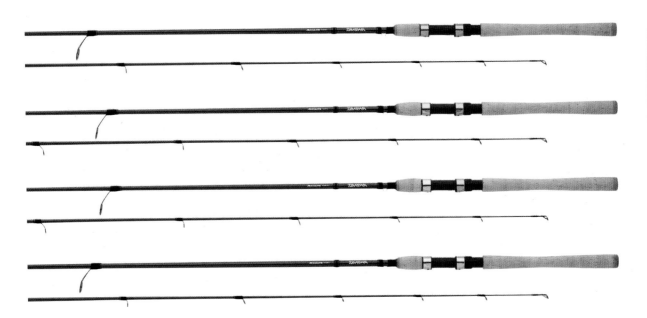

DAIWA ACCULITE SALMON & STEELHEAD
Model: ACSS962LRS, ACSS862MLFS, ACSS862MFS, ACSS962MFS, ACSS902MFS, ACSS902MLFS, ACSS862MHFS
Length: 9'6"; 8'6"; 8'6"; 9'6"; 9'; 9'; 8'6"
Power: L; ML; M; M; M; ML; MH
Action: R; F; F; F; F; F; F
Pieces: 2

Line Weight: 4-10 lbs; 6-12 lbs; 8-17 lbs; 8-17 lbs; 8-17 lbs; 6-12 lbs; 8-20 lbs
Guide Count: 9; 8; 8; 8; 8; 8; 8
Lure Weight: 3/16-1/2 oz; 3/16-1/2 oz; 3/8-1 oz; 3/8-1 oz; 3/8-1 oz; 3/16-1/2 oz; 1/2-1 1/2 oz
Features: IM-6 Graphite Construction; blank-through-handle construction; cut-proof aluminum oxide guides; stainless steel hood reel seat; natural cork grips; hook keeper.
Price: **$49.99**

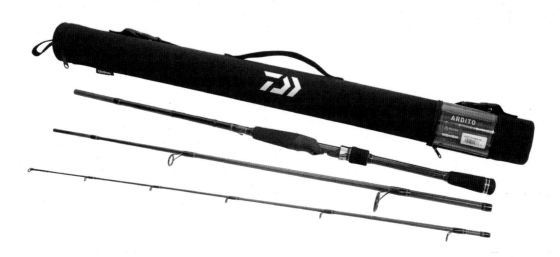

DAIWA ARDITO-TR
Model: ARDT703MFS-TR, ARDT703MHFS-TR, ARDT763MHFS-TR
Length: 7'; 7'; 7'6"
Power: M; MH; MH
Action: F
Pieces: 3
Line Weight: 6-15 lbs; 8-17 lbs; 8-17 lbs
Guide Count: 8

Lure Weight: 1/4-3/4 oz; 1/4-1 oz; 1/4-1 oz
Features: Daiwa's exclusive HVF (High Volume Fiber) Graphite construction; X45 Bias Graphite fiber construction for flexibility, strength and virtually zero blank twist; V-Flex Ferrule Joint System; unsanded micro-pitch taping blank; multi-piece travel design; Fuji aluminum oxide guides; semi-hard travel case.
Price: **$129.99**

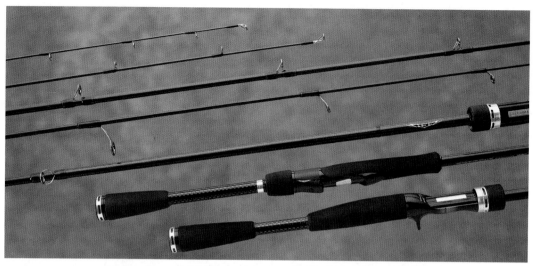

Daiwa Steez AGS Bass casting and spinning rods pictured.

DAIWA STEEZ SVF AGS BASS

Model: STZ701MLFSA-AGS, STZ701MFSA-AGS,
STZ701HFSA-AGS, STZ701MLXSA-AGS
Length: 7'
Power: ML; M; H; ML
Action: F; F; F; XF
Pieces: 1
Line Weight: 4-12 lbs; 6-14 lbs; 8-17 lbs; 3-10 lbs

Guide Count: 9
Lure Weight: 1/16-3/8 oz; 1/8-3/4 oz; 1/4-1 oz; 1/64-1/4 oz
Features: Daiwa's exclusive SVF graphite construction; bias
graphite fiber construction for flexibility, strength and
virtually zero blank twist; Air Guides AGS SiC guides, cut-
proof and corrosion free; Air-Foam lightweight, non-slip
grip; laser-engraved butt cap.
Price:.............................**$529.99–$549.99**

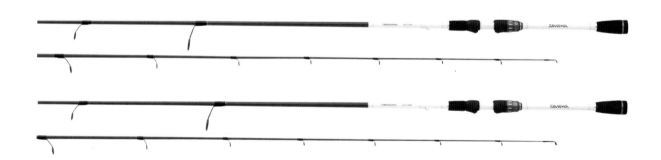

DAIWA TEAM DAIWA S BASS

Model: TDS661MXS, TDS662MXS, TDS701MXS,
TDS721MHXS
Length: 6'6"; 6'6"; 7'; 7'2"
Power: M; M; M; MH
Action: XF
Pieces: 1; 2; 1; 1
Line Weight: 6-15 lbs; 6-15 lbs; 6-15 lbs; 8-17 lbs

Guide Count: 8
Lure Weight: 1/4-3/4 oz
Features: IM-7 graphite construction; un-sanded micro pitch
taping blank; blank-through-handle construction; lightweight
split grip design with non-slip, high-density EVA foam;
machined aluminum reel clamp nut, knurled for sure grip
tightening; Fuji skeleton pipe seat; Fuji aluminum oxide
guides; hook keeper.
Price:....................................**$119.99**

NEW Products: Rods, Freshwater Spinning

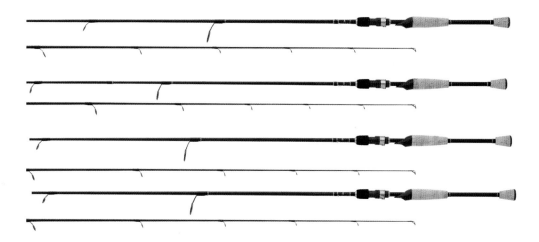

DAIWA TRIFORCE MULTI-PURPOSE

Model: TRF601MFS, TRF602MFS, TRF661MFS, TRF661MHFS, TRF662MFS, TRF701MLFS, TRF701MFS, TRF702MFS, TRF701MHFS
Length: 6'; 6'; 6'6"; 6'6"; 6'6"; 7'; 7'; 7'; 7'
Power: M; M; M; MH; M; ML; M; M; MH
Action: F
Pieces: 1; 2; 1; 1; 2; 1; 1; 2; 1

Line Weight: 6-15 lbs; 6-15 lbs; 6-15 lbs; 8-17 lbs; 6-15 lbs; 4-12 lbs; 6-15 lbs; 6-15 lbs; 8-17 lbs
Guide Count: 7
Lure Weight: 1/8-3/4 oz; 1/8-3/4 oz; 1/8-3/4 oz; 1/4-3/4 oz; 1/8-3/4 oz; 1/8-1/2 oz; 1/8-3/4 oz; 1/8-3/4 oz; 1/4-3/4 oz
Features: IM-6 graphite construction; blank-through-handle construction; stainless steel hooded reel seat; natural split foam and cork grip; cut-proof aluminum oxide guides.
Price: **$34.99**

DAIWA ZILLION BASS

Model: ZIL701MLFS, ZIL721MFS, ZIL731MHFS
Length: 7'; 7'2"; 7'3"
Power: ML; ML; MH
Action: F
Pieces: 1
Line Weight: 4-12 lbs; 6-14 lbs; 8-17 lbs
Guide Count: 8

Lure Weight: 1/16-3/8 oz; 3/16-1/2 oz; 1/4-3/4 oz
Features: Daiwa's exclusive SVF (Super Volume Fiber) graphite technology; X45 bias graphite fiber construction for flexibility, strength and virtually zero blank twist; micro pitch blank finish; Daiwa custom Carbon Air reel seat & machined aluminum reel clamp nut; tangle free Fuji SiC ring K guides; split grip EVA foam design and hook keeper; blank-through-handle construction.
Price: . . . .**$239.99–$249.99**

FALCON LOWRIDER 20

Model: LFS-4-166, LFS-5-167, LFS-2-169, LFS-4-1610
Length: 6'6"; 6'7"; 6'9"; 6'10"
Power: M; MH; L; M
Action: M; XF; F; F
Pieces: N/A

Line Weight: 8-12 lbs; 10-17 lbs; 6-10 lbs; 6-12 lbs
Guide Count: 8
Lure Weight: 1/4-1/2 oz; 3/16-5/8 oz; 1/8-3/8 oz; 3/16-1/2 oz
Features: N/A
Price: . . . . **N/A**

NEW PRODUCTS

NEW Products: **Rods, Freshwater Spinning**

FENWICK EAGLE

Model: EA56MH-MFS-2, EA56UL-MS-2, EA60L-MS-2, EA60ML-MFS, EA60M-MFS, EA60M-MFS-2, EA66L-MS-2, EA66ML-FS, EA66M-FS, EA66M-FS-2, EA66MH-FS, EA66MH-FS-2, EA70UL-MS-2, EA70ML-MFS, EA70ML-MFS-2, EA70M-FS, EA70M-FS-2, EA70MH-FS, EA76UL-MS-2, EA80UL-MS-2
Length: 5'6"; 5'6"; 6'; 6'; 6'; 6'; 6'6"; 6'6"; 6'6"; 6'6"; 6'6"; 6'6"; 7'; 7'; 7'; 7'; 7'; 7'; 7'6"; 8'
Power: MH; UL; L; ML; M; M; L; ML; M; M; MH; MH; UL; ML; ML; M; M; MH; UL; UL
Action: MF; M; M; MF; MF; MF; M; F; F; F; F; F; M; MF; MF; F; F; F; M; M
Pieces: 2; 2; 2; 1; 1; 2; 2; 1; 2; 1; 2; 2; 1; 2; 1; 2; 1; 2; 2
Line Weight: 8-17 lbs; 1-6 lbs; 2-8 lbs; 4-10 lbs; 6-12 lbs; 6-12 lbs; 2-8 lbs; 4-10 lbs; 6-12 lbs; 6-12 lbs; 8-17 lbs; 8-17 lbs; 1-6 lbs; 4-10 lbs; 4-10 lbs; 6-12 lbs; 6-12 lbs; 8-17 lbs; 1-6 lbs; 1-6 lbs
Guide Count: 7; 7; 7; 7; 7; 7; 7; 7; 7; 7; 7; 7; 8; 8; 8; 8; 8; 8; 9; 9
Lure Weight: 3/16-1 oz; 1/32-1/4 oz; 1/16-3/8 oz; 1/8-5/8 oz; 1/8-3/4 oz; 1/8-3/4 oz; 1/16-3/8 oz; 1/8-5/8 oz; 1/4-3/4 oz; 1/8-3/4 oz; 1/4-1 oz; 1/4-1 oz; 1/32-1/4 oz; 1/8-5/8 oz; 1/8-5/8 oz; 1/8-3/4 oz; 1/8-3/4 oz; 1/4-1 oz; 1/32-1/4 oz; 1/32-1/4 oz
Features: B2 burled cork designs provides the feel of traditional cork, but is more chip resistant and durable; stainless steel guides with stainless steel inserts are lightweight, strong, and corrosion resistant.
Price:................................. **$59.95–$69.95**

FENWICK EAGLE SALMON/STEELHEAD

Model: EA86M-MFS-2, EA90M-MS-2, EA96M-MS-2, EA106MH-MS-2
Length: 8'6"; 9'; 9'6"; 10'6"
Power: M; M; M; MH
Action: MF; M; M; M
Pieces: 2
Line Weight: 8-15 lbs; 10-20 lbs; 10-20 lbs; 8-17 lbs
Guide Count: 10; 10; 10; 11
Lure Weight: 3/8-1 oz; 3/8-1 1/2 oz; 3/8-1 1/2 oz; 3/8-1 1/4 oz
Features: B2 burled cork designs provides the feel of traditional cork, but is more chip resistant and durable; stainless steel guides with stainless steel inserts are lightweight, strong, and corrosion resistant.
Price:................................. **$69.95–$79.95**

FENWICK ELITE TECH BASS

Model: ETB69M-MFS, ETB69M-MFS-2, ETB610ML-XFS, ETB70M-FS, ETB70MH-FS, ETB70MH-FS-2, ETB74M-XFS
Length: 6'9"; 6'9"; 6'10"; 7'; 7'; 7'; 7'4"
Power: M; M; ML; M; MH; MH; M
Action: F; MF; XF; F; F; F; F
Pieces: 1; 2; 1; 1; 1; 2; 1
Line Weight: 6-12 lbs; 6-12 lbs; 4-10 lbs; 6-12 lbs; 10-17 lbs; 10-17 lbs; 6-12 lbs
Guide Count: 7; 7; 7; 7; 7; 7; 8
Lure Weight: 1/8-3/4 oz; 1/8-3/4 oz; 1/8-5/8 oz; 1/8-3/4 oz; 1/4-3/4 oz; 1/4-3/4 oz; 1/4-3/4 oz
Features: Hidden handle design reel seat allows function and comfort to co-exist; titanium frame guides are extremely lightweight; EVA and TAC handle design provides a solid grip even when the handle becomes wet; perfected actions designed specifically for bass fishing.
Price:.................................. **$149.95**

FENWICK ELITE TECH RIVER RUNNER

Model: ERR58UL-FS-2, ERR69UL-FS-2, ERR69L-FS-2, ERR72UL-MS-2, ERR72L-MFS-2, ERR76L-MFS-2, ERR80UL-MS-2
Length: 5'8"; 6'9"; 6'9"; 7'2"; 7'2"; 7'6"; 8'
Power: UL; UL; L; UL; L; L; UL
Action: F; F; F; M; MF; MF; M
Pieces: 2
Line Weight: 2-6 lbs; 2-6 lbs; 4-8 lbs; 2-6 lbs; 4-8 lbs; 4-8 lbs; 2-6 lbs

Guide Count: 7; 8; 8; 8; 8; 9; 9
Lure Weight: 1/32-3/16 oz; 1/32-3/16 oz; 1/32-5/16 oz; 1/32-3/16 oz; 1/32-5/16 oz; 1/32-5/16 oz; 1/32-3/16 oz
Features: Hidden Handle Design reel seat allows function and comfort to co-exist; titanium frame guides are extremely lightweight; TAC and cork handle design provides a solid grip even when the handle becomes wet; perfected actions designed specifically for light and ultra light applications.
Price: **$149.95**

FENWICK ELITE TECH WALLEYE

Model: ETW59M-XFS, ETW63ML-XFS, ETW66ML-FS, ETW66M-FS, ETW66M-FS-2, ETW69ML-XFS, ETW69ML-XFS-2, ETW72M-FS, ETW72M-FS-2, ETW72ML-FS, ETW76ML-FS
Length: 5'9"; 6'3"; 6'6"; 6'6"; 6'6"; 6'9"; 6'9"; 7'2"; 7'2"; 7'2"; 7'6"
Power: M; ML; ML; M; M; ML; ML; M; M; ML; ML
Action: XF; XF; F; F; F; XF; XF; F; F; F; F
Pieces: 1; 1; 1; 1; 2; 1; 2; 1; 2; 1; 1
Line Weight: 4-12 lbs; 4-10 lbs; 4-10 lbs; 4-12 lbs; 4-12 lbs; 4-10 lbs; 4-10 lbs; 4-12 lbs; 4-12 lbs; 4-10 lbs; 4-10 lbs

Guide Count: 7; 7; 8; 8; 8; 8; 8; 9; 9; 9; 9
Lure Weight: 1/8-3/4 oz; 1/8-5/8 oz; 1/8-5/8 oz; 1/8-3/4 oz; 1/8-3/4 oz; 1/8-5/8 oz; 1/8-5/8 oz; 1/8-3/4 oz; 1/8-3/4 oz; 1/8-5/8 oz; 1/8-5/8 oz
Features: Hidden handle design reel seat allows function and comfort to co-exist; titanium frame guides are extremely lightweight; TAC and EVA handle design provides a solid grip even when the handle becomes wet; perfected actions designed specifically for walleye fishing.
Price: **$149.95**

G.LOOMIS IMX JIG AND WORM

Model: IMX 802S JWR, IMX 803S JWR, IMX 852S JWR, IMX 853S JWR
Length: 6'8"; 6'8"; 7'1"; 7'1"
Power: M; MH; M; MH
Action: XF

Pieces: 1
Line Weight: 6-12 lbs; 8-14 lbs; 6-12 lbs; 8-14 lbs
Guide Count: N/A
Lure Weight: 1/8-3/8 oz; 3/16-5/8 oz; 1/8-3/8 oz; 3/16-5/8 oz
Features: N/A
Price: **$295**

LAMIGLAS SI SERIES

Model: SI 106 MS
Length: 10'6"
Power: M
Action: F
Pieces: 2
Line Weight: 8-12 lbs

Guide Count: N/A
Lure Weight: N/A
Features: Delivers greater sensitivity by using advanced resins, offering superior stength, as much as 40 percent, with no added weight; features titanium K-frame guides and exposed blank reel seats.
Price: **$500**

NEW PRODUCTS

LAMIGLAS X-11 SALMON/STEELHEAD
Model: LX 79 MS, LX 86 HS
Length: 7'9"; 8'6"
Power: N/A
Action: N/A
Pieces: 2

Line Weight: 8-12 lbs; 12-25 lbs
Guide Count: N/A
Lure Weight: 1/4-3/4 oz; 1/2-1 1/2 oz
Features: Exposed reel seats provide additional sensitivity and feel; glossy merlot color, IM graphite blanks.
Price: **$124**

LEW'S CUSTOM SPEED STICK SERIES
Model: LSRM, LDSS, LSHS, LWS, LMSR1, LMSR2, LMSR3, LTS
Length: 6'8"; 6'10"; 6'10"; 7'; 7'; 7'2"; 7'2"; 7'2"; 7'3"; 7'4"; 7'6"; 7'6"; 7'11"; 6'9"; 7'2"; 7'6"; 6'6"; 6'9"; 7'; 7'
Power: M; ML; M; ML; M; MH; MH; M
Action: F; XF; XF; F; F; F; MF; MF
Pieces: N/A
Line Weight: 6-12 lbs; 4-10 lbs; 6-12 lbs; 4-10 lbs; 6-12 lbs; 8-14 lbs; 8-30 lbs; 8-30 lbs

Guide Count: 8+1; 8+1; 8+1; 9+1; 9+1; 9+1; 11+1; 10+1
Lure Weight: 1/8-1/2 oz; 1/8-1/2 oz; 1/8-3/8 oz; 1/8-3/8 oz; 3/16-5/8 oz; 3/8-3/4 oz; 1/4-1 oz; 1/4-5/8 oz
Features: Lightweight, proprietary, multilayered, multidirectional, HM60 graphite blank construction; stainless steel guide frames with titanium oxide inserts; Lew's exclusive lightweight graphite skeletal reel seat; Lew's built in trigger hook keeper on casting models; spinning models feature patented "No Foul" hook keeper; custom shaped high density EVA grips with Duracork reinforcement.
Price: . . . .**$129.99–$139.99**

OKUMA THUNDER CAT
Model: TC-S-762H, TC-S-802H
Length: 7'6"; 8'
Power: H
Action: MF
Pieces: 2
Line Weight: 15-60 lbs
Guide Count: N/A
Lure Weight: 1-8 oz
Features: Extremely durable E-glass rod blank construction; EVA fore grip for comfort while fighting big Cats; EVA butt

section reduces weight and increases comfort; double foot stainless steel guides for ultimate durability; heavy duty stainless steel hook keeper on all models; graphite pipe reel seat with stainless steel hoods; durable non-skid, rubber gimbals on all models; blank construction, butted in handle for 1-pcs strength and feel; 2-pcs blank design also offers easy transportation; fluorescent wrapped indicator tip for improved visibility at night.
Price: **$79.99**

SHIMANO COMPRE MUSKIE

Model: CPCM70HD, CPCM76MHD, CPCM80XHD, CPCM80XXHD, CPCM86MHD, CPCM86HD, CPCM86XHTD, CPCM90XXHTD, CPCM96XHTD
Length: 7'; 7'6"; 8'; 8'; 8'6"; 8'6"; 8'6"; 9'; 9'6"
Power: H; MH; XH; XXH; MH; H; XH; XXH; XH
Action: F

Pieces: 1
Line Weight: 50-100 lbs; 50-80 lbs; 65-100 lbs; 80-100 lbs; 65-100 lbs; 50-100 lbs; 65-100 lbs; 80-100 lbs; 65-100 lbs
Guide Count: N/A
Lure Weight: N/A
Features: N/A
Price: . . . . **$149.99–$189.99**

ST. CROIX AVID X

Model: AXS66MLF, AXS66MF, AXS68MXF, AXS69MLXF, AXS70MLF, AXS70MLF2, AXS70MF, AXS70MF2, AXS70MHF
Length: 6'6"; 6'6"; 6'8"; 6'9"; 7'; 7'; 7'; 7'; 7'
Power: ML; M; M; ML; ML; ML; M; M; MH
Action: F; F; XF; XF; F; F; F; F; F
Pieces: 1; 1; 1; 1; 1; 2; 1; 2; 1
Line Weight: 4-10 lbs; 6-12 lbs; 6-12 lbs; 6-10 lbs; 4-10 lbs; 4-10 lbs; 6-12 lbs; 6-12 lbs; 8-14 lbs
Guide Count: N/A

Lure Weight: 1/4-3/8 oz; 3/16-5/8 oz; 3/16-5/8 oz; 1/8-1/2 oz; 1/8-3/8 oz; 1/8-3/8 oz; 3/16-5/8 oz; 3/16-5/8 oz; 3/8-3/4 oz
Features: Integrated Poly Curve (IPC) tooling technology; premium, high-modulus SCIII graphite; incredibly light, super sensitive and durable; slim-profile ferrules; Kigan Z micro-guide platform reduces weight while maintaining proper stripper guide ring height for optimum line flow efficiency. Z guides feature slim, strong aluminum-oxide rings with gunsmoke frames; Fuji reel seat with gunsmoke hood(s); split-grip/select-grade cork handle; exclusive Kigan hook-keeper; two coats of Flex Coat slow-cure finish.
Price: . . . . **$200–$210**

ST. CROIX TRIUMPH TRAVEL

Model: TRS66MHF4
Length: 6'6"
Power: MH
Action: F
Pieces: 4
Line Weight: 8-17 lbs
Guide Count: N/A
Lure Weight: 3/8-3/4 oz

Features: Premium-quality SCII graphite; outstanding strength, sensitivity, and hook-setting power; finely tuned actions and tapers for superior performance; hard aluminum-oxide guides with black frames; Fuji DPS reel seat/ frosted silver hoods on spinning models; Fuji ECS or TCS reel seat/ frosted silver hood on casting models; premium-grade cork handle; two coats of Flex Coat slow-cure finish.
Price: **$130**

ST. CROIX TRIUMPH X

Model: TXS50ULM, TXS60LF, TXS66MLF, TXS66MLF2, TXS66MF, TXS66MF2, TXS70MF, TXS70MF2
Length: 5'; 6'; 6'6"; 6'6"; 6'6"; 6'6"; 7'; 7'
Power: UL; L; ML; ML; M; M; M; M
Action: M; F; F; F; F; F; F; F
Pieces: 1; 1; 1; 2; 1; 2; 1; 2
Line Weight: 2-6 lbs; 4-8 lbs; 4-10 lbs; 4-10 lbs; 6-12 lbs; 6-12 lbs; 6-12 lbs; 6-12 lbs

Guide Count: N/A
Lure Weight: 1/16-1/4 oz; 1/16-5/16 oz; 1/8-1/2 oz; 1/8-1/2 oz; 1/4-5/8 oz; 1/4-5/8 oz; 1/4-5/8 oz; 1/4-5/8 oz
Features: Premium-quality SCII graphite; outstanding strength, sensitivity and hook-setting power; hard aluminum-oxide guides with black frames; split-grip/premium EVA handle; Fuji DPS or ECS reel seat with black hood(s); two coats of Flex Coat slow-cure finish.
Price: . . . . **$90–$100**

NEW Products: **Rods, Freshwater Spinning**

WRIGHT & MCGILL SKEET REESE VICTORY PRO CARBON

Model: WMSRSHW611S1, WMSRDSS70S1, WMSRTJ73S1
Length: 6'11"; 7'; 7'3"
Power: N/A
Action: MF; F; F
Pieces: 1
Line Weight: 6-15 lbs; 6-12 lbs; 8-15 lbs
Guide Count: N/A
Lure Weight: 1/8-3/8 oz; 1/8-½ oz; ¼-¾ oz
Features: Features a completely new and redesigned reel seat that optimizes reel placement for balance and features a skeletal design for extreme weight reduction while still providing a solid platform; Pacbay Minima one piece guide frames reduce weight by 20–30% over ceramic ring guides while increasing sensitivity and rod blank return rate; redesigned handles reduce weight and improve all day comfort while providing a solid rod/hand connection; custom fighting butt provides exceptional balance and fish fighting comfort; hook keepers offer both standard and drop shot keeper options; easy to read line and lure weight designations.
Price: **$159.99**

NEW Products: **Rods, Saltwater Spinning**

BERKLEY INSHORE

Model: BSINS661ML-F, BSINS701ML-F, BSINS701M-MF, BSINS701MH-MF, BSINS761ML-F, BSINS761M-MF, BSINS761MH-MF
Length: 6'6"; 7'; 7'; 7'; 7'6"; 7'6"; 7'6"
Power: ML; ML; M; MH; ML; H; MH
Action: F; F; MF; MF; F; MF; MF
Pieces: 1; 1; 1; 1; 1; 1; 1
Line Weight: 6-12 lbs; 6-12 lbs; 8-15 lbs; 10-20 lbs; 6-12 lbs; 8-15 lbs; 10-20 lbs
Guide Count: 8; 9; 9; 9; 9; 9; 9; 9
Lure Weight: 1/16-1/2 oz; 1/16-1/2 oz; 1/4-3/4 oz; 1/2-1 oz; 1/16-1/2 oz; 1/4-3/4 oz; 1/2-1 oz
Features: Blanks and components engineered for saltwater environments; 100 percent carbon fiber blanks; Fuji Guides; durable rubberized cork handles and an ergonomically shaped reel seat for maximum control and minimum fatigue.
Price: **$59.95**

CABELA'S SALT STRIKER ZX INSHORE

Model: SSZX-705MH-F, SSZX-796H-F, SSZX-706H-F, SSZX-706H-F2, SSZX-704M-F2, SSZX-704M-F, SSZX-704M-M2, SSZX-765MH-F2, SSZX-765MH-F, SSZX-705MH-F2, SSZX-704M-M
Length: 7'; 7'9"; 7'; 7'; 7'; 7'; 7'; 7'6"; 7'6"; 7'; 7'
Power: MH; H; H; H; M; M; M; MH; MH; MH; M
Action: F; F; F; F; F; F; M; F; F; F; M
Pieces: 1; 1; 1; 2; 2; 1; 2; 2; 1; 2; 1
Line Weight: 10-17 lbs; 12-25 lbs; 12-20 lbs; 12-20 lbs; 8-15 lbs; 8-15 lbs; 8-17 lbs; 12-20 lbs; 12-20 lbs; 10-17 lbs; 8-17 lbs
Guide Count: N/A
Lure Weight: 1/4-3/4 oz; 3/8-3 oz; 1/4-1 oz; 1/4-1 oz; 1/4-3/4 oz; 1/4-3/4 oz; 1/4-5/8 oz; 1/4-1 oz; 1/4-1 1/2 oz; 1/4-3/4 oz; 1/4-5/8 oz
Features: Features a rugged IM-7 graphite blank that yields phenomenal bending strength; Fuji alconite inserts have stainless steel framed guides for added durability; EVA handles and palm-swell down-locking reel seat (on certain models) provide fatigue-fighting comfort; Winn Grip overlays keep the rod secure in your hands in all conditions; split-grip design for balance and feel.
Price: **$149.99**

CASTAWAY INVICTA

Model: INV-SLS7, INV-SMS7
Length: 7'; 7'
Power: L; M
Action: S; MF
Pieces: N/A
Line Weight: 6-12 lbs; 8-17 lbs

Guide Count: N/A
Lure Weight: 1/16-3/8 oz; 1/16-5/8 oz
Features: 40-ton, 12-toe carbon fiber, carbon intruded resins, ALPS bronze SS316 stainless guides/bronze zirconium rings; custom Winn non-slip floating split grips; ALPS TexTouch triple exposed reel seat; double locking hood; CastAway Static Zoned Guide Spacing.
Price:. **$249.99**

CASTAWAY SKELETON

Model: SKX-SLS7, SKX-SMS7
Length: 7'
Power: L; M
Action: M; M
Pieces: N/A
Line Weight: 6-14 lbs; 8-17 lbs
Guide Count: N/A
Lure Weight: 1/16-1/2 oz; 1/16-5/8 oz

Features: Multi-modulus blended carbon fiber for the ultimate balance of weight and sensitivity; balance induced resins provide superior strength and consistent actions; ALPS SS316 stainless black/black aluminum oxide rings stand up to all of the newest "Super Braids" with strong and corrosion-resistant frames; PY Grade-A custom cork/composite ring split grips; proprietary CastAway Double Exposed Blank-Thru Reel Seat; CastAway Static Zoned Guide Spacing for maximum casting distance and stress distribution.
Price:. **$169.99**

DAIWA COASTAL SALT PRO SURF

Model: CLSP902MFS, CLSP902MHFS, CLSP1002MFS, CLSP1002MHFS, CLSP1062MFS, CLSP1062MHFS, CLSP1102MHFS
Length: 9'; 9'; 10'; 10'; 10'6"; 10'6"; 11'
Power: M; MH; M; MH; M; M; MH
Action: F
Pieces: 2

Line Weight: 10-20 lbs; 12-25 lbs; 10-20 lbs; 12-30 lbs; 10-20 lbs; 15-40 lbs; 15-40 lbs
Guide Count: 5
Lure Weight: 1-4 oz; 2-5 oz; 1-4 oz; 2-6 oz; 1-4 oz; 3-8 oz; 3-8 oz
Features: IM-7 graphite construction with woven carbon construction; Fuji Alconite ring—Low Rider Guide; Fuji DPS stainless hood reel seat; X-Tube Grip; blank-through-handle construction.
Price:. . . . .**$149.99–$169.99**

NEW Products: **Rods, Saltwater Spinning**

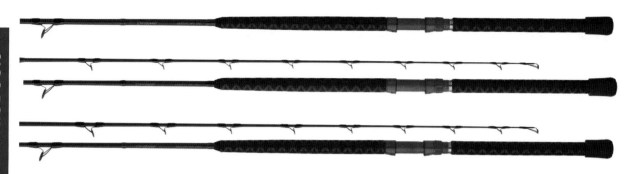

DAIWA PROTEUS BOAT
Model: PRTB76MF, PRTB76MHF, PRTB76HF, PRTB80MF, PRTB80MHF, PRTB80HF
Length: 7′6″; 7′6″; 7′6″; 8′; 8′; 8′
Power: M; MH; H; M; MH; H
Action: F
Pieces: 1

Line Weight: M: 10-25 lbs; 15-30 lbs; 20-50 lbs; 10-25 lbs; 15-30 lbs; 20-50 lbs; B: 20-55 lbs; 40-80 lbs; 55-100 lbs; 20-55 lbs; 40-80 lbs; 55-100 lbs
Guide Count: 10
Lure Weight: N/A
Features: Graphite composite construction; Fuji DPS stainless steel hood reel seat; Fuji alconite tangle-free frame guide; X-Tube grip; blank-through-handle construction.
Price: . . . .**$179.99–$189.99**

LAMIGLAS GRAPHITE SURF AND JETTY
Model: XS 101 MHS, XS 111 MHS
Length: 10′; 11′
Power: N/A
Action: MF
Pieces: 1
Line Weight: 17-40 lbs

Guide Count: N/A
Lure Weight: 3-6 oz
Features: Distinctive high-gloss, clear-coated design with black wraps and gold accents; includes Fuji guides, Fuji graphite reel seats, and functional EVA and cork-tape handle.
Price: . . . . **$350–$390**

LAMIGLAS INSANE SURF SERIES
Model: LIS 9 MS, LIS 10 MS, LIS 10 MHS, LIS 11 MHS
Length: 9′; 10′; 10′; 11′
Power: N/A
Action: F
Pieces: 2

Line Weight: 15-25 lbs; 15-25 lbs; 17-40 lbs; 17-40 lbs
Guide Count: N/A
Lure Weight: 1-3 oz; 1-3 oz; 2-5 oz; 2-6 oz
Features: N/A
Price: . . . . **$170–$194**

LAMIGLAS SUPERSURF 2G SERIES
Model: SSS 9 MHS, SSS 10 MS, SSS 10 MHS, SSS 101 MHS, SSS 11 MHS
Length: 9'; 10'; 10'; 10'; 11'
Power: N/A
Action: F
Pieces: 2; 2; 2; 1; 2

Line Weight: 15-25 lbs; 15-25 lbs; 17-40 lbs; 17-40 lbs; 17-40 lbs
Guide Count: N/A
Lure Weight: 1-3 oz; 1-3 oz; 2-5 oz; 2-5 oz; 2-6 oz
Features: Features Fuji reel seats, lightweight K-frame guides, and a beautiful, aqua-blue finish.
Price:. . . . . **$430–$480**

LEW'S AMERICAN HERO IM6 SPEED STICK SERIES
Model: AH60MFS, AHI70MFS, AHI70MHFS
Length: 6'; 7'; 7'
Power: M; M; MH
Action: F
Pieces: N/A
Line Weight: 4-12 lbs; 8-14 lbs; 8-20 lbs
Guide Count: 7+1; 9+1; 9+1

Lure Weight: 1/8-1/2 oz; 1/16-3/4 oz; 3/8-1 oz
Features: Premium IM6 one-piece graphite blanks; multilayer, multidirectional graphite construction for structural strength; rugged gunsmoke stainless steel guide frames with stainless steel inserts; lightweight graphite reel seats with cushioned stainless steel hoods; great hand/reel stability and comfort; exposed blank for instant vibration transmission; premium, lightweight, durable high-density EVA split-grips; patented "No Foul" hook keeper.
Price:. **$69.99**

LEW'S CUSTOM SPEED STICK SERIES
Model: LSRM, LDSS, LSHS, LWS, LMSR1, LMSR2, LMSR3, LTS, LI-MLS70, LI-MFS70
Length: 6'8"; 6'10"; 6'10"; 7'; 7'; 7'2"; 7'2"; 7'2"; 7'3"; 7'4"; 7'6"; 7'6"; 7'11"; 6'9"; 7'2"; 7'6"; 6'6"; 6'9"; 7'; 7'
Power: M; ML; M; ML; M; MH; MH; M
Action: F; XF; XF; F; F; F; MF; MF
Pieces: N/A

Line Weight: 6-12 lbs; 4-10 lbs; 6-12 lbs; 4-10 lbs; 6-12 lbs; 8-14 lbs; 8-30 lbs; 8-30 lbs
Guide Count: 8+1; 8+1; 8+1; 9+1; 9+1; 9+1; 11+1; 10+1
Lure Weight: 1/8-1/2 oz; 1/8-1/2 oz; 1/8-3/8 oz; 1/8-3/8 oz; 3/16-5/8 oz; 3/8-3/4 oz; 1/4-1 oz; 1/4-5/8 oz
Features: HM60 graphite blank construction; stainless steel guide frames with titanium oxide inserts.
Price:. . . . . **$129.99–$139.99**

OKUMA CALYNN
Model: CY-S-701L, CY-S-701M, CY-S-701MH, CY-S-701ML
Length: 7'
Power: L; M; MH; ML
Action: M/MF; MF; MF; MF
Pieces: 1
Line Weight: 4-10 lbs; 6-15 lbs; 8-17 lbs; 6-12 lbs

Guide Count: N/A
Lure Weight: 1/8-5/8 oz; 1/4-3/4 oz; 1/4-1 oz; 3/16-1/2 oz
Features: Light weight and sensitive 24-ton carbon rod blanks; split neo-cork butt design for reduced weight; custom compressed cork reel seat pipe; designed to match up with Avenger LE or Trio LE spinning reels.
Price:. **$49.99**

NEW PRODUCTS

OKUMA SHADOW STALKER GULF COAST

Model: SSG-S-701H-FG, SSG-S-701M, SSG-S-701MH, SSG-S-701MH-FG, SSG-S-701ML, SSG-S-7101M, SSG-S-7101ML, SSG-S-751M, SSG-S-751MH, SSG-S-751ML

Length: 7'; 7'; 7'; 7'; 7'; 7'10"; 7'10"; 7'5"; 7'5"; 7'5"

Power: H; M; MH; MH; ML; M; ML; M; MH; ML

Action: MF; MF; MF/F; MF/F; M/MF; MF; MF; MF; MF; MF

Pieces: 1

Line Weight: 15-30 lbs; 8-17 lbs; 10-20 lbs; 10-20 lbs; 6-12 lbs; 8-17 lbs; 6-12 lbs; 8-17 lbs; 10-20 lbs; 6-12 lbs

Guide Count: 8+1

Lure Weight: 1/2-2 oz; 3/8-1 oz; 1/2-1 1/2 oz; 1/2-1 1/2 oz; 1/8-3/8 oz; 3/8-1 oz; 1/8-3/8 oz; 3/8-1 oz; 1/2-1 1/2 oz; 1/8-3/8 oz

Features: Lightweight, sensitive 24-ton carbon graphite rod blanks; OC-9 carbon outer wrap: Stripper guide to butt. Improves hoop strength; Fuji hardened aluminum oxide guides for trusted reliability; EVA and compresses cork fore grip for reduced weight and feel; EVA and compressed cork split grip reduces weight and improves balance; FG models feature a full EVA and compressed cork butt section; custom carbon C-40X spinning and casting skeleton reel seats; 701H-FG features a Fuji pipe reel seat; stainless steel hook keepers on all models.

Price:............................$79.99–$109.99

ST. CROIX LEGEND TREK

Model: LTS70MLF3, LTS70MF3, LTS76MHF3, LTS76HF3

Length: 7'; 7'; 7'6"; 7'6"

Power: ML; M; MH; M

Action: F

Pieces: N/A

Line Weight: 6-12 lbs; 8-17 lbs; 10-20 lbs; 15-30 lbs

Guide Count: N/A

Lure Weight: 1/8-1/2 oz; 3/8-3/4 oz; 1/2-1 1/4 oz; 3/4-2 oz

Features: Integrated Poly Curve (IPC) tooling technology; Advanced Reinforcing Technology (ART); high-modulus/high-strain SCIV graphite with FRS for unparalleled strength and durability; slim-profile ferrules; Kigan Master Hand Zero Tangle guides with zirconia rings and titanium frames for the ultimate protection against saltwater corrosion; Fuji reel seats with exclusive E-finish hood(s); super-grade cork handle; corrosion-proof wind check and handle trim pieces; two coats of Flex Coat slow-cure finish; rugged rod case with handle and divided polypropylene liner.

Price:................................$500-$530

NEW Products: **Rods, Freshwater Baitcasting**

ABU GARCIA FANTASISTA REGISTA

Model: FNRC610-4, FNRC70-5, FNRC70-6, FNRC73-6, FNRC76-6, FNRC76-7

Length: 6'10"; 7'; 7'; 7'3"; 7'6"; 7'6"

Power: ML; M; MH; MH; MH; H

Action: F; F; F; F; F; F

Pieces: 1; 1; 1; 1; 1; 1

Line Weight: 6-10 lbs; 8-14 lbs; 10-17 lbs; 10-17 lbs; 10-17 lbs; 10-20 lbs

Guide Count: 9; 10; 10; 11; 11; 11

Lure Weight: 1/8-1/2 oz; 1/4-3/4 oz; 1/4-1 oz; 1/4-1 oz; 1/4-1 oz; 3/8-1 1/2 oz

Features: Tetra axial carbon construction provides an increase in strength and durability; Fuji Titanium frame guides with alconite inserts; high density EVA gives greater sensitivity and durability; Micro Guide system.

Price:.................................... **$499.95**

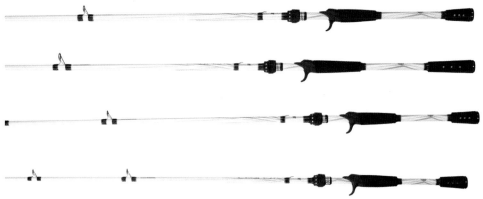

ABU GARCIA VERITAS 2.0

Model: VRTC66-5, VRTC66-6, VRTC69-6, VRTC70-5, VRTC70-6, VRTC70-7, VRTC73-6, VRTC76-6, VRTC79-7, VRTC662-5, VRTC692-6, VRTC711-7, VRTCF76-6, VRTCM66-6, VRTCM69-6, VRTCM70-5, VRTCM70-6, VRTCM73-6, VRTCM76-6, VRTCW70-5, VRTCW76-6, VRTCW711-7, VRTCW711-8

Length: 6'6"; 6'6"; 6'9"; 7'; 7'; 7'; 7'3"; 7'3"; 7'9"; 6'6"; 6'9"; 7'11"; 7'3"; 6'6"; 6'9"; 7'; 7'; 7'3"; 7'3"; 7'; 7'3"; 7'11"; 7'11"

Power: M; MH; MH; M; MH; H; MH; MH; H; M; MH; H; MH; MH; MH; M; MH; MH; MH; M; MH; H; EH

Action: F; MF; F; F; F; EF; F; F; F; F; F; F; M; MF; F; F; F; - ; F; M; M; M; M

Pieces: 1; 1; 1; 1; 1; 1; 1; 1; 1; 2; 2; 1; 1; 1; 1; 1; 1; 1; 1; 1; 1; 1

Line Weight: 8-17 lbs; 12-20 lbs; 12-20 lbs; 8-17 lbs; 12-20 lbs; 12-25 lbs; 12-20 lbs; 12-20 lbs; 12-20 lbs; 8-17 lbs; 12-20 lbs; 12-25 lbs; 12-25 lbs; 12-20 lbs; 12-20 lbs; 8-17 lbs; 12-20 lbs; 12-20 lbs; 12-25 lbs; 8-17 lbs; 12-25 lbs; 12-25 lbs; 14-30 lbs

Guide Count: 9; 9; 9; 9; 9; 9; 9; 9; 9; 9; 9; 10; 9; 9; 9; 10; 10; 10; 10; 9; 9; 10; 10

Lure Weight: 1/4-3/4 oz; 1/4-1 oz; 1/4-1 oz; 1/4-3/4 oz; 1/4-1 oz; 3/8-1 1/2 oz; 1/4-1 oz; 3/8-1 1/4 oz; 5/8-3 oz; 1/4-3/4 oz; 1/4-1 oz; 3/8-1 1/2 oz; 3/8-1 1/4 oz; 1/4-1 oz; 1/4-1 oz; 1/4-3/4 oz; 1/4-1 oz; 1/4-1 oz; 3/8-1 1/4 oz; 1/4-34 oz; 1/2-1 3/8 oz; 3/8-1 1/4 oz; 3/4-2 1/2 oz

Features: Thirty-ton graphite for a lightweight balanced design; spiral carbon core construction provides an increase in break strength of the rod; titanium alloy guides with SiC inserts allow for a lightweight balanced rod; Abu-designed extreme exposure reel seat for increased blank contact and sensitivity; micro click reel seat hood design allows for improved reel fit; high density EVA gives greater sensitivity and durability; Texas rigged hook keeper for all bait applications.

Price:. **$99.95**

ABU GARCIA VERITAS 2.0 FROG SERIES

Model: VRTCF76-6
Length: 7'6"
Power: MH
Action: MF
Pieces: 1
Line Weight: 12-25 lbs
Guide Count: N/A

Lure Weight: 3/8-1 1/4 oz
Features: Specifically designed for fishing lightweight frog baits; extremely lightweight and balanced; 30-ton graphite with Spiral Carbon Core Construction; sensitive tip and stout mid-section; titanium-alloy guides with Zirconium inserts; skeleton reel seat provides high sensitivity transfer; micro click reel seat hood.

Price:. **$99.95**

ABU GARCIA VERITAS 2.0 MICRO-GUIDE SYSTEM

Model: VRTCM66-6, VRTCM69-6, VRTCM70-5, VRTCM70-6, VRTCM73-6, VRTCM76-6
Length: 6'6"; 6'9"; 7'; 7'; 7'3"; 7'6"
Power: MH; MH; H; MH; MH; MH
Action: MF; F; F; F; F; F

Pieces: 1; 1; 1; 1; 1; 1
Line Weight: 12-20 lbs; 12-20 lbs; 8-17 lbs; 12-20 lbs; 12-20 lbs; 12-25 lbs
Guide Count: N/A
Lure Weight: 1/4-1 oz; 1/4-1 oz; 1/4-5/8 oz; 1/4-1 oz; 1/4-1 oz; 3/8-1 1/4 oz
Features: N/A
Price:. **$99.95**

NEW PRODUCTS

NEW Products: Rods, Freshwater Baitcasting

ABU GARCIA VERITAS 2.0 WINCH SERIES
Model: VRTCW70-5, VRTCW76-6, VRTCW711-7, VRTCW711-8
Length: 7'; 7'6"; 7'11"; 7'11"
Power: M; MH; H; XH
Action: M; M; M; M
Pieces: 1; 1; 1; 1

Line Weight: 8-17 lbs; 10-20 lbs; 12-25 lbs; 14-30 lbs
Guide Count: N/A
Lure Weight: 1/4-5/8 oz; 1/2-1 3/8 oz; 3/8-1 1/4 oz; 3/4-1 1/2 oz
Features: N/A
Price: **$99.95**

BASS PRO SHOPS BIONIC BLADE XPS SLIM GRIP
Model: BNB66MTS, BNB66MHTS, BNB70MTS, BNB70MHTS
Length: 6'6"; 6'6"; 7'; 7'
Power: M; MH; M; MH
Action: F; F; F; F
Pieces: 1; 1; 1; 1

Line Weight: 8-17 lbs; 10-20 lbs; 8-17 lbs; 10-20 lbs
Guide Count: N/A
Lure Weight: 1/4-5/8 oz; 3/8-3/4 oz; 1/4-5/8 oz; 3/8-1 1/2 oz
Features: Slim profile grip; minimalist cork fore grip; classic full cork butt; full-contact reel seat with Soft Touch finish; IM8 blank with ArmorCore technology; Pacific Bay Hialoy guides; multi-purpose hook keeper.
Price: **$79.99**

BASS PRO SHOPS JOHNNY MORRIS CARBONLITE SLIM GRIP
Model: N/A
Length: 6'6"; 6'6"; 7'; 7'
Power: M; MH; M; MH
Action: F; F; F; F
Pieces: 1; 1; 1; 1
Line Weight: 8-17 lbs; 10-20 lbs; 8-17 lbs; 10-20 lbs

Guide Count: N/A
Lure Weight: 1/4-5/8 oz; 3/8-1 oz; 1/4-5/8 oz; 3/8-1 oz
Features: Slim profile grip; ergonomic P-Tec polyfoam grip material; 2-piece minimalist reel seat with Soft Touch coatings; RT4 Graphite blank; Carbon Coil Technology; durable Pac Bay titanium guides; A line ID system built into the rod butt.
Price: . . . .**$99.99–$109.99**

BASS PRO SHOPS JOHNNY MORRIS SIGNATURE SERIES
Model: JMR68MT, JMR68MHT, JMR72MT, JMR72MHT, JMR76HT
Length: 6'8"; 6'8"; 7'2"; 7'2"; 7'6"
Power: M; MH; M; MH; H
Action: F; XF; F; F; XF
Pieces: 1; 1; 1; 1; 1
Line Weight: 8-17 lbs; 10-20 lbs; 10-20 lbs; 10-20 lbs; 12-30 lbs
Guide Count: N/A
Lure Weight: 1/4-5/8 oz; 3/8-1 oz; 3/8-1 oz; 3/8-1 oz; 3/8-2 oz
Features: RT5 graphite rod blanks and Carbon Coil Technology maximizes rod strength and weight reduction while minimizing rod blank diameter, resulting in ultra sensitive fishing rods that are also super strong; skeletonized reel seats transfer the lightest strikes directly to the angler's hand by maximizing blank exposure while enhancing weight reduction; Fuji KR Concept guides minimize friction for smooth, long casts while enhancing sensitivity by transferring vibrations from the line through the guide to the rod and to your hand; comfortable cork grips reduce fatigue; the strength for battling heavy fighting northern pike or hauling bass out of the grass as well as the finesse to feel light-biting walleye in late summer.
Price: **$149.99**

BERKLEY E-MOTION PERFORMANCE SERIES

Model: BCEMO641M-MF, BCEMO671MH-F, BCEMO691M-M, BCEMO691M-MF, BCEMO691M-F, BCEMO6101H-XF, BCEMO701MH-F, BCEMO721MH-MF, BCEMO761MH-F, BCEMO761XH-F, BCEMO791MH-M, BSEMO661ML-MF, BSEMO691M-M, BSEMO691M-F, BSEMO701MH-XF

Length: 6'4"; 6'7"; 6'9"; 6'9"; 6'9"; 6'10"; 7'; 7'2"; 7'3"; 7'3"; 7'9"; 6'6"; 6'9"; 6'9"; 7'

Power: M; MH; M; M; M; H; MH; MH; MH; XH; MH; ML; M; M; MH

Action: MF; F; M; MF; F; XF; F; MF; F; F; M; MF; M; F; XF

Pieces: 1

Line Weight: 8-17 lbs; 12-20 lbs; 8-17 lbs; 8-17 lbs; 8-17 lbs; 12-25 lbs; 12-20 lbs; 12-20 lbs; 12-20 lbs; 15-30 lbs; 12-20 lbs; 4-10 lbs; 6-12 lbs; 6-12 lbs; 8-14 lbs

Guide Count: 10; 10; 10; 10; 10; 10; 10; 10; 11; 11; 13; 9; 9; 9; 9

Lure Weight: 1/4-3/4 oz; 1/8-3/4 oz; 1/4-3/4 oz; 1/4-3/4 oz; 1/4-3/4 oz; 3/8-1 1/2 oz; 1/4-1 oz; 1/4-1 oz; 1/4-1 oz; 1/2-3 oz; 1/4-1 oz; 1/16-3/8 oz; 1/8-1/2 oz; 1/8-1/2 oz; 1/4-3/4 oz

Features: A unique blend of 30- and 24-ton graphite; hybrid design guide system; H.E.T. (High Energy Transfer) reel seat with soft coat texture; ergonomically shaped high density EVA split-grip handles.

Price: **$79.95**

BERKLEY HERITAGE

Model: BCH701MH-XF, BCH661ML-XF, BCH662ML-XF, BCH661MH-F, BCH662MH-F, BCH701M-F

Length: 7'; 6'6"; 6'6"; 6;6"; 6'6"; 7';

Power: MH; ML; ML; MH; MH; M;

Action: XF; XF; XF; F; F; F

Pieces: 1; 1; 2; 1; 2; 1

Line Weight: 12-20 lbs; 4-10 lbs; 4-10 lbs; 12-20 lbs; 12-20 lbs; 8-14 lbs

Guide Count: 9; 9; 9; 9; 9; 9; 9

Lure Weight: 3/8-1 oz; 1/16-5/8 oz; 1/16-5/8 oz; 3/8-1 oz; 3/8-1 oz; 1/8-5/8 oz

Features: 100 percent carbon fiber blank construction; stainless steel guides and inserts; traditional full cork handle for durability and comfort.

Price: **$59.95**

BERKLEY INSHORE

Model: BCINS701M-MF, BCINS701MH-MF, BCINS761ML-F, BCINS761M-MF

Length: 7'; 7'; 7'6"; 7'6"

Power: M; MH; ML; M

Action: MF; MF; F; MF

Pieces: 1; 1; 1; 1

Line Weight: 10-17 lbs; 14-20 lbs; 8-15 lbs; 10-17 lbs

Guide Count: 9; 9; 9; 9

Lure Weight: 3/8-3/4 oz; 1/2-1 oz; 1/4-3/4 oz; 3/8-3/4 oz

Features: Blanks and components engineered for saltwater environments; 100 percent carbon fiber blanks; Fuji Guides; durable rubberized cork handles and an ergonomically shaped reel seat for maximum control and minimum fatigue.

Price: **$59.95**

CABELA'S FISH EAGLE 50 TRAVEL

Model: FE50C706-4-B, FE50C665-4-B, FE50C705-4-B

Length: 7'; 6'6"; 7'

Power: H; MH; MH

Action: F

Pieces: 4

Line Weight: 10-20 lbs; 8-17 lbs; 8-17 lbs

Guide Count: N/A

Lure Weight: 3/8-2 1/4 oz; 1/4-1 oz; 1/4-1 oz

Features: 50 million-PSI modulus HM50 graphite blank; Hialoy ceramic inserts are durable and wear-resistant; MagTouch reel seat with more blank exposure for greater sensitivity.

Price: **$119.99**

NEW PRODUCTS

CABELA'S PREDATOR MUSKY
Model: PMUC806-F, PMUC805-F, PMUTR806-MOD, PMUC765-F, PMUC866-F, PMUC867-F, PMUC907-F
Length: 8'; 8'; 8'; 7'6"; 8'6"; 8'6"; 9'
Power: H; MH; H; MH; H; XH; XH
Action: F; F; M; F; F; F; F
Pieces: 1
Line Weight: 30-65 lbs; 20-50 lbs; 20-65 lbs; 20-50 lbs; 30-65 lbs; 35-80 lbs; 35-80 lbs

Guide Count: N/A
Lure Weight: 2-7 oz; 3/4-4 oz; 1-9 oz; 3/4-4 oz; 2-7 oz; 3 1/2-10 oz; 3 1/2-10 oz
Features: IM8 blanks for a combination of heavy-duty strength and castability; Fuji guides and a Pac Bay tip top promote long, smooth casts; handles deliver a strong grip and all-day comfort.
Price:. . . . .**$149.99–$159.99**

CABELA'S TOURNAMENT ZX CRANKSHAFT
Model: TZXCS7106-1, TZXCS755-1, TZXCS704-1
Length: 7'1"; 7'5"; 7'
Power: H; MH; M
Action: F
Pieces: 1

Line Weight: 15-30 lbs; 15-30 lbs; 12-25 lbs
Guide Count: N/A
Lure Weight: 5/8-2 1/4 oz; 3/8-1 1/2 oz; 1/4-1 oz
Features: Technique-specific action designed for crankbaits; IM8 graphite blank construction; ergonomic split-handle design featuring Winn Grip overlays; Pac Bay Hialoy aluminum-oxide guides.
Price:. **$109.99**

CABELA'S TOURNEY TRAIL MUSKIE
Model: N/A
Length: 7'6"; 7'; 7'6"; 8'; 8'
Power: XH; MH; H; H; XH
Action: F
Pieces: 1

Line Weight: 20-50 lbs; 15-30 lbs; 17-40 lbs; 17-40 lbs; 20-50 lbs
Guide Count: N/A
Lure Weight: 2-6 oz; 3/4-2 1/2 oz; 1-3 oz; 1-3 oz; 2-6 oz
Features: Light, responsive IM8 graphite blanks; stainless steel guide frames; titanium-oxide guide-ring material; long-lasting cork grips.
Price:. **$79.99**

CABELA'S TOURNEY TRAIL SALMON/ STEELHEAD
Model: TTCS865-2-B, TTCS906-2-B
Length: 8'6"; 9'
Power: MH; H
Action: F
Pieces: 2

Line Weight: 8-17 lbs; 10-20 lbs
Guide Count: N/A
Lure Weight: 1/2-1 1/2 oz
Features: Light, responsive IM8 graphite blanks; stainless steel guide frames; titanium-oxide guide-ring material; long-lasting cork grips.
Price:. **$79.99**

CABELA'S TOURNEY TRAIL SE
Model: TTSEC665, TTSEC664, TTSEC705, TTSEC705-2, TTSEC706, TTSEC704
Length: 6'6"; 6'6"; 7'; 7'; 7'; 7'
Power: MH; H; MH; MH; H; M
Action: MF; F; MF; MF; F; F
Pieces: 1; 1; 1; 2; 1; 1

Line Weight: 8-17 lbs; 8-17 lbs; 10-17 lbs; 10-17 lbs; 10-20 lbs; 8-17 lbs
Guide Count: N/A
Lure Weight: 1/4-1 oz; 1/4-5/8 oz; 1/4-3/4 oz; 1/4-3/4 oz; 3/8-2 1/4 oz; 1/4-5/8 oz
Features: Sensitive IM7 graphite blanks; stainless steel guide frames; titanium-oxide guide-ring material; weight-reducing EVA split grips.
Price:. **$64.99**

NEW PRODUCTS

CABELA'S XML
Model: XMLC624-1, XMLC664-1, XMLC665-1, XMLC665-2, XMLC704-1, XMLC704-2, XMLC705-1, XMLC705-2, XMLC706-1, XMLC706-2
Length: 6'2"; 6'6"; 6'6"; 6'6"; 7; 7; 7; 7; 7; 7
Power: M; M; MH; MH; M; M; MH; MH; H; H
Action: F
Pieces: 1; 1; 1; 2; 1; 2; 1; 2; 1; 2

Line Weight: 8-17 lbs; 8-17 lbs; 8-17 lbs; 8-17 lbs; 8-17 lbs; 8-17 lbs; 8-17 lbs; 8-17 lbs; 10-20 lbs; 10-20 lbs
Guide Count: N/A
Lure Weight: 1/4-5/8 oz; 1/4-5/8 oz; 1/4-1 oz; 1/4-1 oz; 1/4-5/8 oz; 1/4-5/8 oz;1/4-1 oz; 1/4-1 oz; 3/8-2 1/4 oz; 3/8-2 1/4 oz
Features: Spiral-core-technology graphite blanks; lightweight, super-durable stainless steel Alps guides; precise guide spacing; exposed-blank MagTouch reel seats.
Price:................................. **$149.99**

CABELA'S XML TRAVEL
Model: XMLC664XF-4, XMLC704-4, XMLC705-4, XMLC706-4
Length: 6'6"; 7'; 7'; 7'
Power: M; M; MH; H
Action: XF; F; F; F
Pieces: 4
Line Weight: 8-17 lbs; 8-17 lbs; 8-17 lbs; 10-20 lbs
Guide Count: N/A
Lure Weight: 1/4-5/8 oz; 1/4-5/8 oz; 1/4-1 oz; 3/8-2 1/4 oz
Features: Built on the legendary XML 64 million-modulus, spiral-core-technology graphite blanks; feature lightweight, super-durable stainless steel Alps guides, double-coated with black chrome for maximum corrosion resistance; Concept spacing increases sensitivity while decreasing line drag; exposed-blank MagTouch reel seats; grips made with premium cork and have thread-covering down-locking fore grips; butts compatible with the XML Weight-Balance System; Cordura nylon case and nylon storage sleeve included.
Price:................................. **$159.99**

CASTAWAY INVICTA
Model: INV-TW66, INV-WRH66, INV-SBM610, INV-7MH, INV-7H, INV-GHB73, INV-FP76
Length: 6'6"; 6'6"; 6'10"; 7'; 7'; 7'3"; 7'6"
Power: MH; H; M; MH; H; XH; XH
Action: M; M; M; MF; M; M; F
Pieces: N/A
Line Weight: 8-17 lbs; 10-20 lbs; 8-14 lbs; 8-17 lbs; 12-20 lbs; 10-30 lbs; 15-30 lbs
Guide Count:

Lure Weight: 1/4-8 oz; 1/4-1 oz; 3/8-3/4 pz; 3/8-5/8 oz; 1/4-1 oz; 1/2-1 oz; 1/2-2 oz
Features: 40-ton, 12-toe carbon fiber, carbon intruded resins; ALPS bronze SS316 stainless guides/bronze zirconium rings; custom Winn non-slip floating split grips; ALPS TexTouch triple exposed reel seat; double locking hood; CastAway Static Zoned Guide Spacing.
Price:........................**$249.99–$259.99**

CASTAWAY SKELETON
Model: SKX-TW66, SKX-WRMH66, SKX-WRH66, SKX-WWM68, SKX-SBM610, SKX-7MH, SKX-7H, SKX-GHB73, SKX-FP76, SKX-FR76, SKX-LRC76
Length: 6'6"; 6'6"; 6'6"; 6'8"; 6'10"; 7'; 7'; 7'3"; 7'6"; 7'6"; 7'6"
Power: M; MH; H; M; M; MH; H; XH; XH; H; M
Action: M; M; M; M; F; MF; M; M; F; S; XF
Pieces: N/A
Line Weight: 8-17 lbs; 8-17 lbs; 10-20 lbs; 10-17 lbs; 8-14 lbs; 8-17 lbs; 12-20 lbs; 10-60 lbs; 15-30 lbs; 12-25 lbs; 10-15 lbs

Guide Count:
Lure Weight: 1/4-5/8 oz; 1/4-5/8 oz; 1/4-1 oz; 5/16-3/4 oz; 3/8-3/4 oz; 3/8-5/8 oz; 1/4-1 oz; 1/2-1 oz; 1/2-2 oz; 1/4-3/4 oz; 1/4-3/4 oz
Features: Multi-modulus blended carbon fiber for the ultimate balance of weight and sensitivity; balance induced resins provide superior strength and consistent actions; ALPS SS316 stainless black/black aluminum oxide rings stand up to all of the newest "Super Braids" with strong and corrosion-resistant frames; PY Grade-A custom cork/composite ring split-grips; proprietary CastAway Double Exposed Blank-Thru Reel Seat; CastAway Static Zoned Guide Spacing for maximum casting distance and stress distribution.
Price:........................**$169.99–$179.99**

NEW Products: Rods, Freshwater Baitcasting

DAIWA ARDITO-TR

Model: ARDT703MFB-TR, ARDT703MHFB-TR, ARDT763MHFB-TR
Length: 7'; 7'; 7'6"
Power: M; MH; MH
Action: F
Pieces: 3
Line Weight: 8-17 lbs; 10-20 lbs; 10-20 lbs

Guide Count: 10
Lure Weight: 1/4-3/4 oz; 1/4-1 oz; 1/4-1 oz
Features: Daiwa's exclusive HVF (High Volume Fiber) Graphite construction; X45 Bias Graphite fiber construction for flexibility, strength, and virtually zero blank twist; V-Flex Ferrule Joint System; unsanded micro-pitch taping blank; multi-piece travel design; Fuji aluminum oxide guides; semi-hard travel case.
Price: **$129.99**

DAIWA DXSB SWIMBAIT

Model: DXSB801MHFB, DXSB801HFB, DXSB801XHFB, DXSB801XXHFB
Length: 8'; 8'; 8'; 7'
Power: MH; H; XH; M
Action: F
Pieces: 1
Line Weight: 10-30 lbs; 12-40 lbs; 20-50 lbs; 8-20 lbs

Guide Count: 9
Lure Weight: 1-6 oz; 2-8 oz; 3-10 oz; 1/4-1 oz
Features: IM-7 graphite blank construction; Fuji aluminum oxide guides; Fuji reel seat; natural cork grips; blank-through-handle construction; specially designed hook keeper for large baits.
Price: **$109.99**

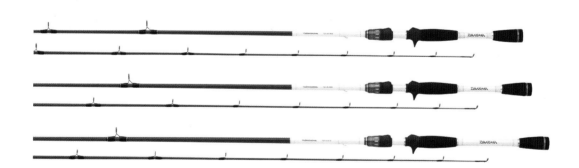

DAIWA TEAM DAIWA S BASS TRIGGER GRIP

Model: TDS661MXB, TDS661MHXB, TDS701MXB, TDS771MRB, TDS701MHXB, TDS701HXB, TDS741HFB
Length: 6'6"; 6'6"; 7'; 7'7"; 7'; 7'; 7'4"
Power: M; MH; M; M; MH; H; H
Action: XF; XF; XF; R; XF; XF; F
Pieces: 1
Line Weight: 8-17 lbs; 10-20 lbs; 8-17 lbs; 8-17 lbs; 10-20 lbs; 12-25 lbs; 55-80 lbs (braid)

Guide Count: 10
Lure Weight: 1/4-3/4 oz; 1/4-1 oz; 1/4-3/4 oz; 1/4-3/4 oz; 1/4-1 oz; 3/8-1 1/2 oz; 1/2-2 oz
Features: IM-7 graphite construction; unsanded micro pitch taping blank; blank-through-handle construction; lightweight split grip design with non-slip, high-density EVA foam; machined aluminum reel clamp nut, knurled for sure grip tightening; Fuji skeleton pipe seat; Fuji aluminum oxide guides; hook keeper.
Price: **$69.99**

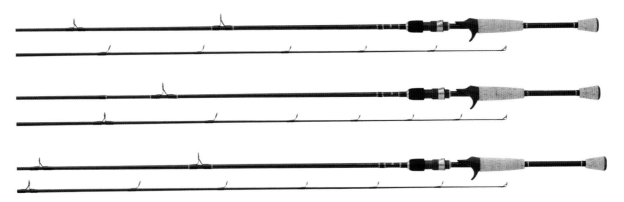

DAIWA TRIFORCE MULTI-PURPOSE
Model: TRF601MHFB, TRF661MFB, TRF661MHFB, TRF662MHFB, TRF701MFB, TRF701MHFB
Length: 6'; 6'6"; 6'6"; 6'6"; 7'; 7'
Power: MH; M; MH; MH; M; MH
Action: F
Pieces: 1; 1; 1; 2; 1; 1
Line Weight: 10-20 lbs; 8-17 lbs; 10-20 lbs; 10-20 lbs; 8-17 lbs; 10-20 lbs

Guide Count: 8
Lure Weight: 1/4-1 oz; 1/4-3/4 oz; 1/4-1 oz; 1/4-1 oz; 1/4-3/4 oz; 1/4-1 oz
Features: IM-6 graphite construction; blank-through-handle construction; stainless steel hooded reel seat; natural split foam and cork grip; cut-proof aluminum oxide guides.
Price: **$34.99**

DAIWA ZILLION BASS
Model: ZIL741HRB, ZIL801MHRB
Length: 7'4"; 8'
Power: H; MH
Action: R
Pieces: 1
Line Weight: 12-25 lbs; 15-30 lbs
Guide Count: 9; 10

Lure Weight: 3/8-1 1/2 oz; N/A
Features: Daiwa's exclusive SVF (Super Volume Fiber) graphite technology; X45 bias graphite fiber construction for flexibility, strength and virtually zero blank twist; micro pitch blank finish; Daiwa custom carbon air reel seat & machined aluminum reel clamp nut; tangle free Fuji SiC ring K guides; split grip EVA foam design and hook keeper; blank-through-handle construction.
Price: **$299.99**

FALCON RODS CARA ST
Model: CCM-5-167, CCM-5-1610, CCM-6-1610, CCM-4-17, CCM-7-173
Length: 6'7"; 6'10"; 6'10"; 7'; 7'3"
Power: MH; MH; H; M; H
Action: XF; F; MF; M; F
Pieces: N/A

Line Weight: 12-20 lbs; 10-20 lbs; 12-25 lbs; 8-12 lbs; 15-30 lbs
Guide Count: 12; 12; 12; 12; 13
Lure Weight: 1/4-3/4 oz; 3/16-5/8 oz; 1/4-3/4 oz; 1/4-1/2 oz; 1/2-1 1/2 oz
Features: N/A
Price: . . . . **$249.99–$329.99**

FALCON RODS LOWRIDER 20
Model: LFC-4-166, LFC-5-166, LFC-5-167S, LFC-5-168S, LFC-5-1610S, LFC-6-1610S, LFC-4-17, LFC-5-17, LFC-6-17, LFC-7-17, LFC-7-173S, LFC-6-179, LFC-5F-17, LFC-7-1610, LFC-7-172
Length: 6'6"; 6'6"; 6'7"; 6'8"; 6'10"; 6'10"; 7'; 7'; 7'; 7'; 7'3"; 7'9"; 7'; 6'10"; 7'2"
Power: M; MH; MH; MH; MH; H; M; MH; H; H; H; H; MH; H; H
Action: M; MF; XF; MF; F; MF; M; MF; F; MF; F; M; F; MF; F
Pieces: N/A

Line Weight: 8-17 lbs; 12-20 lbs; 12-20 lbs; 10-20 lbs; 10-20 lbs; 12-25 lbs; 8-17 lbs; 12-20 lbs; 12-25 lbs; 15-30 lbs; 15-30 lbs; 12-25 lbs; 12-20 lbs; 15-30 lbs; 15-30 lbs
Guide Count: 9; 9; 9; 9; 9; 9; 10; 10; 10; 10; 10; 10; 10; 9; 10
Lure Weight: 1/4-1/2 oz; 1/4-3/4 oz; 1/4-3/4 oz; 1/4-3/4 oz; 3/16-5/8 oz; 1/4-3/4 oz; 1/4-1/2 oz; 1/4-3/4 oz; 3/8-1 oz; 3/8-1 1/4 oz; 1/2-1 1/2 oz; 3/4-2 oz; 1/4-3/4 oz; 3/4-1 1/4 oz; 1/2-1 1/2 oz
Features: N/A
Price:...............................$159.99–$179.99

FENWICK EAGLE
Model: EA66M-FC, EA66M-FC-2, EA66MH-FC, EA70M-FC, EA70MH-FC, EA76MH-FC
Length: 6'6"; 6'6"; 6'6"; 7'; 7'; 7'6"
Power: M; M; MH; M; MH; MH
Action: F
Pieces: 1; 2; 1; 1; 1; 1
Line Weight: 8-17 lbs; 8-17 lbs; 10-20 lbs; 8-17 lbs; 10-20 lbs; 10-20 lbs

Guide Count: 9; 9; 9; 10; 10; 10
Lure Weight: 1/4-3/4 oz; 1/4-3/4 oz; 3/8-1 oz; 1/4-3/4 oz; 1/4-1 oz; 1/4-1 oz
Features: B2 burled cork designs provides the feel of traditional cork, but is more chip resistant and durable; stainless steel guides with stainless steel inserts are lightweight, strong, and corrosion resistant.
Price:.............................. $59.95–$69.95

FENWICK EAGLE SALMON/STEELHEAD
Model: EA86M-MFC-2, EA90M-MC-2, EADR90MH-MC-2, EA96M-MFC-2, EA10MH-MC-2, EA106MH-MC-2, EAM106MH-MC-2
Length: 8'6"; 9'; 9'6"; 10'; 10'6"
Power: M; M; M; MH; MH
Action: MF; M; MF; M; M
Pieces: 2

Line Weight: 8-15 lbs; 12-30 lbs; 10-20 lbs; 12-25 lbs; 15-30 lbs
Guide Count: 11; 11; 11; 12; 12
Lure Weight: 3/8-1 oz; 3/8-2 oz; 3/8-2 oz; 1/2-4 oz; 1-6 oz
Features: B2 burled cork designs provides the feel of traditional cork, but is more chip resistant and durable; stainless steel guides with stainless steel inserts are lightweight, strong, and corrosion resistant.
Price:.............................. $69.95–$79.95

FENWICK ELITE TECH BASS
Model: ETB66M-FC, ETB69MH-FC, ETB70M-FC, ETB70MH-FC, ETB72MH-MC, ETB73MH-XFC, ETB75H-XFC, ETB76MH-FC, ETB78MH-MC, ETB79XH-FC, ETB711H-MC
Length: 6'6"; 6'9"; 7'; 7'; 7'2"; 7'3"; 7'5"; 7'6"; 7'8"; 7'9"; 7'11"
Power: M; MH; M; MH; MH; MH; H; MH; MH; XH; H
Action: F; F; F; F; M; XF; XF; F; M; F; M
Pieces: 1
Line Weight: 8-14 lbs; 10-17 lbs; 8-14 lbs; 10-17 lbs; 10-20 lbs; 10-17 lbs; 12-30 lbs; 10-20 lbs; 10-20 lbs; 17-30 lbs; 12-30 lbs

Guide Count: 8; 9; 9; 9; 9; 9; 9; 9; 11; 9; 10
Lure Weight: 3/8-5/8 oz; 1/4-3/4 oz; 3/8-5/8 oz; 1/4-3/4 oz; 3/8-1 oz; 1/4-3/4 oz; 3/8-1 1/8 oz; 3/8-7/8 oz; 3/8-1 1/2 oz; 1/2-4 oz; 1/2-2 oz
Features: Hidden handle design reel seat allows function and comfort to co-exist; titanium frame guides are extremely lightweight; EVA and TAC handle design provides a solid grip even when the handle becomes wet; perfected actions designed specifically for bass fishing.
Price:.................................... $149.95

FENWICK ELITE TECH PREDATOR

Model: ETPR74MH-FC, ETPR80H-FC, ETPR86XH-FC, ETPR80MH-FC, ETPR90XH-FC
Length: 7'4"; 8'; 8'6"; 8'; 9'; 8'6"
Power: MH; H; XH; MH; XH; H
Action: F; F; F; F; F; MF
Pieces: 1; 1; 1; 1; 1; 2
Line Weight: 15-40 lbs; 20-50 lbs; 20-65 lbs; 15-40 lbs; 20-65 lbs; 20-50 lbs

Guide Count: 9; 10; 11; 10; 11; 11
Lure Weight: 1-4 oz; 2-8 oz; 4-12 oz; 1-4 oz; 4-12 oz; 2-8 oz
Features: Hidden handle design reel seat allows function and comfort to co-exist; titanium frame guides are extremely lightweight; EVA and TAC handle design provides a solid grip even when the handle becomes wet; erfected actions designed specifically for targeting large aggressive species.
Price:.........................**$129.95–$199.95**

FENWICK ELITE TECH WALLEYE

Model: ETW70M-MFC
Length: 7'
Power: M
Action: MF
Pieces: 1
Line Weight: 8-20 lbs

Guide Count: 9
Lure Weight: 1/4-1 oz
Features: Hidden Handle Design reel seat allows function and comfort to coexist; titanium frame guides are extremely lightweight; TAC and EVA handle design provides a solid grip even when the handle becomes wet; perfected actions designed specifically for walleye fishing.
Price:............................ **$149.95**

G.LOOMIS E6X BASS JIG AND WORM

Model: E6X 803C JWR, E6X 852C JWR, E6X 853C JWR, E6X 854C JWR, E6X 893C JWR, E6X 894C JWR
Length: 6'8"; 7'1"; 7'1"; 7'1"; 7'5"; 7'5"
Power: MH; M; MH; H; MH; H
Action: XF; XF; XF; F; XF; F
Pieces: 1
Line Weight: 12-16 lbs; 10-14 lbs; 12-16 lbs; 14-20 lbs; 12-16 lbs; 14-20 lbs

Guide Count: N/A
Lure Weight: 3/16-5/8 oz; 1/8-3/8 oz; 3/16-5/8 oz; 5/16-3/4 oz; 3/16-5/8 oz; 5/16-3/4 oz
Features: Features fast tapers for accuracy, control, and power for more positive hooksets with less effort; extensive range of power-ratings for fishing virtually any size soft plastics baits and jig/trailer combinations.
Price:..........................**$189.99-$199.99**

LAMIGLAS CERTIFIED PRO KWIK SERIES

Model: XCC 793 GH, XCC 885 GH, XCC 965 GH
Length: 7'9"; 8'8"; 9'6"
Power: 2
Action: MF
Pieces: 1; 1; 2

Line Weight: 15-30 lbs; 15-40 lbs; 15-40 lbs
Guide Count: N/A
Lure Weight: 1-6 oz; 4-12 oz; 4-12 oz
Features: Features Fuji reel seats and Fuji Concept Guide System.
Price:...............................**$310–$360**

NEW Products: Rods, Freshwater Baitcasting

LAMIGLAS SI SERIES
Model: SI 98 MC
Length: 9'8"
Power: M
Action: F
Pieces: 2
Line Weight: 8-12 lbs

Guide Count: N/A
Lure Weight: N/A
Features: Delivers greater sensitivity by using advanced resins, offering superior stength, as much as 40 percent, with no added weight; features titanium K-frame guides and exposed blank reel seats.
Price: **$500**

LAMIGLAS X-11 SALMON/STEELHEAD
Model: LX 96 HC, LX 106 HC
Length: 9'6"; 10'6"
Power: 3
Action: N/A
Pieces: 2

Line Weight: 15-30 lbs
Guide Count: N/A
Lure Weight: 1-8 oz
Features: Exposed reel seats provide additional sensitivity and feel; glossy merlot color, IM graphite blanks.
Price: **$124**

LEW'S AMERICAN HERO IM6 SPEED STICK SERIES
Model: AH70MHCBC, AHI69MFC
Length: 7'; 6'9"
Power: MH; M
Action: M; F
Pieces: N/A
Line Weight: 12-30 lbs; 8-15 lbs
Guide Count: 9+1

Lure Weight: 1/2-1 1/4 oz; 1/16-3/4 oz
Features: Premium IM6 one-piece graphite blanks; multilayer, multidirectional graphite construction for structural strength; rugged gunsmoke stainless steel guide frames with stainless steel inserts; lightweight graphite reel seats with cushioned stainless steel hoods; great hand/reel stability and comfort; exposed blank for instant vibration transmission; premium, lightweight, durable high-density EVA split-grips; patented "No Foul" hook keeper.
Price: **$69.99**

LEW'S CUSTOM SPEED STICK SERIES
Model: LTWS, LSPS, LSBR, LWR1, LMBR1, LMGR, LMBR2, LFJR, LFBJR, LMH, LMPS, LMBR3, LMHC, LMCR, LSBC, LCBR1, LMCBR2, LI-MFC66, LI-MC69, LI-MLC70, LI-MC70
Length: 6'8"; 6'10"; 6'10"; 7'; 7'; 7'2"; 7'2"; 7'2"; 7'3"; 7'4"; 7'6"; 7'6"; 7'11"; 6'9"; 7'2"; 7'6"
Power: ML; M; MH; MH; H;; MH; MH; H; MH; H; MH; H; MH; M; MH
Action: F; MF; F; MF; F; F; F; F; MF; F; F; MF; F; MF; MF; MF; MF
Pieces: N/A
Line Weight: 6-10 lbs; 10-20 lbs; 10-20 lbs; 12-20 lbs; 12-25 lbs; 14-65 lbs; 12-20 lbs; 12-20 lbs; 15-30 lbs; 10-25 lbs; 15-65 lbs; 12-30 lbs; 15-65 lbs; 12-30 lbs; 10-17 lbs; 15-30 lbs; 10-25 lbs

Guide Count: 9+1; 9+1; 9+1; 9+1; 9+1; 10+1; 10+1; 10+1; 10+1; 10+1; 10+1; 10+1; 10+1; 11+1; 9+1; 10+1; 10+1
Lure Weight: 1/8-1/2 oz; 3/16-5/8 oz; 3/16-5/8 oz; 3/16-5/8 oz; 1/4-7/8 oz; 3/8-1 oz; 3/8-1 oz; 3/16-5/8 oz; 1/2-1 oz; 1/4-5/8 oz; 1/2-2 oz; 1/2-1 oz; 3/16-1 oz; 1/2-3 oz; 1/4-3/4 oz; 1/2-1 1/4 oz; 1/2-1 3/8 oz
Features: Lightweight, proprietary, multilayered, multidirectional, HM60 graphite blank construction; stainless steel guide frames with titanium oxide inserts; Lew's exclusive lightweight graphite skeletal reel seat; Lew's built in trigger hook keeper on casting models; spinning models feature patented "No Foul" hook keeper; custom shaped high density EVA grips with Duracork reinforcement.
Price: . . . .**$129.99–$149.99**

NEW PRODUCTS

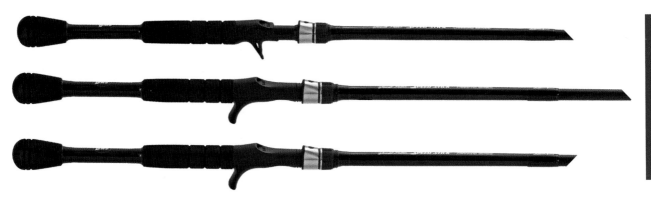

LEW'S DAVID FRITTS PERFECT CRANKBAIT SPEED STICK SERIES

Model: LDFP66M, LDFP70M, LDFP70MH, LDFP76MH
Length: 6′6″; 7′; 7′; 7′6″
Power: M; M; MH; MH
Action: M
Pieces: N/A
Line Weight: 10-17 lbs; 10-25 lbs; 15-30 lbs; 15-30 lbs
Guide Count: 9+1; 9+1; 9+1; 10+1
Lure Weight: 1/4-3/4 oz; 3/8-1 oz; 1/2-1 1/4 oz; 1/2-1 1/4 oz

Features: Premium 42 million modulus graphite/glass composite construction for strength and flexibility; guides are rugged stainless steel frames with aluminum oxide inserts, for smooth and easy line flow while casting; lightweight graphite reel seats with stainless steel cushioned hoods for comfort while making continuous casts; premium cork handles with high density EVA end caps for durability; loop style hook keepers designed especially for crankbait hooks of all sizes.
Price: **$79.99**

LEW'S TEAM LEW'S HM85 MILLION GRAPHITE SERIES

Model: TL711APC
Length: 7′11″
Power: H
Action: MF
Pieces: N/A
Line Weight: 12-25 lbs
Guide Count: 11+1
Lure Weight: 1/2-3 oz

Features: Features Lew's proprietary APT (Advanced Performance Technology) blank construction; multilayer, multidirectional 85 million modulus premium graphite blanks; Fuji KR Concept MICRO guides with stainless steel frames, Alconite Braid Concept tangle-free guides; skeletal graphite reel seat with cushioned black stainless steel hoods; great hand/reel stability and comfort; exposed blank for instant vibration transmission; full premium split-grip cork handles.
Price: **$199.99**

LAMIGLAS INSANE SURF SERIES

Model: LIS 10 MHC, LIS 11 MHC
Length: 10′; 11′
Power: N/A
Action: F
Pieces: 2

Line Weight: 17-40 lbs
Guide Count: N/A
Lure Weight: 2-5 oz; 2-6 oz
Features: Features new X-Flock handles with heat shrunk grips that are tough yet comfortable.
Price: . . . . **$180–$194**

NEW Products: Rods, Freshwater Baitcasting

OKUMA THUNDER CAT

Model: TC-C-762H, TC-C-802H
Length: 7'6"; 8'
Power: H
Action: MF
Pieces: 2
Line Weight: 15-60 lbs
Guide Count: N/A
Lure Weight: 1-8 oz

Features: Extremely durable E-glass rod blank construction; EVA fore grip for comfort while fighting big Cats; EVA butt section reduces weight and increases comfort; double foot stainless steel guides for ultimate durability; heavy duty stainless steel hook keeper on all models; graphite pipe reel seat with stainless steel hoods; durable non-skid, rubber gimbals on all models; 2-pcs blank construction, butted in handle for 1-pcs strength and feel; 2-pcs blank design also offers easy transportation; fluorescent wrapped indicator tip for improved visibility at night.
Price: **$79.99**

SHIMANO ZODIAS

Model: ZDS1610ML, ZDS1610M, ZDS1610MH, ZDS172M, ZDS172MH, ZDS172H
Length: 6'10"; 6'10"; 6'10"; 7'2"; 7'2"; 7'2"
Power: ML; M; MH; M; MH; H
Action: N/A
Pieces: 1
Line Weight: 6-16 lbs; 10-20 lbs; 10-25 lbs; 10-20 lbs; 10-25 lbs; 10-30 lbs

Guide Count: N/A
Lure Weight: 3/16-1/2 oz; 1/4-3/4 oz; 3/8-1 oz; 1/4-3/4 oz; 3/8-1 oz; 1/2-1 1/2 oz
Features: Utilizes Shimano's Hi-Power X construction that significantly reduces blank twist, allowing efficient and easy transfer of energy through the rod; crisp, lightweight blank delivers every tick and vibration down through the custom CI4+ reel seat.
Price: . . . . **$189.99–$199.99**

ST. CROIX AVID X

Model: AXC64MXF, AXC66MF, AXC66MHF, AXC68MXF, AXC70MF, AXC70MM, AXC70MHF, AXC70MHM, AXC74HF
Length: 6'4"; 6'6"; 6'6"; 6'8"; 7'; 7'; 7'; 7'; 7'4"
Power: M; M; MH; M; M; M; MH; MH; H
Action: XF; F; F; XF; F; M; F; M; F
Pieces: 1
Line Weight: 8-14 lbs; 10-17 lbs; 12-20 lbs; 8-14 lbs; 10-17 lbs; 8-14 lbs; 12-20 lbs; 10-20 lbs; 14-25 lbs
Guide Count: N/A

Lure Weight: 1/4-5/8 oz; 1/4-5/8 oz; 3/8-1 oz; 1/4-5/8 oz; 1/4-5/8 oz; 1/4-5/8 oz; 3/8-1/2 oz; 3/8-1/2 oz; 3/8-1 1/2 oz
Features: Integrated Poly Curve (IPC) tooling technology; premium, high-modulus SCIII graphite; incredibly light, super sensitive, and durable; slim-profile ferrules; Kigan Z micro-guide platform reduces weight while maintaining proper stripper guide ring height for optimum line flow efficiency. Z guides feature slim, strong aluminum-oxide rings with gunsmoke frames; Fuji reel seat with gunsmoke hood(s); split-grip/select-grade cork handle; exclusive Kigan hook-keeper; two coats of Flex Coat slow-cure finish.
Price: . . . . **$200–$210**

ST. CROIX LEGEND TOURNAMENT BASS

Model: TBC69MHMF, TBC70MHMF
Length: 6'9"; 7'
Power: MH
Action: MF
Pieces: 1
Line Weight: 10-20 lbs; 12-20 lbs
Guide Count: N/A
Lure Weight: 1/4-5/8 oz; 3/8-3/4 oz
Features: Integrated Poly Curve (IPC) tooling technology; Advanced Reinforcing Technology (ART); high modulus-

high-strain SCIV graphite with FRS for unparalleled strength and durability; technique-specific bass series features unrivaled technology and performance; Fuji K-Series Concept tangle-free guides with Alconite rings and polished frames. Ideal for super braid, mono and fluorocarbon lines, the sloped frame and ring "shed" tangles before they become a problem; Fuji SK2 split reel seat for the ultimate in light weight and sensitivity; machined-aluminum wind check and trim pieces; split-grip /super-grade cork handle; two coats of Flex Coat slow-cure finish.
Price: **$270**

ST. CROIX LEGENDXTREME

Model: LXC70MF2, LXC70MHF2
Length: 7'
Power: M; MH
Action: F
Pieces: 2
Line Weight: 10-17 lbs; 12-20 lbs
Guide Count: N/A
Lure Weight: 1/4-5/8 oz; 3/8-1 oz
Features: Integrated Poly Curve (IPC) tooling technology; Taper Enhancement Technology (TET) blank design provides curved patterns for improved action with increased sensitivity; Advanced Reinforcing Technology (ART); super high-modulus SCVI graphite with FRS in lower section for

maximum power and strength with reduced weight; high-modulus/high-strain SCV graphite with FRS and carbon-matte scrim for unparalleled strength, durability and sensitivity; slim-profile ferrules; Fuji K-R Concept tangle-free guides with SiC rings and exclusive E-color finish frames. Ideal for super braid, mono and fluorocarbon lines, the sloped frame and ring "shed" tangles before they become a problem; Fuji SK2 split reel seat for the ultimate in light weight and sensitivity; Xtreme-Skin handle repels water, dirt, and fish slime and cleans up easily. Manufactured by St. Croix to provide outstanding angler comfort, casting efficiency and sensitivity; machined-aluminum wind check, handle trim pieces and butt cap with logo badge; two coats of Flex Coat slow-cure finish; includes protective rod sack.
Price: **$440**

ST. CROIX TRIUMPH TRAVEL

Model: TRC66MH4
Length: 6'6"
Power: MH
Action: F
Pieces: 4
Line Weight: 10-20 lbs
Guide Count: N/A
Lure Weight: 3/8-1 oz

Features: Premium-quality SCII graphite; outstanding strength, sensitivity, and hook-setting power; finely tuned actions and tapers for superior performance; hard aluminum-oxide guides with black frames; Fuji DPS reel seat/ frosted silver hoods on spinning models; Fuji ECS or TCS reel seat/ frosted silver hood on casting models; premium-grade cork handle; two coats of Flex Coat slow-cure finish.
Price: **$130**

ST. CROIX TRIUMPH X

Model: TXC66MF, TXC66MHF, TXC70MF, TXC70MHF
Length: 6'6"; 6'6"; 7'; 7'
Power: M; MH; M; MH
Action: F
Pieces: 1
Line Weight: 10-17 lbs; 10-20 lbs; 10-17 lbs; 10-20 lbs

Guide Count: N/A
Lure Weight: 1/4-3/4 oz; 3/8-1 oz; 1/4-3/4 oz; 3/8-1 oz
Features: Premium-quality SCII graphite; outstanding strength, sensitivity, and hook-setting power; hard aluminum-oxide guides with black frames; split-grip/ premium EVA handle; Fuji DPS or ECS reel seat with black hood(s); two coats of Flex Coat slow-cure finish.
Price: **$100**

WRIGHT & MCGILL SKEET REESE VICTORY PRO CARBON

Model: WMSRJBW74C1, WMSRSBW70C1, WMSRCR76C1, WMSRFP80C1, WMSRSXL80C1, WMSRSKT76C1, WMSRFS70C1
Length: 7'4"; 7'; 7'6"; 8'; 8'; 7'6"; 7'
Power: N/A
Action: F; F; MF; F; F; MF; F
Pieces: 1
Line Weight: 12-25 lbs; 10-20 lbs; 12-25 lbs; 15-30 lbs; 20-50 lbs; 10-25 lbs; 10-20 lbs
Guide Count: N/A
Lure Weight: 3/8-1 1/4 oz; 1/4-3/4 oz; 1/4-1 1/2 oz; 3/8-2 oz; 2-8 oz; 1/4-1 oz; 1/4-3/4 oz

Features: Features a completely new and redesigned reel seat that optimizes reel placement for balance and features a skeletal design for extreme weight reduction while still providing a solid platform; Pacbay Minima one piece guide frames reduce weight by 20–30% over ceramic ring guides while increasing sensitivity and rod blank return rate; redesigned handles reduce weight and improve all day comfort while providing a solid rod/hand connection; custom fighting butt provides exceptional balance and fish fighting comfort; hook keepers offer both standard and drop shot keeper options; easy to read line and lure weight designations.
Price: **$159.99**

NEW PRODUCTS

NEW Products: Rods, Saltwater Baitcasting

CABELA'S SALT STRIKER ZX INSHORE
Model: SSIC-706H-F, SSIC-796H-F, SSIC-705MH-F, SSIC-765MH-F2
Length: 7'; 7'9"; 7'; 7'6"
Power: H; H; MH; MH
Action: F
Pieces: 1; 1; 1; 2
Line Weight: 12-20 lbs; 12-25 lbs; 10-17 lbs; 12-20 lbs
Guide Count: N/A

Lure Weight: 1/4-1 oz; 3/8-3 oz; 1/4-3/4 oz; 1/2-1 1/2 oz
Features: Features a rugged IM7 graphite blank that yields phenomenal bending strength; Fuji alconite inserts have stainless steel framed guides for added durability; EVA handles and MagTouch down-locking reel seat provide fatigue-fighting comfort; Winn grip overlays keep the rod secure in your hands in all conditions; split-grip design for balance and feel.
Price: $149.99

CASTAWAY INVICTA
Model: INV-SRML85, INV-SRM65, INV-MLC67F, INV-SRTT69, INV-SRL7, INV-SRM7
Length: 6'5"; 6'5"; 6'7"; 6'9"; 7'; 7'
Power: ML; M; ML; L; M
Action: M; MF; F; F; S; MF
Pieces: N/A
Line Weight: 8-14 lbs; 8-17 lbs; 8-14 lbs; 8-14 lbs; 6-12 lbs; 8-17 lbs

Guide Count:
Lure Weight: 1/16-1/2 oz; 1/4-3/4 oz; 1/16-1/2 oz; 1/16-1/2 oz; 1/16-3/8 oz; 1/16-5/8 oz
Features: 40-ton, 12-toe carbon fiber, carbon intruded resins; ALPS bronze SS316 stainless guides/bronze zirconium rings; custom Winn non-slip floating split-grips; ALPS TexTouch triple exposed reel seat; double locking hood; CastAway Static Zoned Guide Spacing.
Price: $249.99

CASTAWAY SKELETON
Model: SKX-SRW65L, SKX-SRW65ML, SKX-SRW65M, SKX-MLC67F, SKX-M69F, SKX-LSH7, SKX-MLH7, SKX-MSH7
Length: 6'5"; 6'5"; 6'5"; 6'7"; 6'9"; 7'; 7'; 7'
Power: L; ML; M; ML; M; L; M; M
Action: F; M; MF; F; F; M; M; M
Pieces: N/A
Line Weight: 8-14 lbs; 8-14 lbs; 8-17 lbs; 8-14 lbs; 8-17 lbs; 6-14 lbs; 8-17 lbs; 8-17 lbs
Guide Count:
Lure Weight: 1/16-1/2 oz; 1/16-1/2 oz; 1/4-3/4 oz; 1/16-1/2 oz; 1/4-5/8 oz; 1/16-1/2 oz; 1/16-5/8 oz; 1/16-5/8 oz

Features: Multi-modulus blended carbon fiber for the ultimate balance of weight and sensitivity; balance induced resins provide superior strength and consistent actions; ALPS SS316 stainless black/black aluminum oxide rings stand up to all of the newest "Super Braids" with strong and corrosion-resistant frames; PY Grade-A custom cork/composite ring split grips; proprietary CastAway Double Exposed Blank-Thru Reel Seat; CastAway Static Zoned Guide Spacing for maximum casting distance and stress distribution.
Price: $169.99

LEW'S CUSTOM SPEED STICK SERIES
Model: LI-MFC66, LI-MC69, LI-MLC70, LI-MC70
Length: 6'6"; 6'9"; 7'; 7'
Power: M; M; ML; M
Action: F; F; MF; MF
Pieces: N/A
Line Weight: 8-14 lbs; 8-15 lbs; 8-20 lbs; 8-20 lbs
Guide Count: 9+1; 9+1; 9+1; 9+1
Lure Weight: 1/16-1/2 oz; 1/16-3/4 oz; 1/16-5/8 oz; 1/16-5/8 oz

Features: Lightweight, proprietary, multilayered, multidirectional, HM60 graphite blank construction; stainless steel guide frames with titanium oxide inserts for reduced corrosion; Lew's exclusive lightweight graphite skeletal reel seat; Lew's built-in trigger hook keeper on casting models; patented "No Foul" hook keeper in front of reel seats on both casting and spinning models for easy storage in saltwater rod holders; custom shaped high density EVA grips with Duracork reinforcement.
Price: $139.99

OKUMA SHADOW STALKER INSHORE

Model: SSG-C-701M, SSG-C-701MH
Length: 7'
Power: M; MH
Action: M/MF; MF
Pieces: 1
Line Weight: 8-17 lbs; 10-20 lbs
Guide Count: 9+1
Lure Weight: 3/8-1 oz; ½-1 ½ oz

Features: Lightweight, sensitive 24-ton carbon graphite rod blanks; OC-9 carbon outer wrap: Stripper guide to butt. Improves hoop strength; Fuji hardened aluminum oxide guides for trusted reliability; EVA and compresses cork fore grip for reduced weight and feel; EVA and compressed cork split grip reduces weight and improves balance; FG models feature a full EVA and compressed cork butt section; custom carbon C-40X spinning and casting skeleton reel seats; 701H-FG features a Fuji pipe reel seat; stainless steel hook keepers.
Price: **$99.99**

ST. CROIX LEGEND TREK

Model: LTC70MF3, LTC76MHF3, LTC76HF3, LTC76XHF3
Length: 7'; 7'6"; 7'6"; 7'6"
Power: M; MH; H; XH
Action: F
Pieces: 3
Line Weight: 8-17 lbs; 10-20 lbs; 15-30 lbs; 17-40 lbs
Guide Count: N/A
Lure Weight: 3/8-3/4 oz; 1/2-1 1/4 oz; 3/4-2 oz; 1-3 oz

Features: Integrated Poly Curve (IPC) tooling technology; Advanced Reinforcing Technology (ART); high-modulus/high-strain SCIV graphite with FRS for unparalleled strength and durability; slim-profile ferrules; Kigan Master Hand Zero Tangle guides with zirconia rings and titanium frames for the ultimate protection against saltwater corrosion; Fuji reel seats with exclusive E-finish hood(s); super-grade cork handle; corrosion-proof wind check and handle trim pieces; two coats of Flex Coat slow-cure finish; rugged rod case with handle and divided polypropylene liner.
Price: . . . . **$460–$500**

NEW Products: **Rods, Freshwater Fly Fishing**

CABELA'S 9-IRON

Model X: 995-4, 996-4, 998-4, 999-4, 9910-4
Length: 9'9"
Power: N/A
Action: N/A
Pieces: 4
Line Weight: 5W–10W
Guide Count: N/A

Lure Weight: N/A
Features: Features Winn's polymer grip technology with handles that reduce fatigue, enhance control, and minimize injuries due to repetitive motion; uniquely formulated polymer offers sensitivity and creates the perfect weight for optimal rod balance; fast-action 9'9" four-piece graphite blank loads easily when nymphing or using heavy sink-tip line for streamers.
Price: **$229.99**

NEW PRODUCTS

NEW Products: Rods, Freshwater Fly Fishing

NEW PRODUCTS

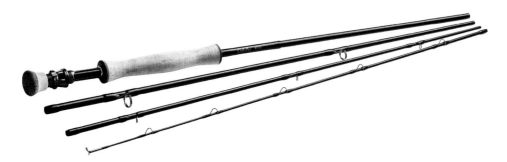

CABELA'S ATOLL

Model X: 908, 909, 910, 912
Length: 9'
Power: N/A
Action: N/A
Pieces: 4
Line Weight: 8W–12W
Guide Count: N/A
Lure Weight: N/A

Features: Features a fast action for casting heavy lines and large flies with precise accuracy in salt water; anodized reel seat withstands harsh saltwater conditions; skeletonized design with a carbon-fiber insert reduces weight for optimal balance; four-piece blank constructed of a high-modulus graphite blend; REC recoil guides always return to their original shape, won't corrode, and are 50 percent lighter than other types of stripper guides; titanium-carbide double-foot snake guides have a high, rounded arch design for smooth casting.
Price: $299.99

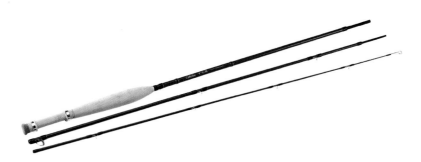

CABELA'S CGR FIBERGLASS

Model X: CGR 262-3, CGR 359-3, CGR 466-3, CGR 570-3, CGR 676-3, CGR 876-3
Length: 6'2"; 5'9"; 6'6"; 7'; 7'6"; 7'6"
Power: N/A
Action: N/A
Pieces: 3

Line Weight: 2W–8W
Guide Count: N/A
Lure Weight: N/A
Features: Features high-grade cork handles with model-specific grips and spigot ferrules; 5/6- and 7/8-weight rods feature fighting butts; 7/8-weight features a saltwater reel seat; all models include a nylon rod case.
Price: $129.99

CABELA'S PRIME FIBERGLASS

Model X: 360-1, 464-4, 471-1, 573-1
Length: 6'; 6'4"; 7'1"; 7'3"
Power: N/A
Action: N/A
Pieces: 1
Line Weight: 3W–5W
Guide Count: N/A
Lure Weight: N/A

Features: Features a one-piece fiberglass blank, eliminating ferrule-induced dead spots; slow full flexing action delivers dry flies gracefully, making it the ideal rod for small- to medium-sized trout streams; the 5-wt. model throws streamers and light poppers well; all models have a snub-nose half-wells cork handle and the 5 wt. has a fighting butt; ceramic stripper guides reduce friction to enhance the smooth feel; includes an olive rod sock.
Price: $159.99

CABELA'S RLS+

Model X: 864-4, 905-4, 906-4, 908-4
Length: 8'6"; 9'; 9'; 9'
Power: N/A
Action: N/A
Pieces: 4
Line Weight: 4W–8W
Guide Count: N/A

Lure Weight: N/A
Features: Features a moderate/fast action that delivers premium performance for a wide range of fishing scenarios; high-quality rod components offer lightweight strength and durability (8 wt. has an aluminum reel seat and fighting butt); models 905, 906, and 908 feature a double stripper, and 864 comes equipped with a single stripper; all models include a rod/reel case.
Price:. **$129.99**

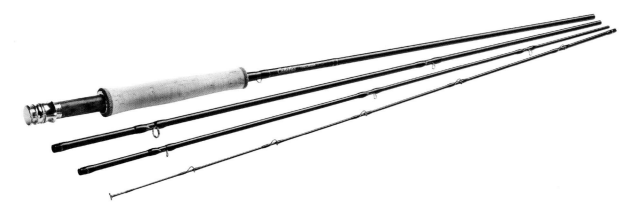

CABELA'S THEOREM

Model X: 763-4, 804-4, 904-4, 905-4, 906-4, 961-4 FB, 908-4
Length: 7'6"; 8'; 9'; 9'; 9'; 9'; 9'
Power: N/A
Action: MF; MF; F; F; F; F; F
Pieces: 4
Line Weight: 3W–8W
Guide Count: N/A

Lure Weight: N/A
Features: Features Generation-II nano-silica resin and a high-modulus graphite blank; four-piece high-modulus graphite blank features lightweight, corrosion-resistant REC recoil guides that always return to their original shape; tapers increase feel yet recover quickly for exceptional accuracy; burl-wood reel seat (3-6 wt.) or high-polish aluminum reel seat (8 wt.) with high-polish aluminum hardware and a modified western cork handle.
Price:. **$259.99**

FENWICK EAGLE FLY

Model X: EAFLY804WT-4, EAFLY865WT-4, EAFLY905WT-4, EAFLY906WT-4, EAFLY908WT-4,
Length: 8'; 8'6"; 9'; 9'; 9'
Power: N/A
Action: N/A

Pieces: 4
Line Weight: 4W–8W
Guide Count: 10; 10; 11; 11; 11
Lure Weight: N/A
Features: Cork handles provide lightweight comfort; classic Fenwick actions; travel tube.
Price:. **$99.95**

ORVIS RECON

Model: SI14ST-51-64, SI14SZ-51-64, SI14S1-51-64, SI14S3-51-64, SI14S5-51-64
Length: 8'4"; 9'; 8'6"; 9'; 9'
Power: N/A
Action: N/A
Pieces: 4
Line Weight: 3W–6W

Guide Count: N/A
Lure Weight: N/A
Features: Helios 2-inspired high-performance tapers; improved, unsanded ferrule design; lightest-weight rod in its class; new US made aluminum rod tube; shadow green blank with black nickel reel seat and dark burl wood insert; heavy-duty black nickel hardware; 7" half wells grip; silver snake and stripping guides.
Price: **$425**

ST. CROIX LEGEND X

Model: LXF9011.4
Length: 9'
Power: N/A
Action: MF
Pieces: 4
Line Weight: 11W
Guide Count: N/A
Lure Weight: N/A
Features: Blanks built with a multi-dynamic blend of four carbon materials provide dialed-in performance for casting big flies to the meanest predatory fish; Integrated Poly Curve (IPC) tooling technology; Advanced Reinforcing Technology

(ART); super high-modulus SCVI graphite with FRS in lower section for maximum power and strength with reduced weight; high-modulus/high-strain SCV graphite with FRS and carbon-matte scrim for unparalleled strength, durability and sensitivity; premium-quality SCII graphite with FRS in the tip section; slim-profile ferrules; Xtreme-Skin handle repels water, dirt, and fish slime and cleans up easily. Manufactured by St. Croix to provide outstanding angler comfort, casting efficiency, and sensitivity; anodized, machined-aluminum reel seat; Fuji K Series Tangle-Free stripper guides with Alconite rings; REC Recoil snake guides; two coats of Flex Coat slow-cure finish; alignment dots; rugged rod case with handle and divided polypropylene liner.
Price: . . . . **$500–$52**

NEW Products: **Rods, Saltwater Fly Fishing**

FENWICK EAGLE FLY

Model: EAFLY804WT-4, EAFLY865WT-4, EAFLY905WT-4, EAFLY906WT-4, EAFLY908WT-4,
Length: 8'; 8'6"; 9'; 9'; 9'
Power: N/A
Action: N/A
Pieces: 4

Line Weight: 4W–8W
Guide Count: 10; 10; 11; 11; 11
Lure Weight: N/A
Features: Cork handles provide lightweight comfort; classic Fenwick actions; travel tube.
Price: **$99.95**

ORVIS RECON

Model #: SI14S8-51-64, SI14TJ-51-64, SI14TS-51-64, SI14T4-51-64
Length: 9'
Power: N/A
Action: N/A
Pieces: 4
Line Weight: 7W–10W

Guide Count: N/A
Lure Weight: N/A
Features: Helios 2-inspired high-performance tapers; improved, unsanded ferrule design; lightest-weight rod in its class; new US made aluminum rod tube; shadow green blank with black nickel reel seat and dark burl wood insert; heavy-duty black nickel hardware; 7" half wells grip; silver snake and stripping guides.
Price: **$450**

ABU GARCIA ORRA S

Model: ORRA2S10; ORRA2S20; ORRA2S30; ORRA2S40
Gear Ratio: 5.8:1; 5.8:1; 5.8:1; 5.8:1
Inches/ Turn: 26.5; 30.5; 33; 37
Spool Cap. (M): 4 lbs/140 yds, 6 lbs/110 yds, 8 lbs/80 yds; 6 lbs/170 yds, 8 lbs/120 yds, 10 lbs/100 yds; 6 lbs/225 yds, 8 lbs/175 yds, 10 lbs/140 yds; 8 lbs/285 yds, 10 lbs/230 yds, 12 lbs/195 yds
Spool Cap. (B): 6 lbs/150 yds; 8 lbs/175 yds; 10 lbs/180 yds; 14 lbs/250 yds
Weight: 7.8 oz; 8.7 oz; 9.2 oz; 10.2 oz
Hand Retrieve: R or L
Max Drag: 10 lbs; 12 lbs; 12 lbs; 18 lbs
Reel Bearings: 7; 7; 7; 7

Features: Six stainless steel HPCR bearings + one roller bearing provides increased corrosion protection; ARC-6 (Aluminum reinforced C6 carbon) body design combines an X-Cräftic gearbox design with a C6 carbon body, which gives a lightweight construction that houses gears in perfect alignment; Rocket line management system provides better control of all types of fishing lines; Rocket spool lip design allows better control of line coming of the spool; machined aluminum braid ready spool allows braid to be tied directly to the spool without any slip; Slow Oscillation provides even line lay with all types of line; Carbon Matrix hybrid drag system for super smooth reliable drag performance; Everlast bail system for improved durability; stainless steel main shaft and components for improved corrosion resistance.
Price:. **$69.95**

ABU GARCIA ORRA SX

Model: ORRA2SX10; ORRA2SX20; ORRA2SX30; ORRA2SX40
Gear Ratio: 5.2:1; 5.8:1; 5.8:1; 5.8:1
Inches/ Turn: 26.5; 30.5; 33; 37
Spool Cap. (M): 4 lbs/140 yds, 6 lbs/110 yds, 8 lbs/80 yds; 6 lbs/170 yds, 8 lbs/120 yds, 10 lbs/100 yds; 6 lbs/225 yds, 8 lbs/175 yds, 10 lbs/140 yds; 8 lbs/285 yds, 10 lbs/230 yds, 12 lbs/195 yds
Spool Cap. (B): 6 lbs/150 yds; 8 lbs/175 yds; 10 lbs/180 yds; 14 lbs/250 yds
Weight: 8.10 oz; 8.30 oz; 8.80 oz; 10 oz
Hand Retrieve: R or L
Max Drag: 10 lbs; 12 lbs; 12 lbs; 18 lbs
Reel Bearings: 9; 9; 9; 9

Features: 8 stainless steel HPCR bearings + 1 roller bearing provides increased corrosion protection; ARC-6 (Aluminum reinforced C6 carbon) body design combines an X-Cräftic gearbox design with a C6 carbon body, which gives a lightweight construction that houses gears in perfect alignment; Rocket line management system provides better control of all types of fishing lines; Rocket spool lip design allows better control of line coming off the spool; machined aluminum braid ready spool allows braid to be tied directly to the spool without any slip; Slow Oscillation provides even line lay with all types of line; Carbon Matrix drag system provides smooth, consistent drag pressure across the entire drag range; Everlast bail system for improved durability; stainless steel main shaft and components for improved corrosion resistance.
Price:. **$99.95**

NEW PRODUCTS

BASS PRO MICRO LITE ELITE

Model: MEX05F, MEX10F
Gear Ratio: 5.2:1; 5.2:1
Inches/ Turn: 23; 24
Spool Cap. (M): 6 lbs/150 yds; 8 lbs/140 yds
Spool Cap. (B): N/A
Weight: 5.8 oz; 5.8 oz
Hand Retrieve: L; R
Max Drag: 6 lbs; 6 lbs

Reel Bearings: 6+1
Features: Perfect for crappie, trout, and panfish; smooth and precise 7-bearing system includes Powerlock instant anti-reverse; machined-aluminum folding handle and double-anodized aluminum spool is corrosion-resistant; carbon fiber drag system applies smooth and consistent pressure; ideal for casting lightweight lures on light line.
Price:. **$39.99**

CABELA'S PRO GUIDE

Model: PG1000, PG2500, PG3000, PG2000, PG4000
Gear Ratio: 4.9:1; 5.3:1; 5.3:1; 5.3:1; 5.3:1
Inches/ Turn: 21.4; 31.1; 31.1; 27.6; 37
Spool Cap. (M): 4 lbs/120 yds; 8 lbs/170 yds; 10 lbs/200 yds; 8 lbs/110 yds; 12 lbs/260 yds
Spool Cap. (B): N/A
Weight: 5.3 oz; 10.8 oz; 10.6 oz; 9.3 oz; 14.3 oz
Hand Retrieve: N/A

Max Drag: 4.4 lbs; 8.8 lbs; 8.8 lbs; 4.4 lbs; 13.2 lbs
Reel Bearings: 7+1; 9+1; 9+1; 9+1; 8+1
Features: Advanced locomotive levelwind promotes even line winding for reduced tangles; DigiGear digital-gear design maximizes winding power and delivers smooth retrieves; infinite anti-reverse and microclick front drag adjustment give you complete control of the action; long-casting ABS aluminum spool.
Price:. **$49.99**

CABELA'S TOURNAMENT ZX

Model: TZX1500, TZX2000, TZX2500, TZX3000, TZX4000
Gear Ratio: 6:1; 6:1; 6:1; 5.6:1; 5.7:1
Inches/ Turn: 27.6; 27.6; 31.1; 31.1; 37
Spool Cap. (M): 6 lbs/100 yds; 8 lbs/110 yds; 8 lbs/170 yds; 10 lbs/200 yds; 12 lbs/260 yds
Spool Cap. (B): N/A
Weight: 8.1 oz; 9.3 oz; 10.8 oz; 10.6 oz; 14.3 oz
Hand Retrieve: N/A
Max Drag: 4.4 lbs; 4.4 lbs; 8.8 lbs; 8.8 lbs; 14.3 lbs
Reel Bearings: 7+1

Features: 7+1 bearings deliver the cast-after-cast tournament-level performance; fine-tune the micro-click front-drag adjustment for precise drag on various sized fish; advanced locomotive levelwind evenly winds mono and braided lines; DigiGear digitally-designed gearing delivers smooth retrieves for season after season of use; infinite anti-reverse for rock-solid hooksets; rigid HardBodyz frame protects internal components from the elements; ABS aluminum spool is engineered for longer casts; lightweight Air Bail.
Price:. **$79.99**

NEW Products: **Reels, Freshwater Spinning**

DAIWA BALLISTIC EX

Model: BLS-EX2000H, BLS-EX2500H, BLS-EX3000H, BLS-EX4000H
Gear Ratio: 5.6:1
Inches/ Turn: 29.5; 33.2; 37.4; 39.9
Spool Cap. (M): 6 lbs/135 yds, 8 lbs/110 yds, 10 lbs/90 yds; 6 lbs/210 yds, 8 lbs/170 yds, 10 lbs/140 yds; 8 lbs/240 yds, 10 lbs/200 yds, 12 lbs/170 yds; 10 lbs/300 yds, 12 lbs/260 yds, 14 lbs/210 yds
Spool Cap. (B): N/A
Weight: 7.9 oz; 8.6 oz; 10.4 oz; 13.9 oz

Hand Retrieve: R, L
Max Drag: 8.8 lbs; 15.4 lbs; 15.4 lbs; 17.6 lbs
Reel Bearings: 1CRBB, 8BB, 1RB
Features: Magsealed construction; lightweight, corrosion-proof Zaion body and side cover; 10 Bearing System (1CRBB + 8BB + 1RB); Air Rotor for lighter weight and greater sensitivity; Air Bail of lightweight, hollow stainless; DigiGear digital gear design; waterproof drag; machine cut aluminum direct screw-in handle; two ball bearing spool support keeps drag washers in perfect alignment; ABS aluminum spool.
Price:. . . . .**$199.99–$209.99**

DAIWA EMCAST BR BITE N' RUN

Model: EMCBR4000A, EMCBR4500A, EMCBR5000A
Gear Ratio: 4.6:1
Inches/ Turn: 31.1; 33.8; 33.8
Spool Cap. (M): 10 lbs/300 yds, 12 lbs/260 yds, 14 lbs/220 yds; 12 lbs/350 yds, 14 lbs/300 yds, 17 lbs/220 yds; 17 lbs/250 yds
Spool Cap. (B): N/A

Weight: 16.8 oz; 17.8 oz; 17.5 oz
Hand Retrieve: R, L
Max Drag: 22 lbs
Reel Bearings: 7BB, 1RB
Features: Lightweight composite body, side cover and rotor; 8-bearing system (7BB + 1RB); machine-cut aluminum handle; Air Bail; Ultimate Tournament Carbon Drag (UTD) with 22 lbs Drag Max.
Price:. **$119.00**

DAIWA EXCELER EXE

Model: EXE1500SH, EXE2500SH, EXE2000SH, EXE3000H, EXE3500H, EXE4000H
Gear Ratio: 6.0:1; 6.0:1; 6.0:1; 5.6:1; 5.7:1; 5.7:1
Inches/ Turn: 30.4; 35.6; 31.6; 37.4; 38.5; 39.9
Spool Cap. (M): 8 lbs/80 yds; 10 lbs/140 yds; 6 lbs/135 yds; 10 lbs/90 yds; 12 lbs/170 yds; 14 lbs/170 yds; 14 lbs/210 yds
Spool Cap. (B): N/A
Weight: 8.1 oz; 9.3 oz; 8.1 oz; 10.8 oz; 13.6 oz; 13.6 oz

Hand Retrieve: R, L
Max Drag: 4.4 lbs; 8.8 lbs; 4.4 lbs; 13.2 lbs; 13.2 lbs; 13.2 lbs
Reel Bearings: 4BB, 1RB
Features: Narrow, rigid aluminum "Hardbodyz" body design; Air Bail; DigiGear digital gear design; Air Rotor for lighter weight and greater sensitivity; machine cut aluminum handle; Infinite Anti-Reverse; ABS aluminum spool; precision-click drag adjustment.
Price:. . . . .**$79.99–$89.99**

DAIWA LEGALIS LGL

Model: LGL1500SH, LGL2000SH, LGL2500SH, LGL3000H, LGL3500H, LGL4000H
Gear Ratio: 6.0:1; 6.0:1; 6.0:1; 5.6:1; 5.7:1; 5.7:1
Inches/ Turn: 30.4; 31.6; 35.6; 37.4; 38.5; 39.9
Spool Cap. (M): 8 lbs/80 yds; 10 lbs/90 yds; 10 lbs/140 yds; 12 lbs/170 yds; 14 lbs/170 yds; 14 lbs/210 yds
Spool Cap. (B): N/A
Weight: 8.1 oz; 8.1 oz; 9.3 oz; 10.8 oz; 13.6 oz; 13.6 oz

Hand Retrieve: R, L
Max Drag: 4.4 lbs; 4.4 lbs; 8.8 lbs; 13.2 lbs; 13.2 lbs; 13.2 lbs
Reel Bearings: 4BB, 1RB
Features: Narrow, rigid aluminum "HardBodyz" body design; Air Rotor for lighter weight and greater sensitivity; machine-cut aluminum handle; DigiGear digital gear design; Infinite Anti-Reverse; ABS aluminum spool; precision-click drag adjustment.
Price: . . . . $59.99–$69.99

DAIWA PROCYON EX

Model: PREX2000SH, PREX2500SH, PREX3000H, PREX4000H
Gear Ratio: 6.0:1; 6.0:1; 5.6:1; 5.7:1
Inches/ Turn: 31.9; 35.6; 37.4; 39.9
Spool Cap. (M): 10 lbs/90 yds; 10 lbs/140 yds; 12 lbs/170 yds; 14 lbs/210 yds
Spool Cap. (B): N/A
Weight: 8.6 oz; 9.2 oz; 10.9 oz; 14.6 oz

Hand Retrieve: R, L
Max Drag: 8.8 lbs; 15.4 lbs; 15.4 lbs; 17.6 lbs
Reel Bearings: 7BB, 1RB
Features: Narrow, rigid aluminum "Hardbodyz" body design; magsealed construction; Air Bail of lightweight, hollow stainless steel; DigiGear digital gear design; Air Rotor for lighter weight and greater sensitivity; waterproof drag; machine-cut aluminum handle; ABS aluminum spool.
Price: . . . . $149.99–$159.99

LEW'S AMERICAN HERO SPINNING SERIES

Model: AH200C, AH300C, AH400C
Gear Ratio: 6.2:1
Inches/ Turn: 26; 31; 34
Spool Cap. (M): 6 lbs/175 yds; 8 lbs/185 yds; 12 lbs/160 yds
Spool Cap. (B): N/A
Weight: 9.2 oz; 10.5 oz; 10.8 oz
Hand Retrieve: R/L
Max Drag: N/A

Reel Bearings: 4+1
Features: Rugged, lightweight, graphite body and rotor; double anodized aluminum spool; strong and balanced thick aluminum bail; thin compact gear box; Zero-Reverse one-way clutch bearing; precision cut solid brass pinion gear; fold down anodized aluminum handle with SoftTouch knob; adjustable handle for right or left hand retrieve; Speed Lube for exceptional smoothness and uninterrupted performance in all weather conditions; over-sized multiple disc drag system for smooth performance.
Price: . . . . $29.99–$31.99

LEW'S LASER LITE SPEED SPIN SERIES

Model: LLS50, LLS75, LLS100
Gear Ratio: 5.2:1
Inches/ Turn: 23; 23.5; 24
Spool Cap. (M): 4 lbs/150 yds; 6 lbs/120 yds; 8 lbs/120 yds
Spool Cap. (B): N/A
Weight: 6 oz; 6.4 oz; 6.7 oz
Hand Retrieve: R/L
Max Drag: N/A
Reel Bearings: 6+1

Features: Lightweight skeletal graphite rotor design; rugged, lightweight, graphite body and skeletal rotor; double anodized aluminum spool with holes; strong and balanced aluminum bail wire; thin compact gear box; Zero-Reverse, one-way clutch bearing; machined aluminum handle with Lew's custom knob. Fold down handle with SoftTouch knob; adjustable for right or left hand retrieve; Speed Lube for exceptional smoothness and uninterrupted performance in all weather conditions; oiled felt multiple disc drag system for smooth performance.
Price: **$29.99**

LEW'S TOURNAMENT PRO HP SPINNING SERIES

Model: TP200HP, TP300HP, TP400HP
Gear Ratio: 5.6:1; 6.1:1; 6.1:1
Inches/ Turn: 36; 42; 46
Spool Cap. (M): 6 lbs/150 yds; 12 lbs/170 yds; 14 lbs/220 yds
Spool Cap. (B):
Weight: 8.9 oz; 10.5 oz; 12.2 oz
Hand Retrieve: R
Max Drag: N/A
Reel Bearings: 9+1
Features: Large spool spinning reel for improved casting distance, improved drag performance, and less line twist; lightweight Carbon C40 high strength body and side cover with sealed body engineering; digi-balanced lightweight carbon skeletal rotor; premium 10-stainless steel bearing system; Zero-Reverse sealed one-way clutch bearing; stainless steel, lightweight hollow bail wire; parallel line lay oscillation system; oversized titanium line roller to reduce line twist; double anodized larger arbor aluminum spool; oversized smooth Carbon Teflon multi-disc sealed drag system; quality solid brass pinion gearing; durable stainless steel main shaft; external stainless steel screws; machine cut aluminum handle with Lew's Performance handle knob; adjustable for right or left hand retrieve; external lube port; Speed Lube for exceptional smoothness and uninterrupted performance in all weather conditions, from extreme heat to freezing cold.
Price: **$99.99**

LEW'S WALLY MARSHALL SIGNATURE SERIES SPINNING REELS

Model: WSP50, WSP75, WSP100
Gear Ratio: 5.2:1
Inches/ Turn: 22; 23.5; 24
Spool Cap. (M): 4 lbs/150 yds; 6 lbs/120 yds; 8 lbs/120 yds
Spool Cap. (B): N/A
Weight: 6 oz; 6.4 oz; 6.7 oz
Hand Retrieve: R/L

Max Drag: N/A
Reel Bearings: 5+1
Features: Lightweight graphite body and new skeletal rotor design; double anodized aluminum spool with gold accent lines; strong and balanced wire aluminum bail; thin, compact gear box; quality six-bearing system; Zero-Reverse one-way clutch bearing; collapsible handle adjusts for right or left hand retrieve.
Price: **$29.99**

NEW PRODUCTS

OKUMA RTX

Model: RTX-55, RTX-65, RTX-80
Gear Ratio: 4.5:1; 4.8:1; 4.8:1
Inches/ Turn: 37.5; 41; 44.5
Spool Cap. (M): 10 lbs/380 yds, 12 lbs/340 yds, 15 lbs/240 yds; 12 lbs/430 yds, 15 lbs/310 yds, 20 lbs/260 yds; 15 lbs/420 yds, 20 lbs/350 yds, 25 lbs/260 yds
Spool Cap. (B): N/A
Weight: 11.9 oz; 17.3 oz; 18 oz
Hand Retrieve: N/A
Max Drag: 20 lbs; 31 lbs; 33 lbs

Reel Bearings: 7+1
Features: Extremely lightweight C-40X carbon frame, sideplate, and rotor; multi-disc, Japanese oiled felt drag system; 7BB + 1RB stainless steel ball bearings; Quick-Set anti-reverse roller bearing; ALG: precision AlumiLite alloy main gear and oscillating gears; machined aluminum, 2-tone anodized spool; Precision Elliptical Gearing system; rigid, forged aluminum handle design with EVA handle knob; Hydro Block watertight drag seal; durable 1-pcs solid aluminum, gun smoke anodized bail wire; RESII: computer balanced Rotor Equalizing System.
Price:. . . . .**$114.99–$134.99**

PFLUEGER PATRIARCH XT

Model: PATXTSP30X, PATXTSP35X
Gear Ratio: 5.2:1
Inches/ Turn: 27; 28.8
Spool Cap. (M): 4 lbs/140 yds, 6 lbs/120 yds, 8 lbs/90 yds; 6 lbs/180 yds, 8 lbs/140 yds, 10 lbs/110 yds
Spool Cap. (B): 6 lbs/150 yds, 8 lbs/115 yds, 10 lbs/90 yds; 8 lbs/200 yds, 10 lbs/150 yds, 14 lbs/110 yds
Weight: 6.1 oz; 7.3 oz
Hand Retrieve: N/A
Max Drag: 10 lbs; 14 lbs

Reel Bearings: 10
Features: Magnesium body and rotor for a feather-light design; skeletonized spool extremely ported aircraft grade aluminum; sealed carbon drag-sealed system, always lubricated, always smooth; carbon handle 21% lighter than aluminum; titanium main shaft reduces weight and improves performance; carbon inlay rotor ultimate in lightweight rotor construction; carbon arbor lightweight spool design that combines carbon and aluminum; suitable for saltwater as well.
Price:. **$249.95**

PFLUEGER SUPREME XT

Model: SUPXTSP25X, SUPXTSP30X, SUPXTSP35X, SUPXTSP40X
Gear Ratio: 5.2:1; 6.2:1; 6.2:1; 6.2:1
Inches/ Turn: 22.8; 31.8; 33.8; 38.6
Spool Cap. (M): 2 lbs/220 yds, 4 lbs/110 yds, 6 lbs/90 yds; 4 lbs/255 yds, 6 lbs/145 yds, 8 lbs/130 yds; 6 lbs/230 yds, 8 lbs/185 yds, 10 lbs/155 yds; 8 lbs/285 yds, 10 lbs/230 yds, 12 lbs/195 yds
Spool Cap. (B): 4 lbs/200 yds, 6 lbs/140 yds, 8 lbs/110 yds; 6 lbs/275 yds, 8 lbs/190 yds, 10 lbs/160 yds; 8 lbs/250 yds, 10 lbs/220 yds, 14 lbs/160 yds; 10 lbs/320 yds, 14 lbs/280 yds, 20 lbs/200 yds

Weight: 6 oz; 6.8 oz; 8 oz; 8.7 oz
Hand Retrieve: N/A
Max Drag: 8; 10; 12; 14
Reel Bearings: 10
Features: Corrosion-resistant stainless steel ball bearings; magnesium body and rotor with feather light design; braid ready spool allows braid to be tied directly to spool; sealed carbon drag sealed system, always lubricated, always smooth; carbon handle is 21 percent lighter than aluminum; EVA knob with high density EVA, lightweight comfort; slow oscillation gearing - improves line lay and minimizes line twist; suitable for saltwater as well.
Price:. **$149.95**

Reels, Freshwater Spinning

SHIMANO STELLA FI

Model: STLC2000SFI, STL2500HGSFI, STLC3000XGFI, STL4000XGFI
Gear Ratio: 5.1:1; 6.0:1; 6.4:1; 6.2:1
Inches/ Turn: 27; 34.6; 36.6; 37.4
Spool Cap. (M): 3 lbs/136 yds, 4 lbs/109 yds, 5 lbs/82 yds; 5 lbs/120 yds, 6 lbs/104 yds, 8 lbs/77 yds; 8 lbs/197 yds,10 lbs/164 yds,12 lbs/109 yds; 10 lbs/186 yds,12 lbs/164 yds,14 lbs/136 yds
Spool Cap. (B): 3 lbs/125 yds, 4 lbs/105 yds, 5 lbs/90 yds; 5 lbs/140 yds, 8 lbs/120 yds, 10 lbs/85 yds; 10 lbs/200 yds, 20 lbs/140 yds, 40 lbs/105 yds; 15 lbs/280 yds, 30 lbs/170 yds, 50 lbs/150 yds
Weight: 6.3 oz; 7.7 oz; 7.9 oz; 9.3 oz
Hand Retrieve: R/L
Max Drag: 6.6 lbs; 8.8 lbs; 19.8 lbs; 24.2 lbs
Reel Bearings: 13
Features: The Stella FI series is more about finesse, making them perfect for light line applications in both fresh and salt water, from inland lakes to the coast; Micromodule Gear Technology delivers a new level of smoothness and reduced vibration for easier winding and better contact with the lure being retrieved; S-Direct Gear means more precise gear component alignment, reducing movement of critical parts within the reel; Coreprotect involves a sealed bail arm line roller, rotor and roller clutch, so the Stella FIs can be fished in a variety of environments without being affected by sand, dirt or water; G Free Body means the reel's center of gravity has been moved closer to the rod by positioning the worm shaft oscillation mechanism at the top of the reel body for less winding fatigue; 13 SA-RB bearings and an all-new design anti-reverse bearing, which generates less friction and lighter handle rotation; Titanium Bail Arm, a larger, ergonomically shaped drag knob for adjusting the new Coil Wave Spring Drag, a longer spool shape for greater casting distance, and a re-designed line clip for when the reel is not in use.
Price: . . . .**$789.99–$819.99**

WAVESPIN LEGEND 250

Model: N/A
Gear Ratio: 5.2:1
Inches/ Turn: N/A
Spool Cap. (M): 6 lbs/205 yds, 8 lbs/155 yds, 10 lbs/125 yds
Spool Cap. (B): 20 lbs/205 yds, 30 lbs/155 yds, 40 lbs/125 yds
Weight: 9.5 oz
Hand Retrieve: N/A
Max Drag: N/A
Reel Bearings: 7+1
Features: N/A
Price: **$139.95**

WRIGHT & MCGILL SÁBALOS PRO CARBON

Model: WMSABPC2000S, WMSABPC3000S, WMSABPC4000S
Gear Ratio: 6.0:1; 6.0:1; 5.5:1
Inches/ Turn: 33.5; 35.5; 37.5
Spool Cap. (M): 10 lbs/160 yds; 12 lbs/140 yds; 14 lbs/140 yds
Spool Cap. (B): N/A
Weight: 8.1 oz; 8.3 oz; 11.6 oz
Hand Retrieve: N/A
Max Drag: 14 lbs
Reel Bearings: 9+1
Features: Lightweight carbon body; 9+1 ball bearings: 2 ceramic, 7 stainless steel; dynamic balanced rotor; titanium coated anti-twist line roller; large diameter bail; ported aluminum spool with carbon ring; ultra cast spool; powerful front drag—14 lbs max drag; titanium main shaft; lightweight carbon handle with EVA paddles.
Price: . . . . **N/A**

NEW Products: **Reels, Freshwater Spinning**

WRIGHT & MCGILL SKEET REESE VICTORY PRO CARBON

Model: WMSRVPC2000S, WMSRVPC3000S, WMSRVPC4000S
Gear Ratio: 6.0:1; 6.0:1; 5.5:1
Inches/ Turn: 33.5; 35.5; 37.5
Spool Cap. (M): 10 lbs/160 yds; 12 lbs/140 yds; 14 lbs/140 yds
Spool Cap. (B): N/A
Weight: 8.1 oz; 8.3 oz; 11.6 oz

Hand Retrieve: N/A
Max Drag: 14 lbs
Reel Bearings: 9+1
Features: Lightweight carbon body; 9+1 ball bearings: 2 ceramic, 7 stainless steel; dynamic balanced rotor; titanium coated anti-twist line roller; large diameter bail; ported aluminum spool with carbon ring; ultra cast spool; powerful front drag—14 lbs max drag; titanium main shaft; lightweight carbon handle with EVA paddles.
Price: N/A

NEW Products: **Reels, Saltwater Spinning**

ABU GARCIA ORRA INSHORE

Model: ORRA2INS30; ORRA2INS35; ORRA2INS40; ORRA2SIN560
Gear Ratio: 5.8:1; 5.8:1; 5.8:1; 5.6:1
Inches/ Turn: 33; 36; 37; 35
Spool Cap. (M): 6 lbs/225 yds, 8 lbs/175 yds, 10 lbs/140 yds; 8 lbs/240 yds, 10 lbs/190 yds, 12 lbs/135 yds; 8 lbs/285 yds, 10 lbs/230 yds, 12 lbs/195 yds; 12 lbs/250 yds, 14 lbs/205 yds, 20 lbs/150 yds
Spool Cap. (B): 10 lbs/180 yds; 14 lbs/190 yds; 14 lbs/250 yds; 20 lbs/220 yds
Weight: 8 oz; 9 oz; 9.80 oz; 13.90 oz
Hand Retrieve: R or L
Max Drag: 12 lbs; 12 lbs; 18 lbs; 20 lbs
Reel Bearings: 9; 9; 9; 9
Features: Eight stainless steel HPCR bearings + one roller bearing provides increased corrosion protection; ARC-6 (Aluminum reinforced C6 carbon) body design combines an X-Cräftic gearbox design with a C6 carbon body, which gives a lightweight construction that houses gears in perfect alignment; Rocket line management system provides better control of all types of fishing lines; Rocket spool lip design allows better control of line coming off the spool; machined aluminum braid ready spool allows braid to be tied directly to the spool without any slip; Slow Oscillation provides even line lay with all types of line; Carbon Matrix drag system provides smooth, consistent drag pressure across the entire drag range; Everlast bail system for improved durability; Everlast bail system for improved durability; stainless steel main shaft and components for improved corrosion resistance; flat EVA knob provide greater comfort and durability; designed for saltwater applications.
Price: . . . . **$129.95–$149.95**

ABU GARCIA ORRA POWER FINESSE
Model: ORRA2PF35
Gear Ratio: 5.8:1
Inches/ Turn: 36
Spool Cap. (M): 8 lbs/240 yds; 10 lbs/190 yds; 12 lbs/135 yds
Spool Cap. (B): 14 lbs/190 yds
Weight: 9.30 oz
Hand Retrieve: R or L
Max Drag: 12
Reel Bearings: 9
Features: Eight stainless steel HPCR bearings + one roller bearing provides increased corrosion protection; ARC-6 (Aluminum reinforced C6 carbon) body design combines an

X-Cräftic gearbox design with a C6 carbon body, which gives a lightweight construction that houses gears in perfect alignment; Rocket line management system provides better control of all types of fishing lines; Rocket spool lip design allows better control of line coming off the spool; machined aluminum braid ready spool allows braid to be tied directly to the spool without any slip; Slow Oscillation provides even line lay with all types of line; Carbon Matrix drag system provides smooth, consistent drag pressure across the entire drag range; Everlast bail system for improved durability; stainless steel main shaft and components for improved corrosion resistance.
Price: **$99.95**

CABELA'S SALT STRIKER INSHORE
Model: SSI4000, SSI2500, SSI3000
Gear Ratio: 5.7:1; 6:1; 5.6:1
Inches/ Turn: 39.9; 35.6; 37.4
Spool Cap. (M): 12 lbs/260 yds; 8 lbs/170 yds; 10 lbs/200 yds
Spool Cap. (B): N/A
Weight: 13.6 oz; 9.3 oz; 10.8 oz
Hand Retrieve: N/A
Max Drag: 13.2 lbs; 8.8 lbs; 13.2 lbs

Reel Bearings: 7+1
Features: Seven ball bearings, three extra corrosion-resistant and one roller bearing, provides a super-smooth drive; narrow rigid aluminum HardBodzy design with effortless rotation; Air Rotor reduces weight and increases sensitivity; DigiGear digital gear system provides a perfect mesh between the rugged surface-treated alloy drive gear and marine bronze pinion gear for optimized speed, power, and durability; machine-cut aluminum handle; ABS aluminum spool; easy-to-adjust precision-click drag.
Price: . . . .**$99.99–$109.99**

CABELA'S SALT STRIKER SURF
Model: SSS5000, SSS6000
Gear Ratio: 5.1:1; 5.1:1
Inches/ Turn: 42.5
Spool Cap. (M): 17 lbs/310 yds; 30 lbs/230 yds
Spool Cap. (B): N/A
Weight: 23.1 oz
Hand Retrieve: N/A
Max Drag: 22 lbs
Reel Bearings: 7+1

Features: Seven ball bearings and one roller bearing provide a super-smooth drive; infinite anti-reverse delivers rock-solid hooksets; precision worm gear levelwind cross wraps your line for smooth releases and better casting; DigiGear digital gear system provides a perfect mesh between the rugged surface-treated alloy drive gear and marine bronze pinion gear for optimized speed, power, and durability; oversized handle knob and machined handle arm; ABS aluminum spool.
Price: . . . . **$79.99–$89.99**

NEW Products: **Reels, Saltwater Spinning**

DAIWA EMCAST PLUS SURF

Model: EMCP4500A, EMCP5000A, EMCP5500A, EMCP6000A
Gear Ratio: 4.6:1
Inches/ Turn: N/A
Spool Cap. (M): 12 lbs/390 yds, 14 lbs/310 yds, 17 lbs/230 yds; 14 lbs/410 yds, 17 lbs/310 yds, 20 lbs/240 yds; 20 lbs/290 yds, 25 lbs/230 yds, 30 lbs/200 yds; 25 lbs/320 yds, 30 lbs/240 yds, 40 lbs/190 yds

Spool Cap. (B): N/A
Weight: 23.3 oz; 23.3 oz; 27.9 oz; 27.9 oz
Hand Retrieve: N/A
Max Drag: 33 lbs
Reel Bearings: 10BB, 1RB
Features: Precision, worm gear levelwind; lightweight composite body, side cover and rotor; one-touch folding handle with oversize, soft touch power handle knob; ABS aluminum spool.
Price: **$89.99**

DAIWA EMCAST SPORT SURF

Model: EMCS4500A, EMCS5000A, EMCS5500A, EMCS6000A
Gear Ratio: 4.6:1
Inches/ Turn: N/A
Spool Cap. (M): 12 lbs/390 yds, 14 lbs/310 yds, 17 lbs/230 yds; 14 lbs/410 yds, 17 lbs/310 yds, 20 lbs/240 yds; 20 lbs/290 yds, 25 lbs/230 yds, 30 lbs/200 yds; 25 lbs/320 yds, 30 lbs/240 yds, 40 lbs/190 yds

Spool Cap. (B): N/A
Weight: 22.6 oz; 22.6 oz; 26.8 oz; 26.8 oz
Hand Retrieve: N/A
Max Drag: 33 lbs
Reel Bearings: 7BB, 1RB
Features: Precision, worm gear levelwind; lightweight composite body, side cover and rotor; one-touch folding handle with oversize, soft touch power handle knob; ABS aluminum spool.
Price: **$79.99**

DAIWA EMBLEM PRO-EX SURF

Model: Emblem Pro-EX Surf
Model: EMPEX5000, EMPEX5500
Gear Ratio: 5.1:1
Inches/ Turn: 48.9
Spool Cap. (M): 14 lbs/410 yds, 20 lbs/240 yds, 25 lbs/190 yds
Spool Cap. (B): 55 lbs/380 yds; 70 lbs/300 yds
Weight: 24 oz

Hand Retrieve: N/A
Max Drag: 33 lbs
Reel Bearings: 1CRBB, 5BB, 1RB
Features: Lightweight composite body, side cover & rotor; ultra tough Dura-Aluminum drive gear; machine-cut aluminum handle; soft touch power handle knob; ABS aluminum spool; line guard prevents line snags behind spool.
Price: . . . . **N/A**

OKUMA AVENGER ABF B-SERIES

Model: ABF-20b, ABF-30b, ABF-40b, ABF-55b, ABF-65b, ABF-80b
Gear Ratio: 5.0:1; 5.0:1; 4.5:1; 4.5:1; 4.5:1; 4.5:1
Inches/ Turn: 25; 25; 29; 30; 36; 40
Spool Cap. (M): 4 lbs/190 yds, 6 lbs/110 yds. 8 lbs/90 yds; 6 lbs/200 yds, 8 lbs/160 yds, 10 lbs/110 yds; 8 lbs/270 yds, 10 lbs/190 yds, 12 lbs/170 yds; 10 lbs/380 yds, 12 lbs/340 yds, 15 lbs/240 yds; 12 lbs/430 yds, 15 lbs/310 yds, 20 lbs/260 yds; 15 lbs/420 yds, 20 lbs/350 yds, 25 lbs/260 yds
Spool Cap. (B): N/A
Weight: 8.9 oz; 9.6 oz; 11.3 oz; 15.6 oz; 22.1 oz; 22.9 oz

Hand Retrieve: N/A
Max Drag: 8 lbs; 12 lbs; 13 lbs; 19 lbs; 33 lbs; 33 lbs
Reel Bearings: 6+1
Features: On/Off auto trip bait feeding system; multi-disc, oiled felt drag system; 6BB + 1RB bearing drive system; one Quick-Set anti-reverse roller bearing; precision machine-cut brass pinion gear; corrosion-resistant graphite body; rigid, diecast aluminum handle design; Precision Elliptical Gearing system; machined aluminum, 2-tone anodized spool; corrosion-resistant, stainless steel bail wire; RESII: computer balanced Rotor Equalizing System.
Price: . . . . **$49.99–$69.99**

OKUMA AZORES

Model: Z-55S, Z-65S, Z-80S
Gear Ratio: 5.8:1; 5.4:1; 5.4:1
Inches/ Turn: 39; 42; 46
Spool Cap. (M): 10 lbs/380 yds, 12 lbs/340 yds, 15 lbs/240 yds; 12 lbs/430 yds, 15 lbs/310 yds, 20 lbs/260 yds; 15 lbs/420 yds, 20 lbs/350 yds, 25 lbs/260 yds
Spool Cap. (B): N/A
Weight: 18.6 oz; 24.7 oz; 25.5 oz
Hand Retrieve: N/A
Max Drag: 29 lbs; 44 lbs; 44 lbs
Reel Bearings: 6+1

Features: DFD: Precision Dual Force Drag system; precision click drag adjustment for more precise settings; multi-disc, carbonite, and felt drag washers for DFD; 6HPB + 1RB corrosion-resistant stainless steel bearings; Quick-Set anti-reverse roller bearing plus ratchet system; dual anti-reverse system for maximum security; precision machine cut brass pinion gear; CRC: corrosion-resistant coating process; HDGII: corrosion-resistant, high-density gearing; ALC: rigid diecast aluminum body, sideplate and rotor; MSS: carbon Mechanical Stabilizing System; machined aluminum, 2-tone anodized spool with LCS lip; machined aluminum handle arm for added strength; Hydro Block watertight drag seal; heavy-duty, solid aluminum bail wire.
Price: . . . .**$119.99–$129.99**

NEW PRODUCTS

OKUMA CASCADE

Model: CA-25-CL, CA-30-CL, CA-40-CL
Gear Ratio: 5.0:1
Inches/ Turn: 25.4; 25.4; 30
Spool Cap. (M): 4 lbs/280 yds, 6 lbs/170 yds, 8 lbs/130 yds; 4 lbs/320 yds, 6 lbs/200 yds, 8 lbs/155 yds; 8 lbs/290 yds, 10 lbs/210 yds, 12 lbs/180 yds
Spool Cap. (B): N/A
Weight: 7.6 oz; 7.4 oz; 8.8 oz

Hand Retrieve: N/A
Max Drag: 15 lbs; 15 lbs; 16 lbs
Reel Bearings: 1BB
Features: Multi-disc, oiled felt drag system; multi-stop anti-reverse system; silver electroplated ABS spool; corrosion-resistant graphite body; corrosion-resistant, stainless steel bail wire; RESII: computer balanced Rotor Equalizing System.
Price:. . . . . **$11.99–$12.99**

OKUMA CAYMUS

Model: C-30, C-40, C-55
Gear Ratio: 5.0:1; 5.0:1; 4.5:1
Inches/ Turn: 25; 29; 30
Spool Cap. (M): 6 lbs/200 yds, 8 lbs/160 yds, 10 lbs/110 yds; 8 lbs/270 yds, 10 lbs/190 yds, 12 lbs/170 yds; 10 lbs/380 yds, 12 lbs/340 yds, 15 lbs/240 yds
Spool Cap. (B): N/A
Weight: 8.2 oz; 10 oz; 14.2 oz
Hand Retrieve: N/A
Max Drag: 13 lbs; 13 lbs; 18 lbs

Reel Bearings: 7+1
Features: Multi-disc, oiled felt drag system; 7 BB + 1RB for ultimate smoothness; Quick-Set anti-reverse roller bearing; precision machine-cut brass pinion gear; corrosion-resistant graphite body; rigid, forged aluminum, black anodized handle design ; lightweight, EVA handle knobs for comfort; Precision Elliptical Gearing system; machined aluminum, 2-tone anodized spool; heavy-duty, solid aluminum bail wire; RESII: computer balanced Rotor Equalizing System; Narrow Blade Body Design for reduced fatigue.
Price:. . . . . **$49.99–$54.99**

OKUMA HELIOS

Model: Hx-30S
Gear Ratio: 6.0:1
Inches/ Turn: 33.5
Spool Cap. (M): 4 lbs/355 yds, 6 lbs/225 yds, 8 lbs/175 yds
Spool Cap. (B): N/A
Weight: 8.8 oz
Hand Retrieve: N/A
Max Drag: 13 lbs
Reel Bearings: 8+1

Features: Lightweight C-40X carbon frame, sideplate and rotor; multi-disc carbonite drag system; 8HPB + 1RB corrosion-resistant stainless steel ball bearings; Quick-Set anti-reverse roller bearing; ALG: precision AlumiLite alloy main gear and oscillating gears; machined aluminum, 2-tone anodized spool; 1-K woven carbon fiber drag knob and sideplate inserts; Precision Elliptical Gearing system; 1-K woven carbon fiber handle design for reduced weight; light weight EVA handle knob; Hydro Block watertight drag seal; durable 1-pcs solid aluminum, gun smoke anodized bail wire; RESII: computer balanced Rotor Equalizing System.
Price: **$139.99**

OKUMA NYTRIX

Model: NX-25, NX-30, NX-40, NX-55, NX-65, NX80
Gear Ratio: 5.0:1; 5.0:1; 5.0:1; 4.5:1; 4.8:1; 4.8:1
Inches/ Turn: 25.4; 25.4; 30; 30; 37; 41
Spool Cap. (M): 4 lbs/280 yds, 6 lbs/160 yds, 8 lbs/130 yds; 4 lbs/320 yds, 6 lbs/200 yds, 8 lbs/155 yds; 8 lbs/290 yds, 10 lbs/210 yds, 12 lbs/180 yds; 10 lbs/340 yds, 12 lbs/300 yds, 14 lbs/255yds; 12 lbs/440 yds, 15 lbs/310 yds, 20 lbs/260 yds; 15 lbs/430 yds, 20 lbs/360 yds, 25 lbs/260 yds
Spool Cap. (B): N/A

Weight: N/A
Hand Retrieve: N/A
Max Drag: 15 lbs; 15 lbs; 16 lbs; 26 lbs; 33 lbs; 33 lbs
Reel Bearings: 1BB
Features: Multi-disc, oiled felt drag system; multi-stop anti-reverse system; machined aluminum, silver anodized spool; corrosion-resistant graphite body; rigid aluminum handle arm for strength; corrosion-resistant, stainless steel bail wire; RESII: computer balanced Rotor Equalizing System.
Price: . . . . **$17.99–$29.99**

NEW PRODUCTS

OKUMA TRIO REX ARENA
Model: TXA-60
Gear Ratio: 4.5:1
Inches/ Turn: 40
Spool Cap. (M): 10 lbs/460 yds, 14 lbs/340 yds, 18 lbs/260 yds
Spool Cap. (B): N/A
Weight: 20.2 oz
Hand Retrieve: N/A

Max Drag: 28 lbs
Reel Bearings: 2+1
Features: Crossover Construction aluminum body; lightweight graphite rotor with brush guards; 2BB+1RB stainless steel bearing system; heavy-duty, rigid aluminum handle arm; Comfortable Ergo Grip handle knob design; long cast, two tone anodized aluminum spool; brass worm shaft oscillation system; external bail trip design for maximum durability.
Price: **$99.99**

PLFUEGER SUPREME
Model: SUPSP25X, SUPSP30X, SUPSP35X, SUPSP40X
Gear Ratio: 5.2:1; 6.2:1; 6.2:1; 6.2:1
Inches/ Turn: 22.8; 31.8; 33.8; 38.6
Spool Cap. (M): 2 lbs/220 yds, 4 lbs/110 yds, 6 lbs/90 yds; 4 lbs/255 yds, 6 lbs/145 yds, 8 lbs/130 yds; 6 lbs/230 yds, 8 lbs/185 yds, 10 lbs/155 yds; 8 lbs/285 yds, 10 lbs/230 yds, 12 lbs/195 yds
Spool Cap. (B): 4 lbs/200 yds, 6 lbs/160 yds, 8 lbs/110 yds; 6 lbs/275 yds, 8 lbs/190 yds, 10 lbs/160 yds; 8 lbs/250 yds, 10 lbs/220 yds, 14 lbs/160 yds; 10 lbs/320 yds, 14 lbs/280 yds, 20 lbs/200 yds
Weight: 6.6 oz; 7.5 oz; 8.8 oz; 9.6 oz

Hand Retrieve: N/A
Max Drag: 8; 10; 12; 14
Reel Bearings: 9
Features: 9-bearing system; corrosion-resistant stainless steel ball bearings; magnesium body and rotor; feather light design; braid ready spool allows braid to be tied directly to spool; stainless steel/oil felt drag; consistent drag pressure, and corrosion-resistant; aluminum handle aircraft grade aluminum, extreme durability; soft touch rubber knob provides excellent grip and comfort; slow oscillation gearing improves line lay and minimizes line twist.
Price: **$99.95**

SHIMANO SARAGOSA SW

Model: SRG5000SW, SRG6000SW, SRG8000SW, SRG10000SW, SRG20000SW, SRG25000SW
Gear Ratio: 5.7:1; 5.7:1; 5.6:1; 4.9:1; 4.4:1; 4.4:1
Inches/ Turn: 38; 40; 42; 40; 41; 45
Spool Cap. (M): 10 lbs/240 yds, 12 lbs/195 yds, 14 lbs/165 yds; 12 lbs/265 yds, 16 lbs/170 yds, 20 lbs/120 yds; 14 lbs/345 yds, 16 lbs/250 yds, 20 lbs/185 yds; 12 lbs/500 yds, 16 lbs/320 yds, 20 lbs/220 yds; 20 lbs/460 yds, 25 lbs/380 yds, 30 lbs/320 yds; 20 lbs/570 yds, 25 lbs/490 yds, 30 lbs/360 yds
Spool Cap. (B): 20 lbs/245 yds, 30 lbs/225 yds, 40 lbs/175 yds; 30 lbs/290 yds, 50 lbs/195 yds, 65 lbs/215 yds; 40 lbs/340 yds, 50 lbs/265 yds, 65 lbs/215 yds; 50 lbs/405 yds, 65 lbs/220 yds, 80 lbs/185 yds; 65 lbs/490 yds, 80 lbs/400 yds, 100 lbs/340 yds; 65 lbs/630 yds, 80 lbs/520 yds, 100 lbs/440 yds
Weight: 18 oz; 19 oz; 22 oz; 24.3 oz; 33.3 oz; 34.2 oz
Hand Retrieve: R/L
Max Drag: 22 lbs; 22 lbs; 27 lbs; 33 lbs; 44 lbs; 44 lbs
Reel Bearings: 5+1; 5+1; 5+1; 6+1; 6+1; 6+1
Features: Super Stopper II anti-reverse uses a one-way roller bearing that eliminates back-play; X-Ship provides improved gear durability; bearings feature shields on both sides that reduce the possibility of salt or sand inhibiting the bearing's rotation; X-TOUGH DRAG with its dramatically enhanced smoothness, control and toughness anticipates the vigorous speed of blue-fin tuna and giant tuna.
Price: . . . .$259.99–$399.99

SHIMANO STELLA SW

Model: STL5000SWBHG, STL5000SWBPG, STL5000SWBXG, STL6000SWBHG, STL6000SWBPG, STL8000SWBHG, STL8000SWBPG, STL10000SWBPG, STL14000SWBXG, STL18000SWBHG, STL20000SWBPG, STL30000SWB
Gear Ratio: 5.7:1; 4.6:1; 6.2:1; 5.7:1; 4.6:1; 5.6:1; 4.9:1; 4.9:1; 6.2:1; 5.7:1; 4.4:1; 4.4:1
Inches/ Turn: 38; 31; 41; 41; 33; 42; 37; 40; 53; 51; 41; 52
Spool Cap. (M): 10 lbs/240 yds, 12 lbs/195 yds, 14 lbs/165 yds; 10 lbs/240 yds, 12 lbs/195 yds, 14 lbs/165 yds; 10 lbs/240 yds, 12 lbs/195 yds, 14 lbs/165 yds; 12 lbs/265 yds, 16 lbs/170 yds, 20 lbs/120 yds; 12 lbs/265 yds, 16 lbs/170 yds, 20 lbs/120 yds; 12 lbs/345 yds, 16 lbs/250 yds, 20 lbs/185 yds; 12 lbs/345 yds, 16 lbs/250 yds, 20 lbs/185 yds; 12 lbs/500 yds, 16 lbs/320 yds, 20 lbs/220 yds; 12 lbs/555 yds, 16 lbs/360 yds, 20 lbs/260 yds; 20 lbs/415 yds, 25 lbs/340 yds, 30 lbs/280 yds; 20 lbs/460 yds, 25 lbs/380 yds, 30 lbs/320 yds; 40 lbs/370 yds, 50 lbs/300 yds, 60 lbs/250 yds
Spool Cap. (B): 20 lbs/245 yds, 30 lbs/225 yds, 40 lbs/175 yds; 20 lbs/245 yds, 30 lbs/225 yds, 40 lbs/175 yds; 20 lbs/245 yds, 30 lbs/225 yds, 40 lbs/175 yds; 30 lbs/290 yds, 50 lbs/195 yds, 65 lbs/140 yds; 30 lbs/290 yds, 50 lbs/195 yds, 65 lbs/140 yds; 40 lbs/ 340 yds, 50 lbs/265 yds, 65 lbs/215 yds; 40 lbs/ 340 yds, 50 lbs/265 yds, 65 lbs/215 yds; 50 lbs/360 yds, 65 lbs/290 yds, 80 lbs/215 yds; 50 lbs/400 yds, 65 lbs/315 yds, 80 lbs/240 yds; 50 lbs/600 yds, 65 lbs/440 yds, 80 lbs/360 yds; 65 lbs/490 yds, 80 lbs/400 yds, 100 lbs/340 yds; 65 lbs/900 yds, 80 lbs/700 yds, 100 lbs/570 yds
Weight: 15.3 oz; 15.3 oz; 15.3 oz; 15.5 oz; 23.8 oz; 23.8 oz; 24.2 oz; 24.3 oz; 30.9 oz; 31.2 oz; 34.9 oz
Hand Retrieve: R/L
Max Drag: 29 lbs; 29 lbs; 29 lbs; 29 lbs; 29 lbs; 62 lbs; 62 lbs; 55 lbs; 55 lbs; 55 lbs; 55 lbs; 44 lbs
Reel Bearings: 14+1
Features: Super Stopper II anti-reverse uses a one-way roller bearing that eliminates back-play; X-Ship provides improved gear durability; X-Shield and X-Protect combine to provide extreme water resistance in the harshest conditions; The POWER ALUMINUM BODY, X-RIGID ROTOR, X-RIGID BAIL, and X-RIGID HANDLE combine to provide ultimate rigidity and eliminate loss of power caused by reel flex; X-TOUGH DRAG with its dramatically enhanced smoothness, control and toughness anticipates the vigorous speed of blue-fin tuna and giant tuna.
Price: . . . . $1059.99–$1259.99

MR. CRAPPIE SLAB SHAKER SPINCAST

Model: MSC1
Gear Ration: 4.3:1
Inches/ Turn: 12
Spool Cap. (M): 6 lbs/70 yds
Spool Cap. (B): N/A
Weight: 4.9 oz
Hand Retrieve: R/L

Max Drag: N/A
Reel Bearings: N/A
Features: Aluminum nose cone and spool; ball bearing drive system; spool-applied adjustable disc drag system; all metal gears, 4.3:1 gear ratio; smooth drag system with easy adjust drag dial; dual grip metal handle with dual soft touch grip knobs; adjustable for right or left hand retrieve.
Price:................................... **$14.99**

MR. CRAPPIE SLAB SHAKER UNDERSPIN

Model: MUS1
Gear Ration: 4.3:1
Inches/ Turn: 12
Spool Cap. (M): 6 lbs/70 yds
Spool Cap. (B): N/A
Weight: 4.9 oz

Hand Retrieve: R/L
Max Drag: N/A
Reel Bearings: N/A
Features: Aluminum nose cone and spool; ball bearing drive system; spool-applied adjustable disc drag system; all metal gears, 4.3:1 gear ratio; smooth drag system with easy adjust drag dial; adjustable for right or left hand retrieve.
Price:................................... **$14.99**

ZEBCO 33 MAX

Model: 33MXK.20C.BX6
Gear Ration: 2.6:1
Inches/ Turn: 16
Spool Cap. (M): 20 lbs/100 yds
Spool Cap. (B): N/A
Weight: 12.4 oz

Hand Retrieve: R/L
Max Drag: N/A
Reel Bearings: 1
Features: Dial-adjustable drag; dual ceramic pick-up pins; lightweight graphite frame; QuickSet anti-reverse; changeable right or left rand retrieve; ball bearing drive; built-in Bite Alert.
Price:................................... **$29.99**

NEW PRODUCTS

ZEBCO 33 MICRO

Model: 33MCK.04C.BX6
Gear Ration: 4.3:1
Inches/ Turn: 16
Spool Cap. (M): 4 lbs/90 yds
Spool Cap. (B): N/A
Weight: 5.6 oz

Hand Retrieve: R/L
Max Drag: N/A
Reel Bearings: 1
Features: Dial-adjustable drag; dual ceramic pick-up pins; lightweight graphite frame; QuickSet anti-reverse; changeable right or left rand retrieve; ball bearing drive; built-in Bite Alert.
Price:. $17.99

ZEBCO 33 MICRO TRIGGERSPIN

Model: 33MTK.04C.BX6
Gear Ration: 4.3:1
Inches/ Turn: 16
Spool Cap. (M): 4 lbs/90 yds
Spool Cap. (B): N/A
Weight: 6 oz
Hand Retrieve: R/L

Max Drag: N/A
Reel Bearings: 1
Features: Dial-adjustable drag; dual ceramic pick-up pins; lightweight graphite frame; QuickSet anti-reverse; changeable right or left rand retrieve; ball bearing drive; built-in Bite Alert.
Price:. $17.99

ZEBCO 33 PLATINUM

Model: 33KPL.10C.BX6
Gear Ration: 4.1:1
Inches/ Turn: 22
Spool Cap. (M): 10 lbs/95 yds
Spool Cap. (B): N/A
Weight: 9.7 oz

Hand Retrieve: R/L
Max Drag: N/A
Reel Bearings: 4+1
Features: Dial-adjustable drag; brass pinion gear; dual ceramic pick-up pins; all-metal body; anodized metal handle; Continuous Anti-Reverse; changeable right or left hand retrieve; 5 bearings (4 + clutch).
Price:. $34.99

NEW PRODUCTS

13 FISHING CONCEPT E
Model: E 5.3:1, E 6.6:1, E 7.3:1, E 8.1:1
Gear Ration: 5.3:1; 6.6:1; 7.3:1; 8.1:1
Inches/ Turn: 21; 26.1; 28.9; 32
Retrieve Speed: N/A
Spool Cap. (M): 12 lbs/100 yds
Spool Cap. (B): N/A
Weight: 5.78 oz
Hand Retrieve: N/A

Max Drag: 22 lbs
Reel Bearings: 3
Features: Hybrid Ceramic + 3 Anti Corrosion + 4 Stainless + 1 A/R Clutch Frame and sideplates are made using 13 Fishing's proprietary Featherweight Magnesium; high spin Ceramic spool bearings; ready for action in both fresh or saltwater; features the stopping power of the Japanese NTN Anti-Reverse roller clutch with a performance milled inner sleeve.
Price: **$380.00**

BASS PRO SHOPS REVOLUTION LOW PROFILE
Model: RNC300H, RNC300S
Gear Ration: 6.2:1; 5.3:1
Inches/ Turn: 28; 24
Retrieve Speed: N/A
Spool Cap. (M): 14 lbs/190 yds
Spool Cap. (B): 65 lbs/125 yds
Weight: 10.5 oz

Hand Retrieve: R
Max Drag: 20 lbs
Reel Bearings: 6+1
Features: 7-bearing system includes Powerlock instant anti-reverse; aluminum frame; double-anodized-aluminum spool with line pin; adjustable dual braking system; carbon washer drag system; cast control knob; Power Crank handle with Soft Touch PVC knobs.
Price: **$99.99**

CABELA'S ARACHNID
Model: ARACHNID 100XSL, ARACHNID 100XS, ARACHNID 100H, ARACHNID 100HL
Gear Ration: 8.1:1; 8.1:1; 6.3:1; 6.3:1
Inches/ Turn: 33.9; 33.9; 26.3; 26.3
Retrieve Speed: N/A
Spool Cap. (M): 14 lbs/120 yds
Spool Cap. (B): N/A
Weight: 7.6 oz
Hand Retrieve: L; R; R; L
Max Drag: 13.2 lbs

Reel Bearings: 11+1
Features: Features a wide-aperture T-Wing System that reduces line angles and friction no matter where it is positioned during the cast; Air Rotation System allows the spool to spin easily for longer casting distances; 12-bearing system; provides up to 13.2 lbs. of maximum drag pressure; durable, corrosion-resistant Zaion star drag; Magforce-Z Cast Control minimizes backlash while improving casting distance; lightweight aluminum frame, spool, and gear housing.
Price: **$179.99**

CABELA'S PRO GUIDE
Model: PG100H, PG100HL
Gear Ration: 6.3:1
Inches/ Turn: 25.7
Retrieve Speed: N/A
Spool Cap. (M): 12 lbs/120 yds
Spool Cap. (B): N/A
Weight: 7.7 oz
Hand Retrieve: R; L
Max Drag: 10 lbs

Reel Bearings: 7+1
Features: Lightweight composite frame and sideplate allow for easy thumbing and line maintenance; 90mm swept handle for less wobble, better feel, and winding power; Magforce cast control quickly adjusts for accurate casting with various lure weights; smooth seven-bearing system (7BB+1RB); I-shaped soft-touch handle knobs are easy to grasp; composite easy-adjust star drag.
Price: **$69.99**

NEW PRODUCTS

DAIWA AIRD AIR

Model: AIR100HA, AIR100HSA, AIR100HSLA, AIR100HLA
Gear Ration: 6.3:1; 7.1:1; 7.1:1; 6.3:1
Inches/ Turn: 25.7; 30; 30; 25.7
Retrieve Speed: N/A
Spool Cap. (M): 12 lbs/120 yds, 14 lbs/100 yds
Spool Cap. (B): 40 lbs/115 yds, 55 lbs/85 yds
Weight: 7.7 oz
Hand Retrieve: N/A

Max Drag: 11 lbs
Reel Bearings: 9BB, 1RB
Features: Brand new re-designed lightweight composite frame and side plate; Magforce cast control; Ultimate Tournament Carbon Drag (UTD) with 11 lbs Drag Max; 90mm Swept Handle for less wobble, better feel, and winding power; I-Shape soft touch handle knob; 10 bearing system (9BB + 1RB).
Price:. **$89.99**

DAIWA TATULA

Model: TATULA-HD200HL, TATULA-HD200HS, TATULA-HD200HSL, TATULA-HD200H
Gear Ration: 6.3:1; 7.3:1; 7.3:1; 6.3:1
Inches/ Turn: 28.1; 32.2; 32.2; 28.1
Retrieve Speed: N/A
Spool Cap. (M): 14 lbs/165 yds, 17 lbs/125 yds, 20 lbs/100 yds
Spool Cap. (B): 40 lbs/190 yds, 55 lbs/145 yds
Weight: 8.1 oz

Hand Retrieve: N/A
Max Drag: 13.2 lbs
Reel Bearings: 2CRBB + 5BB + 1RB
Features: T-Wing System (TWS); rugged, lightweight aluminum frame and side plate (gear side); air rotation; Ultimate Tournament Carbon Drag UTD; Magforce-Z cast control; iInfinite anti-reverse; corrosion resistant clutch mechanism; large, 90mm swept power handle with cutouts for reduced weight; I-shape handle knob.
Price:. **$149.99**

DAIWA ZILLION
Model: ZLNTW100H, ZLNTW100HL, ZLNTW100HS, ZLNTW100HSL, ZLNTW100P, ZLNTW100XXS, ZLNTW100XXSL
Gear Ration: 6.3:1; 6.3:1; 7.3:1; 7.3:1; 5.5:1; 9.1:1; 9.1:1
Inches/ Turn: 28.1; 28.1; 32.2; 32.2; 24.2; 40.3; 40.3
Retrieve Speed: N/A
Spool Cap. (M): 14 lbs/120 yds, 16 lbs/100 yds
Spool Cap. (B): 40 lbs/140 yds, 55 lbs/105 yds
Weight: 7.5 oz
Hand Retrieve: N/A
Max Drag: 13.2 lbs

Reel Bearings: 2CRBB + 7BB + 1RB
Features: T-Wing System (TWS); rugged, lightweight aluminum frame; free-floating A7075 aluminum alloy spool starts faster, spins longer; durable Zaion lightweight side plate (gear side); Ultimate Tournament Carbon Drag (UTD); large, 90mm swept power handle with cutouts for reduced weight; anodized parts coloring system: 9.1:1 XTRA HYPER SPEED: Purple, 7.3:1 HYPER SPEED: Red, 6.3:1 HIGH SPEED: Gold, 5.5:1 POWER: Black; 6-point support system; Magforce-Z cast control; I-shape handle knob; Zaion swept star drag; micro-click tension knob.
Price: **$299.99**

LEW'S AMERICAN HERO SPEED SPOOL BAITCAST REEL
Model: AH1H
Gear Ration: 6.4:1
Inches/ Turn: 28
Retrieve Speed: N/A
Spool Cap. (M): 12 lbs/120 yds
Spool Cap. (B):
Weight: 7.2 oz
Hand Retrieve: R
Max Drag: N/A
Reel Bearings: 4+1

Features: One-piece, lightweight, graphite composite frame and sideplates; five premium double-shielded stainless steel bearing system; Zero-Reverse one-way stainless steel clutch bearing; externally adjustable Magnetic Control System (MCS); machine-forged aluminum anodized blue spool; durable Rulon drag system, provides up to 10 lb. drag power; high strength solid brass main gear and crank shaft; anodized aluminum bowed handle with Lew's custom paddle handle knobs; Zirconia line guide; Quick and easy removable graphite palming sideplate; anodized aluminum blue spool tension adjustment knob; fully adjustable, smooth, bowed graphite star drag system.
Price: **$59.99**

NEW Products: **Reels, Freshwater Baitcasting**

LEW'S BB1 PRO SPEED SPOOL

Model: PS1, PS1HZ, PS1SHZ, PS1HZL, PS1SHZL
Gear Ration: 5.1:1; 6.4:1; 7.1:1; 6.4:1; 7.1:1
Inches/ Turn: 21; 28; 31; 28; 31
Retrieve Speed: N/A
Spool Cap. (M): 12 lbs/160 yds
Spool Cap. (B): N/A
Weight: 6.5 oz
Hand Retrieve: R; R; R; L; L
Max Drag: 14 lbs
Reel Bearings: 10; 9+1; 9+1; 9+1; 9+1
Features: Premium 10-bearing system with double-shielded stainless steel ball bearings; available in multi-stop (PS1) and

Zero-Reverse anti-reverse models (PS1HZ, PS1SHZ, PS1HLZ, PS1SHLZ); one-piece die-cast aluminum frame with graphite sideplates; braid-ready, machined forged, double-anodized, aluminum spool; 27-position externally adjustable SpeedCast Centrifugal Braking System; handle-side double anodized aluminum spool tension knob with audible click; audible click bowed metal star drag; bowed lightweight carbon fiber 95MM reel handle with Lew's custom paddle knobs; oversized titanium line guide positioned farther from the spool to minimize line friction and maximize casting performance; quick release sideplate mechanism provides easy access to spool; external lube port.
Price: **$199.99**

LEW'S BB2 PRO SPEED SPOOL SERIES

Model: PS2HZ, PS2SHZ, PS2SHZL
Gear Ration: 6.4:1; 7.1:1; 7.1:1
Inches/ Turn: 28; 31; 31
Retrieve Speed: N/A
Spool Cap. (M): 14 lbs/190 yds
Spool Cap. (B):
Weight: 6.8 oz
Hand Retrieve: R; R; L
Max Drag: N/A
Reel Bearings: 9+1
Features: One-piece die-cast aluminum frame with graphite sideplates; machine-forged aluminum, double anodized, U

shaped, large capacity, braid ready spool; premium 10-bearing system with double-shielded stainless steel ball bearings; externally adjustable 6-pin 27-position SpeedCast Adjustable Centrifugal Braking system (ACB); double anodized aluminum spool tension knob with audible click; carbon composite drag system with 14 lbs. of drag power; audible click, double anodized, bowed aluminum star drag; bowed, 95mm carbon fiber power handle with Lew's custom double power handle knobs; oversized titanium-coated Zirconia line guide positioned farther away from the spool to minimize line friction and maximize casting performance; quick release sideplate mechanism provides easy and quick access to the spool; external lube port.
Price: **$209.99**

NEW PRODUCTS

LEW'S TEAM LEW'S LITE SPEED SPOOL LFS SERIES

Model: TLL1H, TLL1SH, TLL1SHL
Gear Ration: 6.8:1; 7.5:1; 7.5:1
Inches/ Turn: 28; 31; 31
Retrieve Speed: N/A
Spool Cap. (M): 12 lbs/102 yds
Spool Cap. (B): N/A
Weight: 5.7 oz
Hand Retrieve: R; R; L
Max Drag: 14 lbs
Reel Bearings: 10+1
Features: One-piece die-cast aluminum frame; strong, lightweight Carbon C45 Carbon sideplates; double anodized gold detail finishing; aircraft-grade Duralumin drilled U shape spool, drive gear, crank shaft, and crank shaft; premium 11-bearing system with double-shielded stainless steel ball bearings and Zero-Reverse anti-reverse; externally adjustable 6-pin 27 position SpeedCast® adjustable centrifugal braking system (ACB); double anodized aluminum spool tension adjustment with audible click; rugged carbon composite drag system; double anodized, bowed audible click aluminum star drag; bowed lightweight 85MM carbon fiber handle with Lew's custom EVA foam cork lightweight handle knobs; titanium-coated Zirconia line guide; external lube port.
Price: **$239.99**

LEW'S TOURNAMENT LITE SPEED SPOOL SERIES

Model: LG1H, LG1SH, LG1HL
Gear Ration: 6.4:1; 7.1:1; 6.4:1
Inches/ Turn: 28; 31; 28
Retrieve Speed: N/A
Spool Cap. (M): 12 lbs/120 yds
Spool Cap. (B): N/A
Weight: 5.7 oz
Hand Retrieve: R; R; L
Max Drag: 14 lbs
Reel Bearings: 10+1
Features: One-piece, new lightweight C45 Carbon carbon frame and sideplates; drilled and forged, anodized aluminum U style spool; easily removable palming C45 carbon sideplate; premium 11 double-shielded stainless steel bearing system; Zero-Reverse one-way clutch bearing; externally adjustable 6-pin, 27 position SpeedCast; adjustable Centrifugal Braking (ACB) System; anodized aluminum spool tension adjustment with audible click; rugged carbon composite metal star drag system; bowed, lightweight, aluminum reel handle with Lew's custom paddle handle knobs; titanium-coated Zirconia line guide.
Price: **$179.99**

NEW Products: **Reels, Freshwater Baitcasting**

LEW'S TOURNAMENT MB SPEED SPOOL LFS SERIES

Model: TS1SMB, TS1HMB, TS1SHMB, TS1XHMB, TS1SHMBL
Gear Ration: 5.6:1; 6.8:1; 7.5:1; 8.3:1; 7.5:1
Inches/ Turn: 23; 28; 31; 35; 31
Retrieve Speed: N/A
Spool Cap. (M): 12 lbs/150 yds; 12 lbs/120 yds; 12 lbs/120 yds; 12 lbs/120 yds; 12 lbs/120 yds
Spool Cap. (B): N/A
Weight: 6.7 oz
Hand Retrieve: R; R; R; R; L
Max Drag: 14 lbs
Reel Bearings: 9+1
Features: One-piece die-cast aluminum frame; drilled and forged, double anodized aluminum U style spool; easily removable palming graphite sideplate; high strength solid brass gearing; premium double-shielded stainless steel bearing system; Zero-Reverse one-way clutch bearing; externally adjustable Multi-Setting Brake (MSB) dual cast control system utilizing both an external click-dial for setting the magnetic brake, plus 4 individually disengaging, disk-mounted internal brake shoes that operate on centrifugal force; double anodized aluminum spool tension adjustment with audible click; rugged carbon composite metal star drag system; audible click, bowed, anodized aluminum star drag; bowed, lightweight, aluminum reel handle with Lew's custom paddle handle knobs; Zirconia line guide; external lube port; TS1SMB features high capacity spool and a longer 95MM power crank handle.
Price:. **$139.99**

LEW'S SPEED SPOOL LFS SERIES

Model: SSG1S, SSG1H, SSG1SH, SSG1HL
Gear Ration: 5.6:1; 6.8:1; 7.5:1; 6.8:1
Inches/ Turn: 23; 28; 31; 28
Retrieve Speed: N/A
Spool Cap. (M): 12 lbs/150 yds; 12 lbs/120 yds; 12 lbs/120 yds; 12 lbs/120 yds
Spool Cap. (B): N/A
Weight: 7 oz; 6.9 oz; 6.9 oz; 6.9 oz
Hand Retrieve: R; R; R; L
Max Drag: 10 lbs
Reel Bearings: 9+1
Features: One-piece die-cast aluminum frame; double-shielded premium stainless steel bearing system with Zero-Reverse anti-reverse; drilled, machine forged and anodized aluminum U-style spool; high strength solid brass gearing; externally-adjustable magnetic brake system (MCS); Zero-Reverse one-way clutch bearing; easily removable palming graphite sideplate; rugged Rulon star drag system; anodized aluminum spool tension adjustment; anodized, bowed, aluminum handle with Lew's custom paddle knobs; external lube port; Zirconia line guide; deep-spool SSG1S cranking model with a longer 95MM handle.
Price:. **$99.99**

LEW'S SUPERDUTY SPEED SPOOL SERIES
Model: SD1XH
Gear Ration: 8.0:1
Inches/ Turn: 35
Retrieve Speed: N/A
Spool Cap. (M): 30 lbs/160 yds
Spool Cap. (B): N/A
Weight: 7.8 oz
Hand Retrieve: R
Max Drag: 14 lbs
Reel Bearings: 10+1
Features: Sturdy, lightweight one-piece all aluminum frame and aluminum sideplate on the handle side; double-

shielded premium stainless steel bearing system with Zero-Revere anti-reverse; lightweight machined, double anodized, deep capacity aluminum spool with drilled hole for braided line connection; high strength brass gearing for increased strength and durability; externally-adjustable Magnetic Control System (MCS); Zero-Reverse one-way clutch bearing; easily removable, palming graphite sideplate with SoftTouch armor finish; double anodized aluminum spool tension adjustment with audible click; rugged carbon composite double anodized metal star drag system; anodized, aluminum "power crank" 95MM reel handle with Lew's® custom paddle handle knobs; titanium-coated Zirconia line guide.
Price: **$179.99**

MR. CRAPPIE SLAB DADDY
Model: MC1H
Gear Ration: 6.2:1
Inches/ Turn: 25
Retrieve Speed: N/A
Spool Cap. (M): 12 lbs/125 yds
Spool Cap. (B): N/A
Weight: 7.2 oz
Hand Retrieve: N/A
Max Drag: N/A

Reel Bearings: 3+1
Features: One-piece, lightweight, graphite composite frame and sideplates; 4 stainless steel bearing system (3+1); Zero-Reverse one-way stainless steel clutch bearing; externally adjustable Magnetic Control System (MCS); machine forged anodized aluminum spool; quick and easy removable graphite palming sideplate; fully adjustable, smooth, graphite star drag system; aluminum handle with SoftTouch grip knobs.
Price: **$39.99**

OKUMA COLD WATER LOW PROFILE LINE COUNTER
Model: CW-354D, CW-354DLX
Gear Ration: 5.4:1
Inches/ Turn: 26.1
Retrieve Speed: N/A
Spool Cap. (M): 12 lbs/250 yds, 14 lbs/230 yds, 12 lbs/150 yds
Spool Cap. (B): N/A
Weight: 12.5 oz; 12.7 oz
Hand Retrieve: N/A
Max Drag: 25 lbs

Reel Bearings: 3BB + 1RB
Features: ALC: Rigid diecast aluminum frame and handle side plate; multi-disc, carbonite drag system; balanced aluminum handle arm with Ergo Grip handle knobs; Quick-Set anti-reverse roller bearing; oversized machine cut brass XL drive and pinion gears; machined aluminum, two tone anodized spool; mechanical line counter function measures in feet; CVT: Clear View Technology anti-fogging line counter; aluminum ratcheting drag star for precision drag settings; automatic trip, spool engaging mechanism; DLX represent left hand crank line counter models.
Price: **$159.99**

PFLUEGER PATRIARCH XTLOW PROFILE
Model: PATXT64LPX
Gear Ration: 6.4:1
Inches/ Turn: 26
Retrieve Speed: N/A
Spool Cap. (M): 10 lbs/175 yds, 12 lbs/145 yds, 17 lbs/100 yds
Spool Cap. (B): 20 lbs/190 yds, 30 lbs/140 yds, 50 lbs/100 yds
Weight: 5.8 oz

Hand Retrieve: R
Max Drag: 20 lbs
Reel Bearings: 11
Features: 11-Bearing system; corrosion-resistant stainless steel ball bearings; C45 Carbon Sideplate: 45 percent carbon material, lightweight durability; Ultimate Breaking System: 6-pin centrifugal and magnetic break, ultimate cast control; C-lock Sideplate System: cam locking sideplate allows for quick breaking adjustments.
Price:................................. $249.95

SHIMANO CURADO 200-I
Model: CU200IPG, CU200I, CU200IHG
Gear Ration: 5.5:1; 6.3:1; 7.2:1
Inches/ Turn: 26; 23; 30
Retrieve Speed: N/A
Spool Cap. (M): 8 lbs/180 yds, 10 lbs/155 yds, 14 lbs/110 yds

Spool Cap. (B): 30 lbs/190 yds, 50 lbs/120 yds, 65 lbs/80 yds
Weight: 7.4 oz
Hand Retrieve: R; L; R
Max Drag: 12 lbs
Reel Bearings: 5+1
Features: N/A
Price:....................................$180

WRIGHT & MCGILL SKEET REESE VICTORY II
Model: WMSRVII63RC, WMSRVII63LC, WMSRVII70RC
Gear Ration: 6.3:1; 6.3:1; 7.0:1; 7.0:1
Inches/ Turn: 23.5; 23.5; 27.5; 27.5
Retrieve Speed: N/A
Spool Cap. (M): 10 lbs/195 yds; 12 lbs/165 yds; 14 lbs/125 yds
Spool Cap. (B): 12 lbs/165 yds
Weight: 7.7 oz; 7.7 oz; 7.8 oz; 7.8 oz

Hand Retrieve: R/L
Max Drag: 12 lbs
Reel Bearings: 9+1
Features: Lightweight aluminum frame; unlimited anti-reverse; removable aluminum spool; removable graphite side plate; magnetic casting control; powerful and smooth drag; precision cut brass gears; EVA handle knobs; extra wide power handle; available in right/left retrieve; includes neoprene case.
Price:.................................. $105.99

NEW Products: **Reels, Freshwater Baitcasting**

WRIGHT & MCGILL SKEET REESE VICTORY PRO CARBON
Model: WMSRVPCC64R, WMSRVPCC79R
Gear Ration: 6.4:1; 7.9:1
Inches/ Turn: 26.5; 32.5
Retrieve Speed: N/A
Spool Cap. (M): 10 lbs/135 yds; 12 lbs/120 yds; 14 lbs/95 yds
Spool Cap. (B): 12 lbs/120 yds
Weight: 5.5 oz
Hand Retrieve: N/A
Max Drag: 14 lbs

Reel Bearings: 9+1
Features: Ultra light and strong carbon frame and side plates; 9+1 stainless steel bearings with corrosion resistance; unlimited anti-reverse; magnetic casting control; ultra speed "Triangle" line guide for increased casting distance; removable carbon side plate; removable, high speed, ported aluminum spool; powerful star drag and carbon drag technology—14 lbs max drag; 8mm stainless main shaft; 7075 aluminum main gear for strength and weight reduction; extra wide, ported, and curved carbon handle; comfortable, flat EVA paddles.
Price: **$159.99**

NEW Products: **Reels, Saltwater Baitcasting**

13 FISHING CONCEPT E
Model: E 5.3:1, E 6.6:1, E 7.3:1, E 8.1:1
Gear Ration: 5.3:1; 6.6:1; 7.3:1; 8.1:1
Inches/ Turn: 21; 26.1; 28.9; 32
Retrieve Speed: N/A
Spool Cap. (M): 12 lbs/100 yds
Spool Cap. (B): N/A
Weight: 5.78 oz
Hand Retrieve: N/A

Max Drag: 22 lbs
Reel Bearings: 3
Features: Hybrid Ceramic + 3 Anti Corrosion + 4 Stainless + 1 A/R Clutch   Frame and sideplates are made using 13 Fishing's proprietary Featherweight Magnesium; high spin Ceramic spool bearings; ready for action in both fresh or saltwater; features the stopping power of the Japanese NTN Anti-Reverse roller clutch with a performance milled inner sleeve.
Price: **$380.00**

NEW PRODUCTS

ABU GARCIA AMBASSADEUR 7000 C ROUND

Model: C-7000; C-7001
Gear Ration: 4.1:1; 4.1:1
Inches/ Turn: 22; 22
Retrieve Speed: N/A
Spool Cap. (M): 17 lbs/325 yds, 20 lbs/250 yds, 25 lbs/230 yds
Spool Cap. (B): 30 lbs/515 yds, 40 lbs/420 yds, 50 lbs/360 yds
Weight: 21.50 oz

Hand Retrieve: R; L
Max Drag: 20; 20
Reel Bearings: 2
Features: Corrosion-resistant instant anti-reverse bearing provides greater protection; smooth and consistent multi-disc drag system; Duragear brass gear for extended gear life; 4-pin centrifugal brake gives consistent brake pressure throughout the cast; extended bent handle with power knobs for increased cranking power; synchronized level wind system improves line lay and castability.
Price:. **$149.95**

ABU GARCIA AMBASSADEUR 7000 C3 ROUND

Model: C3-7000
Gear Ration: 4.1:1
Inches/ Turn: 22
Retrieve Speed: N/A
Spool Cap. (M): 17 lbs/325 yds, 20 lbs/250 yds, 25 lbs/230 yds
Spool Cap. (B): 30 lbs/515 yds, 40 lbs/420 yds, 50 lbs/360 yds
Weight: 21.50 oz
Hand Retrieve: R

Max Drag: 20 lbs
Reel Bearings: 3
Features: 2 stainless steel ball bearings + 1 roller bearing provides smooth operation; Duragear brass gear for extended gear life; Carbon Matrix drag system provides smooth, consistent drag pressure across the entire drag range; 4-pin centrifugal brake gives consistent brake pressure throughout the cast; extended bent handle with power knobs for increased cranking power; synchronized level wind system improves line lay and castability; corrosion-resistant instant anti-reverse bearing provides greater protection.
Price:. **$169.95**

ABU GARCIA AMBASSADEUR CS PRO ROCKET
Model: CS-7000
Gear Ration: 4.1:1
Inches/ Turn: 22
Retrieve Speed: N/A
Spool Cap. (M): 17 lbs/325 yds, 20 lbs/250 yds, 25 lbs/230 yds
Spool Cap. (B): 30 lbs/515 yds, 40 lbs/420 yds, 50 lbs/360 yds
Weight: 21.50 oz
Hand Retrieve: R

Max Drag: 20 lbs
Reel Bearings: 3
Features: 2 stainless steel ball bearings + 1 roller bearing provides smooth operation; Duragear brass gear for extended gear life; Carbon Matrix drag system provides smooth, consistent drag pressure across the entire drag range; 4-pin centrifugal brake gives consistent brake pressure throughout the cast; extended bent handle with power knobs for increased cranking power; synchronized level wind system improves line lay and castability; corrosion-resistant instant anti-reverse bearing provides greater protection.
Price:. $179.95

ABU GARCIA AMBASSADEUR STRIPER SPECIAL
Model: C3-6500STSPC
Gear Ration: 5.3:1
Inches/ Turn: 26
Retrieve Speed: N/A
Spool Cap. (M): 14 lbs/275 yds
Spool Cap. (B): 30 lbs/310 yds
Weight: 11.6 oz

Hand Retrieve: R
Max Drag: 15 lbs
Reel Bearings: 4
Features: 3 stainless steel ball bearings + 1 roller bearing; Carbon Matrix drag system provides smooth, consistent drag pressure across the entire drag range; extended bent handle for increased cranking power; 6-pin centrifugal brake gives consistent brake pressure throughout the cast; synchronized level wind system improves line lay and castability.
Price:. $149.95

Reels, Saltwater Baitcasting

NEW PRODUCTS

ABU GARCIA BLUE YONDER

Model: BY-6500; BY-7000
Gear Ration: 6.3:1; 5.3:1
Inches/ Turn: 30; 28
Retrieve Speed: N/A
Spool Cap. (M): 14 lbs/275 yds; 17 lbs/325 yds, 20 lbs/250 yds; 25 lbs/230 yds
Spool Cap. (B): 30 lbs/310 yds; 30 lbs/515 yds, 40 lbs/420 yds, 50 lbs/360 yds
Weight: 12.20 oz; 19.50 oz
Hand Retrieve: R; R

Max Drag: 15 lbs; 20 lbs
Reel Bearings: 3; 3
Features: 2 stainless steel ball bearings + 1 roller bearing provides smooth operation; Duragear brass gear for extended gear life; Carbon Matrix drag system provides smooth, consistent drag pressure across the entire drag range; MagTrax brake system gives consistent brake pressure throughout the cast; extended bent handle with power knobs for increased cranking power; open CT frame for easy line access; corrosion-resistant instant anti-reverse bearing provides greater protection.
Price: **$249.95**

ABU GARCIA REVO BEAST

Model: RVO3 BEAST; RVO3 BEAST-L
Gear Ration: 7.1:1; 7.1:1
Inches/ Turn: 29; 29
Retrieve Speed: N/A
Spool Cap. (M): 10 lbs/225 yds, 12 lbs/180 yds; 17 lbs/130 yds
Spool Cap. (B): 20 lbs/235 yds, 30 lbs/180 yds, 50 lbs/125 yds
Weight: 9.40 oz; 9.40 oz
Hand Retrieve: R; L
Max Drag: 22 lbs; 22 lbs
Reel Bearings: 8; 8
Features: X-Cräftic alloy frame and sideplates for increased corrosion resistance; 7 stainless steel HPCR bearings + 1 roller bearing provides increased corrosion protection; titanium coated sideplates provide increased scratch resistance; extended bent handle for increased cranking power; round EVA knob provides improved grip for improved cranking power; Carbon Matrix drag system provides smooth, consistent drag pressure across the entire drag range; Duragear brass gear for extended gear life; Infini brake system allows almost limitless adjustability to handle any fishing situation; Ti coated line guide reduces friction and improves durability; Infini II spool design for extended castability and extreme loads; D2 Gear Design provides a more efficient gear system while improving gear durability; corrosion-resistant instant anti-reverse bearing provides greater protection.
Price: **$349.95**

DAIWA AIRD COASTAL

Model: AIRCL100HA, AIRCL100HSA, AIRCL100HSLA, AIRCL100HLA
Gear Ration: 6.3:1; 7.1:1; 7.1:1; 6.3:1
Inches/ Turn: 25.7; 30; 30; 25.7
Retrieve Speed: N/A
Spool Cap. (M): 12 lbs/160 yds, 14 lbs/135 yds, 16 lbs/110 yds
Spool Cap. (B): 40 lbs/150 yds, 55 lbs/110 yds
Weight: 7.9 oz

Hand Retrieve: N/A
Max Drag: 11 lbs
Reel Bearings: 2CRBB + 4BB + 1RB
Features: Brand new re-designed lightweight composite frame and side plate; Magforce cast control; Ultimate Tournament Carbon Drag (UTD); A7075 aluminum spool, super lightweight—extra strong (100 size); extra line capacity for strong lines, powerful fish; 100mm swept handle with weight-reducing cutouts; oversized I-shape soft touch handle knob; durable metal star drag.
Price: **$99.99**

DAIWA LAGUNA

Model: LGN100HA, LGN100HSA, LGN100HLA, LGN100HSLA
Gear Ration: 6.3:1; 7.1:1; 6.3:1; 7.1:1
Inches/ Turn: 25.7; 30; 25.7; 30
Retrieve Speed: N/A
Spool Cap. (M): 12 lbs/120 yds, 14 lbs/100 yds
Spool Cap. (B): 40 lbs/115 yds, 55 lbs/85 yds
Weight: 7.7 oz

Hand Retrieve: N/A
Max Drag: 10 lbs
Reel Bearings: 5BB, 1RB
Features: Brand new re-designed lightweight composite frame and side plate; 90mm Swept Handle for less wobble, better feel and winding power; I-Shape soft touch handle knob; 6-bearing system (5BB + 1RB); Magforce cast control; composite easy adjust star drag.
Price: **$59.99**

DAIWA SEALINE SLW LEVELWIND

Model: SLW30HL, SLW20HL
Gear Ration: 6.1:1
Inches/ Turn: 24.4
Spool Cap. (M): 14 lbs/480 yds, 20 lbs/295 yds, 25 lbs/230 yds; 12 lbs/450 yds, 14 lbs/360 yds, 20 lbs/210 yds
Spool Cap. (B): 40 lbs/380 yds, 50 lbs/280 yds; 40 lbs/260 yds, 50 lbs/200 yds

Weight: 15.9 oz; 14.6 oz
Hand Retrieve: N/A
Max Drag: 15.4 lbs
Reel Bearings: 1BB, 1RB
Features: Rugged, corrosion-proof composite frame; 2-bearing system (1BB, 1RB); oversize line guide aperture for copper wire line; 20-pound drag max; fast 6.1 to 1 gear ratio; Power Handle with oversize grip.
Price:.............................$99.99–$119.99

LEW'S BB2 INSHORE SPEED SPOOL SERIES

Model: IS2SH, IS2SHL
Gear Ration: 7.1:1
Inches/ Turn: 31
Retrieve Speed: N/A
Spool Cap. (M): 14 lbs/190 yds
Spool Cap. (B):
Weight: 8.1 oz
Hand Retrieve: R; L
Max Drag: 14 lbs
Reel Bearings: 7+1
Features: One-piece all aluminum frame and handle sideplate with three external drain ports of frame; braid ready, machined forged, double anodized, deep capacity, aluminum spool; high strength brass gearing for durability;

premium 8-bearing system with double-shielded stainless steel ball bearings and Zero-Reverse anti-reverse; externally-adjustable Multi-Setting Brake (MSB) dual cast control system utilizing both an external click-dial for setting the magnetic brake, plus 4 individually disengaging, disk-mounted internal brake shoes that operate on centrifugal force; double anodized aluminum spool tension knob with audible click; rugged carbon composite drag system that provides up to 14 lb. of drag power; audible click bowed anodized metal star drag; bowed 95MM anodized aluminum cranking handle with New EVA power handle knobs; oversized silver titanium line guide positioned farther from the spool to minimize line friction and maximize casting performance; quick release sideplate mechanism provides easy access to spool and centrifugal brake system; external lube port.
Price:.................................. $209.99

OKUMA CAYMUS

Model: C-266W-CL
Gear Ration: 6.6:1
Inches/ Turn: 28.5
Spool Cap. (M): 10 lbs/160 yds, 12 lbs/130 yds, 14 lbs/95 yds
Spool Cap. (B): N/A
Weight: 7.6 oz
Hand Retrieve: N/A

Max Drag: 11 lbs
Reel Bearings: 6BB + 1RB
Features: Corrosion-resistant graphite frame and side plates; A6061-T6 machined aluminum, anodized U-shaped spool; multi-disc composite drag system; external adjustable magnetic cast control system; Quick-Set anti-reverse roller bearing; side plate access port for quick spool changes; ergonomic handle design allows cranking closer to body.
Price:................................... $54.99

Okuma Andros Special Edition

Okuma Andros Two-Speed A-Series

Okuma Metaloid

OKUMA ANDROS SPECIAL EDITION

Model: A-12SSE, A-16SSE
Gear Ratio: 6.4:1
Inches/ Turn: 48.4; 58.5
Spool Cap. (M): 20 lbs/560 yds, 25 lbs/420 yds, 30 lbs/30 yds; 20 lbs/870 yds, 25 lbs/650 yds, 30 lbs/500 yds
Spool Cap. (B): N/A
Weight: 24 oz; 58.5 oz
Hand Retrieve: N/A
Max Drag: 5.7-10 lbs
Reel Bearings: 6BB, 1RB
Features: Optimized for fishing consistent light drag settings; features TDC drag cams for gradual drag curves; rigid 1-pc frame and left sideplate construction; 6061-T6 Machined aluminum frame and sideplates; cold forged, Type-II anodized, machined aluminum spool; CRC: Corrosion Resistant Coating process; dual anti-reverse system (Mechanical and roller bearing); quick-set anti-reverse bearing allows for zero handle back play; Ergo Grip handle knob with anodized aluminum handle arm; one screw right sideplate take down for easy internal access; 17-4 grade stainless steel helical cut gearing; silent retrieve system for ultimate cranking smoothness; carbonite drag system with Cal's drag grease; integrated recessed reel foot design for low profile rod fit; lug and plug system on 12 and 16 sizes; all models feature durable Ergo grip handle knobs; On/Off bait clicker designed for kite fishing.
Price: . . . .**$319.99–$349.99**

OKUMA ANDROS TWO-SPEED A-SERIES

Model: A-12IIa, A-12SIIa, A-16IIa, A-5IIa, A-5NIIa
Gear Ratio: 4.7:1 & 2.1:1; 6.4:1 & 2.1:1; 4.3:1 & 1.3:1; 6.4:1 & 3.8:1; 6.4:1 & 3.8:1
Inches/ Turn: 35.4 & 15.7; 48.4 & 15.7; 39.3 & 11.9; 42.1 & 24.8; 42.1 & 24.8
Spool Cap. (M): 20 lbs/560 yds, 25 lbs/420 yds, 30 lbs/320 yds; 20 lbs/560 yds, 25 lbs/420 yds, 30 lbs/320 yds; 20 lbs/870 yds, 25 lbs/650 yds, 30 lbs/500 yds; 12 lbs/620 yds, 15 lbs/430 yds, 20 lbs/340 yds; 12 lbs/420 yds, 15 lbs/300 yds, 20 lbs/250 yds
Spool Cap. (B): N/A
Weight: 24.7 oz; 24.7 oz; 30.1 oz; 15.2 oz; 14.8 oz
Hand Retrieve: N/A
Max Drag: 27-34 lbs; 27-34 lbs; 27-48 lbs; 15-24 lbs; 15-24 lbs
Reel Bearings: 6BB
Features: Rigid 1-piece frame and left sideplate construction; 6061-T6 machined aluminum frame and sideplates; cold forged, Type-II anodized, machined aluminum spool; CRC: Corrosion Resistant Coating process; external adjustable cast control system; stainless steel ratchet drag lever for precise drag settings; Ergo Grip handle knob with anodized aluminum handle arm; one screw right sideplate take down for easy internal access; 17-4 grade stainless steel helical cut gearing; silent retrieve system for ultimate cranking smoothness; Carbonite Dual Force Drag System with Cal's drag grease; all models feature an anodized aluminum gear shifter housing; integrated recessed reel foot design for low profile rod fit; lug and plug system on 12 and 16 size; all models feature durable Ergo grip handle knobs.
Price: . . . .**$319.99–$389.99**

OKUMA METALOID

Model: M-12II, M-12S, M-5II, M-5NII, M-5NS, M-5S
Gear Ratio: 4.7:1 & 2.1:1; 6.4:1; 6.4:1 & 3.8:1; 6.4:1 & 3.8:1; 6.4:1
Inches/ Turn: 35.4 & 15.7; 48.4; 42.1 & 24.8; 42.1 & 24.8; 42.1
Spool Cap. (M): 20 lbs/560 yds, 25 lbs/420 yds, 30 lbs/320 yds; 20 lbs/560 yds, 25 lbs/420 yds, 30 lbs/320 yds; 12 lbs/620 yds, 15 lbs/430 yds, 20 lbs/340 yds; 12 lbs/420 yds, 15 lbs/300 yds, 20 lbs/250 yds; 12 lbs/420 yds, 15 lbs/300 yds, 20 lbs/250 yds
Spool Cap. (B): N/A
Weight: 24.5 oz; 25.3 oz; 15.9 oz; 15.7 oz; 15.4 oz
Hand Retrieve: N/A
Max Drag: 34 lbs; 34 lbs; 24 lbs; 24 lbs; 24 lbs
Reel Bearings: 4BB
Features: Rigid 1-pcs frame and left sideplate construction; 6061-T6 Machined aluminum frame and sideplates; cold forged, Type-II anodized, machined aluminum spool; CRC: Corrosion Resistant Coating process; available in both 2-speed or single speed versions; Ergo Grip handle knob with anodized aluminum handle arm; 17-4 grade stainless steel helical cut gearing; silent retrieve system for cranking smoothness; carbonite drag system with Cal's drag grease; all models feature durable Ergo grip handle knobs; On/Off bait clicker for all models.
Price: . . . .**$189.99–$299.99**

NEW Products: **Reels, Saltwater Baitcasting**

OKUMA CERROS LOWPROFILE
Model: CR-266V, CR-266VLX, CR-273V
Gear Ration: 6.6:1; 6.6:1; 7.3:1
Inches/ Turn: 28.5; 28.5; 31.6
Retrieve Speed: N/A
Spool Cap. (M): 10 lbs/160 yds, 12 lbs/130 yds, 14 lbs/95 yds
Spool Cap. (B): N/A
Weight: 7.9 oz
Hand Retrieve: R/L
Max Drag: 11 lbs

Reel Bearings: 9BB + 1RB
Features: ALC: Rigid diecast aluminum frame; A6061-T6 machined aluminum, anodized V-shaped spool; multi-disc composite drag system; micro-click drag star for precise drag settings; external adjustable magnetic cast control system; 24-point adjustment on cast control for precise settings; Quick-Set anti-reverse roller bearing; corrosion resistant graphite side plates; side plate access port for quick spool changes; lightweight and comfortable EVA handle knobs.
Price:...................................$99.99

NEW Products: **Freshwater Fly Fishing**

CABELA'S WLX II
Model: 3/4, 5/6, 7/8, 9/10
Diameter (in.): 3.15; 3.3; 3.74; 4.4
Weight (oz.): 4.5 oz; 4.7 oz; 5.8 oz; 7.3 oz
Spool Cap. (M): 20 lbs/75 yds WF4; 20 lbs/100 yds WF6; 20 lbs/225 yds WF8; 30 lbs/250 yds WF10

Hand Retrieve: L or R
Features: Fully sealed, proven conical drag has minimal startup inertia; Torrington Zero-Lash Roller Clutch won't wear out; machined 6061 aluminum with a sleek black-satin anodized finish; unique large arbor results in consistent drag torque.
Price:...........................$199.99–$229.99

HATCH 2 PLUS FINATIC
Diameter (in.): 3
Weight (oz.): 3.7 oz
Spool Cap. (M): N/A
Spool Cap. (B): N/A

Hand Retrieve: N/A
Line Weight: 2W–4W
Features: Fully CNC machined in Vista, CA with a proprietary Rulon/Stainless Steel stacked disk drag; available in five color options and large arbor only.
Price:....................................$380

NEW Products: Freshwater Fly Fishing

NAUTILUS CCF-X2

Model: No. 6/8, No. 8/10, No. 10/12, Silver King
Diameter (in.): 4; 4.5; 4.5; 5
Weight (oz.): 7.6 oz; 8.6 oz; 8.9 oz; 9.1 oz
Spool Cap. (M): 6 lbs/225 yds, 7 lbs/200 yds, 8 lbs/100 yds; 8 lbs/250 yds, 9 lbs/225 yds, 10 lbs/200 yds; 10 lbs/300 yds, 11 lbs/275 yds, 12 lbs/250 yds; 10 lbs/300 yds, 11 lbs/275 yds, 12 lbs/250 yds
Spool Cap. (B): N/A
Hand Retrieve: R/L
Line Weight: 6W–12W
Features: The CCF-X2 Disc Braking System is an upgraded, stronger, lighter version of the Cork and Carbon Fiber brake of its predecessor. It features twice the drag surface in a dual action brake configuration. Coupled with hybrid ceramic bearings, the reel delivers less than 1 percent startup inertia at all drag settings. This brake unit is feather light and can be easily switched from RH to LH retrieve; unique reel design features grooves that let the bottom of the backing breathe to promote faster drying; oversized CCF-X2 drag knob features the InfinAdjust drag control system: six turns of the drag knob take you from zero to 20+ lbs to allow precise adjustments to drag tension without fear of over adjusting.
Price: . . . .**$435-$685**

ORVIS BATTENKILL

Model: Battenkill I, II, III, IV, V
Diameter (in.): 2.75; 3; 3.25; 3.75; 4
Weight (oz.): 2.8 oz; 2.9 oz; 3.2 oz; 8.5 oz; 9.5 oz
Spool Cap. (M): WF2F/75 yds, WF4F/75 yds, WF6F/100 yds; WF8F/200 yds, WF10F/200 yds
Spool Cap. (B): N/A
Hand Retrieve: R/L
Line Weight: 1W–11W
Features: Simple design and flawless construction make this the perfect click-and-pawl fly reel for nearly any freshwater fishing situation; features a classically styled, yet technically enhanced, four-position click-and-pawl drag system that is adjusted internally and is designed to work in tandem with the palm of your hand on those sizzling, screaming runs; constructed with a narrow spool for less line stacking on retrieve and a larger spool diameter for higher line retrieval rates; ultra-lightweight fly reel design balances perfectly on shorter rods; machined from heavy-duty bar-stock aluminium for added durability; easily adjustable left- or right-hand retrieve; black nickel.
Price: . . . . **$98–$149**

NEW Products: **Lures, Hardbait**

BAGLEY BALSA B

Type: Crankbait
Color/Pattern: Black on Silver Foil, Bluegill, Chartreuse Crayfish, Chartreuse Shad, Hot Tiger, Red Crawdad, Sexy Shad
Size: 2 in., 2 1/2 in

Weight: 5/16 oz., 7/16 oz
Running depth: 0 ft–3 ft
Features: Perfect for fishing light to medium cover; mimics the look and motion forage-hungry largemouths prey on; front square-lip design slips through heavy cover without issue.
Price: **$8.79**

BAGLEY BALSA SHAD

Type: Crankbait
Color/Pattern: Chartreuse Shad, Hot Tiger, Purple Shad, Red Crawdad, Sexy Shad, Yellow Perch
Size: 2 1/4 in, 2 3/4 in, 3 1/4 in
Weight: 3/8 oz., 1/2 oz., 5/8 oz

Running depth: 5 ft–7 ft, 7 ft–9 ft, 14 ft–17 ft
Blade size: 5, 7, 8
Features: Enticing underwater vibrations get the attention of hungry predators; precision balanced for easy casting on both fast and slow retrieves; full-wire harness for enhanced strength.
Price: **$8.79**

BAGLEY BANG O B

Type: Crankbait
Color/Pattern: Baby Bass, Bluegill, Black Back/Silver Foil, Chartreuse Shad, Glass Minnow, Hot Tiger, Little Musky On Orange, Little Musky On Yellow, Orange Tiger, Parrot, Sexy Shad, Tennessee Shad, Orange Belly, Yellow Dots
Size: 5 1/4 in., 8 in

Weight: 1 1/2 oz, 2 1/4 oz
Running depth: 15 ft–20 ft, 20 ft–30 ft
Features: Draw strikes from deep-dwelling predators; tough lexan lip takes its solid hardwood body down to 30 feet; hand tuned to run true in a wide speed range; heavy-duty split rings and treble hooks.
Price: . . . . **$15.99–$16.49**

BAGLEY BANG-O-LURE

Type: Stick bait
Color/Pattern: Black/Gold/Orange, Black/Silver Foil, Hot Tiger, Sexy Shad, Tennessee Shad/Orange
Size: 4 1/4 in, 5 1/4 in

Weight: 1/4 oz., 3/8 oz
Running depth: 0 ft–2 ft
Features: Jerk, twitch, and burn for savage strikes from game fish.
Price: **$8.79**

BAGLEY BANG-O-LURE DEEP DIVING

Type: Stick bait
Color/Pattern: Albino Orange Belly, Baby Bass, Black Back/Gold Foil, Black Back On Purple/Purple Tiger Stripe, Black Back/Silver Foil, Blue Tiger, Chartreuse Crayfish On White, Hot Tiger, Purple Back/Chartreuse, Sides/Pink Dots, Purple/Silver Foil, Pistachio, Sexy Shad, Tennessee Shad/Orange Belly, Yellow Perch
Size: 5 1/4 in

Weight: 3/8 oz
Running depth: 14 ft–16 ft
Features: Featuring the legendary Bang-O-Lure frame and hand-selected hardwood delivers both superior action and the toughness needed for aggressive fish; perfectly positioned lip displaces a mass of water while swimming, creating wide, strong action that attracts predators from great distances.
Price: **$9.49**

BAGLEY DEEP-DIVING SHAD

Type: Crankbait
Color/Pattern: Albino Orange Belly, Baby Bass, Black Back on Purple/Purple Tiger Stripe, Black Back, Silver Foil, Blue Tiger, Chartreuse Crayfish on White, Hot Tiger, Purple Back/Chartreuse Sides/Pink Dots, Purple/Silver Foil, Pistachio, Rainbow Trout, Sexy Shad, Tennessee Shad Orange Belly, Yellow Perch

Size: 2 3/4 in
Weight: 1/3 oz
Running depth: 12 ft–14 ft
Features: Wide, wobbling action draws the attention of fish; long-lasting balsa-wood body.
Price: **$7.99**

BAGLEY KNOCKER B

Type: Topwater
Color/Pattern: Baby Bass, Bluegill, Brown Frog, Chartreuse Shad, Green Frog, Shad
Size: 3 1/2 in

Weight: 1/2 oz
Running depth: Topwater
Blade size: 9, 11
Features: Great for all species of freshwater fish; casts incredible distances; emits a loud, fish-attracting knock.
Price: **$7.99**

BAGLEY MINNOW B

Type: Stick bait
Color/Pattern: Baby Bass, Black Stripes on Gold, Black Stripes on Silver, Bluegill, Blue White Orange, Chartreuse Shad, Citrus Shad, Gold, Hot Tiger, Mustard Shad, Olive Shad, Pearl Shad, Sexy Shad, Silver, Tennessee Shad
Size: 4 in., 5 in

Weight: 1/4 oz., 3/8 oz
Running depth: 0 ft–3 ft
Blade size: 4, 5
Features: Built with the unmistakable Bagley action, it's easy to cast and fun to work on top or just sub-surface; designed with internal rattle chambers to produce great fish calling sound.
Price: **$4.99**

NEW Products: Lures, Hardbait

BAGLEY RATTLIN' FINGER MULLET
Type: Rigged plastic
Color/Pattern: Copper Mullet, Glass Minnow, Gold, Natural Mullet, Red Head, Sardine, Silver Blue, Silver Chartreuse, Silver Pink
Size: 3 1/2 in, 4 1/4 in
Weight: 1/2 oz, 3/8 oz

Running depth: Topwater
Blade size: 9, 11
Features: Like its balsa brother, this precisely engineered rattling plastic version allows for farther casts in windy conditions, tremendous sound emanation, and enhanced durability that will stand up to those tough in-shore fighters.
Price: **$4.99**

BAGLEY RATTLIN' KILL'R B
Type: Rigged plastic
Color/Pattern: Baby Bass, Black Stripes Gold, Black Stripes Silver, Bluegill, Blue White Orange, Chartreuse Shad, Citrus Shad, Gold, Hot Tiger, Mustard Shad, Olive Shad, Pearl Shad, Silver, Sexy Shad, Tennessee Shad
Size: 2 1/4 in, 3 1/4 in
Weight: 3/8 oz
Running depth: 3 ft–4 ft, 4 ft–5 ft

Blade size: 1
Features: Bagley introduces the Rattlin' Kill'r B and the Rattlin' Diving Kill'r B; both baits are carefully designed to cast far and to emit a low resonating rattle upon retrieve; each version displays an aggressive hunting action in keeping with its legendary balsa brothers; the diving version has a lead insert in the diving lip that makes this bait get deep—quick.
Price: **$4.99**

BAGLEY RUMBLE B
Type: Stick bait
Color/Pattern: Gold, Gold Perch, Hot Perch, Purple Pearl, Purple Silver, Silver, Silver Blue, Silver Fluorescent Chartreuse, Sexy Shad, Yellow Perch
Size: 4 1/4 in

Weight: 3/8 oz
Running depth: 10 ft–12 ft
Blade size: 11
Features: Rolls and flashes with a low, resonating rattle when trolled; unique swimming lip controls the waterflow around the lure.
Price: **$7.99**

BAGLEY SUNNY B
Type: Crankbait
Color/Pattern: Baby Bass, Bluegill, Chartreuse Bluegill, Chartreuse Shad, Citrus Shad, Green Crawdad, Gold Shad, Hot Tiger, Red Crawdad, Shad, Sexy Shad, Silver Shad, Tennessee Orange Shad
Size: 2 in

Weight: 3/8 oz
Running depth: 7 ft
Blade size: 5
Features: Precision balanced for easy casting on both fast and slow retrieves; maximum action resembles a darting baitfish when twitched; deep-diving lip ensures your lure gets down deep; full-wire harness for enhanced strength.
Price: **$8.79**

BASS PRO XPS SQUARE BILL CRANKBAITS

Type: Crankbait
Color/Pattern: Pearl Splatter Back, Chrome Black Back,Chartreuse Black Back, Crawfish Boil, Pearl Red Eye, Chartreuse Shad, OJ Brown Crawdad, XXX Shad, Texas Shad, Chrome XXX Shad, Gold XXX Shad, Chartreuse Blue Back

Size: 2 1/2 in, 2 3/4 in
Weight: 3/8 oz., 1/2 oz
Running depth: 5 ft, 6 ft
Features: Designed for both trolling and casting; dives to about 10 feet on a long cast and trolls down to 20 feet; rounded lip causes quick dive and creates a wiggling action that attracts fish.
Price: **$4.29**

BERKLEY DOUBLE-HOOK WALLEYE RIG – COLORADO BLADE

Type: Bait rig
Color/Pattern: Blue Silver, Clown, Fire Perch, Firetiger, Hammered Copper, Hammered Gold, Hammered Silver, Lime Chartreuse, Orange Chartreuse, Purple Pearl, Purple Rain, Sunrise, Watermelon, Yellow Perch

Size: 48 in. line
Blade size: 3, 4
Features: Colorado-style blades maximize flash and vibration to lure in big fish, and double hooks ensure a solid hookset; matching beads; rigged with 48″ of 17-lb.-test Trilene XT monofilament line.
Price: **$1.99**

BERKLEY DOUBLE-HOOK WALLEYE RIG– INDIANA BLADE

Type: Bait rig
Color/Pattern: Blue Silver, Clown, Firetiger, Lime Chartreuse, Orange Chartreuse, Purple Rain, Yellow Perch
Size: 48 in. line

Blade size: 4
Features: Indiana-style blades maximize flash and vibration to lure in big fish, and double hooks ensure a solid hookset; matching beads; rigged with 48″ of 17-lb.-test Trilene XT monofilament line.
Price: **$1.99**

BERKLEY WALLEYE RIGS – COLORADO BLADE – SINGLE HOOK

Type: Bait rig
Color/Pattern: Hammered Copper, Hammered Gold, Hammered Silver, Purple Pearl, Sunrise, Watermelon

Size: 42 in. line
Blade size: 3
Features: Attention-grabbing spin and flash of a blade; designed by pros and crafted to handle the toughest tests; professionally tied using Trilene XT 12-lb. monofilament line.
Price: **$1.99**

NEW PRODUCTS

BLAKEMORE ROAD RUNNER BARBED GLOW HEAD

Type: Roundhead/specialty
Color/Pattern: Bubble Gum, Chartreuse, Chartreuse/Lime, Chartreuse/Orange, Orange, White Luminescent
Weight: 1/8 oz., 1/4 oz., 3/8 oz.

Running depth:
Features: N-Tense Glow Paint glows in the dark; hammered brass willow blade for ultimate flash; barbed collar holds plastic trailers firmly in place; great for crappie and walleye; 4 included.
Price: **$3.99**

BOMBER LURES SALTWATER GRADE LONG SHOT

Type: Saltwater
Color/Pattern: Baby Blue Fish, Baby Bunker, Black, Blue Mackerel, Bone, Chartreuse Herring, Menhaden, Mother of Pearl, Mullet, Pearl/Yellow

Size: 5 in., 6 in., 7 in
Weight: 3/4 oz., 13/16 oz., 1 3/4 oz.
Running depth: 2 ft–5 ft, 2 ft–8 ft
Features: Advanced casting system for distance casting; corrosion-resistant hooks ideal for salt water; wide-wobbling swimming action attracts predators.
Price: **$9.99**

BUCKEYE LURES FOOTBALL JIG

Type: Bass jig
Color/Pattern: Black, Black Blue, Brown, Brown Pumpkin, Cinnamon Purple, Gold Craw, Green Pumpkin, Peanut Butter/Jelly, Perfect Craw, Texas Craw, Watermelon Red

Weight: 1/2 oz., 3/4 oz., 1 oz.
Features: Unique, flat head enables jig to stand up when it's dragging on the bottom; Mimics foraging prey or a crawfish; weed guard for fishing heavy cover; high-quality silicone skirt.
Price: **$4.00**

CABELA'S BED JIG

Type: Bass jig
Color/Pattern: Black, Chartreuse, Green Pumpkin, Pearl White
Weight: 3/32 oz., 1/8 oz., 3/16 oz., 1/4 oz.

Features: Perfect for finesse presentations; bed head easily pulls through cover; keeper barb holds plastics in place; 6 included.
Price: **$3.99**

NEW Products: **Lures, Hardbait**

CABELA'S CHARTER SERIES CANADIAN SPOON

Type: Casting/Trolling Spoon
Color/Pattern: Avocado Orange, Bee Nice, Eddy, Firefly, Jump Suit, Messed Up, Passion, Pink Lady Slipper, Stewie, Sherbet, The Doctor, Twisted

Weight: 5/8 oz., 7/8 oz., 1 1/4 oz.
Features: Strike-inducing wobble action; strong nickel plating for long-lasting performance; colors designed for clear waters of lakes and reservoirs.
Price: **$4.99**

CABELA'S CHARTER SERIES WALLEYE RUNNER

Type: Crankbait
Color/Pattern: Avocado Orange, Bee Nice, Eddy, Firefly, Jump Suit, Messed Up, Passion, Pink Lady Slipper, Stewie, Sherbet, The Doctor, Twisted
Size: 3 1/2 in, 4 3/4 in

Weight: 1/3 oz., 5/8 oz.
Running depth: 8 ft–21 ft, 15 ft–28 ft
Features: Floats at rest but quickly dives to anywhere from 8–28 ft.; body has a slow, tantalizing wobble that's tailor-made for finicky walleyes; color options made for clear waters of the largest lakes and reservoirs.
Price: **$4.99**

CABELA'S LIPLESS SIDEKICK

Type: Crankbait
Color/Pattern: Chrome/Black Back, Chrome/Blue, Firetiger, Gold/Black Back, Gizzard Shad, Rad Perch, Red Craw
Size: 2 1/2 in., 3 in

Weight: 1/4 oz., 1/2 oz.
Features: Promotes long casts; side blades emulate schooling baitfish; rattle brings in fish from a distance.
Price: **$4.99**

CABELA'S MEAN-EYE JIG

Type: Roundhead/specialty
Color/Pattern: Black, Chartreuse, Chartreuse/Black, Chartreuse/Green, Chartreuse/Orange, Firetiger, Glow, Pearl White, White/Pink

Weight: 1/8 oz., 1/4 oz., 3/8 oz.
Features: Finesse, balance, and casting weight; ideal for rigging both live and plastic baits; holographic eyes and a glossed paint coating; includes 6.
Price: **$4.49**

NEW Products: **Lures, Hardbait**

CABELA'S REALIMAGE HDS MINNOW

Type: Stick bait
Color/Pattern: Alewife, Chrome Shiner, Dace Minnow, Fathead, Golden Shiner, Perch, Rainbow Trout, Sucker Minnow
Size: 2 in., 2 1/2 in

Weight: 1/8 oz., 3/16 oz.
Running depth: 4 ft–6ft, 8 ft–12 ft
Features: Incredibly lifelike High Definition Series technology; can be cast or trolled; works well on nearly any game fish.
Price: **$5.99**

CABELA'S TWIN ACTION SPINNER

Type: Bait rig
Color/Pattern: Alewife, Chartreuse/Orange, Clown, Firetiger, Gold Perch, Gold Shiner, Purple/Silver, Silver Shiner, Yellow Perch
Size: 60 in. line

Blade size: 3, 4
Features: Twice the flash, vibration, and spinning action; produces an underwater thump that draws fish in from a distance; deep-cup Colorado blades spin to create a larger profile; becomes an underwater beacon for huge walleye.
Price: **$2.99**

DAIWA SALT PRO MINNOW – FLOATING

Type: Saltwater
Color/Pattern: Black Purple, Black Yellow, Blue Mackerel, Bone, Bunker, Green Mackerel, Laser Chartreuse Rainbow, Laser Green Shiner, Laser Red Head, Laser Shiner, Mother of Pearl, Purple Back Silver, Sand Eel, Sardine, Translucent Lime, Yellow Pearl

Size: 6 in
Weight: 1 1/9 oz.
Features: Erratic side-to-side action draws predator's attention; weight-transfer system for easier, longer casts; realistic scale pattern and 3D eyes; #1 heavy-duty saltwater hooks.
Price: **$9.99**

DAIWA SALT PRO MINNOW – SINKING

Type: Saltwater
Color/Pattern: Black Purple, Bone, Bunker, Green Mackerel, Laser Green Shiner, Laser Sardine, Laser Shiner, Sand Eel, Translucent Lime, Yellow Pearl
Size: 6 in

Weight: 1 1/4 oz.
Features: Ideal for casting long distances; erratic side-to-side action draws predator's attention; weight-transfer system for easier, longer casts; realistic scale pattern and 3D eyes; #1 heavy-duty saltwater hooks.
Price: **$10.99**

DAIWA SALT PRO MINNOW BULLET – FAST SINKING

Type: Saltwater
Color/Pattern: Black Purple, Bone, Bunker, Green Mackerel, Laser Green Shiner, Laser Shiner, Sand Eel, Sardine, Translucent Lime, Yellow Pearl

Size: 6 in
Weight: 2 1/8 oz.
Features: Tight S action imitates a real baitfish; sinks level so you will get bites on the fall; heavy weight and small lips for casting in windy conditions; #2/0 heavy-duty saltwater hook.
Price: **$17.99**

DAIWA SALT PRO MINNOW BULLET – SINKING

Type: Saltwater
Color/Pattern: Black Purple, Bone, Bunker, Green Mackerel, Laser Green Shiner, Laser Shiner, Sand Eel, Sardine, Translucent Lime, Yellow Pearl

Size: 6 in
Weight: 1 1/2 oz.
Features: Tight S action imitates a real baitfish; sinks level so you will get bites on the fall; heavy weight and small lips for casting in windy conditions; #2/0 heavy-duty saltwater hook.
Price: **$15.99**

ECO PRO TUNGSTEN FREE BALL JIG

Type: Bass jig
Color/Pattern: Black, Green Pumpkin
Weight: 3/16 oz., 1/4 oz., 3/8 oz., 1/2 oz.

Features: Free-moving action brings life to your plastics; removable clevis makes it super-easy to change hooks; dense tungsten allows you to fish deeper with a smaller profile; equipped with a 4/0 or 3/0 (3/16 oz only) super-sharp EWG hook; includes 2.
Price: . . . . **$5.48–$5.99**

ECO PRO TUNGSTEN KIRA CASTING JIG

Type: Bass jig
Color/Pattern: Black, Black/Blue, DS, Green Pumpkin/Black, Okeechobee Craw, PB&J

Weight: 1/4 oz., 3/8 oz., 1/2 oz., 3/4 oz.
Features: Fiber weedguard easily works through heavy cover; vertical line tie for strong angle of pull; soft skirt for natural presentation.
Price: **$5.79**

ECO PRO TUNGSTEN RAPID FIRE SPINNERBAIT

Type: Spinnerbait
Color/Pattern: Hot Chartreuse/White, Spot Remover, Squirrel, White

Weight: 3/8 oz., 1/2 oz.
Features: Great for pressured fish; perfectly balanced tungsten head; cupped blades engage at any speed; small profile with a heavier weight for long casts.
Price:. **$8.49**

ECO PRO TUNGSTEN WAR CRY BUZZBAIT

Type: Buzzbait
Color/Pattern: Black, Bluegill, Hot Chartreuse, Hot Chartreuse White, White

Weight: 3/8 oz.
Features: Bright prop blade emits a clacking noise to irritate bass; tungsten head delivers an acoustics pitch that bass can't resist; light-wire construction collapses when struck for better hooksets; sticky-sharp 3/0 hook.
Price:. **$7.99**

KOKABOW IN-FLIGHT LAKE TROLLS

Type: Dodgers/flashers
Color/Pattern: Black Eagle, Blue Heron, Eagle, Harpy, Harrier, Hawk, Kestrel, Kingfisher, Merlin, Osprey, Raptor, Talon, Silver

Size: 26 in. line
Features: Extremely light with virtually no drag; colorful rudder and lightweight wire; five willowleaf blades and prism tape; made with premiere crystals and glass beads.
Price:. **$8.99**

LINDY LIL' GUY

Type: Bait rig
Color/Pattern: Aunt Creepy, Black Eye, Chameleon, Coward, Orangeade, Perch
Size: 2 in

Features: Adds crankbait action to your rig; floats when motionless to keep you off the bottom; snell storage unit keeps rig tangle-free; 36-in. 14-lb. Silver Thread Fluorocarbon line.
Price:. **$3.99**

LIVETARGET TROUT FRY

Type: Crankbait
Color/Pattern: Brown Trout, Rainbow
Size: 2 in., 2 3/4 in

Weight: 1/8 oz., 5/16 oz.
Features: Imitates trout fry; shallow, slow-sinking bait; weight-transfer system.
Price: **$13.49**

LIVETARGET YEARLING BAITBALL CRANKBAIT

Type: Crankbait
Color/Pattern: Blue/Chartreuse, Chartreuse/Black, Gold/Black, Pearl/Olive Shad, Pearl/Violet Shad
Size: 1 3/4 in, 2 in, 2 3/8 in
Weight: 1/4 oz., 3/8 oz., 1/2 oz.

Running depth: 0 ft–7 ft
Features: Combines BaitBall design with small crankbait profile; covers midrange water depths and delivers a tantalizing flash; schools of 3D hatchlings entice hungry game fish to strike; well-rounded color selection makes lures visible in any environment.
Price: **$15.99**

LIVETARGET YEARLING BAITBALL JERKBAIT

Type: Jerkbait
Color/Pattern: Blue/Chartreuse, Gold/Black, Pearl/Natural, Pearl/Olive Shad, Pearl/Violet Shad, Silver/Black
Size: 3 3/4 in, 4 1/4 in
Weight: 3/8 oz., 1/2 oz.

Running depth: 3 ft–4 ft, 4 ft–5 ft
Features: Ultrarealistic appearance of a large baitfish school; creates a variety of flash profiles predators can't resist; 3 3/4-in. jerkbait is short and stocky to produce a wide, deep flash; long, sleek 4 1/4-in. jerkbait suspends with the nose down; attractive coloration is effective in variable water conditions.
Price: **$15.99**

LIVETARGET YEARLING BAITBALL RATTLEBAIT

Type: Lipless bait
Color/Pattern: Blue/Chartreuse, Gold/Black, Pearl/Olive Shad, Pearl/Violet Shad, Silver/Black

Size: 2 1/2 in., 3 in
Features: Lures appear as a year-old hatch of fleeing baitfish; two different profiles, running attitudes and fall actions; loud rattle calls made with lead and steel BBs.
Price: **$15.99**

NEW PRODUCTS

LIVETARGET YEARLING BAITBALL SQUAREBILL

Type: Crankbait
Color/Pattern: Blue/Chartreuse, Chrtreuse/Black, Gold/Black, Pearl/Olive Shad, Pearl/Violet Shad, Silver/Black
Size: 1 7/8 in, 2 3/8 in
Weight: 1/4 oz., 1/2 oz.

Running depth: 3 ft–4 ft, 4 ft–5 ft
Features: 3D yearling pattern replicates a school of yearling baitfish; ideal for situations when bass are feeding in shallow water; assortment of colors take on a variety of water conditions; square bill deflects off underwater cover to bring pattern to life.
Price: **$15.99**

LIVETARGET YEARLING BAITBALL WALKING BAIT

Type: Topwater
Color/Pattern: Blue/Chartreuse Shad, Pearl/Natural, Pearl/Violet Shad, Silver/Black
Size: 3 1/2 in, 4 1/2 in

Features: Acts as a cluster of baitfish reconnecting after a predatory assault; two different profiles that generate a traditional walk-the-dog action; added balance enhancement for super-easy retrieves; concave dimple generates a spitting action and blooping sound.
Price: **$16.99**

LUNKERHUNT MAGIC BEAN

Type: InLine spinner
Color/Pattern: 24 Karat, Firetiger, Glow, Neon
Weight: 1/4 oz.

Features: This penny-sized body is ready for vertical jigging, casting, and ice fishing; an irresistible rotating blade on the tail attracts hungry fish.
Price: **$4.99**

MACK'S LURE CHA CHA FLOATING CRAWLER RIG

Type: Bait rig
Color/Pattern: Blue Sparkle/Pearl/Blue Scale, Chartreuse Sparkle/Chartreuse/Green Scale, Green Sparkle/FireTiger, Hot Pink Sparkle/Pearl/Pink Scale, Orange Black Tiger/Chartreuse/Orange Scale

Size: 72 in. line
Features: Two-hook (#4s) floating harness; Smile Blade turns at speeds less than 1/4 mph; perfect for hard-hitting walleye or trout.
Price: **$3.49**

MACK'S LURE DOUBLE WHAMMY CLASSIC SPINNER

Type: Bait rig
Color/Pattern: Chartreuse/Chrome/Flo Chartreuse, Hammered Brass Gold/Gold, Hammered Nickel/Flo Chartreuse/Flo Orange, Rainbow/Flo Green/Flo Orange

Features: Classic Indiana Blade; wedding ring bead; #6 two-hook design.
Price: **$3.09**

MACK'S LURE SMILE BLADE SPINDRIFT FLOATING WALLEYE RIG

Type: Bait rig
Color/Pattern: Black Scale, Blue Scale, Chartreuse Scale, Green Scale, Orange Green, Orange Scale, Red, White Pink
Size: 74 in. line

Blade size: 1
Features: Enticing wobble action at ultraslow speeds; unique swivel-to-hook system; strong VMC Spindrift #1 hook; rigged on 74" of 12 lb. test monofilament.
Price: **$3.59**

MACK'S LURE WEDDING RING PROMISE KEEPER SPINNER

Type: InLine spinner
Color/Pattern: Black/Silver Scale, Chartreuse/Red Dot, Pink/Silver Scale, Red/Black Dot, White/Red Dot

Size: 2 3/8 in
Weight: 1/8 oz.
Features: Great for smallmouth bass, trout, and other species; use with a lightweight spinning outfit; includes #8 treble and #4 single hook.
Price: **$3.79**

NORTHLAND BAITFISH-IMAGE COLORADO BLADE

Type: Blade
Color/Pattern: Cisco Purple, Clown, Dace Pink, Firetiger, Gold Perch, Gold Shiner, Rainbow, Silver Shiner, Sunrise, Yellow Perch

Blade size: 3, 4
Features: Holographic patterns mimic fish scales, producing realistic looks that fish can't resist; the perfect finishing touch to your custom-made rigs; includes 3.
Price: **$2.79**

NEW Products: Lures, Hardbait

NORTHLAND PRO WALLEYE SERIES CRAWLER HARNESS

Type: Bait rig
Color/Pattern: UV Fire Perch, UV Glo Red, UV Glo Shiner, UV Gold Christmas, UV Hot Steel, UV Silver Christmas, UV Tiger, UV Wonderbread White
Size: 3 in

Blade size: 3
Features: Created by legendary guide Jason Mitchell; #3 Colorado blade for optimum thump and vibration; Speed Clevis provides quick blade changes; hand-decorated, bright UV blade and SuperGlo beads.
Price: **$3.69**

NORTHLAND PRO WALLEYE SERIES FLOAT'N CRAWLER HARNESS

Type: Bait rig
Color/Pattern: UV Fire Perch, UV Glo Red, UV Glo Shiner, UV Gold Christmas, UV Hot Steel, UV Silver Christmas, UV Tiger, UV Wonderbread White
Size: 40 in. line

Blade size: 4
Features: UV-brightened blade and Super-Glo beads attract fish; holographic cork float for running near the surface; swap blades quickly with the Speed Clevis; pre-rigged with 40 in. of 15-lb. Bionic monofilament.
Price: **$3.99**

NORTHLAND PRO WALLEYE SERIES LONG-SHANK SPINNER

Type: Bait rig
Color/Pattern: UV Fire Perch, UV Glo Red, UV Glo Shiner, UV Gold Christmas, UV Hot Steel, UV Silver Christmas, UV Tiger, UV Wonderbread White
Size: 40 in. line
Blade size: 3

Features: UV-brightened blade and Super-Glo beads; attracts fish from a distance; #3 deep-cup Colorado blade provides irresistible vibrations; 1/0 long-shank hook is optimized for speed and snake rigging; Speed Clevis makes swapping blades quick and easy; hand-decorated blade; rigged on 40 in. of 15# Northland Bionic Monofilament.
Price: **$3.69**

NORTHLAND PRO WALLEYE SERIES MICRO-BLADE SPINNER

Type: Bait rig
Color/Pattern: UV Fire Perch, UV Glo Red, UV Glo Shiner, UV Gold Christmas, UV Hot Steel, UV Silver Christmas, UV Tiger, UV Wonderbread White
Size: 40 in. line

Blade size: 0
Features: Small #0 blade produces subtle, irresistible flicker and flash; optically brightened UV blade and Super-Glo beads; pre-rigged with 40 in. of 15-lb. line; #2 Crawler Hauler hook.
Price: **$3.29**

NORTHLAND RZ JIG

Type: Roundhead/specialty
Color/Pattern: Assorted, Chartreuse, Crawdad, Firetiger, Glow, Glo Watermelon, Moonlight (Glow), Orange, Shrimp, Sunrise

Weight: 1/32 oz., 1/16 oz., 1/8 oz., 3/16 oz., 1/4 oz., 3/8 oz.
Features: Optically brightened eyes; ultrareflective UV coatings, attracting fish from greater distances; precision-sharpened, black-nickel hooks; includes 4–6 depending on size.
Price: **$2.99**

NORTHLAND SINK'N JIG

Type: Roundhead/specialty
Color/Pattern: Assorted, Black, Chartreuse, Glow, Lime Green, Orange, Pink
Weight: 1/32 oz., 1/16 oz., 1/8 oz., 3/16 oz., 1/4 oz., 3/8 oz.

Features: DuraFinish coating delivers long-lasting like-new appearance; Bait-Saver collar holds both soft plastics and live bait securely; large eye gives fish a target so you get better hookup rates; includes 5–9 depending on size.
Price: **$2.99**

PANTHER MARTIN FISHSEEUV HAMMERED HOOCHIE SKIRT SPINNER

Type: InLine spinner
Color/Pattern: Blue Chartreuse Tiger, Gold Pink, Green Chartreuse Tiger, Purple Flourescent Red Tiger, Yellow Flourescent Red Tiger, Yellow Pink Tiger

Weight: 7/16 oz., 3/4 oz.
Features: Hoochie skirts emulate the motion of small prey; FishSeeUV paint is visible to predators at all depths; hammered blades are highly reflective and visible; sonic vibrations alert fish of the spinner's presence.
Price: **$5.99**

RAT-L-TRAP FLOATING TRAP

Type: Lipless bait
Color/Pattern: Candy Craw, Chrome Black Back, Chrome Blue Back, Sunrise Perch, Tennessee Shad
Size: 3 in

Weight: 1/3 oz.
Features: Conquers cover and weaves through obstructions; outperforms other lipless crankbaits; secret weapon of Bassmaster Pros.
Price: **$6.99**

NEW PRODUCTS

RAT-L-TRAP KNOCK-N-TRAP

Type: Lipless bait
Color/Pattern: Blueberry Patch, Blue Shiner, Candy Craw, Chrome Black Back, Chrome Blue Back, Sunrise Perch
Size: 3 in

Weight: 1/2 oz.
Features: Strike-inducing low-frequency thumping sound; identical body style to the original Rat-L-Trap; tight wobble mimics a panicked minnow.
Price: **$6.99**

RAT-L-TRAP PANFISH SUPER NATURAL CRANKBAIT

Type: Lipless bait
Color/Pattern: Black Caterpillar, Black Pink, Chrome Blue Orange Belly, Gold Black Orange Belly, Grub, Rainbow Trout, Red Caterpillar, Sexy West

Size: 1 3/4 in
Weight: 1/8 oz.
Features: Super Natural laser-color technology brings baits to life; blade, shimmy, and rattle target crappie, white bass, perch, and sunfish; lures even the wariest fish out of hiding.
Price: **$4.99**

REBEL FLOATING MINNOW

Type: Saltwater
Color/Pattern: Gold/Black, Silver/Black, Silver/Blue
Size: 5 1/2 in
Weight: 5/8 oz.

Running depth: 0 ft–4 ft
Features: Attention-grabbing, shallow-diving, floating version; dives to 4 ft upon retrieval; equipped with strong #2 saltwater hooks.
Price: **$6.99**

REBEL JOINTED MINNOW

Type: Saltwater
Color/Pattern: Gold/Black, Silver/Black, Silver/Blue
Size: 4 1/2 in, 5 1/2 in
Weight: 7/16 oz., 11/16 oz.

Running depth: 0 ft–3 ft, 0 ft–4 ft
Features: Modeled after the Original Rebel Minnow; jointed action adds smoothness to the swimming motion; fish it three ways to produce fish-attracting action; #4 or #2 saltwater grade hook.
Price: **$6.99**

REBEL JUMPIN' MINNOW
Type: Topwater
Color/Pattern: Bone, Copper/Black/Orange, Silver/Black, Silver/Blue
Size: 4 1/2 in

Weight: 1/2 oz.
Features: Realistic baitfish appearance; side-to-side action and lead rattle triggers hunting instint; aerodynamic design casts smooth and far.
Price:......................................**$6.99**

REBEL MICRO CRITTERS MICRO CRAWFISH
Type: Barbless
Color/Pattern: Chartreuse Brown, Ditch Brown, Stream Craw
Size: 1 5/16 in

Weight: 1/16 oz.
Running depth: 1 ft–2 ft
Features: Ideal for young, less-experienced anglers; single, barbless hook for enhanced safety; small, super-light construction.
Price:......................................**$3.99**

REBEL MICRO CRITTERS MICRO CRICKHOPPER
Type: Barbless
Color/Pattern: Brown Cricket, Firetiger, Yellow Grasshopper
Size: 1 1/4 in

Weight: 1/16 oz.
Running depth: 2 ft–3 ft
Features: Ideal for young, less-experienced anglers; single, barbless hook for enhanced safety; small, super-light construction.
Price:......................................**$3.99**

REBEL MICRO CRITTERS MICRO MINNOW
Type: Barbless
Color/Pattern: Rainbow Trout, Silver/Black, Tennessee Shad
Size: 1 1/2 in

Weight: 1/16 oz.
Running depth: 0 ft–2 ft
Features: Ideal for young, less-experienced anglers; single, barbless hook for enhanced safety; small, super-light construction.
Price:......................................**$3.99**

REBEL MICRO CRITTERS MICRO POP-R
Type: Barbless
Color/Pattern: Bullfrog, Ole Bass, Silver/Black
Size: 1 1/4 in

Weight: 1/16 oz.
Features: Barbless hooks are safer for youngsters; produces irresistible topwater action; fish-fooling paint schemes.
Price: **$3.99**

SAVAGE GEAR 3D HARD EEL
Type: Saltwater
Color/Pattern: Black/Orange, Cisco, Firetiger, Golden Ambulance, Pike
Size: 10 in

Weight: 4 oz.
Features: Realistic profile based on a 3D scan of a real eel; hard-bodied construction withstands toothy predators; comes with two replaceable tails for the perfect action; can be fished subsurface or as a topwater wake bait.
Price: **$15.99**

SHIMANO SUSPENDING WAXWING
Type: Saltwater jig
Color/Pattern: Bone, Chrome, Sandeel, Sardine
Size: 3 1/2 in, 4 3/5 in
Weight: 1/2 oz., 1 3/4 oz.

Running depth: 3 ft
Features: Suspends at 3 ft.; walk-the-dog motion on retrieve; realistic matte-rubber finish; corrosion-resistant hooks great for saltwater suspension.
Price: **$14.99**

SOUTHERN PRO LIGHT WIRE UNPAINTED JIGHEAD

Type: Panfish jig
Color/Pattern: Unpainted

Weight: 1/32 oz., 1/16 oz., 1/8 oz.
Features: Easily penetrates on light hooksets or when slow trolling crappies; works well on the thin skin in crappie mouths; includes 10.
Price:. **$1.99**

SPRO LITTLE JOHN DEEP DIVER 70

Type: Crankbait
Color/Pattern: Baby Bass, Cell Mate, Citrus Shad, Nasty Shad, Spicy, Spring Craw, Top Perch
Size: 2 3/4 in

Weight: 1 oz.
Running depth: 20 ft
Features: Designed by John Crews; unique tungsten weight-transfer system; equipped with Gamakatsu hooks.
Price:. **$12.99**

SPRO ROCK CRAWLER 55

Type: Crankbait
Color/Pattern: Green Craw, Molting Craw, Mud Bug, Red Craw, Phantom Brown, Phantom Green, Spring Craw
Size: 2 1/8 in

Weight: 1/2 oz.
Running depth: 8 ft–12 ft
Features: Wide, wobbling action; works in a depth range of 8 ft. to 12 ft.; equipped with #5 sharp hooks.
Price:. **$10.99**

STRIKE KING KVD 1.5 SHALLOW CRANKBAIT

Type: Crankbait
Color/Pattern: Black Back Chartreuse, Chartreuse Perch, Chartreuse Sexy Shad, Neon Bluegill, Orange Belly Craw, Sexy Shad, Summer Sexy Shad, Tennessee Shad
Size: 2 1/2 in

Weight: 2/5 oz.
Running depth: 0 ft–3 ft
Features: Slender flat side for erratic thumping action; reaches fish down to 3 ft.; designed by Bassmaster Classic champion Kevin VanDam.
Price:. **$6.99**

NEW PRODUCTS

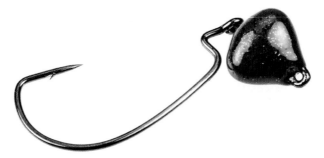

STRIKE KING MARK DAVIS JOINTED STRUCTURE HEAD JIG

Type: Bass jig
Color/Pattern: Black/Blue, Green Pumpkin, Watermelon Red

Weight: 3/8 oz., 1/2 oz., 3/4 oz.
Features: Unique Cobra Head cuts through weeds; free-swinging Z-bend black-nickel hook; chip-resistant powder-coated paint; includes 2.
Price: **$5.49**

STRIKE KING PRO MODEL KVD 8.0 MAGNUM SQUARE BILL

Type: Crankbait
Color/Pattern: Black Back Chartreuse, Citrus Shad, Natural Bream, Sexy Shad, Summer Sexy Shad

Size: 4 in
Weight: 1 1/2 oz.
Features: Built big for big fish; erratic wandering action; silently deflects cover.
Price: **$14.99**

STRIKE KING PRO MODEL LUCKY SHAD

Type: Crankbait
Color/Pattern: Blue Gizzard, Gold Black Back, Natural Bream, Orange Bream, Natural Shad, Sexy Shad
Size: 2 1/2 in

Weight: 3/10 oz.
Running depth: 8 ft
Features: Wobbling shad body with three-dimensional eyes; effortless to cast; 8-ft. diving depth; available in an array of classic Strike King colors.
Price: **$6.99**

STRIKE KING WALLEYE SERIES BANANA SHAD

Type: Stick bait
Color/Pattern: Chrome Blue, Gold Black Back, Hot Tiger, Lemonade, Pink Throat, Purple Tiger, Strobe Shad, Violet Alewife, Yellow Perch

Size: 3 13/16 in
Weight: 1/2 oz.
Running depth: 20 ft
Features: Banana style works deep structure or suspended fish; walleye-specific color patterns; dives down to 20 ft.
Price: **$7.99**

STRIKE KING WALLEYE SERIES BONSAI SHAD

Type: Crankbait
Color/Pattern: Chrome Blue, Ghost w/ Pink Throat, Gold Black Back, Hot Tiger, Lemonade, Purple Tiger, Strobe Shad, Violet Alewife, Yellow Perch
Size: 2 1/2 in

Weight: 3/10 oz.
Running depth: 12 ft
Features: Realistic, rattling minnow body with three-dimensional eyes; 12-ft. diving depth is effective when trolled or cast; available in a range of colors to match conditions.
Price: **$7.49**

SUICK LURES SHACK ATTACK CURLY SUE

Type: Musky/pike bait
Color/Pattern: Dirty Perch, Firetiger, Hot Perch, White/Red Eyes, Wonder Perch
Size: 6 in., 9 in
Weight: 3 oz., 5 oz.

Features: Delivers huge underwater vibrations; super-durable with a lifelike profile; Tough Bond Technology lengthens the life of the lure; long curly tail gives off an aggressive motion that is sure to catch the attention of every fish in the area.
Price: . . . . **$14.99–$19.99**

SUICK LURES SHACK ATTACK SUZY SUCKER

Type: Musky/pike bait
Color/Pattern: Brown Sucker, Chartreuse/Orange Tail, Gold Sucker, Light Sucker, Lumina Black, Red Copper
Size: 6 in., 9 in

Weight: 3 oz., 6 oz.
Features: External breakaway rigging system prolongs the life of the lure; specifically made to withstand ferocious muskie attacks; upside-down paddletail gives off heavy-duty vibrations.
Price: . . . . **$15.99–$19.99**

NEW PRODUCTS

TSUNAMI PLASTIC ZIG JIG PRO
Type: Saltwater
Color/Pattern: Chartreuse Head/White Body, Red Head/ Chartreuse Foil Body, Red Head/Silver Foil Body, Red Head/ White Body,
Size: 3 in

Weight: 1 oz.
Features: Lifelike performance triggers violent strikes; plastic construction and holographic finishes; precise balance delivers unique swimming actions; high-density core casts long and sinks fast; lifelike 3D eyes are inset in a bright, contrasting head.
Price: **$5.99**

TSUNAMI SHORT METAL ZIG JIG PRO
Type: Saltwater
Color/Pattern: Red/Silver/Black Hook, Red/Silver/Gold Hook
Size: 2 1/2 in
Weight: 7/8 oz.

Features: Slim profile creates a darting, vibrating action; fast-sinking high-density core ensures long, tumble-free casts; holographic finish, large 3D eyes and contrasting head color; ultrasharp Mustad treble hooks.
Price: **$4.99**

TSUNAMI SLIM METAL ZIG JIG PRO
Type: Saltwater
Color/Pattern: Chartreuse Head/Chrome, Chartreuse Head/ Gold, Red Head/Chrome, Red Head/Gloss Gold
Size: 2 3/4 in

Weight: 1 oz.
Features: Slim profile creates a darting, vibrating action; fast-sinking high-density core ensures long, tumble-free casts; holographic finish, large 3D eyes and contrasting head color; ultrasharp Mustad treble hooks.
Price: **$4.99**

YO-ZURI 3DB CRAYFISH
Type: Crankbait
Color/Pattern: Blue Black, Brown, Green, Luminous, Parrot, Red
Size: 3 in

Weight: 3/4 oz.
Features: 3D Internal Prism technology delivers powerful flashes; Wave Motion ribbed belly creates enticing vibrations; realistic slow-sinking design.
Price: **$9.99**

NEW Products: **Lures, Hardbait**

YO-ZURI 3DB VIBE
Type: Crankbait
Color/Pattern: Bluegill, Ghost Shad, Sexy Shad, Silver Black, Silver Blue
Size: 2 5/8 in

Weight: 1/2 oz.
Features: 3D Internal Prism technology reflects light to attract fish; ribbed belly creates vibration and sparks a bite response; lifelike body shape peaks the interest of hungry lunkers; large red eye gives predators a target to strike.
Price: **$9.99**

YO-ZURI 3DS MINNOW
Type: Crankbait
Color/Pattern: Ayu, Black/Silver, Ghost Shad, Glow/Chartreuse, Gold/Black, Peanut Bunker, Sardine
Size: 2 3/4 in

Weight: 1/4 oz.
Features: Realistic 3D body technology attracts fish; rolling swimming action, lifelike color; effective in both salt water and fresh water.
Price: **$8.99**

YO-ZURI DEEP DIVER CRYSTAL MINNOW
Type: Saltwater
Color/Pattern: Bronze, Bronze Shiner, Chartreuse, Gold Red, Green Mackerel, Perch, Red Head, Sardine
Size: 3 1/2 in, 4 3/8 in, 5 1/4 in

Weight: 3/8 oz., 9/16 oz., 7/8 oz.
Features: Visible to fish even in murky water; realistic appearance and strong, sharp hooks; dives deep quickly to work structure.
Price: . . . . **$12.99–$15.99**

YO-ZURI FLOATING MAG MINNOW
Type: Saltwater
Color/Pattern: Bronze, Green Mackerel, Pearl Red Head, Sardine
Size: 5 in

Weight: 7/8 oz.
Running depth: 4 ft
Features: Built-in magnetic weight transfer system; mimics the tight wiggling action of a large baitfish; state-of-the-art, scaled holographic foil.
Price: **$14.99**

NEW Products • **91**

NEW Products: **Lures, Hardbait**

YO-ZURI MAG DARTER

Type: Saltwater
Color/Pattern: Bronze, Ghost Black, Green Mackerel, Sardine
Size: 5 in

Weight: 1 oz.
Running depth: 3 ft
Features: Built-in magnetic weight transfer system; mimics the tight wiggling action of a large baitfish; state-of-the-art, scaled holographic foil.
Price: **$14.99**

YO-ZURI MAGNUM CRYSTAL 3D MINNOW

Type: Saltwater
Color/Pattern: Blue Silver, Green Silver, Red Head, Sardine, Silver Black
Size: 6 1/2 in

Weight: 1 1/2 oz.
Running depth: 3 ft
Features: Bright holographic finish attracts predators from long distances; blood-red inserts give fish a target to zero in on; shallow-running; quick, responsive darting action; through-wire construction with sharp, strong treble hooks.
Price: **$19.99**

YO-ZURI ULTRA BAIT LAZER SQUID JIG

Type: Saltwater
Color/Pattern: Green, Pink
Size: 3 3/4 in
Weight: 5/16 oz.

Features: Metallic laser finish with glow-in-the-dark belly accents attract squid; durable eight-tine stainless steel hooks increase hookup rates; reverse-feathered pectoral fins create lifelike swimming action; swivel line-tie promotes easy rigging.
Price: **$7.49**

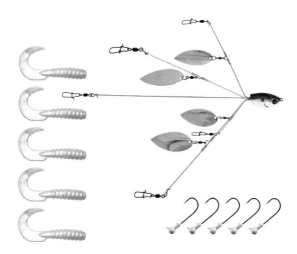

YUM YUMBRELLA ULTRA-LITE FLASH MOB JR. KITS

Type: Umbrella rig
Color/Pattern:
Features: Deadly on game fish; durable stainless steel heat-treated wire construction; great for multilure rigs; three wire includes three 1/8-oz. roundhead jigheads, three 4 in. pearl/silver-flake minnows, and one three-wire rig; five wire: rigged with willowleaf spinning blades positioned at the midpoint of each lure arm; includes five 1/8-oz. round-ball jigheads, five pearl-white curltail grubs, and one five-wire rig.
Price: **$13.49**

Z-MAN EZ SKIRT FINESSE

Type: Jig skirt
Color/Pattern: Black/Blue, Brown/Orange, Green Pumpkin/
Purple, Okeechobee Craw, PB and J, Texas Craw,
Watermelon/Pumpkin

Size: 2 3/4 in
Features: Spider-cut skirt profile; tremendous lifelike action
on jigs of all sizes; solid-hub design for quick skirt
replacement; includes 3.
Price: $2.99

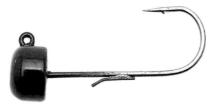

Z-MAN FINESSE SHROOMZ JIG

Type: Bass jig
Color/Pattern: Black, Green Pumpkin
Weight: 1/15 oz., 1/10 oz., 1/6 oz.

Features: Ideal for light techniques, including the Ned rig;
welded-wire keeper holds plastics in place; equipped with
super-sharp black-nickel hooks; includes 5.
Price: . . . . $4.79–$4.99

Z-MAN PROJECT Z FLIP 'N CAST JIG

Type: Bass jig
Color/Pattern: Bayou Craw, Black/Blue, California Craw,
Green Pumpkin Craw, Okeechobee Craw

Weight: 3/8 oz.
Features: Z-Tex skirt for realistic look and action; molded-in
keeper holds plastics in place; durable Mustad UltraPoint
hooks.
Price: $4.49

Z-MAN PROJECT Z FOOTBALL JIG

Type: Bass jig
Color/Pattern: Bayou Craw, Black/Blue, California Craw,
Green Pumpkin Craw, Okeechobee Craw

Weight: 1/2 oz.
Features: Football head minimizes snagging; Z-Tex silicone
skirt for lifelike attraction; custom keeper holds most soft-
plastic trailers; sharp Mustad UltraPoint hooks.
Price: $4.49

BASS PRO 40-PIECE MAGNUM CRAPPIE TUBE KIT

Color/Pattern: Assorted
Quantity: 40
Features: 33–2 1/2 in Magnum Crappie Tubes (4 each of 3 colors and 3 each of 7 colors); 6–1/32 oz Rough Jigheads;

1—Size #0 Jig Spinner Arm; magnum crappie tube's upsized body has hollow body and tentacles that are salt-impregnated for maximum attraction; ensures fish holds bite for solid hookset..
Price: **$5.99**

BASS PRO RIBBONTAIL WORMS - GARLIC SCENT

Color/Pattern: Green Pumpkin, Green Pumpkin Magic Pearl, Red Shad, Texas Red, Sapphire Blue, Watermelon Red Flake

Size: 7 in., 10 in
Quantity: 9
Features: Long, sinuous tail with wiggling and squirming action; durable; infused with garlic, salt, and 8up scent.
Price: **$3.49**

BASS PRO RIVER BUG - GARLIC SCENT

Color/Pattern: Black Blue Flake, Green Pumpkin, Green Pumpkin Magic Pearl, Summer Craw, Watermelon Red Flake
Size: 3 1/2 in, 4 1/4 in
Quantity: 8

Features: Redesigned beaver-style bug-bait made for flippin'; Unique and vivacious appendages to vibrate bass; infused with garlic, salt, and 8up scent.
Price: . . . . **$3.69–$4.19**

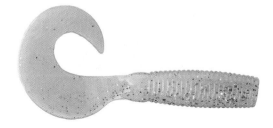

BASS PRO XPS SINGLE TAIL GRUBS - GARLIC SCENT

Color/Pattern: Watermelon Red Flake, White Ice, Houdini, Milky Salt n' Pepper, Smoke Pepper
Size: 4 in., 5 in

Quantity: 9
Features: Designed by pro staff; infused with garlic, salt, and 8up scent; durable.
Price: **$3.49**

BASS PRO XPS SWIMMING MINNOW
Color/Pattern: Pearl, XXX Shad, Perch, Shiner, Blue Black Herring
Size: 4 1/4 in

Quantity: 4
Features: Soft-plastic body with swishing tail; custom paint; 3D eyes.
Price: $5.49

BASS PRO XPS SWIMMING MINNOW–RIGGED
Color/Pattern: Pearl, XXX Shad, Perch, Shiner, Blue Black Herring
Size: 4 1/4 in
Weight: 3/4 oz.

Quantity: 1
Features: Pre-rigged with black nickel treble hook; soft-plastic body with swishing tail action; custom paint; 3D eyes.
Price: $2.79

BERKLEY GULP! ALIVE! HAWG
Type: Grub
Color/Pattern: Bubblegum, Fluorescent Orange, Natural, Pearl/White
Size: 1 1/2 in
Weight: 2.1 oz.

Quantity: 9
Features: Mimics tiny nymphs or underwater bugs; fish-attracting Gulp! Alive! attractant; baits can be recharged for long-lasting performance by placing them back into the liquid in the jar; great for ice fishing or open water.
Price: $3.99

BERKLEY GULP! ALIVE! HOLLOW SHRIMP
Type: Shrimp bait
Color/Pattern: Natural, New Penny, Nuclear Chicken, Pearl White
Size: 3 in

Quantity: 7
Features: Hollow construction falls slowly and collapses on the hookset; Gulp! scent and realistic-looking shrimp body attract hungry fish; can be rigged a variety of ways to match any presentation.
Price: . . . . $6.49–$9.99

BERKLEY HAVOC CRAW FATTY
Type: Craw
Color/Pattern: Black Blue Fleck, Black-Blue Silver Fleck, Black Red Fleck, Green Pumpkin, Green Pumpkin Blue, Green Pumpkin Red, Okochobee Craw, Smokey Green Pumpkin, Watermelon Candy

Size: 4 in
Quantity: 8
Features: Designed by pro angler Bobby Lane; big ribs and a plump body catch the attention of big bass; versatile soft bait, you can rig it a variety of ways.
Price: **$2.99**

BERKLEY HAVOC PIT BOSS
Type: Creature
Color/Pattern: Big Texan, Black-Blue, California, Electric Blue, Green Pumpkin, Green Pumpkin/Green, Green Pumpkin/Purple Fleck, Junebug, Lime-Purple Passion, Okochobee Craw, Plum, Sapphire Blue, Summer Craw, Vampire Orange, Watermelon/Orange Fleck

Size: 3 in., 4 in
Quantity: 10, 8
Features: Developed by pro angler Skeet Reese; mimics baitfish and crawfish; great for flipping techniques.
Price: **$2.99**

BERKLEY HAVOC THE DEUCE
Type: Grub
Color/Pattern: Green Pumpkin, Green Pumpkin/Blue, Green Pumpkin/Sumthin, Smoke Sparkle/Black Flake, Watermelon Red

Size: 3 in
Quantity: 10
Features: Designed by pro angler Gary Klein; unique double-tail design; produces enticing action at any speed.
Price: **$2.99**

BERKLEY POWERBAIT FIGHT'N BUG
Type: Craw
Color/Pattern: Alabama Craw, Black/Blue Fleck, Green Pumpkin, Molting, Okochobee Craw, Rusty Crawfish, Watermelon Candy
Size: 3 1/2 in

Quantity: 8
Features: Gives fish a taste that makes them hold on longer; soft, textured plastic body imitates a crawdad defending itself to drive fish crazy; excellent on a lighter Texas rig or as a jig trailer.
Price: **$4.99**

BLAKEMORE ROAD RUNNER RANDY'S SWIM ROLLIN' RUNNER

Type: Rigged plastic swimbait
Color/Pattern: Alewife, Albino Halo Shad, Albino Shad, Arkansas Halo Shiner, Bluegill, Lemon Shad, Smoke Phantom

Weight: 1/4 oz., 3/8 oz.
Quantity: 1
Features: Scaled body imitates shad or other small baitfish; lifelike holographic finish and 3D eyes; infused with Bang Scent; durable Daiichi forged needlepoint hooks; includes one rigged body and an extra tail.
Price: **$5.99**

CABELA'S ACTION TAIL 51-PIECE STICK BAIT KIT

Type: Stick bait
Color/Pattern: 6 colors included
Size: 5 in

Quantity: 50
Features: Fifty 5-inch stick baits; six fish-enticing colors; comes in a handy Plano 3600 utility box; effective bait when Texas or wacky rigged.
Price: **$19.99**

CABELA'S ACTION TAIL 76-PIECE 4-INCH STICK BAIT KIT

Type: Stick bait
Color/Pattern: 6 colors included

Size: 4 in
Quantity: 75
Features: Seventy-five 4-inch stick baits; six fish-enticing colors; comes in a handy Plano 3600 utility box.
Price: **$19.99**

CABELA'S ACTION TAIL 1,021-PIECE CRAPPIE TUBE KIT

Type: Tube
Color/Pattern: 33 colors

Quantity: 1021
Features: Various colors to match water conditions; 970 tubes in 33 colors; 1/48-oz., 1/32-oz. and 1/16-oz. jigs.
Price: **$44.99**

NEW Products: **Lures, Softbait**

CABELA'S GO-TO TRIP CRAPPIE GRUB
Type: Grub
Color/Pattern: Chartreuse, Black/Opaque Chartreuse, Junebug/Chartreuse, Pink White, Red/White, White, White/Chartreuse

Size: 2 in
Quantity: 20
Features: Triple-tail design produces a fluttering action at slow speeds; attractive color options work well in both clear and cloudy water; unique vibrations draw in hungry panfish.
Price:.....................................**$2.49**

CABELA'S GO-TO TRIP CRAPPIE TUBES
Type: Tube
Color/Pattern: Black/Chartreuse, Black/Chartreuse Sparkle, Glow/Black/Chartreuse, Hot Pink/White, Orange/Chartreuse, Pumpkin Pepper/Chartreuse, Red/Chartreuse Sparkle

Size: 1 1/2 in
Quantity: 20
Features: Accurately imitates minnows or small shad; particularly deadly on crappie, panfish, or trout; ideal colors for clear or stained water.
Price:.....................................**$1.59**

DOCKSIDE BAIT & TACKLE MATRIX SHAD
Type: Unrigged plastic swimbaits
Color/Pattern: Green Hornet, Lemon Head, Magneto, Midnight Mullet, Pink Champagne, Shrimp Creole, Tiger Bait, Ultra Violet

Size: 3 in
Quantity: 8
Features: Paddletail perfectly mimics young prey; ideal for use on a jig or trailer; use for redfish, speckled trout, and other game fish.
Price:.....................................**$4.19**

GENE LAREW BOBBY GARLAND BABY SHAD
Type: Grub
Color/Pattern: Bleeding Shad, Bluegrass, Blue Ice, Blue Thunder, Chartreuse Black Pepper, Crystal, Electric Chicken, Hologram Ghost, Lights Out, Key Lime Pie, Mo' Glo Outlaw Special, Monkey Milk, Pearl White

Size: 2 in
Quantity: 18
Features: Deadly when fishing big slab crappies; baitfish profile; tempting wiggle.
Price:.....................................**$3.19**

JACKALL DARTS HOG

Type: Creature
Color/Pattern: Black Blue Flake Chartreuse Tail, Black Blue Flake Purple Tail, Cola Red Flake Blood Tail, Crawdad, Green Pumpkin Pepper

Size: 3 1/2 in
Quantity: 6
Features: Multiple appendages create lifelike motion; buoyant tail sits higher than the body at rest; imitates a crawdad.
Price: **$5.29**

JOHNSON CRAPPIE BUSTER SHAD TUBE

Type: Tube
Color/Pattern: Clear Chartreuse Sparkle, Grape/Chartreuse, Green/Chartreuse Sparkle, Lemon/White, Midnight/Pink, Neon Blue/Pearl, Purple Blue Sparkle/Chartreuse, Red Yellow Sparkle

Size: 2 in
Quantity: 8
Features: Resembles shad forage; great for all crappie fishing techniques; tentacles offer lifelike action; can be rigged with a jighead, tube jig, or unweighted hook.
Price: **$1.99**

KALIN'S WAC-O-WORM

Type: Stick bait
Color/Pattern: Baby Bass, Black Blue Flake, Green Pumpkin, Green Pumpkin Magic, Watermelon Red Flake, Watermelon Red/Pearl, Watermelon Seed

Size: 5 in
Quantity: 10
Features: Loaded with salt for weight and flavor; versatile design for finesse presentations; great for Carolina, Texas, or wacky-style rigs.
Price: **$4.99**

LIVETARGET HOLLOW FROG

Type: Frog bait
Color/Pattern: Albino White, Black/Yellow, Brown/Black, Brown/Fluorescent Yellow, Emerald/Brown, Fluorescent Green/Yellow, Green/Yellow, Tan/Brown, Tan/Yellow, Yellow/Black

Size: 1 3/4 in, 2 1/4 in, 2 5/8 in
Weight: 1/4 oz., 5/8 oz., 3/4 oz.
Quantity: 1
Features: Effortless action; realistic hollow-body; works deep in heavy cover.
Price: . . . . **$10.99–$11.99**

NEW PRODUCTS

LUNKERHUNT CORE STRENGTH LUNKER CRAW

Type: Craw
Color/Pattern: Black Blue, Black Red, Pearl, Pumpkin

Size: 4 in
Quantity: 5
Features: Core strength mylar skeleton; mimics a crawfish as it drops; great for bass, pike, and muskie.
Price: **$5.59**

LUNKERHUNT MAYBUG BAIT JAR

Type: Creature
Color/Pattern: Black, Bubble Gum, Olive
Size: N/A

Quantity: 45
Features: Infused with Lunker Attractant; will not dry out in the sun; great for panfish, trout, and other freshwater fish; use in open water or for ice fishing.
Price: **$5.99**

MISTER TWISTER CURLY TAIL

Type: Grub
Color/Pattern: Smoke/Purple Flake (new color)
Size: 3 in

Quantity: 50
Features: Flutter-tail movement; great for everything from crappie to lunker pike; perfect fish-catching action.
Price: **$5.99**

MISTER TWISTER POC'IT HAWG RAISER

Type: Grub
Color/Pattern: Black Neon, Green Pumpkin, Green Pumpkin Blue, Hematoma, Louisiana 220, Penetration, Red Bug, Watermelon Candy, Watermelon Seed
Quantity: 1
Features: Twister has incorporated two oversized Curly Tails on longer, flexible legs, positioned fully behind the two Side Tabs. Up front, there are two smaller Curly Tail arms for added visual attraction as well as lift and glide, especially when Carolina-rigged. Plus, the body is covered with a series of Poc'it chambers to increase water disturbance and slow the bait's swim while releasing an attention-getting trail of bubbles.
Price: **$4.54**

NORTHLAND IMPULSE PADDLE SHAD

Type: Unrigged plastic swimbaits
Color/Pattern: Blue, Brown Crawdad, Fluorescent
Chartreuse, Silver, Firetiger, Perch, Hot Steel, Purpledescent
Size: 3 in, 3 1/2 in

Quantity: 4
Features: Unique shape produces a crankbait-like wobble;
super-sensitive tail amplifier allows the bait to swim slowly;
fortified with proven fish-attracting Impulse scent.
Price: **$3.99**

SAVAGE GEAR 3D LINE THRU PIKE

Type: Unrigged plastic swimbait
Color/Pattern: Pike
Size: 8 in, 12 in
Weight: 2 1/4 oz, 6 1/2 oz
Quantity: 1

Features: Based on 3D scans of real pike for incredible
detail; line-thru design makes it easier to land fish; great for
fishing in clear water; 8 in. model comes rigged on
0.7mm/60-lb.-test wire with #2 treble hooks; 12 in. model
comes rigged with 0.9mm/80-lb.-test wire with #1/0 treble
hooks.
Price: . . . . **$9.99–$18.99**

SÉBILE ACTION FIRST PIVOT FROG

Type: Frog bait
Color/Pattern: Brown, Black/Yellow, Firetiger, Green, Spot
Mess, White Lime, Yellow
Size: 2 1/2 in
Weight: 1/2 oz.
Quantity: 1

Features: Features an innovative Gravity Hook System that
allows razor-sharp weighted hooks to move side to side for
more realistic action; teamed with a collapsible construction,
these hooks produce reliable hooksets; weighted design gives
the lure a keeled posture making it super easy to walk
whether you're fishing open water or heavy cover.
Price: **$7.99**

SOUTHERN PRO RAINBOW TUBE

Type: Tube
Color/Pattern: Black/Limeade, Bleeding Shad, Blue Passion,
Clown, Crawfish, Firetiger, Red/Limeade, Sunrise
Size: 1 1/2 in

Quantity: 25
Features: Unique three-color combinations; patterns for
both stained and clear water; fish with a standard jighead or
tube jig.
Price: **$2.59**

NEW Products: **Lures, Softbait**

STRIKE KING MR. CRAPPIE SHADPOLE CURLY TAIL

Type: Grub
Color/Pattern: Chartreuse Shiner, Glimmer Blue, Hotchicken.com, Pepper Shad, Purple Sage, Refrigerator White, Tuxedo Black/Chartreuse

Size: 2 in
Quantity: 15
Features: Swimming action of a threadfin shad; fat curly tail produces vibration; specifically made to target crappie.
Price:. **$2.79**

TIGHTLINES UV WHISKER TEXAS RIG

Type: Craw
Color/Pattern: Blue/Black, Craw, Green Pumpkin/PBJ
Size: 4 in

Quantity: 3
Features: Poured with an isolated UV-absorbing coloring; fluttering crawfish profile with a soft silicone skirt; works for almost any jig or Texas rig.
Price:. **$5.99**

UNCLE JOSH PORK BABY NIGHTCRAWLER

Type: Worm
Color/Pattern: Canadian Crawler, Great Lakes Crawler, Natural

Size: 3 in
Quantity: 14
Features: Filled with extracted worm scent; realistic fishtail swimming action; durable design won't get bitten off.
Price:. **$6.49**

UNCLE JOSH PORK REDWORM

Type: Worm
Color/Pattern: Canadian Crawler, Natural
Size: 4 in

Quantity: 8
Features: Made from natural pork for live-bait taste; filled with scent from real worms; easy to thread on a hook; lifelike action.
Price:. **$6.49**

YUM BAD JAMMA

Type: Creature
Color/Pattern: Black/Blue Shadow, Black/Blue Flake, Black/Red Flake, Green Pumpkin, Green Pumpkin/Blue, Green Pumpkin/Purple, Junebug, Watermelon Candy

Size: 3 1/4 in
Quantity: 12
Features: Twin curltails and a wide, ribbed body; presents the right action and look to fool big bass; Texas rigged and flipped, pitched and punched, or used as a trailer.
Price: **$3.49**

YUM CRAWBUG

Type: Craw
Color/Pattern: Carolina Pumpkin, Crawdad, Green Pumpkin, Watermelon/Red Flake, Watermelon Seed
Size: 2 1/2 in, 3 1/4 in

Quantity: 8
Features: Designed with realistic 3D details; hollow body and soft texture imitate a fleeing crawfish; entices hungry largemouths whether you flip it, rig it, or jig it.
Price: **$2.99**

YUM CRAW PAPI

Type: Craw
Color/Pattern: Green Pumpkin/Purple, Ultimate Craw, Virgo Blue, Virgo Red
Size: 3 3/4 in

Quantity: 8
Features: Durable plastic withstands aggressive strikes; ultrarealistic crawfish profile fools leery fish; oversized pinchers create attention-grabbing action.
Price: **$3.49**

YUM DINGER

Type: Stick bait
Color/Pattern: Bama Bug, Bama Magic, Bream, Black/Blue Flake, Cajun Neon, Carolina Pumpkin/Chartreuse, Green Pumpkin, Green Pumpkin/Chartreuse, Melon Pie, Watermelon/Pearl Laminate, Watermelon/Red Flake, Watermelon Seed

Size: 4 in, 5 in
Quantity: 10, 8
Features: Soft-plastic wormlike stick bait delivers slow, subtle action; realistic texture makes bass hang on for the hookset; inactive fish strike whether they're feeding or not.
Price: **$2.99**

NEW Products: **Lures, Softbait**

YUM MIGHTY BUG

Type: Creature
Color/Pattern: Black Neon, Green Pumpkin, Watermelon Red

Size: 3 3/4 in
Quantity: 7
Features: Tri-segmented body with six appendages; infused with attractant; slight twitch creates a panicked action.
Price: **$3.49**

YUM MIGHTY WORM

Type: Worm
Color/Pattern: Blue Flek, Green Pumpkin, Grape/Red, Ultimate Craw, Watermelon/Red, Watermelon Seed,
Size: 10-1/2 in

Quantity: 5
Features: A straight-tail softbait with plenty of dancing and writhing action; fish it on a Texas rig or jighead for large lifelike actions, or put it on a Carolina rig for more-subtle swimming motions.
Price: **$3.49**

YUM MONEY CRAW

Type: Craw
Color/Pattern: Cajun Neon, Crawdad, Green Pumpkin, Junebug, Ultimate Craw
Size: 3 3/4 in

Quantity: 7
Features: Paddle-like claws produce extreme action; crawdad profile entices lunkers; effective when rigged, jigged, or as a trailer.
Price: **$3.49**

YUM RIBBONTAIL WORM

Type: Worm
Color/Pattern: Black/Blue Fleck, Black Neon, Red Shad, Tequila Sunrise, Watermelon Seed
Size: 7 1/2 in

Quantity: 12
Features: Curly-tail soft bait with a built-in difference—the curl is longer than most, so it delivers an extra-furious swimming action; solid body takes on slamming strikes without tearing.
Price: **$2.99**

YUM SHARP SHOOTER

Type: Worm
Color/Pattern: Bold Bluegill, Ghost Shad, Green Pumpkin, Green Pumpkin/Purple, Morning Dawn, Ox/Red, Watermelon Candy, Watermelon Seed

Size: 4 1/2 in, 6 in
Quantity: 20, 15
Features: Bladelike tail produces an undulating motion underwater; soft consistency increases action; fish as a drop-shot or with a jighead.
Price: **$2.99**

YUM SWURM

Type: Worm
Color/Pattern: Green Pumpkin, Pearl Rainbow, Smoke Red Pepper, Swurm'n Shad, Watermelon Pearl Laminate, Watermelon Seed

Size: 4 3/4 in, 6 1/4 in
Quantity: 7
Features: Glides and undulates when twitched; works on a multitude of species.
Price: **$3.49**

YUM THUMP'N DINGER

Type: Worm
Color/Pattern: Black, Black/Blue Flake, Black/Blue Laminate, Green Pumpkin, Green Pumpkin Neon, Junebug, Pearl/Silver Flake, Red Bug, Watermelon/Pearl Laminate, Watermelon/Red Flake

Size: 6 in
Quantity: 10
Features: Excellent when Texas rigged or as swimming worm; produces a panicky swimming motion; emits a vibrating, thumping sound.
Price: **$2.99**

YUM TUBE

Type: Tube
Color/Pattern: Watermelon Seed, Green Pumpkin, White/Silver Flake, Ultimate Craw, Melon Candy
Size: 4 in

Quantity: 6
Features: Soft plastic construction ensures natural movement; durable enough to withstand punishing strikes; free-moving tentacles entice even the most lethargic fish.
Price: **$3.49**

NEW Products: **Lures, Softbait**

YUM WARNING SHOT

Type: Worm
Color/Pattern: Bold Bluegill, Ghost Shad, Green Pumpkin, Green Pumpkin/Purple, Morning Dawn, Ox/Red Flake, Watermelon Candy, Watermelon Seed
Size: 3 3/4 in

Quantity: 10
Features: Ribbed body, flat bottom, and a long, thin bladelike tail moves with every current or twitch of the rod tip; great for drop-shot rigs and as a finesse jig when threaded on a jighead.
Price: **$2.99**

Z-MAN FINESSE T.R.D. STICK BAIT

Type: Stick bait
Color/Pattern: Canada Craw, Coppertreuse, Green Pumpkin, PB&J
Size: 2 3/4 in

Quantity: 8
Features: Soft, durable ElaZtech construction for realistic feel; ideal for the Ned rig; great for beginning and experienced anglers.
Price: **$4.19**

Z-MAN POP SHADZ

Type: Frog bait
Color/Pattern: Bad Shad, Breaking Bream, Mud Minnow, Pearl, Redbone, Smoky Shad
Size: 5 in

Quantity: 1
Features: Cupped face catches air to spit water and create a popping sound; ElaZtech material has a natural buoyancy; works great in saltwater too.
Price: **$5.49**

ROD & REEL ROUNDUP FOR 2015
By Frank Sargeant

The remarkable thing about the new crop of tackle is that many manufacturers continue to make their gear lighter without sacrificing strength and performance. Improvements in engineering and materials, plus increased input from anglers as to exactly what they want, have made it possible to find pretty much exactly the rod and reel combo you want for every imaginable application. Here's a look at some that caught our eye:

ABU GARCIA REVO BEAST

The **Abu Garcia Revo Beast** is one of the more powerful new baitcasters on the market, and it bucks the trend toward lightness at 9.35 ounces. But that's by design—the reel is aimed at anglers who heave giant swimbaits and big topwaters for lunker bass, as well as for stripers, muskies, and other heavyweights. It boasts a maximum drag of 22 pounds, and the extra deep spool holds up to 180 yards of 12-pound-test. A brass main gear and titanium-coated line guide adds to durability. It's a top-ender, priced at $359.95.

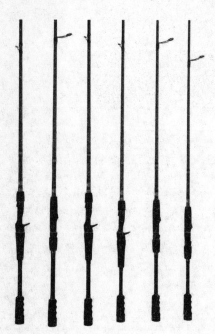

ABU GARCIA FANTASISTA REGISTA FAMILY OF RODS

Also new is the **Abu Garcia Fantasista** rod lineup with what the company calls "tetra-axial carbon construction"—a special carbon wrapping process that provides strength and sensitivity in a lightweight design. Fuji skeletal reel seat and split handles keep the rod light, as do the low-profile Fuji Titanium Alconite K micro-guides. It's a cosmetic match for Abu's Revo reel lineup, and is also premium priced at $499.95; www.abugarcia.com.

CASTAWAY INVICTA

CastAway's **Invicta** is an upper-end series that includes split grips built from the same composite material used on high-end golf clubs. The blanks are 40-ton carbon with a new "carbon-intruded" resin that increases power and strength while cutting weight. CastAway will offer the series in a wide range of spinning and baitcasting models, with actions fine-tuned for specific fresh and saltwater fishing techniques and angling situations. The rods feature ALPS Bronze SS316 Stainless/Bronze guides with Zirconium rings and CastAway's Static Zoned Guide Spacing for superior casting, line control, and fish-fighting performance. The handles of the Invicta rods are particularly innovative, featuring custom Tour Star/Winn non-slip split grips and new CastAway/ALPS double-finger, blank-exposed reel seats with double-locking hoods. This unique handle design provides anglers with a comfortable and secure grip—even with wet hands—along with the sensitivity to feel what's going on with their baits at all times. And it also provides flotation for the rod if dropped overboard—an important added benefit for a rod of this value. MSRP is $250 to $260, depending on the model; www.castawayrods.com.

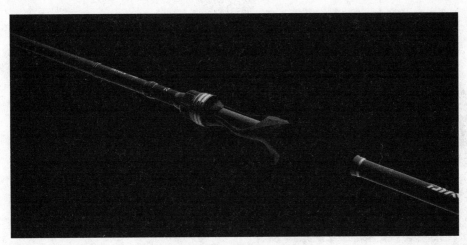

DAIWA TATULA CASTING GRIP

Daiwa now offers a full lineup of **Tatula rods** to match their Tatula reels. The rods feature bias-ply carbon fiber construction which spokesman Curt Arakawa says provides great hoop strength and stiffness plus zero blank twist without an increase in weight. The rods feature Daiwa custom reel seats with machined aluminum locking nut, Fuji Alconite ring guides, and EVA foam grips. There are nine trigger-grip casting rods in the series, a froggin' rod, a flippin' rod, three standard spinning rods, and two drop-shot spinning rods in the series. A five-year limited warranty gives customer assurance. MSRP is $149.95 to $169.95; www.daiwa.com.

EAGLE CLAW WRIGHT & MCGILL VICTORY PRO CARBON CASTING ROD

Al Noraker, VP of Product Development for Eagle Claw Wright & McGill, says their new **Victory Pro Carbon Series rods**, developed with lots of input from top bassing pro Skeet Reese, features a new taping material called "EBS" (Extreme Binding Substrate) that delivers a 78 percent increase in tensile strength. Using a hyper pressure process, the new material encircles the blank after rolling and forces the nano resins into every cavity and space in the carbon material during the baking process, eliminating weak spots and fracture points, and delivering up to 40 percent more strength without increasing weight or reducing sensitivity. And, says Noraker, the blanks have a carbon content of 77.5 percent of the total weight versus the normal construction that averages at 67 percent—more fiber and less resin equals lighter weight. The skeletal reel seat also keeps weight down, and the Pacbay Minima one-piece guide frames reduce weight by 20–30 percent over ceramic-ring guides while increasing sensitivity and rod blank return rate. There are seven casting models and three spinning, all at an MSRP of $159.95.

AL NORAKER, VICE PRESIDENT OF PRODUCT DEVELOPMENT FOR EAGLE CLAW WRIGHT & MCGILL, SHOWS OFF A BEAUTIFUL LAKE TROUT.

EAGLE CLAW WRIGHT & MCGILL VICTORY PRO CARBON SPINNING REEL.

Also new from Wright & McGill is the **Skeet Reese Victory Pro Carbon spinning reel series**, which Al Noraker calls the highest-performance spinning reels the company has ever introduced. The reels are available in 20, 30, and 40 sizes; and thanks to features like the carbon frame, ported aluminum spool, and graphite handle, all three weigh in at less than 9 ounces, remarkably light for full-featured premium spinning reels. All feature 6.0:1 gearing. Two ceramic bearings plus seven stainless steel bearings make these reels remarkably smooth, says Noraker, and the titanium main shaft and titanium-coated line roller make them far more durable than most in the size classes. Despite the light weight, these front-drag reels deliver up to 14 pounds of drag. Suggested price is an affordable $159.95; www.wright-mcgill.com.

FALCON RODS LOWRIDER 20 CASTING ROD

Falcon Rods president Chris Beckwith says the company's venerable **LowRider** is celebrating its 20th anniversary in the 2015 lineup, which inspired a complete redesign of the series. Fourteen casting and nine spinning models complete the new lineup. The distinctive red blanks will come with new Fuji Concept O guides and Fuji ECS reel seats, both state of the art components to help anglers make even longer casts and maximize strike sensitivity.

CHRIS BECKWITH, PRESIDENT OF FALCON RODS, SMILES AFTER CATCHING A GIGANTIC PEACOCK BASS.

Beckwith said the 2015 **LowRider-20** models will have new, lighter handle designs for casting and retrieving utility, and to let the fingers better feel the lure action on the retrieve. Depending on their function, some models will feature natural cork, split-grip handles. Others will have one-piece rear grips of natural cork but without fore grips. The saltwater models feature chromed stainless steel guides for lifetime durability. MSRP is $159 to $200, depending on the model; www.falconrods.com.

FENWICK ELITE TECH BASS CASTING ROD

Fenwick has redesigned their entire **Elite Series** lineup, with technique-specific rods in the Bass, Walleye, River Runner, and heavy-duty Predator specials. There are 18 different rods in the bass series alone, and 11 more for walleyes, allowing the perfect fit for anything from throwing heavy-weight swimbaits for big California bass to finessing walleyes or smallmouth in clear northern lakes. "Hidden Handle" mounts wrap around the base of the reel for a more comfortable grip, and titanium guides have "deep-pressed" inserts to protect against pop-out. Prices range from $149.95 for the Bass, Walleye, and River Runner series to as high as $199.95 for the Predator series; www.fenwickfishing.com.

G.LOOMIS IMX MAG BASS CASTING ROD

G.Loomis has one of the widest selections of top-shelf rods in the bassing industry with their new **IMX lineup**, which includes a remarkable 34 different technique-specific rods providing a broad range of power and action. Offered in "Jig & Worm" casting and spinning rods, "Mag Bass" casting rods, Carolina rig, Flip/Punch technique, swimbait, umbrella rig, spinnerbait, topwater, and jerkbait casting rods, plus spinning models for DropShot and ShakyHead use, the IMX bass rods "provide a new level in weight reduction, sensitivity, and strength so more bass anglers can enjoy the G.Loomis experience," says Bruce Holt with the company's product development team. He said the rods are as much as 15 percent lighter than former versions in the respective actions thanks to new manufacturing processes. They're priced at $295 to $315; www.gloomis.com.

LEW'S BB1 PRO SPEED SPOOL

The Lew's **BB1 Pro Speed Spool** low-profile baitcaster comes in gearing from a powerful 5.1:1 to a speedy 7.1:1 ratio, and the entire series includes ten ball bearings and click-dial centrifugal cast control. An over-sized titanium line guide positioned further away from the spool than in most reels minimizes line friction and maximizes casting performance. The spool holds 160 yards of 12-pound-test mono, and maximum drag is 14 pounds. MSRP is $199.99.

LEW'S SPEED STICK 365 CARBON NANOLAR SERIES

Also new from Lew's is the **Speed Stick 365 rod series**; 50 million-modulus graphite blanks get strength from a multilayer, multidirectional construction process using premium resins. There are seven baitcasting models, from a 6-foot, 6-inch medium action trigger stick to a heavy action 7-foot, 6-inch flippin' rod, plus four spinning models, all with MSRP of $99.99; www.lews.com.

PFLUEGER PATRIARCH XTLOW PROFILE

The Pflueger **Patriarch XTLow Profile** is a lightweight baitcasting reel at just 6.28 ounces, yet it delivers a remarkable 20 pounds of drag when fully locked down, ideal for taking on big bass in heavy cover. Main gears and shaft are aircraft aluminum and the line guide is titanium for maximum durability. Gearing is 6.4:1 and the line capacity is 145 yards of 12-pound-test mono. It's a 10-bearing reel, and the side plate flips up for easy cast control. Price is $249.95; www.pfluegerfishing.com.

SHIMANO CURADO 200-I

Shimano's new **Curado 200-I** is an update of one of the favorite bassing reels of all time, the Curado 200. The new version scales 7.4 ounces and is available in 5.5:1, 6.3:1, and 7.2:1 gearing. The new **SVS Infinity Brake System** provides infinitely adjustable spool control and brake force. Five ball bearings and one Super Stopper Anti-Reverse roller bearing keep the reel super-smooth, and all parts are saltwater-proof. The company's solid X-Ship design improves gear durability and enhances casting performance for longer casts and when using lighter lures.

"With X-Ship, we support the pinion gear on both ends with bearings, keeping it in precise alignment with the drive gear, even under heavy loads," says Product Manager Robby Gant. "It's proven technology from our Tranx and Calcutta D series—reels primarily used with big baits to target big fish."

The Curado 200-I has an externally-adjustable dial with six settings, and Shimano's new **S3D Stable Spool Design** also improves casting capabilities by reducing spool vibration. Line capacity is 115 yards of 14-pound-test mono. It's available in right or left hand retrieve at an MSRP of about $180.

SHIMANO COMPRE MUSKIE

Shimano also has new additions to the **Compre series** of muskie rods, available in lengths from 7 to 9 feet, 6 inches long, all in heavy, extra-heavy, or extra-extra-heavy action with big two-hander handles on IM-8 graphite blanks.

"We're able to offer smaller-diameter blanks that are not only durable, but also lightweight and sensitive," says Robby Gant.

The three models 8-6 and up telescope for an easier fit in the rod box or car. The 8-foot X-Heavy and 8-6 XX-Heavy feature Shimano's TC4 construction process with an inner layer of dynamic T-glass wrapped with an inner and outer layer of graphite for maximum strength; fish.shimano.com.

JIM SARIC, PROFESSIONAL ANGLER AND PUBLISHER AND EDITOR OF *MUSKY HUNTER MAGAZINE,* **HOLDS A TROPHY-SIZED MUSKELLUNGE.**

ST. CROIX TRIUMPH X CASTING ROD

St. Croix's new **Triumph series** reportedly delivers high-level performance at an affordable price. The twelve rods in the series are built on SC-II graphite blanks and get a unique paint that makes them easy to spot on the water. A premium EVA split-grip handle combined with Fuji reel seat provides casting comfort. They retail for $90 to $100. The **Avid-X series** includes eighteen bass and walleye rods with low-profile guides and high-grade cork split-grips with Fuji gunsmoke reel seats. A wide variety of actions are available to fit any angling situation. They're $200 to $230.

ST. CROIX LEGEND TREK TRAVEL ROD

Also new from St. Croix is the **Legend Trek travel rod series**, premium rods that come in travel cases. They're built with SC-IV graphite with slim-profile ferrules and Kigan Master Hand Zero Tangle guide with zirconia rings and titanium frames, and have top-grade cork handles. Pricing is $460 to $530 and a 15-year warranty protects the investment; www.stcroixrods.com.

13 FISHING E 7.3:1 LOW-PROFILE BAITCASTING REEL

13 Fishing is a small, relatively new company, but they're producing some impressive reels, particularly in their high-end **E-Series baitcasters**. These reels, with a MSRP at $380, feature flyweight magnesium frame and sideplates, cork grips, and other weight-saving materials and designs that trim the weight down to a scant 5.78 ounces—one of the lightest in the industry—yet the drag system can be clamped down to deliver an impressive 22 pounds of drag. They also feature the same ceramic bearings used in distance-casting tournament reels; incredible smoothness and wear-resistance; a total of 11 bearings in all; and a Japanese NTN Dead Stop anti-reverse system roller clutch with a performance-milled inner sleeve. The 6.1:1 geared model delivers 26.1 inches of line per turn, and the spool holds up to 100 yards of 12-pound-test mono. The E series is also available in 5.3:1, 7.3:1, and 8.1:1 versions. The company also makes **A-Series reels** in the four versions for about $170, and **C-Series reels** for about $230; www.13fishing.com.

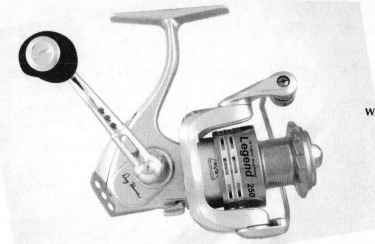

WAVESPIN LEGEND 250 SPINNING REEL

The **WaveSpin Legend** spinning reel is a final tribute to designer Doug Hannon, "The Bass Professor," who passed away in March of 2013. The Legend was the final invention of this unique Florida angler who designed the weedless trolling motor prop and many other patented devices that are now part of the daily life of fishermen everywhere. The reel features the unique star-point spool, which Hannon designed to cut friction over standard round-lip spools—a side benefit is the spool greatly reduces "wind knots" that are common when using thin braids on spinning gear. The striking anodized gold-and-pearl finish on these reels makes them look much more expensive than their $139.95 MSRP, and the two-year warranty should help make them an easy sell. Weight is 9.5 ounces, gear ratio 5.2:1, and line capacity 125 yards of 10-pound-test mono. Eight sealed bearings make this a butter-smooth fishing tool. The company also offers 1500-, 3000-, and 4000-sized reels, all with the unique WaveSpin spool; www.wavespinreel.com.

THE LATE DOUG HANNON INSPECTING
A GOOD-SIZED BASS CAUGHT WITH HIS WAVESPIN
LEGEND 250-EQUIPPED ROD.

Parts of this report appeared originally in *Fishing Tackle Retailer*; www.fishingtackleretailer.com.

RODS: Freshwater Spinning

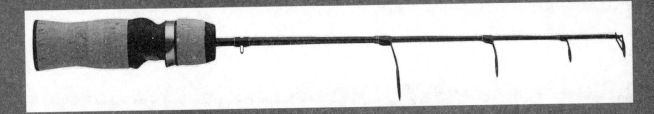

ABU GARCIA VENGEANCE

Model: VNGS56-3, VNGS66-4, VNGS66-5, VNGS66-6, VNGS70-5, VNGS70-6
Length: 5'6''; 6'6''; 6'6''; 6'6''; 7'; 7'
Power: L; ML; M; MH; M; MH
Action: MF; F; MF; F; F; F
Pieces: 1
Line Weight: 2-10 lbs; 6-10 lbs; 6-12 lbs; 8-14 lbs; 6-12 lbs; 6-14 lbs
Guide Count: 6+tip; 7+tip; 7+tip; 7+tip; 7+tip; 7+tip

Lure Weight: 1/16-5/16 oz; 1/8-1/2 oz; 1/8-1/2 oz; 1/4-3/4 oz; 3/16-5/8 oz; 1/4-3/4 oz
Features: 24-ton graphite construction for a lightweight and balanced design; high-density EVA handles are more durable and comfortable; soft-touch sea guide reel seats for increased comfort; zirconium coated guides are perfect for braided line usage; Texas-rigged hook keeper for all bait applications; one-piece rod.
Price: **$49.99**

ABU GARCIA VENGEANCE 2PC

Model: VNGS662-4, VNGS662-5, VNGS662-6, VNGS702-5
Length: 6'6''; 6'6''; 6'6''; 7'
Power: ML; M; MH; M
Action: F; MF; F; F
Pieces: 2
Line Weight: 6-10 lbs; 6-12 lbs; 8-14 lbs; 6-12 lbs
Guide Count: 7+tip
Lure Weight: 1/8-1/2 oz; 1/8-1/2 oz; 1/4-3/4 oz; 3/16-5/8 oz

Features: 24-ton graphite construction for a lightweight and balanced design; high-density EVA handles are more durable and comfortable; soft-touch sea guide reel seats for increased comfort; zirconium coated guides are perfect for braided line usage; Texas-rigged hook keeper for all bait applications.
Price: **$49.99**

ACTION	POWER	
M=Moderate	UL=Ultra Light	H=Heavy
MF=Moderate Fast	L=Light	MH=Medium-Heavy
F=Fast	ML=Medium-Light	XH=Extra Heavy
XF=Extra Fast		

ABU GARCIA VERACITY–MICRO-GUIDE

Model: VERS69-4, VERS70-5, VERS70-6, VERS76-5
Length: 6'9''; 7'; 7'; 7'6''
Power: ML; M; MH; M
Action: F
Line Weight: 6-10 lbs; 8-14 lbs; 8-14 lbs; 6-12 lbs
Guide Count: 6+tip; 7+tip; 7+tip; 8+tip
Lure Weight: 1/8-1/2 oz; 3/16-5/8 oz; 1/4-3/4 oz; 3/16-5/8 oz
Features: 36-ton graphite with nanotechnology for decreased weight and increased impact resistance; titanium alloy guides with titanium inserts allow for a super lightweight guide giving the ultimate in rod performance; high-density EVA gives greater sensitivity and durability; micro-guide system provides improved balance and sensitivity; Texas-rigged hook keeper for all bait applications.
Price: **$149.95**

ABU GARCIA VERACITY–WINCH MODEL

Model: VERSW70-5
Length: 7'
Power: M
Action: M
Line Weight: 8-14 lbs
Guide Count: 7+tip
Lure Weight: 3/16-5/8 oz
Features: 36-ton graphite with nanotechnology for decreased weight and increased impact resistance; titanium alloy guides with titanium inserts allow for a super lightweight guide giving the ultimate in rod performance; high-density EVA gives greater sensitivity and durability; micro-guide system provides improved balance and sensitivity; Texas-rigged hook keeper for all bait applications.
Price: **$149.95**

ACTION	**POWER**	
M=Moderate	UL=Ultra Light	H=Heavy
MF=Moderate Fast	L=Light	MH=Medium-Heavy
F=Fast	ML=Medium-Light	XH=Extra Heavy
XF=Extra Fast		

ABU GARCIA VERITAS SPINNING

Model: VRS66-5, VRS66-6, VRS69-4, VRS70-5, VRS70-6
Length: 6'6''; 6'6''; 6'9''; 7'; 7'
Power: M; MH; ML; M; MH
Action: XF; F; MF; F; F
Pieces: 1
Line Weight: 6-12 lbs; 8-14 lbs; 6-10 lbs; 6-12 lbs; 8-14 lbs
Guide Count: 7+tip
Lure Weight: 1/8-1/2 oz; 1/4-3/4 oz; 1/8-1/2 oz; 3/16-5/8 oz; 1/4-3/4 oz
Features: 30-ton graphite construction with

nanotechnology for decreased weight and increased compression strength; one-piece double-anodized aluminum screw down creates a secure connection with the reel; high-density EVA handles are more durable and comfortable; Abu-designed extreme exposure reel seats provide direct finger to rod contact for increased sensitivity; titanium alloy guides with SiC inserts create a lightweight, balanced rod design; Texas-rigged hook keeper for all bait applications; one-piece rod.
Price: **$99.95**

ABU GARCIA VERITAS SPINNING 2PC

Model: VRS662-5, VRS662-6, VRS702-5
Length: 6'6''; 6'6''; 7'
Power: M; MH; M
Action: F; F; XF
Pieces: 2
Line Weight: 6-12 lbs; 8-14 lbs; 6-12 lbs
Guide Count: 7+tip
Lure Weight: 1/8-1/2 oz; 1/4-3/4 oz; 3/16-5/8 oz
Features: 30-ton graphite construction with nanotechnology for decreased weight and increased compression strength;

one-piece double-anodized aluminum screw down creates a secure connection with the reel; high-density EVA handles are more durable and comfortable; Abu-designed extreme exposure reel seats provide direct finger to rod contact for increased sensitivity; titanium alloy guides with SiC inserts create a lightweight, balanced rod design; Texas-rigged hook keeper for all bait applications.
Price: **$99.95**

ACTION	**POWER**	
M=Moderate	**UL=Ultra Light**	**H=Heavy**
MF=Moderate Fast	**L=Light**	**MH=Medium-Heavy**
F=Fast	**ML=Medium-Light**	**XH=Extra Heavy**
XF=Extra Fast		

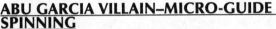

ABU GARCIA VILLAIN–MICRO-GUIDE SPINNING

Model: VLSM610-5, VLSM69-4, VLSM71-5
Length: 6'10"; 6'9"; 7'1"
Power: M; ML; M
Action: MF; F; F
Pieces: 1
Line Weight: 6-12 lbs; 6-10 lbs; 6-12 lbs
Guide Count: 7+tip

Lure Weight: 3/16-5/8 oz; 1/8-1/2 oz; 3/16-5/8 oz
Features: Titanium alloy guides, with titanium inserts allow for a super lightweight guide, giving the ultimate in rod performance; C6 total exposure reel seat gives complete contact to the rod for the ultimate sensitivity; high-density EVA gives greater sensitivity and durability; carbon-wrapped guides reduce weight; Texas-rigged hook keeper for all bait applications; split-grip design; one-piece rod.
Price: **$179.95**

ABU GARCIA VILLAIN–SPINNING

Model: VLS610-5, VLS66-6, VLS69-4, VLS71-5, VLS71-6
Length: 6'10"; 6'6"; 6'9"; 7'1"; 7'1"
Power: M; MH; ML; M; MH
Action: MF; F; F; F; F
Pieces: 1
Line Weight: 6-12 lbs; 8-14 lbs; 6-10 lbs; 6-12 lbs; 8-14 lbs
Guide Count: 7+tip
Lure Weight: 3/16-5/8 oz; 1/4-3/4 oz; 1/8-1/2 oz; 3/16-5/8 oz; 1/4-3/4 oz

Features: Titanium alloy guides with titanium inserts allow for a super lightweight guide, giving the ultimate in rod performance; C6 total exposure reel seat gives complete contact to the rod for the ultimate sensitivity; high-density EVA gives greater sensitivity and durability; carbon-wrapped guides reduce weight; Texas-rigged hook keeper for all bait applications; split-grip design; one-piece rod.
Price: **$179.95**

ACTION	POWER	
M=Moderate	**UL**=Ultra Light	**H**=Heavy
MF=Moderate Fast	**L**=Light	**MH**=Medium-Heavy
F=Fast	**ML**=Medium-Light	**XH**=Extra Heavy
XF=Extra Fast		

RODS: Freshwater Spinning

ABU GARCIA VILLAIN–SPINNING 2PC
Model: VLS6102-5, VLS662-6
Length: 6'10''; 6'6''
Power: M; MH
Action: MF; F
Pieces: 2
Line Weight: 6-12 lbs; 8-14 lbs
Guide Count: 7+tip
Lure Weight: 3/16-5/8 oz; 1/4-3/4 oz

Features: Titanium alloy guides with titanium inserts allow for a super lightweight guide giving the ultimate in rod performance; C6 total exposure reel seat gives complete contact to the rod for the ultimate sensitivity; high-density EVA gives greater sensitivity and durability; carbon wrapped guides reduce weight; Texas-rigged hook keeper for all bait applications; split grip design.
Price:................................... $179.95

ABU GARCIA VOLATILE
Model: VOLS70-4, VOLS70-5, VOLS70-6, VOLS76-5
Length: 7'; 7'; 7'; 7'6''
Power: M; M; MH; M
Action: F
Pieces: 1
Line Weight: 6-12 lbs; 8-17 lbs; 10-20 lbs; 8-17 lbs
Guide Count: 7+tip
Lure Weight: 1/16-3/8 oz; 1/4-5/8 oz; 3/8-1 oz; 1/4-5/8 oz

Features: 30-ton graphite with NanoTechnology for decreased weight and increased impact resistance; high-density EVA gives greater sensitivity and durability; Texas-rigged hook keeper for all bait applications; stainless steel guides with Zirconium inserts; Fuji IPS (spinning) and Fuji EPS (casting) reel seat for greater comfort; split grip design.
Price:................................... $99.95

ACTION	POWER	
M=Moderate	UL=Ultra Light	H=Heavy
MF=Moderate Fast	L=Light	MH=Medium-Heavy
F=Fast	ML=Medium-Light	XH=Extra Heavy
XF=Extra Fast		

BASS PRO SHOPS 3' GRAPHITE

Model: 3' Graphite
Length: 3'
Power: M
Action: F
Pieces: 1
Line Weight: 6–12 lb
Lure Weight: 1/8-1/2 oz

Features: An excellent rod for pitching lures under docks, working areas with thick brush, kayak fishing, and ice fishing for larger fish; great for children; features high-performing IM6 graphite blanks for the strength and sensitivity you need to take your limit; complete with aluminum oxide guides and our comfortable cork handles with a graphite reel seat.
Price:................................... $21.99

BASS PRO SHOPS JOHNNY MORRIS CARBONLITE

Model: CL66MSF, CL66MHSF, CL68MSXF, 69MLSDS, CL70MSF, CL70MHSF, CL72MSDS, CL90MLSM-2PC, CL56ULS, CL60LS, CL66MLS, CL66MSF-2, CL70MHSF-2
Length: 6'6''; 6'6''; 6'8''; 6'9''; 7'; 7'; 7'2''; 9'; 5'6''; 6'; 6'6''; 6'6''; 7'
Power: M; MH; M; ML; M; MH; M; ML; UL; L; ML; M; MH
Action: F; F; XF; F; F; F; F; F; F; F; F; F; F
Pieces: 1; 1; 1; 1; 1; 1; 1; 2; 1; 1; 1; 2; 2
Line Weight: 4-12 lbs; 6-17 lbs; 4-12 lbs; 4-10 lbs; 4-12 lbs; 6-17 lbs; 4-12 lbs; 4-10 lbs; 1-6 lbs; 2-8 lbs; 4-10 lbs; 4-12 lbs; 6-17 lbs

Lure Weight: 1/8-1/2 oz; 1/4-5/8 oz; 1/8-1/2 oz; 1/16-3/8 oz; 1/8-1/2 oz; 1/4-5/8 oz; 1/8-1/2 oz; 1/16-3/8 oz; 1/32-1/4 oz; 1/16-1/4 oz; 1/16-3/8 oz; 1/8-1/2 oz; 1/4-5/8 oz
Features: 85 million-modulus carbon fiber blank; Pac Bay DLC stainless steel framed guides; works great with mono, fluoro, or superlines; almost weightless space-age P-Tec polyfoam grips; two-piece soft-touch reel seat with maximum blank exposure.
Price:................................... $99.99

ACTION	POWER	
M=Moderate	UL=Ultra Light	H=Heavy
MF=Moderate Fast	L=Light	MH=Medium-Heavy
F=Fast	ML=Medium-Light	XH=Extra Heavy
XF=Extra Fast		

BASS PRO SHOPS JOHNNY MORRIS SIGNATURE SERIES II

Model: 68MS, 68MHS, 72MS, 72MHS
Length: 6'8"; 6'8"; 7'2"; 7'2"
Power: M; MH; M; MH
Action: XF; XF; F; F
Pieces: 1
Line Weight: 4–12 lbs; 6–17 lbs; 4-12 lbs; 6-17 lbs
Lure Weight: 1/8-½ oz; ¼-5/8 oz; 1/8-½ oz; ¼-5/8 oz

Features: Super-high-grade 85 million-modulus graphite blank; industry leading Type 1 slit carbon powerwall construction; exclusive carbon cloth butt wrap for unprecedented strength; Fuji new concept stainless steel K-guides with Alconite rings; premium molded split handles with ultra-comfortable P-Tec polyfoam grips; our super-low-profile two-piece exposed-blank reel seat with a soft-touch finish.
Price: **$139.99**

BASS PRO SHOPS MICRO LITE GRAPHITE

Model: ML36/4-T, 46ULS, 50ULS, 56ULS-2, 56LS, 60ULS-2, 60LS, 60MLS, 66ULS-2, 66LS-2, 66MLS-2, 70ULS-2, 70LS-2, 70MLS-2, 76ULS-2
Length: 3'6"; 4'6"; 5'; 5'6"; 5'6"; 6'; 6'; 6'; 6'6"; 6'6"; 6'6"; 7'; 7'; 7'; 7'6"
Power: L; UL; UL; UL; L; UL; L; ML; UL; L; ML; UL; L; ML; UL
Action: Fast
Pieces: 1; 1; 1; 2; 1; 2; 1; 1; 2; 2; 2; 2; 2; 2; 2
Line Weight: 2-8 lbs; 1-6 lbs; 1-6 lbs; 1-6 lbs; 2-8 lbs; 1-6 lbs; 2-8 lbs; 4-10 lbs; 1-6 lbs; 2-8 lbs; 4-10 lbs; 2-6 lbs; 2-8 lbs; 4-10 lbs; 2-6 lbs

Lure Weight: 1/32-1/4 oz; 1/64-1/8 oz; 1/32-1/4 oz; 1/32-1/4 oz; 1/16-1/4 oz; 1/32-1/4 oz; 1/16-1/4 oz; 1/16-3/8 oz; 1/32-1/4 oz; 1/16-1/4 oz; 1/16-3/8 oz; 1/16-1/4 oz; 1/16-1/4 oz; 1/16-3/8 oz; 1/16-1/4 oz
Features: Another excellent rod for light tackle; features IM6 graphite blanks with real solid carbon tip sections for incredible sensitivity and toughness; ultra-thin, lightweight guides that balance almost weightlessly on the spline and deliver a truly awesome feel; complete with gold anodized reel seats; contoured cork handles.
Price: **$49.99**

ACTION	POWER	
M=Moderate	**UL**=Ultra Light	**H**=Heavy
MF=Moderate Fast	**L**=Light	**MH**=Medium-Heavy
F=Fast	**ML**=Medium-Light	**XH**=Extra Heavy
XF=Extra Fast		

BASS PRO SHOPS MICRO LITE GRAPHITE FLOAT 'N' FLY

Model: 80MLS-2, 86MLS-2, 96MLS-2
Length: 8'; 8'6''; 9'6''
Power: ML
Action: F
Pieces: 2
Line Weight: 4-10 lbs
Lure Weight: 1/16–3/8 oz

Features: A perfect rod for light tackle; features IM6 graphite blanks with real solid carbon tip sections for incredible sensitivity and toughness; ultra-thin, lightweight guides balance almost weightlessly on the spline and deliver a truly awesome feel; complete with gold anodized reel seats; contoured cork handles; pre-equipped for use with balance kit (sold separately).
Price: **$54.99**

BERKLEY AIR IM8

Model: A94-8-6M, A94-9MH, A94-9L, A94-9M, A94-9-6M, A94-99ML, A94-10-6XL, A94-109ML
Length: 8'6''; 9'; 9'; 9'; 9'6''; 9'9''; 10'6''; 10'6''
Power: M; MH; L; M; M; ML; XL; ML
Pieces: 2
Line Weight: 8-12 lbs; 10-20 lbs; 6-10 lbs; 8-14 lbs; 8-12 lbs; 6-10 lbs; 4-10 lbs; 6-10 lbs
Guide Count: 9; 9; 9; 9; 10; 10; 10; 10
Lure Weight: 3/8-3/4 oz; 1/2-1 1/2 oz; 1/8-1/2 oz; 3/8-3/4 oz; 3/8-3/4 oz; 1/8-1/2 oz; 1/8-1/2 oz; 1/8-1/2 oz

Features: Constructed of IM8 advanced-modulus graphite; air IM8 rods are lightweight and have a sensitive blank that provides the ultimate in feel with enough power to land big fish with ease; titanium-coated SS304 guides for increased durability and abrasion resistance when fishing with braided line; perfect for casting to big steelhead or trolling for giant lake trout; concept guide spacing improves sensitivity and maximizes blank strength; air IM8 gives anglers the length, power, and performance they need for demanding conditions.
Price: . . . . **$99.99–$109.99**

ACTION	POWER	
M=Moderate	UL=Ultra Light	H=Heavy
MF=Moderate Fast	L=Light	MH=Medium-Heavy
F=Fast	ML=Medium-Light	XH=Extra Heavy
XF=Extra Fast		

RODS: Freshwater Spinning

BERKLEY AMP
Model: AS562L, AS601M, AS662ML, AS661M, AS662M, AS701M, AS702M
Length: 5'6''; 6'; 6'6''; 6'6''; 6'6''; 7'; 7'
Power: L; M; ML; M; M; M; M
Pieces: 2; 1; 2; 1; 2; 1; 2
Line Weight: 2-8 lbs; 4-12 lbs; 4-10 lbs; 4-12 lbs; 4-12 lbs; 4-12 lbs; 4-12 lbs
Guide Count: 4; 4; 5; 5; 5; 5; 5
Lure Weight: 1/16-3/8 oz; 1/8-3/4 oz; 1/8-5/8 oz; 1/8-3/4 oz; 1/8-3/4 oz; 1/8-3/4 oz; 1/8-3/4 oz

Features: Lighter, faster, and more sensitive than the average rod; features X-posed reel seats and split-grip cork handles on both spinning and casting models, allowing the hand to remain in constant contact with the rod blank and taking sensitivity and light weight to a new level; comes with an armadillo hide finish that eliminates cut fibers and ensures the blank is free from imperfections.
Price: $29.99

BERKLEY CHERRYWOOD HD
Model: CWD461ULS, CWD501ULS, CWD561ULS, CWD562LS, CWD601MS, CWD601MHS, CWD662MLS, CWD661MS, CWD662MS, CWD701MS, CWD702MS, CWD702MHS
Length: 4'6''; 5'; 5'6''; 5'6''; 6'; 6'; 6'6''; 6'6''; 6'6''; 7'; 7'; 7'
Power: UL; UL; UL; L; M; MH; ML; M; M; M; M; MH
Pieces: 1; 1; 1; 2; 1; 1; 2; 1; 2; 1; 2; 2
Line Weight: 1-4 lbs; 1-4 lbs; 2-6 lbs; 2-6 lbs; 6-14 lbs; 8-17 lbs; 4-12 lbs; 6-14 lbs; 6-14 lbs; 6-14 lbs; 6-14 lbs; 8-17 lbs
Guide Count: 4; 4; 5; 5; 5; 5; 6; 6; 6; 6; 6; 6

Lure Weight: 1/32-1/8 oz; 1/32-1/8 oz; 1/32-1/8 oz; 1/16-1/4 oz; 1/8-3/4 oz; 1/4-1 oz; 1/8-5/8 oz; 1/8-3/4 oz; 1/8-3/4 oz; 1/8-3/4 oz; 1/8-3/4 oz; 1/4-1 oz
Features: Graphite technology; remarkable value; offers a balanced graphite composition blank and quality construction for excellent responsiveness and durability; comes with a chromium guide system that is 20 times tougher and up to 55 percent lighter than conventional oxide guides.
Price: $24.99

ACTION	**POWER**	
M=Moderate	UL=Ultra Light	H=Heavy
MF=Moderate Fast	L=Light	MH=Medium-Heavy
F=Fast	ML=Medium-Light	XH=Extra Heavy
XF=Extra Fast		

BERKLEY C-SERIES

Model: BCS902L, BCS1002L, BCS1102L, BCS1202L, BCS1403L
Length: 9'; 10'; 11'; 12'; 14'
Power: L
Pieces: 2
Line Weight: 4-12 lbs
Guide Count: 9; 9; 10; 10; 11

Features: Solid carbon fiber tip allows for quick reaction on even the lightest bite; 24-ton carbon fiber blank creates a lightweight and sensitive feeling rod; EVA power grip ergonomically designed for more control and less hand fatigue; durable, high strength-to-weight titanium oxide insert; stainless steel guides; bell-shaped tapered rear handle for secure rod holder placement.
Price: . . . . **$44.99–$49.99**

BERKLEY GLOWSTIK

Model: GSS702M, GSS802MH, GSS902MH, GSS1002MH
Length: 7'; 8'; 9'; 10'
Power: M; MH; MH; MH
Pieces: 2
Line Weight: 10-20 lbs; 10-25 lbs; 10-30 lbs; 10-30 lbs
Guide Count: 5; 5; 6; 7

Lure Weight: 1/2-3 oz; 1-4 oz; 1-5 oz; 1-5 oz
Features: The right rod for any nighttime fishing adventure; features super strong, super tough E-glass technology, making it nearly indestructible; exclusive lighted blank design can be activated to glow continuously for great night bite detection.
Price: . . . . **$39.99–$49.99**

ACTION	POWER	
M=Moderate	UL=Ultra Light	H=Heavy
MF=Moderate Fast	L=Light	MH=Medium-Heavy
F=Fast	ML=Medium-Light	XH=Extra Heavy
XF=Extra Fast		

RODS: Freshwater Spinning

BERKLEY LIGHTNING ROD–ICE

Model: LR24ULS, LR28MLS, LR28MS, LR32MHS, LR32HS, LR32MHC
Length: 2'; 2'4''; 2'4''; 2'8''; 2'8''; 2'8''
Power: UL; ML; M; MH; H; MH
Pieces: 1
Line Weight: 1-6 lbs; 2-6 lbs; 4-8 lbs; 6-10 lbs; 8-14 lbs
Guide Count: 3; 4; 4; 4; 4; 4

Features: Fore-grip uses hidden thread technology to reduce wear and tear on your fingers; skeleton reel seat provides increased sensitivity and reduces overall weight; guides are 20X tougher and 55 percent lighter than traditional aluminum oxide guides and are factory tested for dependability.
Price: . . . . **$14.99–$19.99**

BERKLEY LIGHTNING ROD

Model: LR502ULS, LR562LS, LR601MHS, LR601MLS, LR602MLS, LR601MS, LR662MLS, LR661MS, LR662MS, LR701MS, LR702MS
Length: 5'; 5'6''; 6'; 6'; 6'; 6'; 6'6''; 6'6''; 6'6''; 7'; 7'
Power: UL; L; MH; ML; ML; ML; ML; M; M; M; M
Pieces: 2; 2; 1; 1; 2; 1; 2; 1; 2; 1; 2
Line Weight: 2-6 lbs; 4-8 lbs; 10-17 lbs; 6-12 lbs; 6-12 lbs; 8-14 lbs; 6-12 lbs; 8-14 lbs; 8-14 lbs; 8-14 lbs; 8-14 lbs
Guide Count: 5; 5; 6; 6; 6; 6; 6; 6; 6; 6; 6

Lure Weight: 1/32-1/4 oz; 1/16-3/8 oz; 3/8-3/4 oz; 1/16-1/2 oz; 1/16-1/2 oz; 1/4-5/8 oz; 1/16-1/2 oz; 1/4-5/8 oz; 1/4-5/8 oz; 1/4-5/8 oz; 1/4-5/8 oz
Features: #1 selling graphite rod; unique combination of strength and sensitivity; the fastest, strongest, and lightest rod in its class; features chrome-plated SS304 guides.
Price: **$39.99**

ACTION	POWER	
M=Moderate	UL=Ultra Light	H=Heavy
MF=Moderate Fast	L=Light	MH=Medium-Heavy
F=Fast	ML=Medium-Light	XH=Extra Heavy
XF=Extra Fast		

BERKLEY LIGHTNING ROD SHOCK

Model: SHS601M, SHS662ML, SHS661M, SHS701ML, SHS701M, SHS761ML
Length: 6'; 6'6''; 6'6''; 7'; 7'; 7'6''
Power: M; ML; M; ML; M; ML
Pieces: 1; 2; 1; 1; 1; 1
Line Weight: 4-12 lbs; 4-10 lbs; 4-12 lbs; 4-10 lbs; 4-12 lbs; 4-10 lbs
Guide Count: 5
Lure Weight: 1/8-3/4 oz; 1/8-5/8 oz; 1/8-3/4 oz; 1/8-5/8 oz; 1/4-3/4 oz; 1/8-5/8 oz
Features: Near zero-stretch line with plenty of strength in a small diameter; designed specifically for superline fishing; aluminum oxide guides are diamond polished to a rich, black surface for strength, durability, and reduced friction; downsized guides help decrease wind knots while remaining lightweight and tough; strike-amplifying tip blends fiberglass with graphite to produce a slower-reacting tip; split-grip design delivers more sensitivity and better balance with less weight; suspended reel seat dampens reel vibration, ensuring maximum sensitivity; 1K power helix construction produces extra strength in the backbone while remaining light weight, to handle the stress loads inherent to fishing with superline.
Price:. . . . . **$49.99–$54.99**

BERKLEY TROUT DOUGH

Model: TDS461UL, TDS501UL, TDS562UL, TDS602UL, TDS662UL, TDS702UL, TDS702L, TDS762UL, TDS802UL
Length: 4'6''; 5'; 5'6''; 6'; 6'6''; 7'; 7'; 7'6''; 8'
Power: UL; UL; UL; UL; UL; UL; L; UL; UL
Pieces: 1; 1; 2; 2; 2; 2; 2; 2; 2
Line Weight: 1-4 lbs; 1-4 lbs; 1-6 lbs; 1-6 lbs; 1-6 lbs; 1-6 lbs; 2-8 lbs; 1-6 lbs; 1-6 lbs
Guide Count: 5; 6; 7; 7; 8; 8; 8; 9; 10
Lure Weight: 1/32-1/8 oz; 1/32-1/8 oz; 1/32-3/16 oz; 1/32-3/16 oz; 1/32-1/4 oz; 1/32-1/4 oz; 1/16-3/8 oz; 1/32-1/4 oz; 1/32-1/4 oz
Features: Engineered specifically to cast farther and with more accuracy without losing your bait; cork split-grip handle construction helps to reduce overall weight; uni-directional fiberglass technology delivers the strength required to fish for trout without compromising the diameter or weight of the rod.
Price:. **$39.99**

ACTION	POWER	
M=Moderate	UL=Ultra Light	H=Heavy
MF=Moderate Fast	L=Light	MH=Medium-Heavy
F=Fast	ML=Medium-Light	XH=Extra Heavy
XF=Extra Fast		

RODS: Freshwater Spinning

CABELA'S FISH EAGLE 50 TRAVEL

Model: FE50S704-4
Length: 7'
Power: M
Action: F
Pieces: 4
Line Weight: 8-12 lbs
Lure Weight: 1/4-3/4 oz
Features: High-quality HM50 graphite, 50 million-PSI modulus blanks; Pacific Bay stainless steel guide frames with

durable wear-resistant Hialoy ceramic inserts, to reduce line friction for consistently longer casts and smoother retrieves; down-locking fore grips for flawless security, eliminating exposed reel seat threads; cork grips with rubberized accents for a better grasp; pearl gray-green color has a matte finish; travel rods break down into four pieces for easy portability (case sold separately).
Price: **$199.99**

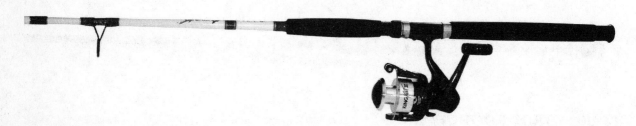

CABELA'S KING KAT

Model: CKKS702, CKKS802, CKKS102, CKKS602-M, CKKS662-M
Length: 7'; 8'; 10'; 6'; 6'6''
Power: MH; MH; MH; M; M
Pieces: 2
Line Weight: 12-25 lbs; 14-30 lbs; 14-30 lbs; 6-15 lbs; 6-15 lbs

Features: This rod stands up to the long fights big flatheads and blues are known for; constructed from ultratough E-glass; bright tip to help you detect nighttime bites; rugged double-foot ceramic guides and stainless steel hoods on the reel seats add to the performance and durability of our King Kat rods; sure-grip EVA handles offer no-slip confidence during long fights in bad weather.
Price: **$29.99**

ACTION	POWER	
M=Moderate	UL=Ultra Light	H=Heavy
MF=Moderate Fast	L=Light	MH=Medium-Heavy
F=Fast	ML=Medium-Light	XH=Extra Heavy
XF=Extra Fast		

CABELA'S PLATINUM ZX

Model: PZXS663-1, PZXS663-2, PZXS664-1, PZXS664-2, PZXS693-1, PZXS702-2, PZXS703-1, PZXS703-2, PZXS704-1, PZXS704-2, PZXS705-2, PZXS763-2
Length: 6'6''; 6'6''; 6'6''; 6'6''; 6'9''; 7'; 7'; 7'; 7'; 7'; 7'; 7'6''
Power: ML; ML; M; M; M; L; ML; ML; M; M; MH; ML
Action: F
Pieces: 1; 2; 1; 2; 1; 2; 1; 2; 1; 2; 2; 2

Line Weight: 4-8 lbs; 4-8 lbs; 6-12 lbs; 6-12 lbs; 6-12 lbs; 2-8 lbs; 4-8 lbs; 4-8 lbs; 6-12 lbs; 6-12 lbs; 8-20 lbs; 4-8 lbs
Lure Weight: 1/8-3/8 oz; 1/8-3/8 oz; 1/4-5/8 oz; 1/4-5/8 oz; 1/4-5/8 oz; 1/16-3/8 oz; 1/8-3/8 oz; 1/8-3/8 oz; 1/4-5/8 oz; 1/4-5/8 oz; 3/8-1 oz; 1/8-3/8 oz
Features: 3M Powerlux matrix resin; Fuji's tangle-eliminating K-Series guides; up to 30 percent stronger and 15 percent lighter; diamond-polished SiC inserts; palm-swell seats.
Price: **$199.99**

CABELA'S TOURNEY TRAIL SB

Model: TTS664-2
Length: 6'6''
Power: M
Action: F
Pieces: 2
Line Weight: 6-12 lbs

Lure Weight: 1/4-5/8 oz
Features: IM7 construction; graphite reel seat; aluminum oxide guides; high-quality cork handle; steel-blue blank color.
Price: **$64.99**

ACTION	POWER	
M=Moderate	UL=Ultra Light	H=Heavy
MF=Moderate Fast	L=Light	MH=Medium-Heavy
F=Fast	ML=Medium-Light	XH=Extra Heavy
XF=Extra Fast		

RODS: **Freshwater Spinning**

CABELA'S WHUPPIN' STICK

Model: WSSM60-2, WSSH72-2, WSSH80-2, WSSM10-2, WSSL56-2, WSSMH60-1, WSSMH90-2, WSSM90-2, WSSM66-2, WSSM80-2, WSSM70-2, WSSML66-2
Length: 6'; 7'2''; 8'; 10'; 5'6''; 6'; 9'; 9'; 6'6''; 8'; 7'; 6'6''
Power: M; H; H; M; L; MH; MH; M; M; M; M; M
Pieces: 2; 2; 2; 2; 2; 1; 2; 2; 2; 2; 2; 2
Line Weight: 6-15 lbs; 12-50 lbs; 14-50 lbs; 4-20 lbs; 4-10 lbs; 6-15 lbs; 14-30 lbs; 4-20 lbs; 6-15 lbs; 4-20 lbs; 6-15 lbs; 4-12 lbs

Features: This rod is known for its nearly indestructible, advanced polymer fiberglass blanks; graphite reel seats securely lock reel in place without adding significant weight to the rod; blank-through-handle construction makes it easy to feel even the light biters; stainless steel frame guides with ceramic inserts will stand up to the toughest fish; cork grips ensure all-day comfort.
Price: **$29.99**

CABELA'S XML

Model: XMLS601-2, XMLS602-1, XMLS604-1, XMLS663-1, XMLS663-2, XMLS664-1, XMLS664XF-1, XMLS664-2, XMLS665-1, XMLS702-2, XMLS703-1, XML703-2, XMLS704-1, XMLS704-2, XMLS705-1, XMLS705-2
Length: 6'; 6'; 6'; 6'6''; 6'6''; 6'6''; 6'6''; 6'6''; 6'6''; 7'; 7'; 7'; 7'; 7'; 7'; 7'
Power: UL; ML; M; ML; ML; M; M; M; MH; L; ML; ML; M; M; MH; MH
Action: F; F; F; F; F; F; XF; F; F; F; F; F; F; F; F; F
Pieces: 2; 1; 1; 1; 2; 1; 1; 2; 1; 2; 1; 2; 1; 2; 1; 2
Line Weight: 2-6 lbs; 4-8 lbs; 6-12 lbs; 4-8 lbs; 4-8 lbs; 6-12 lbs; 6-12 lbs; 6-12 lbs; 8-20 lbs; 2-8 lbs; 4-8 lbs; 4-8 lbs; 6-12 lbs; 6-12 lbs; 8-20 lbs; 8-20 lbs
Lure Weight: 1/16-3/8 oz; 1/8-3/8 oz; 1/4-5/8 oz; 1/8-3/8 oz; 1/8-3/8 oz; 1/4-5/8 oz; 1/4-5/8 oz; 1/4-5/8 oz; 3/8-1 oz; 1/16-3/8 oz; 1/8-3/8 oz; 1/8-3/8 oz; 1/4-5/8 oz; 1/4-5/8 oz; 3/8-1 oz; 3/8-1 oz

Features: These updated rods are built on our legendary XML 64 million-modulus, spiral-core-technology graphite blanks. They feature lightweight, super-durable SS316 stainless steel Alps guides, double-coated with black chrome for maximum corrosion resistance. Precise guide spacing compacts the distance between guides from the middle to the tip of the rod. This increases sensitivity and decreases line drag. Rods have a palm-swell American Tackle Aero reel seat. Grips are made of premium cork and have thread-covering downlocking fore grips. Butts are compatible with our Weight-Balancing System, available separately.
Price: **$149.99**

ACTION		POWER	
M=Moderate	UL=Ultra Light		H=Heavy
MF=Moderate Fast	L=Light		MH=Medium-Heavy
F=Fast	ML=Medium-Light		XH=Extra Heavy
XF=Extra Fast			

CABELA'S XML TRAVEL

Model: XMLS603-4, XMLS665XF-4, XMLS663-4, XMLS703-4, XMLS704-4
Length: 6'; 6'6"; 6'6"; 7'; 7'
Power: ML; M; ML; ML; M
Action: F; XF; F; F; F
Pieces: 4
Line Weight: 4-8 lbs; 6-12 lbs; 4-8 lbs; 4-8 lbs; 6-12 lbs
Lure Weight: 1/8-3/8 oz; 1/4-5/8 oz; 1/8-3/8 oz; 1/8-3/8 oz; 1/4-5/8 oz

Features: Four-piece rods are built on the legendary XML 64 million-modulus, spiral-core-technology graphite blanks; features lightweight, super-durable stainless steel Alps guides, double-coated with black chrome for maximum corrosion resistance; concept spacing increases sensitivity while decreasing line drag; palm-swell Aero reels seats; premium cork grips and thread-covering downlocking fore grips; butts are compatible with the XML weight-balance system (sold separately); Cordura nylon case and nylon storage sleeve included.
Price: **$159.99**

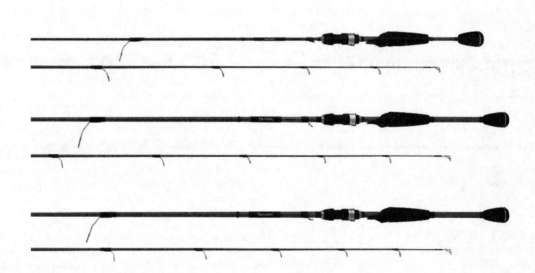

DAIWA AIRD

Model: AIRD562ULFS, AIRD602MXS, AIRD661MHXS, AIRD662MXS, AIRD701MXS
Length: 5'6"; 6'; 6'6"; 6'6"; 7'
Power: UL; M; MH; M; M
Action: F; XF; XF; XF; XF
Pieces: 2; 2; 1; 2; 1
Line Weight: 1-4 lbs; 4-10 lbs; 8-17 lbs; 6-15 lbs; 6-15 lbs

Guide Count: 6; 7; 8; 8; 8
Lure Weight: 1/32-1/2 oz; 1/8-1/2 oz; 1/4-1 oz; 1/4-3/4 oz; 1/4-3/4 oz
Features: IM6 graphite blank; minimized, direct contact reel seat for reduced weight and greater sensitivity with stainles steel hood; lightweight split-grip design with non-slip, high-density EVA foam; stainless steel guides; folding hook keeper.
Price: . . . . **$44.95–$59.95**

ACTION	POWER	
M=Moderate	UL=Ultra Light	H=Heavy
MF=Moderate Fast	L=Light	MH=Medium-Heavy
F=Fast	ML=Medium-Light	XH=Extra Heavy
XF=Extra Fast		

RODS: **Freshwater Spinning**

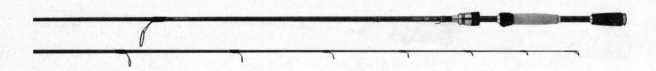

DAIWA CIELO BASS

Model: CEL6101MLXS, CEL711MFS, CEL721MLFS, CEL731MHFS
Length: 6'10''; 7'1''; 7'2''; 7'3''
Power: ML; M; ML; MH
Action: XF; F; F; F
Pieces: 1
Line Weight: 4-12 lbs; 6-14 lbs; 4-12 lbs; 8-17 lbs
Guide Count: 8

Lure Weight: 1/16-3/8 oz; 1/8-3/4 oz; 1/16-3/8 oz; 1/4-3/4 oz
Features: 3D cross reinforced Bias Graphite or GlaTech construction; unsanded blank with micro pitch taping pattern; Fuji skeleton pipe reel seat for lighter weight and greater sensitivity; machined aluminum reel clamp with graphite insert; Minima black ring guides; 20 percent to 30 percent lighter than ceramics split-grip design with natural cork and EVA foam; hook keeper; five-year limited warranty.
Price:.............................$129.95–$139.95

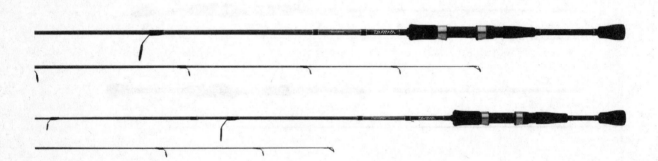

DAIWA CROSSFIRE CFE

Model: CFE562ULFS, CFE602MFS, CFE661MHFS, CFE662MFS, CFE701MHFS, CFE701MLFS, CFE702MFS
Length: 5'6''; 6'; 6'6''; 6'6''; 7'; 7'; 7'
Power: UL; M; MH; M; MH; ML; M
Action: F
Pieces: 2; 2; 1; 2; 1; 1; 2

Line Weight: 1-4 lbs; 6-15 lbs; 8-17 lbs; 6-15 lbs; 8-17 lbs; 4-12 lbs; 6-15 lbs
Guide Count: 5; 5; 6; 6; 6; 6; 6
Lure Weight: 1/32-1/8 oz; 1/8-3/4 oz; 1/4-3/4 oz; 1/8-3/4 oz; 1/4-3/4 oz; 1/8-1/2 oz; 1/8-3/4 oz
Features: 26-ton IM6 graphite blank construction; aluminum oxide guides; stainless hooded reel seat; split-design foam grip; hook keeper.
Price:.................................. $24.95

ACTION	POWER	
M=Moderate	UL=Ultra Light	H=Heavy
MF=Moderate Fast	L=Light	MH=Medium-Heavy
F=Fast	ML=Medium-Light	XH=Extra Heavy
XF=Extra Fast		

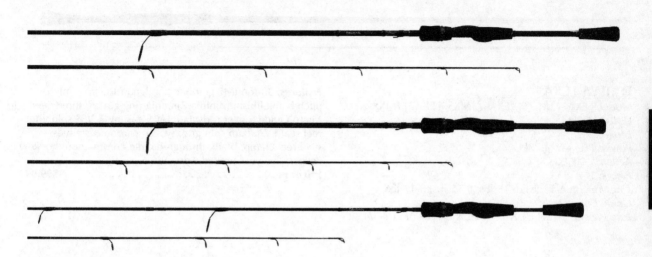

DAIWA EXCELER EXE

Model: EXE562ULFS, EXE602MFS, EXE661MLXS, EXE661MXS, EXE662MFS, EXE661MHXS, EXE702MFS, EXE701MLXS, EXE701MHXS
Length: 5'6''; 6'; 6'6''; 6'6''; 6'6''; 6'6''; 7'; 7'; 7'
Power: UL; M; ML; M; M; MH; M; ML; MH
Action: F; F; XF; XF; F; XF; F; XF; XF
Pieces: 2; 2; 1; 1; 2; 1; 2; 1; 1
Line Weight: 1-4 lbs; 6-15 lbs; 4-12 lbs; 6-15 lbs; 6-15 lbs; 8-17 lbs; 6-15 lbs; 4-12 lbs; 8-17 lbs

Guide Count: 6; 7; 8; 7; 7; 7; 7; 7; 7
Lure Weight: 1/32-1/8 oz; 1/8-3/4 oz; 1/8-1/2 oz; 1/8-3/4 oz; 1/8-3/4 oz; 1/4-1 oz; 1/8-3/4 oz; 1/8-1/2 oz; 1/4-1 oz
Features: 26-ton IM6 graphite blank with woven carbon accent; aluminum oxide guides; Daiwa custom reel seat; split-design foam grip; hook keeper.
Price: **$44.95**

ACTION	POWER	
M=Moderate	UL=Ultra Light	H=Heavy
MF=Moderate Fast	L=Light	MH=Medium-Heavy
F=Fast	ML=Medium-Light	XH=Extra Heavy
XF=Extra Fast		

RODS: Freshwater Spinning

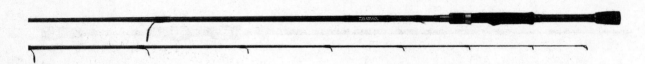

DAIWA LEXA

Model: LEXA721MLFS, LEXA671MXS, LEXA711MXS, LEXA731MHXS
Length: 7'2"; 6'7"; 7'1"; 7'3"
Power: ML; M; M; MH
Action: F; XF; XF; XF
Pieces: 1
Line Weight: 4-12 lbs; 6-15 lbs; 6-15 lbs; 8-17 lbs
Guide Count: 9; 8; 9; 9
Lure Weight: 1/16-3/8 oz; 1/4-3/4 oz; 1/4-3/4 oz; 1/4-3/4 oz

Features: 30-ton IM7 graphite blank construction; micro pitch blank finish; Minima Zirconia ring guides; three new Micro Guide trigger rods; Fuji (ACS casting & VSS spinning) reel seat EVA foam split grip; woven carbon & stainless steel reel clamp; blank-through-handle construction; hook keeper; five-year limited warranty.
Price:.................................... **$99.99**

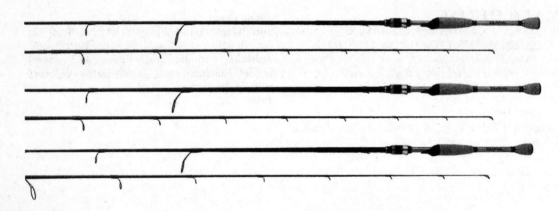

DAIWA PROCYON

Model: PRCN661MLXS, PRCN701MLXS, PRCN601MXS, PRCN661MXS, PRCN701MXS, PRCN661MHXS, PRCN701MHXS, PRCN662MFS, PRCN602MHFS, PRCN702MHFS
Length: 6'6"; 7'; 6'; 6'6"; 7'; 6'6"; 7'; 6'6"; 6'; 7'
Power: ML; ML; M; M; M; MH; MH; M; MH; MH
Action: XF; XF; XF; XF; XF; XF; XF; F; F; F
Pieces: 1; 1; 1; 1; 1; 1; 1; 2; 2; 2
Line Weight: 4-12 lbs; 4-12 lbs; 6-15 lbs; 6-15 lbs; 6-15 lbs; 8-17 lbs; 8-17 lbs; 8-17 lbs; 6-14 lbs; 8-17 lbs

Guide Count: 8; 9; 7; 8; 9; 9; 9; 7; 8; 9
Lure Weight: 1/8-1/2 oz; 1/8-1/2 oz; 1/4-3/4 oz; 1/4-3/4 oz; 1/4-3/4 oz; 1/4-1 oz; 1/4-1 oz; 1/4-1 oz; 1/8-3/4 oz; 1/4-1 oz
Features: IM7 graphite construction; micro pitch blank taping; Minima reel seat with machined clamp nut; woven graphite insert; Minima black ring guides; lightweight split-grip cork handles; hook keeper; five-year limited warranty.
Price:............................. **$59.95–$69.95**

ACTION		POWER	
M=Moderate		UL=Ultra Light	H=Heavy
MF=Moderate Fast		L=Light	MH=Medium-Heavy
F=Fast		ML=Medium-Light	XH=Extra Heavy
XF=Extra Fast			

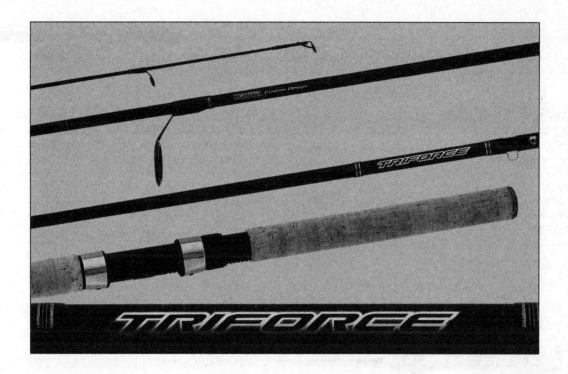

DAIWA TRIFORCE-E

Model: TFE562ULFS, TFE562LFS, TFE602ULFS, TFE602LFS, TFE602MFS, TFE662MFS, TFE702MFS, TFE501ULFS, TFE601MFS, TFE661MFS, TFE661MHFS, TFE701MFS
Length: 5'6''; 5'6''; 6'; 6'; 6'; 6'6''; 7'; 5'; 6'; 6'6''; 6'6''; 7'
Power: UL; L; UL; L; M; M; M; UL; M; M; MH; M
Action: F
Pieces: 2; 2; 2; 2; 2; 2; 2; 1; 1; 1; 1; 1
Line Weight: 1-4 lbs; 2-6 lbs; 1-4 lbs; 2-6 lbs; 6-14 lbs; 6-14 lbs; 6-14 lbs; 1-4 lbs; 6-14 lbs; 6-14 lbs; 8-17 lbs; 8-17 lbs

Guide Count: 6; 6; 7; 7; 7; 7; 7; 6; 7; 7; 7; 7
Lure Weight: 1/32-1/8 oz; 1/16-3/8 oz; 1/32-1/8 oz; 1/16-3/8 oz; 1/8-3/4 oz; 1/8-3/4 oz; 1/8-3/4 oz; 1/32-1/8 oz; 1/8-3/4 oz; 1/8-3/4 oz; 1/4-1 oz; 1/4-3/4 oz
Features: High-quality graphite blank; strong, blank-through-handle construction; cut-proof aluminum oxide guides; custom thread wrap with durable multi-coat finish; protective foam butt cap and grip check.
Price: **$29.95**

ACTION	POWER	
M=Moderate	UL=Ultra Light	H=Heavy
MF=Moderate Fast	L=Light	MH=Medium-Heavy
F=Fast	ML=Medium-Light	XH=Extra Heavy
XF=Extra Fast		

RODS: Freshwater Spinning

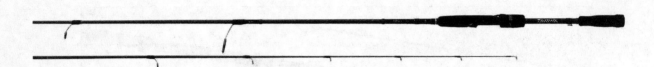

DAIWA TATULA BASS

Model: TAT701MFS, TAT711MLXS, TAT721MHXS
Length: 7'; 7'1''; 7'2''
Power: M; ML; MH
Action: F; XF; XF
Pieces: 1
Line Weight: 6-14 lbs; 4-12 lbs; 8-17 lbs
Guide Count: 8
Lure Weight: 1/8-3/4 oz; 1/16-3/8 oz; 1/4-3/4 oz

Features: Daiwa's exclusive SVF (Super Volume Fiber) graphite technology; graphite fiber construction for flexibility, strength, and virtually zero blank twist; micro pitch blank finish; Daiwa custom reel seat & machined aluminum reel clamp nut; Fuji Alconite ring guides; split grip design with EVA foam; hook keeper; blank-through-handle construction.
Price: **$149.95**

FENWICK AETOS

Model: A631MHXFS, A631MXFS, A661MFS, A662MFS, A671MHFS, A681MHXFS, A701MFS, A701MHFS, A702MFS, A721MXFS, A741MHXFS, A761MHFS, A761MLXFS
Length: 6'3''; 6'3''; 6'6''; 6'6''; 6'7''; 6'8''; 7'; 7'; 7'; 7'2''; 7'4''; 7'6''; 7'6''
Power: MH; M; M; M; MH; MH; M; MH; M; M; MH; MH; ML
Action: XF; XF; F; F; F; XF; F; F; F; XF; XF; F; XF
Pieces: 1; 1; 1; 2; 1; 1; 1; 1; 2; 1; 1; 1; 1

Line Weight: 8-17 lbs; 4-12 lbs; 6-14 lbs; 6-14 lbs; 8-17 lbs; 10-17 lbs; 6-14 lbs; 6-14 lbs; 6-14 lbs; 6-14 lbs; 10-17 lbs; 12-20 lbs; 4-10 lbs
Guide Count: 8; 8; 8; 8; 8; 8; 8; 8; 8; 8; 8; 9; 9
Lure Weight: 1/4-3/4 oz; 1/8-5/8 oz; 1/8-5/8 oz; 1/8-5/8 oz; 1/4-3/4 oz; 1/4-3/4 oz; 1/8-5/8 oz; 3/8-1 oz; 1/8-5/8 oz; 1/8-5/8 oz; 3/8-1 oz; 3/8-1 oz; 1/16-1/2 oz
Features: Fuji Skeleton reel seats for a reduced weight and increase in sensitivity; combination of TAC and cork split grip handle constructions; titanium framed guides with lightweight titanium inserts.
Price: **$179.95**

ACTION	POWER	
M=Moderate	**UL**=Ultra Light	**H**=Heavy
MF=Moderate Fast	**L**=Light	**MH**=Medium-Heavy
F=Fast	**ML**=Medium-Light	**XH**=Extra Heavy
XF=Extra Fast		

FENWICK AETOS ICE
Model: AICE18LXFS, AICE21LXFS, AICE25MXFS, AICE25ULXFS, AICE28MLXFS, AICE29MXFTS, AICE30MHXFS
Length: 18''; 21''; 25''; 25''; 28''; 28''; 30''
Power: L; L; M; UL; ML; M; MH
Action: XF
Pieces: 1

Line Weight: 2-4 lbs; 2-4 lbs; 4-8 lbs; 2-4 lbs; 2-6 lbs; 4-8 lbs; 6-10 lbs
Guide Count: 4; 4; 5; 5; 6; 6; 6
Features: High-modulus solid graphite blanks; hidden handle design reel seats with carbon fiber hoods; combination of TAC and cork handle construction; stainless steel guides with stainless steel inserts.
Price: **$49.95**

FENWICK ELITETECH ICE
Model: ETI23UL, ETI24ML, ETI25UL, ETI26ML, ETI27M, ETI28MH, ETI28ML
Length: 23''; 24''; 25''; 26''; 27''; 28''; 28''
Power: UL; ML; UL; ML; M; MH; ML
Action: F
Pieces: 1

Line Weight: 2-4 lbs; 2-6 lbs; 2-4 lbs; 2-6 lbs; 4-8 lbs; 6-10 lbs; 2-6 lbs
Guide Count: 4; 4; 4; 5; 5; 5; 5
Features: High-modulus graphite blanks; TAC handle delivers increased grip and durability in even the most rigid conditions; twist-lock reel seat with stainless steel hood.
Price: **$39.95**

ACTION	POWER	
M=Moderate	UL=Ultra Light	H=Heavy
MF=Moderate Fast	L=Light	MH=Medium-Heavy
F=Fast	ML=Medium-Light	XH=Extra Heavy
XF=Extra Fast		

FENWICK ELITETECH RIVER RUNNER

Model: ESMS632MH-F, ESMS63M-F, ESMS63MH-F, ESMS692M-XF, ESMS69M-XF, ESMS69ML-F, ESMS74M-F
Length: 6'3''; 6'3''; 6'3''; 6'9''; 6'9''; 6'9''; 7'4''
Power: MH; M; MH; M; M; ML; M
Action: F; F; F; XF; XF; F; F
Pieces: 2; 1; 1; 2; 1; 1; 1
Line Weight: 10-17 lbs; 6-12 lbs; 10-17 lbs; 6-12 lbs; 6-12 lbs; 4-10 lbs; 6-12 lbs
Guide Count: 7; 7; 7; 8; 8; 8; 9

Lure Weight: 1/4-3/4 oz; 1/8-3/4 oz; 1/4-3/4 oz; 1/8-3/4 oz; 1/8-3/4 oz; 1/16-5/8 oz; 1/8-3/4 oz
Features: Titanium framed guides with lightweight zirconium inserts reduce overall blank weight and line wear with extreme heat dispersion; TAC inlay reel seat allows function and comfort to coexist; outstanding control with minimum weight not seen on the market today; high-modulus graphite blank designed specifically for smallmouth applications.
Price:.....................................**$149.95**

FENWICK ELITETECH WALLEYE

Model: EWS63M-XF, EWS66M-F, EWS66ML-F, EWS69ML-F, EWS72M-F, EWS72ML-F, EWS592MH-MF, EWS662M-F, EWS692MH-MF, EWS722M-F
Length: 6'3''; 6'6''; 6'6''; 6'9''; 7'2''; 7'2''; 5'9''; 6'6''; 6'9''; 7'2''
Power: M; M; ML; ML; M; ML; MH; M; MH; M
Action: XF; F; F; F; F; F; MF; F; MF; F
Pieces: 1; 1; 1; 1; 1; 1; 1; 2; 2; 2
Line Weight: 4-12 lbs; 4-12 lbs; 4-10 lbs; 4-10 lbs; 4-12 lbs; 4-10 lbs; 6-12 lbs; 4-10 lbs; 6-12 lbs; 4-10 lbs
Guide Count: 8; 8; 8; 10; 10; 10; 8; 8; 10; 10

Lure Weight: 1/8-3/4 oz; 1/8-3/4 oz; 1/8-5/8 oz; 1/8-5/8 oz; 1/8-3/4 oz; 1/8-5/8 oz; 1/8-1 oz; 1/8-3/4 oz; 1/8-1 oz; 1/8-3/4 oz
Features: Fuji Alconite guides and Fuji reel seat TAC handles provide increased grip in all fishing conditions, are more durable than cork, and provide enhanced grip when wet; FDS graphite-crafted from multi-laminate lay-up for lightweight strength and increased sensitivity; tips soft enough to cast your ultra-light jigs or feel the lightest tap when you go vertical.
Price:.....................................**$149.95**

ACTION	**POWER**	
M=Moderate	UL=Ultra Light	H=Heavy
MF=Moderate Fast	L=Light	MH=Medium-Heavy
F=Fast	ML=Medium-Light	XH=Extra Heavy
XF=Extra Fast		

FENWICK HMG

Model: HMG60L-MS-2, HMG60M-FS, HMG60M-FS-2, HMG60ML-FS, HMG66L-MFS-2, HMG66M-FS, HMG66M-FS-2, HMG66MH-FS, HMG69ML-FS, HMG69ML-FS-2, HMG70M-FS, HMG70M-FS-2, HMG70MH-FS, HMG70ML-FS, HMG70UL-MS-2, HMG76L-MS-2, HMG76ML-FS
Length: 6'; 6'; 6'; 6'; 6'6''; 6'6''; 6'6''; 6'6''; 6'9''; 6'9''; 7'; 7'; 7'; 7'; 7'; 7'6''; 7'6''
Power: L; M; M; ML; L; M; M; MH; ML; ML; M; M; MH; ML; UL; L; ML
Action: M; F; F; F; MF; F; F; F; F; F; F; F; F; F; M; M; F
Pieces: 2; 1; 2; 1; 2; 1; 2; 1; 1; 2; 1; 2; 1; 1; 2; 2; 1
Line Weight: 4-8 lbs; 8-14 lbs; 8-14 lbs; 6-12 lbs; 4-8 lbs; 8-14 lbs; 8-14 lbs; 10-17 lbs; 6-12 lbs; 6-12 lbs; 8-14 lbs; 8-14 lbs; 10-17 lbs; 6-12 lbs; 2-6 lbs; 4-8 lbs; 6-12 lbs

Guide Count: 7; 7; 7; 7; 8; 8; 8; 8; 8; 8; 9; 9; 9; 9; 9; 9; 9
Lure Weight: 1/16-3/8 oz; 1/4-3/4 oz; 1/4-3/4 oz; 1/8-5/8 oz; 1/16-3/8 oz; 1/4-3/4 oz; 1/4-3/4 oz; 3/8-1 oz; 1/8-5/8 oz; 1/8-5/8 oz; 1/4-3/4 oz; 1/4-3/4 oz; 3/8-1 oz; 1/8-5/8 oz; 1/32-1/4 oz; 1/16-3/8 oz; 1/8-5/8 oz
Features: Blanks spiraled with carbon thread creating unparalleled strength and precise action; sculpted TAC and EVA-blended handle combine for a feeling of outstanding control, while keeping weight to an absolute minimum; deep pressed titanium guides help eliminate insert pop-out and are virtually bullet proof; soft-touch Fuji reel seat designs.
Price:....................................**$99.95**

LAMIGLAS X-11

Model: LX 562 ULS, LX 602 LS, LX 622 LS, LX 702 ULS
Length: 5'6''; 6'; 6'6''; 7'
Action: MF
Pieces: 2
Line Weight: 2-8 lbs; 4-8 lbs; 4-8 lbs; 2-8 lbs
Lure Weight: 1/8-1/4 oz; 1/8-3/8 oz; 1/8-1/2 oz; 1/8-1/2 oz
Features: All the value and performance of our new X-11 Series for salmon and steelhead are pared down to specialty applications for smaller species like trout, bass, walleye, panfish, and kokanee. These fast-action blanks feature our durable IM graphite and deep pressed guides with zirconia inserts. The darker maroon color sets a very nice contrast between the reel seat and premium cork handles (one-year limited warranty).
Price:....................................**$100**

ACTION	POWER	
M=Moderate	UL=Ultra Light	H=Heavy
MF=Moderate Fast	L=Light	MH=Medium-Heavy
F=Fast	ML=Medium-Light	XH=Extra Heavy
XF=Extra Fast		

RODS

RODS: **Freshwater Spinning**

LEW'S AMERICAN HERO IM6 SPEED STICK

Model: AH66MS, AH70MS, AH70MHS
Length: 6'6''; 7'; 7'
Power: M; M; MH
Action: F
Pieces: 1
Line Weight: 4-12 lbs; 4-12 lbs; 8-14 lbs
Guide Count: 8; 9; 10
Lure Weight: 1/8-1/2 oz; 1/8-1/2 oz; 3/8-3/4 oz

Features: Premium IM6 one-piece graphite blanks; multilayer, multidirectional graphite construction for structural strength; rugged gunsmoke stainless steel guide frames with stainless steel inserts; lightweight graphite reel seats with cushioned stainless steel hoods; great hand/reel stability and comfort; exposed blank for instant vibration transmission; premium, durable high-density EVA split grips; split grip lightweight EVA handles; exclusive "No Foul" hook keeper; Lew's limited one-year warranty.
Price:..................................... **$69.99**

LEW'S LASER LG GRAPHITE

Model: LGA56ULFS, LGA56LFS, LGA60MLFS, LGA60MFS, LGA66MFS, LGA66MHFS, LGA70MLFS, LGA70MFS
Length: 5'6''; 5'6''; 6'; 6'; 6'6''; 6'6''; 7'; 7'
Power: UL; L; ML; M; M; MH; ML; M
Action: F
Pieces: 1
Line Weight: 1-6 lbs; 2-8 lbs; 4-10 lbs; 4-12 lbs; 4-12 lbs; 6-17 lbs; 4-10 lbs; 4-12 lbs
Guide Count: 7; 7; 7; 7; 8; 8; 9; 9
Lure Weight: 1/32-1/4 oz; 1/16-1/2 oz; 1/16-5/16 oz; 1/8-3/8 oz; 1/8-1/2 oz; 1/4-5/8 oz; 1/16-5/16 oz; 1/8-1/2 oz

Features: Premium IM6 graphite blank; multi layer, multidirectional graphite one-piece blanks reinforced with premium resins; Lew's proprietary advanced performance technology blank construction; black-coated stainless steel frame with titanium oxide guide rings; lightweight graphite reel seat with cushioned stainless steel hoods; great hand/reel stability and comfort; exposed blank for instant vibration transmission on casting models; natural cork split-grip handles offer reduced weight without compromising rod control; limited one-year warranty.
Price:..................................... **$49.99**

ACTION		POWER	
M=Moderate	**UL**=Ultra Light	**H**=Heavy	
MF=Moderate Fast	**L**=Light	**MH**=Medium-Heavy	
F=Fast	**ML**=Medium-Light	**XH**=Extra Heavy	
XF=Extra Fast			

LEW'S SPEED STICK 365 CARBON NANOLAR

Model: SFS66M, SFS70ML, SFS70M, SFS70MH
Length: 6'6''; 7'; 7'; 7'
Power: M; ML; M; MH
Action: MF
Pieces: 1
Line Weight: 6-12 lbs; 6-10 lbs; 6-12 lbs; 8-14 lbs
Guide Count: 9; 10; 10; 10
Lure Weight: 3/16-5/8 oz; 1/8-1/2 oz; 1/8-5/16 oz; 3/8-3/4 oz

Features: Proprietary multilayer, multidirectional Carbon Nanolar premium HM50; rugged gunsmoke stainless steel guide frames with stainless steel inserts; great hand/reel stability and comfort; exposed blank for instant vibration transmission; Lew's exclusive lightweight graphite skeletal casting reel seat with ceramic hook holder in trigger; premium high-density EVA split grips; Lew's limited one-year warranty.
Price: $99.99

LEW'S TOURNAMENT SL MICRO GUIDE

Model: TS66MFS, TS66MHFS, TS70MLFS, TS70MFS
Length: 6'6''; 6'6''; 7'; 7'
Power: M; MH; ML; M
Action: F
Pieces: 1
Line Weight: 6-12 lbs; 8-14 lbs; 6-14 lbs; 8-14 lbs
Guide Count: 9
Lure Weight: 3/16-5/8 oz; 3/16-3/4 oz; 1/8-5/8 oz; 1/4-5/8 oz
Features: Premium HM60 graphite blanks; multilayer, multidirectional 60 million-modulus graphite blank

reinforced with premium resins; Lew's proprietary advanced performance technology blank construction; black-coated stainless steel frames with hard aluminum oxide micro guides, which reduce rod weight, enhance casting distance, and increase sensitivity; lightweight skeletal graphite reel seats with cushioned black stainless steel hoods; great hand/reel stability and comfort; exposed blank for instant vibration transmission; high-density EVA foam split-grip handles reduce weight without sacrificing control; limited lifetime warranty.
Price: $119.99

ACTION	POWER	
M=Moderate	**UL**=Ultra Light	**H**=Heavy
MF=Moderate Fast	**L**=Light	**MH**=Medium-Heavy
F=Fast	**ML**=Medium-Light	**XH**=Extra Heavy
XF=Extra Fast		

G.LOOMIS CLASSIC SPIN JIG

Model: SJR 6400 IMX, SJR 642 IMX, SJR 700 GL3, SJR 720 IMX, SJR 721 GLX, SJR 721 IMX, SJR 721 GL3, SJR 722 GLX, SJR 722 IMX, SJR 722 GL3, SJR 723 IMX, SJR 724 IMX, SJR 781 IMX, SJR 782 GLX, SJR 782 IMX, SJR 782 GL3, SJR 783 GLX, SJR 783 IMX, SJR 783 GL3, SJR 783-2 GLX, SJR 783-2 GL3, SJR 842 GL3, SJR 843 IMX, SJR 843 GL3, SJR 844 IMX, SJR 902 IMX

Length: 5'4''; 5'4''; 5'10''; 6'; 6'; 6'; 6'; 6'; 6'; 6'; 6'; 6'; 6'6''; 6'6''; 6'6''; 6'6''; 6'6''; 6'6''; 6'6''; 6'6''; 6'6''; 7'; 7'; 7'; 7'; 7'6''

Power: ML; M; ML; ML; L; L; L; M; M; M; MH; H; L; M; M; M; MH; MH; MH; MH; MH; M; MH; MH; H; M

Action: XF; F; XF; XF; F; F; F; F; F; F; F; F; F; F; F; F; F; F; F; F; F; F; F; F; F; F

Pieces: 1; 1; 1; 1; 1; 1; 1; 1; 1; 1; 1; 1; 1; 1; 1; 1; 1; 1; 2; 2; 1; 1; 1; 1; 1

Line Weight: 2-6 lbs; 6-12 lbs; 4-8 lbs; 4-8 lbs; 6-10 lbs; 6-10 lbs; 6-10 lbs; 6-12 lbs; 6-12 lbs; 6-12 lbs; 8-15 lbs; 10-17 lbs; 6-10 lbs; 6-12 lbs; 6-12 lbs; 6-12 lbs; 8-15 lbs; 8-15 lbs; 8-15 lbs; 8-15 lbs; 8-15 lbs; 6-12 lbs; 8-15 lbs; 8-15 lbs; 10-17 lbs; 8-17 lbs

Lure Weight: 1/64-1/8 oz; 1/8-3/8 oz; 1/32-1/4 oz; 1/32-1/4 oz; 1/16-5/16 oz; 1/16-5/16 oz; 1/16-5/16 oz; 1/8-3/8 oz; 1/8-3/8 oz; 1/8-3/8 oz; 3/16-5/8 oz; 1/4-1 oz; 1/16-5/16 oz; 1/8-3/8 oz; 1/8-3/8 oz; 1/8-3/8 oz; 3/16-5/8 oz; 3/16-5/8 oz; 3/16-5/8 oz; 3/16-5/8 oz; 3/16-5/8 oz; 1/8-3/8 oz; 3/16-5/8 oz; 3/16-3/4 oz; 3/16-3/4 oz; 1/4-1 oz; 1/4-5/8 oz

Features: These are special, fast-action rods designed to give warm-water spin fishermen the power and performance of a casting rod in a spinning configuration; rated for slightly lighter line because spinning reels traditionally don't handle heavier line as well as a casting reel, even with oversized guides; originally developed for fishing soft plastics for bass, but have since been discovered by walleye anglers for vertical jigging as well as grubs and light bottom-bounce rigs; many of these rods are suitable for light saltwater use; light, sensitive, and extremely accurate; the more popular models are available in GLX, IMX, and GL3.

Price: . . . . $210–$380

G.LOOMIS GL2 JIG & WORM

Model: GL2 802S JWR, GL2 803S JWR, GL2 804S JWR, GL2 852S JWR, GL2 853S JWR, GL2 854S JWR

Length: 6'8''; 6'8''; 6'8''; 7'1''; 7'1''; 7'1''

Power: MW; MH; H; M; MH; H

Action: XF

Pieces: 1

Line Weight: 6-12 lbs; 8-14 lbs; 12-20 lbs; 6-12 lbs; 8-14 lbs; 12-20 lbs

Lure Weight: 1/8-3/8 oz; 3/16-5/8 oz; 5/16-3/4 oz; 1/8-3/8 oz; 3/16-5/8 oz; 5/16-3/4 oz

Features: These rods are most effective for really big bass; nice tip to give smooth, accurate casts and a powerful butt-section to help set the hook and land the fish; handles feature split grips; uniquely comfortable reel seat; Fuji concept guides.

Price: . . . . $200–$205

ACTION	POWER	
M=Moderate	**UL**=Ultra Light	**H**=Heavy
MF=Moderate Fast	**L**=Light	**MH**=Medium-Heavy
F=Fast	**ML**=Medium-Light	**XH**=Extra Heavy
XF=Extra Fast		

G.LOOMIS GLX JIG & WORM

Model: GLX 722S JWR, GLX 782S JWR, GLX 783S JWR, GLX 801S JWR, GLX 802S JWR, GLX 803S JWR, GLX 852S JWR, GLX 853S JWR, GLX 902S JWR
Length: 6'; 6'6''; 6'6''; 6'8''; 6'8''; 6'8''; 7'1''; 7'1''; 7'6''
Power: M; M; MH; ML; M; MH; M; MH; M
Action: F; F; F; XF; XF; XF; XF; XF; F
Pieces: 1
Line Weight: 6-12 lbs; 6-12 lbs; 8-14 lbs; 6-10 lbs; 6-12 lbs; 8-14 lbs; 6-12 lbs; 8-14 lbs; 6-12 lbs

Lure Weight: 1/8-3/8 oz; 1/8-3/8 oz; 3/16-5/8 oz; 1/16-3/16 oz; 1/8-3/8 oz; 3/16-5/8 oz; 1/8-3/8 oz; 3/16-5/8 oz; 1/8-3/8 oz
Features: Designed specifically for fishing jigs and soft plastics; features a split-grip handle with our unique cork comfort grip; Fuji titanium SIC guides and tip-top; legendary for their sensitivity; extra-fast actions, allowing accurate, low trajectory casts with plenty of power to handle even the biggest bass; made with a gorgeous dark green blank.
Price: .... **$410–$450**

G.LOOMIS NRX JIG & WORM

Model: NRX 802S JWR, NRX 802S JWR G, NRX 803S JWR, NRX 803S JWR G, NRX 852S JWR, NRX 852S JWR G, NRX 872S JWR, NRX 872S JWR G, NRX 901S JWR, NRX 901S JWR G, NWR 902S JWR, NRX 902S JWR G
Length: 6'8''; 6'8''; 6'8''; 6'8''; 7'1''; 7'1''; 7'3''; 7'3''; 7'6''; 7'6''; 7'6''; 7'6''
Power: M; M; MH; MH; M; M; M; M; ML; ML; M; M
Action: XF; XF; XF; XF; XF; XF; XF; XF; F; F; F; F
Pieces: 1
Line Weight: 6-10 lbs; 6-10 lbs; 8-14 lbs; 8-14 lbs; 6-12 lbs; 6-12 lbs; 6-12 lbs; 6-12 lbs; 4-10 lbs; 4-10 lbs; 6-12 lbs; 6-12 lbs

Lure Weight: 1/8-1/4 oz; 1/8-1/4 oz; 1/8-5/16 oz; 1/8-5/16 oz; 1/8-3/8 oz; 1/8-3/8 oz; 1/8-3/8 oz; 1/8-3/8 oz; 1/16-5/16 oz; 1/16-5/16 oz; 1/8-3/8 oz; 1/8-3/8 oz
Features: Designed specifically for fishing jigs and soft plastics; insanely light, unbelievably sensitive, and strong; feature split-grip cork handles; Fuji titanium SIC stripper guides, with the ultra-lite, ultra-strong RECOIL guides the rest of the way.
Price: .... **$500–$575**

ACTION	POWER	
M=Moderate	UL=Ultra Light	H=Heavy
MF=Moderate Fast	L=Light	MH=Medium-Heavy
F=Fast	ML=Medium-Light	XH=Extra Heavy
XF=Extra Fast		

OKUMA C3-40X

Model: C3x-S-6101L, C3x-S-661M, C3x-S-661MH, C3x-S-691ML, C3x-S-701M, C3x-S-701MH, C3x-S-701ML, C3x-S-741ML, C3x-S-761M
Length: 6'10''; 6'10''; 6'6''; 6'6''; 6'9''; 7'; 7'; 7'; 7'4''; 7'6''
Power: L; MH; M; MH; ML; M; MH; ML; ML; M
Action: F
Pieces: 1
Line Weight: 4-8 lbs; 6-14 lbs; 8-17 lbs; 10-20 lbs; 6-10 lbs; 8-17 lbs; 10-20 lbs; 6-12 lbs; 6-12 lbs; 8-17 lbs
Guide Count: 8; 8; 7; 7; 8; 8; 8; 8; 8; 9
Lure Weight: 3/8-3/4 oz; 3-12 oz; 1/8-3/8 oz; 1/16-5/8 oz; 1/4-5/8 oz; 1/4-5/8 oz; 1/4-1 oz; 1/8-3/8 oz; 1/8-3/8 oz; 3/8-3/4 oz

Features: 40-ton carbon, ultra-sensitive blank construction; custom 1K woven carbon cone grip configuration; customized ported Fuji reel seats for reduced weight; ultra-hard zirconium guide inserts for braided line; titanium guide frames on all spinning models; titanium guide frames on all double foot casting guides; ALPS low profile frames on all single foot casting guides; split-grip butt for reduced weight and improved balance; C3 rods are backed by a limited lifetime warranty.
Price:.............................**$154.99–$174.99**

OKUMA CITRIX

Model: Ci-S-661M, Ci-S-661MH, Ci-S-661ML, Ci-S-662M, Ci-S-691ML, Ci-S-701M, Ci-S-701MH
Length: 6'6''; 6'6''; 6'6''; 6'6''; 6'9''; 7'; 7
Power: M; MH; ML; M; ML; M; MH
Action: F
Pieces: 1; 1; 1; 2; 1; 1; 1
Line Weight: 8-17 lbs; 10-20 lbs; 6-12 lbs; 8-17 lbs; 6-10 lbs; 8-17 lbs; 10-20 lbs
Guide Count: 8
Lure Weight: 1/4-1 oz; 1/8-3/8 oz; 1/4-5/8 oz; 1/8-1/2 oz; 1/4-5/8 oz; 1/4-1 oz

Features: IM8 graphite blank construction; lightweight EVA split grips for reduced weight; zero foregrip design for improved balance and weight reduction; ALPS stainless steel guide frames; zirconium line guide inserts for use with braid or mono lines; Pacific Bay Minima reel seat for reduced weight; custom anodized aluminum reel seat threads for strength and balance; stainless steel hook keeper; citrix rods are backed by a limited lifetime warranty.
Price:.................................. **$119.99**

ACTION	POWER	
M=Moderate	UL=Ultra Light	H=Heavy
MF=Moderate Fast	L=Light	MH=Medium-Heavy
F=Fast	ML=Medium-Light	XH=Extra Heavy
XF=Extra Fast		

OKUMA CRAPPIE HIGH PERFORMANCE

Model: CHP-S-501L, CHP-S-561L, CHP-S-601L, CHP-S-661L
Length: 5'; 5'6"; 6'; 6'6"
Power: L
Action: M
Pieces: 1
Line Weight: 4-8 lbs
Guide Count: 6; 6; 7; 7

Lure Weight: 1/16-5/16 oz
Features: Premium IM8 graphite rod blanks; crappie-specific rod actions; low-profile stainless steel guide frames; split-grip butt design reduces weight and improves balance; premium cork fore and rear grips; custom skeleton reel seat design on spinning models; one-year limited warranty.
Price: **$64.99**

OKUMA HELIOS

Model: HS-CM-701H, HS-CM-701M, HS-CM-701MH, HS-CM-761H, HS-CM-761XH, HS-SKR-701M, HS-SKR-701MH, HS-SKR-701ML
Length: 7'; 7'; 7'; 7'6"; 7'6"; 7'; 7'; 7'
Power: H; M; MH; H; XH; M; MH; ML
Action: F
Pieces: 1
Line Weight: 12-25 lbs; 8-17 lbs; 10-20 lbs; 12-25 lbs; 15-30 lbs; 8-17 lbs; 10-20 lbs; 6-10 lbs
Guide Count: 10; 10; 10; 11; 11; 8; 8; 8
Lure Weight: 3/8-1 1/4 oz; 1/4-5/8 oz; 1/4-1 oz; 3/8-1 1/4 oz; 1/2-2 oz; 1/4-5/8 oz; 1/4-1 oz; 1/8-1/2 oz

Features: 40-ton carbon, ultra-sensitive blank construction; rods starting in the 3.6 oz range; designed with ALPS mini guide system; ultra-hard zirconium inserts for braided line; zero foregrip design for improved balance and weight reduction; machined aluminum reel seat thread with Fuji hood; durable, lightweight Pacific Bay Minima reel seat and trigger; split-grip butt design for reduced weight and improved balance; comfortable EVA rear grips; Fuji movable hook keeper for precise keeper placement; helios rods are backed by a limited lifetime warranty.
Price: . . . .**$174.99–$179.99**

ACTION		POWER	
M=Moderate	UL=Ultra Light		H=Heavy
MF=Moderate Fast	L=Light		MH=Medium-Heavy
F=Fast	ML=Medium-Light		XH=Extra Heavy
XF=Extra Fast			

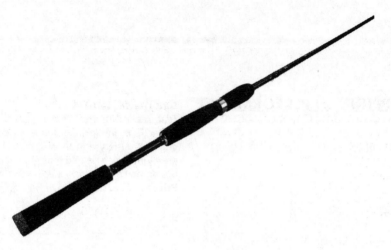

OKUMA TARVOS

Model: TV-S-601M, TV-S-602M, TV-S-661M, TV-S-661ML, TV-S-662M, TV-S-662ML, TV-S-701M, TV-S-701MH, TV-S-702M
Length: 6'; 6'; 6'6''; 6'6''; 6'6''; 6'6''; 7'; 7'; 7'
Power: M; M; M; ML; M; ML; M; MH; M
Action: M/MF
Pieces: 1; 2; 1; 1; 2; 2; 1; 1; 2
Line Weight: 6-15 lbs; 6-15 lbs; 6-15 lbs; 4-10 lbs; 6-15 lbs; 4-10 lbs; 6-15 lbs; 6-15 lbs; 6-15 lbs

Guide Count: 7
Lure Weight: 1/8-5/8 oz; 1/8-5/8 oz; 1/8-5/8 oz; 1/8-5/16 oz; 1/8-5/8 oz; 1/8-5/16 oz; 1/4-3/4 oz; 1/4-3/4 oz; 1/4-3/4 oz
Features: Graphite composite rod blank construction; stainless steel guide frames; titanium oxide guide inserts; stainless steel hooded reel seat; split-grip butt design; comfortable EVA fore and rear grips; stainless steel hook keeper; one-year limited warranty.
Price: **$42.99**

SHIMANO CLARUS

Model: CSSW60MLB, CSSWX60MLB, CSSW60MB, CSSWX60MB, CSSW66MLB, CSSWX66MLB, CSSWX66ML2B, CSSW66MB, CSSWX66MB, CSSWX66M2B, CSSW70MLB, CSSW70MB, CSSW76MLB, CSSW76MB
Length: 6'; 6'; 6'; 6'; 6'6''; 6'6''; 6'6''; 6'6''; 6'6''; 6'6''; 7'; 7'; 7'6''; 7'6''
Power: ML; ML; M; M; ML; ML; ML; M; M; M; ML; M; ML; M
Action: F; XF; F; XF; F; XF; XF; F; XF; XF; F; F; F; F
Pieces: 1; 1; 1; 1; 1; 1; 2; 1; 1; 2; 1; 1; 1; 1

Line Weight: 4-10 lbs; 4-10 lbs; 6-10 lbs; 6-10 lbs; 4-10 lbs; 4-10 lbs; 4-10 lbs; 6-10 lbs; 6-10 lbs; 6-12 lbs; 4-10 lbs; 6-10 lbs; 4-12 lbs; 6-12 lbs
Guide Count: 7; 7; 7; 7; 8; 8; 8; 8; 8; 8; 9; 9; 9; 9
Lure Weight: 1/16-5/16 oz; 1/16-5/16 oz; 3/16-5/8 oz; 3/16-5/8 oz; 1/16-3/8 oz; 1/16-3/8 oz; 1/16-3/8 oz; 3/16-5/8 oz; 3/16-5/8 oz; 3/16-5/8 oz; 1/16-3/8 oz; 3/16-5/8 oz; 1/16-5/8 oz; 3/16-5/8 oz
Features: IM8 graphite construction; Fuji aluminum oxide guides; custom reel seats.
Price: . . . . **$89.99–$99.99**

ACTION	POWER	
M=Moderate	UL=Ultra Light	H=Heavy
MF=Moderate Fast	L=Light	MH=Medium-Heavy
F=Fast	ML=Medium-Light	XH=Extra Heavy
XF=Extra Fast		

SHIMANO COMPRE

Model: CPSW60MLC, CPSWX60MLC, CPSW60MC, CPSWX60MC, CPSW66MLC, CPSWX66MLC, CPSW66MC, CPSWX66MC, CPSW70MLC, CPSW70MC, CPSW70M2C, CPSW76MLC, CPSW76MC
Length: 6'; 6'; 6'; 6'; 6'6''; 6'6''; 6'6''; 6'6''; 7'; 7'; 7'; 7'6''; 7'6''
Power: ML; ML; M; M; ML; ML; M; M; ML; M; M; ML; M
Action: F; XF; F; XF; F; XF; F; XF; F; F; F; F; F
Pieces: 1
Line Weight: 4-10 lbs; 4-10 lbs; 6-10 lbs; 6-10 lbs; 4-10 lbs; 4-10 lbs; 6-10 lbs; 6-10 lbs; 4-10 lbs; 6-10 lbs; 6-12 lbs; 4-12 lbs; 6-12 lbs
Guide Count: 7; 7; 7; 7; 8; 8; 8; 8; 9; 9; 9; 9; 9
Lure Weight: 1/16-5/16 oz; 1/16-5/16 oz; 3/16-5/8 oz; 3/16-5/8 oz; 1/16-3/8 oz; 1/16-3/8 oz; 3/16-5/8 oz; 3/16-5/8 oz; 1/16-3/8 oz; 3/16-5/8 oz; 3/16-5/8 oz; 1/16-5/8 oz; 3/16-5/8 oz
Features: IM9 graphite construction; Fuji aluminum oxide guides; custom reel seats.
Price:..........................**$99.99–$119.99**

SHIMANO CUMARA

Model: CUS68MA, CUS68MHA, CUS72MA, CUS72MHA, CUS76MA, CUSX76MA, CUSDX68MA, CUSCX72MA, CUSS71MLA, CUSS71MA
Length: 6'8''; 6'8''; 7'2''; 7'2''; 7'6''; 7'6''; 6'8''; 7'2''; 7'1''; 7'1''
Power: M; MH; M; MH; M; M; M; M; ML; M
Action: F; F; F; F; F; XF; XF; XF; F; F
Line Weight: 6-12 lbs; 8-14 lbs; 6-12 lbs; 8-14 lbs; 8-16 lbs; 8-17 lbs; 5-10 lbs; 5-10 lbs; 6-10 lbs; 8-12 lbs
Lure Weight: 1/8-3/8 oz; 3/16-5/8 oz; 1/8-3/8 oz; 3/16-5/8 oz; 1/4-5/8 oz; 1/4-5/8 oz; 1/8-3/8 oz; 1/8-3/8 oz; 1/16-1/4 oz; 1/8-5/16 oz
Features: Convenient hook keeper; Fuji KR-concept Alconite guides; custom Shimano reel seat; shaped EVA foam grips; micro guides; technique specific actions; laser-etched badge.
Price:..........................**$249.99–$259.99**

ACTION	POWER	
M=Moderate	UL=Ultra Light	H=Heavy
MF=Moderate Fast	L=Light	MH=Medium-Heavy
F=Fast	ML=Medium-Light	XH=Extra Heavy
XF=Extra Fast		

RODS: Freshwater Spinning

SHIMANO FX

Model: FXS50ULB2, FXS56ULB2, FXS56MB2, FXS60MB2, FXS66MB2, FXS70MB2, FXS70MHB2, FXS66MHB2, FXS80MHB2, FXS90MHB2
Length: 5'; 5'6''; 5'6''; 6'; 6'6''; 6'6''; 7'; 7'; 8'; 9'
Power: UL; UL; M; M; M; MH; M; MH; MH; MH
Action: F
Pieces: 2
Line Weight: 1-4 lbs; 2-6 lbs; 6-14 lbs; 6-14 lbs; 6-14 lbs; 8-17 lbs; 6-14 lbs; 12-25 lbs; 12-25 lbs; 14-25 lbs

Guide Count: 5; 5; 5; 5; 5; 6; 6; 7; 7; 7
Lure Weight: 1/32-3/16 oz; 1/32-3/16 oz; 1/8-1/2 oz; 1/8-1/2 oz; 1/4-5/8 oz; 1/4-3/4 oz; 1/4-5/8 oz; 1/2-3 oz; 3/4-4 oz; 3/4-4 oz
Features: Durable aeroglass blank construction; features reinforced aluminum oxide guides; solid locking graphite reel seat; comfortable EVA handles.
Price:................................ **$12.99–$19.99**

SHIMANO SOJOURN

Model: SJS50UL2A, SJS56UL2A, SJS60MA, SJS60M2A, SJS60ML2A, SJS66MA, SJS66M2A, SJS66MHA, SJS70HA, SJS70MA, SJS70M2A, SJS70MHA
Length: 5'; 5'6''; 6'; 6'; 6'; 6'6''; 6'6''; 6'6''; 7'; 7'; 7'; 7'
Power: UL; UL; M; M; ML; M; M; MH; H; M; M; MH
Action: F
Pieces: 2; 2; 1; 2; 2; 1; 2; 1; 1; 1; 2; 1
Line Weight: 1-4 lbs; 2-6 lbs; 6-12 lbs; 6-12 lbs; 4-10 lbs; 6-14 lbs; 6-14 lbs; 8-17 lbs; 12-25 lbs; 6-14 lbs; 6-14 lbs; 10-20 lbs

Lure Weight: 1/32-3/16 oz; 1/32-3/16 oz; 1/8-1/2 oz; 1/8-1/2 oz; 1/16-3/8 oz; 1/8-5/8 oz; 1/8-5/8 oz; 1/4-3/4 oz; 1/2-3 oz; 1/4-3/4 oz; 1/4-3/4 oz; 1/4-1 oz
Features: Graphite composite blank; low-profile aluminum oxide guides; custom reel seat; custom-shaped cork handle; EVA butt cap; multi-purpose hook keeper.
Price:................................ **$29.99–$34.99**

ACTION	POWER	
M=Moderate	UL=Ultra Light	H=Heavy
MF=Moderate Fast	L=Light	MH=Medium-Heavy
F=Fast	ML=Medium-Light	XH=Extra Heavy
XF=Extra Fast		

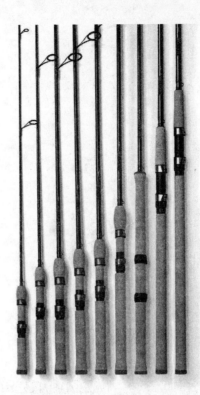

ST. CROIX AVID SERIES

Model: AVS46ULF, AVS50ULF, AVS56ULF2, AVS59MXF, AVS60ULF, AVS60ULF2, AVS60LF, AVS60MLF, AVS60MF, AVS63MLXF, AVS63MXF, AVS66ULF, AVS66ULF2, AVS66LF, AVS66LF2, AVS66MLF, AVS66MLF2, AVS66MF, AVS66MF2, AVS66MHF, AVS66MHF2, AVS68MXF, AVS69MLXF, AVS70ULF, AVS70ULM2, AVS70MLF, AVS7070MLF2, AVS70MF, AVS70MF2, AVS70MHF, AVS76MLXF, AVS76MLXF2, AVS80MLM2

Length: 4'6"; 5'; 5'6"; 5'9"; 6'; 6'; 6'; 6'; 6'; 6'3"; 6'3"; 6'6"; 6'6"; 6'6"; 6'6"; 6'6"; 6'6"; 6'6"; 6'6"; 6'6"; 6'6"; 6'8"; 6'9"; 7'; 7'; 7'; 7'; 7'; 7'; 7'; 7'6"; 7'6"; 8'

Power: UL; UL; UL; M; UL; UL; L; ML; M; ML; M; UL; UL; L; L; ML; ML; M; M; MH; MH; M; ML; UL; UL; ML; ML; M; M; MH; ML; ML; ML

Action: F; F; F; XF; F; F; F; F; F; XF; XF; F; F; F; F; F; F; F; F; F; F; XF; XF; F; M; F; F; F; F; F; XF; XF; M

Pieces: 1; 1; 2; 1; 1; 2; 1; 1; 1; 1; 1; 1; 2; 1; 2; 1; 2; 1; 2; 1; 2; 1; 1; 1; 2; 1; 2; 1; 2; 1; 1; 2; 2

Line Weight: 2-6 lbs; 2-6 lbs; 2-6 lbs; 6-10 lbs; 2-6 lbs; 2-6 lbs; 4-8 lbs; 4-10 lbs; 6-12 lbs; 4-8 lbs; 6-10 lbs; 2-6 lbs; 2-6 lbs; 4-8 lbs; 4-8 lbs; 4-10 lbs; 4-10 lbs; 6-12 lbs; 6-12 lbs; 8-14 lbs; 8-14 lbs; 6-12 lbs; 6-10 lbs; 2-6 lbs; 2-6 lbs; 4-10 lbs; 4-10 lbs; 6-12 lbs; 6-12 lbs; 8-14 lbs; 4-10 lbs; 4-10 lbs; 4-8 lbs

Lure Weight: 1/32-3/16 oz; 1/32-3/16 oz; 1/32-3/16 oz; 1/8-1/2 oz; 1/32-3/16 oz; 1/32-3/16 oz; 1/16-1/4 oz; 1/8-3/8 oz; 3/16-5/8 oz; 1/16-3/8 oz; 1/8-1/2 oz; 1/32-3/16 oz; 1/32-3/16 oz; 1/16-1/4 oz; 1/16-1/4 oz; 1/8-3/8 oz; 1/8-3/8 oz; 3/16-5/8 oz; 3/16-5/8 oz; 3/8-3/4 oz; 3/8-3/4 oz; 3/16-5/8 oz; 1/8-1/2 oz; 1/32-3/16 oz; 1/32-3/16 oz; 1/8-3/8 oz; 1/8-3/8 oz; 3/16-5/8 oz; 3/16-5/8 oz; 3/8-3/4 oz; 1/8-3/8 oz; 1/8-3/8 oz; 1/16-5/16 oz

Features: Integrated Poly Curve tooling technology; premium, high-modulus SCIII graphite; superb sensitivity, extreme strength and durability, incredibly light, and an outstanding value; specialized, technique-specific, and species-specific designs; slim-profile ferrules; Fuji Alconite concept guide system with black frames; Fuji SKM reel seat/gunsmoke hoods; Fuji DPS reel seat/gunsmoke hoods on carp models; select-grade cork handle; two coats of Flex Coat slow-cure finish; lifetime limited warranty.

Price: . . . . **$150–$210**

ACTION	POWER	
M=Moderate	**UL**=Ultra Light	**H**=Heavy
MF=Moderate Fast	**L**=Light	**MH**=Medium-Heavy
F=Fast	**ML**=Medium-Light	**XH**=Extra Heavy
XF=Extra Fast		

ST. CROIX LEGEND ELITE

Model: LES60ULF2, LES60MLF, LES60MF, LES63MXF, LES66LF, LES66LF2, LES66MLF, LES66MLF2, LES66MF, LES66MF2, LES66MHF, LES68MXF, LES70ULM2, LES70LF, LES70LF2, LES70MLF, LES70MLF2, LES70MF, LES70MF2, LES70MHF, LES70MHF2, LES76MLXF, LES76MLXF2, LES76MF, LES76MF2

Length: 6'; 6'; 6'; 6'3"; 6'6"; 6'6"; 6'6"; 6'6"; 6'6"; 6'6"; 6'6"; 6'8"; 7'; 7'; 7'; 7'; 7'; 7'; 7'; 7'; 7'6"; 7'6"; 7'6"; 7'6"

Power: UL; ML; M; M; L; L; ML; ML; M; M; MH; M; UL; L; L; ML; ML; M; M; MH; MH; ML; ML; M; M

Action: F; F; F; XF; F; F; F; F; F; F; F; XF; M; F; F; F; F; F; F; F; F; XF; XF; F; F

Pieces: 2; 1; 1; 1; 1; 2; 1; 2; 1; 2; 1; 1; 2; 1; 2; 1; 2; 1; 2; 1; 2; 1; 2; 1; 2

Line Weight: 2-6 lbs; 4-10 lbs; 6-12 lbs; 6-10 lbs; 4-8 lbs; 4-8 lbs; 4-10 lbs; 4-10 lbs; 6-12 lbs; 6-12 lbs; 8-14 lbs; 6-12 lbs; 2-6 lbs; 4-8 lbs; 4-8 lbs; 4-10 lbs; 4-10 lbs; 6-12 lbs; 6-12 lbs; 8-14 lbs; 8-14 lbs; 4-10 lbs; 4-10 lbs; 6-12 lbs; 6-12 lbs

Lure Weight: 1/32-3/16 oz; 1/8-3/8 oz; 3/16-5/8 oz; 1/8-1/2 oz; 1/16-1/4 oz; 1/16-1/4 oz; 1/8-3/8 oz; 1/8-3/8 oz; 3/16-5/8 oz; 3/16-5/8 oz; 3/8-3/4 oz; 3/16-5/8 oz; 1/32-3/16 oz; 1/16-1/4 oz; 1/16-1/4 oz; 1/8-3/8 oz; 1/8-3/8 oz; 3/16-5/8 oz; 3/16-5/8 oz; 3/8-3/4 oz; 3/8-3/4 oz; 1/8-3/8 oz; 1/8-3/8 oz; 3/16-5/8 oz; 3/16-5/8 oz

Features: Integrated Poly Curve tooling technology; Advanced Reinforcing Technology; super high-modulus SCVI graphite with FRS in lower section for maximum power and strength with reduced weight; high-modulus/high-strain SCV graphite with FRS and carbon-matte scrim for unparalleled strength and durability; slim-profile ferrules; phenomenally sensitive, light, and smooth casting; Fuji SiC Concept Guide System with titanium-finished frames; Fuji VSS reel seat/frosted silver hood on spinning models; Fuji ACS reel seat/frosted silver hood on casting models; machined-aluminum wind check; super-grade cork handle; two coats of Flex Coat slow-cure finish; includes deluxe rod sack; lifetime limited warranty.

Price: . . . . $330–$380

ACTION	POWER	
M=Moderate	UL=Ultra Light	H=Heavy
MF=Moderate Fast	L=Light	MH=Medium-Heavy
F=Fast	ML=Medium-Light	XH=Extra Heavy
XF=Extra Fast		

ST. CROIX LEGENDXTREME

Model: LXS59MXF, LXS63MXF, LXS68MXF, LXS610MLXF, LXS610MXF, LXS70LF, LXS70LF2, LXS70MLF, LXS70MLF2, LXS70MF, LXS70MF2, LXS70MHF, LXS70MHF2, LXS76MLXF, LXS76MLXF2, LXS76MF, LXS76MF2

Length: 5'9''; 6'3''; 6'8''; 6'10''; 6'10''; 7'; 7'; 7'; 7'; 7'; 7'; 7'; 7'; 7'6''; 7'6''; 7'6''; 7'6''

Power: M; M; M; ML; M; L; L; ML; ML; M; M; MH; MH; ML; ML; M; M

Action: XF; XF; XF; XF; XF; F; F; F; F; F; F; F; F; XF; XF; F; F

Pieces: 1; 1; 1; 1; 1; 1; 2; 1; 2; 1; 2; 1; 2; 1; 2; 1; 2

Line Weight: 6-10 lbs; 6-10 lbs; 6-12 lbs; 6-10 lbs; 6-12 lbs; 4-8 lbs; 4-8 lbs; 4-10 lbs; 4-10 lbs; 6-12 lbs; 6-12 lbs; 8-14 lbs; 8-14 lbs; 4-10 lbs; 4-10 lbs; 6-12 lbs; 6-12 lbs

Lure Weight: 1/8-1/2 oz; 1/8-1/2 oz; 3/16-5/8 oz; 1/8-1/2 oz; 1/8-5/16 oz; 1/16-1/4 oz; 1/16-1/4 oz; 1/8-3/8 oz; 1/8-3/8 oz; 3/16-5/8 oz; 3/16-5/8 oz; 3/8-3/4 oz; 3/8-3/4 oz; 1/8-3/8 oz; 1/8-3/8 oz; 3/16-5/8 oz; 3/16-5/8 oz

Features: Integrated Poly Curve tooling technology; Taper Enhancement Technology blank design provides curved patterns for improved action with increased sensitivity; Advanced Reinforcing Technology; super high-modulus SCVI graphite with FRS in lower section for maximum power and strength with reduced weight; high-modulus/high-strain SCV graphite with FRS and carbon-matte scrim for unparalleled strength, durability, and sensitivity; slim-profile ferrules; Fuji K-R Concept Tangle Free guides with SiC rings and exclusive E-color finish frames. Ideal for super braid, mono, and fluorocarbon lines, the sloped frame and ring shed tangles before they become a problem; Fuji SK2 split reel seat for the ultimate in light weight and sensitivity; Xtreme-Skin handle repels water, dirt, and fish slime and cleans up easily; manufactured by St. Croix to provide outstanding angler comfort, casting efficiency, and sensitivity; machined-aluminum wind check, handle trim pieces and butt cap with logo badge; two coats of Flex Coat slow-cure finish; includes protective rod sack; lifetime limited warranty.

Price: . . . . $370–$440

RODS

ACTION	POWER	
M=Moderate	UL=Ultra Light	H=Heavy
MF=Moderate Fast	L=Light	MH=Medium-Heavy
F=Fast	ML=Medium-Light	XH=Extra Heavy
XF=Extra Fast		

RODS: Freshwater Spinning

ST. CROIX PREMIER SPINNING

Model: PS46ULM, PS50ULM, PS56ULF2, PS56LF, PS56MF, PS60ULF, PS60ULF2, PS60LF, PS60MLF, PS60MLF2, PS60MF, PS60MF2, PS60MHF, PS66ULF, PS66ULF2, PS66LF, PS66LF2, PS66MLF, PS66MLF2, PS66MF, PS66MF2, PS66MHF, PS66MHF2, PS70ULF2, PS70MLF, PS70MLF2, PS70MF, PS70MF2, PS70MHF, PS70HF, PS70HF2, PS70XHF, PS76MLF, PS76MLF2, PS76MF, PS76MF2, PS86LM2

Length: 4'6''; 5'; 5'6''; 5'6''; 5'6''; 6'; 6'; 6'; 6'; 6'; 6'; 6'; 6'; 6'6''; 6'6''; 6'6''; 6'6''; 6'6''; 6'6''; 6'6''; 6'6''; 6'6''; 6'6''; 7'; 7'; 7'; 7'; 7'; 7'; 7'; 7'; 7'; 7'6''; 7'6''; 7'6''; 7'6''; 8'6''

Power: UL; UL; UL; L; M; UL; UL; L; ML; ML; M; M; MH; UL; UL; L; L; ML; ML; M; M; MH; MH; UL; ML; ML; M; M; MH; H; H; XH; ML; ML; M; M; L

Action: M; M; F; F; F; F; F; F; F; F; F; F; F; F; F; F; F; F; F; F; F; F; F; F; F; F; F; F; F; F; F; F; F; F; F; F; M

Pieces: 1; 1; 2; 1; 1; 1; 2; 1; 1; 2; 1; 2; 1; 1; 2; 1; 2; 1; 2; 1; 2; 1; 2; 2; 1; 2; 1; 2; 1; 1; 2; 1; 1; 2; 1; 2; 2

Line Weight: 2-6 lbs; 2-6 lbs; 2-6 lbs; 4-8 lbs; 6-12 lbs; 2-6 lbs; 2-6 lbs; 4-8 lbs; 4-10 lbs; 4-10 lbs; 6-12 lbs; 6-12 lbs; 8-14 lbs; 2-6 lbs; 2-6 lbs; 4-8 lbs; 4-8 lbs; 4-10 lbs; 4-10 lbs; 6-12 lbs; 6-12 lbs; 8-14 lbs; 8-17 lbs; 2-6 lbs; 4-10 lbs; 4-10 lbs; 6-12 lbs; 6-12 lbs; 8-14 lbs; 10-20 lbs; 10-20 lbs; 12-25 lbs; 4-10 lbs; 4-10 lbs; 6-12 lbs; 6-12 lbs; 4-8 lbs

Lure Weight: 1/16-1/4 oz; 1/16-1/4 oz; 1/32-3/16 oz; 1/16-5/16 oz; 1/4-5/8 oz; 1/32-3/16 oz; 1/32-3/16 oz; 1/16-5/16 oz; 1/8-1/2 oz; 1/8-1/2 oz; 1/4-5/8 oz; 1/4-5/8 oz; 3/8-3/4 oz; 1/32-3/16 oz; 1/32-3/16 oz; 1/16-5/16 oz; 1/16-5/16 oz; 1/8-1/2 oz; 1/8-1/2 oz; 1/4-5/8 oz; 1/4-5/8 oz; 3/8-1/4 oz; 1/2-1 oz; 1/32-3/16 oz; 1/8-1/2 oz; 1/8-1/2 oz; 1/4-5/8 oz; 1/4-5/8 oz; 3/8-3/4 oz; 1/2-1 1/2 oz; 1/2-1 1/2 oz; 3/4-2 oz; 1/8-1/2 oz; 1/8-1/2 oz; 1/4-5/8 oz; 1/4-5/8 oz; 1/16-5/16 oz

Features: Premium-quality SCII graphite; outstanding strength, sensitivity and hook-setting power; finely tuned actions and tapers for superior performance; Kigan Master Hand 3D guides featuring slim, strong aluminum-oxide rings with black frames; Fuji DPS reel seat/frosted silver hoods; premium-grade cork handle; two coats of Flex Coat slow-cure finish; five-year warranty.

Price: . . . . **$110–$170**

ACTION	POWER	
M=Moderate	UL=Ultra Light	H=Heavy
MF=Moderate Fast	L=Light	MH=Medium-Heavy
F=Fast	ML=Medium-Light	XH=Extra Heavy
XF=Extra Fast		

ST. CROIX RAGE SERIES

Model: RS68MXF, RS610MLXF, RS610MXF, RS71MF, RS71MHF
Length: 6'8''; 6'10''; 6'10''; 7'1''; 7'1''
Power: M; ML; M; M; MH
Action: XF; XF; XF; F; F
Pieces: 1
Line Weight: 6-12 lbs; 6-10 lbs; 6-12 lbs; 6-12 lbs; 8-14 lbs
Lure Weight: 3/16-5/8 oz; 1/8-1/2 oz; 1/8-5/16 oz; 3/16-5/8 oz; 3/8-3/4 oz
Features: Integrated Poly Curve (IPC) tooling technology; premium, high-modulus SCIII graphite; incredibly lightweight and sensitive with superb balance and extreme strength; Pac Bay Minima micro guide configuration for high performance and improved durability by eliminating insert

failure, plus 20 percent to 30 percent weight savings compared to ceramic guides; Pacific Bay Minima casting reel seat/black hood provides maximum rod blank exposure and is 30 percent lighter than conventional trigger reel seats; Pacific Bay Minima spinning reel seat/black hood provides maximum rod blank exposure and is 10 percent to 20 percent lighter than conventional spinning reel seats; contoured handle provides split-grip performance; featuring a precision-shaped core wrapped with a neoprene skin for maximum comfort and sensitivity; EVA trim pieces provide additional refinement; two coats of Flex Coat slow-cure finish; five-year warranty.
Price: **$150**

ST. CROIX TROUT SERIES

Model: TSS54ULF, TSS56ULF2, TSS60ULF2, TSS64LF2, TSS70LXF2
Length: 5'4''; 5'6''; 6'; 6'4''; 7'
Power: UL; UL; UL; L; L
Action: F; F; F; F; XF
Pieces: 1; 2; 2; 2; 2
Line Weight: 2-6 lbs; 2-6 lbs; 2-6 lbs; 4-8 lbs; 4-8 lbs
Lure Weight: 1/32-3/16 oz; 1/32-3/16 oz; 1/32-3/16 oz; 1/16-1/4 oz; 1/16-1/4 oz

Features: To paraphrase Theodore Roosevelt, it's not the size of the fish in the fight, but the size of the fight in the fish. You have to figure Teddy would have had his eyes keenly focused on our new Trout Series spinning rods. Like the popular Panfish Series, our new Trout rods offer the perfect blend of weight, sensitivity, and balance. Both series serve up incredibly dialed-in, specialized performance for fish that require the utmost finesse and delicacy.
Price: . . . . **$110–$130**

ACTION	POWER	
M=Moderate	UL=Ultra Light	H=Heavy
MF=Moderate Fast	L=Light	MH=Medium-Heavy
F=Fast	ML=Medium-Light	XH=Extra Heavy
XF=Extra Fast		

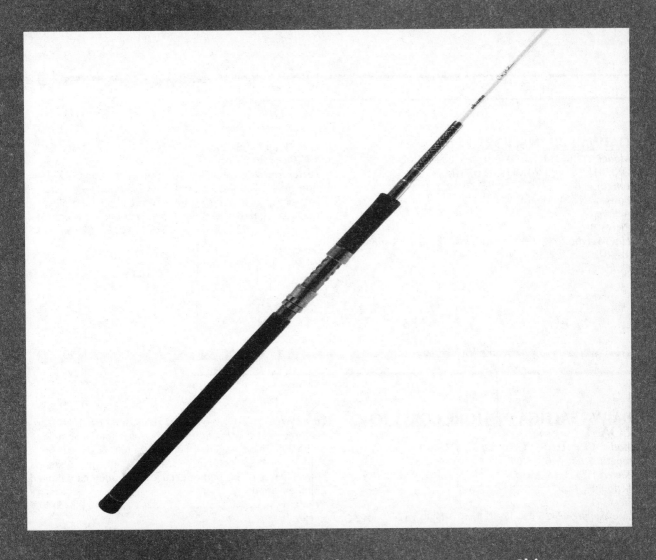

162 Daiwa

163 G.Loomis

164 Lamiglas

165 Okuma

167 Shimano

168 St. Croix

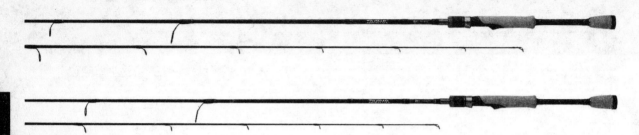

DAIWA DXI INSHORE

Model: DXI661MLFS, DXI661MFS, DXI701MLFS, DXI701MFS, DXI761MLFS, DXI761MFS
Length: 6'6''; 6'6''; 7'; 7'; 7'6''; 7'6''
Power: ML; M; ML; M; ML; M
Action: F
Pieces: 1
Line Weight: 8-17 lbs; 8-20 lbs; 8-17 lbs; 8-20 lbs; 8-17 lbs; 8-20 lbs
Guide Count: 8; 8; 8; 8; 9; 9

Lure Weight: 1/8-3/4 oz; 1/4-1 oz; 1/8-3/4 oz; 1/4-1 oz; 1/8-3/4 oz; 1/4-1 oz
Features: IM6 graphite blank construction; Minima Zirconia ring guides; Fuji (ACS casting & VSS spinning) reel seat; split-design natural cork grip; woven carbon & stainless steel reel clamp; hook keeper; five-year limited warranty.
Price:.............................$89.95–$99.95

DAIWA SALTIGA INSHORE COAST-TO-COAST

Model: CC701HFS, CC701XHFS, CC761MFS, CC761MHFS
Length: 7'; 7'; 7'6''; 7'6''
Power: H; XH; M; MH
Action: F
Pieces: 1
Line Weight: 15-25 lbs; 17-30 lbs; 10-17 lbs; 12-20 lbs
Guide Count: 8; 8; 7; 7

Lure Weight: 1/2-1 1/2 oz; 1/2-2 oz; 3/8-3/4 oz; 1/4-1 oz
Features: Bias construction high-modulus graphite blank; tough Fuji Alconite guides; Fuji SiC tip-top (Northeast models only); genuine Fuji reel seat; high-quality cork grip; convenient hook keeper; protective rubber butt cap; limited lifetime warranty.
Price:.................................. $149.95

ACTION		**POWER**	
M=Moderate	UL=Ultra Light	H=Heavy
MF=Moderate Fast	L=Light	MH=Medium-Heavy
F=Fast	ML=Medium-Light	XH=Extra Heavy
XF=Extra Fast		

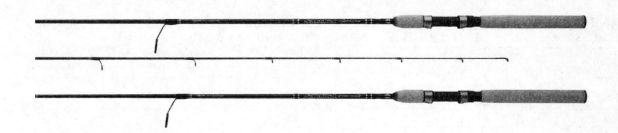

DAIWA SALTIGA INSHORE GULF COAST

Model: GC661MFS, GC701MFS, GC701MLXS, GC761MLXS, GC801MLXS
Length: 6'6''; 7'; 7'; 7'6''; 8'
Power: M; M; ML; ML; ML
Action: F; F; XF; XF; XF
Pieces: 1
Line Weight: 8-20 lbs; 8-20 lbs; 8-17 lbs; 8-17 lbs; 8-17 lbs
Guide Count: 8; 9; 9; 9; 10

Lure Weight: 1/4-1 oz; 1/4-1 oz; 1/8-3/4 oz; 1/8-3/4 oz; 1/8-3/4 oz
Features: Bias construction high-modulus graphite blank; tough Fuji Alconite guides; Fuji SiC tip-top (Northeast models only); genuine Fuji reel seat; high-quality cork grip; convenient hook keeper, protective rubber butt cap; limited lifetime warranty.
Price: . . . .$139.95–$149.95

G.LOOMIS NRX INSHORE

Model: NRX 804S XMR, NRX 803S XMR, RX 842S MR, NRX 843S MR, NRX 882S MR, NRX 883S MR, NRX 921S MR, NRX 922S MR, NRX 923S MR
Length: 6'8''; 6'8''; 7'; 7'; 7'4''; 7'4''; 7'8''; 7'8''; 7'8''
Power: MH; M; M; MH; M; MH; ML; M; MH
Action: XF; XF; F; F; F; F; F; F; F
Pieces: 1
Line Weight: 10-20 lbs; 8-15 lbs; 8-15 lbs; 10-20 lbs; 8-15 lbs; 10-20 lbs; 6-12 lbs; 8-15 lbs; 10-20 lbs
Lure Weight: 1/2-1 1/2 oz; 3/8-1 oz; 3/16-5/8 oz; 3/16-3/4 oz; 3/16-5/8 oz; 3/16-3/4 oz; 1/8-3/8 oz; 3/16-5/8 oz; 3/16-3/4 oz
Features: Most inshore fishing is done on the flats or in shallow bays around docks or mangroves where getting a bait to the fish and then getting that fish to the boat is a real challenge. You need everything on your side. It's about the tide and the affect it has on the flats, the reeds, the rocks, and the mangroves. It's about being in the right place at the right time and making the right presentation. Basically, it's

about NRX "Mag Rod" Inshore spinning rods . . . a series of fast and extra-fast, magnum power spinning rods featuring the new nano-silica resin system that allows us to use less material without losing strength. Rods that are very light, incredibly—no—insanely sensitive and stronger than any high-performance, high-modulus rod we've ever made. These rods are rated for braid. It's the ultimate connection for sensitivity, fish-fighting control, and taking vegetation and heavy cover out of the equation. Another great feature on these new rods is the hybrid guide train. We use titanium-framed, SIC K-frame stripper guides that are designed to keep braided line from tangling on the frames at the stiffest point of the rod. After the first three K-frame guides, we've added nickle-titanium RECOIL guides to reduce weight and increase the rate of recovery for the tip, creating unequaled casting distance! All feature split-grip handle configurations and are backed with a limited-lifetime warranty.
Price: . . . .$610–$675

ACTION	POWER	
M=Moderate	UL=Ultra Light	H=Heavy
MF=Moderate Fast	L=Light	MH=Medium-Heavy
F=Fast	ML=Medium-Light	XH=Extra Heavy
XF=Extra Fast		

RODS: Saltwater Spinning

RODS

LAMIGLAS BLACK SALT
Model: BS 722 S, BS 723 S, BS 724 S, BS 725 S, BS 773 S, BS 774 S, BS 775 S, BS 806 TARPON
Length: 7'2''; 7'2''; 7'2''; 7'2''; 7'7''; 7'7''; 7'7''; 8'
Action: F; F; F; F; F; F; F; MF
Pieces: 1
Line Weight: 4-10 lbs; 6-15 lbs; 8-17 lbs; 10-20 lbs; 6-15 lbs; 8-17 lbs; 10-20 lbs; 15-40 lbs

Lure Weight: 1/8-3/8 oz; 1/4-1/2 oz; 3/8-3/4 oz; 3/8-1 oz; 1/4-1/2 oz; 3/8-3/4 oz; 3/8-1 oz; 1-3 oz
Features: These rods offer the smooth agility to cast accurately and the raw power to pull fish to the boat; deep pressed guides with zirconia inserts; AmTack Areo reel seats; graphite handles; made in the USA.
Price: **$270**

LAMIGLAS EXCEL INSHORE
Model: XLS 702 S, XLS 703 S, XLS 704 S, XLS 763 S, XLS 764 S, XLS 7114 S, XLS 823 S
Length: 7'; 7'; 7'; 7'6''; 7'6''; 7'11''; 8'2''
Action: MF; F; F; F; F; MF; F
Pieces: 1
Line Weight: 6-10 lbs; 8-12 lbs; 8-17 lbs; 8-12 lbs; 8-17 lbs; 8-17 lbs; 8-17 lbs

Lure Weight: 1/8-3/8 oz; 1/4-1/2 oz; 3/8-3/4 oz; 1/4-1/2 oz; 3/8-3/4 oz; 3/8-3/4 oz; 3/8-3/4 oz
Features: Lightweight blanks with deep pressed stainless guides are ideal for all inshore species; lighter models feature split-grip handles; finished in a metallic copper tone; made in USA.
Price: **$230**

LAMIGLAS TRI-FLEX GRAPHITE
Model: TFX 6015 S, TFX 6615 S
Length: 6'; 6'6''
Action: F
Pieces: 1
Line Weight: 8-17 lbs
Lure Weight: 1/4-1 oz
Features: Cork handles immediately categorize these rods as inshore, but don't overlook these highly capable models

wherever the need for refined power of tri-flex graphite exists; latest editions are precision-balanced rods for throwing bucktails for striped bass, fluke, and bluefish; others are equally at home casting swim baits to tuna as they are throwing eels to stripers or crabs to tarpon; easy handling and can-do nature.
Price: . . . . **$260–$400**

ACTION	POWER	
M=Moderate	UL=Ultra Light	H=Heavy
MF=Moderate Fast	L=Light	MH=Medium-Heavy
F=Fast	ML=Medium-Light	XH=Extra Heavy
XF=Extra Fast		

OKUMA CRUZ POPPING

Model: CRP-S-762M, CRP-S-792H, CRP-S-792MH
Length: 7'6''; 7'9''; 7'9''
Power: M; H; MH
Action: M
Pieces: 1
Line Weight: 30-65 lbs; 65-150 lbs; 50-100 lbs
Guide Count: 7; 8; 7
Lure Weight: 1-5 1/2 oz; 5 1/2-11 1/2 oz; 3-7 oz
Features: Extremely durable carbon and glass blank mixture for ultimate strength; ALPS 316-grade stainless steel double-footed guide frames; smaller diameter guide inserts allow line to shoot out of rod for longer cast; ALPS hard zirconium guide inserts, perfect for braided line; custom ALPS machined aluminum, two-tone anodized reel seats; EVA fore and rear grips for all day casting comfort; one-piece rod blank construction, butted into handle for uninterrupted rod tapers; machined tapered hood transitions above and below reel seat; low-profile butt cap design for unobstructed fishing; heavy model features a machined aluminum gimbal; all Cruz popping rods are one-piece blanks plus the handle configuration; limited lifetime warranty.
Price:. . . . .**$179.99–$189.99**

ACTION	POWER	
M=Moderate	UL=Ultra Light	H=Heavy
MF=Moderate Fast	L=Light	MH=Medium-Heavy
F=Fast	ML=Medium-Light	XH=Extra Heavy
XF=Extra Fast		

OKUMA PEZ VELA

Model: PV-S-661MH, PV-S-701M, PV-S-701MH
Length: 6'6''; 7'; 7'
Power: MH; M; MH
Action: MF
Pieces: 1
Line Weight: 15-30 lbs; 15-25 lbs; 20-30 lbs
Guide Count: 6; 7; 7

Features: Extremely durable carbon and glass rod blank mixture; EVA fore and rear grips on spinning models; casting models feature EVA fore grip and a graphite butt; double-footed stainless steel guide frames; polished titanium oxide guide inserts; cushioned stainless steel hooded reel seat; durable non-skid, rubber gimbals on all models; all Pez Vela rods are one-piece blank construction; one-year warranty.
Price: **$69.99**

OKUMA SARASOTA

Model: Sr-S-661M, Sr-S-661ML, Sr-S-701M, Sr-S-701ML
Length: 6'6''; 6'6''; 7'; 7'
Power: M; ML; M; ML
Action: MF
Pieces: 1
Line Weight: 20-40 lbs; 15-30 lbs; 20-40 lbs; 15-30 lbs
Guide Count: 6; 6; 7; 7
Features: Durable E-glass blank construction; glass fiber outer wrap increases hoop strength; double-footed stainless steel guide frames; HD model uses heavy duty-style guide frames; use Pacific Bay roller stripper and tip guides; polished titanium oxide guide inserts; stainless steel hooded reel seats; heavy duty aluminum hooded reel seat on HD/T models; graphite gimbals on all models; custom epoxy-wrapped foregrip transition cone; one-year warranty.
Price: **$49.99**

ACTION	POWER	
M=Moderate	UL=Ultra Light	H=Heavy
MF=Moderate Fast	L=Light	MH=Medium-Heavy
F=Fast	ML=Medium-Light	XH=Extra Heavy
XF=Extra Fast		

SHIMANO SAGUARO

Model: SGS66M, SGS66MH, SGS70ML, SGS70M, SGS70MH, SGS70H, SGS80MH2, SGS90MH2
Length: 6'6''; 6'6''; 7'; 7'; 7'; 7'; 8'; 9'
Power: M; MH; ML; M; MH; H; MH; MH
Action: F
Pieces: 1; 1; 1; 1; 1; 1; 2; 2

Line Weight: 14-30 lbs; 20-40 lbs; 8-14 lbs; 12-20 lbs; 14-30 lbs; 20-40 lbs; 14-30 lbs; 14-30 lbs
Guide Count: 7; 7; 7; 7; 7; 7; 8; 8
Features: Aluminum O ring; T-glass; graphite reel seat with stainless steel hoods; comfortable EVA handles; one-year warranty.
Price: . . . . **$39.99–$44.99**

SHIMANO TALAVERA

Model: TES66MH, TES66H, TES70ML, TES70M, TES70MH, TES70H
Length: 6'6''; 6'6''; 7'; 7'; 7'; 7'
Power: MH; H; ML; M; MH; H
Action: F
Pieces: 1
Line Weight: 14-30 lbs; 20-40 lbs; 8-14 lbs; 12-20 lbs; 14-30 lbs; 20-40 lbs

Guide Count: 7
Features: Graphite reel seat; Fuji aluminum oxide guides; EVA grip; AFTCO roller stripper; tip with Fuji heavy duty aluminum oxide boat guides (trolling models only); graphite gimbal with cap (on selected models); black aluminum reel seat (trolling models only).
Price: . . . . **$79.99–$89.99**

ACTION	POWER	
M=Moderate	UL=Ultra Light	H=Heavy
MF=Moderate Fast	L=Light	MH=Medium-Heavy
F=Fast	ML=Medium-Light	XH=Extra Heavy
XF=Extra Fast		

RODS

RODS: Saltwater Spinning

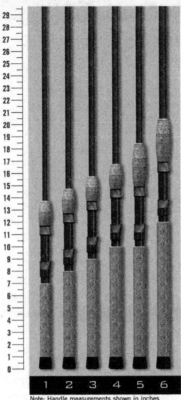

Note: Handle measurements shown in inches

ST. CROIX AVID SERIES INSHORE
Model: AIS66MF, AIS66MHF, AIS70LM, AIS70MLF, AIS70MF, AIS70MM, AIS70MHF, AIS70HF, AIS76MLF, AIS76MF, AIS76MHF, AIS76HF, AIS80MLF, AIS80MF, AIS80MHF, AIS80HF
Length: 6'6''; 6'6''; 7'; 7'; 7'; 7'; 7'; 7'; 7'6''; 7'6''; 7'6''; 7'6''; 8'; 8'; 8'; 8'
Power: M; MH; L; ML; M; M; MH; H; ML; M; MH; H; ML; M; MH; H
Action: F; F; M; F; F; M; F; F; F; F; F; F; F; F; F; F
Pieces: 1
Line Weight: 8-17 lbs; 10-20 lbs; 6-12 lbs; 6-12 lbs; 8-17 lbs; 8-17 lbs; 10-20 lbs; 15-30 lbs; 6-12 lbs; 8-17 lbs; 10-20 lbs; 15-30 lbs; 6-12 lbs; 8-17 lbs; 14-30 lbs; 17-40 lbs

Lure Weight: 3/8-3/4 oz; 1/2-1 1/4 oz; 1/8-3/8 oz; 1/8-1/2 oz; 3/8-3/4 oz; 1/4-5/8 oz; 1/2-1 1/4 oz; 3/4-2 oz; 1/8-1/2 oz; 3/8-3/4 oz; 1/2-1 1/4 oz; 3/4-2 oz; 1/8-1/2 oz; 3/8-3/4 oz; 1/2-2 oz; 3/4-3 oz
Features: Integrated Poly Curve tooling technology; premium, high-modulus SCIII graphite; designed specifically for inshore saltwater angling; ALPS zirconium guides with 316 stainless steel frames for outstanding protection from saltwater corrosion; Fuji DPS reel seat/frosted silver hoods on spinning models; ECS or TCS reel seat/frosted silver hood on casting models; machined-aluminum wind check; super-grade cork handle; two coats of Flex Coat slow-cure finish; lifetime limited warranty.
Price: . . . . $210–$270

ACTION	POWER	
M=Moderate	UL=Ultra Light	H=Heavy
MF=Moderate Fast	L=Light	MH=Medium-Heavy
F=Fast	ML=Medium-Light	XH=Extra Heavy
XF=Extra Fast		

ST. CROIX LEGEND INSHORE

Model: LIS70MLF, LIS70MF, LIS70MHF, LIS76MLF, LIS76MF
Length: 7'; 7'; 7'; 7'6''; 7'6''
Power: ML; M; MH; ML; M
Action: F
Pieces: 1
Line Weight: 6-12 lbs; 8-17 lbs; 10-20 lbs; 6-12 lbs; 8-17 lbs
Lure Weight: 1/8-1/2 oz; 3/8-3/4 oz; 1/2-1 1/4 oz; 1/8-1/2 oz; 3/8-3/4 oz
Features: Integrated Poly Curve tooling technology; Advanced Reinforcing Technology; high-modulus/high-strain SCIV graphite with FRS for unparalleled strength and durability; designed specifically for inshore saltwater angling; Kigan Master Hand Zero Tangle guides with zirconia rings and titanium frames for the ultimate protection against saltwater corrosion; the sloped, wide-leg design prevents line tangles with mono, fluorocarbon, and super braid lines; Fuji SK2 split reel seat for the ultimate in light weight and sensitivity; super-grade cork handle on spinning models; split-grip/super-grade cork handle on casting models; corrosion-proof wind check and reel seat trim pieces; two coats of Flex Coat slow-cure finish; lifetime limited warranty.
Price:. . . . . **$350–$380**

ST. CROIX LEGENDXTREME INSHORE

Model: XIS70MLF, XIS70MF, XIS70MHF
Length: 7'
Power: ML; M; MH
Action: F
Pieces: 11
Line Weight: 6-12 lbs; 8-17 lbs; 10-20 lbs
Lure Weight: 1/8-1/2 oz; 3/8-3/4 oz; 1/2-1 1/4 oz
Features: The middle school hallway. The Red Zone. The checkout line at Costco. There are places that test your wherewithal—but none as decisively as the inshore saltwater arena. Venture in there and you better be ready to man-up. It might also be a good idea to carry one of our new LegendXtreme Inshore rods. Hyper-performance rods for intense inshore fishing. Loaded with proprietary technologies, built on high-modulus SCVI and SCV graphite blanks, and finished with cutting edge fittings, these are the rods you go to when your intensity level hits high tide.
Price:. . . . . **$390–$400**

ACTION		POWER	
M=Moderate	UL=Ultra Light	H=Heavy	
MF=Moderate Fast	L=Light	MH=Medium-Heavy	
F=Fast	ML=Medium-Light	XH=Extra Heavy	
XF=Extra Fast			

RODS: **Saltwater Spinning**

ST. CROIX MOJO INSHORE

Model: MIS70MLF, MIS70MF, MIS70MHF, MIS70HF, MIS76MLF, MIS76MF, MIS76MHF, MIS76HF
Length: 7'; 7'; 7'; 7'; 7'6''; 7'6''; 7'6''; 7'6''
Power: ML; M; MH; H; ML; M; MH; H
Action: F
Pieces: 1
Line Weight: 6-14 lbs; 8-17 lbs; 10-20 lbs; 15-30 lbs; 6-14 lbs; 8-17 lbs; 10-20 lbs; 15-30 lbs
Lure Weight: 1/8-1/2 oz; 3/8-3/4 oz; 1/2-1 1/4 oz; 3/4-2 oz; 1/8-1/2 oz; 3/8-3/4 oz; 1/2-1 1/4 oz; 3/4-2 oz

Features: Premium-quality SCII graphite; specialized inshore saltwater series designed and built for superior performance; Batson Forecast hard aluminum-oxide guides with 316 stainless-steel frames for dramatically improved corrosion resistance compared to 304 stainless-steel frames; Fuji DPS reel seat/black hoods on spinning models; Fuji ECS reel seat/black hood on casting models; split-grip/premium-grade cork handle; two coats of Flex Coat slow-cure finish; five-year warranty.
Price: . . . . **$130–$150**

ACTION	POWER	
M=Moderate	UL=Ultra Light	H=Heavy
MF=Moderate Fast	L=Light	MH=Medium-Heavy
F=Fast	ML=Medium-Light	XH=Extra Heavy
XF=Extra Fast		

ST. CROIX TRIUMPH SURF

Model: TSR70M, TSRS80M2, TSRS90M2, TSRS100M2, TSRS106MH2
Length: 7'; 8'; 9'; 10'; 10'6''
Power: M; M; M; M; MH
Action: MF
Pieces: 1; 2; 2; 2; 2
Line Weight: 8-17 lbs; 8-17 lbs; 8-20 lbs; 8-20 lbs; 10-25 lbs

Lure Weight: 1/2-2 oz; 1/2-2 oz; 1/2-2 1/2 oz; 3/4-4 oz; 2-6 oz
Features: Premium-quality SCII graphite; designed for long-distance casting; lightweight, hard aluminum-oxide surf guides; Fuji DPS reel seat/frosted silver hoods; custom cork tape handle; two coats of Flex Coat slow-cure finish; five-year warranty.
Price: . . . . **$110–$180**

ACTION	POWER	
M=Moderate	UL=Ultra Light	H=Heavy
MF=Moderate Fast	L=Light	MH=Medium-Heavy
F=Fast	ML=Medium-Light	XH=Extra Heavy
XF=Extra Fast		

174 Eagle Claw

RODS: Saltwater Spincasting

EAGLE CLAW BRAVE EAGLE
Model: BRV100-3, BRV100-4, BRV100-5
Length: 3'; 4'; 5'
Power: M
Pieces: 1; 1; 2
Line Weight: 4-15 lbs
Guide Count: 3

Lure Weight: 1/4-5/8 oz; 3/16-1/2 oz; 1/8-3/8 oz
Features: Available in spinning and spincast models; durable, solid glass construction for years of trouble free fishing; soft foam handles for all day comfort; stainless steel guides; one-year warranty.
Price:. $19.99

RODS

ACTION	POWER	
M=Moderate	UL=Ultra Light	H=Heavy
MF=Moderate Fast	L=Light	MH=Medium-Heavy
F=Fast	ML=Medium-Light	XH=Extra Heavy
XF=Extra Fast		

ABU GARCIA VENDETTA

Model: VNTC63-5, VNTC66-5, VNTC66-6, VNTC69-6, VNTC70-5, VNTC70-6, VNTC73-6, VNTC73-7, VNTC76-6, VNTC76-7
Length: 6'3''; 6'6''; 6'6''; 6'9''; 7'; 7'; 7'3''; 7'3''; 7'6''; 7'6''
Power: M; M; MH; M; M; MH; MH; H; MH; H
Action: F; F; XF; F; MF; F; XF; M; F; F
Pieces: 1
Line Weight: 8-17 lbs; 8-17 lbs; 12-20 lbs; 12-20 lbs; 8-17 lbs; 12-20 lbs; 12-20 lbs; 14-30 lbs; 12-25 lbs; 14-30 lbs
Guide Count: 8; 8; 8; 8; 8; 8; 9; 8; 8; 8

Lure Weight: 1/4-5/8 oz; 1/4-5/8 oz; 1/4-1 oz; 1/4-2 oz; 1/4-5/8 oz; 1/4-1 oz; 1/4-1 oz; 3/8-1 1/2 oz; 3/8-1 1/4 oz; 3/8-1 1/2 oz
Features: 30-ton graphite for a lightweight balanced design; one-piece aluminum screw down hood creates a secure connection; high-density EVA gives greater sensitivity and durability; Texas-rigged hook keeper for all bait applications; stainless steel guides with zirconium inserts; Abu designed extreme exposure reel seat for increased blank contact and sensitivity; IntraCarbon technology provides a lightweight barrier to improve durability without adding weight.
Price: **$79.95**

ABU GARCIA VENDETTA 2PC

Model: VNTC662-6
Length: 6'6''
Power: MH
Action: XF
Pieces: 2
Line Weight: 12-20 lbs
Guide Count: 8
Lure Weight: 1/4-1 oz

Features: 30-ton graphite for a lightweight balanced design; one-piece aluminum screw down hood creates a secure connection; high-density EVA gives greater sensitivity and durability; Texas-rigged hook keeper for all bait applications; stainless steel guides with zirconium inserts; Abu-designed extreme exposure reel seat for increased blank contact and sensitivity; IntraCarbon technology provides a lightweight barrier to improve durability without adding weight.
Price: **$79.95**

ABU GARCIA VENGEANCE

Model: VNGC66-5, VNGC66-6, VNGC70-5, VNGC70-6, VNGC76-7
Length: 6'6''; 6'6''; 7'; 7'; 7'6''
Power: M; MH; M; MH; H
Action: MF; F; MF; F; XF
Pieces: 1
Line Weight: 8-17 lbs; 12-20 lbs; 8-17 lbs; 12-20 lbs; 14-30 lbs
Guide Count: 8; 8; 8; 8; 9

Lure Weight: 1/4-5/8 oz; 1/4-1 oz; 1/4-5/8 oz; 1/4-1 oz; 3/8-1 1/2 oz
Features: 24-ton graphite construction for a lightweight and balanced design; high-density EVA handles are more durable and comfortable; soft-touch sea guide reel seats for increased comfort; zirconium-coated guides are perfect for braided line usage; Texas-rigged hook keeper for all bait applications; one-piece rod.
Price: . . . . **$49.99–$59.99**

ACTION	POWER	
M=Moderate	UL=Ultra Light	H=Heavy
MF=Moderate Fast	L=Light	MH=Medium-Heavy
F=Fast	ML=Medium-Light	XH=Extra Heavy
XF=Extra Fast		

ABU GARCIA VENGEANCE 2PC

Model: VNGC662-5
Length: 6'6''
Power: M
Action: F
Pieces: 1
Line Weight: 8-17 lbs
Guide Count: 8

Lure Weight: 1/4-5/8 oz
Features: 24-ton graphite construction for a lightweight and balanced design; high-density EVA handles are more durable and comfortable; soft-touch sea guide reel seats for increased comfort; zirconium-coated guides are perfect for braided line usage; Texas-rigged hook keeper for all bait applications; one-piece rod.
Price: **$49.99**

ABU GARCIA VERACITY

Model: VERC66-6, VERC69-6, VERC70-5, VERC70-6, VERC73-6, VERC76-6, VERC76-7, VERC79-7
Length: 6'6''; 6'6''; 7'; 7'; 7'3''; 7'6''; 7'6''; 7'9''
Power: MH; MH; M; MH; MH; MH; H; H
Action: MF; F; MF; F; F; F; F; F
Pieces: 1
Line Weight: 12-20 lbs; 12-20 lbs; 8-17 lbs; 12-20 lbs; 12-20 lbs; 12-25 lbs; 14-30 lbs; 14-30 lbs
Guide Count: 10; 10; 10; 10; 11; 11; 11; 10

Lure Weight: 1/4-1 oz; 1/4-1 oz; 1/4-5/8 oz; 1/4-1 oz; 1/4-1 oz; 3/8-1 1/2 oz; 1/2-2 oz; 5/8-3 oz
Features: 36-ton graphite with NanoTechnology for decreased weight and increased impact resistance; titanium alloy guides with Ti inserts allow for a super lightweight guide giving the ultimate in rod performance; high-density EVA gives greater sensitivity and durability; Micro Guide system provides improved balance and sensitivity; Texas rigged hook keeper for all bait applications.
Price: **$149.95**

ACTION	POWER	
M=Moderate	UL=Ultra Light	H=Heavy
MF=Moderate Fast	L=Light	MH=Medium-Heavy
F=Fast	ML=Medium-Light	XH=Extra Heavy
XF=Extra Fast		

RODS: **Freshwater Baitcasting**

ABU GARCIA VERITAS

Model: VRC66-5, VRC66-6, VRC69-6, VRC70-5, VRC70-6, VRC70-7, VRC711-7, VRC73-6, VRC76-6
Length: 6'6"; 6'6"; 6'9"; 7'; 7'; 7'; 7'11"; 7'3"; 7'6"
Power: M; MH; MH; M; MH; H; H; MH; MH
Action: F; F; XF; MF; F; XF; MF; F; F
Pieces: 1
Line Weight: 8-17 lbs; 12-20 lbs; 12-20 lbs; 8-17 lbs; 12-20 lbs; 12-25 lbs; 12-25 lbs; 12-20 lbs; 12-25 lbs
Guide Count: 10
Lure Weight: 1/4-5/8 oz; 1/4-1 oz; 1/4-1 oz; 1/4-5/8 oz; 1/4-1 oz; 3/8-1 1/2 oz; 3/8-1 1/2 oz; 1/4-1 oz; 3/8-1 1/4 oz

Features: 30-ton graphite construction with nanotechnology for decreased weight and increased compression strength; one-piece double-anodized aluminum screw down creates a secure connection with the reel; high-density EVA handles are more durable and comfortable; Abu-designed extreme exposure reel seats provide direct finger to rod contact for increased sensitivity; titanium alloy guides with SiC inserts create a lightweight, balanced rod design; Texas-rigged hook keeper for all bait applications; one-piece rod.
Price: **$99.95**

ABU GARCIA VILLAIN

Model: VLC66-5, VLC66-6, VLC69-4, VLC69-6, VLC71-5, VLC71-6, VLC73-7, VLC76-6, VLC80-7
Length: 6'6"; 6'6"; 6'9"; 6'9"; 7'1"; 7'1"; 7'3"; 7'6"; 8'
Power: M; MH; ML; MH; M; MH; H; MH; H
Action: F; F; MF; F; M; F; F; F; MF
Pieces: 1
Line Weight: 8-17 lbs; 12-20 lbs; 6-10 lbs; 12-20 lbs; 8-17 lbs; 12-20 lbs; 14-30 lbs; 12-25 lbs; 14-30 lbs
Guide Count: 10

Lure Weight: 1/4-5/8 oz; 1/4-1 oz; 1/8-1/2 oz; 1/4-1 oz; 1/4-5/8 oz; 1/4-1 oz; 3/4-1 1/2 oz; 3/8-1 1/4 oz; 3/8-1 1/2 oz
Features: Titanium alloy guides with titanium inserts allow for a super lightweight guide giving the ultimate in rod performance; C6 total exposure reel seat gives complete contact to the rod for the ultimate sensitivity; high-density EVA gives greater sensitivity and durability; carbon-wrapped guides reduces weight; Texas-rigged hook keeper for all bait applications; split-grip design; one-piece rod.
Price: **$179.95**

ACTION		**POWER**	
M=Moderate	UL=Ultra Light	H=Heavy
MF=Moderate Fast	L=Light	MH=Medium-Heavy
F=Fast	ML=Medium-Light	XH=Extra Heavy
XF=Extra Fast		

ABU GARCIA VOLATILE

Model: VOLC69-4, VOLC70-5, VOLC70-6, VOLC72-5, VOLC79-5, VOLC80-6, VOLC80-7
Length: 6'9''; 7'; 7'; 7'2''; 7'9''; 8'; 8'
Power: ML; M; MH; M; M; MH; H
Action: XF; F; F; M; F; F; F
Pieces: 1
Line Weight: 6-12 lbs; 8-17 lbs; 12-20 lbs; 8-17 lbs; 10-20 lbs; 12-25 lbs; 15-30 lbs
Guide Count: 9; 9; 8; 9; 10; 10; 11

Lure Weight: 1/16-3/8 oz; 1/4-5/8 oz; 1/2-1 oz; 3/8-3/4 oz; 3/8-2 oz; 1/2-3 oz; 3/4-4 oz
Features: 30-ton graphite with nanotechnology for decreased weight and increased impact resistance; high-density EVA gives greater sensitivity and durability; Texas-rigged hook keeper for all bait applications; stainless steel guides with zirconium inserts; Fuji IPS (spinning) and Fuji EPS (casting) reel seat for greater comfort; split-grip design.
Price:. . . . . **$99.95–$139.95**

ABU GARCIA VOLATILE MUSKIE

Model: VOLCMU79-6, VOLCMU80-6, VOLCMU80-7, VOLCMU86-8
Length: 7'9''; 8'; 8'; 8'6''
Power: MH; MH; H; XH
Action: F
Pieces: 1
Line Weight: 25-30 lbs; 30-60 lbs; 40-60 lbs; 50-100 lbs
Guide Count: 10; 11; 11; 12

Lure Weight: 1/4-1 oz; 2-6 oz; 4-10 oz; 6-16 oz
Features: 30-ton graphite with nanotechnology for decreased weight and increased impact resistance; high-density EVA gives greater sensitivity and durability; Texas-rigged hook keeper for all bait applications; stainless steel guides with zirconium inserts; Fuji IPS (spinning) and Fuji EPS (casting) reel seat for greater comfort; split-grip design.
Price:. . . . .**$129.95–$149.95**

ACTION	POWER	
M=Moderate	UL=Ultra Light	H=Heavy
MF=Moderate Fast	L=Light	MH=Medium-Heavy
F=Fast	ML=Medium-Light	XH=Extra Heavy
XF=Extra Fast		

RODS

BASS PRO SHOPS BIONIC BLADE XPS MICRO GUIDE TRIGGER
Model: BBM66MT, BBM66MHT, BBM70MT, BBM70MHT, BBM70HT
Length: 6'6''; 6'6''; 7'; 7'; 7'
Power: M; MH; M; MH; H
Action: F
Pieces: 1
Line Weight: 8-17 lbs; 10-20 lbs; 8-17 lbs; 10-20 lbs; 12-30 lbs

Lure Weight: 1/4-5/8 oz; 3/8-3/4 oz; 1/4-5/8 oz; 3/8-3/4 oz; 3/8-2 oz
Features: Engineered for sensitivity and Pacific Bay micro guides for smooth casting and virtually friction-free line flow; revolutionary IM8 blank is created with innovative ArmorCore Technology—a stronger-than-steel aramid fiber core that is wrapped with ultra-light, superpowerful IM8 graphite to make this one of the most powerful, lightweight rods; EVA split grips add to control and fishing comfort.
Price: **$79.99**

BASS PRO SHOPS CLASSIC 200
Model: BPCL-205, BPCL-207, BPCL-208
Length: 5'6''; 6'; 6'6''
Power: L; M; M
Pieces: 2
Line Weight: 4-8 lbs; 6-12 lbs; 6-12 lbs

Lure Weight: 1/16–1/2 oz; 1/8-1/2 oz; 1/8-1/2 oz
Features: Durable, strong, and very affordable fiberglass rods; two-piece blanks for easy transport; comfortable EVA handles.
Price: **$10.99**

ACTION		**POWER**	
M=Moderate	UL=Ultra Light	H=Heavy	
MF=Moderate Fast	L=Light	MH=Medium-Heavy	
F=Fast	ML=Medium-Light	XH=Extra Heavy	
XF=Extra Fast			

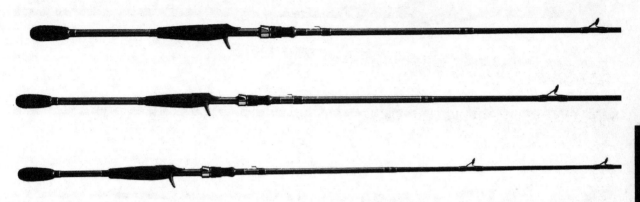

BASS PRO SHOPS JOHNNY MORRIS CARBONLITE MICRO GUIDE

Model: CLM66MTF, CLM66MHTF, CLM69MHTXF, CLM70MTF, CLM70MHTF, CLM70HTXF, CLM76MHTF, CLM76HTXF
Length: 6'6''; 6'6''; 6'9''; 7'; 7'; 7'; 7'6''; 7'6"
Power: M; MH; MH; M; MH; H; MH; H
Action: F; F; XF; F; F; XF; F; F
Pieces: 1

Line Weight: 8-17 lbs; 10-20 lbs; 10-20 lbs; 8-17 lbs; 10-20 lbs; 12-30 lbs; 10-20 lbs; 12-30 lbs
Lure Weight: 1/4-5/8 oz; 3/8-1 oz; 3/8-1 oz; 1/4-5/8 oz; 3/8-1 oz; 3/8-1 1/2 oz; 3/8-1 1/2 oz; 3/8-2 oz
Features: Ultra-rich carbon fiber blank; extreme high-tech Pacific Bay micro guides; split handles; advanced P-Tec polyfoam grips; super light two-piece; soft-touch reel seat is bridgeless.
Price: **$119.99**

BASS PRO SHOPS JOHNNY MORRIS CARBONLITE TRIGGER

Model: CL66MTF, CL66MHTF, CL69MHTXF, CL70MTF, CL70MTM, CL70MHTF, CL70HTXF, CL76HTXF, CL76MHTF, CL66MLTF, CL66MTF-2, CL70MHTF-2
Length: 6'6''; 6'6''; 6'9''; 7'; 7'; 7'; 7'; 7'6''; 7'6''; 6'6''; 6'6''; 7'
Power: M; MH; MH; M; M; MH; H; H; MH; ML; M; MH
Action: F; F; XF; F; M; F; XF; XF; F; F; F; F
Pieces: 1; 1; 1; 1; 1; 1; 1; 1; 1; 1; 2; 2

Line Weight: 8-17 lbs; 10-20 lbs; 10-20 lbs; 8-17 lbs; 8-17 lbs; 10-20 lbs; 12-30 lbs; 12-30 lbs; 10-20 lbs; 6-14 lbs; 8-17 lbs; 10-20 lbs
Lure Weight: 1/4-5/8 oz; 3/8-1 oz; 3/8-1 oz; 1/4-5/8 oz; 1/4-5/8 oz; 3/8-1 oz; 3/8-1 1/2 oz; 3/8-2 oz; 3/8-1 1/2 oz; 1/16-1/2 oz; 1/4-5/8 oz; 3/8-1 oz
Features: 85 million-modulus carbon fiber blank; Pac Bay DLC stainless steel–framed guides; almost weightless space-age P-Tec polyfoam grips; two-piece Soft Touch reel seat with maximum blank exposure.
Price: . . . . **$99.99–$119.99**

ACTION	POWER	
M=Moderate	UL=Ultra Light	H=Heavy
MF=Moderate Fast	L=Light	MH=Medium-Heavy
F=Fast	ML=Medium-Light	XH=Extra Heavy
XF=Extra Fast		

RODS: Freshwater Baitcasting

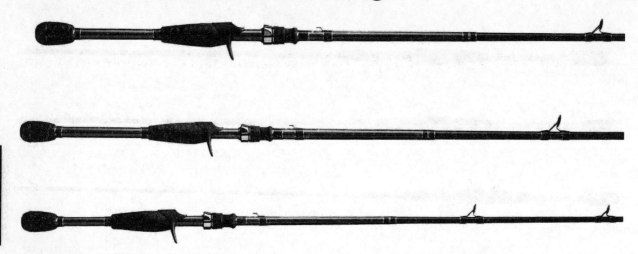

BASS PRO SHOPS JOHNNY MORRIS SIGNATURE SERIES II TRIGGER

Model: JML68MT, JML68MHT, JML72MHT, JML72MT, JML76HT
Length: 6'8"; 6'8"; 7'2"; 7'2"; 7'6"
Power: M; MH; MH; M; H
Action: XF; XF; F; F; XF
Pieces: 1
Line Weight: 8-17 lbs; 10-20 lbs; 10-20 lbs; 10-20 lbs; 12-30 lbs
Lure Weight: ¼-5/8 oz; 3/8-1 oz; 3/8-1 oz; 3/8-1 oz; 3/8-2 oz

Features: Super high-grade 85 million-modulus graphite blank; industry leading Type 1 slit carbon powerwall construction; exclusive carbon cloth butt wrap for unprecedented strength; Fuji new concept stainless steel K-guides with Alconite rings; premium molded split handles with ultra-comfortable P-Tec polyfoam grips; our super-low-profile two-piece exposed-blank reel seat with a soft-touch finish.
Price: **$139.99**

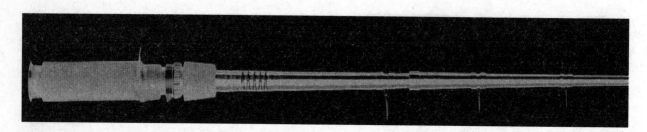

BASS PRO SHOPS POWER PLUS TROPHY CLASS TRIGGER

Model: 1051, 1052, 1053, 1054, 1055, 1056
Length: 6'6"; 6'6"; 7'; 7'; 7'6"; 7'6"
Power: MH; H; MH; H; MH; H
Pieces: 2
Line Weight: 10-25 lbs; 12-30 lbs; 10-25 lbs; 12-30 lbs; 10-25 lbs; 12-30 lbs
Lure Weight: 1/2-2 oz; 1-4 oz; 1/2-2 oz; 1-4 oz; 1/2-2 oz; 1-4 oz

Features: Unidirectional fiberglass construction eliminates the layering normally found in fiberglass rods, adding flexibility and eliminating premature breakage and stress on the wrist; features an extended EVA foam handle, for extra power and fighting leverage, that easily fits in rod holders; heavy duty double foot aluminum oxide guides; hook keeper for pre-rigging; sensitive graphite reel seat; all rods are 2 pieces; guide number includes tip.
Price: **$29.99**

ACTION	POWER	
M=Moderate	UL=Ultra Light	H=Heavy
MF=Moderate Fast	L=Light	MH=Medium-Heavy
F=Fast	ML=Medium-Light	XH=Extra Heavy
XF=Extra Fast		

BERKLEY AIR IM8
Model: A92-7-9HB, A92-8-6MH, A92-8-6H, A92-8-6XH, A92-8-6M, A92-9XH, A92-9-6M, A92-10-6XH
Length: 7'9''; 8'6''; 8'6''; 8'6''; 8'6''; 9'; 9'6''; 10'6''
Power: H; MH; H; XH; M; XH; M; XH
Pieces: 1; 2; 2; 2; 2; 2; 2; 2
Line Weight: 15-50 lbs; 10-20 lbs; 12-25 lbs; 15-50 lbs; 8-12 lbs; 20-65 lbs; 8-14 lbs; 20-80 lbs
Guide Count: 9; 10; 10; 10; 10; 10; 10; 12
Lure Weight: 1/2-4 oz; 1/2-1 1/2 oz; 1/2-1 3/4 oz; 3/4-3 oz; 3/8-3/4 oz; 3/4-3 oz; 3/8-3/4 oz; 2-8 oz

Features: Constructed of IM8 advanced-modulus graphite; air IM8 rods are lightweight and have a sensitive blank that provides the ultimate in feel with enough power to land big fish with ease; titanium-coated SS304 guides are found on all air IM8 spinning and casting models for increased durability and abrasion resistance when fishing with braided line; concept guide spacing improves sensitivity and maximizes blank strength; air IM8 gives anglers the length, power, and performance they need for demanding conditions.
Price:............................ **$99.99–$109.99**

BERKLEY AMP
Model: AC601MH, AC661M, AC701M
Length: 6'; 6'6''; 7'
Power: MH; M; M
Pieces: 1
Line Weight: 10-25 lbs; 8-20 lbs; 8-20 lbs
Guide Count: 6
Lure Weight: 1/4-1 1/4 oz; 1/4-3/4 oz; 1/4-3/4 oz

Features: X-posed reel seats; split-grip cork handles on both spinning and casting models, allowing the hand to remain in constant contact with the rod blank, and taking sensitivity and light weight to a new level; comes with an armadillo hide finish that eliminates cut fibers and ensures the blank is free from imperfections.
Price:................................. **$29.99**

ACTION		POWER	
M=Moderate	UL=Ultra Light	H=Heavy	
MF=Moderate Fast	L=Light	MH=Medium-Heavy	
F=Fast	ML=Medium-Light	XH=Extra Heavy	
XF=Extra Fast			

RODS

BERKLEY CHERRYWOOD HD

Model: CWD561MC, CWD601MHC, CWD661MHC, CWD661MC, CWD662MC, CWD701MHC, CWD701MLC, CWD701MC
Length: 5'6''; 6'; 6'6''; 6'6''; 6'6''; 7'; 7'; 7'
Power: M; MH; MH; M; M; MH; ML; M
Pieces: 1; 1; 1; 1; 2; 1; 1; 1
Line Weight: 8-17 lbs; 10-20 lbs; 10-20 lbs; 8-17 lbs; 8-17 lbs; 10-20 lbs; 6-14 lbs; 8-17 lbs

Guide Count: 6; 7; 7; 7; 7; 7; 7; 7
Lure Weight: 1/4-3/4 oz; 1/4-1 oz; 1/4-1 oz; 1/4-3/4 oz; 1/4-3/4 oz; 1/4-1 oz; 1/8-5/8 oz; 1/4-3/4 oz
Features: Balanced graphite composition blank and quality construction for excellent responsiveness and durability; chromium guide system that is 20 times tougher and up to 55 percent lighter than conventional oxide guides.
Price: $24.99

BERKLEY GLOWSTIK

Model: GSC702M, GSC802MH, GSC902MH, GSC1002MH
Length: 7'; 8'; 9'; 10'
Power: M; MH; MH; MH
Pieces: 2
Line Weight: 10-20 lbs; 10-25 lbs; 10-30 lbs; 10-30 lbs
Guide Count: 7; 8; 9; 10
Lure Weight: 1/2-3 oz; 1-4 oz; 1-5 oz; 1-5 oz

Features: This is the right rod for any nighttime fishing adventure; super strong, super tough E-glass technology makes this blank nearly indestructible; exclusive lighted blank design can be activated to glow continuously for great night bite detection.
Price: . . . . $39.99–$49.99

ACTION		POWER	
M=Moderate	UL=Ultra Light	H=Heavy	
MF=Moderate Fast	L=Light	MH=Medium-Heavy	
F=Fast	ML=Medium-Light	XH=Extra Heavy	
XF=Extra Fast			

BERKLEY LIGHTNING ROD IM6

Model: LR561MC-SH, LR601MHC-SH, LR601MHC, LR601MC, LR661MHC, LR661MC, LR701MHC, LR701MC, LR761HTC
Length: 5'6''; 6'; 6'; 6'; 6'6''; 6'6''; 7'; 7'; 7'6''
Power: M; MH; MH; M; MH; M; MH; M; H
Pieces: 1
Line Weight: 8-14 lbs; 10-17 lbs; 10-17 lbs; 8-14 lbs; 10-17 lbs; 8-14 lbs; 10-20 lbs; 8-14 lbs; 12-25 lbs
Guide Count: 6; 6; 6; 6; 7; 7; 7; 7; 8

Lure Weight: 1/4-5/8 oz; 3/8-3/4 oz; 3/8-3/4 oz; 1/4-5/8 oz; 3/8-3/4 oz; 1/4-5/8 oz; 1/2-1 oz; 1/4-5/8 oz; 5/8-1 1/2 oz
Features: North America's #1 selling graphite rod; a unique combination of strength and sensitivity; the fastest, strongest, and lightest rod in its class; chrome-plated SS304 guides have made the rod lighter, stronger, and more sensitive than ever.
Price: **$39.99**

CABELA'S KING KAT

Model: CKKC08, CKKC09, CKKS662-M
Length: 8'; 9'; 6'6''
Power: MH; MH; M
Pieces: 2
Line Weight: 14-30 lbs; 14-30 lbs; 8-20 lbs

Features: Ultra-tough E-glass; a bright tip to help detect nighttime bites; rugged double-foot ceramic guides; stainless steel hoods on the reel seats add to the performance and durability of the King Kat rods; sure-grip EVA handles offer no-slip confidence during long fights in bad weather.
Price: **$29.99**

ACTION	POWER	
M=Moderate	UL=Ultra Light	H=Heavy
MF=Moderate Fast	L=Light	MH=Medium-Heavy
F=Fast	ML=Medium-Light	XH=Extra Heavy
XF=Extra Fast		

RODS

CABELA'S TOURNEY TRAIL

Model: PTTC564-1, TTC604-1, TTC665-1, TTC665-2, TTC705-1, TTC705-2, TTCS865-2, TTC666-1, TTC706-2, TTCS906-2, TTCM705-1, TTCM766-1, TTCM767-1, TTC706-1, TTC704-2, TTC664-2
Length: 5'6''; 6'; 6'6''; 6'6''; 7'; 7'; 8'6''; 6'6''; 7'; 9'; 7'; 7'6''; 7'6''; 7'; 7'; 6'6''
Power: M; M; MH; MH; MH; MH; MH; H; H; H; MH; H; XH; H; M; M
Action: F; F; MF; MF; MF; MF; MF; F; F; MF; F; F; F; F; F; F
Pieces: 1; 1; 1; 2; 1; 2; 2; 1; 2; 2; 1; 1; 1; 1; 2; 2
Line Weight: 8-17 lbs; 8-17 lbs; 8-17 lbs; 8-17 lbs; 10-17 lbs; 10-17 lbs; 8-17 lbs; 15-25 lbs; 10-20 lbs; 10-20 lbs; 15-30 lbs; 17-40 lbs; 20-50 lbs; 10-20 lbs; 8-14 lbs; 8-17 lbs

Lure Weight: 1/4-5/8 oz; 1/4-5/8 oz; 1/4-1 oz; 1/4-1 oz; 1/4-3/4 oz; 1/4-3/4 oz; 1/2-1 1/2 oz; 5/8-1 1/2 oz; 3/8-2 1/4 oz; 1/2-1 1/2 oz; 3/4-2 1/2 oz; 1-3 oz; 2-6 oz; 3/8-2 1/4 oz; 1/4-5/8 oz; 1/4-5/8 oz
Features: Small, yet strong aluminum-oxide guides that are perfectly sized and wrapped to the new steel-blue blanks in a seamless bond; heavy duty graphite reel seats with cushioned hoods secure the reel; screw-down locking fore grips were added to eliminate exposed threads when the reel is snugged; higher-quality cork handles to make casting for fish more comfortable; built around IM7 100 percent graphite blanks that have fast tip-sensitive actions; limited two-year warranty.
Price:. **$64.99**

CABELA'S TOURNAMENT ZX BASS

Model: TZXC-71MH (Spinnerbait/Swim Jig), TZXC-79H (Swimbait/Umbrella Rig), TZXC-69M (Jerkbait/Topwater), TZXC-76HXF (Flippin), TZXC-72MH (Jig & Worm), TZXC-73H (Topwater Frog), TZXC-71M (Crankbait)
Length: 7'1''; 7'9''; 6'9''; 7'6''; 7'2''; 7'3''; 7'1''
Power: MH; H; M; H; MH; H; M
Action: F; MF; F; XF; XF; F; MF
Lure Weight: 1/4-5/8 oz; 1-4 oz; 1/4-3/8 oz; 1/2-1 1/2 oz; 3/16-5/8 oz; 1/4-1 1/4 oz; 1/4-5/8 oz
Features: Built with technique-specific actions, these bass fishing rods are constructed using HM64 graphite rod blanks. The result is the optimum balance of power, light weight, and responsiveness. Black Pac Bay stainless steel–framed guides with Hialoy ceramic guide inserts virtually eliminate line friction without tacking extra weight on the blank. Split-grip handles with MagTouch reel seats for all day fishing comfort. Down-locking woven carbon-fiber hood eliminates exposed reel-seat threads. EVA grips with Winn Grip overlays provide a custom, secure grip even when wet. Each technique is clearly displayed on the exposed portion of the split-grip handle for easy identification in the rod locker.
Price:. **$99.99**

ACTION		POWER	
M=Moderate	UL=Ultra Light	H=Heavy	
MF=Moderate Fast	L=Light	MH=Medium-Heavy	
F=Fast	ML=Medium-Light	XH=Extra Heavy	
XF=Extra Fast			

CABELA'S WHUPPIN' STICK

Model: WSCM66-2, WSCH80-2, WSCMH66-2, WSCM60-2, WSCMH90-2, WSCML70-2, WSCM70-2
Length: 6'6''; 8'; 6'6''; 6'; 9'; 7'; 7'
Power: M; H; MH; M; MH; ML; M
Pieces: 2
Line Weight: 8-20 lbs; 14-50 lbs; 12-25 lbs; 12-20 lbs; 14-30 lbs; 8-20 lbs; 8-20 lbs

Features: Nearly indestructible, advanced polymer fiberglass blanks; graphite reel seats securely lock your reel in place without adding significant weight to the rod; blank through-handle construction makes it easy to feel even the light biters; stainless steel frame guides with ceramic inserts will stand up to the toughest fish; cork grips ensure all-day comfort.
Price: **$29.99**

CABELA'S XML

Model: XMLC624-1, XMLC664-1, XMLC665-1, XMLC665-2, XMLC704-1, XMLC704-2, XMLC705-1, XMLC705-2, XMLC706-1, XMLC706-2
Length: 6'2''; 6'6''; 6'6''; 6'6''; 7'; 7'; 7'; 7'; 7'; 7'
Power: M; M; MH; MH; M; M; MH; MH; H; H
Action: F
Pieces: 1; 1; 1; 2; 1; 2; 1; 2; 1; 2
Line Weight: 8-17 lbs; 8-17 lbs; 8-17 lbs; 8-17 lbs; 8-17 lbs; 8-17 lbs; 8-17 lbs; 8-17 lbs; 10-20 lbs; 10-20 lbs
Lure Weight: 1/4-5/8 oz; 1/4-5/8 oz; 1/4-1 oz; 1/4-1 oz; 1/4-5/8 oz; 1/4-5/8 oz; 1/4-1 oz; 1/4-1 oz; 3/8-2 1/4 oz; 3/8-2 1/4 oz

Features: These updated rods are built on our legendary XML 64 million-modulus, spiral-core-technology graphite blanks. They feature lightweight, super-durable SS316 stainless steel Alps guides, double coated with black chrome for maximum corrosion resistance. Precise guide spacing compacts the distance between guides from the middle to the tip of the rod. This increases sensitivity and decreases line drag. Exposed-blank MagTouch reel seats. Grips are made of premium cork and have thread-covering down-locking fore grips. Butts are compatible with our Weight-Balancing System, available separately.
Price: **$149.99**

ACTION	POWER	
M=Moderate	UL=Ultra Light	H=Heavy
MF=Moderate Fast	L=Light	MH=Medium-Heavy
F=Fast	ML=Medium-Light	XH=Extra Heavy
XF=Extra Fast		

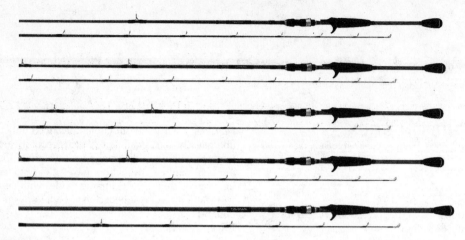

DAIWA AIRD

Model: AIRD661MXB, AIRD661MHXB, AIRD662MHXB, AIRD701MLXB, AIRD701MHXB, AIRD701HXB
Length: 6'6''; 6'6''; 6'6''; 7'; 7'; 7'
Power: M; MH; MH; ML; MH; H
Action: XF
Pieces: 1; 1; 2; 1; 1; 1
Line Weight: 8-17 lbs; 10-20 lbs; 10-20 lbs; 6-15 lbs; 10-20 lbs; 12-25 lbs

Guide Count: 10
Lure Weight: 1/4-3/4 oz; 1/4-1 oz; 1/4-1 oz; 1/8-1/2 oz; 1/4-1 oz; 3/8-1 1/2 oz
Features: IM6 graphite blank; minimized, direct contact reel seat for reduced weight and greater sensitivity with stainless hood; lightweight split-grip design with non-slip, high-density EVA foam; stainless steel guides; folding hook keeper.
Price:...........................**$44.95–$59.95**

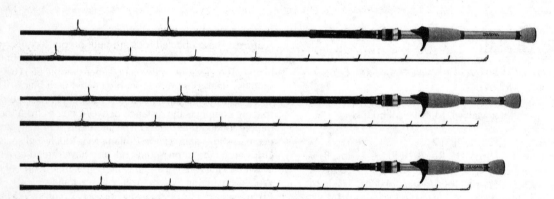

DAIWA PROCYON TRIGGER GRIP

Model: PRCN601MFB, PRCN661MXB, PRCN701MLFB, PRCN701MXB, PRCN661MHXB, PRCN701MHXB, PRCN701HFB
Length: 6'; 6'; 7'; 7'; 6'6''; 7'; 7'
Power: M; M; ML; M; MH; MH; H
Action: F; XF; F; XF; XF; XF; F
Pieces: 1
Line Weight: 8-17 lbs; 10-20 lbs; 6-14 lbs; 8-17 lbs; 10-20 lbs; 8-17 lbs; 12-25 lbs

Guide Count: 9; 9; 10; 10; 10; 10; 10
Lure Weight: 1/4-3/4 oz; 1/4-1 oz; 1/4-1/2 oz; 1/4-3/4 oz; 1/4-1 oz; 1/4-3/4 oz; 3/8-1 1/2 oz
Features: IM7 graphite construction micro pitch blank; taping Minima reel seat with machined clamp nut; woven graphite insert Minima black ring guides; lightweight split-grip cork handles; hook keeper; five-year limited warranty.
Price:...........................**$59.95–$69.95**

ACTION		**POWER**	
M=Moderate	UL=Ultra Light	H=Heavy
MF=Moderate Fast	L=Light	MH=Medium-Heavy
F=Fast	ML=Medium-Light	XH=Extra Heavy
XF=Extra Fast		

DAIWA STEEZ FLE-X-LITE

Model: STZ651MLRBA-FL, STZ701MRBA-FL, STZ721MHRBA-FL
Length: 6'5''; 7'; 7'2''
Power: ML; M; MH
Action: R
Pieces: 1
Line Weight: 6-16 lbs; 8-20 lbs; 12-25 lbs
Guide Count: 9

Lure Weight: 3/32-3/4 oz; 1/8-1 oz; 1/4-3/8 oz
Features: Exclusive SVF Fle-X-Lite graphite blank construction; Air-Beam reel seat; machined aluminum fore-screw nut; Fuji titanium-framed SiC guides; cut-proof and corrosion-free Air-Foam grips are noticeably lighter than cork or ordinary EVA foam yet offer a firm, non-slip grip; laser-engraved butt cap; limited lifetime warranty.
Price:. . . . .$479.95–$509.95

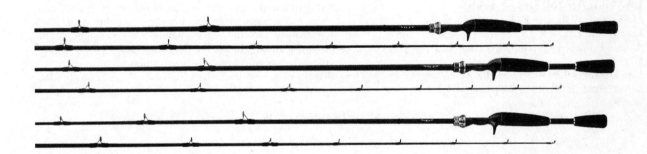

DAIWA STEEZ SVF GRAPHITE

Model: STZ601MFBA, STZ631MHFBA, STZ671MHFBA, STZ701MHFBA
Length: 6'; 6'3''; 6'7''; 7'
Power: M; MH; MH; MH
Action: F
Pieces: 1
Line Weight: 8-16 lbs; 8-20 lbs; 12-20 lbs; 12-20 lbs
Guide Count: 8; 9; 9; 9
Lure Weight: 1/8-5/8 oz; 3/16-1 oz; 1/4-1 oz; 1/4-1 oz

Features: Exclusive SVF graphite construction; bias graphite fiber construction for flexibility, strength, and virtually zero blank twist; Air-Beam reel seat; machined aluminum fore-screw nut; Fuji titanium-framed SiC guides; cut-proof and corrosion-free Air-Foam grips are noticeably lighter than cork or ordinary EVA foam yet offer a firm, non-slip grip; laser-engraved butt cap; limited lifetime warranty.
Price:. . . . .$419.95–$509.95

ACTION	POWER	
M=Moderate	UL=Ultra Light	H=Heavy
MF=Moderate Fast	L=Light	MH=Medium-Heavy
F=Fast	ML=Medium-Light	XH=Extra Heavy
XF=Extra Fast		

LAMIGLAS EXCEL II BASS
Model: EXL 703 C, EXL 704 C, EXL 705 C, EXL 705 Glass, EXL 733 C, EXL 734 C, EXL 735 C, EXL 736 C, EXL 765 C, EXL 766 Flip
Length: 7'; 7'; 7'; 7'; 7'3''; 7'3''; 7'3''; 7'3''; 7'6''; 7'6''
Action: F; F; F; MF; F; F; F; F; F; F
Pieces: 1
Line Weight: 8-15 lbs; 10-20 lbs; 12-25 lbs; 8-20 lbs; 10-17 lbs; 10-20 lbs; 12-25 lbs; 15-30 lbs; 12-25 lbs; 12-30 lbs

Lure Weight: 3/16-5/8 oz; 1/4-3/4 oz; 1/4-1 oz; 1/4-1 oz; 1/4-3/4 oz; 1/4-1 oz; 1/4-1 1/2 oz; 3/8-2 oz; 1/4-1 1/2 oz; 1/4-2 oz
Features: Beautiful, aqua-blue finish; feature Lamiglas IM graphite construction; split grips; Fuji SK2 reel seats; deep pressed hybrid guide system.
Price:. **$120**

LAMIGLAS INFINITY BASS
Model: INF 723C, INF 724C, INF 735C
Length: 7'2''; 7'2''; 7'3''
Action: F
Pieces: 1
Line Weight: 10-20 lbs; 12-25 lbs; 12-25 lbs
Lure Weight: 1/4-3/4 oz; 1/4-1 oz; 1/4-1 1/2 oz

Features: Infinity graphite composite blanks made with resins can achieve incredible strength, durability, and sensitivity, while enabling the lightest weight designs; deep pressed titanium guides; Fuji reel seats and counterbalanced woven graphite handles.
Price:. **$360**

ACTION	POWER	
M=Moderate	UL=Ultra Light	H=Heavy
MF=Moderate Fast	L=Light	MH=Medium-Heavy
F=Fast	ML=Medium-Light	XH=Extra Heavy
XF=Extra Fast		

LAMIGLAS X-11

Model: LX 702 ULC
Length: 7'
Action: MF
Pieces: 2
Line Weight: 2-8 lbs
Lure Weight: 1/8-1/2 oz
Features: All the value and performance of our new X-11 Series for salmon and steelhead are pared down to specialty applications for smaller species like trout, bass, walleye, panfish, and kokanee. These fast-action blanks feature our durable IM graphite and deep pressed guides with zirconia inserts. The darker maroon color sets a very nice contrast between the reel seat and premium cork handles (one-year limited warranty).
Price: **$100**

LEW'S AMERICAN HERO IM6 SPEED STICK

Model: AH66MHC, AH70MC, AH70MHC, AH76HC
Length: 6'6''; 7'; 7'; 7'6''
Power: MH; M; MH; H
Action: F
Pieces: 1
Line Weight: 10-20 lbs; 8-17 lbs; 10-20 lbs; 20-40 lbs
Guide Count: 9; 9; 10; 10
Lure Weight: 3/8-1 oz; 1/4-5/8 oz; 3/8-1 1/2 oz; 3/4-6 oz

Features: Premium IM6 one-piece graphite blanks; multilayer, multidirectional graphite construction for structural strength; rugged gunsmoke stainless steel guide frames with stainless steel inserts; lightweight graphite reel seats with cushioned stainless steel hoods; great hand/reel stability and comfort; exposed blank for instant vibration transmission; premium, durable high-density EVA split grips; split-grip lightweight EVA handles; exclusive "No Foul" hook keeper; Lew's limited one-year warranty.
Price: **$69.99**

ACTION	POWER	
M=Moderate	UL=Ultra Light	H=Heavy
MF=Moderate Fast	L=Light	MH=Medium-Heavy
F=Fast	ML=Medium-Light	XH=Extra Heavy
XF=Extra Fast		

LEW'S LASER LG GRAPHITE

Model: LGA60MFPC, LGA66MFC, LGAMHFC, LGA70MFC, LGA70MHFC
Length: 6'; 6'6''; 6'6''; 7'; 7'
Power: M; M; MH; M; MH
Action: F
Pieces: 1
Line Weight: 8-17 lbs; 8-17 lbs; 10-20 lbs; 8-17 lbs; 10-20 lbs
Guide Count: 9; 10; 10; 10; 10
Lure Weight: 1/4-5/8 oz; 1/4-5/8 oz; 3/8-1 oz; 1/4-5/8 oz; 3/8-1 1/2 oz

Features: Premium IM6 graphite blank; multilayer, multidirectional graphite one-piece blanks reinforced with premium resins; Lew's proprietary APT (Advanced Performance Technology) blank construction; black-coated stainless steel frame with titanium oxide guide rings; lightweight graphite reel seat with cushioned stainless steel hoods; great hand/reel stability and comfort; exposed blank for instant vibration transmission on casting models; natural cork split-grip handles offer reduced weight without compromising rod control.
Price:. **$49.99**

LEW'S SPEED STIC 365 CARBON NANOLAR

Model: SFC66M, SFC66MH, SFC70ML, SFC70M, SFC70MH, SFC72XH, SFC76H
Length: 6'6''; 6'6''; 7'; 7'; 7'; 7'2''; 7'6''
Power: M; MH; ML; M; MH; XH; H
Action: MF
Pieces: 1
Line Weight: 10-14 lbs; 10-20 lbs; 6-10 lbs; 10-17 lbs; 12-20 lbs; 17-30 lbs; 14-30 lbs
Guide Count: 9; 9; 9; 9; 9; 9; 10

Lure Weight: 1/4-5/8 oz; 3/8-1 oz; 1/8-1/2 oz; 1/4-5/8 oz; 3/8-1 oz; 1/2-2 1/2 oz; 1/2-2 oz
Features: Proprietary multilayer, multidirectional Carbon Nanolar premium HM50; rugged gunsmoke stainless steel guide frames with stainless steel inserts; great hand/reel stability and comfort; exposed blank for instant vibration transmission; Lew's exclusive lightweight graphite skeletal casting reel seat with ceramic hook holder in trigger; premium high-density EVA split grips; Lew's limited one-year warranty.
Price:. **$99.99**

ACTION		POWER	
M=Moderate	UL=Ultra Light	H=Heavy	
MF=Moderate Fast	L=Light	MH=Medium-Heavy	
F=Fast	ML=Medium-Light	XH=Extra Heavy	
XF=Extra Fast			

LEW'S TOURNAMENT SL MICRO GUIDE
Model: TS66MFC, TS66MHFC, TS70MLFC, TS70MFC, TS70MHFC, TS72XHXFC
Length: 6'6''; 6'6''; 7'; 7'; 7'; 7'2''
Power: M; MH; ML; M; MH; XH
Action: F; F; F; F; F; XF
Pieces: 1
Line Weight: 8-17 lbs; 10-20 lbs; 8-14 lbs; 8-17 lbs; 10-20 lbs; 14-30 lbs
Guide Count: 12
Lure Weight: 1/4-5/8 oz; 3/8-3/4 oz; 3/16-5/8 oz; 1/4-3/4 oz; 3/8-1 oz; 1/2-2 oz
Features: Premium HM60 graphite blanks; multilayer, multidirectional 60 million-modulus graphite blank reinforced with premium resins; Lew's proprietary APT (Advanced Performance Technology) blank construction; black-coated stainless steel frames with hard aluminum oxide micro guides, which reduce rod weight, enhance casting distance, and increase sensitivity; lightweight skeletal graphite reel seats with cushioned black stainless steel hoods; great hand/reel stability and comfort; exposed blank for instant vibration transmission; high-density EVA foam split-grip handles reduce weight without sacrificing control.
Price: $119.99

G.LOOMIS BASS SPINNERBAIT
Model: 11274-01, 11275-01, 11276-01, 11277-01, 11278-01, 11279-01
Length: 6'3''; 6'3''; 6'9''; 6'9''; 6'9''; 7'2''
Power: L; M; L; M; M; MH
Action: XF
Pieces: 1
Line Weight: 8-12 lbs; 10-17 lbs; 8-12 lbs; 10-17 lbs; 12-20 lbs; 12-25 lbs
Lure Weight: 1/4-3/8 oz; 3/8-1/2 oz; 1/4-3/8 oz; 3/8-1/2 oz; 1/2-3/4 oz; 3/4-1 1/2 oz
Features: These rods are designed specifically to fish spinnerbaits; feature extra-fast tips to help improve accuracy and lower the trajectory, so the wind has less affect on bait, loading effortlessly, allowing quick underhand snap casts to help cover a lot of water; combination of accuracy and control give an added advantage when fighting fish in heavy cover; feature fiber blend technology; Fuji guides and Fuji's ECS exposed blank trigger reel seat; SBR864C utilizes a much larger blank so it has a standard Fuji trigger real seat.
Price: . . . . $225–$260

ACTION	POWER	
M=Moderate	UL=Ultra Light	H=Heavy
MF=Moderate Fast	L=Light	MH=Medium-Heavy
F=Fast	ML=Medium-Light	XH=Extra Heavy
XF=Extra Fast		

RODS: **Freshwater Baitcasting**

G.LOOMIS CLASSIC

Model: CR 721 IMX, CR 722 IMX, CR 722 GL3, CR 723
GLX, CR 723 IMX, CR 723 GL3, CR 724 IMX
Length: 6'
Power: L; M; M; MH; MH; MH; H
Action: F
Pieces: 1
Line Weight: 6-12 lbs; 8-14 lbs; 8-14 lbs; 10-17 lbs; 10-17
lbs; 10-17 lbs; 12-20 lbs
Lure Weight: 3/16-1/2 oz; 1/4-5/8 oz; 1/4-5/8 oz; 1/4-3/4
oz; 1/4-3/4 oz; 1/4-3/4 oz; 1/4-1 oz

Features: Designed for accurate, low-trajectory casting
which makes them ideal for fishing in tight quarters,
around low overhanging limbs and cover; Fuji's ECS
(exposed blank—trigger reel seats) and 7-inch, straight cork
rear-grips; anglers use them for topwater baits, spinnerbaits,
small jigs, and worms where accuracy is more important
than distance; these rods remain on the cutting edge of
graphite technology today. The most popular models are
available in three levels of graphite performance: GL3,
IMX, and GLX.
Price: . . . .$210–$340

G.LOOMIS GL2 JIG & WORM

Model: GL2 722C JWR, GL2 723C JWR, GL2 724C JWR,
GL2 802C JWR, GL2 803C JWR, GL2 804C JWR, GL2
805C JWR, GL2 852C JWR, GL2 853C JWR, GL2 854C
JWR, GL2 855C JWR, GL2 893C JWR, GL2 894C JWR
Length: 6'; 6'; 6'; 6'8"; 6'8"; 6'8"; 6'8"; 7'1"; 7'1"; 7'1";
7'1"; 7'5"; 7'5"
Power: M; MH; H; M; MH; H; XH; M; MH; H; XH; MH; H
Action: F; F; F; XF; XF; XF; XF; XF; XF; XF; XF; XF; XF
Pieces: 1

Line Weight: 10-14 lbs; 12-16 lbs; 14-20 lbs; 10-14 lbs;
12-16 lbs; 14-20 lbs; 17-25 lbs; 10-14 lbs; 12-16 lbs;
14-20 lbs; 17-25 lbs; 12-16 lbs; 14-20 lbs
Lure Weight: 1/4-5/8 oz; 1/4-3/4 oz; 1/4-1 oz; 1/8-3/8 oz;
3/16-5/8 oz; 5/16-3/4 oz; 1/4-1 oz; 1/8-3/8 oz; 3/16-5/8 oz;
5/16-3/4 oz; 1/4-1 oz; 3/16-5/8 oz; 5/16-3/4 oz
Features: GL2 Jig & Worm casting rods offer a unique
blend of power, sensitivity, and fishability; handles feature
split-grips, Fuji trigger reel seat, and Concept guides.
Price: . . . .$195–$220

ACTION	POWER	
M=Moderate	UL=Ultra Light	H=Heavy
MF=Moderate Fast	L=Light	MH=Medium-Heavy
F=Fast	ML=Medium-Light	XH=Extra Heavy
XF=Extra Fast		

G.LOOMIS GLX JIG & WORM CASTING

Model: GLX 802C JWR, GLX 803C JWR, GLX 804C JWR, GLX 805C JWR, GLX 852C JWR, GLX 853C JWR, GLX 854C JWR, GLX 855C JWR, GLX 893C JWR, GLX 894C JWR, GLX 895C JWR
Length: 6'8''; 6'8''; 6'8''; 6'8''; 7'1''; 7'1''; 7'1''; 7'1''; 7'5''; 7'5''; 7'5''
Power: M; MH; H; XH; M; MH; H; XH; MH; H; H
Action: XF; XF; F; F; XF; XF; F; F; XF; F; F
Pieces: 1
Line Weight: 10-14 lbs; 12-16 lbs; 14-20 lbs; 17-25 lbs; 10-14 lbs; 12-16 lbs; 14-20 lbs; 17-25 lbs; 12-16 lbs; 14-20 lbs; 17-25 lbs

Lure Weight: 1/8-3/8 oz; 3/16-5/8 oz; 5/16-3/4 oz; 1/4-1 oz; 1/8-3/8 oz; 3/16-5/8 oz; 5/16-3/4 oz; 1/4-1 oz; 3/16-5/8 oz; 5/16-3/4 oz; 1/4-1 oz
Features: Designed specifically for fishing jigs and soft plastics; feature a split-grip handle with a mag touch trigger reel seat; Fuji titanium SIC guides and tip-tops; legendary for their sensitivity, these rods will tell you everything that's going on with that bait, no matter how deep the water or how thick the cover; they have extra-fast actions for accurate, low trajectory casts with plenty of power to handle even the biggest bass; made with a gorgeous dark green blank.
Price: . . . .$410–$460

G.LOOMIS NRX JIG & WORM

Model: NRX 802C JWR, NRX 802C JWR G, NRX 803C JWR, NRX 803C JWR G, NRX 804C JWR, NRX 804C JWR G, NRX 852C JWR, NRX 852C JWR G, NRX 854C JWR, NRX 854C JWR G, NRX 853C JWR, NRX 853C JWR G, NRX 893C JWR, NRX 893C JWR G, NRX 894C JWR, NRX 894C JWR G, NRX 895 JWR, NRX 895C JWR G
Length: 6'8''; 6'8''; 6'8''; 6'8''; 6'8''; 6'8''; 7'1''; 7'1''; 7'1''; 7'1''; 7'1''; 7'1''; 7'5''; 7'5''; 7'5''; 7'5''; 7'5''; 7'5''
Power: M; M; MH; MH; H; H; M; M; H; H; MH; MH: MH; MH; H; H; XH; XH
Action: XF; XF; XF; XF; F; F; XF; XF; F; F; XF; XF; XF; XF; XF; XF; XF; XF
Pieces: 1

Line Weight: 10-14 lbs; 10-14 lbs; 12-16 lbs; 12-16 lbs; 14-20 lbs; 14-20 lbs; 10-14 lbs; 10-14 lbs; 14-20 lbs; 14-20 lbs; 12-16 lbs; 12-16 lbs; 12-16 lbs; 12-16 lbs; 14-20 lbs; 14-20 lbs; 17-25 lbs; 17-25 lbs
Lure Weight: 1/8-3/8 oz; 1/8-3/8 oz; 3/16-3/4 oz; 3/16-3/4 oz; 5/16-3/4 oz; 5/16-3/4 oz; 1/8-3/8 oz; 1/8-3/8 oz; 5/16-3/4 oz; 5/16-3/4 oz; 3/16-5/8 oz; 3/16-5/8 oz; 3/16-5/8 oz; 3/16-5/8 oz; 5/16-3/4 oz; 5/16-3/4 oz; 1/4-1 oz; 1/4-1 oz
Features: Designed specifically for fishing jigs and soft plastics; insanely light, unbelievably sensitive, and strong; feature split-grip cork handles; Fuji titanium SIC stripper guides, with the ultra-lite, ultra-strong RECOIL guides the rest of the way.
Price: . . . .$500–$600

ACTION	POWER	
M=Moderate	UL=Ultra Light	H=Heavy
MF=Moderate Fast	L=Light	MH=Medium-Heavy
F=Fast	ML=Medium-Light	XH=Extra Heavy
XF=Extra Fast		

RODS: Freshwater Baitcasting

OKUMA C3-40X

Model: C3x-C-6101MH, C3x-C-661M, C3x-C-661MH, C3x-C-681H, C3x-C-681MH, C3x-C-701M, C3x-C-701MH, C3x-C-701ML, C3x-C-7101M, C3x-C-7111H, C3x-C-721H, C3x-C-721XH, C3x-C-761M, C3x-C-761XXH
Length: 6'10''; 6'6''; 6'6''; 6'8''; 6'8''; 7'; 7'; 7'; 7'10''; 7'11''; 7'11''; 7'2''; 7'2''; 7'6''; 7'6''
Power: MH; M; MH; H; MH; M; MH; ML; M; H; XH; H; XH; M; XXH
Action: F
Pieces: 1
Line Weight: 12-20 lbs; 8-17 lbs; 10-20 lbs; 12-20 lbs; 10-20 lbs; 8-17 lbs; 10-20 lbs; 6-12 lbs; 8-17 lbs; 15-30 lbs; 20-40 lbs; 12-20 lbs; 15-30 lbs; 8-17 lbs; 30-60 lbs

Guide Count: 10; 9; 9; 9; 10; 10; 10; 10; 12; 11; 11; 10; 10; 12; 11
Lure Weight: 1/4-1 oz; 1/4-5/8 oz; 1/4-1 oz; 3/8-1 oz; 3/16-3/4 oz; 1/4-5/8 oz; 1/4-1 oz; 1/8-3/8 oz; 1/4-1 oz; 1-5 oz; 2-8 oz; 3/8-1 oz; 3/8-1 oz; 1/2-2 oz; 3/8-3/4 oz; 3-12 oz
Features: 40-ton carbon, ultra sensitive blank construction; custom 1K woven carbon cone grip configuration; customized ported Fuji reel seats for reduced weight; ultra hard zirconium guide inserts for braided line; titanium guide frames on all spinning models; titanium guide frames on all double foot casting guides; ALPS low-profile frames on all single foot casting guides; split-grip butt for reduced weight and improved balance; limited lifetime warranty.
Price: . . . . **$154.99–$194.99**

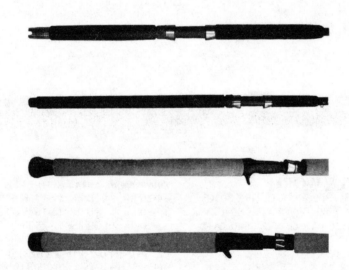

OKUMA CELILO SPECIALTY

Model: CE-C-1102Ha, CE-C-461Ha, CE-C-561Ha, CE-C-701Ha, CE-C-701XHa, CE-C-702L
Length: 11'; 4'6''; 5'6''; 7'; 7'; 7'
Power: H; H; H; H; XH; L
Action: M/MF; XF; F/XF; F; F; M
Pieces: 2; 1; 1; 1; 1; 2
Line Weight: 15-40 lbs; 40-100 lbs; 50-100 lbs; 20-50 lbs; 30-80 lbs; 2-8 lbs

Guide Count: 8; 5; 6; 10; 10; 8
Features: Sensitive graphite composite blanks; aluminum oxide guide inserts; Fuji guides on 701H and 701XH; stainless steel hooded reel seats; aluminum gimbal on halibut and sturgeon rods; rugged graphite butt section on halibut rod; one-year warranty.
Price: . . . . **$44.99–$79.99**

ACTION	POWER	
M=Moderate	UL=Ultra Light	H=Heavy
MF=Moderate Fast	L=Light	MH=Medium-Heavy
F=Fast	ML=Medium-Light	XH=Extra Heavy
XF=Extra Fast		

OKUMA EVX
Model: EVx-C-601Ma, EVx-C-661Ha, EVx-C-661Ma, EVx-C-661MHa, EVx-C-661MLa, EVx-C-681MHa, EVx-C-691MHa, EVx-C-701Ma, EVx-C-701MHa, EVx-C-701MLa, EVx-C-751Ha, EVx-C-751MHa, EVx-C-761H-Ta
Length: 6'; 6'6''; 6'6''; 6'6''; 6'6''; 6'8''; 6'9''; 7'; 7'; 7'; 7'5''; 7'5''; 7'6''
Power: M; H; M; MH; ML; MH; MH; M; MH; ML; H; MH; H
Action: MF; MF; MF; F; MF; MF; MF; F; F; MF; F; MF; MF
Pieces: 1
Line Weight: 8-17 lbs; 12-25 lbs; 8-17 lbs; 10-20 lbs; 6-12 lbs; 10-20 lbs; 12-25 lbs; 8-17 lbs; 10-20 lbs; 6-12 lbs; 12-25 lbs; 10-20 lbs; 12-25 lbs

Guide Count: 10; 11; 11; 11; 11; 11; 11; 11; 11; 11; 10; 10; 11
Lure Weight: 1/4-5/8 oz; 3/8-1 1/4 oz; 1/4-5/8 oz; 1/4-1 oz; 1/8-3/8 oz; 1/4-1 oz; 3/8-1 1/2 oz; 1/4-5/8 oz; 1/4-1 oz; 1/8-3/8 oz; 3/8-1 1/4 oz; 1/4-1 oz; 3/8-1 1/4 oz
Features: IM8 graphite blank construction; crank bait rods are glass blank construction; ALPS stainless steel guide frames; zirconium guide inserts for braided line; Fuji ACS trigger reel seat on casting models; Fuji DPS carbon reel seat on spinning models; premium cork full or split grips; casting rods with rear split grip and no foregrip; spinning rods with rear split grip and no foregrip; crank bait rods with full rear cork butt; no foregrip; integrated compressed cork butt cap; limited lifetime warranty.
Price:. . . . .$84.99–$119.99

OKUMA REFLEXIONS
Model: Rx-C-661M, Rx-C-661MH, Rx-C662M, Rx-C-701M, Rx-C-701MH, Rx-C-701ML, Rx-C-7101M-T
Length: 6'6''; 6'6''; 6'6''; 7'; 7'; 7'; 7'10''
Power: M; MH; M; M; MH; ML; M
Action: MF; MF; MF; F; MF; MF; MF
Pieces: 1; 1; 2; 1; 1; 1; 1
Line Weight: 8-17 lbs; 10-20 lbs; 8-17 lbs; 8-17 lbs; 12-25 lbs; 6-15 lbs; 10-20 lbs

Guide Count: 9; 9; 8; 9; 9; 9; 9
Lure Weight: 1/4-5/8 oz; 1/4-1 oz; 1/4-5/8 oz; 1/4-5/8 oz; 3/8-1 1/4 oz; 1/8-5/8 oz; 1/4-1 oz
Features: IM6 rod blanks and low-profile stainless steel guide frames with braid-ready zirconium inserts; split-grip cork handles; stainless steel hooded reel seat; thru-blank reel seats on casting models to reduce weight and increase sensitivity; limited lifetime warranty.
Price:. $64.99

ACTION	POWER	
M=Moderate	UL=Ultra Light	H=Heavy
MF=Moderate Fast	L=Light	MH=Medium-Heavy
F=Fast	ML=Medium-Light	XH=Extra Heavy
XF=Extra Fast		

OKUMA TARVOS

Model: TV-C-661M, TV-C-661MH, TV-C-701M, TV-C-701MH
Length: 6'6''; 6'6''; 7'; 7'
Power: M; MH; M; MH
Action: M/MF
Pieces: 1
Line Weight: 6-15 lbs; 8-17 lbs; 6-15 lbs; 6-15 lbs

Guide Count: 9; 9; 10; 10
Lure Weight: 1/4-3/4 oz; 1/4-1 oz; 1/4-3/4 oz; 1/4-3/4 oz
Features: Graphite composite rod blank construction; stainless steel guide frames; titanium oxide guide inserts; stainless steel hooded reel seat; split-grip butt design; comfortable EVA fore and rear grips; stainless steel hook keeper; one-year limited warranty.
Price: **$42.99**

SHIMANO COMPRE BASS CASTING WORM & JIG

Model: CPC68MC, CPCX68MC, CPC68MHC, CPCX68MHC, CPC72MC, CPCX72MC, CPC72MHC, CPCX72MHC, CPC72HC
Length: 6'8''; 6'8''; 6'8''; 6'8''; 7'2''; 7'2''; 7'2''; 7'2''; 7'2''
Power: M; M; MH; MH; M; M; MH; MH; H
Action: F; XF; F; XF; F; XF; F; XF; F

Line Weight: 6-12 lbs; 8-14 lbs; 10-17 lbs; 12-20 lbs; 6-12 lbs; 8-14 lbs; 10-17 lbs; 12-20 lbs; 12-25 lbs
Lure Weight: 1/8-1/4 oz; 1/4-3/8 oz; 1/4-3/4 oz; 1/4-1 oz; 1/8-1/4 oz; 1/4-3/8 oz; 1/4-3/4 oz; 1/4-1 oz; 1/2-1 1/2 oz
Features: IM9 graphite construction; Fuji aluminum oxide guides; custom Shimano reel seats.
Price: . . . . **$99.99–$109.99**

ACTION	POWER	
M=Moderate	UL=Ultra Light	H=Heavy
MF=Moderate Fast	L=Light	MH=Medium-Heavy
F=Fast	ML=Medium-Light	XH=Extra Heavy
XF=Extra Fast		

SHIMANO CUMARA

Model: CUC68MA, CUCX68MA, CUC68MHA, CUCX68MHA, CUC72MA, CUCX72MA, CUC72MHA, CUCX72MHA, CUCX711HA, CUC711XHA, CUCSB610MHA, CUCSBX610MHA, CUCSBX72MHA, CUCC70MA, CUCC70MHA, CUCC76MA, CUCC76MHA, CUCC711MA, CUCC711MHA, CUCU79HA
Length: 6'8''; 6'8''; 6'8''; 6'8''; 7'2''; 7'2''; 7'2''; 7'2''; 7'11''; 7'11''; 6'10''; 6'10''; 7'2''; 7'; 7'; 7'6''; 7'6''; 7'11''; 7'11''; 7'9''
Power: M; M; MH; MH; M; M; MH; MH; H; XH; MH; MH; MH; M; MH; M; MH; M; MH; H
Action: F; XF; F; XF; F; XF; F; XF; XF; F; F; XF; XF; MF; MF; MF; MF; MF; F; F

Line Weight: 6-12 lbs; 8-14 lbs; 10-17 lbs; 12-20 lbs; 6-12 lbs; 8-14 lbs; 10-17 lbs; 12-20 lbs; 15-30 lbs; 15-30 lbs; 8-17 lbs; 10-20 lbs; 12-25 lbs; 8-14 lbs; 10-20 lbs; 8-17 lbs; 10-20 lbs; 10-20 lbs; 12-25 lbs; 15-30 lbs
Lure Weight: 1/8-1/4 oz; 1/4-3/8 oz; 1/4-3/4 oz; 1/4-1 oz; 1/8-1/4 oz; 1/4-3/8 oz; 1/4-3/4 oz; 1/4-1 oz; 3/8-1 oz; 1-3 oz; 3/8-1/2 oz; 1/2-1 oz; 3/4-1 1/4 oz; 1/4-5/8 oz; 3/8-1 oz; 1/4-3/4 oz; 3/8-1 oz; 3/8-3/4 oz; 3/8-1 oz; 1-3 oz
Features: Convenient hook keeper; Fuji KR-concept Alconite guides; custom Shimano reel seat; shaped EVA foam grips; micro guides technique-specific actions; laser-etched badge.
Price: . . . . **$249.99–$259.99**

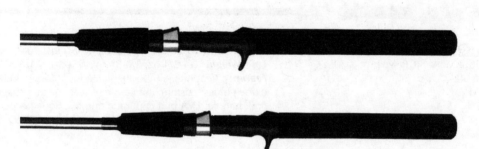

SHIMANO FX

Model: FXC60MB-2, FXC66MHB2, FXC70MB-2
Length: 6'; 6'6''; 7'
Power: M; MH; M
Action: F
Pieces: 2
Line Weight: 6-15 lbs; 10-20 lbs; 8-17 lbs

Lure Weight: 1/4-3/4 oz; 1/4-1 oz; 1/4-5/8 oz
Features: Durable aeroglass blank construction features; reinforced aluminum oxide guides; solid locking graphite reel seat; comfortable EVA handles.
Price: **$12.99**

ACTION	POWER	
M=Moderate	UL=Ultra Light	H=Heavy
MF=Moderate Fast	L=Light	MH=Medium-Heavy
F=Fast	ML=Medium-Light	XH=Extra Heavy
XF=Extra Fast		

SHIMANO SELLUS

Model: SUC68MH, SUCX68MH, SUC72MH, SUCX72MH, SUCSB610M, SUCSB610MH, SUCT68M, SUCCB68M, SUCC870M, SUCC870MH, SUCX76MH
Length: 6'8''; 6'8''; 7'2''; 7'2''; 6'10''; 6'10''; 6'8''; 6'8''; 7'; 7'; 7'6''
Power: MH; MH; MH; MH; M; MH; M; M; M; MH; MH
Action: F; XF; F; XF; F; F; F; F; F; F; XF
Line Weight: 10-17 lbs; 12-20 lbs; 10-17 lbs; 12-20 lbs; 8-15 lbs; 10-20 lbs; 10-20 lbs; 8-14 lbs; 8-17 lbs; 10-20 lbs; 15-30 lbs

Lure Weight: 1/4-3/4 oz; 1/4-1 oz; 1/4-3/4 oz; 1/4-1 oz; 1/4-1/2 oz; 1/2-1 oz; 3/8-1 oz; 1/4-5/8 oz; 1/4-3/4 oz; 3/8-1 oz; 3/8-1 oz
Features: 24-ton graphite blank technique specific actions; low-profile aluminum oxide guides; custom Shimano reel seat; custom-shaped EVA split-grip handle; laser-etched technique badge; multipurpose hook keeper.
Price: . . . .**$49.99–$59.99**

SHIMANO SOJOURN

Model: SJC66MA, SJC66M2A, SJC66MHA, SJC70MA
Length: 6'6''; 6'6''; 6'6''; 7'
Power: M; M; MH; M
Action: F
Pieces: 1; 2; 1; 1

Line Weight: 10-20 lbs; 10-20 lbs; 15-30 lbs; 10-20 lbs
Lure Weight: 1/4-3/4 oz; 1/4-3/4 oz; 1/4-1 oz; 1/4-3/4 oz
Features: Graphite composite blank; low-profile aluminum oxide guides; custom Shimano reel seat; custom-shaped cork handle; EVA butt cap; multipurpose hook keeper.
Price: . . . .**$29.99–$34.99**

ACTION	**POWER**	
M=Moderate	UL=Ultra Light	H=Heavy
MF=Moderate Fast	L=Light	MH=Medium-Heavy
F=Fast	ML=Medium-Light	XH=Extra Heavy
XF=Extra Fast		

RODS: Freshwater Baitcasting

ST. CROIX LEGEND ELITE

Model: LEC60MF, LEC66MF, LEC66MHF, LEC68MXF, LEC70MF, LEC70MHF, LEC70HF
Length: 6'; 6'6''; 6'6''; 6'8''; 7'; 7'; 7'
Power: M; M; MH; M; M; MH; H
Action: F; F; F; XF; F; F; F
Pieces: 1
Line Weight: 10-17 lbs; 10-17 lbs; 12-20 lbs; 8-14 lbs; 10-17 lbs; 12-20 lbs; 14-25 lbs
Lure Weight: 1/4-5/8 oz; 1/4-5/8 oz; 3/8-1 oz; 1/4-5/8 oz; 1/4-5/8 oz; 3/8-1 oz; 3/8-1 1/2 oz
Features: Integrated Poly Curve tooling technology; Advanced Reinforcing Technology; super high-modulus

SCVI graphite with FRS in lower section for maximum power and strength with reduced weight; high-modulus/high-strain SCV graphite with FRS and carbon-matte scrim for unparalleled strength and durability; slim-profile ferrules; phenomenally sensitive, light, and smooth casting; Fuji SiC Concept Guide System with titanium-finished frames; Fuji VSS reel seat/frosted silver hood on spinning models; Fuji ACS reel seat/frosted silver hood on casting models; machined-aluminum wind check; super-grade cork handle; two coats of Flex Coat slow-cure finish; includes deluxe rod sack; lifetime limited warranty.
Price: . . . .$330–$380

ST. CROIX LEGEND TOURNAMENT BASS

Model: TBC68MF, TBC68MXF, TBC68MHF, TBC610MLXF, TBC610MXF, TBC71MF, TBC71MHF, TBC71MHXF, TBC72MM, TBC73MHF, TBC73XHF, TBC74HF, TBC76MHMF, TBC78MHM, TBC79HMF, TBC710HF, TBC710HM, TBC711HMF
Length: 6'8''; 6'8''; 6'8''; 6'10''; 6'10''; 7'1''; 7'1''; 7'1''; 7'2''; 7'3''; 7'3''; 7'4''; 7'6''; 7'8''; 7'9''; 7'10''; 7'10''; 7'11''
Power: M; M; MH; ML; M; M; MH; MH; M; MH; XH; H; MH; MH; H; H; H; H
Action: F; XF; F; XF; XF; F; F; XF; M; F; F; F; MF; M; MF; F; M; MF
Pieces: 1
Line Weight: 10-17 lbs; 8-14 lbs; 12-20 lbs; 6-10 lbs; 10-14 lbs; 10-17 lbs; 12-20 lbs; 12-17 lbs; 8-14 lbs; 12-25 lbs; 17-30 lbs; 14-25 lbs; 12-25 lbs; 10-20 lbs; 14-30 lbs; 14-30 lbs; 12-25 lbs; 14-30 lbs

Lure Weight: 1/4-5/8 oz; 1/4-5/8 oz; 3/8-1 oz; 1/8-1/2 oz; 1/8-5/16 oz; 1/4-5/8 oz; 3/8-1 oz; 5/16-3/4 oz; 1/4-5/8 oz; 5/8-1 1/4 oz; 1-2 1/2 oz; 3/8-1 1/2 oz; 3/8-1 1/4 oz; 3/8-1 oz; 1/2-2 oz; 1-4 oz; 1/2-1 3/8 oz; 1/2-2 oz
Features: Integrated Poly Curve tooling technology; Advanced Reinforcing Technology; high-modulus/high-strain SCIV graphite with FRS for unparalleled strength and durability; technique-specific bass series features unrivaled technology and performance; Fuji K-Series Concept Tangle Free guides with Alconite rings and polished frames; ideal for super braid, mono, and fluorocarbon lines, the sloped frame and ring shed tangles before they become a problem; Fuji SK2 split reel seat for the ultimate in light weight and sensitivity; machined-aluminum wind check and trim pieces; split-grip/super-grade cork handle; two coats of Flex Coat slow-cure finish; lifetime limited warranty.
Price: . . . .$260–$290

ACTION	POWER	
M=Moderate	UL=Ultra Light	H=Heavy
MF=Moderate Fast	L=Light	MH=Medium-Heavy
F=Fast	ML=Medium-Light	XH=Extra Heavy
XF=Extra Fast		

ST. CROIX LEGENDXTREME

Model: LXC68MF, LXC68MXF, LXC68MHF, LXC610MXF, LXC70MF, LXC70MHF, LXC71MHXF, LXC72MM, LXC74HF, LXC76MHMF, LXC78MHM, LXC711HMF
Length: 6'8''; 6'8''; 6'8''; 6'10''; 7'; 7'; 7'1''; 7'2''; 7'4''; 7'6''; 7'8''; 7'11''
Power: M; M; MH; M; M; MH; MH; M; H; MH; MH; H
Action: F; XF; F; XF; F; F; XF; M; F; MF; M; MF
Pieces: 1
Line Weight: 10-17 lbs; 8-14 lbs; 12-20 lbs; 10-14 lbs; 10-17 lbs; 12-20 lbs; 12-20 lbs; 8-14 lbs; 14-25 lbs; 12-25 lbs; 10-20 lbs; 14-30 lbs
Lure Weight: 1/4-5/8 oz; 1/4-5/8 oz; 3/8-1 oz; 1/8-5/16 oz; 1/4-5/8 oz; 3/8-1 oz; 1/4-3/4 oz; 1/4-5/8 oz; 3/8-1 1/2 oz; 3/8-1 1/4 oz; 3/8-1 oz; 1/2-2 oz
Features: Integrated Poly Curve tooling technology; Taper Enhancement Technology blank design provides curved patterns for improved action with increased sensitivity; Advanced Reinforcing Technology; super high-modulus SCVI graphite with FRS in lower section for maximum power and strength with reduced weight; high-modulus/high-strain SCV graphite with FRS and carbon-matte scrim for unparalleled strength, durability, and sensitivity; slim-profile ferrules; Fuji K-R Concept Tangle Free guides with SiC rings and exclusive E-color finish frames; ideal for super braid, mono, and fluorocarbon lines, the sloped frame and ring shed tangles before they become a problem; Fuji SK2 split reel seat for the ultimate in light weight and sensitivity; Xtreme-Skin handle repels water, dirt, and fish slime and cleans up easily; manufactured by St. Croix to provide outstanding angler comfort, casting efficiency, and sensitivity; machined-aluminum wind check, handle trim pieces, and butt cap with logo badge; two coats of Flex Coat slow-cure finish; includes protective rod sack; lifetime limited warranty.
Price:. . . . .**$410–$450**

ACTION	POWER	
M=Moderate	UL=Ultra Light	H=Heavy
MF=Moderate Fast	L=Light	MH=Medium-Heavy
F=Fast	ML=Medium-Light	XH=Extra Heavy
XF=Extra Fast		

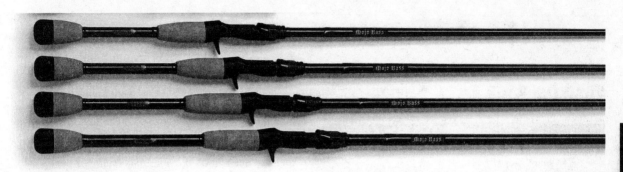

ST. CROIX MOJO BASS

Model: MBC66MF, MBC66MHF, MBC68MXF, MBC70MF, MBC70MHF, MBC70MHM, MBC70HF, MBC76MHMF, MBC79HF, MBC711HMF
Length: 6'6''; 6'6''; 6'8''; 7'; 7'; 7'; 7'; 7'6''; 7'9''; 7'11''
Power: M; MH; M; M; MH; MH; H; MH; H; H
Action: F; F; XF; F; F; M; F; MF; F; MF
Pieces: 1
Line Weight: 10-17 lbs; 12-20 lbs; 8-14 lbs; 10-17 lbs; 12-20 lbs; 10-20 lbs; 14-25 lbs; 12-25 lbs; 14-30 lbs; 14-30 lbs
Lure Weight: 1/4-5/8 oz; 3/8-1 oz; 1/4-5/8 oz; 1/4-5/8 oz; 3/8-1 oz; 3/8-1 oz; 3/8-1 1/2 oz; 3/8-1 1/4 oz; 1-4 oz; 1/2-2 oz

Features: Premium-quality SCII graphite; super premium, 100 percent linear S-glass on Mojo Bass Glass models; technique-specific bass series designed and built for superior performance; Kigan Master Hand 3D guides featuring slim, strong aluminum-oxide rings with black frames; Fuji ECS reel seat/black hood on casting models; Fuji DPS reel seat/black hoods on spinning models; split-grip/premium-grade cork handle; two coats of Flex Coat slow-cure finish; five-year warranty.
Price:................................$110–$130

ST. CROIX PREMIER

Model: PC56MF, PC60MF, PC60MHF, PC66MF, PC66MF2, PC66MHF, PC66MHF2, PC70MLF, PC70MF, PC70MHF, PC70HF, PC70HF2
Length: 5'6''; 6'; 6'; 6'6''; 6'6''; 6'6''; 6'6''; 7'; 7'; 7'; 7'; 7'
Power: M; M; MH; M; M; MH; MH; ML; M; MH; H; H
Action: F
Pieces: 1; 1; 1; 1; 2; 1; 2; 1; 1; 1; 1; 2
Line Weight: 8-14 lbs; 10-17 lbs; 10-20 lbs; 10-17 lbs; 10-17 lbs; 10-20 lbs; 10-20 lbs; 8-14 lbs; 10-17 lbs; 10-20 lbs; 12-25 lbs; 12-25 lbs
Lure Weight: 1/4-5/8 oz; 1/4-3/4 oz; 3/8-1 oz; 1/4-3/4 oz; 1/4-3/4 oz; 3/8-1 oz; 3/8-1 oz; 3/16-5/8 oz; 1/4-3/4 oz; 3/8-1 oz; 1/2-1 1/2 oz; 1/2-1 1/2 oz

Features: Let's take a moment and thank genetics. And, because it's a well-known fact musky fishermen possess above average intelligence, combined with a knack for vanishing for long lengths of time, it's nice for us all that genetics does the work of passing that intelligence down. You'll still have to do the honors of handing down the intelligence on the premium SCII graphite blanks and top-grade components that make up the Premier casting rods. Be sure to let them know they are not only fast, light, and loaded with genuine fortitude—but have earned a bit of their own honor over the years, too.
Price:................................. $130–$170

ACTION	POWER	
M=Moderate	**UL=Ultra Light**	**H=Heavy**
MF=Moderate Fast	**L=Light**	**MH=Medium-Heavy**
F=Fast	**ML=Medium-Light**	**XH=Extra Heavy**
XF=Extra Fast		

ST. CROIX RAGE

Model: RC68MF, RC68MXF, RC68MHF, RC610MXF, RC71MF, RC71MHF, RC71MHXF, RC72MM, RC74HF, RC76MHMF, RC78MHM, RC11HMF
Length: 6'8''; 6'8''; 6'8''; 6'10''; 7'1''; 7'1''; 7'1''; 7'2''; 7'4''; 7'6''; 7'8''; 7'11''
Power: M; M; MH; M; M; MH; MH; M; H; MH; MH; H
Action: F; XF; F; XF; F; F; XF; M; F; MF; M; MF
Pieces: 1
Line Weight: 10-17 lbs; 8-14 lbs; 12-20 lbs; 10-14 lbs; 10-17 lbs; 12-20 lbs; 12-17 lbs; 8-14 lbs; 14-25 lbs; 12-25 lbs; 10-20 lbs; 14-30 lbs
Lure Weight: 1/4-5/8 oz; 1/4-5/8 oz; 3/8-1 oz; 1/8-5/16 oz; 1/4-5/8 oz; 3/8-1 oz; 5/16-3/4 oz; 1/4-5/8 oz; 3/8-1 1/2 oz; 3/8-1 1/4 oz; 3/8-1 oz
Features: Integrated Poly Curve tooling technology; premium, high-modulus SCIII graphite; incredibly lightweight and sensitive with superb balance and extreme strength; Pacific Bay Minima micro guide configuration for high performance and improved durability by eliminating insert failure, plus 20 percent to 30 percent weight savings compared to ceramic guides; Pacific Bay Minima casting reel seat/black hood provides maximum rod blank exposure and is 30 percent lighter than conventional trigger reel seats; Pacific Bay Minima spinning reel seat/black hood provides maximum rod blank exposure and is 10 percent to 20 percent lighter than conventional spinning reel seats; contoured handle provides split-grip performance; featuring a precision-shaped core wrapped with a neoprene skin for maximum comfort and sensitivity; EVA trim pieces provide additional refinement; two coats of Flex Coat slow-cure finish; five-year warranty.
Price: . . . .**$150–$170**

ST. CROIX WILD RIVER

Model: WRC80HF2, WRC86MF2, WRC86MHF2, WRC86HF2, WR90MF2, WRC90MLF2, WRC90MHF2, WRC90HF2, WRC90HM2, WRC90XHM2, WRC96HM2, WRC96XHM2, WRC106MF2, WRC106MHM2, WRC106HM2, WRC106XHM2
Length: 8'; 8'6''; 8'6''; 8'6''; 9'; 9'; 9'; 9'; 9'; 9'; 9'6''; 9'6''; 10'6''; 10'6''; 10'6''; 10'6''
Power: H; M; MH; H; ML; M; MH; H; H; XH; H; XH; M; MH; H; XH
Action: F; F; F; F; F; F; F; F; M; M; M; M; F; M; M; M
Pieces: 2
Line Weight: 15-40 lbs; 8-12 lbs; 10-17 lbs; 12-25 lbs; 6-10 lbs; 8-12 lbs; 10-17 lbs; 12-25 lbs; 15-30 lbs; 15-40 lbs; 15-30 lbs; 15-40 lbs; 8-12 lbs; 10-17 lbs; 12-25 lbs; 15-40 lbs
Lure Weight: 3/4-3 oz; 1/4-3/4 oz; 3/8-1 oz; 1/2-2 oz; 1/8-5/8 oz; 1/4-3/4 oz; 3/8-1 oz; 1/2-2 oz; 1-6 oz; 4-12 oz; 1-6 oz; 4-12 oz; 1/4-3/4 oz; 3/8-1 oz; 1/2-2 oz; 4-12 oz
Features: Salmon and steelhead fishing is not the NBA. It doesn't just go on and on, day after day with no end. When the fish are running, it's time to hit it—and preferably with a St. Croix Wild River rod. Thirty-eight unique, specialized lengths, actions, and powers to cover any situation, Wild River rods are built on rich gold dust green metallic finish blanks and are even available in Downrigging and Kokanee categories. Remember, there's no shame in letting a little dust collect around the house.
Price: . . . .**$190–$240**

ACTION	POWER	
M=Moderate	UL=Ultra Light	H=Heavy
MF=Moderate Fast	L=Light	MH=Medium-Heavy
F=Fast	ML=Medium-Light	XH=Extra Heavy
XF=Extra Fast		

          www.skyhorsepublishing.com

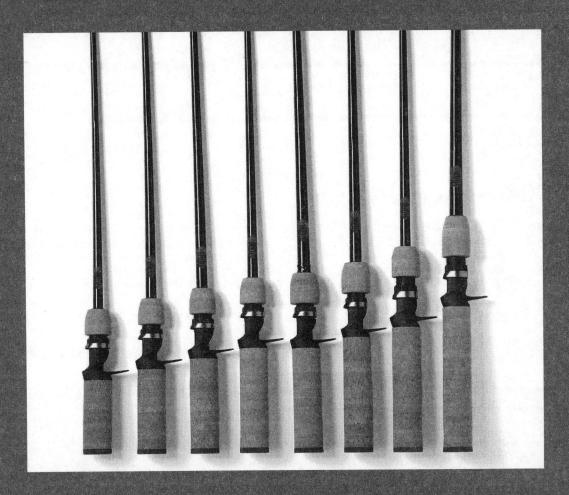

206 Daiwa
207 Lamiglas

208 G.Loomis
209 Okuma

211 Shimano
212 St. Croix

RODS: **Saltwater Baitcasting**

RODS

DAIWA SALTIGA INSHORE COAST-TO-COAST

Model: CC701HFB, CC701XHFB, CC761HFB, CC761XHFB, CC801HFB, CC801XHFB
Length: 7'; 7'; 7'6''; 7'6''; 8'; 8'
Power: H; XH; H; XH; H; XH
Action: F
Pieces: 1
Line Weight: 15-25 lbs; 17-30 lbs; 15-25 lbs; 17-30 lbs; 15-25 lbs; 17-30 lbs

Guide Count: 9
Lure Weight: 1/2-1 1/2 oz; 1/2-2 oz; 1/2-1 1/2 oz; 1/2-2 oz; 1/2-1 1/2 oz; 1/2-2 oz
Features: Bias construction high-modulus graphite blank; tough Fuji Alconite guides; Fuji SiC tip-top (Northeast models only); genuine Fuji reel seat; high-quality cork grip; convenient hook keeper; protective rubber butt cap; limited lifetime warranty.
Price: **$94.95**

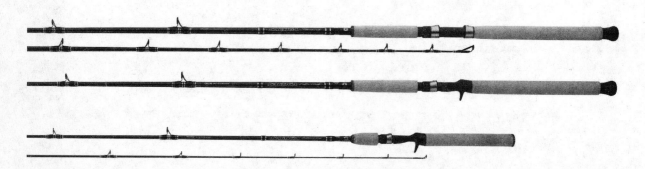

DAIWA SALTIGA INSHORE GULF COAST

Model: GC661MLFB, GC701MLXB, GC701MXB, GC761MXB
Length: 6'6''; 7'; 7'; 7'6''
Power: ML; ML; M; M
Action: F; XF; XF; XF
Pieces: 1
Line Weight: 6-14 lbs; 6-14 lbs; 8-20 lbs; 8-20 lbs

Guide Count: 9; 10; 10; 10
Lure Weight: 1/8-1/2 oz; 1/8-1/2 oz; 1/4-1 oz; 1/4-1 oz
Features: Bias construction high-modulus graphite blank; tough Fuji Alconite guides; Fuji SiC tip-top (Northeast models only); genuine Fuji reel seat; high-quality cork grip; convenient hook keeper, protective rubber butt cap; limited lifetime warranty.
Price: . . . . **$139.95–$149.95**

ACTION	POWER	
M=Moderate	**UL**=Ultra Light	**H**=Heavy
MF=Moderate Fast	**L**=Light	**MH**=Medium-Heavy
F=Fast	**ML**=Medium-Light	**XH**=Extra Heavy
XF=Extra Fast		

LAMIGLAS BIG FISH
Model: BFC 5610, BFC 5610 RT, BFC 70 H
Length: 5'6''; 5'6''; 7'
Power: XH; XH; H
Action: F
Pieces: 1
Line Weight: 50-100 lbs; 50-100 lbs; 20-50 lbs

Features: Smooth, balanced designs are focused on 20- to 100-pound pound line classes, placing them in the heart of halibut, tuna, shark, large striper, and wreck fisheries; features aluminum reel seats; slick butts; roller tip; wireline rod with silicon nitrate guides; premier cod rod.
Price: . . . .**$180–$220**

LAMIGLAS TRI-FLEX GRAPHITE INSHORE
Model: TFX 6015 C, TFX 7020 CT, TFX 7030 C, TFX 7030 CT, TFX 7040 CT, TFX 7650 CT
Length: 6'; 7'; 7'; 7'; 7'; 7'6''
Action: F
Pieces: 1
Line Weight: 8-17 lbs; 8-20 lbs; 15-30 lbs; 15-30 lbs; 20-40 lbs; 20-50 lbs
Lure Weight: 1/4-1 oz; 1-4 oz; 3/4-3 oz; 3-6 oz; 4-10 oz; 6-16 oz

Features: Cork handles immediately categorize these rods as inshore, but don't overlook these nine highly capable models wherever the need for refined power of tri-flex graphite exists (specifically, the new TFX 6015 C, TFX 6015 S, and TRX 6615 S); latest editions are precision-balanced rods for throwing bucktails for striped bass, fluke, and bluefish; others are equally at home casting swim baits to tuna as they are throwing eels to stripers or crabs to tarpon; easy handling and can-do nature.
Price: . . . .**$220–$310**

ACTION	POWER	
M=Moderate	UL=Ultra Light	H=Heavy
MF=Moderate Fast	L=Light	MH=Medium-Heavy
F=Fast	ML=Medium-Light	XH=Extra Heavy
XF=Extra Fast		

RODS

LAMIGLAS TRI-FLEX GRAPHITE SALTWATER

Model: BL 5630 C, BL 7020 C, BL 7030 C, BL 7040 C, BL 7050 LB, BL 7640 C
Length: 5'6''; 7'; 7'; 7'; 7'; 7'6''
Action: F; MF: MF; M; MF; M
Pieces: 1
Line Weight: 20-40 lbs; 10-20 lbs; 15-30 lbs; 20-40 lbs; 20-50 lbs; 20-50 lbs

Lure Weight: 1-6 oz; 1-3 oz; 1-6 oz; 2-8 oz; 2-10 oz; 6-12 oz
Features: A combination of lightweight power, durability, sensitivity, and structural integrity that will provide years, and perhaps decades, of exciting battles.
Price:.................................$260–$400

G.LOOMIS ESCAPE GLX

Model: ETR 84-3 MLS-10 GLX, ETR 84-3 MS-12 GLX
Length: 7'
Power: ML; M
Action: F
Pieces: 3
Line Weight: 6-12 lbs
Lure Weight: 1/4-1/2 oz; 1/4-5/8 oz

Features: Three-piece, high-performance, technical fishing tools; has specific line and lure ratings as well as the optimum line recommended; guides on the GLX models are nickel-titanium RECOIL, making it virtually impossible to experience any issues with rings popping out or frames fracturing; handles feature cork grips with fixed reel seats; comes in a handsome, protective rod sock and travel case.
Price:.................................$655–$665

ACTION	POWER	
M=Moderate	UL=Ultra Light	H=Heavy
MF=Moderate Fast	L=Light	MH=Medium-Heavy
F=Fast	ML=Medium-Light	XH=Extra Heavy
XF=Extra Fast		

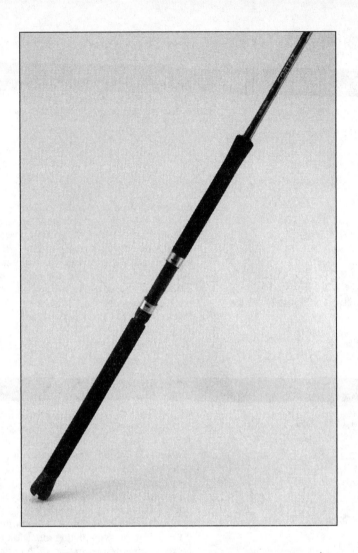

OKUMA CORTEZ

Model: CZ-C-661M, CZ-C-661MH, CZ-C-701M, CZ-C-701MH

Length: 6'6''; 6'6''; 7'; 7'

Power: M; MH; M; MH

Action: MF

Pieces: 1

Line Weight: 20-30 lbs; 30-50 lbs; 20-30 lbs; 30-50 lbs

Guide Count: 9; 9; 10; 10

Features: Extremely durable carbon and glass blank mixture for ultimate strength; EVA fore and rear grips for comfort and durability; double-footed stainless steel guide frames; polished titanium oxide guide inserts; cushioned stainless steel hooded reel seat; graphite gimbals on all models; durable non-skid, rubber gimbals on all models; all Cortez rods are one-piece blank construction; one-year warranty.

Price: . . . . **$139.99–$244.99**

ACTION	POWER	
M=Moderate	UL=Ultra Light	H=Heavy
MF=Moderate Fast	L=Light	MH=Medium-Heavy
F=Fast	ML=Medium-Light	XH=Extra Heavy
XF=Extra Fast		

RODS: **Saltwater Baitcasting**

OKUMA PEZ VELA

Model: PV-C-661M, PV-C-661MH, PV-C-701M, PV-C-701MH
Length: 6'6''; 6'6''; 7'; 7'
Power: M; MH; M; MH
Action: MF
Pieces: 1
Line Weight: 12-25 lbs; 15-30 lbs; 12-25 lbs; 15-30 lbs
Guide Count: 7

Features: Extremely durable carbon and glass rod blank mixture; EVA fore and rear grips on spinning models; casting models feature EVA fore grip and a graphite butt; double-footed stainless steel guide frames; polished titanium oxide guide inserts; cushioned stainless steel hooded reel seat; durable non-skid, rubber gimbals on all models; all Pez Vela rods are one-piece blank construction; one-year warranty.
Price:............................$49.99–$74.99

OKUMA SARASOTA

Model: Sr-C-661M, Sr-C-661MH, Sr-C-661ML, Sr-C-701M, Sr-C-701ML
Length: 6'6''; 6'6''; 6'6''; 7'; 7'
Power: M; MH; ML; M; ML
Action: MF
Pieces: 1
Line Weight: 20-40 lbs; 30-50 lbs; 15-30 lbs; 20-40 lbs; 15-30 lbs
Guide Count: 9; 9; 9; 10; 10

Features: Durable E-glass blank construction; glass fiber outer wrap increases hoop strength; double-footed stainless steel guide frames; HD model uses heavy duty-style guide frames; use Pacific Bay roller stripper and tip guides; polished titanium oxide guide inserts; stainless steel hooded reel seats; heavy duty aluminum hooded reel seat on HD/T models; graphite gimbals on all models; custom epoxy wrapped foregrip transition cone; one-year warranty.
Price:...................................$49.99

ACTION	POWER	
M=Moderate	UL=Ultra Light	H=Heavy
MF=Moderate Fast	L=Light	MH=Medium-Heavy
F=Fast	ML=Medium-Light	XH=Extra Heavy
XF=Extra Fast		

SHIMANO SAGUARO
Model: SGC66M, SGC66MH, SGC70ML, SGC70M, SGC70MH
Length: 6'6''; 6'6''; 7'; 7'; 7'
Power: M; MH; ML; M; MH
Action: F
Pieces: 1
Line Weight: 15-30 lbs; 20-50 lbs; 10-20 lbs; 15-30 lbs; 20-50 lbs

Guide Count: 7; 7; 8; 8; 8
Features: Composite rod blank; aluminum O ring; T-glass; graphite reel seat with stainless steel hoods; comfortable EVA handles; one-year warranty.
Price: **$39.99**

SHIMANO TALAVERA
Model: TEC60H, TEC60XH, TEC66M, TEC70ML, TEC70M, TEC70MH
Length: 6'; 6'; 6'6''; 7'; 7'; 7'
Power: H; XH; M; ML; M; MH
Action: F
Pieces: 1
Line Weight: 20-50 lbs; 30-80 lbs; 15-30 lbs; 10-20 lbs; 15-30 lbs; 20-50 lbs

Features: Shimano aeroglass or graphite composite (on selected models); graphite reel seat; Fuji heavy duty aluminum oxide boat guides (on selected models); EVA grip; AFTCO roller stripper and tip; graphite gimbal with cap (on selected models); black aluminum reel seat (trolling models only).
Price: . . . . **$79.99–$99.99**

ACTION	POWER	
M=Moderate	UL=Ultra Light	H=Heavy
MF=Moderate Fast	L=Light	MH=Medium-Heavy
F=Fast	ML=Medium-Light	XH=Extra Heavy
XF=Extra Fast		

ST. CROIX LEGEND INSHORE GULF COAST

Model: LGCC66XLM, LGCC66LM, LGCC66MLM, LGCC70MLM
Length: 6'6''; 6'6''; 6'6''; 7'
Power: XL; L; ML; ML
Action: M
Pieces: 1
Line Weight: 6-10 lbs; 8-12 lbs; 8-14 lbs; 8-14 lbs
Lure Weight: 1/32-1/8 oz; 1/16-1/4 oz; 1/8-3/8 oz; 1/8-3/8 oz
Features: Integrated Poly Curve tooling technology; Advanced Reinforcing Technology; high-modulus/high-strain SCIV graphite with FRS for unparalleled strength and durability; designed specifically for inshore saltwater angling; Kigan Master Hand Zero Tangle guides with zirconia rings and titanium frames for the ultimate protection against saltwater corrosion; the sloped, wide-leg design prevents line tangles with mono, fluorocarbon, and super braid lines; Fuji SK2 split reel seat for the ultimate in light weight and sensitivity; super-grade cork handle on spinning models; split-grip/super-grade cork handle on casting models; corrosion-proof wind check and reel seat trim pieces; two coats of Flex Coat slow-cure finish; lifetime limited warranty.
Price: . . . .**$300–$310**

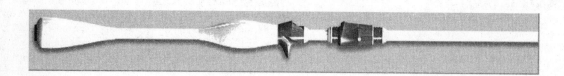

ST. CROIX LEGENDXTREME INSHORE

Model: XIC70MHF
Length: 7'
Power: MH
Action: F
Pieces: 1
Line Weight: 10-20 lbs
Lure Weight: 1/2-1 1/4 oz
Features: The middle school hallway. The Red Zone. The checkout line at Costco. There are places that test your wherewithal—but none as decisively as the inshore saltwater arena. Venture in there and you better be ready to man-up. It might also be a good idea to carry one of our new LegendXtreme Inshore rods. Hyper-performance rods for intense inshore fishing. Loaded with proprietary technologies, built on high-modulus SCVI and SCV graphite blanks, and finished with cutting edge fittings, these are the rods you go to when your intensity level hits high tide.
Price: **$390**

ACTION	POWER	
M=Moderate	UL=Ultra Light	H=Heavy
MF=Moderate Fast	L=Light	MH=Medium-Heavy
F=Fast	ML=Medium-Light	XH=Extra Heavy
XF=Extra Fast		

ST. CROIX LEGEND SURF

Model: LSC100MMF2, LSC106MHMF2, LSC110MHMF2
Length: 10'; 10'6''; 11'
Power: M; MH; MH
Action: MF
Pieces: 2
Line Weight: 10-20 lbs; 12-25 lbs; 15-40 lbs
Lure Weight: 1-4 oz; 2-6 oz; 3-8 oz
Features: Integrated Poly Curve tooling technology; Advanced Reinforcing Technology; high-modulus/high-strain SCIV graphite with FRS for unparalleled strength and durability; off-set, slim-profile ferrules on two-piece models provide one-piece performance; designed for extreme surf fishing performance; Fuji LC surf guides with Alconite ring for greater casting distance and accuracy; sloped frame reduces line tangling; Fuji DPS reel seat/frosted silver hoods; custom X-grip neoprene handle provides comfort and durability while reducing weight; positive grip improves when wet; two coats of Flex Coat slow-cure finish; lifetime limited warranty.
Price: . . . .**$430–$470**

ACTION	POWER	
M=Moderate	UL=Ultra Light	H=Heavy
MF=Moderate Fast	L=Light	MH=Medium-Heavy
F=Fast	ML=Medium-Light	XH=Extra Heavy
XF=Extra Fast		

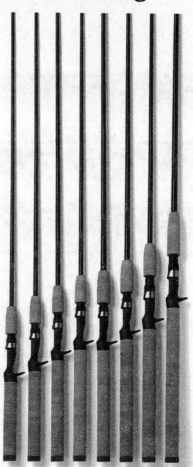

ST. CROIX TIDEMASTER INSHORE

Model: TIC66MHF, TIC66HF, TIC70LM, TIC70MLF, TIC70MF, TIC70MM, TIC70MHF, TIC70HF, TIC76MF, TIC76MHF, TIC76HF, TIC80MHF, TIC80HF

Length: 6'6''; 6'6''; 7'; 7'; 7'; 7'; 7'; 7'; 7'6''; 7'6''; 7'6''; 8'; 8'

Power: MH; H; L; ML; M; M; MH; H; M; MH; H; MH; H

Action: F; F; M; F; F; M; F; F; F; F; F; F; F

Pieces: 1

Line Weight: 10-20 lbs; 12-25 lbs; 6-12 lbs; 8-14 lbs; 8-17 lbs; 8-17 lbs; 10-20 lbs; 12-25 lbs; 8-17 lbs; 10-20 lbs; 12-25 lbs; 14-30 lbs; 17-40 lbs

Lure Weight: 1/2-1 1/4 oz; 3/4-2 oz; 1/8-3/8 oz; 1/8-1/2 oz; 3/8-3/4 oz; 1/4-5/8 oz; 1/2-1 1/4 oz; 3/4-2 oz; 3/8-3/4 oz; 1/2-1 1/4 oz; 3/4-2 oz; 1/2-2 oz; 3/4-3 oz

Features: Premium-quality SCII graphite; outstanding strength, sensitivity, and hook-setting power; designed specifically for inshore saltwater angling; Batson Forecast hard aluminum-oxide guides with 316 stainless-steel frames for dramatically improved corrosion resistance compared to 304 stainless-steel frames; Fuji DPS reel seat/frosted silver hoods on spinning models; Fuji ECS or TCS reel seat/frosted silver hood on casting models; premium-grade cork handle; two coats of Flex Coat slow-cure finish; five-year warranty.
Price: . . . .**$150–$210**

ACTION	POWER	
M=Moderate	UL=Ultra Light	H=Heavy
MF=Moderate Fast	L=Light	MH=Medium-Heavy
F=Fast	ML=Medium-Light	XH=Extra Heavy
XF=Extra Fast		

RODS: Freshwater Fly Fishing

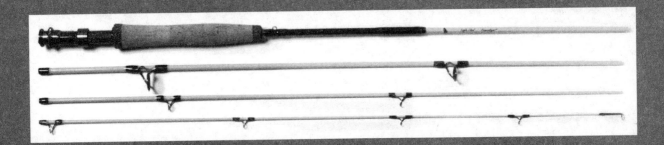

216 Beaverkill

217 Daiwa

218 Eagle Claw

219 Lamiglas

220 L. L. Bean

222 G.Loomis

225 Okuma

226 Orvis

227 Redington

229 Rise

230 Sage

232 Scott

236 Shakespeare

236 St. Croix

239 Temple Fork

242 Wright & McGill

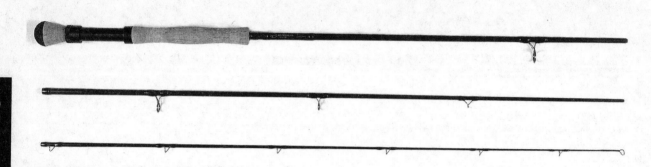

BEAVERKILL FULL FLEX—LEGACY

Model: F703-3-3, F763-3-3, F804-3-3, F864-3-3, F904-3-3, F905-3-3
Length: 7'; 7'6''; 8'; 8'6''; 9'; 9'
Pieces: 3
Line Weight: 3W–5W
Features: Super-grade Portuguese cork grips; stripping guides are high-frame, three-leg, one-piece stainless steel with a silicon carbide molded ring; snake guides, the sidemounted hook keeper, and tip-tops are stainless-steel-coated with groove-resistant titanium carbide; lustrous emerald green proprietary blanks using a slip ferrule system are hand-crafted in the USA; forest green Beaverkill nylon-covered carrying case with integral dual-pocket rod pouch.
Price: **$395**

BEAVERKILL MID FLEX—LEGACY

Model: F703-2-3, F763-2-3, F804-2-3, F864-2-4-3, F904-2-3, F905-2-3, F906-2-3, F907-2-3, F908-2-3, F1008-2-3, F909-2-3
Length: 7'; 7'6''; 8'; 8'6''; 9'; 9'; 9'; 9'; 9'; 10'; 9'
Pieces: 3
Line Weight: 3W–9W
Features: Super-grade Portuguese cork grips; stripping guides are high-frame, three-leg, one-piece stainless steel with a silicon carbide molded ring; snake guides, the sidemounted hook keeper, and tip-tops are stainless-steel-coated with groove-resistant titanium carbide; lustrous emerald green proprietary blanks using a slip ferrule system are hand-crafted in the USA; forest green Beaverkill nylon-covered carrying case with integral dual-pocket rod pouch.
Price: **$395**

ACTION	POWER	
M=Moderate	UL=Ultra Light	H=Heavy
MF=Moderate Fast	L=Light	MH=Medium-Heavy
F=Fast	ML=Medium-Light	XH=Extra Heavy
XF=Extra Fast		

BEAVERKILL TIP FLEX—LEGACY

Model: F904-1-3, F905-1-3, F906-1-3, F907-1-3, F908-1-3, F909-1-3, F9010-1-3, F9012-1-3
Length: 9'
Pieces: 3
Line Weight: 4W–12W
Features: Super-grade Portuguese cork grips; stripping guides are high-frame, three-leg, one-piece stainless steel with a

silicon carbide molded ring; snake guides, the sidemounted hook keeper, and tip-tops are stainless-steel-coated with groove-resistant titanium carbide; lustrous emerald green proprietary blanks using a slip ferrule system are hand-crafted in the USA; forest green Beaverkill nylon-covered carrying case with integral dual-pocket rod pouch.
Price: $395

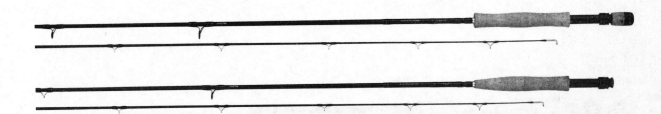

DAIWA ALGONQUIN

Model: AQF905A, AQF906A, AQF907A, AQF908EBA, AQF969EBA
Length: 9'; 9'; 9'; 9'; 9'6''
Pieces: 2
Line Weight: 4W–9W

Guide Count: 11
Features: High-quality graphite blank; aluminum oxide stripper and quality-plated snake guides; machined aluminum reel seat; removable extension butt on eight and nine weight models; natural cork grips.
Price: **$44.95**

ACTION	POWER	
M=Moderate	UL=Ultra Light	H=Heavy
MF=Moderate Fast	L=Light	MH=Medium-Heavy
F=Fast	ML=Medium-Light	XH=Extra Heavy
XF=Extra Fast		

RODS: Freshwater Fly Fishing

EAGLE CLAW FEATHERLIGHT

Model: FL300-6'6, FL300-7, FL300-8
Length: 6'6''; 7'; 8'
Action: L
Pieces: 2
Line Weight: 3W–6W
Guide Count: 9
Features: Classic featherlight action has been updated for a slightly quicker response; traditional fiberglass construction for the ultimate in feel, durability, and forgiveness; beautiful cork handles fit comfortably in your hand and provide a sure grip every time; perfectly matched components such as reel seats and guides complement every rod; one-year warranty.

Price:.................................... **$22.99**

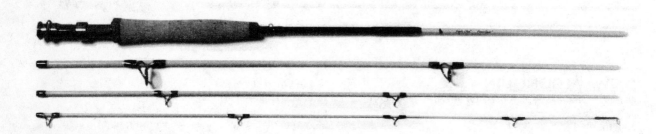

EAGLE CLAW POWERLIGHT

Model: PLF8644, PLF954
Length: 8'6''; 9'
Action: MF
Pieces: 4
Line Weight: 4W–5W
Guide Count: 9; 10
Features: Powerful IM7 graphite is the backbone of this entirely new series of performance rods; ultra-light to medium-heavy actions are available for just about any species you are targeting; custom cork handles provide exceptional performance while maintaining their beautiful appearance and incredible durability; gun smoke finished guides and reel seats; fly rods feature four-piece construction for easy travel and storage; one-year warranty.

Price:.................................... **$39.99**

ACTION	POWER	
M=Moderate	UL=Ultra Light	H=Heavy
MF=Moderate Fast	L=Light	MH=Medium-Heavy
F=Fast	ML=Medium-Light	XH=Extra Heavy
XF=Extra Fast		

LAMIGLAS INFINITY SI

Model: ISI 904, ISI 905, ISI 906, ISI 907, ISI 908, ISI 909, ISI 910, ISI 1178 SW
Length: 9'; 9'; 9'; 9'; 9'; 9'; 9'; 11'
Action: F
Pieces: 1; 1; 1; 2; 2; 2; 2; 2
Line Weight: 4 W–10 W
Features: Endless opportunity awaits with our new Infinity Fly series. Fifteen state-of-the-art new blanks, with lighter faster actions, including 4 ultra long casting models. Of special note, the 1178 is the first ever "switch" rod in our collection. A unique new hybrid cross of traditional casting and spey casting design. Its balance and handle design accommodates both methods to confidently swing steelhead flies on large rivers in the morning and work the brushy shores in the evening. Finished with exotic machined aluminum and carbon fiber reel seats.
Price: . . . .**$310–$400**

LAMIGLAS X-11

Model: LX 905, LX 906, LX 908, LX 909, LX 910
Length: 9'
Action: MF
Pieces: 2
Line Weight: 5 W–9 W
Features: Our new X-11 Series teaches another valuable lesson: high performance doesn't have to come with a high price tag. These moderate/fast action blanks feature our durable IM graphite and deep pressed guides with zirconia inserts. You'll have years, and likely decades, of exceptional casting and catches. The darker maroon color sets a very nice contrast between the reel seat and premium cork handles (one-year limited warranty).
Price: **$160**

ACTION	POWER	
M=Moderate	UL=Ultra Light	H=Heavy
MF=Moderate Fast	L=Light	MH=Medium-Heavy
F=Fast	ML=Medium-Light	XH=Extra Heavy
XF=Extra Fast		

RODS: **Freshwater Fly Fishing**

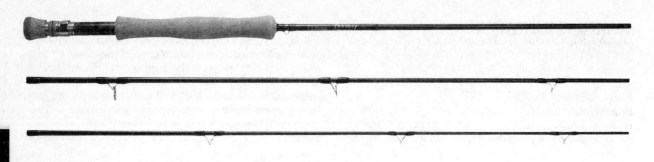

L. L. BEAN DOUBLE L

Model: 8'6'', 4 wt; 8'6'', 5 wt; 8'6'', 6 wt; 9', 4 wt; 9', 5 wt; 9', 6 wt; 9', 7 wt; 9', 8 wt
Length: 8'6''; 8'6''; 8'6''; 9'; 9'; 9'; 9'; 9'
Pieces: 4
Line Weight: 4W–8W
Features: The fastest, lightest, and strongest Double L Rod

ever offered; perfect blend of tradition and performance; fluid, medium action for ease of casting and delicate presentations.
Price: . . . .$245–$275

L. L. BEAN QUEST II FOUR-PIECE

Model: 9', 5 wt; 9', 6 wt; 9', 8 wt; 9', 9 wt
Length: 9'
Pieces: 4
Line Weight: 5W–9W

Features: Fine-tuned for beginner to intermediate casters; just tie on a fly and you're ready to fish; includes a rod, a reel loaded with backing, fly line, and a leader.
Price: **$109**

ACTION	**POWER**	
M=Moderate	UL=Ultra Light	H=Heavy
MF=Moderate Fast	L=Light	MH=Medium-Heavy
F=Fast	ML=Medium-Light	XH=Extra Heavy
XF=Extra Fast		

L. L. BEAN QUEST II TWO-PIECE

Model: 6'6'', 3 wt; 7'6'', 4 wt; 8'6'', 5 wt; 9', 5 wt; 8'6'', 6 wt
Length: 6'6''; 7'6''; 8'6''; 9'; 8'6''
Pieces: 2
Line Weight: 3W–6W

Features: Fine-tuned for beginner to intermediate casters; fish effectively on streams, lakes, and rivers; will grow with you, providing years of angling performance.
Price: **$99.99**

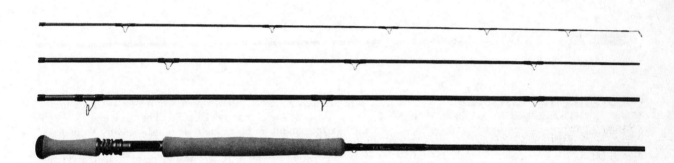

L. L. BEAN SILVER GHOST

Model: 10', 4 wt; 10', 5 wt; 10', 6 wt; 10', 7 wt; 10', 8 wt
Length: 10'
Pieces: 4
Line Weight: 4W–8W

Features: Lightweight design is durable and delivers outstanding performance; effectively handles heavier nymph rigs; great choice for big streamers in fast-moving water.
Price: . . . . **$300–$380**

ACTION	POWER	
M=Moderate	UL=Ultra Light	H=Heavy
MF=Moderate Fast	L=Light	MH=Medium-Heavy
F=Fast	ML=Medium-Light	XH=Extra Heavy
XF=Extra Fast		

L. L. BEAN STREAMLIGHT ULTRA TWO-PIECE

Model: 5'9'', 3 wt; 6'11'', 4 wt; 6'6'', 3 wt; 8', 5 wt; 8'6'', 5 wt; 9', 5 wt; 8'6'', 6 wt; 9', 6 wt; 9'7'', 7 wt; 9', 8 wt; 9', 9 wt
Length: 5'9''; 6'11''; 6'6''; 8'; 8'6''; 9'; 8'6''; 9'; 9'7''; 9'; 9'
Pieces: 2

Line Weight: 3W–9W
Features: Redesigned to be lighter with an improved taper; a rod you won't outgrow as your casting improves; reel-on-rod case included.
Price: . . . . **$99–$125**

G.LOOMIS GLX CLASSICS

Model: FR 1084-2 GLX, FR 1085-2 GLX, FR 1086-2 GLX, FR 1088-2 GLX
Length: 9'
Power: MS
Action: F
Pieces: 2
Line Weight: 4W–8W

Features: Lighter and more efficient than ever; made for the fanatical angler that specializes and has exacting expectations for his or her style of fishing; very accurate in line size, but their biggest attribute may be their versatility; they load as well at 15 feet as they do at 60 feet, and they are extremely powerful given their extreme light weight.
Price: . . . .**$600–$620**

ACTION	POWER	
M=Moderate	UL=Ultra Light	H=Heavy
MF=Moderate Fast	L=Light	MH=Medium-Heavy
F=Fast	ML=Medium-Light	XH=Extra Heavy
XF=Extra Fast		

G.LOOMIS NRX LITE PRESENTATION

Model: NRX 903-4 LP G, NRX 1043-4 LP G, NRX 1084-4 LP G, NRX 1085-4 LP G, NRX 903-4 LP, NRX 1043-4 LP, NRX 1084-4 LP, NRX 1085-4 LP

Length: 7'6''; 8'8''; 9'; 9'; 7'6''; 8'8''; 9'; 9'

Power: M

Action: M

Pieces: 4

Line Weight: 3W–5W

Features: For when conditions call for long, delicate casts using extremely light leaders; they are smooth casting, soft tapers for managing long, whisper-thin leaders and small- to medium-sized dry flies; they track true for exceptional accuracy and control, plus they are light as a feather with beautiful lines; featuring select species cork and your choice of our original, stealthy look in matte black with bright blue wraps or a more traditional evergreen with subtle green wraps and silver trim.

Price:.............................**$720–$755**

G.LOOMIS NRX NYMPH

Model: NRX 1203-4 Nymph G, NRX 1204-4 Nymph G, NRX 1203-4 Nymph, NRX 1204-4 Nymph

Length: 10'

Power: XS

Action: XF

Pieces: 4

Line Weight: 3W–4W

Features: Extremely fast, 10-foot, four-piece rods with light, sensitive tips to help anglers make short, accurate casts for drifting nymphs; long, light leaders guide the flies along the bottom, almost pulling the rig downstream; extra length and extra fast action helps improve casting accuracy and line mending while giving you quick hooksets and positive fish-fighting control.

Price:.............................**$775–$785**

ACTION	POWER	
M=Moderate	UL=Ultra Light	H=Heavy
MF=Moderate Fast	L=Light	MH=Medium-Heavy
F=Fast	ML=Medium-Light	XH=Extra Heavy
XF=Extra Fast		

RODS

G.LOOMIS NRX TROUT

Model: NRX 1083-4 G, NRX 1084-4 G, NRX 1085-4 G, NRX 1086-4 G, NRX 1083-4, NRX 1084-4, NRX 1085-4, NRX 1086-4
Length: 9'
Power: MS
Action: MF; F; F; F; MF; F; F; F
Pieces: 4
Line Weight: 3W–6W

Features: Black ion-coated REC recoil guides; each rod's custom reel seat has no exposed threads so as to make it easy to lock the reel to the reel seat; grips feature HD cork design, where the cork transitions to provide more sensitivity where needed, and more durability where needed.
Price:................................$730–$745

G.LOOMIS PRO4X TROUT

Model: PRO4x 963-4, PRO4x 964-4, PRO4x 1084-4, PRO4x 1085-4, PRO4x 1086-4, PRO 4X 1146-4 FR, PRO 4X 1147-4 FR, PRO 4X 1148-4 FR, PRO 4X 1203-4 FR, PRO 4X 1204-4 FR
Length: 8'; 8'; 9'; 9'; 9'; 9'6''; 9'6''; 9'6''; 10'; 10'
Power: M; M; MS; MS; MS; MS; MS; MS; MS; MS
Action: MF; MF; F; F; F; F; F; F; F; F
Pieces: 4
Line Weight: 3 W–8 W
Features: We took a page from our NRX blank technology to develop a new series of fly rods that "new-to-the-sport" and intermediate flyfishers will learn to appreciate and will have expert anglers wondering how this much performance gets packed into such an affordable package. A new taper design along with a noticeable weight-reduction in the upper half of the blank allows us to make a fly rod that is incredibly light, recovers quickly, and casts with unbelievable precision. It's the G.Loomis way . . . reduce as much weight as possible, take total advantage of the materials, and create a taper that is dynamic, efficient, and user-friendly. They are as beautiful to look at as they are to cast. A rod any flyfisher would be proud to own!
Price:................................$345–$375

ACTION	**POWER**	
M=Moderate	UL=Ultra Light	H=Heavy
MF=Moderate Fast	L=Light	MH=Medium-Heavy
F=Fast	ML=Medium-Light	XH=Extra Heavy
XF=Extra Fast		

OKUMA CRISIUM

Model: CRF-34-70-2, CRF-45-86-2, CRF-56-90-2, CRF-67-86-2, CRF-67-96-2, CRF-78-90-2
Length: 7'; 8'6''; 9'; 8'6''; 9'6''; 9'
Action: MF
Pieces: 2
Line Weight: 3W–8W

Guide Count: 7; 10; 10; 10; 10; 10
Features: Lightweight graphite construction; two-piece rod design; titanium oxide stripper guide; stainless steel snake guides; rosewood reel seat; Okuma rod bag; one-year warranty.
Price:.............................$59.99–$64.99

RODS

OKUMA SLV

Model: SLV-10-90-4, SLV-3-80-4, SLV-4-86-4, SLV-5-90-4, SLV-6-90-4, SLV-7-90-4, SLV-8-90-4, SLV-8-96-4
Length: 8'; 8'; 8'; 9'; 9'; 9'; 9'6''; 9'6''
Action: MF
Pieces: 4
Line Weight: 3W–10W

Guide Count: 10; 9; 10; 10; 10; 10; 10; 11
Features: Lightweight graphite construction; four-piece rod design; titanium oxide stripper guide; stainless steel snake guides; aluminum pipe reel seat with aluminum hoods; Okuma rod bag; one-year warranty.
Price:.............................$79.99–$89.99

ACTION	**POWER**	
M=Moderate	UL=Ultra Light	H=Heavy
MF=Moderate Fast	L=Light	MH=Medium-Heavy
F=Fast	ML=Medium-Light	XH=Extra Heavy
XF=Extra Fast		

Freshwater Fly Fishing

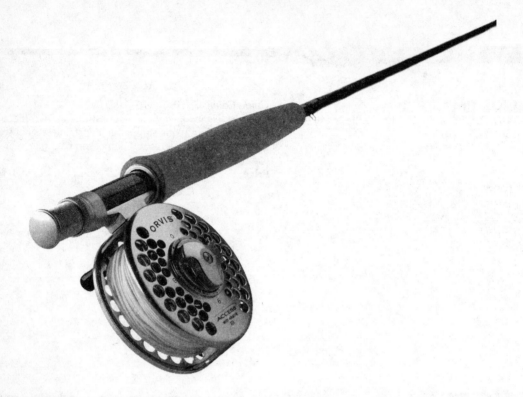

ORVIS ACCESS

Model: 3-weight 8'4" Fly Rod—Mid Flex, 4-weight 7' Fly Rod—Mid Flex, 4-weight 8' Fly Rod—Mid Flex, 4-weight 8'6" Fly Rod—Mid Flex, 4-weight 9' Fly Rod—Mid Flex, 4-weight 9' Fly Rod—Tip Flex, 4-weight 10' Fly Rod—Tip Flex, 5-weight 8'6" Fly Rod—Mid Flex, 5-weight 8'6" Fly Rod—Mid Flex, 2-piece, 5-weight 9' Fly Rod—Mid Flex, 5-weight 9' Fly Rod—Tip Flex, 5-weight 9' Fly Rod—Mid Flex (2-piece), 5-weight 10' Fly Rod—Tip Flex, Switch 5-weight 11' Fly Rod—Tip Flex, 6-weight 9' Fly Rod—Tip Flex, 6-weight 9' Fly Rod—Tip Flex, 2-piece, Switch

6-weight 11' Fly Rod—Tip Flex
Length: 8'4''; 7'; 8'; 8'6''; 9'; 9'; 10'; 8'6''; 8'6''; 9'; 9'; 9'; 10'; 11'; 9'; 9'; 11'
Action: M; M; M; M; M; F; F; M; M; M; F; M; F; F; F; F; F
Pieces: 4
Line Weight: 3W–6W
Features: Incredibly lightweight and offers remarkably smooth, precise, and balanced casting performance.
Price: **$425**

ACTION	POWER	
M=Moderate	UL=Ultra Light	H=Heavy
MF=Moderate Fast	L=Light	MH=Medium-Heavy
F=Fast	ML=Medium-Light	XH=Extra Heavy
XF=Extra Fast		

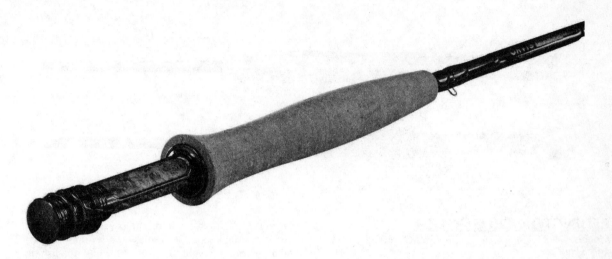

ORVIS HELIOS 2

Model: 2-weight 6' Fly Rod—Mid Flex, 2-weight 8'4" Fly Rod—Mid Flex, 3-weight 7'6" Fly Rod—Mid Flex, 3-weight 8'4" Fly Rod—Mid Flex, 3-weight 10' Fly Rod—Tip Flex, 4-weight 7' Fly Rod—Mid Flex, 4-weight 8'6" Fly Rod—Mid Flex, 4-weight 9' Fly Rod—Mid Flex, 4-weight 9' Fly Rod—Tip Flex, 4-weight 10' Fly Rod—Tip Flex, 5-weight 7'9" Fly Rod—Mid Flex, 5-weight 8'6" Fly Rod—Mid Flex, 5-weight 8'6" Fly Rod—Tip Flex, 5-weight 9' Fly Rod—Mid Flex, 5-weight 9' Fly Rod—Tip Flex, 5-weight 10' Fly Rod—Tip Flex, 6-weight 9' Fly Rod—Mid Flex, 6-weight 9' Fly Rod—Tip Flex

Length: 6'; 8'4"; 7'6"; 8'4"; 10'; 7'; 8'6"; 9'; 9'; 10'; 7'9"; 8'6"; 8'6"; 9'; 9'; 10'; 9'; 9'
Action: M; M; M; M; F; M; M; M; F; F; M; M; F; M; F; F; M; F
Pieces: 3; 4; 4; 4; 4; 4; 4; 4; 4; 4; 4; 4; 4; 4; 4; 4; 4
Line Weight: 2W–6W
Features: Lightweight, sensitive, and extremely powerful; 20 percent stronger than the original Helios; 20 percent lighter in hand; 100 percent increase in tip-impact strength; fine-tuned tapers for unrivaled tracking, accuracy, and lifting power.
Price: **$795**

REDINGTON CLASSIC TROUT

Model: 276-4, 376-4, 386-4, 480-4, 486-4, 490-4, 586-4, 590-4, 690-4, 380-6, 590-6
Length: 7'6"; 7'6"; 8'6"; 8'; 8'6"; 9'; 8'6"; 9'; 9'; 8'; 9'
Action: M
Pieces: 4; 6
Line Weight: 2W–6W

Features: Medium action. Offered in 4-piece and 6-piece configurations. Six-piece offers extreme packability for the backpacking and traveling angler. Titanium oxide stripping guides. Dark clay brown blank with matching Rosewood reel seat insert. Custom machined reel seat components. Alignment dots for easy rod set up. Divided brown ballistic Nylon rod tube.
Price: . . . . **$149.95–$169.95**

ACTION		POWER	
M=Moderate		UL=Ultra Light	H=Heavy
MF=Moderate Fast		L=Light	MH=Medium-Heavy
F=Fast		ML=Medium-Light	XH=Extra Heavy
XF=Extra Fast			

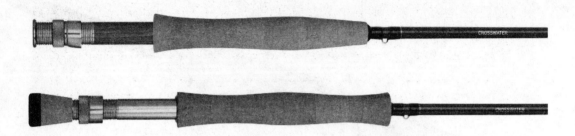

REDINGTON CROSSWATER

Model: 476-2, 580-2, 586-2, 590-2, 690-2, 890-2, 990-2, 590-4, 890-4
Length: 7'6"; 8'; 8'6"; 9'; 9'; 9'; 9'; 9'; 9'
Action: MF
Pieces: 2; 4
Line Weight: 4W–9W

Features: Medium-fast action. Attractive trim details and cosmetics. Alignment dots for easy rod set-up. Weights available from 4-weight to 9-weight for multiple fishing needs. Durable anodized aluminum reel seat, ideal for all fresh and saltwater applications. Rod comes with black cloth rod sock.
Price: . . . . **$119.95–$139.95**

REDINGTON VOYANT

Model: 376-4, 486-4, 490-4, 586-4, 590-4, 596-4, 5100-4, 690-4, 696-4, 6100-4, 790-4, 7100-4, 890-4, 990-4, 1090-4
Length: 7'6"; 8'6"; 9'; 8'6"; 9'; 9'6"; 10'; 9'; 9'6"; 10'; 9'; 10'; 9'; 9'; 9'
Action: F
Pieces: 4
Line Weight: 3W–10W
Features: Fast action. Smooth casting, high-performing, and versatile enough for the beginner to the more advanced anglers. Alignment dots for easy rod set-up. Half-wells grip (3wt–6wt). Full-wells grip (7wt–10wt). Durable anodized aluminum and wood reel seat. Comes in a cloth tube with zippered closure and a black cloth rod bag. Lifetime warranty.
Price: **$189.95**

ACTION		POWER	
M=Moderate		**UL**=Ultra Light	**H**=Heavy
MF=Moderate Fast		**L**=Light	**MH**=Medium-Heavy
F=Fast		**ML**=Medium-Light	**XH**=Extra Heavy
XF=Extra Fast			

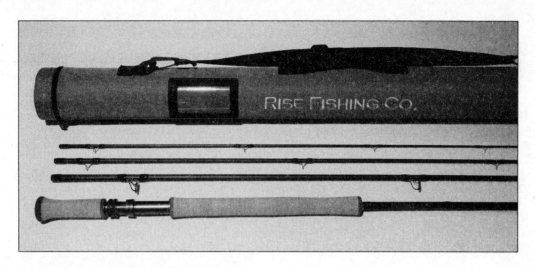

RISE BLACKWATER SPEY AND SWITCH

Model: 11-6/7wt, 11-7/8wt, 119-8wt, 126-8wt, 133-8wt, 14-9wt
Length: 11'; 11'; 11'9''; 12'6''; 13'3''; 14'

Action: MF
Pieces: 4
Line Weight: 6W–9W
Price: . . . .$450–$580

RISE IN-STREAM SERIES

Model: 80-4wt, 86-4wt, 90-4wt, 86-5wt, 90-5wt
Length: 8'; 8'6''; 9'; 8'6''; 9'
Action: M; M; M; MF; MF
Pieces: 4
Line Weight: 4W–5W
Features: Made from IM7 and IM8 graphite makes these lightweight, crisp-feeling rods; the reel seat is a nickel silver uplocking seat with burled rosewood glossy finish; all guides are lightweight titanium carbide; the In-Stream series is a beautiful dark red finish with black wraps; all In-Stream series fly rods come with a case and a lifetime warranty.
Price: . . . . $189.99–$199.99

ACTION	POWER	
M=Moderate	UL=Ultra Light	H=Heavy
MF=Moderate Fast	L=Light	MH=Medium-Heavy
F=Fast	ML=Medium-Light	XH=Extra Heavy
XF=Extra Fast		

RODS: **Freshwater Fly Fishing**

SAGE BASS II

Model: Bluegill, Smallmouth, Largemouth, Peacock
Length: 7'11''
Action: F
Pieces: 4
Line Weight: 230 gr; 290 gr; 330 gr; 390 gr
Features: Fast-action graphite III construction; built within tournament specifications; Fuji ceramic stripping guides; hard chromed snake guides; saltwater safe, red anodized aluminum reel seat; custom, pre-shaped cork handle 6½" full-wells grip; fighting butt; olive ballistic cloth rod/reel case; Sage BASS II taper line included.
Price: **$550**

SAGE CIRCA

Model: 7'9'', 3 wt; 8'9'', 3 wt; 7'9'', 4 wt; 8'9'', 4 wt; 8'9'', 5 wt
Length: 7'9''; 8'9''; 7'9''; 8'9''; 8'9''
Line Weight: 3W–5W
Features: A soft-action premium fly rod featuring Sage's groundbreaking Konnetic technology; designed for intermediate to advanced casters; built for delicate, accurate presentations.
Price: **$775**

ACTION	POWER	
M=Moderate	UL=Ultra Light	H=Heavy
MF=Moderate Fast	L=Light	MH=Medium-Heavy
F=Fast	ML=Medium-Light	XH=Extra Heavy
XF=Extra Fast		

SAGE ONE ELITE 590-4
Model: One Elite 590-4
Length: 9'
Action: F
Pieces: 4
Line Weight: 5W
Features: All-water rod; fast-action Konnetic technology construction; black ice shaft color; black primary thread wraps with gray titanium trim wraps; elite, Flor-grade, snubnose, half-wells cork handle; titanium reel seat with laser-etched logo on end cap; titanium winding check; titanium stripper guides with ceramic insert; black hook keeper; extra (spare) tip section.
Price:. **$1,350**

SAGE ONE SERIES
Model: 376-4, 390-4, 486-4, 490-4, 496-4, 4100-4, 586-4, 590-4, 596-4, 5100-4, 690-4, 691-4, 696-4, 697-4, 6100-4, 6101-4, 790-4, 796-4, 7100-4, 890-4, 896-4, 8100-4, 990-4, 1090-4, 1190-4, 1290-4
Length: 7'6''; 9'; 8'6''; 9'; 9'6''; 10'; 8'6''; 9'; 9'6''; 10'; 9'; 9'; 9'6''; 9'6''; 10'; 10'; 9'; 9'6''; 10'; 9'; 9'6''; 10'; 9'; 9'; 9'; 9'
Action: F
Pieces: 4
Line Weight: 3W–12W
Features: Fast-action Konnetic technology construction; Fuji ceramic stripping guides; hard chromed snake guides; high-grade, custom-tapered, shaped cork handles; walnut wood and golden bronze-colored aluminum anodized freshwater reel seat; weights 6 through 10 have an all golden bronze-colored aluminum anodized reel seat; black powder-coated aluminum rod tube with Sage medallion.
Price:. **$795**

ACTION	POWER	
M=Moderate	UL=Ultra Light	H=Heavy
MF=Moderate Fast	L=Light	MH=Medium-Heavy
F=Fast	ML=Medium-Light	XH=Extra Heavy
XF=Extra Fast		

RODS: Freshwater Fly Fishing

SAGE TXL-F
Model: 000710-4, 00710-4, 0710-4, 1710-4, 2710-4, 3610-4, 3710-4, 4610-4, 4710-4
Length: 7'10''; 7'10''; 7'10''; 7'10''; 7'10''; 6'10''; 7'10''; 6'10''; 7'10''
Action: MF
Pieces: 4
Line Weight: 0W–4W
Features: Moderate-fast action G5 technology exclusive; Sage TXL-F ultra-light guide package; greater sensitivity using micro ferrule technology; smooth, more efficient power transfer between sections; increased feel and control with an ergonomic handle; snub nose, half-wells grip; bronze anodized reel seat with natural walnut insert; 1 5/8" antique bronze powder-coated aluminum tube with black cloth bag.
Price:....................................**$625**

SCOTT A4
Model: 753/4, 803/4, 804/4, 854/4, 904/4, 1004/4, 855/4, 905/4, 905/4W, 1005/4, 906/4, 956/4, 1006/4, 907/4, 957/4, 1007/4, 908/4, 958/4, 1008/4, 909/4, 9010/4, 9012/4
Length: 7'6''; 8'; 8'; 8'6''; 9'; 10'; 8'6''; 9'; 9'; 10'; 9'; 9'6''; 10'; 9'; 9'6''; 10'; 9'; 9'6''; 10'; 9'; 9'; 9'
Pieces: 4
Line Weight: 3W–12W
Features: Multi-modulus design for fine-tuned flex and recovery; natural finish—naturally stronger, naturally lighter; handcrafted in the USA—built from beginning to end in Montrose, Colorado.
Price:....................................**$395**

ACTION		POWER	
M=Moderate	UL=Ultra Light	H=Heavy
MF=Moderate Fast	L=Light	MH=Medium-Heavy
F=Fast	ML=Medium-Light	XH=Extra Heavy
XF=Extra Fast		

SCOTT F2
Model: 602/3, 653/3; 703/3; 774/3
Length: 6'; 6'6''; 7'; 7'7''
Pieces: 3
Line Weight: 2W–4W

Features: A continuous taper and smooth progressive action; proprietary S2 high-performance fiberglass epoxy composite; faster recovery and greater feel; handcrafted in the USA—built from beginning to end in Montrose, Colorado.
Price: **$645**

SCOTT G2
Model: 772/4, 842/4, 773/4, 843/4, 883/4, 774/4, 844/4, 884/4, 904/4, 845/4, 885/4, 905/4, 906/4
Length: 7'7''; 8'4''; 7'7''; 8'4''; 8'8''; 7'7''; 8'4''; 8'8''; 9'; 8'4''; 8'8''; 9'; 9'
Pieces: 4
Line Weight: 2W–6W
Features: X-core technology offers enhanced feel with unequalled stability; multi-modulus design for fine-tuned

flex and recovery; natural finish—naturally stronger, naturally lighter; Scott hollow internal ferrule allows for continuous taper and smooth progressive action; Advanced Reinforced Carbon reduces torque and increases strength; handcrafted in the USA—built from beginning to end in Montrose, Colorado.
Price: **$745**

ACTION	POWER	
M=Moderate	UL=Ultra Light	H=Heavy
MF=Moderate Fast	L=Light	MH=Medium-Heavy
F=Fast	ML=Medium-Light	XH=Extra Heavy
XF=Extra Fast		

SCOTT L2H

Model: 1105/4, 1106/4, 1256/4, 1157/4, 1257/4, 1158/4, 1308/4, 1409/4, 1510/4
Length: 11'; 11'; 12'6''; 11'6''; 12'6''; 11'6''; 13'; 14'; 15'
Pieces: 4
Line Weight: 5W–10W

Features: Multi-modulus design for fine-tuned flex and recovery; natural finish—naturally stronger, naturally lighter; Advanced Reinforced Carbon reduces torque and increases strength; handcrafted in the USA—built from beginning to end in Montrose, Colorado.
Price: . . . .**$545–$645**

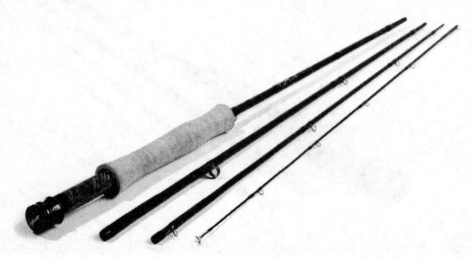

SCOTT M

Model: 803/4, 884/4, 904/4, 885/4, 905/4, 906/4
Length: 8'; 8'8''; 9'; 8'8''; 9'; 9'
Pieces: 4
Line Weight: 3W–6W
Features: X-Core technology enhances feel, incredible stability, and unequalled performance; the finest cork, components and craftsmanship; natural finish—naturally stronger, naturally lighter; Advanced Reinforced Carbon reduces torque and increases strength; handcrafted in the USA—built from beginning to end in Montrose, Colorado.
Price: **$995**

ACTION	POWER	
M=Moderate	UL=Ultra Light	H=Heavy
MF=Moderate Fast	L=Light	MH=Medium-Heavy
F=Fast	ML=Medium-Light	XH=Extra Heavy
XF=Extra Fast		

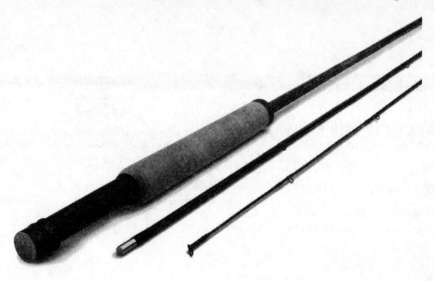

SCOTT SC
Model: 653, 6114, 754, 7105
Length: 6'5''; 6'11''; 7'5''; 7'10''
Pieces: 2
Line Weight: 3W–5W

Features: Hollow blanks with butt swells; Hariki handmade nickel silver ferrules; agate guides in handmade nickel silver frames; handcrafted in the USA—built from beginning to end in Montrose, Colorado.
Price: **$3,250**

SCOTT T3H
Model: 1064/4, 1106/4, 1286/4, 1287/4, 1357/4, 1108/4, 1288/4, 1358/4, 1409/4, 1509/4, 1510/4, 1610/4
Length: 10'6''; 11'; 12'8''; 12'8''; 13'6''; 11'; 12'8''; 13'6''; 14'; 15'; 15'; 16'
Pieces: 4
Line Weight: 4W–10W
Features: X-Core technology enhances feel, incredible stability, and unequalled performance; Advanced

Reinforced Carbon for reducing torque and increasing strength; multi-modulus design for fine-tuned flex and recovery; natural finish—naturally stronger, naturally lighter; Mil-Spec III anodized reel seats and titanium guides offer the highest levels of corrosion resistance; handcrafted in the USA—built from beginning to end in Montrose, Colorado.
Price: . . . .**$925–$995**

ACTION	POWER	
M=Moderate	UL=Ultra Light	H=Heavy
MF=Moderate Fast	L=Light	MH=Medium-Heavy
F=Fast	ML=Medium-Light	XH=Extra Heavy
XF=Extra Fast		

SHAKESPEARE UGLY STIK BIGWATER

Model: BWF11009089, BWF11009010
Length: 9'
Pieces: 2
Line Weight: 8W–10W
Guide Count: 9
Features: Howald process and Ugly Stik Clear Tip design for guaranteed strength and sensitivity; double-footed Fuji stainless steel guides with aluminum oxide inserts; durable EVA grips and graphite Fuji reel seats with corrosion-resistant stainless steel hoods; epoxy-coated blanks for protection from UV rays; exclusive ugly back; 60-day/five-year warranty.
Price: . . . . **$44.95–$199.95**

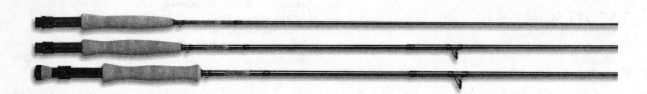

ST. CROIX AVID SERIES FLY

Model: A762.4, A603.2, A663.4, A703.2, A793.4, A664.4, A704.2, A794.4, A864.4, A904.2, A904.4, A805.4, A865.4, A905.2, A905.4, A906.2, A906.4, A907.4
Length: 7'6''; 6'; 6'6''; 7'; 7'9''; 6'6''; 7'; 7'9''; 8'6''; 9'; 9'; 8'; 8'6''; 9'; 9'; 9'; 9'; 9'
Pieces: 4; 2; 4; 2; 4; 4; 2; 4; 4; 2; 4; 4; 2; 4; 2; 4; 4
Line Weight: 2W–7W
Features: Integrated Poly Curve tooling technology; premium, high-modulus SCIII graphite; slim-profile ferrules; Fuji Alconite stripper guides with black frames; hard chrome, single-foot fly guides on 2, 3, 4, 5, 6 wt models; hard chrome snake guides on 7 wt model; uplocking, anodized aluminum reel seat with an ebony wood insert on 2, 3, 4, 5, 6 wt models; uplocking, anodized aluminum reel seat on 7 wt model; select-grade cork handle; two coats of Flex Coat slow-cure finish; rugged rod case with handle and divided polypropylene liner; lifetime limited warranty.
Price: . . . . **$250–$310**

ACTION	POWER	
M=Moderate	UL=Ultra Light	H=Heavy
MF=Moderate Fast	L=Light	MH=Medium-Heavy
F=Fast	ML=Medium-Light	XH=Extra Heavy
XF=Extra Fast		

ST. CROIX BANK ROBBER

Model: BR905.4, BR906.4, BR907.4
Length: 9'
Action: F
Pieces: 4
Line Weight: 5W–7W
Features: Integrated Poly Curve tooling technology; Advanced Reinforcing Technology; super high-modulus SCVI graphite with FRS in lower section for maximum power and strength with reduced weight; high-modulus/ high-strain SCV graphite with FRS and carbon-matte scrim for unparalleled strength, durability, and sensitivity; designed with Kelly Galloup especially for streamer fishing; slim-profile ferrules; one-piece performance in four-piece designs; Fuji K Series Tangle-Free stripper guides with Alconite rings; REC Recoil snake guides; anodized, machined-aluminum reel seat with built-in hook-keeper; Flora-grade cork handle; two coats of Flex Coat slow-cure finish; alignment dots; rugged rod case with handle and divided polypropylene liner; lifetime limited warranty.
Price: **$460**

ST. CROIX HIGH STICK DRIFTER

Model: HSD964.4, HSD1004.4, HSD1005.4
Length: 9'6''; 10'; 10'
Action: F
Pieces: 4
Line Weight: 4W–5W
Features: Integrated Poly Curve tooling technology; Advanced Reinforcing Technology; super high-modulus SCVI graphite with FRS in lower section for maximum power and strength with reduced weight; high-modulus/ high-strain SCV graphite with FRS and carbon-matte scrim for unparalleled strength, durability, and sensitivity; designed with Kelly Galloup especially for nymph fishing; slim-profile ferrules; one-piece performance in four-piece designs; Fuji K series tangle-free stripper guides with Alconite rings; REC Recoil snake guides; anodized, machined-aluminum reel seat with built-in hook-keeper; Flora-grade cork handle; two coats of Flex Coat slow-cure finish; alignment dots; rugged rod case with handle and divided polypropylene liner; lifetime limited warranty.
Price: **$460**

ACTION	POWER	
M=Moderate	UL=Ultra Light	H=Heavy
MF=Moderate Fast	L=Light	MH=Medium-Heavy
F=Fast	ML=Medium-Light	XH=Extra Heavy
XF=Extra Fast		

RODS

RODS

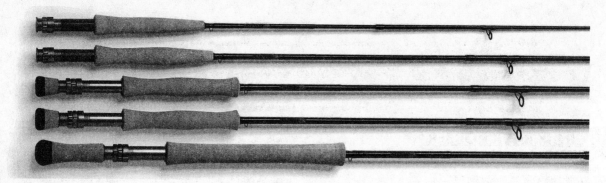

ST. CROIX IMPERIAL

Model: 1602.2, 1663.2, 1703.4, 1863.4, 1764.2, 1764.4, 1804.2, 1804.4, 1864.4, 1904.2, 1904.4, 1805.2, 1805.4, 1865.2, 1865.4, 1905.2, 1905.4, 1906.2, 1906.4, 11006.4, 1907.4, 11007.4, 1908.2, 1908.4, 1968.4, 11008.4, 1909.2, 1909.4, 19010.2, 19010.4

Length: 6'; 6'6''; 7'; 8'6''; 7'6''; 7'6''; 8'; 8'; 8'6''; 9'; 9'; 8'; 8'; 8'6''; 8'6''; 9'; 9'; 9'; 9'; 10'; 9'; 10'; 9'; 9'; 9'6''; 10'; 9'; 9'; 9'; 9'

Action: F

Pieces: 2; 2; 4; 4; 2; 4; 2; 4; 4; 2; 4; 2; 4; 2; 4; 2; 4; 2; 4; 4; 4; 4; 2; 4; 4; 4; 2; 4; 2; 4

Line Weight: 2W–10W

Features: Dynamic blend of high-modulus/high-strain SCIV graphite and premium-quality SCII graphite; lightweight, fast-action fly rods designed for maximum performance and value; aluminum-oxide stripper guides with black frames; hard chrome snake guides; uplocking, machined-aluminum reel seat with a rosewood insert on 2, 3, 4, 5 & 6 wt models; uplocking, machined-aluminum reel seat on 7, 8, 9 & 10 wt models; premium-grade cork handle; two coats of Flex Coat slow-cure finish; rugged rod case with handle and divided polypropylene liner; lifetime limited warranty.

Price:..................................**$210–$280**

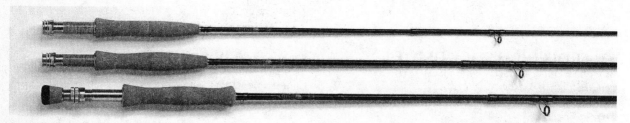

ST. CROIX LEGEND ELITE

Model: EFW793.4, EFW864.4, EFW904.4, EFW865.4, EFW905.4, EFW906.4, EFW907.4, EFW967.4, EFW908.4, EFW968.4, EFW909.4, EFW9010.4

Length: 7'9''; 8'6''; 9'; 8'6''; 9'; 9'; 9'; 9'6''; 9'; 9'6''; 9'; 9'

Action: F

Pieces: 4

Line Weight: 3W–10W

Features: Integrated Poly Curve tooling technology; Advanced Reinforcing Technology; super high-modulus SCVI graphite with FRS in lower section for maximum power and strength with reduced weight; high-modulus/high-strain SCV graphite with FRS and carbon-matte scrim for unparalleled strength and durability; slim-profile ferrules; phenomenally sensitive, light, and smooth casting; Fuji SiC Concept Guide System with titanium-finished frames; Fuji VSS reel seat/frosted silver hood on spinning models; Fuji ACS reel seat/frosted silver hood on casting models; machined-aluminum wind check; super-grade cork handle; two coats of Flex Coat slow-cure finish; includes deluxe rod sack; lifetime limited warranty.

Price:..................................**$430–$500**

ACTION	**POWER**	
M=Moderate	UL=Ultra Light	H=Heavy
MF=Moderate Fast	L=Light	MH=Medium-Heavy
F=Fast	ML=Medium-Light	XH=Extra Heavy
XF=Extra Fast		

ST. CROIX RIO SANTO

Model: RS804.2, RS804.4, RS765.2, RS865.2, RS865.4, RS905.2, RS905.4, RS906.2, RS906.4, RS908.2, RS908.4
Length: 8'; 8'; 7'6''; 8'6''; 8'6''; 9'; 9'; 9'; 9'; 9'; 9'
Action: MF
Pieces: 2; 4; 2; 2; 4; 2; 4; 2; 4; 2; 4
Line Weight: 4W–8W

Features: Premium-quality SCII graphite; smooth, versatile, moderate-fast actions; aluminum-oxide stripper guides with black frames; stainless steel snake guides; uplocking, aluminum reel seat; premium-grade cork handle; two coats of Flex Coat slow-cure finish; includes cloth rod sack; five-year warranty.
Price: . . . .**$110–$140**

RODS

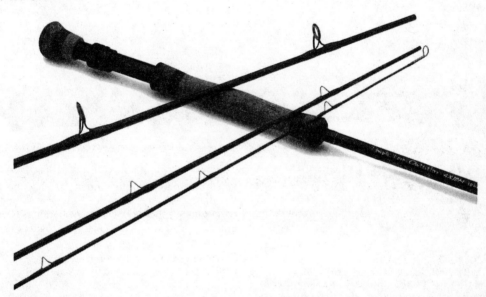

TEMPLE FORK AXIOM

Model: TF 05 90 4 A, TF 06 90 4 A, TF 07 90 4 A , TF 08 90 4 A, TF 09 90 4 A, TF 10 90 4 A
Length: 9'
Action: F
Pieces: 4
Line Weight: 5W–10W
Features: Kevlar is sandwiched between two layers of carbon fiber to reduce the ovaling effect a rod blank experiences under load, creating an exceptionally smooth, powerful rod with remarkable damping (tip bounce) qualities; ultra-high line speed with crisp, clean, accurate loops; features a rich translucent blue blank accentuated with gold script and accents; Flor-grade cork (reverse half wells on the 4 and 5, full wells with decorative burl rings on the 6–10); gun metal blue uplocking reel seat; large stripping guides with gold titanium oxide inserts.
Price: . . . .**$275–$300**

ACTION	POWER	
M=Moderate	**UL**=Ultra Light	**H**=Heavy
MF=Moderate Fast	**L**=Light	**MH**=Medium-Heavy
F=Fast	**ML**=Medium-Light	**XH**=Extra Heavy
XF=Extra Fast		

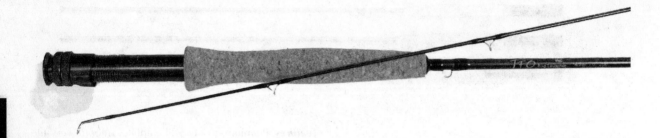

TEMPLE FORK BUG LAUNCHERS

Model: TF BL 4/5, TF BL 5/6
Length: 7'; 8'
Action: F
Pieces: 2
Line Weight: 4W–6W

Features: Thinner diameter compressed cork grips for a better fit in smaller hands; made from general graphite; extended reel seat allows smaller anglers to use two hands for more control.
Price:................................. **$89.95**

TEMPLE FORK LEFTY KREH FINESSE

Model: TF .5 50 3 F, TF 01 69 4 F, TF 02 73 4 F, TF 03 79 4 F, TF 03 89 4 F, TF 04 79 4 F, TF 04 89 4 F, TF 05 79 4 F, TF 05 89 4 F
Length: 5'; 6'9''; 7'3''; 7'9''; 8'9''; 7'9''; 8'9''; 7'9''; 8'9''
Action: M
Pieces: 3; 4; 4; 4; 4; 4; 4; 4; 4
Line Weight: 0.5W–5W
Features: Ideal rods for meadow streams, limestone creeks, and spring creeks; at short to medium distances, these rods cast effortlessly, turning over long leaders easily; shorter lengths are perfect for tight quarters, while the longer length rods will keep a back cast well above tall grasses; handsomely appointed with rosewood inserts on an uplocking reel seat, which nicely accentuates the deep olive finish.
Price:........................... **$179.95–$189.95**

ACTION	POWER	
M=Moderate	UL=Ultra Light	H=Heavy
MF=Moderate Fast	L=Light	MH=Medium-Heavy
F=Fast	ML=Medium-Light	XH=Extra Heavy
XF=Extra Fast		

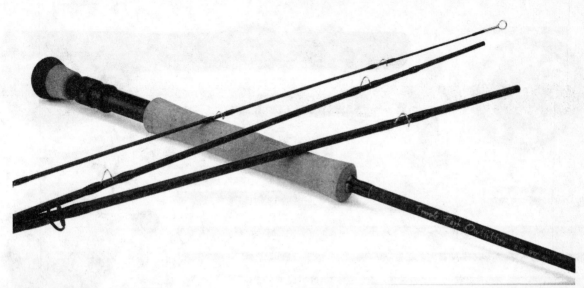

TEMPLE FORK LEFTY KREH PROFESSIONAL SERIES II

Model: TFO 02 80 3 P2, TFO 03 76 4 P2, TFO 04 80 4 P2, TFO 04 86 4 P2, TFO 04 90 4 P2, TFO 05 76 4 P2, TFO 05 86 4 P2, TFO 05 90 4 P2, TFO 05 10 4 P2, TFO 06 90 4 P2, TFO 06 10 4 P2
Length: 8'; 7'6''; 8'6''; 8'; 8'6''; 9'; 7'6''; 8'6''; 9'; 10'; 9'; 10'
Action: MF
Pieces: 3; 4; 4; 4; 4; 4; 4; 4; 4; 4; 4; 4
Line Weight: 2W–6W

Features: Smooth casting and powerful, yet forgiving; perfect rods for all anglers and skill levels; include matte black finished blanks and subtle gold logos; feature alignment dots color coded by line weight, premium grade cork with burled accents, and oversized stripper guides; new anodized reel seats with braided carbon fiber inserts make these rods as forgiving on the eyes as they are in the hand; each rod comes with an attractive rod sock with the logo.
Price: . . . . **$149.95–$199.95**

ACTION		POWER	
M=Moderate		UL=Ultra Light	H=Heavy
MF=Moderate Fast		L=Light	MH=Medium-Heavy
F=Fast		ML=Medium-Light	XH=Extra Heavy
XF=Extra Fast			

RODS

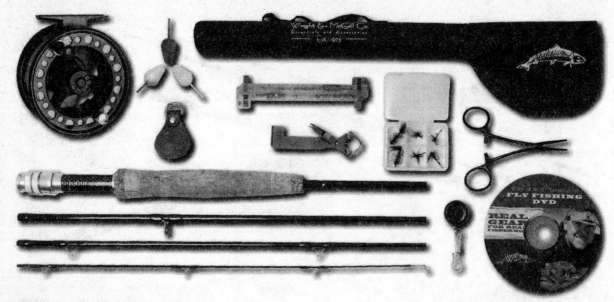

WRIGHT & MCGILL PLUNGE

Model: WMEPC8644, WMEPC954, WMEPC984
Length: 8'6''; 9'; 9'
Power: S
Action: MF
Pieces: 4
Line Weight: 4W–8W
Features: High-modulus graphite, four-piece fly rod in one of two lengths and actions; floating fly line, fly line backing, tapered leader; W & M Power L Nipper, Qwik Drop Shot Dispenser; 5" black forceps; tool retractor; leader straightener; fly box; high float strike indicators; Umpqua fly assortment; travel case; Wright & McGill Essentials of Fly Fishing DVD included.
Price: . . . . $159.99–$169.99

ACTION	POWER	
M=Moderate	UL=Ultra Light	H=Heavy
MF=Moderate Fast	L=Light	MH=Medium-Heavy
F=Fast	ML=Medium-Light	XH=Extra Heavy
XF=Extra Fast		

244 G.Loomis

244 Lamiglas

245 Orvis

246 Redington

248 Rise

249 Sage

251 Scott

252 St. Croix

G.LOOMIS NRX PRO-1
Model: NRX 1068-1 PRO-1, NRX 1068-1 PRO-1 G, NRX 1069-1 PRO-1, NRX 1069-1 PRO-1 G, NRX 10610-1 PRO-1, NRX 10610-1 PRO-1 G, NRX 10611-1 PRO-1, NRX 10611-1 PRO-1 G, NRX 10612-1 PRO-1, NRX 10612-1 PRO-1 G

Length: 8'10"
Power: S
Action: XF
Pieces: 1
Line Weight: 8 W–12 W
Price: . . . .$725–$815

G.LOOMIS NRX SALTWATER
Model: NRX 1087-4 G, NRX 1088-4 G, NRX 1089-4 G, NRX 10810-4 G, NRX 10811-4 G, NRX 10812-4 G, NRX 1087-4, NRX 1088-4, NRX 1089-4, NRX 10810-4, NRX 10811-4, NRX 10812-4
Length: 9'
Power: S
Action: F
Pieces: 4
Line Weight: 7W–12W

Features: Utilize a stiffer, lighter, and higher-density carbon married with Nano Silica resin systems, to create a material that makes the rods lighter, yet more durable; extremely sensitive, and yet stiffer; feature black ion-coated REC recoil guides; custom reel seat has no exposed threads, to make it easy to lock the reel to the reel seat; grips feature HD cork design, where the cork transitions to provide more sensitivity where needed, and more durability where needed.
Price: . . . .$795–$900

LAMIGLAS BUG SLINGER
Model: BS908, BS909, BS910, BS911, BS912
Length: 9'
Action: F
Pieces: 1
Line Weight: 8 W–12 W
Features: We'll place our new Bug Slinger Fly rods up against anything and be highly confident of the outcome.

Smooth, long, effortless casts with perfect balance and control. These are powerful, 1-piece, saltwater specialty fly rods with a backbone tough enough for big tarpon and wily bonefish. A custom machined aluminum reel seat with woven carbon fiber insert anchors the natural black polished graphite blank.
Price: . . . .$425–$495

ACTION		POWER	
M=Moderate	**UL**=Ultra Light	**H**=Heavy	
MF=Moderate Fast	**L**=Light	**MH**=Medium-Heavy	
F=Fast	**ML**=Medium-Light	**XH**=Extra Heavy	
XF=Extra Fast			

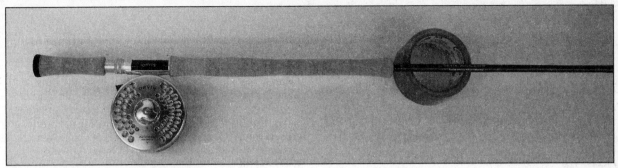

RODS

ORVIS ACCESS SALTWATER
Model: 6-weight 9' Fly Rod—Tip Flex, 6-weight 9'6" Fly Rod—Tip Flex, 7-weight 9' Fly Rod—Tip Flex, 7-weight 10' Fly Rod—Tip Flex, Switch 7-weight 11' Fly Rod—Tip Flex, 8-weight 9' Fly Rod—Mid Flex, 8-weight 9' Fly Rod—Tip Flex, 8-weight 10' Fly Rod—Tip Flex, Switch 8-weight 11' Fly Rod—Tip Flex, 9-weight 9' Fly Rod—Tip Flex, 2-piece, 9-weight 9' Fly Rod—Tip Flex, 10-weight 9' Fly Rod—Tip Flex, 12-weight 9' Fly Rod—Tip Flex
Length: 9' 9'6''; 9'; 10'; 11'; 9'; 9'; 10'; 11'; 9'; 9'; 9'; 9'
Action: F; F; F; F; F; M; F; F; F; F; F; F; F
Pieces: 4; 4; 4; 4; 4; 4; 4; 4; 4; 2; 4; 4; 4
Line Weight: 6W–12W
Features: Contain proprietary carbon-based composite graphite and use a brand-new epoxy-based plasticized

resin system, making the rods very light and very strong; the blank uses tapers that were previously perfected with the Helios; graphite modulus is higher than almost every premium rod on the market; glossy, rootbeer, graphite blank is complemented by the woven graphite reel seat; milled aluminum hardware on the reel seat is anodized in champagne; the reel seat is lightweight, simple, and attractive; sunburst rod wrapping with gold tipping; gold alignment ticks by the rod maker; snake guides are all-chrome, and the stripping guides are black anodized steel; two oversized black anodized stripping guides for distance casting; low-profile cork/rubber fighting butt; super-grade cork handle-half wells shape.
Price: **$425**

ORVIS HELIOS 2 SALTWATER
Model: 6-weight 9' Fly Rod—Tip Flex, 6-weight 9'6" Fly Rod—Tip Flex, 6-weight 10' Fly Rod—Tip Flex, 7-weight 9' Fly Rod—Tip Flex, 7-weight 10' Fly Rod—Tip Flex, 8-weight 9' Fly Rod—Mid Flex, 8-weight 9' Fly Rod—Tip Flex, 8-weight 10' Fly Rod—Tip Flex, 9-weight 9' Fly Rod—Tip Flex, 10-weight 9' Fly Rod—Tip Flex, 11-weight 9' Fly Rod—Tip Flex, 12-weight 9' Fly Rod—Tip Flex, 14-weight 8'6" Fly Rod—Tip Flex
Length: 9'; 9'6''; 10'; 9'; 10'; 9'; 9'; 10'; 9'; 9'; 9'; 9'; 8'6''
Action: F; F; F; F; F; M; F; F; F; F; F; F; F
Pieces: 4
Line Weight: 6W–14W
Features: Winner of six industry awards; 20 percent lighter in hand; 20 percent stronger; 100 percent increase in tip impact; fine-tuned tapers for unrivaled tracking, accuracy, and lifting power.
Price: **$850**

ACTION	POWER	
M=Moderate	UL=Ultra Light	H=Heavy
MF=Moderate Fast	L=Light	MH=Medium-Heavy
F=Fast	ML=Medium-Light	XH=Extra Heavy
XF=Extra Fast		

REDINGTON CLASSIC TROUT
Model: 276-4, 376-4, 386-4, 480-4, 486-4, 490-4, 586-4, 590-4, 690-4, 380-6, 590-6
Length: 7'6''; 7'6''; 8'6''; 8'; 8'6''; 9'; 8'6''; 9'; 9'; 8'; 9'
Action: M
Pieces: 4; 6
Line Weight: 2W–6W

Features: Medium action. Offered in 4-piece and 6-piece configurations. Six-piece offers extreme packability for the backpacking and traveling angler. Titanium oxide stripping guides. Dark clay brown blank with matching rosewood reel seat insert. Custom machined reel seat components. Alignment dots for easy rod set up. Divided brown ballistic Nylon rod tube.
Price:...........................**$149.95–$169.95**

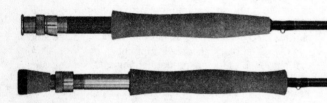

REDINGTON CROSSWATER
Model: 476-2, 580-2, 586-2, 590-2, 690-2, 890-2, 990-2; 590-4; 890-4
Length: 7'6''; 8'; 8'6''; 9'; 9'; 9'; 9'; 9'; 9'
Action: MF
Pieces: 2; 4
Line Weight: 4W–9W
Features: Medium-fast action, attractive trim details and cosmetics. Alignment dots for easy rod set up. Weights

available from 4wt to 9wt for multiple fishing needs. Durable anodized aluminum reel seat, ideal for all fresh- and saltwater applications. Rod comes with black cloth rod sock. Outfits come complete and ready to fish with a Crosswater reel that's prespooled with backing, RIO Mainstream WF fly line, and knotless leader.
Price:...........................**$69.95–$89.95**

ACTION	POWER	
M=Moderate	**UL=Ultra Light**	**H=Heavy**
MF=Moderate Fast	**L=Light**	**MH=Medium-Heavy**
F=Fast	**ML=Medium-Light**	**XH=Extra Heavy**
XF=Extra Fast		

REDINGTON PREDATOR
Model: 6710-4, 690-4, 790-4, 8710-4, 890-4, 983-4, 990-4, 1083-4, 1090-4, 1190-4, 1290-4, 1480-4
Length: 7'10''; 9'; 9'; 7'10''; 9'; 8'3''; 9'; 8'3''; 9'; 9'; 9'; 9'
Action: F
Pieces: 4
Line Weight: 6W–14W
Features: Fast-action power for picking up line and fighting large fish; carbon fiber weave in butt section and at ferrules for improved strength and durability; 54 and 42 million modulus, red core blank; anodized machined aluminum reel seat, ideal for all saltwater applications; durable oversized guides, titanium oxide ring, robust for saltwater and for shooting line for extra distance; gun smoke frame snake and stripping guides, titanium oxide ring; comes with fabric rod tube with dividers.
Price:....................................**$249.95**

REDINGTON VOYANT
Model: 376-4, 486-4, 490-4, 586-4, 590-4, 596-4, 5100-4, 690-4, 696-4, 6100-4, 790-4, 7100-4, 890-4, 990-4, 1090-4
Length: 7'6''; 8'6''; 9'; 8'6''; 9'; 9'6''; 10'; 9'; 9'6''; 10'; 9'; 10'; 9'; 9'; 9'
Action: F
Pieces: 4
Line Weight: 3W–10W
Features: Fast action. Alignment dots for easy rod set up. Half-wells grip (3wt–6wt). Full-wells models (7wt–10wt). Durable anodized aluminum and wood reel seat. Comes in a cloth tube with zippered closure and a black cloth rod bag. Lifetime warranty.
Price:.................................**$189.95**

ACTION	POWER	
M=Moderate	UL=Ultra Light	H=Heavy
MF=Moderate Fast	L=Light	MH=Medium-Heavy
F=Fast	ML=Medium-Light	XH=Extra Heavy
XF=Extra Fast		

RODS: Saltwater Fly Fishing

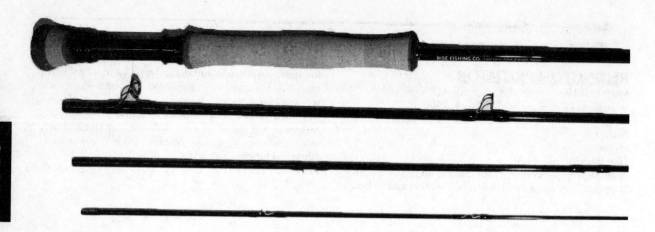

RISE LEVEL SERIES

Model: 90-5wt, 90-6wt, 90-7wt, 90-8wt, 90-9wt, 90-10wt, 90-12wt, 90-14wt
Length: 9'
Action: F
Pieces: 4
Line Weight: 5W–14W
Features: Made from IM8 and IM10 graphite; black

anodized saltwater-safe seat with oversized lightweight chrome guides; fighting butt and cork handle are made from super-grade cork with composite cork accents; rich blue with black wraps; four-piece and comes with a case and lifetime warranty.
Price:. . . . .**$199.99–$299.99**

ACTION	POWER	
M=Moderate	UL=Ultra Light	H=Heavy
MF=Moderate Fast	L=Light	MH=Medium-Heavy
F=Fast	ML=Medium-Light	XH=Extra Heavy
XF=Extra Fast		

SAGE BASS II

Model: Bluegill, Smallmouth, Largemouth, Peacock
Length: 7'11''
Action: F
Pieces: 4
Line Weight: 230 gr; 290 gr; 330 gr; 390 gr
Features: Fast-action graphite III construction, built within tournament specifications; Fuji ceramic stripping guides; hard chromed snake guides; saltwater safe; red anodized aluminum reel seat; custom, pre-shaped cork handle 6½" full-wells grip; fighting butt; olive ballistic cloth rod/reel case; Sage BASS II taper line included.
Price: **$550**

SAGE ONE ELITE 590-4

Model: One Elite 590-4
Length: 9'
Action: F
Pieces: 4
Line Weight: 5W
Features: All-water rod; fast-action Konnetic technology construction; black ice shaft color; black primary thread wraps with gray titanium trim wraps; elite, Flor-grade, snubnose, half-wells cork handle; titanium reel seat with laser-etched logoed end cap; titanium winding check, titanium stripper guides with ceramic insert black hook keeper; extra (spare) tip section.
Price: **$1,350**

ACTION	**POWER**	
M=Moderate	UL=Ultra Light	H=Heavy
MF=Moderate Fast	L=Light	MH=Medium-Heavy
F=Fast	ML=Medium-Light	XH=Extra Heavy
XF=Extra Fast		

RODS

SAGE ONE SERIES

Model: 376-4, 390-4, 486-4, 490-4, 496-4, 4100-4, 586-4, 590-4, 596-4, 5100-4, 690-4, 691-4, 696-4, 697-4, 6100-4, 6101-4, 790-4, 796-4, 7100-4, 890-4, 896-4, 8100-4, 990-4, 1090-4, 1190-4, 1290-4
Length: 7'6''; 9'; 8'6''; 9'; 9'6''; 10'; 8'6''; 9'; 9'6''; 10'; 9'; 9'; 9'6''; 9'6''; 10'; 10'; 9'; 9'6''; 10'; 9'; 9'6''; 10'; 9'; 9'; 9'; 9'
Action: F
Pieces: 4

Line Weight: 3W–12W
Features: Fast-action Konnetic Technology construction; Fuji ceramic stripping guides; hard chromed snake guides; high-grade, custom-tapered, shaped cork handles; walnut wood and golden bronze-colored aluminum anodized freshwater reel seat; weights 6 through 10 have an all golden bronze colored aluminum anodized reel seat; black powder coated aluminum rod tube with Sage medallion.
Price: **$795**

SAGE MOTIVE

Model: 890-4, 990-4, 1090-4, 1190-4, 1290-4
Length: 9'
Action: F
Pieces: 4
Line Weight: 8 W–12 W

Features: Saltwater series; fast action; new taper design; bluefin blue color blank; blue primary thread wraps with royal blue and black trim wraps; aluminum reel seat with hidden hook keepers; full-wells grip; blue steel divided ballistic nylon rod tube with divided liner.
Price: **$425**

ACTION		POWER	
M=Moderate	**UL**=Ultra Light	**H**=Heavy	
MF=Moderate Fast	**L**=Light	**MH**=Medium-Heavy	
F=Fast	**ML**=Medium-Light	**XH**=Extra Heavy	
XF=Extra Fast			

SCOTT S4S

Model: 908/2, 909/2; 9010/2; 9011/2; 9012/2; 905/4; 806/4; 906/4; 907/4; 808/4; 908/4; 909/4; 8010/4; 9010/4; 9011/4; 9012/4; 8813/4
Length: 9'; 9'; 9'; 9'; 9'; 9'; 8'; 9'; 9'; 8'; 9'; 9'; 8'; 9'; 9'; 9'; 8'8''
Pieces: 2; 2; 2; 2; 2; 4; 4; 4; 4; 4; 4; 4; 4; 4; 4; 4; 4
Line Weight: 8W–13W

Features: X-core technology; enhanced feel, incredible stability, and unequalled performance; Mil-Spec III anodized reel seats and titanium; titanium guides offer the highest levels of corrosion resistance; Advanced Reinforced Carbo reduces torque and increases strength; handcrafted in the USA—built from beginning to end in Montrose, Colorado.
Price: **$775**

ACTION	POWER	
M=Moderate	UL=Ultra Light	H=Heavy
MF=Moderate Fast	L=Light	MH=Medium-Heavy
F=Fast	ML=Medium-Light	XH=Extra Heavy
XF=Extra Fast		

RODS: Saltwater Fly Fishing

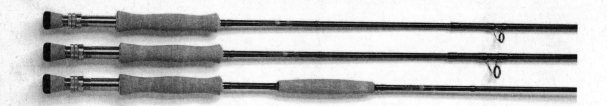

ST. CROIX LEGEND ELITE SALTWATER

Model: ESW906.4, ESW907.4, ESW908.4, ESW909.4, ESW9010.4, ESW9012.4, ESW9012.4.FG
Length: 9'
Action: F
Pieces: 4
Line Weight: 6W–12W
Features: Integrated Poly Curve tooling technology; Advanced Reinforcing Technology; super high-modulus SCVI graphite with NSi resin in lower section for added power with reduced weight; featuring 3M Powerlux resin for unparalleled strength and durability; high-modulus/high-strain SCV graphite with NSi resin and carbon-matte scrim; slim-profile ferrules; one-piece performance in four-piece designs; max-power butt sections for handling powerful fish and stiff winds; Fuji MN Saltwater Alconite stripper guides with chrome frames; hard chrome snake guides; REC hard-anodized aluminum reel seat; Flora-grade cork handle; two coats of Flex Coat slow-cure finish; alignment dots; rugged rod case with handle and divided polypropylene liner; lifetime limited warranty.
Price:................................$470–$540

ST. CROIX LEGEND X SALTWATER

Model: LXF907.4, LXF908.4, LXF909.4, LXF9010.4
Length: 9'
Action: MF
Pieces: 4
Line Weight: 7 W–10 W
Features: To the gentle readers who still think fly fishing is nothing more than the quiet pastime of stately figures in tweed, we have someone we'd like you to meet. Yeah, that's right, the guy over there with the musky on his line, a buzz from the action, and a brand new St. Croix Legend X fly rod in his hand. This revolutionary fly rod series is just what the counter-fly-culture crowd has been craving. A beefy, multi-dynamic blend of four carbon materials capable of getting big flies out to the meanest predatory fish—bass, pike, and musky. Loaded with IPC and ART, these bad boys put it all right there, and then some. Wrap your hands around the grip of a Legend X and hang on.
Price:................................$500–$520

ACTION	POWER	
M=Moderate	UL=Ultra Light	H=Heavy
MF=Moderate Fast	L=Light	MH=Medium-Heavy
F=Fast	ML=Medium-Light	XH=Extra Heavy
XF=Extra Fast		

ABU GARCIA CARDINAL S

Model: 5, 10, 20, 30, 40, 60
Gear Ratio: 5.2:1; 5.2:1; 5.1:1; 5.1:1; 5.1:1; 4.8:1
Inches/Turn: 20.5; 21; 27; 29; 29; 30
Retrieve Speed: Std
Spool Cap. (M): 4 lbs/100 yds; 6 lbs/110 yds; 8 lbs/130 yds; 8 lbs/175 yds; 12 lbs/180 yds; 14 lbs/205 yds
Spool Cap. (B): 4 lbs/160 yds; 6 lbs/150 yds; 8 lbs/190 yds; 10 lbs/180 yds; 14 lbs/210 yds; 20 lbs/200 yds
Weight: 6.3 oz; 6.8 oz; 8.68 oz; 9.1 oz; 9.6 oz; 13.1 oz

Hand Retrieve: R or L
Max Drag: 6 lbs; 6 lbs; 14 lbs; 14 lbs; 14 lbs; 20 lbs
Features: Three ball bearings plus one roller bearing provides smooth operation; lightweight graphite body and rotor; machined aluminum spool provides strength without adding excess weight; Everlast bail system for improved durability; slow oscillation provides even line lay with all types of line.
Price:.............................$29.99–$39.99

ABU GARCIA CARDINAL STX

Model: 5, 10, 20, 30, 40
Gear Ratio: 5.2:1; 5.2:1; 5.1:1; 5.1:1; 5.1:1
Inches/Turn: 20.5; 21; 27; 29; 29
Retrieve Speed: Std
Spool Cap. (M): 4 lbs/100 yds; 6 lbs/110 yds; 8 lbs/130 yds; 8 lbs/175 yds; 12 lbs/180 yds
Spool Cap. (B): 4 lbs/160 yds; 6 lbs/150 yds; 8 lbs/190 yds; 10 lbs/180 yds; 14 lbs/210 yds
Weight: 6.4 oz; 6.9 oz; 8.9 oz; 9.2 oz; 9.7 oz

Hand Retrieve: R or L
Max Drag: 6 lbs; 6 lbs; 14 lbs; 14 lbs; 14 lbs
Features: Six ball bearings plus one roller bearing provides smooth operation; lightweight graphite body and rotor; machined aluminum spool provides strength without adding excess weight; Everlast bail system for improved durability; slow oscillation provides even line lay with all types of line.
Price:...................................$49.99

ABU GARCIA CARDINAL SX

Model: 5, 10, 20, 30, 40
Gear Ratio: 5.2:1; 5.2:1; 5.1:1; 5.1:1; 5.1:1
Inches/Turn: 20.5; 21; 27; 29; 29
Retrieve Speed: Std
Spool Cap. (M): 4 lbs/100 yds; 6 lbs/110 yds; 8 lbs/130 yds; 8 lbs/175 yds; 12 lbs/180 yds
Spool Cap. (B): 4 lbs/160 yds; 6 lbs/150 yds; 8 lbs/190 yds; 10 lbs/180 yds; 14 lbs/210 yds
Weight: 6.4 oz; 6.9 oz; 8.8 oz; 9.2 oz; 9.7 oz

Hand Retrieve: R or L
Max Drag: 6 lbs; 6 lbs; 14 lbs; 14 lbs; 14 lbs
Features: Five ball bearings plus one roller bearing provides smooth operation; lightweight graphite body and rotor; machined aluminum spool provides strength without adding excess weight; Everlast bail system for improved durability; slow oscillation provides even line lay with all types of line.
Price: **$39.99**

ABU GARCIA ORRA S

Model: 10, 20, 30, 40
Gear Ratio: 5.2:1; 5.8:1; 5.8:1; 5.8:1
Inches/Turn: 24.5; 31; 33; 33
Retrieve Speed: Std
Spool Cap. (B): 6 lbs/150 yds; 8 lbs/130 yds; 8 lbs/175 yds; 10 lbs/210 yds
Weight: 7.8 oz; 8.7 oz; 9.2 oz; 10.2 oz
Hand Retrieve: R or L
Max Drag: 10 lbs; 12 lbs; 12 lbs; 18 lbs
Features: Six stainless steel HPCR bearings plus one roller bearing provides increased corrosion protection; one-piece gear box design allows for more precise gear alignment for smoother operation; machined aluminum braid ready spool allows braid to be tied directly to the spool without any slip; Hybrid Carbon Matrix drag system for super smooth reliable drag performance; slow oscillation provides even line lay with all types of line; X-Cräftic alloy frame for increased corrosion resistance; Duragear brass gear for extended gear life; Everlast bail system for improved durability; stainless steel main shaft and components for improved corrosion resistance.
Price: **$69.95**

ABU GARCIA ORRA SX

Model: 10, 20, 30, 40, 60
Gear Ratio: 5.2:1; 5.8:1; 5.8:1; 5.8:1; 4.8:1
Retrieve Speed: Std
Spool Cap. (M): 4 lbs/110 yds; 4 lbs/135 yds; 6 lbs/125 yds; 8 lbs/125 yds; 17 lbs/250 yds
Spool Cap. (B): 6 lbs/125 yds; 8 lbs/125 yds; 10 lbs/125 yds; 14 lbs/125 yds; 20 lbs/200 yds
Weight: 8.1 oz; 9.1 ozs; 9.5 oz; 10.8 oz; 13.6 oz
Hand Retrieve: R or L

Max Drag: 10 lbs; 12 lbs; 12 lbs; 18 lbs; 20 lbs
Features: Seven stainless steel ball bearings plus one roller bearing provides smooth operation; X-Cräftic alloy frame for increased corrosion resistance; graphite sideplates; Power Disk drag system gives smooth drag performance; MagTrax brake system gives consistent brake pressure throughout the cast; compact bent handle and star provide a more ergonomic design; Duragear brass gear for extended gear life.
Price:.................................... $99.95

ABU GARCIA REVO S

Model: 20, 40, 10, 30
Gear Ratio: 5.1:1; 5.8:1; 5.2:1; 5.8:2
Inches/Turn: 27; 33; 25; 33
Retrieve Speed: Std
Spool Cap. (M): 8 lbs/130 yds; 12 lbs/180 yds; 6 lbs/110 yds; 10 lbs/140 yds
Spool Cap. (B): 8 lbs/190 yds; 14 lbs/210 yds; 6 lbs/150 yds; 10 lbs/180 yds
Weight: 8.2 oz; 10.1 oz; 7.44 oz; 9.0 oz
Hand Retrieve: R or L

Max Drag: 12 lbs; 18 lbs; 9 lbs; 12 lbs
Features: Seven stainless steel ball bearings plus one roller bearing provides smooth operation; X2-Cräftic alloy frame for increased corrosion resistance; lightweight graphite sideplates; Carbon Matrix drag system provides smooth, consistent drag pressure across the entire drag range; D2 Gear Design provides a more efficient gear system while improving gear durability; pitch centrifugal brake system; compact bent handle and star provide a more ergonomic design.
Price:....................................$129.95

ABU GARCIA REVO SX
Model: 10, 20, 30, 40
Gear Ratio: 5.2:1; 5.1:1; 5.8:1; 5.8:1
Inches/Turn: 25; 27; 33; 33
Retrieve Speed: Std
Spool Cap. (M): 4 lbs/110 yds; 4 lbs/135 yds; 6 lbs/125 yds; 8 lbs/125 yds
Spool Cap. (B): 6 lbs/125 yds; 8 lbs/125 yds; 10 lbs/125 yds; 14 lbs/125 yds
Weight: 7.44 oz; 8.2 oz; 8.9 oz; 10.2 oz
Hand Retrieve: R or L
Max Drag: 9 lbs; 12 lbs; 12 lbs
Features: Nine stainless steel ball bearings plus one roller bearing provides smooth operation; X2-Cräftic alloy frame for increased corrosion resistance; C6 carbon handle sideplate provides significant weight reduction without sacrificing strength and durability; Carbon Matrix drag system provides smooth, consistent drag pressure across the entire drag range; D2 Gear Design provides a more efficient gear system while improving gear durability; MagTrax brake system gives consistent brake pressure throughout the cast; Infini II spool design for extended castability and extreme loads; compact bent handle and star provide a more ergonomic design; titanium-coated line guide reduces friction and improves durability.
Price: $159.95

BASS PRO SHOPS CATMAXX
Model: 70, 80
Gear Ratio: 4.5:1
Inches/Turn: 22
Spool Cap. (M): 25 lbs/190 yds; 25 lbs/290 yds
Weight: 25.2 oz; 26.3 oz
Hand Retrieve: R or L
Max Drag: 37.4 lbs; 39.6 lbs
Reel Bearings: 3+1
Features: Built on abuse-absorbing graphite bodies; 100 percent aluminum spools; feature a quality four-bearing system including PowerLock instant anti-reverse; easy handling, great drag system, big line capacity, and oversized machined-aluminum handle.
Price: $49.99

REELS: Freshwater Spinning

BASS PRO SHOPS CRAPPIE MAX
Model: 750, 1000
Gear Ratio: 5.6:1
Inches/Turn: 24
Spool Cap. (M): 4 lbs/160 yds; 6 lbs; 160 yds
Weight: 5.1 oz; 6.9 oz
Hand Retrieve: R or L
Reel Bearings: 3

Features: Full graphite frame and sidecover; gold-anodized aluminum spool; stainless steel bail wire; hard chrome-plated line roller; ultra-smooth with three chrome-plated steel ball bearings, plus 18-point multi-stop anti-reverse for lightning-fast response time; die-cast handle, soft rubber paddle, and free graphite spare spool.
Price: **$21.99**

BASS PRO SHOPS EXTREME
Model: 10B, 20B, 40B, 50B
Gear Ratio: 5.6:1; 5.1:1; 5.1:1; 5.1:1
Inches/Turn: 31; 33; 36; 40
Spool Cap. (M): 6 lbs/90 yds; 8 lbs/80 yds; 12 lbs/115 yds; 12 lbs/200 yds
Weight: 7.5 oz; 10.4 oz; 11 oz; 11 oz
Hand Retrieve: R or L

Max Drag: 19.5 lbs; 19.5 lbs; 22 lbs; 22 lbs
Reel Bearings: 5+1
Features: Standard features include: one-piece aluminum frame with sealed sideplates; ported, forged aluminum spool; super-light graphite rotor; left- or right-hand retrieve; stainless steel shaft and bail wire; titanium nitride-coated roller; machined-aluminum handle with soft-touch knob.
Price: **$59.99**

BASS PRO SHOPS PRO QUALIFIER
Model: 10, 20, 20H, 40, 40H, 50
Gear Ratio: 5.6:1; 5.1:1; 6.1:1; 5.1:1; 6.1:1; 5.1:1
Inches/Turn: 31; 33; 39; 36; 43; 40
Spool Cap. (M): 6 lbs/90 yds; 8 lbs/80 yds; 8 lbs/80 yds; 12 lbs/115 yds; 12 lbs/115 yds; 14 lbs/160 yds
Weight: 7.5 oz; 10.4 oz; 10.4 oz; 11 oz; 11 oz; 11 oz
Hand Retrieve: R or L
Max Drag: 19.5 lbs; 19.5 lbs; 19.5 lbs; 22 lbs; 22 lbs; 22 lbs

Reel Bearings: 7+1
Features: Ultra-slim body design, popular Mag Spool Technology and premium eight-bearing system with double-shielded stainless steel ball bearings and Powerlock instant anti-reverse; carbon fiber sealed drag, a major upgrade for long-term smoothness, power, and consistency; lightweight anodized-aluminum body/sidecovers; forged-aluminum spool; stainless steel bail wire and mainshaft; strong machined-aluminum handle.
Price:. **$69.99**

CABELA'S FISH EAGLE TOURNAMENT II
Model: 1000A, 2000A, 25000A, 3000A
Gear Ratio: 5.2:1
Spool Cap. (M): 4 lbs/115 yds; 6 lbs/115 yds; 8 lbs/145 yds; 10 lbs/195 yds
Weight: 8.4 oz; 9.9 oz; 11.7 oz; 12.4 oz
Hand Retrieve: R or L
Reel Bearings: 5+1

Features: The aluminum spool with its titanium-coated spool lip combines power with the anti-twist titanium line roller for superior winding and even line lay that translates into longer casts with less kinks; the five-bearing system and one-way clutch bearing offer amazingly smooth retrieves; lightweight, sturdy graphite body and rotor; aluminum fold-down handle.
Price:. **$39.99**

REELS: Freshwater Spinning

CABELA'S FISH EAGLE UL
Model: 500ULX, 2000X, 2500X, 3000X
Gear Ratio: 5.2:1
Spool Cap. (M): 6 lbs/110 yds; 8 lbs/140 yds; 12 lbs/180 yds; 4 lbs/100 yds.
Weight: 6.8 oz; 8.8 oz; 10 oz; 6.3 oz
Hand Retrieve: R or L
Reel Bearings: 4+1

Features: 4+1 bearings for ultrasmooth retrieves. Instant anti-reverse with on/off switch. Everlast oversized bail system. Aluminum spool and Stealth Oscillation for even line lay. Aluminum handle with soft-touch paddle knob. Adjustable for left- or right-hand retrieve. Graphite body and rotor.
Price: **$29.99**

CABELA'S PRO GUIDE
Model: 3000
Gear Ratio: 6.2:1
Spool Cap. (M): 10 lbs/195 yds
Weight: 11 oz
Hand Retrieve: R or L
Max Drag: 14 lbs
Reel Bearings: 9+1

Features: Ten-bearing system for smooth casts and a one-way instant anti-reverse clutch for solid hooksets; the main spool is aluminum, while the body is a hybrid of metal and graphite for lightweight strength; anti-twist, titanium-coated line roller; convertible aluminum fold-down handle.
Price: **$49.99**

CABELA'S VERANO
Model: 2000VRN, 2500VRN, 3500VRN
Gear Ration: 6.0:1; 6.0:1; 6.2:1
Inches/Turn: 31.1; 35; 41.3
Spool Cap. (M): 6 lbs/135 yds; 8 lbs/170 yds; 16 lbs/220 yds
Weight: 7.6 oz; 8.5 oz; 17.6 oz

Hand Retrieve: R or L
Max Drag: 8.8 lbs; 15.4 lbs; 17.6 lbs
Reel Bearings: 9+1
Features: Engineered by Daiwa Lightweight; corrosion-resistant Zaion body; spool's rearward taper helps prevent tangles; waterproof drag with click adjustment.
Price:....................................**$149.99**

DAIWA LEXA
Model: 1500SH, 2500SH, 3500SH
Gear Ratio: 6.0:1; 6.0:1; 6.2:1
Inches/Turn: 29.9; 35; 41.3
Spool Cap. (M): 4 lbs/155 yds; 6 lbs/210 yds
Weight: 8.1 oz; 8.9 oz; 12.2 oz
Hand Retrieve: R or L
Max Drag: 8.8 lbs; 8.8 lbs; 17.6 lbs
Reel Bearings: 4+1

Features: A hollow air bail is super strong yet light in weight, with no protrusions to snag line; air rotor weighs up to 15 percent less than ordinary rotors; features aluminum construction, a felt-sealed body, and digital gear design; advanced locomotive levelwind promotes precise, even line winding; smooth performance and feel from a five-bearing system; infinite anti-reverse; an ABS aluminum spool, for long casts with fewer snarls; Twist Buster II line twist reduction; and a lifetime bail spring.
Price:........................ **$119.95–$129.95**

DAIWA SS TOURNAMENT
Model: 700, 1300, 1600, 2600
Gear Ratio: 4.9:1; 5.1:1; 4.9:1; 4.6:1
Inches/Turn: 26; 32; 28.7; 29.9
Spool Cap. (M): 4 lbs/145 yds; 6 lbs/240 yds; 10 lbs/210 yds; 10 lbs/210 yds
Weight: 7 oz; 8.5 oz; 11.5 oz; 13.7 oz
Hand Retrieve: R or L
Max Drag: 8.8 lbs; 15.4 lbs; 15.4 lbs; 17.6 lbs

Reel Bearings: 3
Features: Long-cast technology; exclusive worm gear for perfect line winding; three stainless steel bearings; aluminum spool; super-smooth drag with oversized felt/stainless discs and precision click adjustment; SiC line roller; lifetime bail spring; right- or left-hand retrieve.
Price:. . . . . **$104.95–$114.95**

DAIWA STEEZ
Model: 2500, 2508
Gear Ratio: 4.8:1
Inches/Turn: 27.9
Spool Cap. (M): 8 lbs/110 yds; 8 lbs/170 yds
Weight: 6.9 oz; 7 oz
Hand Retrieve: R or L
Max Drag: 15.4 lbs
Reel Bearings: 11+1
Features: The lightest reels of their kind; air metal magnesium body, side-cover, and rotor; air spool (ultra-lightweight composite) with reverse-taper (ABS) design; Digigear digital gear design; eleven CRBB; super corrosion-resistant ball bearings plus roller bearing; tubular stainless air bail; infinite anti-reverse; advanced locomotive levelwind; washable design with sealed, waterproof drag system; precision, super micro-pitch drag adjustment; pillar-type tight oscillation system; ultra-quiet and smooth precision; stainless main shaft.
Price:. **$529.95**

DAIWA STEEZ EX

Model: 2508H, 3012H
Gear Ratio: 5.6:1
Inches/Turn: 33
Spool Cap. (M): 8 lbs/110 yds; 8 lbs/170 yds
Weight: 6.8 oz; 8.5 oz
Hand Retrieve: R or L
Max Drag: 15.4 lbs
Reel Bearings: 12+1
Features: Built for fresh or salt water with ultra-lightweight, corrosion-proof Zaion body and air rotor; mag-sealed construction (body and line roller); max drag 15.4 pounds; 13 bearing system (7 CRBB/5BB+1RB); Digigear digital gear design for speed, power and durability; lightweight, hollow, stainless steel air bail; machined aluminum handle with cork knob; silent oscillation; ABS air spool with cut-proof, titanium nitride spool lip; infinite anti-reverse; and neoprene reel bag.
Price: . . . . $749.95–$799.95

DAIWA TOURNAMENT BASIA QD

Model: 45QDA
Gear Ratio: 4.1:1
Inches/Turn: 34.7
Spool Cap. (M): 12 lbs/260 yds
Weight: 18.5 oz
Hand Retrieve: R or L
Max Drag: 22 lbs
Features: Large diameter aluminum ABS long-cast spool has been combined with immaculate line lay to deliver a casting experience that seems more like a dream than reality; features include a machined alloy handle and a magnesium alloy body and rotor; superb quick drag offers the perfect crossover from front drag to free spool, without the need for conversions; drilled holes on the spool skirt allow light in for identifying the running reel much more quickly; extreme durability with superior performance.
Price: $599.95

DAIWA WINDCAST Z CARP
Model: 5000, 5500
Gear Ratio: 4.9:1
Inches/Turn: 40
Spool Cap. (M): 17 lbs/310 yds; 25 lbs/230 yds
Weight: 20.5 oz
Hand Retrieve: R or L
Max Drag: 20.5 lbs
Reel Bearings: 8+1
Features: Designed primarily for carp fishing, these are fast, distance-casting reels that are well matched to a variety of fishing styles; a tapered spool delivers high-speed line release for distance casting—a feature that's also enhanced by a traveling line guard; a quick drag allows big fish anglers to cross over between the free spool mode and the drag engaged, with less than one turn of the drag knob; eight corrosion-resistant ball bearings and long-cast spool make it ideal for the surf as well; other features include an aluminum wishbone handle, a high-impact HIP clip, and a built-in cushion on the pin for forgiving but secure line location.
Price: **$229.95**

LEW'S GOLD SPIN HIGH SPEED SPIN
Model: 1000H, 2000H, 3000H, 4000H
Gear Ratio: 5.6:1; 6.1:1; 6.1:1; 6.1:1
Inches/Turn: 25; 31; 34; 38
Spool Cap. (M): 6 lbs/150 yds; 8 lbs/140 yds; 10 lbs/140 yds; 12 lbs/160 yds
Weight: 6.3 oz; 7.3 oz; 7.4 oz; 8.5 oz
Hand Retrieve: R or L
Reel Bearings: 9+1
Features: The high-speed Gold series features the lightweight high-strength C40 carbon body and side cover to meet anglers' most demanding expectations for spinning reels that are lighter, faster, and stronger.
Price: **$129.99**

LEW'S LASER SPEED SPIN

Model: 100, 200, 300, 400
Gear Ratio: 5.2:1
Inches/Turn: 22; 26; 31; 33
Spool Cap. (M): 6 lbs/170 yds; 6 lbs/150 yds; 10 lbs/180 yds; 12 lbs/195 yds.
Weight: 8.7 oz; 8.9 oz; 9.9 oz; 10.4 oz
Hand Retrieve: R or L
Reel Bearings: 9+1

Features: Quality ten-bearing system; rugged graphite body and rotor with metallic paint; double-anodized aluminum spool with holes and gold accent lines; larger diameter spool for longer casting and faster line retrieve; strong and balanced thick aluminum bail; thin compact gear box; zero-reverse one-way clutch bearing; aluminum handle with performance handle knob; adjustable for right- or left-hand retrieve; speed lube for exceptional smoothness and performance in all temperatures.
Price: **$39.99**

LEW'S LASER LITE SPEED SPIN

Model: 50, 75, 100
Gear Ratio: 5.2:1
Inches/Turn: 22; 23; 24
Spool Cap. (M): 4 lbs/80 yds; 6 lbs/80 yds; 6 lbs/90 yds
Weight: 6.0 oz; 6.4 oz; 6.7 oz
Hand Retrieve: R or L
Reel Bearings: 6+1

Features: Rugged graphite body and rotor; double-anodized aluminum spool with holes and gold accent lines; larger diameter spool for longer casts and faster line retrieve; strong and balanced thick aluminum bail; thin compact gear box; seven-bearing system, zero-reverse one-way clutch bearing; machined aluminum handle with soft-touch knob; adjustable for right- or left-hand retrieve; speed lube for exceptional smoothness and uninterrupted performance in all weather conditions; oversized multiple disc drag system for smooth performance.
Price: **$29.99**

LEW'S TOURNAMENT HIGH-SPEED SPEED SPIN

Model: 100H; 200H; 300H; 400H
Gear Ratio: 5.6:1; 6.1:1; 6.1:1; 6.1:1
Inches/Turn: 25; 31; 34; 38
Spool Cap. (M): 6 lbs/150 yds; 8lbs/140 yds; 10 lbs/140 yds; 12 lbs/160 yds
Weight: 6.9 oz; 8.3 oz; 8.4 oz; 9.6 oz
Hand Retrieve: R or L
Reel Bearings: 9+1
Features: Premium ten stainless steel bearing system; zero-reverse one-way clutch bearing; rugged graphite body and side cover; Digi-balanced graphite rotor with stainless; durable stainless steel main shaft; external stainless steel screws; machine-cut aluminum handle; smooth carbon Teflon multi-disc sealed drag system; quality solid brass pinion gearing; durable stainless steel main shaft; parallel line lay oscillation system; oversized titanium line roller to reduce line twist; double-anodized ported aluminum spool; external stainless steel; screws; adjustable right- or left-hand retrieve; speed lube for exceptional smoothness and performance in all temperatures; designed for use in fresh and salt water.
Price: **$79.99**

OKUMA DEAD EYE

Model: 25, 30
Gear Ratio: 5.0:1
Inches/Turn: 25
Spool Cap. (M): 4 lbs/310 yds; 4 lbs/355 yds
Weight: 8 oz; 7.8 oz
Hand Retrieve: R or L
Max Drag: 8 lbs; 13 lbs
Reel Bearings: 5+1
Features: Multi-disc, Japanese-oiled felt drag system; rigid, forged aluminum handle design with EVA handle knob; 5BB+1RB ball bearings for ultimate smoothness; quick-set anti-reverse roller bearing; precision machine-cut brass pinion gear; lightweight, corrosion-resistant frame & sideplates; machined aluminum, two-tone anodized spool; precision elliptical gearing system; Hydro Block watertight drag seal; RESII: computer-balanced rotor equalizing system; corrosion-resistant, stainless steel bail wire; one-year limited warranty.
Price: . . . . **$42.99–$99.99**

OKUMA EPIXOR

Model: 20b, 25b, 30b, 40b, 55b
Gear Ratio: 5.0:1; 5.0:1; 5.0:1; 5.0:1; 4.9:1
Inches/Turn: 22; 24.5; 25; 28; 30
Spool Cap. (M): 4 lbs/190 yds; 6 lbs/180 yds; 6 lbs/200 yds; 8 lbs/270 yds; 10 lbs/380 yds
Weight: 8 oz; 8.7 oz; 10.1 oz; 10.6 oz; 14.8 oz
Hand Retrieve: R or L
Max Drag: 8 lbs; 8 lbs; 13 lbs; 13 lbs; 18 lbs
Reel Bearings: 9+1

Features: Multi-disc, Japanese-oiled felt drag system; rigid, forged aluminum handle design with EVA handle knob; 5BB+1RB ball bearings for ultimate smoothness; quick-set anti-reverse roller bearing; precision machine-cut brass pinion gear; lightweight, corrosion-resistant frame and sideplates; machined aluminum, two-tone anodized spool; precision elliptical gearing system; Hydro Block watertight drag seal; RESII: computer balanced rotor equalizing system; corrosion-resistant, stainless steel bail wire; one-year limited warranty.
Price: . . . . **$64.99–$74.99**

OKUMA EPIXOR BAITFEEDER

Model: 30, 50, 65, 80
Gear Ratio: 5.0:1; 4.5:1; 4.5:1; 4.5:1
Inches/Turn: 27; 31; 36; 40
Spool Cap. (M): 6 lbs/330 yds; 10 lbs/440 yds ; 12 lbs/540 yds; 15 lbs/510 yds
Weight: 12.2 oz; 17.4 oz; 26.7 oz; 28.1 oz
Hand Retrieve: R or L
Max Drag: 12 lbs; 17 lbs; 22 lbs; 22 lbs
Reel Bearings: 9+1

Features: On/off auto-trip bait feeding system; multi-disc, Japanese-oiled felt drag system; nine stainless steel ball bearings; one quick-set anti-reverse roller bearing; precision machine-cut brass pinion gear; corrosion-resistant graphite body; machined aluminum, two-tone anodized and ported spool; rigid, forged aluminum handle design; S-curve oscillation system; Hydro Block water tight drag seal; corrosion-resistant, stainless steel bail wire; RESII: computer balanced rotor equalizing system; one-year warranty.
Price: . . . . **$99.99–$109.99**

REELS: **Freshwater Spinning**

OKUMA RTX HIGH SPEED
Model: 25S, 30S, 35S, 40S
Gear Ratio: 6.0:1
Inches/Turn: 29.5; 30; 33.5; 34
Spool Cap. (M): 4 lbs/310 yds; 4 lbs/355 yds; 6 lbs/325 yds; 8 lbs/325 yds
Weight: 6.6 oz; 6.6 oz; 8.6 oz; 8.2 oz
Hand Retrieve: R or L
Max Drag: 8 lbs; 13 lbs; 13 lbs; 13 lbs
Reel Bearings: 7+1

Features: Extremely lightweight C-40X carbon frame, sideplate and rotor; multi-disc, Japanese-oiled felt drag system; 7BB+1RB stainless steel ball bearings; quick-set anti-reverse roller bearing; precision Alumilite alloy main gear and oscillating gears; machined aluminum, two-tone anodized spool; precision elliptical gearing system; rigid, forged aluminum handle design with EVA handle knob; Hydro Block watertight drag seal; durable one-piece solid aluminum, gun smoke anodized bail wire; RESII: computer balanced rotor equalizing system; one-year limited warranty.
Price:. . . . . **$99.99–$134.99**

OKUMA TRIO HIGH SPEED
Model: 30S, 40S, 55S
Gear Ratio: 6.0:1
Inches/Turn: 30; 34; 40
Spool Cap. (M): 6 lbs/200 yds; 8 lbs/270 yds; 10 lbs/380 yds
Weight: 10.4 oz; 10.8 oz; 14.7 oz
Hand Retrieve: R or L
Max Drag: 18 lbs; 20 lbs; 24 lbs
Reel Bearings: 9+1
Features: An intelligently designed, agile, and rugged performer for all freshwater and inshore saltwater fishing applications; available in both standard gearing and high-speed models; multi-disc, Japanese-oiled felt drag washers; dual force drag system; 9BB+1RB stainless steel bearings; quick-set anti-reverse roller bearing; precision machine-cut brass pinion gear; corrosion-resistant coating process; corrosion-resistant, high-density gearing; crossover aluminum and graphite hybrid body design; crossover aluminum and graphite hybrid rotor design; patented elliptical oscillation system; hybrid spool design with graphite arbor and aluminum lip; aluminum drag chamber precision spool system; rigid, forged aluminum handle design; Hydro Block watertight drag seal; heavy-duty, solid aluminum, anodized bail wire; RESII: computer balanced rotor equalizing system; one-year warranty.
Price:. . . . . **$74.99–$89.99**

PENN Z SERIES

Model: 704Z; 706Z (bail-less)
Gear Ratio: 3.8:1
Inches/Turn: 30; 33
Spool Cap. (M): 15 lbs/345 yds; 20 lbs/295 yds
Spool Cap. (B): 30 lbs/465 yds; 50 lbs/400 yds
Weight: 23.5 oz; 22.8 oz
Hand Retrieve: L

Max Drag: 15 lbs
Reel Bearings: 1; 3
Features: Full metal body with graphite sideplate; HT-100 carbon fiber drag washers; machine-cut brass main gear with stainless steel pinion gear; machined and anodized aluminum spool.
Price: $199.99

PFLUEGER ARBOR

Model: 7430X; 7435X; 7440X; 7450X
Gear Ratio: 4.3:1
Inches/Turn: 25; 26.6; 29.7; 32.4
Spool Cap. (M): 6 lbs/120 yds; 8 lbs/155 yds; 10 lbs/150 yds; 12 lbs/225 yds
Spool Cap. (B): 8 lbs/160 yds; 10 lbs/195 yds; 15 lbs/250 yds; 15 lbs/330 yds
Hand Retrieve: R or L
Max Drag: 10 lbs; 10 lbs; 18 lbs; 25 lbs
Reel Bearings: 7+1

Features: Seven stainless steel ball bearings; on/off instant anti-reverse bearing; lightweight hybrid construction provides the strength of an aluminum body without the weight; lightweight graphite rotor; large arbor spool design for maximum line control; machined, ported, and double anodized braid ready aluminum spool; smoothed sealed carbon fiber drag system; solid aluminum bail wire; sure-click bail provides an audible signal when bail is fully opened and ready to cast; spare aluminum spool; convertible right- or left-hand retrieve.
Price: $79.95

REELS: Freshwater Spinning

REELS

PFLUEGER PATRIARCH

Model: 9525X; 9530X; 9535X; 9540X
Gear Ratio: 05:02.1
Inches/Turn: 24.5; 27; 28.8; 32.7
Spool Cap. (M): 4 lbs/110 yds; 6 lbs/120 yds; 8 lbs/140 yds; 10 lbs/170 yds
Spool Cap. (B): 6 lbs/110 yds; 8 lbs/115 yds; 10 lbs/150 yds; 14 lbs/160 yds
Hand Retrieve: R or L
Max Drag: 8 lbs; 8 lbs; 16 lbs; 16 lbs
Reel Bearings: 9+1

Features: The ultra lightweight, magnesium body, rotor, and sideplate are protected with proprietary three-step coating to provide premium corrosion resistance and durability; its solid titanium main shaft is 30 percent stronger and 43 percent lighter than comparable stainless steel shafts; carbon handle with EVA knob is 20 percent lighter than comparable aluminum handles; sealed carbon drag system and durable titanium-coated line roller.
Price:. $199.95

PFLUEGER PRESIDENT

Model: 6920X; 6925X; 6930X; 6935X; 6940X
Gear Ratio: 5.2:1
Inches/Turn: 20.7; 22.4; 25.2; 27.4; 30.2
Spool Cap. (M): 4 lbs/100 yds; 4 lbs/110 yds; 6 lbs/145 yds; 8 lbs/185 yds; 10 lbs/230 yds
Spool Cap. (B): 6 lbs/125 yds; 6 lbs/140 yds; 8 lbs/190 yds; 10 lbs/220 yds; 14 lbs/280 yds
Weight: 5.9 oz; 7.2 oz; 8.3 oz; 9.9 oz; 10.9 oz
Hand Retrieve: R or L
Max Drag: 6 lbs; 6 lbs; 9 lbs; 10 lbs; 12 lbs;
Reel Bearings: 7+1; 9+1; 9+1; 9+1; 9+1

Features: Lightweight graphite body; corrosion-resistant; stainless steel main shaft and components; nine stainless steel ball bearings (model 6920 has seven); one instant anti-reverse bearing; machined, ported, double-anodized aluminum spool; braid-ready spool; titanium-coated spool lip and line roller; smooth multi-disc drag; solid aluminum bail wire; Sure-Click Bail with audible signal; soft-touch knob; on/off anti-reverse; converts to left- or right-hand retrieve.
Price:. . . . .$49.95–$59.95

PFLUEGER TRION
Model: 20X; 25X; 30X; 35X; 40X
Gear Ratio: 5.2:1
Inches/Turn: 20.8; 23; 25.9; 28.5; 31.9
Spool Cap. (M): 4 lbs/100 yds; 4 lbs/110 yds; 6 lbs/145 yds; 8 lbs/185 yds; 10 lbs/230 yds
Spool Cap. (B): 6 lbs/125 yds; 6 lbs/140 yds; 8 lbs/190 yds; 10 lbs/220 yds; 14 lbs/280 yds
Weight: 5.9 oz; 7.1 oz; 8.6 oz; 10.4 oz; 11.4 oz
Hand Retrieve: R or L
Max Drag: 6 lbs; 6 lbs; 9 lbs; 10 lbs; 12 lbs

Reel Bearings: 5; 7; 7; 7; 7
Features: 6+1 bearings (4+1 bearings on TRI20B); double-anodized aluminum spool; on/off instant anti-reverse bearing; lightweight graphite body and rotor; long-cast aluminum spool with titanium lip; smooth multi-disc drag system with stainless steel and oiled felt washer; sure-click bail provides an audible signal when bail is fully opened and ready to cast; anti-twist titanium line roller; aluminum handle with soft-touch knob.
Price:.............................$29.95–$39.95

QUANTUM CATALYST PTI
Model: 15, 25, 30
Gear Ratio: 5.3:1; 5.2:1; 5.2:1
Inches/Turn: 26; 28; 31
Spool Cap. (M): 6 lbs/140 yds; 8 lbs/150 yds; 10 lbs/150 yds
Weight: 7.5 oz; 8.6 oz; 8.9 oz
Hand Retrieve: R or L
Max Drag: 8 lbs; 19 lbs; 19 lbs

Reel Bearings: 10
Features: ThinLine aluminum body and side cover; TiMag titanium bail with magnetic trip; polymer-stainless hybrid PT bearings; line management system; extra-hard PT gears; lightweight, machined aluminum crank handle; MAGLOK magnetic continuous anti-reverse; aluminum long stroke spool design; smooth front-adjustable drag system.
Price:................................$119.99

REELS: Freshwater Spinning

QUANTUM ENERGY PTI

Model: 15, 25, 30
Gear Ratio: 5.3:1; 5.2:1; 5.2:1
Inches/Turn: 26; 28; 31
Spool Cap. (M): 6 lbs/140 yds; 8 lbs/150 yds; 10 lbs/150 yds
Weight: 7.0 oz; 8.3 oz; 8.6 oz
Hand Retrieve: R or L

Max Drag: 8 lbs; 19 lbs; 19 lbs
Reel Bearings: 11
Features: Polymer-stainless hybrid PT bearings; LMS line management system; continuous anti-reverse; machined aluminum handle; double-anodized aluminum spool; new SCR aluminum frame and side cover.
Price:. $139.99

QUANTUM EXO PTI

Model: 15, 25, 30, 40, 50
Gear Ratio: 5.3:1; 5.2:1; 5.2:1; 5.2:1; 5.2:1
Inches/Turn: 26; 28; 31; 33; 36
Spool Cap. (M): 8 lbs/100 yds; 8 lb./150 yds; 10 lbs/150 yds; 10 lbs/230 yds; 12 lbs/225yds
Weight: 6.0 oz; 6.9 oz; 7.4 oz; 9.4 oz; 9.7 oz
Hand Retrieve: R or L

Max Drag: 6 lbs; 16 lbs; 20 lbs; 20 lbs; 20 lbs
Reel Bearings: 10+1
Features: Stacked ceramic front-adjustable drag system; polymer-stainless hybrid PT bearings; line management system; extra-hard PT gears; lightweight, machined aluminum crank handle; continuous anti-reverse.
Price:. . . . .$199.95–$209.95

QUANTUM HELLCAT

Model: 20, 30, 40
Gear Ratio: 5.1:1
Inches/Turn: 27; 28; 30
Spool Cap. (M): 6 lbs/130 yds; 8 lbs/190 yds; 10 lbs/170 yds
Weight: 10.0 oz; 11.1 oz; 11.8 oz
Hand Retrieve: R or L

Reel Bearings: 11
Features: Line management system; continuous anti-reverse; aluminum long stroke spool design; smooth front-adjustable drag system; corrosion-resistant stainless steel bail wire.
Price: **$79.99**

QUANTUM SMOKE

Model: 10, 15, 25, 30, 40, 50
Gear Ratio: 5.3:1; 5.3:1; 5.2:1; 5.2:1; 5.2:1; 5.2:1;
Inches/Turn: 24; 26; 28; 31; 33; 36
Spool Cap. (M): 4 lbs/125 yds; 6 lbs/140 yds; 8 lbs/150 yds; 10 lbs/150 yds; 10 lbs/230 yds; 12 lbs/ 225 yds
Weight: 6.2 oz; 6.3 oz; 7.5 oz; 7.8 oz; 9.7 oz; 10.0 oz
Hand Retrieve: R or L
Max Drag: 6 lbs; 6 lbs; 16 lbs; 16 lbs; 20 lbs; 20 lbs

Reel Bearings: 9+1
Features: ThinLine aluminum body and side cover; stacked ceramic front-adjustable drag system; polymer stainless hybrid; PT bearings; line management system; extra-hard PT gears; continuous anti-reverse; aluminum long stroke spool design.
Price: .... **$169.95–$179.95**

QUANTUM SNAPSHOT
Model: 10FC; 20FC; 30FC; 40FC
Gear Ratio: 5.2:1; 5.2:1; 5.2:1; 4.7:1
Spool Cap. (M): 4 lbs/125 yds; 6 lbs/140 yds; 8 lbs/160 yds; 10 lbs/230 yds
Weight: 6.7 oz; 8.6 oz; 9.1 oz; 11.7 oz
Hand Retrieve: R or L

Max Drag: 4 lbs; 8 lbs; 8 lbs
Reel Bearings: 1
Features: Aluminum long stroke spool design; smooth front-adjustable drag system; corrosion-resistant stainless steel bail wire; multi-stop anti-reverse.
Price: **$24.99**

QUANTUM TOUR KVD
Model: 25, 30, 40, 50
Gear Ratio: 5.2:1
Inches/Turn: 28; 31; 33; 36
Spool Cap. (M): 8 lbs/150 yds; 10 lbs/150 yds; 10 lbs/230 yds; 12 lbs/225 yds
Weight: 7.3 oz; 7.6 oz; 9.5 oz; 9.8 oz
Hand Retrieve: R or L
Max Drag: 16 lbs; 20 lbs; 20 lbs; 20 lbs
Reel Bearings: 10

Features: Dual PT continuous anti-reverse; super free spool pinion design; titanium-coated line guide reduces friction on casts and retrieves; MaxCast skeletal spool; one-piece aluminum frame and side cover; quick-release side cover; drag with ceramic, stainless, and carbon fiber discs for smooth, fish-fighting power; high-performance polymer-stainless hybrid PT bearings; adjustable infinite cast control; all metal frame and side covers keep components in perfect alignment; soft-touch laser-etched EVA handle grips; fully machined aluminum handle.
Price: . . . . **$179.99–$189.99**

SHIMANO SAHARA
Model: 500, 1000, 2500, 3000, 4000
Gear Ratio: 4.7:1; 6.0:1; 6.2:1; 6.2:1; 5.8:1
Inches/Turn: 21; 29; 35; 35; 36
Spool Cap. (M): 4 lbs/100 yds; 4 lbs/140 yds; 8 lbs/140 yds; 10 lbs/140 yds; 12 lbs/160 yds
Spool Cap. (B): 8 lbs/105 yds; 10 lbs/95 yds; 15 lbs/145 yds; 20 lbs/145 yds; 30 lbs/175 yds
Weight: 6.2 oz; 7.4 oz; 9.2 oz; 9.2 oz; 12.5 oz
Hand Retrieve: R or L
Max Drag: 6 lbs; 7 lbs; 11 lbs; 15 lbs; 15 lbs
Reel Bearings: 4+1; 3+1; 3+1; 3+1; 3+1
Features: New XGT7 graphite frame and sideplate; three SS ball, one roller; front drag; Super Stopper II; cold-forged aluminum spool; new M compact body; stamping bail; floating shaft; oversized power roller line roller; approved for use in salt water.
Price:.............................**$79.99–$89.99**

SHIMANO SAROS
Model: 1000, 2500, 3000, 4000
Gear Ratio: 6.0:1; 6.0:1; 6.0:1; 5.8:1
Inches/Turn: 29; 34; 34; 37
Spool Cap. (M): 4 lbs/140 yds; 10 lbs/120 yds; 10 lbs/140 yds; 12 lbs/160 yds
Spool Cap. (B): 10 lbs/95 yds; 15 lbs/145 yds; 20 lbs/145 yds; 30 lbs/175 yds
Weight: 7.1 oz; 9.3 oz; 9.5 oz; 11.5 oz
Hand Retrieve: R or L
Max Drag: 7 lbs; 11 lbs; 15 lbs; 15 lbs
Reel Bearings: 5+1
Features: X-ship technology for increased cranking efficiency and more power; lightweight XT-7 frame/rotor/sideplate; rapid fire drag adjustment; six-bearing system.
Price:.........................**$139.99–$149.99**

SHIMANO SEDONA FD

Model: 500; 1000; 2500; 4000
Gear Ratio: 4.7:1; 6.2:1; 6.2:1; 5.7:1
Inches/Turn: 21; 28; 32; 33
Spool Cap. (M): 2 lbs/190 yds; 2 lbs/270 yds; 10 lbs/120 yds; 10 lbs/200 yds
Weight: 6.2 oz; 7.7 oz; 9.5 oz; 12.5 oz
Hand Retrieve: R or L

Max Drag: 4 lbs; 7 lbs; 15 lbs; 20 lbs
Reel Bearings: 4+1
Features: Exclusive S-concept technology propulsion line management system lightweight graphite frame, sideplate and rotor; propulsion line management system; four-shielded ball bearings plus one roller bearing; cold-forged aluminum spool; Power Roller III; Dyna-Balance system.
Price: **$59.99**

SHIMANO SPIREX FG

Model: 1000, 2500, 4000
Gear Ratio: 6.2:1; 6.2:1; 5.7:1
Inches/Turn: 28; 32; 33
Spool Cap. (M): 2 lbs/270 yds; 10 lbs/120 yds; 10 lbs/200 yds
Weight: 8.8 oz; 10.6 oz; 13.9 oz
Hand Retrieve: R or L

Max Drag: 7 lbs; 15 lbs; 20 lbs
Reel Bearings: 5
Features: Rock-solid reliability meets advanced technology; hands-down favorite for walleye and smallmouth anglers; S-concept; graphite frame, sideplate, and rotor; cold-forged aluminum spool; propulsion line management system; Dyna-Balance; Fluidrive.
Price: **$59.99**

SHIMANO SPIREX RG
Model: 1000, 2500, 4000
Gear Ratio: 6.2:1; 6.2:1; 5.7:1
Inches/Turn: 28; 33; 33
Spool Cap. (M): 6 lbs/110 yds; 8 lbs/140 yds; 12 lbs/160 yds
Weight: 9.9 oz; 11.3 oz; 14.5 oz
Hand Retrieve: R or L
Max Drag: 6 lbs; 7 lbs; 9 lbs

Reel Bearings: 5
Features: Rock-solid reliability meets advanced technology; hands-down favorite for walleye and smallmouth anglers; S-concept; graphite frame, sideplate, and rotor; cold-forged aluminum spool; propulsion line management system; Dyna-Balance; Fluidrive.
Price: **$59.99**

SHIMANO STELLA FE
Model: 1000, 2500, 3000, 4000
Gear Ratio: 25; 35; 35; 38
Spool Cap. (M): 4 lbs/140 yds; 8 lbs/140 yds; 8 lbs/170 yds; 10 lbs/200 yds
Spool Cap. (B): 15 lbs/85 yds; 15 lbs/145 yds; 20 lbs/140 yds; 30 lbs/170 yds
Weight: 6.0 oz; 8.0 oz; 8.1 oz; 9.5 oz
Hand Retrieve: R or L
Max Drag: 7 lbs; 20 lbs; 20 lbs; 24 lbs

Reel Bearings: 14+1
Features: A fresh/salt hybrid that is both lightweight and incredibly smooth, with plenty of power for finessing large fish on light line; features Paladin gear durability enhancement and propulsion line management system; Aero Wrap II worm gear oscillation; cold-forged machined aluminum spool with titanium lip; Power Roller III with diamond-like carbon coating.
Price: . . . . **$699.99–$749.99**

REELS: Freshwater Spinning

SHIMANO STRADIC CI4+

Model: 1000, 2500, 3000, 4000
Gear Ratio: 6.0:1; 6.0:1; 6.0:1; 5.8:1
Inches/Turn: 34; 34; 35; 37
Spool Cap. (M): 4 lbs/140 yds; 8 lbs/140 yds; 8 lbs/170 yds; 10 lbs/200 yds
Spool Cap. (B): 15 lbs/85 yds; 15 lbs/145 yds; 20 lbs/145 yds; 30 lbs/175 yds
Weight: 6.0 oz; 7.0 oz; 7.0 oz; 9.0 oz
Hand Retrieve: R or L
Max Drag: 7 lbs; 15 lbs; 15 lbs; 20 lbs
Reel Bearings: 6+1

Features: Ultra-lightweight CI4+ frame, sideplate, and rotor construction; X-ship; Paladin gear durability enhancement; propulsion line management system: propulsion spool lip, Power Roller III, redesigned bail trip; Aero Wrap II oscillation; SR-concept: SR 3D gear, SR handle, SR one-piece bail wire; S A-RB ball bearings; aluminum spool; S-concept: S-rotor, S-guard, S-arm cam; machined aluminum handle; direct drive mechanism (thread in handle attachment); round EVA handle grip; waterproof drag; Magnumlite rotor; maintenance port; Fluidrive II; floating shaft; Dyna-Balance; Super Stopper II; repairable clicker; approved for use in salt water; rated for use with mono, fluorocarbon, and PowerPro lines.
Price:........................**$219.99–$239.99**

SHIMANO STRADIC FJ

Model: 1000, 2500, 3000, 4000, 5000, 6000, 8000
Gear Ratio: 6.0:1; 6.0:1; 6.0:1; 6.2:1; 6.2:1; 4.8:1; 4.8:1
Inches/Turn: 30; 34; 35; 39; 41; 35; 35
Spool Cap. (M): 4 lbs/140 yds; 8 lbs/140 yds; 8 lbs/170 yds; 10 lbs/200 yds; 12 lbs/195 yds; 16 lbs/170 yds; 16 lbs/250 yds
Spool Cap. (B): 15 lbs/85 yds; 15 lbs/145 yds; 20 lbs/145 yds; 30 lbs/175 yds; 30 lbs/200 yds; 50 lbs/240 yds; 50 lbs/265 yds
Weight: 7.5 oz; 9.2 oz; 9.3 oz; 10.8 oz; 10.8 oz; 20.8 oz; 20.5 oz
Hand Retrieve: R or L
Max Drag: 7 lbs; 15 lbs; 15 lbs; 20 lbs; 20 lbs; 29 lbs; 29 lbs
Reel Bearings: 5+1
Features: X-ship for easier turning handle under load; propulsion line management system; SA-RB bearings; aluminum frame (graphite on 1000); lightweight graphite sideplate and rotor; cold-forged aluminum spool; S-concept rotor, guard, and arm cam; machined-aluminum handle; Fluidrive II floating shaft; Dyna-Balance; Super Stopper II; salt water approved; rated for use with mono, fluorocarbon, or braid.
Price:........................**$179.99–$239.99**

SHIMANO SUSTAIN FG
Model: 1000, 2500, 3000, 4000, 5000, 6000, 10000
Gear Ratio: 6.0:1; 6.0:1; 6.0:1; 6.2:1; 6.2:1; 4.8:1; 4.8:1
Inches/Turn: 30; 34; 35; 39; 41; 35; 37
Spool Cap. (M): 4 lbs/140 yds; 8 lbs/140 yds; 10 lbs/140 yds; 12 lbs/160 yds; 12 lbs/195 yds; 16 lbs/170 yds; 16 lbs/340 yds
Spool Cap. (B): 15 lbs/145 yds; 15 lbs/145 yds; 20 lbs/145 yds; 15 lbs/265 yds; 20 lbs/220 yds; 30 lbs/290 yds; 65 lbs/260 yds
Weight: 6.5 oz; 8.3 oz; 8.3 oz; 9.9 oz; 10.6 oz; 19.6 oz; 19.0 oz

Hand Retrieve: R or L
Max Drag: 7 lbs; 20 lbs; 15 lbs; 24 lbs; 20 lbs; 28 lbs; 28 lbs
Reel Bearings: 7+1; 8+1; 8+1; 8+1; 8+1; 8+1; 8+1;
Features: X-ship design; Magnumlite CI4 rotor; aluminum sideplate; rapid fire drag; Paladin gear durability enhancement; propulsion line management system; Aero Wrap II oscillation; aluminum spool; machined aluminum handle; direct drive mechanism (thread-in attachment); EVA handle knob; maintenance port; Fluidrive II; floating shaft; Dyna-Balance; Super Stopper II.
Price: . . . . **$329.99–$399.99**

SHIMANO SYMETRE FL
Model: 500, 1000, 2500, 3000, 4000
Gear Ratio: 4.7:1; 6.0:1; 6.2:1; 6.2:1; 5.8:1
Inches/Turn: 21; 29; 35; 35; 36
Spool Cap. (M): 4 lbs/100 yds; 6 lbs/110 yds; 8 lbs/140 yds; 10 lbs/140 yds; 12 lbs/160 yds;
Spool Cap. (B): 8 lbs/105 yds; 10 lbs/95 yds; 15 lbs/145 yds; 20 lbs/145 yds; 30 lbs/175 yds
Weight: 6.1 oz; 6.5 oz; 9 oz; 9 oz; 11.8 oz

Hand Retrieve: R or L
Max Drag: 6 lbs; 7 lbs; 11 lbs; 15 lbs; 15 lbs
Reel Bearings: 4+1
Features: Four A-RB plus one A-RB stainless steel bearings; X-ship technology; XGT7 stronger and lighter frame technology; aluminum cold-forged spool; Super Stopper II; Dyna-Balance; propulsion line management system; Varispeed II oscillation system.
Price: . . . . **$99.99–$109.99**

SHIMANO SYNCOPATE FG

Model: 1000, 2500, 4000
Gear Ratio: 5.2:1; 5.2:1; 5.1:1
Inches/Turn: 25; 29; 32
Spool Cap. (M): 4 lbs/140 yds; 8 lbs/140 yds; 10 lbs/200 yds
Spool Cap. (B): 15 lbs/85 yds; 15 lbs/145 yds; 30 lbs/175 yds
Weight: 7.6 oz; 9.2 oz; 12.7 oz

Hand Retrieve: R or L
Max Drag: 7 lbs; 7 lbs; 13 lbs
Reel Bearings: 4
Features: Propulsion spool lip; graphite frame; graphite sideplate; graphite rotor; aluminum spool; Varispeed oscillation ported handle shank; Quick Fire II; Dyna-Balance; Power Roller II; fresh water or salt water; use with mono, fluoro, and braid.
Price:.................................. **$29.99**

ABU GARCIA ORRA S
Model: 10, 20, 30, 40
Gear Ratio: 5.2:1; 5.8:1; 5.8:1; 5.8:1
Inches/Turn: 24.5; 31; 33; 33
Retrieve Speed: Std
Spool Cap. (B): 6 lbs/150 yds; 8 lbs/130 yds; 8 lbs/175 yds; 10 lbs/210 yds
Weight: 7.8 oz; 8.7 oz; 9.2 oz; 10.2 oz
Hand Retrieve: R or L
Max Drag: 10 lbs; 12 lbs; 12 lbs; 18 lbs

Features: Stunning design and a sleek look highlight the advancement in spinning reel technology; smooth performing sealed Hybrid Carbon Matrix drag system and includes a durable braid-ready aluminum spool that eliminates the need for a mono backing; unique corkscrew design of the spool allows braid to be tied directly to the spool without the line slipping.
Price: **$69.95**

CABELA'S SALT STRIKER BAITFEEDER
Model: 40B, 65B, 80B
Gear Ratio: 5.0:1; 4.8:1; 4.8:1
Spool Cap. (M): 10 lbs/190 yds; 15 lbs/310 yds; 20 lbs/350 yds
Weight: 12.1 oz; 24.4 oz; 25.6 oz
Hand Retrieve: R or L

Reel Bearings: 9+1
Features: Nine ball bearing drive provides an unbeatably smooth retrieve; quick-set instant anti-reverse; lightweight graphite body and sideplate; anodized-aluminum spool with holes minimizes weight and dissipates heat; striking blue highlights.
Price: . . . . **$69.99–$79.99**

CABELA'S SALT STRIKER SURF
Model: 6000
Gear Ratio: 4.6:1
Inches/Turn: 37.2
Spool Cap. (M): 30 lbs/240 yds
Weight: 24.6 oz
Hand Retrieve: R or L
Max Drag: 33 lbs
Reel Bearings: 7+1

Features: Smooth, eight-bearing system and anodized aluminum surf-casting spool offer long-line control for deep casts and retrieves; one-way clutch instant anti-reverse bearing eliminates back-play for responsive hooksetting power; super-tough, titanium-coated line roller resists abrasion from sand and debris; corrosion-resistant aluminum body and graphite rotor; high-strength aluminum handle with a soft-touch grip.
Price:............................$79.99–$89.99

DAIWA ISLA
Model: 4000H, 5000H, 7000H, 7000HBULL
Gear Ratio: 5.7:1; 5.7:1; 5.7:1; 4.3:1
Inches/Turn: 39.9; 47.6; 54.7; 40.9
Spool Cap. (M): 12 lbs/260 yds; 17 lbs/310 yds; 25 lbs/350 yds; 25 lbs/350 yds
Spool Cap. (B): 40 lbs/320 yds; 55 lbs/440 yds; 80 lbs/550yds; 80 lbs/550 yds
Weight: 15.2 oz; 21.2 oz; 29.4 oz; 29.4 oz
Hand Retrieve: R or L
Max Drag: 22 lbs; 33 lbs; 66 lbs; 66 lbs
Reel Bearings: 8+1

Features: The spool-to-rotor seam is Mag Sealed—permanently sealed via magnetic oil in conjunction with powerful magnets which bar entry to water and debris while maintaining nearly friction-free rotation; the Zaion air rotor is 15 percent lighter than normal rotor designs, better balanced, and extraordinarily strong; features a protrusion-free air bail; forged aluminum spool; Digigear gear design; ultra-smooth nine-bearing system (2 CRBB, 6 BB, 1 RB); ultimate tournament drag; oversized soft-touch handle knob.
Price:.......................... $699.99–$899.99

REELS: Saltwater Spinning

DAIWA STEEZ
Model: 2500, 2508
Gear Ratio: 4.8:1
Inches/Turn: 27.9
Spool Cap. (M): 8 lbs/110 yds; 8 lbs/170 yds
Weight: 6.9 oz; 7 oz
Hand Retrieve: R or L
Max Drag: 15.4 lbs
Reel Bearings: 11+1
Features: Weighs 5.5 ounces; magnesium frame and handle-side sideplate; swept handle for less wobble, better feel and maximum winding leverage; tough, A7075 tempered aluminum drive gear and phosphor bronze pinion; eleven precision ball bearings, plus roller bearing; free-floating A7075 aluminum alloy spool starts faster, spins longer; fast spool change; Magforce-V automatic magnetic spool brake; eight-disc wet drag with precision click adjustment; precision click-free spool adjustment; infinite anti-reverse; Digigear digital gear design; eleven super corrosion-resistant ball bearings plus roller bearing; tubular stainless air Bail; infinite anti-reverse; advanced locomotive levelwind washable design with sealed, waterproof drag system; precision, super micro-pitch drag adjustment; pillartype tight oscillation system, ultra-quiet, and smooth; precision, stainless main shaft.
Price:...................................**$529.95**

DAIWA STEEZ EX
Model: 2508H, 3012H
Gear Ratio: 5.6:1
Inches/Turn: 33
Spool Cap. (M): 8 lbs/110 yds; 8 lbs/170 yds
Weight: 6.8 oz; 8.5 oz
Hand Retrieve: R or L
Max Drag: 15.4 lbs
Reel Bearings: 12+1
Features: Built for fresh or salt water with a corrosion-proof Zaion body; ultra lightweight, corrosion-proof Zaion body and air rotor; mag-sealed construction (body and line roller); max drag 15.4 pounds; thirteen bearing system (7 CRBB/5BB+1RB); Digigear digital gear design for speed, power, and durability; lightweight, hollow, stainless steel air bail; machined aluminum handle with cork knob; silent oscillation; ABS air spool with cut-proof, titanium nitride spool lip; infinite anti-reverse; and neoprene reel bag.
Price:...........................**$749.95–$799.95**

LEW'S GOLD SPIN HIGH SPEED SPIN
Model: 1000H, 2000H, 3000H, 4000H
Gear Ratio: 5.6:1; 6.1:1; 6.1:1; 6.1:1
Inches/Turn: 25; 31; 34; 38
Spool Cap. (M): 6 lbs/150 yds; 8 lbs/140 yds; 10 lbs/140 yds; 12 lbs/160 yds
Weight: 6.3 oz; 7.3 oz; 7.4 oz; 8.5 oz

Hand Retrieve: R or L
Reel Bearings: 9+1
Features: The high-speed Gold series features the lightweight high strength C40 carbon body and side cover to meet anglers' most demanding expectations for spinning reels that are lighter, faster, and stronger.
Price: **$129.99**

LEW'S SPEED SPIN INSHORE
Model: 3000, 4000, 5000
Gear Ratio: 6.1:1; 6.1:1; 5.6:1
Inches/Turn: 34; 38; 40
Spool Cap. (M): 12 lbs/170 yds; 14 lbs/220 yds; 17 lbs/220 yds
Weight: 9.6 oz; 10.0 oz; 15.8 oz
Hand Retrieve: R or L
Reel Bearings: 5+1
Features: Solid aluminum body and sideplate; includes sealed body engineering design; lightweight graphite rotor; premium six stainless steel bearing system; sealed zero-reverse anti-reverse clutch bearing, plus three sealed ball bearings in key locations; oversized hard chrome-plated line roller to reduce line twist; stainless steel, lightweight hollow bail wire; double-anodized aluminum spool; smooth carbon Teflon multi-disc sealed drag system; quality solid brass pinion gearing; high-strength zinc alloy drive gear; durable stainless steel main shaft; external stainless steel screws; machine-cut aluminum handle; power knob on model INS5000; adjustable right- or left-hand retrieve; designed for salt water.
Price: **$99.99**

LEW'S TOURNAMENT HIGH-SPEED SPEED SPIN

Model: 100H; 200H; 300H; 400H
Gear Ratio: 5.6:1; 6.1:1; 6.1:1; 6.1:1
Inches/Turn: 25; 31; 34; 38
Spool Cap. (M): 6 lbs/150 yds; 8lbs/140 yds; 10 lbs/140 yds; 12 lbs/160 yds.
Weight: 6.9 oz; 8.3 oz; 8.4 oz; 9.6 oz
Hand Retrieve: R or L
Reel Bearings: 9+1
Features: Premium ten stainless steel bearing system; zeroreverse one-way clutch bearing; rugged graphite body and side cover; Digi-balanced graphite rotor with stainless; durable stainless steel main shaft; external stainless steel screws; machine-cut aluminum handle; smooth carbon Teflon multi-disc sealed drag system; quality solid brass pinion gearing; durable stainless steel main shaft; parallel line lay oscillation system; oversized titanium line roller to reduce line twist; double-anodized ported aluminum spool; external stainless steel screws; adjustable right- or left-hand retrieve; speed lube for exceptional smoothness and performance in all temperatures; designed for use in fresh and salt water.
Price: **$79.99**

OKUMA CEDROS

Model: 30S, 40S, 45S, 55S, 65S, 80S
Gear Ratio: 6.2:1; 6.2:1; 6.2:1; 6.2:1; 5.7:1; 5.7:1
Inches/Turn: 30; 34; 35; 40; 42; 46
Spool Cap. (M): 6 lbs/200 yds; 8 lbs/270 yds; 10 lbs/240 yds; 10 lbs/380 yds; 12 lbs/430 yds; 15 lbs/420 yds
Weight: 11.1 oz; 12.1 oz; 16.5 oz; 16.9 oz; 22.8 oz; 23 oz
Hand Retrieve: R or L
Max Drag: 18 lbs; 20 lbs; 24 lbs; 24 lbs; 31 lbs; 33 lbs
Reel Bearings: 4+1
Features: Precision dual force drag system; multi-disc, Japanese-oiled felt drag system; 4HPB+1RB corrosion-resistant stainless steel ball bearings; quick-set anti-reverse roller bearing; precision machine-cut brass pinion gear; corrosion-resistant coating process; corrosion-resistant, high-density gearing; rigid die-cast aluminum frame and sideplate; precision elliptical gearing system; machined aluminum, two-tone anodized and ported spool; custom blue anodized machined aluminum handle knob; EVA handle knob on 30-size; Hydro Block water tight drag seal; heavy-duty, solid aluminum, gold anodized bail wire; RESII: Computer balanced rotor equalizing system; narrow blade body design for reduced fatigue; one-year warranty.
Price: . . . . **$109.99–$149.99**

OKUMA CEDROS BAITFEEDER
Model: 55, 65
Gear Ratio: 4.5:1; 4.8:1
Inches/Turn: 30; 34
Spool Cap. (M): 10 lbs/380 yds; 12 lbs/430 yds
Weight: 19.1 oz; 26.6 oz
Hand Retrieve: R or L
Max Drag: 24 lbs; 31 lbs
Reel Bearings: 4+1
Features: On/off auto-trip bait feeding system; precision dual force drag system; multi-disc, Japanese-oiled felt drag system; 4HPB+1RB corrosion-resistant stainless steel ball bearings; quick-set anti-reverse roller bearing; precision machine-cut brass pinion gear; corrosion-resistant coating process; corrosion-resistant, high-density gearing; rigid die-cast aluminum frame and sideplate; precision elliptical gearing system; machined aluminum, two-tone anodized and ported spool; custom blue anodized machined aluminum handle knob; Hydro Block watertight drag seal; heavy-duty, solid aluminum, gold anodized bail wire; RESII: computer balanced rotor equalizing system; narrow blade body design for reduced fatigue; one-year warranty.
Price: . . . .**$159.99–$164.99**

OKUMA CORONADO BAITFEEDER
Model: 40a, 55a, 65a, 80a
Gear Ratio: 4.5:1; 4.5:1; 4.8:1; 4.8:1
Inches/Turn: 28; 30; 34; 34
Spool Cap. (M): 8 lbs/410 yds; 10 lbs/380 yds; 12 lbs/540 yds; 15 lbs/420 yds
Weight: 12 oz; 16.7 oz; 23.6 oz; 24.7 oz
Hand Retrieve: R or L
Max Drag: 20 lbs; 24 lbs; 31 lbs; 33 lbs
Reel Bearings: 4+1
Features: On/off auto-trip bait feeding system; precision dual force drag system; multi-disc, Japanese-oiled felt drag system; 4BB+1RB corrosion-resistant stainless steel ball bearings; quick-set anti-reverse roller bearing; precision machine-cut brass pinion gear; corrosion-resistant coating process; corrosion-resistant, high-density gearing; lightweight, corrosion-resistant graphite body and rotor; precision elliptical gearing system; machined aluminum, two-tone anodized spool; Hydro Block water tight drag seal; heavy-duty, solid aluminum, anodized bail wire; RESII: computer balanced rotor equalizing system; narrow blade body design for reduced fatigue; one-year warranty.
Price: . . . .**$89.99–$99.99**

OKUMA RAW II

Model: 30, 40, 55, 65, 80
Gear Ratio: 5.0:1; 5.0:1; 4.5:1; 4.8:1; 4.8:1
Inches/Turn: 25; 28; 30; 34; 38
Spool Cap. (M): 6 lbs/200 yds; 8 lbs/270 yds; 10 lbs/380 yds; 12 lbs/430 yds; 15 lbs/420 yds
Weight: 10.5 oz; 11 oz; 17 oz; 23.4 oz; 24.2 oz
Hand Retrieve: R or L
Max Drag: 25 lbs; 30 lbs; 35 lbs; 50 lbs; 50 lbs
Reel Bearings: 7+1
Features: Precision dual force drag system; multi-disc, carbonite drag washers; 7 HPB+1RB corrosion-resistant stainless steel ball bearings; quick-set anti-reverse roller bearing; precision machine-cut brass pinion gear; corrosion-resistant coating process; corrosion-resistant, high-density gearing; rigid die-cast aluminum frame, sideplate, and rotor; precision elliptical gearing system; machined aluminum, two-tone anodized spool; carbon fiber handle system on the 30/40 sizes; standard EVA handle knob on 30/40 sizes; heavy-duty aluminum handle on 55/65/80 sizes; oversized round EVA handle grip on 55/65/80 size; Hydro Block water tight drag seal; heavy-duty, solid aluminum bail wire; one-year warranty.
Price: .... **$149.99–$174.99**

PENN CONFLICT

Model: 1000; 2000; 2500; 3000; 4000; 5000; 6000; 8000
Gear Ratio: 5.2:1; 6.2:1; 6.2:1; 6.2:1; 6.2:1; 5.6:1; 5.6:1; 5.3:1
Inches/Turn: 22; 30; 33; 35; 37; 36; 41; 44
Spool Cap. (M): 4 lbs/135 yds; 6 lbs/180 lbs; 8 lbs/175 yds; 10 lbs/165 yds; 10 lbs/220 yds; 15 lbs/200 yds; 20 lbs/230 yds; 25 lbs/310 yds.
Spool Cap. (B): 8 lbs/130 yds; 10 lbs/180 yds; 15 lbs/220 yds; 20 lbs/180 yds; 20 lbs/260 yds; 30 lbs/300 yds; 40 lbs/390 yds; 65 lbs/390 yds
Weight: 7.8 oz; 9.5 oz; 9.8 oz; 11.3 oz; 12 oz; 19 oz; 21.5 oz; 28.1 oz
Hand Retrieve: R or L
Max Drag: 9 lbs; 10 lbs; 12 lbs; 15 lbs; 15 lbs; 25 lbs; 25 lbs; 30 lbs
Reel Bearings: 7+1
Features: HT-100 carbon fiber drag washers; full metal body and sideplate; sealed stainless steel ball bearings; line capacity rings; Superline spool; infinite anti-reverse; Techno-Balanced rotor gives smooth retrieves; heavy-duty aluminum bail wire.
Price: .... **$129.95–$159.95**

PENN CONQUER

Model: 2000; 4000; 5000; 7000; 8000
Gear Ratio: 5.1:1; 5.8:1; 4.8:1; 4.8:1; 4.7:1
Inches/Turn: 28; 32; 31; 37; 40
Spool Cap. (M): 6 lbs/185 yds; 10 lbs/200 yds; 15 lbs/190 yds; 17 lbs/210 yds; 20 lbs/310 yds
Spool Cap. (B): 10 lbs/210 yds; 15 lbs/280 yds; 20 lbs/250 yds; 30 lbs/325 yds; 50 lbs/420 yds
Weight: 9.9 oz; 11.1 oz; 14.6 oz; 18.1 oz; 23.4 oz

Hand Retrieve: R or L
Max Drag: 12 lbs; 19 lbs; 22 lbs; 32 lbs; 32 lbs
Reel Bearings: 10+1
Features: One-piece machined aluminum gear box; forged, machined, and anodized aluminum spool; ten-shielded stainless steel ball bearings; infinite anti-reverse; braid-ready to handle the strain that superlines puts on a reel; friction trip ramp prevents premature bait trip when casting.
Price: **$219.95**

PENN FIERCE

Model: 1000; 2000; 3000; 4000; 5000; 6000; 7000; 8000
Gear Ratio: 5.2:1; 6.2:1; 6.2:1; 6.2:1; 5.6:1; 5.6:1; 5.3:1; 5.3:1
Inches/Turn: 20; 29; 31; 34; 37; 39; 39; 41
Spool Cap. (M): 4 lbs/115 yds; 6 lbs/210 yds; 8 lbs/170 yds; 10 lbs/230 yds; 15 lbs/220 yds; 17 lbs/280 yds; 20 lbs/310 yds; 25 lbs/350 yds
Spool Cap. (B): 8 lbs/130 yds; 10 lbs,/225 yds; 15 lbs/205 yds; 20 lbs/275 yds; 30 lbs/305 yds; 40 lbs/365 yds; 50 lbs/430 yds; 65 lbs/450 yds

Weight: 7.7 oz; 8.8 oz; 11.7 oz; 12.5 oz; 19 oz; 20.6 oz; 26.4 oz; 27.4 oz;
Hand Retrieve: R or L
Max Drag: 7 lbs; 7 lbs; 10 lbs; 13 lbs; 20 lbs; 20 lbs; 25 lbs; 25 lbs
Reel Bearings: 4+1
Features: Machined and anodized aluminum spool; infinite anti-reverse; stainless steel main shaft; four stainless steel ball bearings; Techno-balanced rotor gives smooth retrieves; machined and anodized handle with soft-touch knob.
Price: . . . . **$59.95–$79.95**

PENN TORQUE
Model: S5; S7; S9
Gear Ratio: 5.9:1; 5.1:1; 5.1:1
Inches/Turn: 38; 40; 50
Spool Cap. (M): 15 lbs/300 yds; 20 lbs/340 yds; 25 lbs/440 yds
Spool Cap. (B): 30 lbs/400 yds; 65 lbs/390 yds; 80 lbs/490 yds
Weight: 21.3 oz; 28.6 oz; 30.8 oz
Hand Retrieve: R or L
Max Drag: 38 lbs; 41 lbs; 50 lbs

Reel Bearings: 7+1
Features: One-piece aluminum frame; forged and machined aluminum spool, sideplates, and one-piece handle arm; integral clutch sleeve eliminates any back play during hook set; seven sealed stainless steel ball bearings; machine-cut marine grade bronze main gear; hardened stainless steel pinion gear; innovative bail trip switch allows the angler to choose between manual and auto mode.
Price: . . . . **$659.95–$699.95**

QUANTUM BOCA PTS
Model: 40, 50, 60, 80
Gear Ratio: 5.3:1; 5.3:1; 4.9:1; 4.9:1
Inches/Turn: 33; 36; 37; 41
Spool Cap. (M): 10 lbs/230 yds; 12 lbs/225 yds; 14 lbs/300 yds; 20 lbs/330 yds
Weight: 13.9 oz; 14.1 oz; 24 oz; 25 oz
Hand Retrieve: R or L
Max Drag: 25 lbs; 28 lbs; 30 lbs; 45 lbs
Reel Bearings: 6+1

Features: TiMag titanium bail with magnetic trip; polymer-stainless hybrid PT bearings; extra-hard PT gears; MAGLOK magnetic continuous anti-reverse; SaltGuard seven-layer corrosion protection finish; forged aluminum concave spool; Magnum ceramic drag; aluminum long stroke spool design; smooth front-adjustable drag system; machined aluminum handle.
Price: . . . . **$139.95–$179.95**

QUANTUM CABO PTS

Model: 40, 50, 60, 80
Gear Ratio: 5.3:1; 5.3:1; 4.9:1; 4.9:1
Inches/Turn: 33; 36; 37; 41
Spool Cap. (M): 10 lbs/230 yds; 12 lbs/225 yds; 14 lbs/300 yds; 20 lbs/330 yds
Weight: 13.9 oz; 14.1 oz; 24 oz; 25 oz
Hand Retrieve: R or L
Max Drag: 30 lbs; 35 lbs; 40 lbs; 50 lbs
Reel Bearings: 7+1

Features: Eight PT bearings; hybrid ceramic bearings in high-load areas; sealed Magnum CSC drag; sealed Magnum clutch; TiMag titanium fail-proof bail system with magnetic trip; line management system with ball-bearing line roller; SaltGuard 2.0 multi-layer corrosion protection; SCR alloy body and side cover; SCR alloy rotor on 60 and 80 models; carbon fiber composite rotor on 40 and 50 models; super-hard PT gears.
Price: . . . . **$189.95–$229.95**

QUANTUM SMOKE PTS INSHORE

Model: 25, 30, 40, 50
Gear Ratio: 5.2:1; 5.2:1; 5.3:1; 5.3:1
Inches/Turn: 28; 31; 33; 36
Spool Cap. (M): 8 lbs/150 yds; 10 lbs/150 yds; 10 lbs/250 yds; 12 lbs/225 yds
Weight: 7.6 oz; 7.9 oz; 9.7 oz; 10.0 oz
Hand Retrieve: R or L
Max Drag: 16 lbs; 18 lbs; 20 lbs; 25 lbs

Reel Bearings: 9+1
Features: Sealed CSC drag system SCR base; alloy aluminum body and sidecovers; rigid and lightweight; C4LF carbon fiber rotor; MaxCast II spool; sealed clutch; fail-proof titanium bail wire; SaltGuard 2.0 multi-layer corrosion protection.
Price: . . . . **$179.95–$199.95**

Saltwater Spinning

SHIMANO SAHARA

Model: 500, 1000, 2500, 3000, 4000
Gear Ratio: 4.7:1; 6.0:1; 6.2:1; 6.2:1; 5.8:1
Inches/Turn: 21; 29; 35; 35; 36
Spool Cap. (M): 4 lbs/100 yds; 4 lbs/140 yds; 8 lbs/140 yds; 10 lbs/140 yds; 12 lbs/160 yds
Spool Cap. (B): 8 lbs/105 yds; 10 lbs/95 yds; 15 lbs/145 yds; 20 lbs/145 yds; 30 lbs/175 yds
Weight: 6.2 oz; 7.4 oz; 9.2 oz; 9.2 oz; 12.5 oz
Hand Retrieve: R or L

Max Drag: 6 lbs; 7 lbs; 11 lbs; 15 lbs; 15 lbs
Reel Bearings: 4+1; 3+1; 3+1; 3+1; 3+1
Features: New XGT7 graphite frame and sideplate; three SS ball, one roller; front drag; Super Stopper II; cold-forged aluminum spool; new M compact body; stamping bail; floating shaft; oversized power roller line roller; approved for use in salt water.
Price: . . . .**$79.99–$89.99**

SHIMANO SARAGOSA

Model: 5000, 6000, 8000, 10000, 20000, 25000
Gear Ratio: 5.7:1; 5.7:1; 5.6:1; 4.9:1; 4.4:1; 4.4:1
Inches/Turn: 38.2; 40.6; 42.2; 40; 41; 45
Spool Cap. (M): 12 lbs/195 yds; 12 lbs/265 yds; 14 lbs/270 yds; 16 lbs/300 yds; 20 lbs/380 yds; 50 lbs/230 yds
Spool Cap. (B): 20 lbs/255 yds; 30 lbs/245 yds; 40 lbs/300 yds; 50 lbs/405 yds; 65 lbs/525 yds; 80 lbs/520 yds
Weight: 20 oz; 21 oz; 24 oz; 24 oz; 29 oz; 30 oz
Hand Retrieve: R or L
Max Drag: 22 lbs; 22 lbs; 27 lbs; 33 lbs; 44 lbs; 44 lbs
Reel Bearings: 5+1; 5+1; 5+1; 5+1; 6+1; 6+1
Features: SW concept design with X-ship and X-tough drag; durable cam oscillation system for better drag performance; rigid support drag on 20000 and 25000 sizes; Paladin gear durability enhancement; propulsion line management system; S A-RB shielded ball bearings; 5+1 bearings (6+1 on 20000 & 25000); high-speed retrieves; Stopperless design (no anti-reverse switch); aluminum frame; graphite rotor (aluminum on 10000, 20000 & 25000); Power Roller III line roller; S-arm cam; Super Stopper II anti-reverse; direct drive mechanism; machined aluminum handle shank; Dyna-Balance; Fluidrive II; cold-forged aluminum spool; titanium spool lip; waterproof drag; easy-access drag washers; Dartainium drag (6000-25000); Septon handle grips; rated for use with mono, fluoro, and braided lines.
Price: . . . . $259.99–$399.99

SHIMANO SAROS

Model: 1000, 2500, 3000, 4000
Gear Ratio: 6.0:1; 6.0:1; 6.0:1; 5.8:1
Inches/Turn: 29; 34; 34; 37
Spool Cap. (M): 4 lbs/140 yds; 10 lbs/120 yds; 10 lbs/140 yds; 12 lbs/160 yds
Spool Cap. (B): 10 lbs/95 yds; 15 lbs/145 yds; 20 lbs/145 yds; 30 lbs/175 yds

Weight: 7.1 oz; 9.3 oz; 9.5 oz; 11.5 oz
Hand Retrieve: R or L
Max Drag: 7 lbs; 11 lbs; 15 lbs; 15 lbs
Reel Bearings: 5+1
Features: X-ship technology for increased cranking efficiency and more power; lightweight XT-7 frame/rotor/sideplate; rapid fire drag adjustment; six-bearing system.
Price:........................$139.99–$149.99

SHIMANO SEDONA FD

Model: 500; 1000; 2500; 4000
Gear Ratio: 4.7:1; 6.2:1; 6.2:1; 5.7:1
Inches/Turn: 21; 28; 32; 33
Spool Cap. (M): 2 lbs/ 190 yds; 2 lbs/270 yds; 10 lbs/120 yds; 10 lbs/200 yds
Weight: 6.2 oz; 7.7 oz; 9.5 oz; 12.5 oz
Hand Retrieve: R or L
Max Drag: 4 lbs; 7 lbs; 15 lbs; 20 lbs

Reel Bearings: 4+1
Features: Enjoy high-end performance for affordable price; exclusive S-concept technology; propulsion line management system; lightweight graphite frame, sideplate, and rotor; four-shielded ball bearings plus one roller bearing; cold-forged aluminum spool; Power Roller III; Dyna-Balance system.
Price:...................................$59.99

SHIMANO SPHEROS

Model: 5000, 6000, 8000, 10000, 20000
Gear Ratio: 4.7:1; 4.7:1; 4.7:1; 4.7:1; 4.9/1; 4.9/1
Inches/Turn: 31; 33; 33
Spool Cap. (M): 12 lbs/195 yds; 12 lbs/265 yds; 14 lbs/270 yds; 20 lbs/350 yds; 20 lbs/380 yds
Spool Cap. (B): 20 lbs/255 yds; 30 lbs/245 yds; 40 lbs/300 yds; 50 lbs/600 yds; 50 lbs/655 yds
Weight: 19.6 oz; 20.1 oz; 19.6 oz; 23 oz; 28 oz
Hand Retrieve: R or L
Max Drag: 22 lbs; 27 lbs; 27 lbs; 27 lbs; 41 lbs

Reel Bearings: 3+1
Features: Aluminum frame graphite sideplate; graphite rotor; Power Roller III line roller; S-arm cam; Aero Wave oscillation (8000 sizes only); Aero Wrap oscillation; 3+1 bearings; Super Stopper II anti-reverse; direct drive mechanism; Dyna-Balance; Fluidrive II; cold-forged aluminum Spool; waterproof drag; easy access drag washers; Dartainium drag (6000 to 20000 sizes only); rubber handle grips; repairable clicker.
Price: . . . . **$199.99–$259.99**

SHIMANO SPIREX FG

Model: 1000, 2500, 4000
Gear Ratio: 6.2:1; 6.2:1; 5.7:1
Inches/Turn: 28; 32; 33
Spool Cap. (M): 2 lbs/270 yds; 10 lbs/120 yds; 10 lbs/200 yds
Weight: 8.8 oz; 10.6 oz; 13.9 oz
Hand Retrieve: R or L

Max Drag: 7 lbs; 15 lbs; 20 lbs
Reel Bearings: 5
Features: Rock-solid reliability meets advanced technology; hands-down favorite for walleye and smallmouth anglers; S-concept; graphite frame, sideplate, and rotor; cold-forged aluminum spool; propulsion line management system; Dyna-Balance; Fluidrive.
Price: **$59.99**

SHIMANO SPIREX RG

Model: 1000, 2500, 4000
Gear Ratio: 6.2:1; 6.2:1; 5.7:1
Inches/Turn: 28; 33; 33
Spool Cap. (M): 6 lbs/110 yds; 8 lbs/140 yds; 12 lbs/160 yds
Weight: 9.9 oz; 11.3 oz; 14.5 oz
Hand Retrieve: R or L

Max Drag: 6 lbs; 7 lbs; 9 lbs
Reel Bearings: 5
Features: Rock-solid reliability meets advanced technology; hands-down favorite for walleye and smallmouth anglers; S-concept; graphite frame, sideplate, and rotor; cold-forged aluminum spool; propulsion line management system; Dyna-Balance; Fluidrive.
Price: **$59.99**

SHIMANO STELLA FE

Model: 1000, 2500, 3000, 4000
Gear Ratio: 5.0:1; 6.0:1; 6.0:1; 6.2:1
Inches/Turn: 25; 35; 35; 38
Spool Cap. (M): 4 lbs/140 yds; 8 lbs/140 yds; 8 lbs/170 yds 10 lbs/200 yds
Spool Cap. (B): 15 lbs/85 yds; 15 lbs/145 yds; 20 lbs/140 yds; 30 lbs/170 yds
Weight: 6.0 oz; 8.0 oz; 8.1 oz; 9.5 oz
Hand Retrieve: R or L
Max Drag: 7 lbs; 20 lbs; 20 lbs; 24 lbs
Reel Bearings: 14+1
Features: Paladin gear durability enhancement; X-ship double-bearing supported pinion gear; ultra-light handle rotation; increased gearing efficiency and power propulsion line management system: propulsion spool lip, SR one-piece bail wire, Power Roller III with diamond-like carbon coating; EI surface treatment for extreme corrosion protection on spool; Aero Wrap II oscillation; SR-concept: SR 3D gear, SR handle, SR 3BB oscillation, SR balanced body, SR floating shaft, SR boltless magnesium body, SR one-piece bail wire, SR slider; shielded A-RB bearings; magnesium frame and sideplate; aluminum rotor (1000 size is magnesium); cold-forged and machined aluminum spool with titanium lip; S-concept: S-rotor, S-guard, S-shield roller clutch, S-arm cam; rigid support system: rigid support drag, SR slider; machined aluminum handle; direct drive mechanics (thread in handle attachment); Septon handle grips; waterproof drag; maintenance port; Fluidrive II; Dyna-Balance; Super Stopper II; repairable clicker; approved for use in salt water; rated for use with mono, fluorocarbon, and PowerPro lines.
Price: .... **$699.99–$749.99**

REELS

SHIMANO STELLA SW

Model: 5000, 6000, 8000, 10000, 14000, 18000, 20000
Gear Ratio: 6.2:1; 5.7:1; 5.6:1; 4.9:1; 6.2:1; 5.7:1; 4.4:1
Inches/Turn: 41; 41; 42; 40; 53; 51; 41
Spool Cap. (M): 12 lbs/195 yds; 16 lbs/170 yds; 12 lbs/325 yds; 20 lbs/220 yds; 16 lbs/360 yds; 20 lbs/415 yds; 20 lbs/460 yds
Spool Cap. (B): 20 lbs/245 yds; 30 lbs/290 yds; 40 lbs/340 yds; 50 lbs/360 yds; 65 lbs/315 yds; 50 lbs/600 yds; 80 lbs/445 yds
Weight: 15.3 oz; 15.5 oz; 23.8 oz; 24.2 oz; 24.3 oz; 30.9 oz; 31.2 oz
Hand Retrieve: R or L
Max Drag: 28.7 lbs; 28.7 lbs; 61.7 lbs; 55.1 lbs; 55.1 lbs; 55.1 lbs; 55.1 lbs
Reel Bearings: 14+1

Features: X-touch drag to handle big, fast, fish; X-ship enhances power transmission through the gear; X-shield and X-protect combine to provide extreme water resistance; power aluminum body, X-rigid rotor, X-rigid body and X-rigid handle; propulsion line management system; propulsion spool lip; SR one-piece bail wire; Power Roller IV oversized roller with over-flange; redesigned bail trip; S-arm cam; Aero Wrap II oscillation; Paladin gear durability enhancement; low wear rate pinion gear; cold-forged aluminum spool; ceramic coating on entire spool; diamond-like carbon line roller coating; shielded A-RB bearings; Super Stopper II; Stopperless design (no anti-reverse switch); Septon handle grip (models 10000 and up); direct drive mechanism (thread-in handle attachment); Fluidrive II; Dyna-Balance; approved for use in salt water; rated for use with PowerPro, fluorocarbon, and mono lines.
Price: . . . . **$1059.99–$1259.99**

SHIMANO STRADIC CI4+

Model: 1000, 2500, 3000, 4000
Gear Ratio: 6.0:1; 6.0:1; 6.0:1; 5.8:1
Inches/Turn: 34; 34; 35; 37
Spool Cap. (M): 4 lbs/140 yds; 8 lbs/140 yds; 8 lbs/170 yds; 10 lbs/200 yds
Spool Cap. (B): 15 lbs/85 yds; 15 lbs/145 yds; 20 lbs/145 yds; 30 lbs/175 yds
Weight: 6.0 oz; 7.0 oz; 7.0 oz; 9.0 oz
Hand Retrieve: R or L
Max Drag: 7 lbs; 15 lbs; 15 lbs; 20 lbs
Reel Bearings: 6+1
Features: Ultra-lightweight CI4+ frame, sideplate, and rotor construction; X-ship; Paladin gear durability enhancement; propulsion line management system: propulsion spool lip, Power Roller III, redesigned bail trip; Aero Wrap II Oscillation; SR-concept: SR 3D gear, SR handle, SR one-piece bail wire; S A-RB ball bearings; aluminum spool; S-concept: S-rotor, S-guard, S-arm cam; machined aluminum handle; direct drive mechanism (thread in handle attachment); round EVA handle grip; waterproof drag; Magnumlite rotor; maintenance port; Fluidrive II; floating shaft; Dyna-Balance; Super Stopper II; repairable clicker; approved for use in salt water; rated for use with mono, fluorocarbon, and PowerPro lines.
Price: . . . . **$219.99–$239.99**

SHIMANO STRADIC FJ

Model: 1000, 2500, 3000, 4000, 5000, 6000, 8000
Gear Ratio: 6.0:1; 6.0:1; 6.0:1; 6.2:1; 6.2:1; 4.8:1; 4.8:1
Inches/Turn: 30; 34; 35; 39; 41; 35; 35
Spool Cap. (M): 4 lbs/140 yds; 8 lbs/140 yds; 8 lbs/170 yds; 10 lbs/200 yds; 12 lbs/195 yds; 16 lbs/170 yds; 16 lbs/250 yds
Spool Cap. (B): 15 lbs/85 yds; 15 lbs/145 yds; 20 lbs/145 yds; 30 lbs/175 yds; 30 lbs/200 yds; 50 lbs/240 yds; 50 lbs/265 yds
Weight: 7.5 oz; 9.2 oz; 9.3 oz; 10.8 oz; 10.8 oz; 20.8 oz; 20.5 oz
Hand Retrieve: R or L

Max Drag: 7 lbs; 15 lbs; 15 lbs; 20 lbs; 20 lbs; 29 lbs; 29 lbs
Reel Bearings: 5+1
Features: X-ship for easier turning handle under load; propulsion line management system; SA-RB bearings; aluminum frame (graphite on 1000); lightweight graphite sideplate and rotor; cold-forged aluminum spool; S-concept rotor, guard, and arm cam; machined-aluminum handle; Fluidrive II floating shaft; Dyna-Balance; Super Stopper II; salt water approved; rated for use with mono, fluorocarbon, or braid.
Price: . . . . **$179.99–$239.99**

SHIMANO SUSTAIN FG

Model: 1000, 2500, 3000, 4000, 5000, 6000, 10000
Gear Ratio: 6.0:1; 6.0:1; 6.0:1; 6.2:1; 6.2:1; 4.8:1; 4.8:1
Inches/Turn: 30; 34; 35; 39; 41; 35; 37
Spool Cap. (M): 4 lbs/140 yds; 8 lbs/140 yds; 10 lbs/140 yds; 12 lbs/160 yds; 12 lbs/195 yds; 16 lbs/170 yds; 16 lbs/340 yds
Spool Cap. (B): 15 lbs/145 yds; 15 lbs/145 yds; 20 lbs/145 yds; 15 lbs/265 yds; 20 lbs/220 yds; 30 lbs/290 yds; 65 lbs/260 yds
Weight: 6.5 oz; 8.3 oz; 8.3 oz; 9.9 oz; 10.6 oz; 19.6 oz; 19.0 oz
Hand Retrieve: R or L
Max Drag: 7 lbs; 20 lbs; 15 lbs; 24 lbs; 20 lbs; 28 lbs; 28 lbs

Reel Bearings: 7+1; 8+1; 8+1; 8+1; 8+1; 8+1; 8+1;
Features: X-ship; new Magnumlite CI4 rotor (1000-4000); aluminum sideplate; rapid fire drag; new reel stand on 1000-5000 only; Paladin gear durability enhancement; propulsion line management system: propulsion spool lip, power roller III; redesigned bail trip; aero wrap II oscillation; SR-concept: SR 3D gear, SR one-piece bail wire; shielded A-RB ball bearings; aluminum spool; S-concept: S rotor, S guard, S arm cam; new machined aluminum handle; direct drive mechanism (thread in handle attachment); EVA handle knob; waterproof drag; maintenance port; Fluidrive II; floating shaft; Dyna-Balance Super Stopper II; repairable clicker; approved for use in salt water; rated for use with mono, fluorocarbon, and PowerPro lines.
Price: . . . . **$329.99–$399.99**

SHIMANO SYMETRE FL

Model: 500, 1000, 2500, 3000, 4000
Gear Ratio: 4.7:1; 6.0:1; 6.2:1; 6.2:1; 5.8:1
Inches/Turn: 21; 29; 35; 35; 36
Spool Cap. (M): 4 lbs/100 yds; 6 lbs/110 yds; 8 lbs/140 yds; 10 lbs/140 yds; 12 lbs/160 yds;
Spool Cap. (B): 8 lbs/105 yds; 10 lbs/95 yds; 15 lbs/145 yds; 20 lbs/145 yds; 30 lbs/175 yds
Weight: 6.1 oz; 6.5 oz; 9 oz; 9 oz; 11.8 oz

Hand Retrieve: R or L
Max Drag: 6 lbs; 7 lbs; 11 lbs; 15 lbs; 15 lbs
Reel Bearings: 4+1
Features: New XGT7 graphite frame and sideplate; four bearings, one roller bearing; front drag; Super Stopper anti-reverse; cold-forged aluminum spool; approved for use in salt water.
Price:.............................**$99.99–$109.99**

SHIMANO SYNCOPATE FG

Model: 1000, 2500, 4000
Gear Ratio: 5.2:1; 5.2:1; 5.1:1
Inches/Turn: 25; 29; 32
Spool Cap. (M): 4 lbs/140 yds; 8 lbs/140 yds; 10 lbs/200 yds
Spool Cap. (B): 15 lbs/85 yds; 15 lbs/145 yds; 30 lbs/175 yds
Weight: 7.6 oz; 9.2 oz; 12.7 oz

Hand Retrieve: R or L
Max Drag: 7 lbs; 7 lbs; 13 lbs
Reel Bearings: 4
Features: Propulsion spool lip; graphite frame; graphite sideplate; graphite rotor; aluminum spool; Varispeed oscillation; ported handle shank; Quick Fire II; Dyna-Balance; Power Roller II; P3; approved for use in salt water; rated for use with mono, fluorocarbon, and PowerPro lines.
Price:.................................**$29.99**

SHIMANO THUNNUS

Model: 4000, 6000, 8000, 12000
Gear Ratio: 4.8:1; 4.8:1; 4.8:1; 4.4:1
Inches/Turn: 30; 35; 36; 37
Spool Cap. (M): 12 lbs/160 yds; 20 lbs/120 yds; 20 lbs/195 yds; 20 lbs/265 lbs
Spool Cap. (B): 40 lbs/145 yds; 65 lbs/130 yds; 65 lbs/180 yds; 80 lbs/230 yds
Weight: 12.7 oz; 18 oz; 19.4 oz; 27.7 oz
Hand Retrieve: R or L
Max Drag: 15 lbs; 20 lbs; 20 lbs; 25 lbs
Reel Bearings: 6+1
Features: Lightweight CI4 frame and rotor (AL on 12000); aluminum sideplate; Paladin gear durability enhancement; propulsion line management system: propulsion spool lip, SR one-piece bail wire, Power Roller III; redesigned bail trip; Varispeed oscillation; S-concept, S-rotor, S-arm cam, direct drive mechanism (thread-in handle attachment); oversized Septon grips for power and comfort; waterproof drag; machined aluminum handle; Dartainium II drag washers (cross carbon); repairable clicker; shielded A-RB ball bearings; Super Stopper II anti-reverse; Dyna-Balance; floating shaft; Fluidrive II gearing; approved for use in salt water; rated for use with mono, fluorocarbon, and PowerPro lines.
Price: . . . . **$259.99–$299.99**

304 Abu Garcia
307 Bass Pro Shops

308 Daiwa
308 Eagle Claw

309 Pflueger
310 Zebco

ABU GARCIA ABUMATIC 276I

Model: Abumatic 276i
Gear Ratio: 3.6:1
Inches/Turn: 19
Spool Cap. (M): 8 lbs/110 yds
Weight: 9.2 oz
Hand Retrieve: R or L

Max Drag: 8 lbs
Reel Bearings: 1+1
Features: Duragear drive; instant anti-reverse; ultra-smooth spool drag system; titanium nitride line guide; dual rotating swing-arm pick-up pins.
Price:. . . . .**$29.95–$34.95**

ABU GARCIA ABUMATIC 276UI

Model: Abumatic 276Ui
Gear Ratio: 3.6:1
Inches/Turn: 19
Spool Cap. (M): 8 lbs/110 yds
Weight: 10.1 oz
Hand Retrieve: R or L

Max Drag: 8 lbs
Reel Bearings: 1+1
Features: Dual bearing Duragear drive; instant anti-reverse; ultra-smooth spool drag system; titanium nitride line guide; dual rotating swing-arm pick-up pins.
Price:. **$34.95**

REELS

ABU GARCIA ABUMATIC 476I

Model: Abumatic 476i
Gear Ratio: 3.6:1
Inches/Turn: 19
Spool Cap. (M): 12 lbs/100 yds
Weight: 10.1 oz
Hand Retrieve: R or L

Max Drag: 10 lbs
Reel Bearings: 1+1
Features: Duragear drive; instant anti-reverse; ultra-smooth spool drag system; titanium nitride line guide; dual rotating swing-arm pick-up pins.
Price: **$34.95**

ABU GARCIA ABUMATIC 576I

Model: Abumatic 576i
Gear Ratio: 3.6:1
Inches/Turn: 19
Spool Cap. (M): 8 lbs/110 yds
Weight: 9.4 oz
Hand Retrieve: R or L

Max Drag: 8 lbs
Reel Bearings: 3+1
Features: Duragea drive; instant anti-reverse; ultra-smooth spool drag system; titanium nitride line guide; dual rotating swing-arm pick-up pins; fresh and salt water ready.
Price: **$44.95**

REELS: Freshwater Spincasting

ABU GARCIA ABUMATIC 1276SLI
Model: Abumatic 1276SLI
Gear Ratio: 3.6:1
Inches/Turn: 22
Spool Cap. (M): 14 lbs/100 yds
Weight: 10.2 oz
Hand Retrieve: R or L

Max Drag: 10 lbs
Reel Bearings: 4+1
Features: Four-bearing Duragear drive; instant anti-reverse bearing; ultra-smooth spool drag system; titanium nitride front cone, rotor, and line guide; dual rotating swing-arm titanium nitride pick-up pin; fresh and salt water ready.
Price:..................................... **$64.95**

ABU GARCIA ABUMATIC 170I
Model: Abumatic Classic 170i
Gear Ratio: 3.9:1
Inches/Turn: 25
Spool Cap. (M): 12 lbs/140 yds
Weight: 11.8 oz
Hand Retrieve: R
Max Drag: 10 lbs

Reel Bearings: 3+1
Features: Three-bearing Duragear drive; instant anti-reverse; ultra-smooth carbon matrix SYNCRO drag system; aluminum die-cast and machined body and front cone; dual rotating swing-arm pick-up pins; oscillating far-cast spool with no-twist line system; easy one-touch casting; fresh and salt water ready.
Price:..................................... **$54.95**

BASS PRO SHOPS TINYLITE
Model: TinyLite MCB
Gear Ratio: 4.1:1
Inches/Turn: 16
Spool Cap. (M): 4 lbs/70 yds
Weight: 5.2 oz
Hand Retrieve: R or L

Reel Bearings: 1
Features: Trouble-free handling and loads of fun; polished stainless steel front and rear cones; smooth ball bearing drive system; multi-stop anti-reverse allows quick on/off adjustment; pre-spooled with 70 yards of 4-pound mono.
Price:. **$17.99**

BASS PRO SHOPS TINYLITE TRIGGER
Model: TinyLite Trigger SB
Gear Ratio: 4.1:1
Inches/Turn: 16
Spool Cap. (M): 4 lbs/70 yds
Weight: 5.5 oz
Hand Retrieve: R or L

Reel Bearings: 1
Features: Trouble-free handling and loads of fun; polished stainless steel front and rear cones; smooth ball bearing drive system; multi-stop anti-reverse allows quick on/off adjustment; pre-spooled with 70 yards of 4-pound mono.
Price:. **$17.99**

REELS

DAIWA GOLDCAST

Model: 80, 100, 120
Gear Ratio: 4.1:1
Inches/Turn: 18.3, 20.8, 21.3
Spool Cap. (M): 8 lbs/75 yds; 10 lbs/80 yds; 12 lbs/100 lbs
Weight: 9.2 oz; 9.9 oz; 12 oz
Hand Retrieve: R or L
Reel Bearings: 1

Features: Ball bearing drive; rotating tungsten carbide line pickup; rugged metal body, gearing and nose\cone Fast 4.1: 1 right/left retrieve; oscillating spool levelwind; optimized line aperture for maximum casting; pre-wound with premium line; ultra-smooth, multi-disc drag.
Price: . . . .**$52.95–$54.95**

EAGLE CLAW TITAN

Model: SC100, SC200, SC400
Gear Ratio: 3.3:1
Spool Cap. (M): 8 lbs/100 yds; 10 lbs/100 yds; 20 lbs/205 yds
Weight: 8 oz; 9 oz; 14 oz

Hand Retrieve: R or L
Reel Bearings: 1+1
Features: SC100 & SC200 have star drag system; two ball bearings with one-way clutch; stainless steel front and rear cover; one-year warranty.
Price: **$21.99**

PFLUEGER PRESIDENT
Model: MSSCX, MCSCX, 6USCX, 6SCX, 10SCX
Gear Ratio: 4.1:1; 4.1:1; 3.4:1; 3.4:1; 3.8:1
Inches/Turn: 14; 14; 14.5; 14.5; 18.5
Spool Cap. (M): 2 lbs/90 yds; 2 lbs/90 yds; 4 lbs/110 yds; 4 lbs/110 yds; 8 lbs/90 yds
Hand Retrieve: R or L
Reel Bearings: 5

Features: Four ball bearings; instant anti-reverse bearing; rigid aluminum frame; ported machined aluminum front cone; aluminum handle with soft-touch knob; titanium-coated line guide and dual pick-up pins; spool applied, adjustable disc-drag system; heavy-duty metal gears; convertible left- and right-hand retrieve; pre-spooled with line.
Price: **$39.99**

PFLUEGER TRION
Model: CSCX, SSCX, 6SCB, USCB, 0SCX, 10USCB
Gear Ratio: 4.1:1; 4.1:1; 3.4:1; 3.4:1; 3.8:1; 3.8:1;
Inches/Turn: 14; 14; 14.5; 14.5; 18.5; 18.5
Spool Cap. (M): 2 lbs/90 yds; 2 lbs/90 yds; 4 lbs/110 yds; 4 lbs/110 yds; 8 lbs/90 yds; 8 lbs/90 yds
Hand Retrieve: R or L

Reel Bearings: 2
Features: Two ball bearings; ported machined aluminum front cone; aluminum handle with soft-touch handle knob; titanium pick-up pins; heavy-duty metal gears; convertible left- and right-hand retrieve; pre-spooled with line.
Price: **$29.99**

ZEBCO 33 AUTHENTIC
Model: 33
Gear Ration: 3.6:1
Inches/Turn: 19
Spool Cap. (M): 10 lbs/110 yds
Weight: 8.5 oz
Hand Retrieve: R or L

Reel Bearings: 2+1
Features: Three-bearing drive; industrial-grade stainless steel covers; reversible for right- or left-hand retrieve; quick-set multi-stop anti-reverse; micro-fine adjustment drag control; improved line management system; TPR over-molded rubber knobs.
Price:..................................... **$24.99**

ZEBCO 33 AUTHENTIC LADIES
Model: 33 Lady
Gear Ration: 3.6:1
Inches/Turn: 19
Spool Cap. (M): 10 lbs/110 yds
Weight: 8.5 oz
Hand Retrieve: R or L
Reel Bearings: 1

Features: Ball bearing drive; quick-set multi-stop anti-reverse; industrial-grade stainless steel covers; reversible for right- or left-hand retrieve; micro-fine adjustment drag control; improved line management system; PVC rubber knobs.
Price:..................................... **$24.99**

ZEBCO DELTA
Model: ZD3, ZD2
Gear Ratio: 2.9:1; 3.4:1
Inches/Turn: 14; 16
Spool Cap. (M): 6 lbs/85 yds; 10 lbs/85 yds
Weight: 9.5 oz; 13 oz
Hand Retrieve: R or L
Reel Bearings: 5

Features: Ideal for light to medium fishing situations; double-anodized aircraft-grade aluminum covers; 5 bearing system; triple-cam multi-disc drag; multi-point positive pickup system; ceramic line guide; positive worm-gear drive train; Continuous Anti-Reverse.
Price: **$44.99**

ZEBCO GOLD
Model: 11, 11T, 22
Gear Ratio: 4.3:1; 4.3:1; 3.4:1
Spool Cap. (M): 4 lbs/75 yds; 4 lbs/75 yds; 8 lbs/125 yds
Hand Retrieve: R or L
Reel Bearings: 3

Features: Ball-bearing drive; dual ceramic pickup pins for instant line recovery; classic design with updated components.
Price: . . . .**$26.99–$34.99**

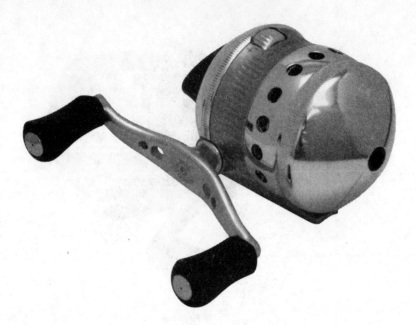

ZEBCO OMEGA

Model: Z02, Z03
Gear Ratio: 3.4:1
Spool Cap. (M): 6 lbs/85 yds; 10 lbs/85 yds
Weight: 10.5 oz
Hand Retrieve: R or L

Reel Bearings: 6+1
Features: The pinnacle of spincast performance; all-metal gears; aircraft aluminum covers; triple-cam multi-disc drag system; 3X positive line pickup; oscillating spool.
Price:. . . . .**$64.99–$69.99**

ZEBCO OMEGA PRO

Model: Omega Pro
Gear Ratio: 2.9:1
Spool Cap. (M): 10 lbs/90 yds
Hand Retrieve: R or L

Reel Bearings: 7
Features: Pro-level spincast performance; all-metal gears; aircraft aluminum covers; 3X positive line pickup (ZO3); oscillating spool.
Price:. . . . .**$74.99–$84.99**

REELS

ZEBCO PLATINUM 733
Model: Platinum 733
Gear Ratio: 2.6:1
Inches/Turn: 14
Spool Cap. (M): 20 lbs/90 yds
Weight: 14

Hand Retrieve: R or L
Reel Bearings: 1
Features: Ideal for catfish and other large species; powerful ball bearing drive and selective anti-reverse; dual ceramic pickup pins.
Price:................................... **$39.99**

ZEBCO PRO STAFF
Model: PS2010B, PS2020B
Gear Ratio: 3.9:1; 3.6:1
Inches/Turn: 16; 17
Spool Cap. (M): 6 lbs/90 yds; 8 lbs/90 yds
Weight: 5.6 oz; 8 oz
Hand Retrieve: R or L

Reel Bearings: 4
Features: Some of the most popular reels of all time; built to last with corrosion-resistant brass and stainless steel components; 3-bearing ball bearing drive system; positive pickup design; selective multi-stop anti-reverse with premium mono line.
Price:.............................**$24.99–$29.99**

316 Abu Garcia   **319 Zebco**

ABU GARCIA ABUMATIC 276I

Model: Abumatic 276i
Gear Ratio: 3.6:1
Inches/Turn: 19
Spool Cap. (M): 8 lbs/110 yds
Weight: 9.2 oz
Hand Retrieve: R or L

Max Drag: 8 lbs
Reel Bearings: 1+1
Features: Duragear drive; instant anti-reverse; ultra-smooth spool drag system; titanium nitride line guide; dual rotating swing-arm pick-up pins.
Price:....................................$29.95

ABU GARCIA ABUMATIC 276UI

Model: Abumatic 276Ui
Gear Ratio: 3.6:1
Inches/Turn: 19
Spool Cap. (M): 8 lbs/110 yds
Weight: 10.1 oz
Hand Retrieve: R or L

Max Drag: 8 lbs
Reel Bearings: 1+1
Features: Dual-bearing Duragear drive; instant anti-reverse; ultra-smooth spool drag system; titanium nitride line guide; dual rotating swing-arm pick-up pins.
Price:....................................$34.95

REELS

ABU GARCIA ABUMATIC 476I

Model: Abumatic 476i
Gear Ratio: 3.6:1
Inches/Turn: 19
Spool Cap. (M): 12 lbs/100 yds
Weight: 10.1 oz
Hand Retrieve: R or L
Max Drag: 10 lbs

Reel Bearings: 1+1
Features: Duragear drive; instant anti-reverse; ultra-smooth spool drag system; titanium nitride line guide; dual rotating swing-arm pick-up pins.
Price: **$34.95**

ABU GARCIA ABUMATIC 576I

Model: Abumatic 576i
Gear Ratio: 3.6:1
Inches/Turn: 19
Spool Cap. (M): 8 lbs/110 yds
Weight: 9.4 oz
Hand Retrieve: R or L

Max Drag: 8 lbs
Reel Bearings: 3+1
Features: Duragear drive; instant anti-reverse; ultra-smooth spool drag system; titanium nitride line guide; dual rotating swing-arm pick-up pins; fresh and salt water ready.
Price: **$44.95**

REELS

REELS: Saltwater Spincasting

ABU GARCIA ABUMATIC 1276SLI
Model: Abumatic 1276SLI
Gear Ratio: 3.6:1
Inches/Turn: 22
Spool Cap. (M): 14 lbs/100 yds
Weight: 10.2 oz
Hand Retrieve: R or L

Max Drag: 10 lbs
Reel Bearings: 4+1
Features: Four-bearing Duragear drive; instant anti-reverse bearing; ultra-smooth spool drag system; titanium nitride front cone, rotor, and line guide; dual rotating swing-arm; titanium nitride pick-up pin; fresh and salt water ready.
Price: **$64.95**

ABU GARCIA ABUMATIC CLASSIC 170I
Model: Abumatic Classic 170i
Gear Ratio: 3.9:1
Inches/Turn: 25
Spool Cap. (M): 12 lbs/140 yds
Weight: 11.8 oz
Hand Retrieve: R
Max Drag: 10 lbs
Reel Bearings: 3+1

Features: Three-bearing Duragear drive; instant anti-reverse; ultra-smooth carbon Matrix SYNCRO drag system; aluminum die-cast and machined body and front cone; dual rotating swing-arm pick-up pins; oscillating far-cast spool with no-twist line system; easy one-touch casting; fresh and salt water ready.
Price: **$54.95**

ZEBCO SALTFISHER 808
Gear Ratio: 2.58:1
Spool Cap. (M): 20 lbs/150 yds
Weight: 22
Hand Retrieve: R

Reel Bearings: 1
Features: Salt water grade spincast products; large-sized combos and reels; true salt water protection.
Price:. **$39.99**

REELS

ABU GARCIA PRO MAX

Model: 2, 2-L
Gear Ratio: 7.1:1
Inches/Turn: 31
Retrieve Speed: High
Spool Cap. (M): 12 lbs/145 yds
Spool Cap. (B): 30 lbs/130 yds
Weight: 7.9 oz
Hand Retrieve: R; L
Max Drag: 15 lbs
Reel Bearings: 8

Features: Seven stainless steel ball bearings plus one roller bearing provides smooth operation; machined double anodized aluminum spool provides strength without adding excess weight; Power Disk drag system gives smooth drag performance; Duragear brass gear for extended gear life; MagTrax brake system gives consistent brake pressure throughout the cast; recessed reel foot plus a compact bent handle and star provide a more ergonomic design; lightweight one-piece graphite frame and graphite sideplates.
Price: **$79.95**

ABU GARCIA REVO MGX

Model: MGX, MGX-L, MGX-SHS, MGX-SHS-L
Gear Ratio: 7.1:1; 7.1:1; 7.9:1; 7.9:1
Inches/Turn: 28; 28; 31; 31
Retrieve Speed: Std; std; high; super high
Spool Cap. (M): 12 lbs/115 yds
Spool Cap. (B): 30 lbs/110 yds
Weight: 5.4 oz
Hand Retrieve: R; L; R; L
Max Drag: 12 lbs
Reel Bearings: 10
Features: Nine stainless steel high-performance corrosion-resistant bearings plus one roller bearing provides increased corrosion protection; one-piece X-mag alloy frame provides a super light yet extremely strong frame; Infini II spool design for extended castability and extreme loads; C6 carbon sideplates provide significant weight reduction without sacrificing strength and durability; carbon matrix drag system provides smooth, consistent drag pressure across the entire drag range; aircraft-grade aluminum main gear provides weight reduction without sacrificing durability; IVCB-IV infinitely variable centrifugal brake gives very precise brake adjustments allowing anglers to easily cast a wide variety of baits; compact bent carbon handle provides a more ergonomic design that is extremely lightweight; flat EVA knobs provide greater comfort and durability; titanium coated line guide reduces friction and improves durability; recessed reel foot allows for a more ergonomic reel design.
Price: **$349.95**

ABU GARCIA REVO MGXTREME
Model: MGXTREME, MGXTREME-L
Gear Ratio: 7.1:1
Inches/Turn: 28
Retrieve Speed: Std
Spool Cap. (M): 12 lbs/115 yds
Spool Cap. (B): 30 lbs/130 yds
Weight: 4.9 oz
Hand Retrieve: R; L
Max Drag: 12 lbs

Reel Bearings: 10
Features: Ten-bearing system; seven stainless high-performance corrosion-resistant bearings plus one roller bearing; two additional CeramiLite spool bearings; one-piece X-Mag alloy frame; aircraft-grade aluminum main gear; Carbon Matrix drag system; C6 carbon sideplates; infinitely variable centrifugal brake; Infini II spool design; compact bent carbon handle; round EVA knob.
Price: $499.99

ABU GARCIA REVO PREMIER
Model: PRM, PRM-HS, PRM-L
Gear Ratio: 6.4:1; 7.1:1; 6.4:1
Inches/Turn: 26; 29; 26
Retrieve Speed: Std; High; Std
Spool Cap. (M): 12 lbs/145 yds
Spool Cap. (B): 30 lbs/140 yds
Weight: 5.87 oz
Hand Retrieve: R; R; L
Max Drag: 20 lbs
Reel Bearings: 11
Features: Ten stainless steel high-performance corrosion-resistant bearings plus one roller bearing provides increased corrosion protection; X2-Cräftic alloy frame for increased corrosion resistance; C6 carbon sideplates provide significant weight reduction without sacrificing strength and durability; carbon matrix drag system provides smooth, consistent drag pressure across the entire drag range; D2 Gear Design provides a more efficient gear system while improving gear durability; Infinitely Variable Centrifugal Brake gives very precise brake adjustments allowing anglers to easily cast a wide variety of baits; Infini II spool design for extended castability and extreme loads; compact bent carbon handle provides a more ergonomic design that is extremely lightweight; flat EVA knob provides greater comfort and durability; titanium-coated line guide reduces friction and improves durability; right- or left-hand models available.
Price: $299.95

ABU GARCIA REVO S

Model: S, S-L
Gear Ratio: 6.4:1
Inches/Turn: 26
Retrieve Speed: Std
Spool Cap. (M): 12 lbs/145 yds
Spool Cap. (B): 30 lbs/140 yds
Weight: 7.44 oz
Hand Retrieve: R; L
Max Drag: 20 lbs
Reel Bearings: 7+1

Features: Seven stainless steel ball bearings plus one roller bearing provides smooth operation; X2-Cräftic alloy frame for increased corrosion resistance; lightweight graphite sideplates; carbon matrix drag system provides smooth, consistent drag pressure across the entire drag range; D2 Gear Design provides a more efficient gear system while improving gear durability; pitch centrifugal brake system; compact bent handle and star provide a more ergonomic design.
Price:.....................................$129.95

ABU GARCIA REVO STX

Model: STX, STX-HS, STX-HS-L, STX-L, STX-SHS
Gear Ratio: 6.4:1; 7.1:1; 7.1:1; 6.4:1; 8.0:1
Inches/Turn: 26; 29; 29; 26; 33
Retrieve Speed: Std; High; High; Std; Super High
Spool Cap. (M): 12 lbs/145 yds
Spool Cap. (B): 30 lbs/140 yds
Weight: 6.35 oz
Hand Retrieve: R; R; L; L; R
Max Drag: 20 lbs
Reel Bearings: 10+1
Features: Ten high-performance corrosion-resistant bearings plus one roller bearing provides increased corrosion protection; X2-Cräftic alloy frame for increased corrosion resistance; C6 carbon sideplates provide significant weight reduction without sacrificing strength and durability; Carbon Matrix drag system provides smooth, consistent drag pressure across the entire drag range; D2 gear design provides a more efficient gear system while improving gear durability; Infini brake system allows almost limitless adjustability to handle any fishing situation; Infini II spool design for extended castability and extreme loads; compact bent handle and star provide a more ergonomic design; titanium-coated line guide reduces friction and improves durability.
Price:.....................................$199.95

ABU GARCIA REVO SX
Model: SX, SX-HS, SX-HS-L, SX-L
Gear Ratio: 6.4:1; 7.1:1; 7.1:1; 6.4:1
Inches/Turn: 26; 29; 29; 26
Retrieve Speed: Std; High; High; Std
Spool Cap. (M): 12 lbs/145 yds
Spool Cap. (B): 30 lbs/140 yds
Weight: 6.66 oz
Hand Retrieve: R; R; L; L
Max Drag: 20 lbs
Reel Bearings: 10
Features: Nine stainless steel ball bearings plus one roller bearing provides smooth operation; X2-Cräftic alloy frame for increased corrosion resistance; C6 carbon handle sideplate provides significant weight reduction without sacrificing strength and durability; carbon matrix drag system provides smooth, consistent drag pressure across the entire drag range; D2 Gear Design provides a more efficient gear system while improving gear durability; MagTrax brake system gives consistent brake pressure throughout the cast; Infini II spool design for extended castability and extreme loads; compact bent handle and star provide a more ergonomic design; titanium-coated line guide reduces friction and improves durability.
Price: **$159.95**

BASS PRO SHOPS BIONIC PLUS
Model: 10HE, 10HLE, 10SE, 10SHE, 10SHLE
Gear Ratio: 6.3:1; 6.3:1; 5.3:1; 7.0:1; 7.0:1
Inches/Turn: 25; 25; 20; 27; 27
Spool Cap. (M): 12 lbs/130 yds
Spool Cap. (B): 30 lbs/190 yds
Weight: 8.1 oz
Hand Retrieve: R; L; R; R; L
Max Drag: 12 lbs
Reel Bearings: 5+1
Features: All-aluminum frame; striking white finish; smart cast anti-backlash system; six-bearing system including Powerlock instant anti-reverse; forged double-anodized aluminum V-grooved spool; aluminum recurve handle and drag star.
Price: $79.99

REELS

BASS PRO SHOPS EXTREME
Model: 10SHA, 10HA, 10SA, 10SHLA, 10HLA,
Gear Ratio: 7.1:1; 6.3:1; 5.3:1; 7.1:1; 6.3:1
Inches/Turn: 27; 24; 20; 27; 24
Spool Cap. (M): 12 lbs/120 yds
Weight: 7.2 oz
Hand Retrieve: R; R; R; L; L
Max Drag: 12 lbs
Reel Bearings: 6+1

Features: Tournament-proven dual braking system; double-anodized V-grooved spool is free-floating; 4-disc aramid fiber/stainless steel washer drag system; one-piece cast, then CNC-machined aluminum frame; easy-access sideplate with push-button release; titanium nitride-coated line guide seven-bearing system; recurve handle; click drag star.
Price: **$89.99**

BASS PRO SHOPS JOHNNY MORRIS CARBONLITE
Model: 10SHA, 10HA, 10HLA, 10SA
Gear Ratio: 7.1:1; 6.4:1; 6.4:1; 5.4:1
Inches/Turn: 29; 26; 26; 22
Spool Cap. (M): 12 lbs/120 yds
Weight: 5.6 oz
Hand Retrieve: R; R; L; R
Max Drag: 14 lbs
Reel Bearings: 9+1

Features: Weighs just 5.9 ounces; one-piece machined aircraft-grade frame; Duralumin gears and shaft V-grooved, ported, machined; Duralumin spool; nine stainless steel, double-shielded ball bearings; a powerlock anti-reverse bearing dual braking system; titanium nitride-coated line guide; carbon fiber recurve handle; drag system with six alternating carbon fiber and stainless washers.
Price: **$129.99**

BASS PRO SHOPS MEGACAST
Model: 1000, 2000
Gear Ratio: 5.2:1
Inches/Turn: 23
Spool Cap. (M): 12 lbs/200 yds
Weight: 9.7 oz
Hand Retrieve: R; L
Max Drag: 8.8 lbs

Reel Bearings: 2+1
Features: Versatile, dependable, and strong; unyielding all-metal frame; three-bearing system includes PowerLock instant anti-reverse; on/off bait clicker switch; easy-adjusting star drag.
Price: **$39.99**

BASS PRO SHOPS PRO QUALIFIER
Model: 10SD, 10SLD, 10SSD, 10SHLA, 10SHD, 10HD, 10HLA
Gear Ratio: 5.2:1; 5.2:1; 4.7:1; 7.1:1; 7.1:1; 6.4:1; 6.4:1
Inches/Turn: 21; 21; 19; 29; 29; 26; 26
Spool Cap. (M): 12 lbs/150 yds; 12 lbs/150 yds; 12 lbs/150 yds; 12 lbs/120 yds; 12 lbs/120 yds; 12 lbs/120 yds; 12 lbs/120 yds;
Weight: 8.8 oz
Hand Retrieve: R; L; R; L; R; R; L

Max Drag: 10 lbs
Reel Bearings: 6+1
Features: Built to put you at the top of your game; one-piece machined-aluminum frame; double-anodized, machined-aluminum drilled spool; seven-bearing system with Powerlock instant anti-reverse dual braking system; pin-release sideplate for quick brake adjustments; built-in lube port.
Price: **$99.99**

REELS: Freshwater Baitcasting

BASS PRO SHOPS TOURNEY SPECIAL
Model: 10HC, 10SC, 10SHC
Gear Ratio: 6.3:1; 5.3:1; 7.0:1
Inches/Turn: 26; 21; 28
Spool Cap. (M): 12 lbs/130 yds
Spool Cap. (B): 30 lbs/185 yds
Weight: 7.6 oz
Hand Retrieve: R

Max Drag: 12 lbs
Reel Bearings: 4+1
Features: Smart cast dual centrifugal brake; five bearing system includes instant anti-reverse; available in right- or left-hand retrieve; striking new black and silver finish.
Price: **$49.99**

CABELA'S TOURNAMENT ZX
Model: BCR-1, BCL-1, BCRHS-1, BCLHS-1
Gear Ratio: 6.5:1; 6.5:1; 7.2:1; 7.2:1
Inches/Turn: 25.7; 25.7; 28.5; 28.5
Spool Cap. (M): 10 lbs/110 yds
Weight: 6.1 oz
Hand Retrieve: R; L; R; L
Max Drag: 8 lbs
Reel Bearings: 8+1

Features: Eight stainless steel ball bearings for smooth performance; externally controlled magnetic braking system; high-strength, one-piece aluminum frame; aircraft-grade graphite side covers; ported aluminum spool; aluminum handle with EVA handle knobs; carbon-fiber drag washer.
Price: **$79.99**

DAIWA AIRD

Model: 100P, 100H, 100HL, 100HS
Gear Ratio: 4.9:1; 6.3:1; 6.3:1; 7.1:1
Inches/Turn: 20.6; 25.7; 25.7; 30
Spool Cap. (M): 12 lbs/120 yds
Spool Cap. (B): 40 lbs/140 yds; 40 lbs/135 yds; 40 lbs/140 yds; 40 lbs/135 yds
Weight: 7.7 oz
Hand Retrieve: L; R; L; R
Max Drag: 8.8 lbs
Reel Bearings: 8+1

Features: Open access, low-profile design for easy thumbing and line maintenance; weighs just 7.7 ounces; ultimate tournament carbon drag with 8.8-pound drag max nine-bearing system (8BB+1RB); Magforce cast control swept handle for less wobble, better feel, and winding power; machined aluminum perforated spool; oversized soft-touch grips.
Price: **$89.95**

DAIWA EXCELER EXE

Model: 100HA, 100HSA, 100HLA, 100HSLA, 100PA
Gear Ratio: 6.3:1; 7.3:1; 6.3:1; 7.3:1; 4.9:1
Inches/Turn: 25.7; 30.6; 25.7; 30.6; 20.6
Spool Cap. (M): 14 lbs/120 yds
Spool Cap. (B): 40 lbs/140 yds
Weight: 7.9 oz
Hand Retrieve: R; R; L; R; R
Max Drag: 11 lbs

Reel Bearings: 5+1
Features: Aluminum frame and sideplate; gear ratios from 4.9 power cranking to 7.3:1 hyper speed; ultimate tournament drag with 11-pound drag max; Magforce cast control; oversized, I-shape grips; infinite, dual anti-reverse; cut-away swept handle for greater power, less wobble, lighter weight.
Price: **$99.99**

Freshwater Baitcasting

DAIWA LAGUNA

Model: 100H, 100HL, 100HS
Gear Ratio: 6.3:1; 6.3:1; 7.1:1
Inches/Turn: 25.7; 25.7; 30
Spool Cap. (M): 12 lbs/120 yds
Weight: 7.4 oz
Hand Retrieve: R; L; R
Max Drag: 8.8
Reel Bearings: 5+1

Features: Open access, low-profile frame for easy thumbing and line maintenance; lightweight composite frame and sideplates; swept handle for less wobble, better feel, and winding power; five ball bearings plus roller bearing; Magforce magnetic anti-backlash control; lightweight, drilled aluminum spool; dual-system infinite; anti-reverse.
Price:................................. **$59.95**

DAIWA LEXA HIGH CAPACITY

Model: 100H, 400HS-P, 300HS-P, 300HS, 100HS, 300H, 400HL, 400HSL, 400HSL-P, 300PWRL, 300HSL-P, 300HSL, 300HL, 100HSL, 100HL, 100PL, 300PWR, 100P, 400H, 400HS, 400PWR-P
Gear Ratio: 6.3:1; 7.1:1; 7.1:1; 7.1:1; 7.1:1; 6.3:1; 6.3:1; 7.1:1:1; 7.1:1:1 5.1:1; 7.1:1; 7.1:1; 6.3:1; 7.1:1; 6.3:1; 4.9:1; 5.1:1; 4.9:1; 6.3:1; 7.1:1; 5.1:1
Inches/Turn: 25.7; 37.7; 32.4; 32.4; 30.0; 28.8; 33.4; 37.7; 37.7; 23.3; 32.4; 32.4; 28.8; 30.0; 25; 20.6; 23.3; 20.6; 33.4; 37.7; 27.1
Spool Cap. (M): 14 lbs/120 yds; 17 lbs/245 yds; 12 lbs/240 yds; 12 lbs/240 yds; 14 lbs/120 yds; 12 lbs/240 yds; 17 lbs/245 yds; 17 lbs/245 yds; 17 lbs/245 yds; 12 lbs/240 yds; 12 lbs/240 yds; 12 lbs/240 yds; 12 lbs/240 yds; 14 lbs/120 yds; 14 lbs/120 yds; 14 lbs/120 yds; 12 lbs/240 yds; 14 lbs/120 yds; 17 lbs/245 yds; 17 lbs/245 yds; 17 lbs/245 yds
Spool Cap. (B): 40 lbs/140 yds; 44 lbs/300 yds; 40 lbs/240 yds; 40 lbs/240 yds; 40 lbs/140 yds; 55 lbs/140 yds; 40 lbs/140 yds; 40 lbs/140 yds; 40 lbs/240 yds; 40 lbs/240 yds; 55 lbs/300 yds; 55 lbs/300 yds; 55 lbs/300 yds; 40 lbs/240 yds; 40 lbs/240 yds; 40 lbs/240 yds; 40 lbs/240 yds; 40 lbs/140 yds; 55 lbs/300 yds; 55 lbs/300 yds; 55 lbs/300 yds

Weight: 8 oz; 16.2 oz; 11.3 oz; 10.5 oz; 8 oz; 10.5 oz; 15.3 oz; 15.3 oz; 16.2 oz; 10.5 oz; 11.3 oz; 10.5 oz; 10.5 oz; 8 oz; 8 oz; 8 oz; 10.5 oz; 8 oz; 15.3 oz; 15.3 oz; 16.2 oz
Hand Retrieve: R; R; R; R; R; L; L; L; L; L; L; L; L; L; L; R; R; R; R; R
Max Drag: 11 lbs; 25 lbs; 22 lbs; 22 lbs; 11 lbs; 22lbs; 25 lbs; 25 lbs; 25 lbs; 22 lbs; 22 lbs; 22 lbs; 22 lbs; 11 lbs; 11 lbs; 11 lbs; 22 lbs; 11 lbs; 25 lbs; 25 lbs; 25 lbs
Reel Bearings: 7+1
Features: Aluminum frame and sideplate (gear side); seven-bearing system (2CRBB, 4BB+1RB); Magforce cast control; infinite anti-reverse; swept handle with weight-reducing cutouts; counter-balanced power handle on P models; super-leverage 120mm handle on 400 size models; A7075 aluminum spool, super lightweight and extra strong (100 size); extra line capacity for strong lines; ultimate tournament carbon drag.
Price:............................ **$129.99–$249.99**

DAIWA MEGAFORCE THS (WITH TWITCHIN' BAR)

Model: 100THS, 100THSL
Gear Ratio: 7.3:1
Inches/Turn: 31.5
Spool Cap. (M): 12 lbs/150 yds
Weight: 8.8 oz
Hand Retrieve: R; L

Max Drag: 8.8 lbs
Reel Bearings: 6
Features: Twitchin' Bar six ball bearings; hyper speed 7.3: 1 gear ratio; swept handle Magforce-Z automatic antibacklash control; precision click drag adjustment.
Price: **$89.95**

DAIWA PX TYPE-R

Model: PX-R, PXL-R
Gear Ratio: 6.8:1
Inches/Turn: 26
Spool Cap. (M): 6 lbs/95 yds
Weight: 5.8 oz
Hand Retrieve: R; L
Max Drag: 13 lbs

Reel Bearings: 10
Features: Weighs just 5.8 ounces; magnesium body; ten ball bearings; carbon swept handle; cork handle knobs; hyper speed 6.8:1 gear ratio; UT drag with a drag max of 13 pounds.; Magforce-Z cast control.
Price: **$499.95**

DAIWA STEEZ EX

Model: 100XS, 100HS, 100H, 100HSL, 100HL
Gear Ratio: 7.9:1; 7.1:1; 6.3:1; 7.1:1; 6.3:1
Inches/Turn: 33.2; 29.8; 26; 29.8; 26
Spool Cap. (M): 14 lbs/120 yds
Weight: 5.8 oz; 5.8 oz; 5.4 oz; 5.8 oz; 5.4 oz
Hand Retrieve: R; R; R; L; L
Max Drag: 13.2 lbs
Reel Bearings: 11+1
Features: Super lightweight magnesium frame and sideplate; swept handle with cutouts for reduced weight; oversized, lightweight 100 MM handle on 7.1 and 7.9 models; ultimate tournament carbon drag with 13.2-pound drag max; free-floating A7075 aluminum alloy spool starts faster, spins longer; fast spool change; eleven precision ball bearings plus roller bearing; tough Dura-Loc pinion; Magforce-Z cast control; precision, micro-click adjustment on star drag and free-spool cap; infinite anti-reverse; free neoprene reel cover included.
Price: **$599.95**

DAIWA T3

Model: 1016HS, 1016H, 1016HSL, 1016HL
Gear Ratio: 7.1:1; 6.3:1; 7.1:1; 6.3:1
Inches/Turn: 29.5; 26.3; 29.5; 26.3
Spool Cap. (M): 14 lbs/120 yds
Weight: 6.5 oz
Hand Retrieve: R; R; L; L
Max Drag: 13.2 lbs
Reel Bearings: 8+1
Features: T-wing system; Magforce 3D cast control system; weighs just 6.5 ounces; ultra-low profile; Zaion frame, clutch cover and sideplate; ultimate tournament drag with micro-click adjustment; available with 6.3:1 or 7.1:1 gear ratios; eight ball bearings (including 4 CRBB) plus roller bearing; aluminum swept handle arm with urethane-covered cork grips; free-floating, lightweight aluminum spool; infinite anti-reverse; fast, one-touch spool change.
Price: **$429.95**

DAIWA T3 BALLISTIC
Model: S100XS, S100HS, S100H, S100XSL, S100HSL, S100HL
Gear Ratio: 8.1:1; 7.1:1; 6.3:1; 8.1:1; 7.1:1; 6.3:1
Inches/Turn: 34; 29.5; 26.3; 34; 29.5; 26.3
Spool Cap. (M): 14 lbs/120 yds
Weight: 7.9 oz; 7.8 oz; 7.8 oz; 7.9 oz; 7.8 oz; 7.8 oz
Hand Retrieve: R; R; R; L; L; L
Max Drag: 11 lbs; 13.2 lbs; 13.2 lbs; 11 lbs; 13.2 lbs; 13.2 lbs
Reel Bearings: 5+1

Features: T-wing system; Magforce 3D cast control system; ultra-low profile Zaion frame, clutch cover, and sideplate; natural black marble Zaion finish; ultimate tournament drag with micro-click adjustment; available with 6.3:1 or 7.1:1 gear ratios; five ball bearings plus roller bearing; aluminum swept handle; free-floating, lightweight aluminum spool; infinite anti-reverse; fast, one-touch spool change.
Price: . . . . **$249.95–$269.95**

DAIWA TATULA
Model: 100HL, 100HSL, 100H, 100HS, R100H, R100XS, R100HL, R100XSL, 100P
Gear Ratio: 6.3:1; 7.3:1; 6.3:1; 7.3:1; 6.3:1; 8.1:1; 6.3:1; 8.1:1; 5.4:1
Inches/Turn: 26.3; 30.5; 26.3; 30.5; 26.3; 33.9; 26.3; 33.9; 22.9
Spool Cap. (M): 14 lbs/120 yds
Spool Cap. (B): 40 lbs/140 yds
Weight: 7.9; 7.9; 7.9; 7.9; 7.6; 7.6; 7.6; 7.6; 7.9
Hand Retrieve: L; L; R; R; R; R; L; L; R

Max Drag: 13.2 lbs
Reel Bearings: 7+1
Features: New T-wing system; rugged, lightweight aluminum frame and sideplate (gear side); air rotation; ultimate tournament carbon drag with 13.2-pound drag max; Magforce-Z cast control; 5.4:1, 6.3:1, and 7.3:1 gear ratios; seven ball bearings plus roller bearing; infinite anti-reverse; corrosion-resistant clutch mechanism; large, 90mm swept power handle with cutouts for reduced weight; new I-shape handle knob.
Price: **$149.95**

DAIWA TD LUNA
Model: 253, 300, 253L, 300L
Gear Ratio: 5.1:1
Inches/Turn: 23.6
Spool Cap. (M): 12 lbs/235 yds; 14 lbs/320 yds; 12 lbs/235 yds; 14 lbs/320 yds
Weight: 11.1 oz; 12.9 oz; 11.1 oz; 12.9 oz
Hand Retrieve: R; R; L; L
Max Drag: 11 lbs; 15.3 lbs; 11 lbs; 15.3 lbs
Reel Bearings: 5+1
Features: Frame and sideplates machined from solid bar stock aluminum; five CRBB super corrosion-resistant ball bearings, plus roller bearing; free-floating spool for maximum casting performance; Magforce-Z automatic magnetic anti-backlash control (Centriflex automatic centrifugal system on 300 size); ultra-smooth, multi-disc drag with Daiwa's exclusive fiber composite and stainless washers; infinite anti-reverse Dura-Loc pinion for solid gear engagement; rugged, six-point drive train support; machined aircraft aluminum spool; cut proof titanium nitrided stainless steel line guide; spool click on 300 size; hard anodized to resist corrosion.
Price: . . . . $279.95–$289.95

DAIWA TD ZILLION HIGH POWER
Model: 100PA, 100PLA
Gear Ratio: 4.9:1
Inches/Turn: 22
Spool Cap. (M): 14 lbs/120 yds
Weight: 8.8 oz
Hand Retrieve: R; L
Max Drag: 8.8 lbs
Reel Bearings: 6+1
Features: High-torque 4.9:1 gear ratio—ideal for crankbait applications; six ball bearings, including four anti-corrosion CRBB ball bearings, plus roller bearing; roller bearing; swept handle for less wobble, better feel, and maximum winding leverage; fast spool change; Magforce-Z automatic anti-backlash system; eight-disc wet drag with precision click adjustment; rigid aluminum frame and handle-side sideplate firmly support the drive train; aluminum guard plate protects finish on top of reel; soft-touch grips.
Price: $319.95

DAIWA TD ZILLION

Model: 100HA, 100SHLA, 100HLA, 100SHA
Gear Ratio: 6.3:1; 7.1:1; 6.3:1; 7.1:1
Inches/Turn: 28; 31.6; 28; 31.6
Spool Cap. (M): 12 lbs/150 yds
Weight: 8.6 oz; 8.8 oz; 8.6 oz; 8.8 oz
Hand Retrieve: R; R; L; R
Max Drag: 8.8 lbs
Reel Bearings: 6+1
Features: Choice of ultra-fast 7.1:1 retrieve or all-purpose 6.3:1; six ball bearings (including CRBB), plus roller bearing; swept handle for less wobble, better feel, and maximum winding leverage; free-floating perforated aluminum spool starts faster, spins longer; fast spool change Magforce-Z automatic anti-backlash system; eight-disc wet drag with precision click adjustment; aluminum guard plate protects finish on top of reel; rigid aluminum frame and handle-side sideplate firmly support the drive train; soft-touch grips.
Price: **$319.95**

DAIWA TD ZILLION HYPER SPEED TYPE R

Model: 100HSHR, 100HSHLR
Gear Ratio: 7.3:1
Inches/Turn: 32
Spool Cap. (M): 14 lbs/120 yds
Weight: 8.5 oz
Hand Retrieve: R; L
Max Drag: 8.5 lbs
Reel Bearings: 11
Features: Hyper Speed 7.3:1 retrieve; eleven hyper speed ball bearings; carbon swept handle; ultimate tournament carbon drag; super rigid aluminum frame and sideplate; Magforce-Z anti-backlash control; free-floating perforated aluminum spool; infinite anti-reverse.
Price: **$439.95**

REELS: Freshwater Baitcasting

DAIWA Z SERIES
Model: HS, H, HL
Gear Ratio: 7.2:1; 6.4:1; 6.4:1
Inches/Turn: 33.5; 29.5; 29.5
Spool Cap. (M): 14 lbs/155 yds
Weight: 9.9 oz
Hand Retrieve: R; R; L
Max Drag: 16.5 lbs
Reel Bearings: 8+1
Features: Magforce-3D; hyper speed 7.2:1 or all-around 6.4:1 gear ratio models; seven-disc carbon UT drag with a drag max of 16.5 pounds–click adjustment; eight CRBB corrosion-resistant ball bearings plus roller bearing; rugged, dual system anti-reverse combines infinite anti-reverse with a multi-stop system; low-friction, titanium-nitrided line guide; aluminum swept handle with large, ball bearing grips; tough aluminum frame; precision high brass drive gear and ultratough aluminum bronze alloy pinion; high-leverage, aluminum star drag with precise click adjustment; super lightweight perforated aluminum alloy spool.
Price: **$649.95**

LEW'S BB1 PRO SPEED SPOOL
Model: PS1; PS1HZ, PS1SHZ, PS1HZL, PS1SHZL
Gear Ratio: 5.1:1; 6.4:1; 7.1:1; 6.4:1; 7.1:1
Inches/Turn: 21; 28; 31; 28; 31
Spool Cap. (M): 12 lbs/160 yds
Weight: 6.5 oz
Hand Retrieve: R; R; R; L; L
Max Drag: 14 lbs
Reel Bearings: 9+1
Features: Premium ten-bearing system with double-shielded stainless steel ball bearings; available in multi-stop (PS1) and zero-reverse anti-reverse models (PS1HZ, PS1SHZ, PS1HLZ, PS1SHLZ); one-piece die-cast aluminum frame with graphite sideplates; braid-ready machined forged double-anodized; aircraft-grade machine-forged Duralumin spools and drive train; externally adjustable SpeedCast centrifugal braking system; right-side aluminum spool tension knob with audible clicker; carbon composite metal star drag system with 14 pounds of drag power; audible click bowed metal star drag; bowed lightweight carbon fiber reel handle with custom paddle knobs; oversized titanium line guide positioned farther from the spool to minimize line friction and maximize casting performance; quick release sideplate mechanism provides easy access to spool; external lube port.
Price: **$199.99**

LEW'S BB1 SPEED SPOOL

Model: 1, 1H, 1L, 1HZ, 1HZL, 1SHZ, 1SHZL
Gear Ratio: 5.1:1; 7.1:1; 5.1:1; 6.4:1; 6.4:1; 7.1:1; 7.1:1
Inches/Turn: 21; 28; 21; 28; 28; 31; 31
Spool Cap. (M): 12 lbs/160 yds
Weight: 7.1 oz; 7.1 oz; 7.1 oz; 7.2 oz; 7.2 oz; 7.2 oz; 7.2 oz;
Hand Retrieve: R; R; L; R; L; R; L
Max Drag: 14 lbs
Reel Bearings: 10
Features: One-piece die-cast aluminum frame; machined forged aluminum, double anodized, U-shaped large capacity spool; premium ten-bearing system with double-shielded ball bearings and multi-stop anti-reverse (BB1 and BB1L models); premium ten-bearing system with double-shielded ball bearings and zero-reverse anti-reverse (BB1HZ, BB1SHZ, BB1HZL, BB1SHZL); positive on/off SmartPlus; six-pin centrifugal braking system; aluminum spool tension knob with audible clicker; carbon composite metal star drag system with 14 pounds of drag power; bowed 95mm aluminum cranking handle with Lew's custom soft-touch contoured paddle handle knob; oversized titanium line guide positioned further away from the spool to minimize line friction and maximize casting performance; quick release sideplate mechanism provides easy access to centrifugal brake system.
Price: $159.99

LEW'S BB2 WIDE SPEED SPOOL

Model: 2HZ, 2SHZ, 2SHZL
Gear Ratio: 6.4:1; 7.1:1; 7.1:1
Inches/Turn: 28; 31; 31
Spool Cap. (M): 14 lbs/190 yds
Weight: 7.4 oz
Hand Retrieve: R; R; L
Max Drag: 14 lbs
Reel Bearings: 9+1
Features: Premium ten-bearing system with double-shielded ball bearings and zero-reverse anti-reverse; one-piece die-cast aluminum frame; machine-forged aluminum double-anodized U-shaped large capacity spool; external lube port; quick release sideplate mechanism provides easy access to spool and centrifugal brake system; positive on/off SmartPlus; six-pin, positive on/off centrifugal braking system; right-side aluminum spool tension knob with audible clicker; rugged carbon composite drag system provides up to 14 pounds of drag power; audible click bowed metal star drag; 95mm bowed aluminum cranking handle with soft-touch paddles.
Price: $169.99

REELS

LEW'S SPEED SPOOL TOURNAMENT

Model: 1H, 1HL, 1SH
Gear Ratio: 6.4:1; 6.4:1; 7.1:1
Inches/Turn: 28; 28; 31
Spool Cap. (M): 12 lbs/120 yds
Weight: 7.9 oz
Hand Retrieve: R; L; R
Max Drag: 14 lbs
Reel Bearings: 9+1
Features: One-piece die-cast aluminum frame; ten double-shielded premium stainless steel bearings; drilled and forged, double anodized aluminum U-style spool; high-strength solid brass gearing; external-adjust multi-setting brake dual magnetic/centrifugal cast control; zero-reverse one-way clutch bearing; easily removable palming graphite sideplate; metal spool tension adjustment with audible click metal star drag delivers up to 14 pounds of drag power; lightweight graphite sideplate; rugged carbon composite drag system with audible click; lightweight aluminum bowed handle with Lew's custom paddle knobs; external lube port; titanium-coated zirconia line guide.
Price: **$199.99**

LEW'S SUPERDUTY SPEED SPOOL

Model: 1S, 1H, 1SH, 1HL, 1SHL
Gear Ratio: 5.4:1; 6.4:1; 7.1:1; 6.4:1; 7.1:1
Inches/Turn: 23; 28; 31; 28; 31
Spool Cap. (M): 12 lbs/150 yds
Weight: 7.8 oz
Hand Retrieve: R; R; R; L; L
Max Drag: 14 lbs
Reel Bearings: 10+1
Features: Sturdy, lightweight one-piece all aluminum frame and aluminum handle sideplate; eleven double-shielded premium stainless steel bearing system with zero-reverse anti-reverse; lightweight machined, anodized, deep-capacity aluminum spool with braid line connection; high-strength brass gearing for increased strength and durability; external-adjust magnetic control system; zero-reverse one-way clutch bearing; easily removable palming graphite side plate with soft-touch armor finish; external handle side metal spool tension adjustment with audible click; rugged carbon composite metal star drag system that provides up to 14 pounds of drag power; bent anodized aluminum power crank 95 mm reel handle with Lew's custom paddle handle knobs; titanium-coated line guide.
Price: **$179.99**

LEW'S TEAM LEW'S GOLD SPEED SPOOL

Model: 1H, 1SH
Gear Ratio: 6.4:1; 7.1:1
Inches/Turn: 28; 31
Spool Cap. (M): 12 lbs/120 yds
Weight: 7 oz
Hand Retrieve: R; R
Max Drag: 14 lbs
Reel Bearings: 10+1
Features: One-piece die-cast aluminum frame and sideplates; titanium deposition finish on metal sideplates; double anodized gold detail finishing; premium double-shielded eleven-bearing system with zero-reverse anti-reverse; aircraft-grade Duralumin drilled U-shaped spool, drive gear, crank shaft and worm shaft; external-adjust multi-setting brake dual cast control system, using both an external click-dial for setting the magnetic brake, plus four individually, disc-mounted adjustable internal brake shoes that operate on centrifugal force; metal spool tension adjustment with audible click; rugged carbon composite drag system; provides up to 14 pounds of drag power; audible click metal star drag system; bowed, lightweight carbon handle with Lew's custom soft-touch contoured handle knobs; titanium-coated zirconia line guide.
Price: $249.99

LEW'S TEAM LEW'S PRO SPEED SPOOL

Model: 1HZ, 1SHZ, 1HZL, 1SHZL
Gear Ratio: 6.4:1; 7.1:1; 6.4:1; 7.1:1
Inches/Turn: 28; 31; 28; 31
Spool Cap. (M): 12 lbs/120 yds
Weight: 6.1 oz
Hand Retrieve: R; R; L; L
Max Drag: 14 lbs
Reel Bearings: 10+1
Features: One-piece die-cast aluminum frame and sideplates; titanium deposition finish on sideplates for ultimate durability; double-anodized gold detail finishing; aircraft-grade Duralumin; twelve-hole drilled U-style spool, drive gear, crank shaft, and worm shaft; premium, double-shielded, stainless steel, eleven-bearing system with zero-reverse anti-reverse; frictionless titanium-coated zirconia line guide; multi-setting brake utilizing both an external click dial to adjust the magnetic brake system, and an internal four-pin positive on/off centrifugal brake system; anodized aluminum spool tension adjustment with audible click; rugged carbon composite drag system, provides up to 14 pounds of drag power, audible click metal star drag; premium bowed light weight 85mm carbon handle with custom soft-touch contoured paddles.
Price: $299.99

LEW'S TOURNAMENT PRO SPEED SPOOL

Model: 1H, 1HL, 1SH, 1SHL
Gear Ratio: 6.4:1; 6.4:1; 7.1:1; 7.1:1
Inches/Turn: 28; 28; 31; 31
Spool Cap. (M): 12 lbs/120 yds
Weight: 6.7 oz
Hand Retrieve: R; L; R; L
Max Drag: 14 lbs
Reel Bearings: 10+1
Features: One-piece die-cast aluminum frame; eleven double-shielded premium stainless steel bearing system with zero-reverse anti-reverse; aircraft-grade machine-forged Duralumin drilled and anodized U-shaped spool and gear system; external-adjust multi-setting brake dual cast control system, using both an external click-dial for setting the magnetic brake, plus four individually, disc-mounted adjustable internal brake shoes that operate on centrifugal force; zero-reverse one-way clutch bearing; easily removable palming graphite sideplate metal spool tension adjustment with audible click; rugged carbon composite metal drag system with audible click metal star; bowed lightweight carbon reel handle with Lew's custom paddle handle knob; external lube port; titanium-coated zirconia line guide.
Price: **$199.99**

OKUMA AKENA

Model: 400
Gear Ratio: 5.1:1
Inches/Turn: 23
Spool Cap. (M): 14 lbs/270 yds
Weight: 12.7 oz
Hand Retrieve: R or L
Max Drag: 10 lbs
Reel Bearings: 5+1
Features: Aluminum left and right sideplates; machined aluminum, gold anodized spool; multi-disc carbonite drag system; 5BB+1RB Stainless steel bearing drive system; quick-set anti-reverse roller bearing; precision machine-cut brass main and pinion gear; adjustable 6-pin velocity control system; non-disengaging levelwind system 400 size; disengaging levelwind on the 250 size; aluminum twin paddle handle with oversized knobs; on/off bait clicker function on 400-size reels; one-year warranty program.
Price: **$109.99**

OKUMA CALERA

Model: 266W, 266WLX
Gear Ratio: 6.6:1
Inches/Turn: 28.5
Spool Cap. (M): 10 lbs/160 yds
Weight: 8.2 oz
Hand Retrieve: R; L
Max Drag: 11 lbs
Reel Bearings: 4+1
Features: Corrosion-resistant graphite frame and sideplates; A6061-T6 machined aluminum, anodized V-shaped spool;

multi-disc composite drag system; 4BB+1RB bearing drive system; micro-click drag star for precise drag settings; external adjustable magnetic cast control system; internal eight-position velocity control system; quick-set anti-reverse roller bearing; easy change palm sideplates access port; ergonomic handle design allows cranking closer to body; zirconium line guide inserts for use with braided line; available gear ratio: 6.6:1; available in both right- and left-hand retrieve; one-year warranty.

Price:. **$79.99**

OKUMA CITRIX

Model: 254a, 273a, 273LXa
Gear Ratio: 5.4; 7.3:1; 5.4:1
Inches/Turn: 23.4; 31.6; 31.6
Spool Cap. (M): 10 lbs/160 yds
Weight: 8.4 oz
Hand Retrieve: R; R; L
Max Drag: 11 lbs
Reel Bearings: 9+1
Features: Rigid die-cast aluminum frame; A6061-T6 machined aluminum, anodized spool; multi-disc carbonite drag system; 9BB+1RB bearing drive system; micro-click

drag star for precise drag settings; external adjustable centrifugal cast control system; quick-set anti-reverse roller bearing; graphite left and right sideplates; easy change palm sideplates access port; ergonomic handle design allows cranking closer to body; available gear ratios 7.3:1 and 5.4:1; 7.1:1 gear ratio available in left-hand retrieve; one-year warranty.

Price:. **$119.99**

REELS

OKUMA CITRIX 350

Model: 364a, 364LXa, 364Pa, 364PLXa
Gear Ratio: 6.4:1
Inches/Turn: 31
Spool Cap. (M): 12 lbs/250 yds
Weight: 11 oz
Hand Retrieve: R; L; R; L
Max Drag: 25 lbs
Reel Bearings: 7+1
Features: Rigid die-cast aluminum frame and sideplates; corrosion-resistant coating process; durable brass main and pinion gear system; A6061-T6 machined aluminum, anodized spool; multi-disc carbonite drag system with 25-pounds max drag; micro-click drag star for precise drag settings; 7BB+1RB stainless steel bearing drive system; precision Japanese ABEC-5 spool bearings; dual anti-reverse system for maximum reliability; synchronized levelwind optimized for braided line; seven-position velocity control system under palm cover; zirconium line guide inserts for use with braided line; on/off bait clicker for trolling, chunking, or bait fishing; available in both right- and left-hand retrieve; one-year warranty program.
Price: . . . . **$169.99–$184.99**

OKUMA HELIOS 2013

Model: 273VA, 273VLXA
Gear Ratio: 7.3:1
Inches/Turn: 31.5
Spool Cap. (M): 10 lbs/160 yds
Weight: 6.3 oz
Hand Retrieve: R; L
Max Drag: 14 lbs
Reel Bearings: 8+1
Features: Rigid die-cast aluminum frame and sideplates; corrosion-resistant coating process; A6061-T6 machined aluminum, anodized spool; heavy duty, aluminum gears and shafts; multi-disc carbonite drag system; micro-click drag star for precise drag settings; 8BB+1RB stainless steel bearing drive system; precision Japanese ABEC-5 spool bearings; quick-set anti-reverse roller bearing; new lightweight seven-position velocity control system; ergonomic handle design allows cranking closer to body; easy change left side plate access port; lightweight at only 6.3 ounces; zirconium line guide inserts for use with braided line; available in both right- and left-hand retrieve; three-year warranty.
Price: **$199.99**

OKUMA HELIOS AIR

Model: 273, 273LX
Gear Ratio: 7.3:1
Inches/Turn: 31.6
Spool Cap. (M): 10 lbs/160 yds
Weight: 5.7 oz
Hand Retrieve: R; L
Max Drag: 14 lbs
Reel Bearings: 8+1
Features: Extremely light magnesium frame and sideplates; this tournament reel was designed for freshwater use; A6061-T6 machined aluminum, anodized spool; heavy duty, aluminum gears and shafts; multi-disc carbonite drag system; micro-click carbon fiber drag star for precise drag settings; 8BB+1RB stainless steel bearing drive system; precision Japanese ABEC-5 spool bearings; quick-set anti-reverse roller bearing; seven-position velocity control system under palm cover; ergonomic swept carbon fiber handle design; easy change palm sideplate access port; lightweight at only 5.7 ounces; zirconium line guide inserts for use with braided line; available in both right- and left-hand retrieve; three-year limited warranty.
Price: **$269.99**

OKUMA ISIS

Model: 250, 400, 400LX
Gear Ratio: 5.1:1
Inches/Turn: 23
Spool Cap. (M): 8 lbs/380 yds; 14 lbs/270 yds; 14 lbs/270 yds
Weight: 11.4 oz; 12.6 oz; 12.6 oz
Hand Retrieve: R; R; L
Max Drag: 10 lbs
Reel Bearings: 4+1
Features: A6061-T6 extruded aluminum, anodized frame; ported frame design for reduced weight; forged aluminum, gun smoke anodized sideplates; machined aluminum, gold anodized spool; multi-disc carbonite drag system; ratcheting drag star for precise drag settings; 4BB+1RB stainless steel bearing drive system; quick-set anti-reverse roller bearing; dual anti-reverse; silent ratcheting and quick-set roller bearing; precision machine-cut brass main and pinion gear; adjustable six-pin velocity control system; engaged levelwind on all models; forged aluminum twin paddle handle on all models; on/off bait clicker function on 400 models; titanium-coated line guide insert; one-year warranty program.
Price: **$209.99**

REELS: Freshwater Baitcasting

OKUMA TORMENTA
Model: 266WLX
Gear Ratio: 6.6:1
Inches/Turn: 28.5
Spool Cap. (M): 10 lbs/160 yds
Weight: 8 oz
Hand Retrieve: R or L
Max Drag: 11 lbs
Reel Bearings: 2+1
Features: Corrosion-resistant graphite frame and sideplate; A6061-T6 machined aluminum, anodized U-shaped spool; multi-disc composite drag system; 2BB+1RB bearing drive system; micro-click drag star for precise drag settings; external adjustable magnetic cast control system; quick-set anti-reverse roller bearing; easy change palm sideplate access port; ergonomic handle design allows cranking closer to body; zirconium line guide inserts for use with braided line; available gear ratio: 6.6:1; available in both right- and left-hand retrieve; one-year warranty.
Price: **$64.99**

PFLUEGER PATRIARCH LOW PROFILE
Model: 71LPX, 71LHLPX, 79LPX
Gear Ratio: 7.1:1; 7.1:1; 7.9:1
Inches/Turn: 29; 29; 32
Spool Cap. (M): 10 lbs/175 yds
Spool Cap. (B): 20 lbs/190 yds
Weight: 6.28 oz
Hand Retrieve: R; L; R
Max Drag: 20 lbs
Reel Bearings: 11
Features: Ten double-shielded stainless steel ball bearings; instant anti-reverse bearing; C45 carbon-infused sideplates, lightweight with unmatched strength; bent carbon fiber handle with EVA handle knobs; rigid aluminum frame; non-detachable cam locking sideplate allows quick break adjustments without loosing the sideplate; double anodized, ported, machined aircraft aluminum spool; ultimate brake system combines centrifugal and magnetic brakes for limitless range of cast control; smooth carbon fiber drag system; titanium line guide; aircraft aluminum main gear and main shaft.
Price: **$199.95**

PFLUEGER SUPREME LOW PROFILE
Model: 54LPX, 64LPX, 64LHLPX, 71LPX
Gear Ratio: 5.4:1; 6.4:1; 6.4:1; 7.1:1
Inches/Turn: 22; 26; 26; 29
Spool Cap. (M): 10 lbs/175 yds
Spool Cap. (B): 20 lbs/190 yds
Weight: 7.83 oz
Hand Retrieve: R; R; L; R
Max Drag: 20 lbs

Reel Bearings: 9
Features: Eight double-shielded stainless steel ball bearings; instant anti-reverse bearing; hybrid gaphite sideplates, lightweight and incredibly durable; rigid aluminum frame; non-detachable cam locking sideplate allows quick break adjustments without loosing the sideplate.
Price: $99.95

PFLUEGER SUPREME XT
Model: 64LPX, 71LPX, 71HLPX
Gear Ratio: 6.4:1; 7.1:1; 7.1:1
Inches/Turn: 26; 29; 29
Spool Cap. (M): 10 lbs/175 yds
Spool Cap. (B): 20 lbs/190 yds
Weight: 6.53 oz
Hand Retrieve: R; R; L
Max Drag: 20 lbs
Reel Bearings: 10
Features: Nine double-shielded stainless steel ball bearings; instant anti-reverse bearing; C45 carbon-infused sideplates, lightweight with unmatched strength; double anodized aluminum handle with EVA knobs; rigid aluminum frame; non-detachable cam locking sideplate allows quick break adjustments without loosing the sideplate; double anodized, ported, machined aircraft aluminum spool; CBS six-pin adjustable centrifugal brake system; smooth carbon fiber drag system; titanium line guide; aircraft aluminum main gear and main shaft.
Price: $149.95

QUANTUM ANTIX
Model: 100H, 100S, 101S
Gear Ratio: 7.0:1; 6.3:1; 6.3:1
Inches/Turn: 30; 27; 27
Spool Cap. (M): 12 lbs/125 yds
Weight: 8.3 oz
Hand Retrieve: R; R; L
Reel Bearings: 9+1

Features: Ultralight skeletal V spool; ACS external adjustable centrifugal braking; continuous anti-reverse; one-piece aluminum frame; MaxCast skeletal spool; flippin' switch; DynaMag magnetic cast control; quick-release side cover.
Price:................................... **$99.95**

QUANTUM AURA
Model: 360CX
Gear Ratio: 6.2:1
Inches/Turn: 28
Spool Cap. (M): 12 lbs/125 yds
Weight: 7.6 oz
Hand Retrieve: R
Max Drag: 12 lbs

Reel Bearings: 3
Features: Durable multi-coated finish; lightweight aluminum crank handle; continuous anti-reverse; titanium-coated line guide reduces friction on casts and retrieves; DynaMag magnetic cast control; forged aluminum spool; quick-release side cover.
Price:................................... **$49.99**

QUANTUM CODE

Model: 860CXB, 870CXB
Gear Ratio: 6.3:1; 7.0:1
Inches/Turn: 29; 32
Spool Cap. (M): 12 lbs/110 yds
Weight: 9 oz; 9.1 oz
Hand Retrieve: R
Reel Bearings: 7+1

Features: Right- and left-hand models; lightweight aluminum crank handle; ACS external adjustable centrifugal braking; continuous anti-reverse; titanium-coated line guide reduces friction on casts and retrieves; one-piece aluminum frame; MaxCast skeletal spool; flippin' switch; quick-release side cover.
Price: **$89.95**

QUANTUM EXO PT 100/200

Model: 100HPT, 100PPT, 100SPT, 200HPT, 200PPT, 200SPT, 201HPT, 201SPT, 101HPT, 101SPT
Gear Ratio: 7.3:1; 5.3:1; 6.6:1; 7.3:1; 5.3:1; 6.6:1; 7.3:1; 6.6:1; 7.3:1; 6.6:1
Inches/Turn: 31; 24; 28; 35; 25; 32; 35; 32; 31; 28
Spool Cap. (M): 12 lbs/145 yds; 12 lbs/145 yds; 12 lbs/145 yds; 14 lbs/175 yds; 14 lbs/175 yds; 14 lbs/175 yds; 14 lbs/175 yds; 14 lbs/175 yds; 12 lbs/145 yds; 12 lbs/145 yds
Weight: 5.9 oz; 5.9 oz; 5.9 oz; 6.8 oz; 6.8 oz; 6.8 oz; 6.8 oz; 6.8 oz; 5.9 oz; 5.9 oz

Hand Retrieve: R; R; R; R; R; R; L; L; L; L
Reel Bearings: 10+1
Features: Ceramic drag system; polymer-stainless hybrid PT bearings; lightweight aluminum crank handle; continuous anti-reverse; one-piece aluminum frame; MaxCast skeletal spool; quick-release side cover; adjustable centrifugal cast control.
Price: . . . . **$249.95–$269.95**

QUANTUM EXO PT 300
Model: 300HPT, 300PPT, 300SPT, 301HPT, 301SPT
Gear Ratio: 7.3:1; 5.3:1; 6.6:1; 7.3:1; 6.6:1
Inches/Turn: 35; 25; 32; 35; 32
Spool Cap. (M): 20 lbs/200 yds
Weight: 7.5 oz
Hand Retrieve: R; R; R; L; L
Reel Bearings: 6+1

Features: Ceramic drag system; polymer-stainless hybrid PT bearings; lightweight aluminum crank handle; MaxCast skeletal spool; quick-release side cover; adjustable centrifugal cast control.
Price: **$299.95**

QUANTUM KINETIC PT
Model: 100HPTA, 100SPTA, 101HPTA, 101SPTA
Gear Ratio: 7.0:1; 6.3:1; 7.0:1; 6.3:1
Inches/Turn: 28; 26; 28; 26
Spool Cap. (M): 12 lbs/145 yds
Weight: 7.5 oz
Hand Retrieve: R; R; L; L
Max Drag: 16 lbs; 18 lbs; 16 lbs; 18 lbs
Reel Bearings: 7+1
Features: Ceramic drag system; polymer-stainless hybrid PT bearings; easy access lubrication port; right- and left-hand models; durable multi-coated finish; lightweight aluminum crank handle; ACS external adjustable centrifugal braking; continuous anti-reverse; titanium-coated line guide reduces friction on casts and retrieves; one-piece aluminum frame; MaxCast skeletal spool; quick-release side cover.
Price: **$119.95**

QUANTUM SMOKE PT

Model: 100HPT, 100SPT, 101HPT, 101SPT, 150HPT, 150PPT, 150SPT, 151HPT
Gear Ratio: 7.0:1; 6.3:1; 7.0:1; 6.3:1; 7.3:1; 5.3:1; 6.6:1; 7.3:1
Inches/Turn: 28; 26; 28; 26; 34; 23; 28; 34
Spool Cap. (M): 12 lbs/105 yds; 12 lbs/135 yds; 12 lbs/105 yds; 12 lbs/135 yds; 12 lbs/165 yds; 12 lbs/165 yds; 12 lbs/165 yds; 12 lbs/165 yds
Weight: 6.2 oz; 6.2 oz; 6.2 oz; 6.2 oz; 6.8 oz; 6.8 oz; 6.8 oz; 6.8 oz
Hand Retrieve: R; R; L; L; R; R; R; L

Max Drag: 15 lbs; 17 lbs; 15 lbs; 17 lbs; 15 lbs; 19 lbs; 17 lbs; 15 lbs
Reel Bearings: 7+1; 7+1; 7+1; 7+1; 8+1; 8+1; 8+1; 8+1
Features: Ceramic drag system; polymer-stainless hybrid PT bearings; super free spool pinion design; right- and left-hand models; ultralight skeletal V spool; durable multi-coated finish; ACS external adjustable centrifugal braking; continuous anti-reverse; titanium-coated line guide reduces friction on casts and retrieves; one-piece aluminum frame and side cover; quick-release side cover.
Price: . . . . **$199.95–$219.95**

QUANTUM ULTREX

Model: 100S
Gear Ratio: 6.3:1
Inches/Turn: 26
Spool Cap. (M): 12 lbs/100 yds
Weight: 7.7 oz
Hand Retrieve: R

Reel Bearings: 1+1
Features: Right- and left-hand models; continuous anti-reverse; DynaMag magnetic cast control; ultra-smooth stainless steel bearings.
Price: **$39.99**

REELS

SHIMANO ANTARES
Model: 100, 101, 100HG, 101HG
Gear Ratio: 5.6:1; 5.6:1; 7.4:1; 7.4:1
Inches/Turn: 26; 26; 34; 34
Spool Cap. (M): 8 lbs/140 yds
Weight: 7.9 oz
Hand Retrieve: R; L; R; L
Reel Bearings: 10+1

Features: Micro module gear; SVS infinity brake system; X-ship; shielded S-ARB ball bearings; Super Stopper II roller bearing; gear ratios of 5.6:1 and 7.4:1; cross carbon drag washers; escape hatch; cold-forged aluminum handle shank; Septon grips; recessed reel seat foot; magnesium frame with aluminum sideplates; G Free-Spool III magnesium spool; not recommended for salt water.
Price:....................................$599.99

SHIMANO CAENAN
Model: 100, 101
Gear Ratio: 6.5:1
Inches/Turn: 27
Spool Cap. (M): 8 lbs/180 yds
Weight: 7.2 oz
Hand Retrieve: R; L
Max Drag: 10 lbs
Reel Bearings: 6+1

Features: Aluminum lo-mass spool system; super stopper; assist stopper; high-speed 6.5:1 retrieve; high-density EVA power grips; six-shielded stainless steel ball bearings; variable brake system with reduced mass hub; disengaging levelwind system; Quickfire II clutch bar; 1/8 turn easy access attached sideplate; drilled handle shank; ceramic line guide; recessed reel foot; metal cast control knob; rated for use with mono, fluorocarbon, and PowerPro lines; approved for use in salt water.
Price:.................................. $89.99

SHIMANO CAIUS
Model: 200, 201
Gear Ratio: 6.5:1
Inches/Turn: 27
Spool Cap. (M): 8 lbs/180 yds
Weight: 7.9 oz; 7.2 oz
Hand Retrieve: R; L
Max Drag: 11 lbs
Reel Bearings: 3+1

Features: Aluminum lo-mass spool system; super stopper; high-speed 6.5:1 retrieve; three-shielded stainless steel ball bearings; new easy MAG II brake system; disengaging levelwind system; Quickfire II clutch bar; drilled handle shank; ceramic line guide; recessed reel foot; rated for use with mono, fluorocarbon, and PowerPro lines; approved for use in salt water.
Price: **$69.99**

SHIMANO CALAIS DC
Model: 200DC, 201DC
Gear Ratio: 7.0:1
Inches/Turn: 31
Spool Cap. (M): 30 lbs/150 yds
Weight: 9.5 oz
Hand Retrieve: R; L
Max Drag: 12 lbs
Reel Bearings: 10+1
Features: 4x8 digital control; S A-RB bearings; magnumlite spool; septon handle material; super free; high-efficiency gearing; tapered titanium levelwind insert; greaseless spool support bearings; super stopper; assist stopper; escape hatch; septon handle material; PV power handles; cold-forged handle shank; drilled, cold-forged drag star; dartainium drag; recessed reel foot; clicking drag adjustment; metal plated finish; asymmetrical spool window; aluminum frame and sideplates; platinum premiere service plan; metal series; approved for use in salt water; rated for use with mono, fluorocarbon, and PowerPro lines.
Price: **$649.99**

REELS

REELS

SHIMANO CALCUTTA TE DC

Model: 100DC, 200DC, 201DC, 250DC
Gear Ratio: 5.8:1; 5.0:1; 5.0:1; 5.0:1
Inches/Turn: 23
Spool Cap. (M): 30 lbs/115 yds; 40 lbs/95 yds; 40 lbs/95 yds; 40 lbs/115 yds
Weight: 8.6 oz; 9.9 oz; 9.9 oz; 10.2 oz
Hand Retrieve: R; R; L; R
Max Drag: 8.5 lbs; 10 lbs; 10 lbs; 10 lbs
Reel Bearings: 10+1
Features: Anti-rust bearings; lo-mass drilled spool system; A7075 aluminum spool; super free; digital control; high-efficiency gearing; super stopper with assist stopper; dartainium drag; clicking drag adjustment; clicking cast control adjustment; recessed reel foot; drilled crossbar; cold-forged handle shank; adjustable handle shank; rubber handle grip (except 250); septon handle grip (250 only); paddle-style grip (except 250); PV power paddles (250 only); machined aluminum frame; stamped aluminum handle side sideplate; titanium levelwind insert; metal series; platinum service plan; approved for use in salt water; rated for use with mono, fluorocarbon, and PowerPro lines.
Price: $529.99

SHIMANO CARDIFF

Model: 200A, 201A, 300A, 301A, 400A, 401A
Gear Ratio: 5.8:1; 5.8:1; 5.8:1; 5.8:1; 5.2:1; 5.2:1
Inches/Turn: 24; 24; 24; 24; 22; 22
Spool Cap. (M): 8 lbs/230 yds; 8 lbs/230 yds; 12 lbs/230 yds; 12 lbs/230 yds; 12 lbs/330 yds; 12 lbs/330 yds
Weight: 8.6 oz; 8.6 oz; 8.9 oz; 8.9 oz; 11.9 oz; 11.9 oz
Hand Retrieve: R; L; R; L; R; L
Max Drag: 10 lbs; 10 lbs; 10 lbs; 10 lbs; 11 lbs; 11 lbs
Reel Bearings: 4+1
Features: Anti-rust bearings; one-piece die-cast aluminum frame; handle side variable brake system; super stopper with assist stopper; non-disengaging levelwind system (400 and 401 only); recessed reel foot (except on models 400A and 401A); three-post quick take down (except on 2-post models, CDF100A); rubber handle grip; aluminum sideplates and spool; clicker (400A and 401A only); metal series; approved for use in salt water; rated for use with mono, fluorocarbon, and PowerPro lines.
Price: . . . . $109.99–$119.99

SHIMANO CHRONARCH CI4+
Model: 150CI4, 150CI4HG, 151CI4, 151CI4HG
Gear Ratio: 6.2:1; 7.6:1; 6.2:1; 7.6:1
Inches/Turn: 26; 31; 26; 32
Spool Cap. (M): 10 lbs/145 yds
Weight: 6.5 oz
Hand Retrieve: R; R; L; L
Max Drag: 11 lbs
Reel Bearings: 7+1

Features: CI4+ frame; CI4+ sideplates; recessed reel foot; high-efficiency gearing; super free bearing supported pinion gear system; X-ship; Dartanium II (cross carbon) drag washers; seven bearings; 6 S A-RB BB; 1 A-RB roller clutch bearing; SVS infinity braking system; magnumlite spool; septon PV grips; disengaging levelwind system; Quickfire II clutch bar; made in Japan; approved for use in salt water.
Price: **$269.99**

SHIMANO CITICA
Model: 200G7, 200G6, 201G6, 200G5
Gear Ratio: 7.1:1; 6.5:1; 6.5:1; 5.5:1
Inches/Turn: 30; 27; 27; 23
Spool Cap. (M): 8 lbs/180 yds
Weight: 7.5 oz
Hand Retrieve: R; R; L; R
Max Drag: 11 lbs
Reel Bearings: 3+1

Features: Aluminum frame; lightweight graphite sideplates; recessed reel foot; high-efficiency gearing; super free bearing supported pinion gear system; variable brake system with reduced mass hub; super stopper; assist stopper; 1/8 turn easy access attached sideplate; metal cast control knob; anodized spool and handle; disengaging levelwind system; Quickfire II clutch bar; lo-mass drilled spool system; dartainium drag; four bearings; three-shielded stainless steel BB; approved for use in salt water.
Price: **$129.99**

SHIMANO CORE

Model: 50MG7, 51MG7, 100MG, 101MG, 100MG7
Gear Ratio: 7.0:1; 7.0:1; 6.2:1; 6.2:1; 7.0:1
Inches/Turn: 28; 28; 26; 26; 30
Spool Cap. (M): 20 lbs/115 yds
Weight: 5.5 oz; 5.5 oz; 6.1 oz; 6.1 oz; 6.7 oz
Hand Retrieve: R; L; R; L; R
Max Drag: 10 lbs; 10 lbs; 11 lbs; 11 lbs; 11 lbs
Reel Bearings: 8+1; 8+1; 4+1; 4+1; 4+1
Features: Ultra-lightweight magnesium frame and sideplate (CORE50 and 51MG7) has graphite sideplates); ultra-lightweight A7075 aluminum spool construction; magnumlite spool design; S A-RB ball bearings; A-RB roller bearing; high-efficiency gearing; super stopper; super free; variable brake system; reduced mass VBS hub; escape hatch; dartanium drag; cold-forged aluminum drag star; clicking drag adjustment; aluminum cast control knob; rubber-shielded cast control knob; tapered titanium levelwind insert; cold-forged aluminum handle shank; drilled handle shank; septon handle grips; recessed reel foot; high-speed 6.2:1 gear ratio (CORE100MG only); lightweight aluminum drive gear; paddle grips (CORE100MG only); super high-speed 7.0:1 gear ratio (CORE100MG7 and CORE50/51MG7); heavy duty brass drive gear (CORE100MG7 only); PV power grips (CORE100MG7 only); 1/8 turn easy access attached sideplate (CORE50/51MG only); approved for use in salt water; rated for use with mono, fluorocarbon, and PowerPro lines.
Price: . . . . **$349.99–$399.99**

SHIMANO METANIUM

Model: 100, 101, 100HG, 101HG, 100XG, 101XG
Gear Ratio: 6.2:1; 6.2:1; 7.4:1; 7.4:1; 8.5:1; 8.5:1
Inches/Turn: 26; 26; 31; 31; 36; 36
Spool Cap. (M): 8 lbs/140 yds
Weight: 6.0 oz; 6.0 oz; 6.0 oz; 6.0 oz; 6.2 oz; 6.2 oz
Hand Retrieve: R; L; R; L; R; L
Reel Bearings: 9+1
Features: Micro module gear; SVS infinity; X-ship; shielded S-ARB ball bearings; gear ratios of 6.2:1, 7.4:1, and 8.5:1; Super Stopper II roller clutch bearing; Dartanium 2 drag washers; MET XG 96mm handle with PV paddle grips; tapered line guide; escape hatch; cold-forged aluminum drag star; Septon handle grip; aluminum cast control knob; recessed reel seat foot; lightweight aluminum drive gear; ultra lightweight magnesium frame; magnesium handle sideplate; carbon onside sideplate; approved for use in salt water.
Price: **$499.99**

ABU GARCIA ORRA 2 SX
Model: SX, SX-HS, SX-L
Gear Ratio: 6.4:1; 7.1:1; 6.4:1
Inches/Turn: 26; 29; 26
Retrieve Speed: Std; High; Std
Spool Cap. (M): 12 lbs/145 yds
Spool Cap. (B): 30 lbs/140 yds
Weight: 7.3 oz
Hand Retrieve: R; R; L
Max Drag: 15 lbs
Reel Bearings: 8

Features: Seven stainless steel ball bearings plus one roller bearing provides smooth operation; X-Cräftic alloy frame for increased corrosion resistance; graphite sideplates; Power Disk drag system gives smooth drag performance; MagTrax brake system gives consistent brake pressure throughout the cast; compact bent handle and star provide a more ergonomic design; Duragear brass gear for extended gear life.
Price:. **$99.99**

ABU GARCIA ORRA WINCH
Model: Winch, Winch-L
Gear Ratio: 5.4:1
Inches/Turn: 22
Retrieve Speed: Low
Spool Cap. (M): 12 lbs/180 yds
Spool Cap. (B): 30 lbs/180 yds
Weight: 7.6 oz
Hand Retrieve: R; L
Max Drag: 15 lbs

Reel Bearings: 8
Features: Seven stainless steel ball bearings plus one roller bearing provides smooth operation; X-Cräftic alloy frame for increased corrosion resistance; graphite sideplates; Power Disk drag system gives smooth drag performance; MagTrax brake system gives consistent brake pressure throughout the cast; Duragear brass gear for extended gear life; extended bent handle for increased cranking power; large PVC knobs provide greater grip.
Price:. **$99.95**

ABU GARCIA REVO INSHORE

Model: Revo Inshore
Gear Ratio: 7.1:1
Inches/Turn: 29
Retrieve Speed: High
Spool Cap. (M): 12 lbs/180 yds
Spool Cap. (B): 30 lbs/180 yds
Weight: 8.7 oz
Hand Retrieve: R
Max Drag: 20 lbs
Reel Bearings: 6+1
Features: Six high-performance corrosion-resistant bearings plus one roller bearing provides increased corrosion protection; X2-Cräftic alloy frame for increased corrosion resistance; C6 carbon sideplates provide significant weight reduction without sacrificing strength and durability; Carbon Matrix drag system provides smooth, consistent drag pressure across the entire drag range; D2 gear design provides a more efficient gear system while improving gear durability; pitch centrifugal brake system; large EVA knobs provide improved grip; extended bent handle for increased cranking power; titanium-coated line guide reduces friction and improves durability; dual anti-reverse provides additional backup for high-pressure situations.
Price: **$249.95**

ABU GARCIA REVO ROCKET

Model: ROCKET, ROCKET-L
Gear Ratio: 9.0:1
Inches/Turn: 37
Retrieve Speed: Super High
Spool Cap. (M): 12 lbs/145 yds
Spool Cap. (B): 30 lbs/140 yds
Weight: 6.75 oz
Hand Retrieve: R; L
Max Drag: 20 lbs
Reel Bearings: 10+1
Features: Ten stainless steel high-performance corrosion-resistant bearings plus one roller bearing provides increased corrosion protection; rocket fast gear ratio of 9.0:1 provides superfast line retrieve of 37 inches per turn, for picking up line quickly; X-Cräftic alloy frame and sideplates for increased corrosion resistance; Carbon Matrix drag system provides smooth, consistent drag pressure across the entire drag range; D2 gear design provides a more efficient gear system while improving gear durability; Infini brake system allows almost limitless adjustability to handle any fishing situation; Infini II spool design for extended castability and extreme loads; extended bent carbon handle for increased cranking power; large EVA knobs provide improved grip; titanium-coated line guide reduces friction and improves durability.
Price: **$299.99**

ABU GARCIA REVO TORO NACL
Model: 50, 50-HS, 51, 60, 60-HS, 61
Gear Ratio: 5.4:1; 6.4:1; 5.4:1; 5.4:1; 6.4:1; 5.4:1
Inches/Turn: 26; 30.9; 26; 26; 30.9; 26
Retrieve Speed: Std; High; Std; Std; High; Std
Spool Cap. (M): 14 lbs/200 yds; 14 lbs/200 yds; 14 lbs/200 yds; 14 lbs/250 yds; 14 lbs/250 yds; 14 lbs/250 yds
Spool Cap. (B): 30 lbs/250 yds; 30 lbs/250 yds; 30 lbs/250 yds; 30 lbs/330 yds; 30 lbs/330 yds; 30 lbs/330 yds
Weight: 10.9 oz; 10.9 oz; 10.9 oz; 11 oz; 11 oz; 11 oz
Hand Retrieve: R; R; L; R; R; L
Max Drag: 22 lbs
Reel Bearings: 6+1
Features: Six stainless steel high-performance corrosion-resistant bearings plus one roller bearing provides increased corrosion protection; X2-Cräftic alloy frame and sideplate for increased corrosion resistance; carbon matrix drag system provides smooth, consistent drag pressure across the entire drag range; aircraft-grade aluminum spool allows for a high-strength spool that is extremely lightweight for greater casting performance; pitch centrifugal brake system; Duragear brass gear for extended gear life; lube port for easy access maintenance; synchronized level wind system improves line lay and castability; titanium-coated line guide reduces friction and improves durability; extended bent handle with power knobs for increased cranking power; dual anti-reverse provides additional backup for high-pressure situations.
Price: **$299.95**

BASS PRO SHOPS JOHNNY MORRIS SIGNATURE SERIES
Model: 10 HD, 10HLD, 10SHD, 20HD
Gear Ratio: 6.4:1; 6.4:1; 7.1:1; 6.4:1
Inches/Turn: 28; 28; 31; 28
Spool Cap. (M): 12 lbs/120 yds
Weight: 8.6 oz
Hand Retrieve: R; L; R; R
Max Drag: 14 lbs
Reel Bearings: 10+1

Features: Die-cast aluminum frame and sideplates; black carbon-titanium deposition finish; double-anodized-aluminum spool; premium Japanese stainless steel ball bearings; 100 percent double-shielded ten-bearing system; Powerlock instant anti-reverse; Duralumin drive gear; dual braking system; beefed-up, super-smooth carbon drag system; lightweight carbon-fiber recurve handle with ribbed silicon knob; padded clutch bar; titanium-nitride guide.
Price: **$159.99**

BASS PRO SHOPS SNAGGING SPECIAL LEVELWIND
Model: SS-30
Gear Ratio: 4.4:1
Inches/Turn: 31.7
Spool Cap. (M): 30 lbs/380 yds
Weight: 24.8 oz
Hand Retrieve: R

Max Drag: 22 lbs
Reel Bearings: 2
Features: Rugged, lightweight graphite frame; deep anodized, machined aluminum spool; two stainless steel ball bearings; audible bait clicker; stainless steel levelwind; smooth, multi-disc drag system; metal line guide; cast control knob; powerful gear ratio of 4.4:1.
Price: $49.99

DAIWA AIRD
Model: 100P, 100H, 100HL, 100HS
Gear Ratio: 4.9:1; 6.3:1; 6.3:1; 7.1:1
Inches/Turn: 20.6; 25.7; 25.7; 30
Spool Cap. (M): 12 lbs/120 yds
Spool Cap. (B): 40 lbs/140 yds; 40 lbs/135 yds; 40 lbs/140 yds; 40 lbs/135 yds
Weight: 7.7 oz
Hand Retrieve: L; R; L; R
Max Drag: 8.8 lbs

Reel Bearings: 8+1
Features: Open access, low-profile design for easy thumbing and line maintenance; weighs just 7.7 ounces; ultimate tournament carbon drag with 8.8-pound drag max; nine bearing system (8BB+1RB); Magforce cast control; swept handle for less wobble, better feel and winding power; machined aluminum perforated spool; oversized soft-touch grips.
Price: $89.95

DAIWA EXCELER EXE

Model: 100HA, 100HSA, 100HLA, 100HSLA, 100PA
Gear Ratio: 6.3:1; 7.3:1; 6.3:1; 7.3:1; 4.9:1
Inches/Turn: 25.7; 30.6; 25.7; 30.6; 20.6
Spool Cap. (M): 14 lbs/120 yds
Spool Cap. (B): 40 lbs/140 yds
Weight: 7.9 oz
Hand Retrieve: R; R; L; R; R
Max Drag: 11 lbs

Reel Bearings: 5+1
Features: Aluminum frame and sideplate; gear ratios from 4.9 power cranking to 7.3:1 hyper speed; ultimate tournament drag with 11-pound drag max; Magforce cast control; oversized, I-shape grips; infinite, dual anti-reverse; cut-away swept handle for greater power, less wobble, lighter weight.
Price: **$99.99**

DAIWA LAGUNA

Model: 100H, 100HL, 100HS
Gear Ratio: 6.3:1; 6.3:1; 7.1:1
Inches/Turn: 25.7; 25.7; 30
Spool Cap. (M): 12 lbs/120 yds
Weight: 7.4 oz
Hand Retrieve: R; L; R
Max Drag: 8.8
Reel Bearings: 5+1

Features: Open-access, low-profile frame for easy thumbing and line maintenance; lightweight composite frame and sideplates; swept handle for less wobble, better feel, and winding power; five ball bearings plus roller bearing; Magforce magnetic anti-backlash control; lightweight, drilled aluminum spool; dual-system infinite anti-reverse.
Price: **$59.95**

DAIWA LEXA HIGH CAPACITY

Model: 100H, 400HS-P, 300HS-P, 300HS, 100HS, 300H, 400HL, 400HSL, 400HSL-P, 300PWRL, 300HSL-P, 300HSL, 300HL, 100HSL, 100HL, 100PL, 300PWR, 100P, 400H, 400HS, 400PWR-P

Gear Ratio: 6.3:1; 7.1:1; 7.1:1; 7.1:1; 7.1:1; 6.3:1; 6.3:1; 7.1:1; 7.1:1; 5.1:1; 7.1:1; 7.1:1; 6.3:1; 7.1:1; 6.3:1; 4.9:1; 5.1:1; 4.9:1; 6.3:1; 7.1:1; 5.1:1

Inches/Turn: 25.7; 37.7; 32.4; 32.4; 30.0; 28.8; 33.4; 37.7; 37.7; 23.3; 32.4; 32.4; 28.8; 30.0; 25; 20.6; 23.3; 20.6; 33.4; 37.7; 27.1

Spool Cap. (M): 14 lbs/120 yds; 17 lbs/245 yds; 12 lbs/240 yds; 12 lbs/240 yds; 14 lbs/120 yds; 12 lbs/240 yds; 17 lbs/245 yds; 17 lbs/245 yds; 17 lbs/245 yds; 12 lbs/240 yds; 12 lbs/240 yds; 12 lbs/240 yds; 12 lbs/240 yds; 14 lbs/120 yds; 14 lbs/120 yds; 14 lbs/120 yds; 12 lbs/240 yds; 14 lbs/120 yds; 17 lbs/245 yds; 17 lbs/245 yds; 17 lbs/245 yds

Spool Cap. (B): 40 lbs/140 yds; 55 lbs/300 yds; 40 lbs/240 yds; 40 lbs/240 yds; 40 lbs/140 yds; 40 lbs/240 yds; 55 lbs/300 yds; 55 lbs/300 yds; 55 lbs/300 yds; 40 lbs/240 yds; 40 lbs/240 yds; 40 lbs/240 yds; 40 lbs/240 yds; 40 lbs/140 yds; 40 lbs/140 yds; 40 lbs/140 yds; 40 lbs/240 yds; 40 lbs/140 yds; 55 lbs/300 yds; 55 lbs/300 yds; 55 lbs/300 yds

Weight: 8 oz; 16.2 oz; 11.3 oz; 10.5 oz; 8 oz; 10.5 oz; 15.3 oz; 15.3 oz; 16.2 oz; 10.5 oz; 11.3 oz; 10.5 oz; 10.5 oz; 8 oz; 8 oz; 8 oz; 10.5 oz; 8 oz; 15.3 oz; 15.3 oz; 16.2 oz

Hand Retrieve: R; R; R; R; R; R; L; L; L; L; L; L; L; L; L; L; R; R; R; R; R

Max Drag: 11 lbs; 25 lbs; 22 lbs; 22 lbs; 11 lbs; 22 lbs; 25 lbs; 25 lbs; 25 lbs; 22 lbs; 22 lbs; 22 lbs; 22 lbs; 11 lbs; 11 lbs; 11 lbs; 22 lbs; 11 lbs; 25 lbs; 25 lbs; 25 lbs

Reel Bearings: 7+1

Features: Aluminum frame and sideplate (gear side); seven-bearing system (2CRBB, 4BB+1RB); Magforce cast control; infinite anti-reverse; swept handle with weight-reducing cutouts; counter-balanced power handle on P models; super-leverage 120mm handle on 400 size models; A7075 aluminum spool, super lightweight and extra strong (100 size); extra line capacity for strong lines; ultimate tournament carbon drag.
Price:. . . . .**$129.99–$249.99**

DAIWA MEGAFORCE THS (WITH TWITCHIN' BAR)

Model: 100THS, 100THSL
Gear Ratio: 7.3:1
Inches/Turn: 31.5
Spool Cap. (M): 12 lbs/150 yds
Weight: 8.8 oz

Hand Retrieve: R; L
Max Drag: 8.8 lbs
Reel Bearings: 6
Features: Twitchin' bar; six ball bearings; hyper speed 7.3:1 gear ratio; swept handle; Magforce-Z automatic anti-backlash control; precision click drag adjustment.
Price: **$89.95**

DAIWA MILLIONAIRE LONG DISTANCE SURF

Model: Millionaire M7HTMAG
Gear Ratio: 5.8:1
Inches/Turn: 28
Spool Cap. (M): 15 lbs/330 yds
Weight: 12.2 oz
Hand Retrieve: R
Max Drag: 11 lbs
Reel Bearings: 5+1

Features: Six ball bearings (5 CRBB) plus roller bearing; lightweight aluminum spool; counter-balanced power handle; fast 5.8:1 retrieve picks up 28" per crank; high-grade brass drive gear and stainless steel pinion; infinite anti-reverse; rigid, one-piece frame; smooth star-adjust drag; Magforce-Z.
Price: **$299.95**

REELS

DAIWA MILLIONAIRE SUPER TUNED SURF

Model: Millionaire M7HTMAGST
Gear Ratio: 5.8:1
Inches/Turn: 28
Spool Cap. (M): 15 lbs/330 yds
Weight: 11.5 oz
Hand Retrieve: R
Max Drag: 11 lbs
Reel Bearings: 8+1

Features: Factory super tuned for optimum performance; super tuned machine-cut spool made of super-balanced, super-lightweight aluminum alloy; carbon swept handle for reduced weight, maximum leverage and control; EVA double handle knob; fast 5.8:1 retrieve picks up 28" per crank; high-grade brass drive gear and stainless steel pinion; nine ball bearings (8 CRBB) plus roller bearing; rigid, one-piece aluminum frame; smooth star-adjust drag; advanced design, super tuned, Magforce-Z.
Price: **$499.95**

DAIWA PX TYPE-R

Model: PX-R, PXL-R
Gear Ratio: 6.8:1
Inches/Turn: 26
Spool Cap. (M): 6 lbs/95 yds
Weight: 5.8 oz
Hand Retrieve: R; L
Max Drag: 13 lbs

Reel Bearings: 10
Features: Weighs just 5.8 ounces; magnesium body; ten ball bearings; carbon swept handle; cork handle knobs; hyper speed 6.8:1 gear ratio; UT drag with a drag max of 13 pounds; Magforce-Z cast control.
Price: **$499.95**

DAIWA STEEZ EX
Model: 100XS, 100HS, 100H, 100HSL, 100HL
Gear Ratio: 7.9:1; 7.1:1; 6.3:1; 7.1:1; 6.3:1
Inches/Turn: 33.2; 29.8; 26; 29.8; 26
Spool Cap. (M): 14 lbs/120 yds
Weight: 5.8 oz; 5.8 oz; 5.4 oz; 5.8 oz; 5.4 oz
Hand Retrieve: R; R; R; L; L
Max Drag: 13.2 lbs
Reel Bearings: 11+1

Features: Super lightweight magnesium frame and sideplate; swept handle with cutouts for reduced weight; oversized, lightweight 100 MM handle on 7.1 and 7.9 models; ultimate tournament carbon drag with 13.2-pound drag max; free-floating A7075 aluminum alloy spool starts faster, spins longer; fast spool change; eleven precision ball bearings plus roller bearing; tough Dura-Loc pinion; Magforce-Z cast control; precision, micro-click adjustment on star drag and free-spool cap; infinite anti-reverse; free neoprene reel cover included.
Price:...................................**$599.95**

DAIWA T3
Model: 1016HS, 1016H, 1016HSL, 1016HL
Gear Ratio: 7.1:1; 6.3:1; 7.1:1; 6.3:1
Inches/Turn: 29.5; 26.3; 29.5; 26.3
Spool Cap. (M): 14 lbs/120 yds
Weight: 6.5 oz
Hand Retrieve: R; R; L; L
Max Drag: 13.2 lbs
Reel Bearings: 8+1

Features: T-wing system; Magforce 3D cast control system; weighs just 6.5 ounces; ultra-low profile; Zaion frame, clutch cover, and sideplate; ultimate tournament drag with micro-click adjustment; available with 6.3:1 or 7.1:1 gear ratios; eight ball bearings (including 4 CRBB) plus roller bearing; aluminum swept handle arm with urethane-covered cork grips; free-floating, lightweight aluminum spool; infinite anti-reverse; fast, one-touch spool change.
Price:...................................**$599.95**

DAIWA T3 BALLISTIC

Model: S100XS, S100HS, S100H, S100XSL, S100HSL, S100HL
Gear Ratio: 8.1:1; 7.1:1; 6.3:1; 8.1:1; 7.1:1; 6.3:1
Inches/Turn: 34; 29.5; 26.3; 34; 29.5; 26.3
Spool Cap. (M): 14 lbs/120 yds
Weight: 7.9 oz; 7.8 oz; 7.8 oz; 7.9 oz; 7.8 oz; 7.8 oz
Hand Retrieve: R; R; R; L; L; L
Max Drag: 11 lbs; 13.2 lbs; 13.2 lbs
Reel Bearings: 5+1

Features: T-wing system; Magforce 3D cast control system; ultra-low profile; Zaion frame, clutch cover, and sideplate; natural black marble Zaion finish; ultimate tournament drag with micro-click adjustment; available with 6.3:1 or 7.1:1 gear ratios; five ball bearings plus roller bearing; aluminum swept handle; free-floating, lightweight aluminum spool; infinite anti-reverse; fast, one-touch spool change.
Price:. . . . . $249.95–$269.95

DAIWA TATULA

Model: 100HL, 100HSL, 100H, 100HS, R100H, R100XS, R100HL, R100XSL, 100P
Gear Ratio: 6.3:1; 7.3:1; 6.3:1; 7.3:1; 6.3:1; 8.1:1; 6.3:1; 8.1:1; 5.4:1
Inches/Turn: 26.3; 30.5; 26.3; 30.5; 26.3; 33.9; 26.3; 33.9; 22.9
Spool Cap. (M): 14 lbs/120 yds
Spool Cap. (B): 40 lbs/140 yds
Weight: 7.9; 7.9; 7.9; 7.9; 7.6; 7.6; 7.6; 7.6; 7.9
Hand Retrieve: L; L; R; R; R; R; L; L; R
Max Drag: 13.2 lbs
Reel Bearings: 7+1
Features: New T-wing system; rugged, lightweight aluminum frame and sideplate (gear side); air rotation; ultimate tournament carbon drag with 13.2-pound drag max; Magforce-Z cast control; gear ratios of 5.4:1, 6.3:1, and 7.3:1; seven ball bearings plus roller bearing; infinite anti-reverse; corrosion resistant clutch mechanism; large, 90mm swept power handle with cutouts for reduced weight; new I-shape handle knob.
Price:. $149.95

REELS: Saltwater Baitcasting

DAIWA TD LUNA
Model: 253, 300, 253L, 300L
Gear Ratio: 5.1:1
Inches/Turn: 23.6
Spool Cap. (M): 12 lbs/235 yds; 14 lbs/320 yds; 12 lbs/235 yds; 14 lbs/320 yds
Weight: 11.1 oz; 12.9 oz; 11.1 oz; 12.9 oz
Hand Retrieve: R; R; L; L
Max Drag: 11 lbs; 15.3 lbs; 11 lbs; 15.3 lbs
Reel Bearings: 5+1
Features: Frame and sideplates machined from solid bar stock aluminum; five CRBB super corrosion-resistant ball bearings, plus roller bearing; free-floating spool for maximum casting performance; Magforce-Z automatic magnetic anti-backlash control (Centriflex automatic centrifugal system on 300 size); ultra-smooth, multi-disc drag with Daiwa's exclusive fiber composite and stainless washers; infinite anti-reverse; Dura-Loc pinion for solid gear engagement; rugged, six-point drive train support; machined aircraft aluminum spool; cut-proof titanium nitrided stainless steel line guide; spool click on 300 size; hard anodized to resist corrosion.
Price:.......................... $279.95–$289.95

DAIWA TD ZILLION HIGH POWER
Model: 100PA, 100PLA
Gear Ratio: 4.9:1
Inches/Turn: 22
Spool Cap. (M): 14 lbs/120 yds
Weight: 8.8 oz
Hand Retrieve: R; L
Max Drag: 8.8 lbs
Reel Bearings: 6+1
Features: Choice of ultra-fast 7.1:1 retrieve or all-purpose 6.3:1; six ball bearings (including CRBB), plus roller bearing; swept handle for less wobble, better feel, and maximum winding leverage; free-floating perforated aluminum spool starts faster, spins longer; fast spool change; Magforce-Z automatic anti-backlash system; eight-disc wet drag with precision click adjustment; aluminum guard plate protects finish on top of reel; rigid aluminum frame and handle-side sideplate firmly support the drive train; soft-touch grips.
Price:................................. $319.95

DAIWA TD ZILLION HYPER SPEED
Model: 100HA, 100SHLA, 100HLA, 100SHA
Gear Ratio: 6.3:1; 7.1:1; 6.3:1; 7.1:1
Inches/Turn: 28; 31.6; 28; 31.6
Spool Cap. (M): 12 lbs/150 yds
Weight: 8.6 oz; 8.8 oz; 8.6 oz; 8.8 oz
Hand Retrieve: R; R; L; R
Max Drag: 8.8 lbs
Reel Bearings: 6+1
Features: Choice of ultra-fast 7.1:1 retrieve or all-purpose 6.3:1; six ball bearings (including CRBB), plus roller bearing; swept handle for less wobble, better feel, and maximum winding leverage; free-floating perforated aluminum spool starts faster, spins longer; fast spool change; Magforce-Z automatic anti-backlash system; eight-disc wet drag with precision click adjustment; aluminum guard plate protects finish on top of reel; rigid aluminum frame and handle-side sideplate firmly support the drive train; soft-touch grips.
Price:. **$439.95**

DAIWA TD ZILLION TYPE R
Model: 100HSHR, 100HSHLR
Gear Ratio: 7.3:1
Inches/Turn: 32
Spool Cap. (M): 14 lbs/120 yds
Weight: 8.5 oz
Hand Retrieve: R; L
Max Drag: 8.5 lbs
Reel Bearings: 11
Features: Hyper speed 7.3:1 retrieve; eleven hyper speed ball bearings; carbon swept handle; ultimate tournament carbon drag; super rigid aluminum frame and sideplate; Magforce-Z anti-backlash control; free-floating perforated aluminum spool; infinite anti-reverse.
Price:. **$439.95**

REELS: Saltwater Baitcasting

DAIWA Z SERIES

Model: HS, H, HL
Gear Ratio: 7.2:1; 6.4:1; 6.4:1
Inches/Turn: 33.5; 29.5; 29.5
Spool Cap. (M): 14 lbs/155 yds
Weight: 9.9 oz
Hand Retrieve: R; R; L
Max Drag: 16.5 lbs
Reel Bearings: 8+1
Features: Magforce-3D; hyper speed 7.2:1 or all-around 6.4:1 gear ratio models; seven-disc carbon UT drag with a drag max of 16.5 pound–click adjustment; eight CRBB corrosion-resistant ball bearings plus roller bearing; rugged, dual system anti-reverse combines infinite anti-reverse with a multi-stop system; low-friction, titanium-nitrided line guide; aluminum swept handle with large, ball bearing grips; tough aluminum frame; precision high brass drive gear and ultra-tough aluminum bronze alloy pinion; high-leverage, aluminum star drag with precise click adjustment; super lightweight perforated aluminum alloy spool.
Price: **$649.95**

LEW'S BB1 INSHORE SPEED SPOOL

Model: 1H, 1SH
Gear Ratio: 6.4:1; 7.1:1
Inches/Turn: 28; 31
Spool Cap. (M): 12 lbs/160 yds
Weight: 7.8 oz
Hand Retrieve: R
Max Drag: 14 lbs
Reel Bearings: 7+1
Features: Premium eight-bearing system with double-shielded stainless steel ball bearings; sturdy one-piece all aluminum frame, handle, and sideplate with three external drain ports on frame; braid-ready machined double-anodized deep-capacity aluminum spool; high-strength brass gearing for durability zero-reverse anti-reverse; multi-setting brake features an external-adjust magnetic braking system and an internal four-pin positive on/off centrifugal brake system; double-anodized aluminum spool tension knob with audible clicker; rugged carbon composite drag system that provides up to 14 pounds of drag power; audible click bowed metal star drag; bowed 95mm aluminum cranking handle with soft-touch paddles; oversized silver titanium line guide positioned farther from the spool to minimize line friction and maximize casting performance; quick release sideplate mechanism provides easy access to spool and centrifugal brake system.
Price: **$199.99**

OKUMA CALERA
Model: 266W, 266WLX
Gear Ratio: 6.6:1
Inches/Turn: 28.5
Spool Cap. (M): 10 lbs/160 yds
Weight: 8.2 oz
Hand Retrieve: R; L
Max Drag: 11 lbs
Reel Bearings: 4+1
Features: Corrosion-resistant graphite frame and sideplates; A6061-T6 machined aluminum, anodized V-shaped spool; multi-disc composite drag system; 4BB+1RB bearing drive system; micro-click drag star for precise drag settings; external adjustable magnetic cast control system; internal eight-position velocity control system; quick-set anti-reverse roller bearing; easy change palm sideplate access port; ergonomic handle design allows cranking closer to body; zirconium line guide inserts for use with braided line; available gear ratio is 6.6:1; available in both right- and left-hand retrieve; one-year warranty.
Price: **$79.99**

OKUMA AKENA
Model: 400
Gear Ratio: 5.1:1
Inches/Turn: 23
Spool Cap. (M): 14 lbs/270 yds
Weight: 12.7 oz
Hand Retrieve: R or L
Max Drag: 10 lbs
Reel Bearings: 5+1
Features: Rigid one-piece anodized aluminum frame; aluminum left and right sideplates; machined aluminum, gold anodized spool; multi-disc carbonite drag system; 5BB+1RB stainless steel bearing drive system; quick-set anti-reverse roller bearing; precision machine-cut brass main and pinion gear; adjustable six-pin velocity control system; non-disengaging levelwind system 400 size; disengaging levelwind on the 250 size; aluminum twin paddle handle with oversized knobs; on/off bait clicker function on 400-size reels; one-year warranty.
Price: **$109.99**

REELS

REELS: Saltwater Baitcasting

OKUMA CEDROS SALT WATER

Model: 273
Gear Ratio: 7.3:1
Inches/Turn: 31.5
Spool Cap. (M): 10 lbs/205 yds
Weight: 8.4 oz
Hand Retrieve: R or L
Max Drag: 14 lbs
Reel Bearings: 6+1
Features: Rigid die-cast aluminum frame and sideplates constructed with T-480 aluminum alloy; titanium coating process on sideplates; corrosion-resistant coating process; heavy duty, aluminum gearing and shafts; A6061-T6 machined aluminum, anodized spool; unique stainless steel clutch slider; multi-disc carbonite drag system; micro-click drag star for precise drag settings; 6BB+1RB stainless steel bearing drive system; precision Japanese ABEC-5 spool bearings; quick-set anti-reverse roller bearing; seven-position velocity control system; heavy duty custom aluminum handle design; durable EVA handle knobs for comfort; easy change left sideplate access port; zirconium line guide inserts for use with braided line; designed specifically for salt water use; available in right- and left-hand retrieve; three-year limited warranty.
Price: $249.99

OKUMA CITRIX

Model: 254a, 273a, 273LXa
Gear Ratio: 5.4; 7.3:1; 5.4:1
Inches/Turn: 23.4; 31.6; 31.6
Spool Cap. (M): 10 lbs/160 yds
Weight: 8.4 oz
Hand Retrieve: R; R; L
Max Drag: 11 lbs
Reel Bearings: 9+1
Features: Rigid die-cast aluminum frame; A6061-T6 machined aluminum, anodized spool; multi-disc carbonite drag system; 9BB+1RB bearing drive system; micro-click drag star for precise drag settings; external adjustable centrifugal cast control system; quick-set anti-reverse roller bearing; graphite left and right sideplates; easy change palm sideplate access port; ergonomic handle design allows cranking closer to body; available gear ratios of 7.3:1 and 5.4:1; 7.3:1 gear ratio available in left-hand retrieve; one-year warranty.
Price: $124.99

OKUMA CITRIX 350
Model: 364a, 364LXa, 364Pa, 364PLXa
Gear Ratio: 6.4:1
Inches/Turn: 31
Spool Cap. (M): 12 lbs/250 yds
Weight: 11 oz
Hand Retrieve: R; L; R; L
Max Drag: 25 lbs
Reel Bearings: 7+1
Features: Rigid die-cast aluminum frame and sideplates; corrosion-resistant coating process; durable brass main and pinion gear system; A6061-T6 machined aluminum, anodized spool; multi-disc carbonite drag system with 25-pound max drag; micro-click drag star for precise drag settings; 7BB+1RB stainless steel bearing drive system; precision Japanese ABEC-5 spool bearings; dual anti-reverse system for maximum reliability; synchronized levelwind optimized for braided line; seven-position velocity control system under palm cover; zirconium line guide inserts for use with braided line; on/off bait clicker for trolling, chunking or bait fishing; available in both right- and left-hand retrieve; one-year warranty.
Price: . . . .**$169.99–$184.99**

OKUMA ISIS
Model: 250, 400, 400LX
Gear Ratio: 5.1:1
Inches/Turn: 23
Spool Cap. (M): 8 lbs/380 yds; 14 lbs/270 yds; 14 lbs/270 yds
Weight: 11.4 oz; 12.6 oz; 12.6 oz
Hand Retrieve: R; R; L
Max Drag: 10 lbs
Reel Bearings: 4+1
Features: A6061-T6 extruded aluminum, anodized frame; ported frame design for reduced weight; forged aluminum, gun smoke anodized sideplates; machined aluminum, gold anodized spool; multi-disc carbonite drag system; ratcheting drag star for precise drag settings; 4BB+1RB stainless steel bearing drive system; quick-set anti-reverse roller bearing; dual anti-reverse with silent ratcheting and quick-set roller bearing; precision machine-cut brass main and pinion gear; adjustable six-pin velocity control system; engaged levelwind on all models; forged aluminum twin paddle handle on all models; on/off bait clicker function on 400 models; titanium-coated line guide insert; one-year warranty.
Price: **$209.99**

REELS

OKUMA SERRANO

Model: 200, 200W
Gear Ratio: 6.2:1
Inches/Turn: 26
Spool Cap. (M): 10 lbs/205 yds; 10 lbs/160 yds
Weight: 7.2 oz
Hand Retrieve: R; L
Max Drag: 11 lbs
Reel Bearings: 10+1
Features: Rigid die-cast aluminum frame; corrosion-resistant coating process; aluminum sideplate holds gears in perfect alignment; A6061-T6 machined aluminum, anodized spool; lightweight inertia-free hi-rise spool on SR-200W; heavy duty, machine-cut, Dura brass gearing; multi-disc carbonite drag system; micro-click drag star for precise drag settings; 10BB+1RB stainless steel bearing drive system; precision Japanese ABEC-5 spool bearings; quick-set anti-reverse roller bearing; seven-position velocity control system; ergonomic handle design allows cranking closer to body; easy change left sideplate access port; zirconium line guide inserts for use with braided line; three-year warranty.
Price:. $174.99

PFLUEGER PATRIARCH LOW PROFILE

Model: 71LPX, 71LHLPX, 79LPX
Gear Ratio: 7.1:1; 7.1:1; 7.9:1
Inches/Turn: 29; 29; 32
Spool Cap. (M): 10 lbs/175 yds
Spool Cap. (B): 20 lbs/190 yds
Weight: 6.28 oz
Hand Retrieve: R; L; R
Max Drag: 20 lbs
Reel Bearings: 11

Features: Ten double-shielded stainless steel ball bearings; instant anti-reverse bearing; C45 carbon infused sideplates, lightweight with unmatched strength; bent carbon fiber handle with EVA handle knobs; rigid aluminum frame; non-detachable cam locking side plate allows quick break adjustments without loosing the sideplate; double anodized, ported, machined aircraft aluminum spool; ultimate brake system combines centrifugal and magnetic brakes for limitless range of cast control; smooth carbon fiber drag system; titanium line guide; aircraft aluminum main gear and main shaft.
Price:. $199.95

PFLUEGER SUPREME LOW PROFILE

Model: 54LPX, 64LPX, 64LHLPX, 71LPX
Gear Ratio: 5.4:1; 6.4:1; 6.4:1; 7.1:1
Inches/Turn: 22; 26; 26; 29
Spool Cap. (M): 10 lbs/175 yds
Spool Cap. (B): 20 lbs/190 yds
Weight: 7.83 oz
Hand Retrieve: R; R; L; R

Max Drag: 20 lbs
Reel Bearings: 9
Features: Eight double-shielded stainless steel ball bearings; instant anti-reverse bearing hybrid graphite sideplates that are lightweight and incredibly durable; rigid aluminum frame; non-detachable cam locking sideplate allows quick break adjustments without loosing the sideplate.
Price: **$99.95**

PFLUEGER SUPREME XT

Model: 64LPX, 71LPX, 71HLPX
Gear Ratio: 6.4:1; 7.1:1; 7.1:1
Inches/Turn: 26; 29; 29
Spool Cap. (M): 10 lbs/175 yds
Spool Cap. (B): 20 lbs/190 yds
Weight: 6.53 oz
Hand Retrieve: R; R; L
Max Drag: 20 lbs
Reel Bearings: 10

Features: Nine double-shielded stainless steel ball bearings; instant anti-reverse bearing; C45 carbon infused sideplates that are lightweight with unmatched strength; double-anodized aluminum handle with EVA knobs; rigid aluminum frame; non-detachable cam locking sideplate allows quick break adjustments without loosing the sideplate; double-anodized, ported, machined aircraft aluminum spool; six-pin adjustable centrifugal brake system; smooth carbon fiber drag system; titanium line guide; aircraft aluminum main gear and main shaft.
Price: **$149.95**

REELS: Saltwater Baitcasting

QUANTUM SMOKE INSHORE
Model: 100HPTs, 101HPTs
Gear Ratio: 7.0:1
Inches/Turn: 28
Spool Cap. (M): 12 lbs/135 yds
Weight: 6.2 oz

Hand Retrieve: R; L
Reel Bearings: 7+1
Features: New and improved SCR base alloy aluminum body and side covers protected by our exclusive SaltGaurd 2.0 multilayer corrosion protection.
Price:.................................$219.95

SHIMANO CAENAN
Model: 100, 101
Gear Ratio: 6.5:1
Inches/Turn: 27
Spool Cap. (M): 8 lbs/180 yds
Weight: 7.2 oz
Hand Retrieve: R; L
Max Drag: 10 lbs
Reel Bearings: 6+1

Features: Aluminum lo-mass spool system; super stopper; assist stopper; high-speed 6.5:1 retrieve; high-density EVA power grips; six-shielded stainless steel ball bearings; variable brake system with reduced mass hub; disengaging levelwind system; Quickfire II clutch bar; 1/8 turn easy access attached sideplate; drilled handle shank; ceramic line guide; recessed reel foot; metal cast control knob; rated for use with mono, fluorocarbon, and PowerPro lines; approved for use in salt water.
Price:.................................. **$89.99**

SHIMANO CAIUS

Model: 200, 201
Gear Ratio: 6.5:1
Inches/Turn: 27
Spool Cap. (M): 8 lbs/180 yds
Weight: 7.9 oz; 7.2 oz
Hand Retrieve: R; L
Max Drag: 11 lbs
Reel Bearings: 3+1

Features: Aluminum lo-mass spool system; super stopper; high-speed 6.5:1 retrieve; three-shielded stainless steel ball bearings; new easy MAG II brake system; disengaging levelwind system; Quickfire II clutch bar; drilled handle shank; ceramic line guide; recessed reel foot; rated for use with mono, fluorocarbon, and PowerPro lines; approved for use in salt water.
Price: **$69.99**

SHIMANO CALAIS DC

Model: 200DC, 201DC
Gear Ratio: 7.0:1
Inches/Turn: 31
Spool Cap. (M): 30 lbs/150 yds
Weight: 9.5 oz
Hand Retrieve: R; L
Max Drag: 12 lbs
Reel Bearings: 10+1
Features: 4x8 digital control; S A-RB bearings; magnumlite spool; septon handle material; super free; high-efficiency gearing; tapered titanium levelwind insert; greaseless spool support bearings; super stopper; assist stopper; escape hatch; septon handle material; PV power handles; cold-forged handle shank; drilled, cold-forged drag star; dartainium drag; recessed reel foot; clicking drag adjustment; metal plated finish; asymmetrical spool window; aluminum frame and sideplates; platinum premiere service plan; metal series; approved for use in salt water; rated for use with mono, fluorocarbon, and PowerPro lines.
Price: **$649.99**

Saltwater Baitcasting

SHIMANO CALCUTTA TE DC

Model: 100DC, 200DC, 201DC, 250DC
Gear Ratio: 5.8:1; 5.0:1; 5.0:1; 5.0:1
Inches/Turn: 23
Spool Cap. (M): 30 lbs/115 yds; 40 lbs/95 yds; 40 lbs/95 yds; 40 lbs/115 yds
Weight: 8.6 oz; 9.9 oz; 9.9 oz; 10.2 oz
Hand Retrieve: R; R; L; R
Max Drag: 8.5 lbs; 10 lbs; 10 lbs; 10 lbs
Reel Bearings: 10+1
Features: Anti-rust bearings; lo-mass drilled spool system; A7075 aluminum spool; super free; digital control; high-efficiency gearing; super stopper with assist stopper; dartainium drag; clicking drag adjustment; clicking cast control adjustment; recessed reel foot; drilled crossbar; cold-forged handle shank; adjustable handle shank; rubber handle grip (except 250); septon handle grip (250 only); paddle-style grip (except 250); PV power paddles (250 only); machined aluminum frame; stamped aluminum handle side sideplate; titanium levelwind insert; metal series; platinum service plan; approved for use in salt water; rated for use with mono, fluorocarbon, and PowerPro lines.
Price: **$529.99**

SHIMANO CARDIFF

Model: 200A, 201A, 300A, 301A, 400A, 401A
Gear Ratio: 5.8:1; 5.8:1; 5.8:1; 5.8:1; 5.2:1; 5.2:1
Inches/Turn: 24; 24; 24; 24; 22; 22
Spool Cap. (M): 8 lbs/230 yds; 8 lbs/230 yds; 12 lbs/230 yds; 12 lbs/230 yds; 12 lbs/330 yds; 12 lbs/330 yds
Weight: 8.6 oz; 8.6 oz; 8.9 oz; 8.9 oz; 11.9 oz; 11.9 oz
Hand Retrieve: R; L; R; L; R; L
Max Drag: 10 lbs; 10 lbs; 10 lbs; 10 lbs; 11 lbs; 11 lbs
Reel Bearings: 4+1
Features: Anti-rust bearings; one-piece die-cast aluminum frame; handle side variable brake system; super stopper with assist stopper; non-disengaging levelwind system (400 and 401 only); recessed reel foot (except on models 400A and 401A); three post quick take down (except on 2-post models, CDF100A); rubber handle grip; aluminum sideplates and spool; clicker (400A and 401A only); metal series; approved for use in salt water; rated for use with mono, fluorocarbon, and PowerPro lines.
Price: . . . . **$109.99–$119.99**

SHIMANO CHRONARCH CI4+

Model: 150CI4, 150CI4HG, 151CI4, 151CI4HG
Gear Ratio: 6.2:1; 7.6:1; 6.2:1; 7.6:1
Inches/Turn: 26; 31; 26; 32
Spool Cap. (M): 10 lbs/145 yds
Weight: 6.5 oz
Hand Retrieve: R; R; L; L
Max Drag: 11 lbs
Reel Bearings: 7+1

Features: CI4+ frame; CI4+ sideplates; recessed reel foot; high-efficiency gearing; super free bearing supported pinion gear system; X-ship; Dartanium II (cross carbon) drag washers; seven bearings; 6 S A-RB BB; 1 A-RB roller clutch bearing; SVS infinity braking system; magnumlite spool; septon PV grips; disengaging levelwind system; Quickfire II clutch bar; made in Japan; approved for use in salt water.
Price: **$269.99**

SHIMANO CITICA

Model: 200G7, 200G6, 201G6, 200G5
Gear Ratio: 7.1:1; 6.5:1; 6.5:1; 5.5:1
Inches/Turn: 30; 27; 27; 23
Spool Cap. (M): 8 lbs/180 yds
Weight: 7.5 oz
Hand Retrieve: R; R; L; R
Max Drag: 11 lbs
Reel Bearings: 3+1

Features: Aluminum frame; lightweight graphite sideplates; recessed reel foot; high-efficiency gearing; super free bearing supported pinion gear system; variable brake system with reduced mass hub; super stopper; assist stopper; 1/8 turn easy access attached sideplate; metal cast control knob; anodized spool and handle; disengaging levelwind system; Quickfire II clutch bar; lo-mass drilled spool system; dartainium drag; four bearings; three-shielded stainless steel BB; approved for use in salt water.
Price: **$129.99**

REELS

SHIMANO CORE

Model: 50MG7, 51MG7, 100MG, 101MG, 100MG7
Gear Ratio: 7.0:1; 7.0:1; 6.2:1; 6.2:1; 7.0:1
Inches/Turn: 28; 28; 26; 26; 30
Spool Cap. (M): 20 lbs/115 yds
Weight: 5.5 oz; 5.5 oz; 6.1 oz; 6.1 oz; 6.7 oz
Hand Retrieve: R; L; R; L; R
Max Drag: 10 lbs; 10 lbs; 11 lbs; 11 lbs; 11 lbs
Reel Bearings: 8+1; 8+1; 4+1; 4+1; 4+1
Features: Ultra-lightweight magnesium frame and sideplates; (CORE50 and 51MG7) has graphite sideplates; ultra-lightweight A7075 aluminum spool construction; magnumlite spool design; S A-RB ball bearings; A-RB roller bearing; high-efficiency gearing; super stopper; super free; variable brake system; reduced mass VBS hub; escape hatch; dartainium drag; cold-forged aluminum drag star; clicking drag adjustment; aluminum cast control knob; rubber-shielded cast control knob; tapered titanium levelwind insert; cold-forged aluminum handle shank; drilled handle shank; septon handle grips; recessed reel foot; high-speed 6.2:1 gear ratio (CORE100MG only); lightweight aluminum drive gear; paddle grips (CORE100MG only); super high-speed 7.0:1 gear ratio (CORE100MG7 and CORE50/51MG7); heavy duty brass drive gear (CORE100MG7 only); PV power grips (CORE100MG7 only); 1/8 turn easy access attached sideplate (CORE50/51MG only); approved for use in salt water; rated for use with mono, fluorocarbon, and PowerPro lines.
Price:..........................$349.99–$399.99

SHIMANO METANIUM

Model: 100, 101, 100HG, 101HG, 100XG, 101XG
Gear Ratio: 6.2:1; 6.2:1; 7.4:1; 7.4:1; 8.5:1; 8.5:1
Inches/Turn: 26; 26; 31; 31; 36; 36
Spool Cap. (M): 8 lbs/140 yds
Weight: 6.0 oz; 6.0 oz; 6.0 oz; 6.0 oz; 6.2 oz; 6.2 oz
Hand Retrieve: R; L; R; L; R; L
Reel Bearings: 9+1
Features: Micro module gear; SVS infinity; X-ship; shielded S-ARB ball bearings; gear ratios of 6.2:1, 7.4:1, and 8.5:1; Super Stopper II roller clutch bearing; Dartanium 2 drag washers; MET XG 96mm handle with PV paddle grips; tapered line guide; escape hatch; cold-forged aluminum drag star; Septon handle grip; aluminum cast control knob; recessed reel seat foot; lightweight aluminum drive gear; ultra-lightweight magnesium frame; magnesium handle sideplate; carbon onside sideplate; approved for use in salt water.
Price:.................................$499.99

CABELA'S PRESTIGE PLUS
Model: 1, 2, 3
Gear Ratio: 3; 3.38; 3.75
Weight: 5.4 oz; 6.4 oz; 6.1 oz
Spool Cap. (M): 20 lbs/70 yds WF4; 20 lbs/100 yds WF6;
30 lbs/200 yds WF8

Hand Retrieve: L or R
Line Weight: 3-4; 5-6; 7-8
Features: Mid-arbor design for plenty of backing capacity;
molded, paddle-style handle; three sizes available.
Price:. **$49.99**

CABELA'S PRESTIGE PREMIER
Model: 1, 2, 3, 4
Gear Ratio: 2.99; 3.38; 3.81; 4.34
Weight: 4.23 oz; 4.58 oz; 5.64 oz; 8.28 oz
Spool Cap. (M): 20 lbs/80 yds WF4; 20 lbs/100 yds WF6;
20 lbs/200 yds WF8; 30 lbs/270 yds WF10
Hand Retrieve: L or R

Line Weight: 1-4; 5-6; 7-8; 9-10
Features: Mid-arbor design for plenty of backing capacity;
molded, paddle-style handle; four sizes available.
Price:. **$89.99**

CABELA'S RLS+
Model: 1, 2, 3, 4
Gear Ratio: 3.23; 3.46; 3.7; 4.13
Weight: 4.9 oz; 5.22 oz; 5.54 oz; 6.31 oz
Spool Cap. (M): 20 lbs/70 yds WF4; 20 lbs/100 yds WF6;
20 lbs/150 yds WF8; 20 lbs/250 yds WF10

Hand Retrieve: L or R
Line weight: 3-4; 5-6; 7-8; 8-10
Features: New lighter weight design; Rulon drag system;
large-arbor for a quicker retrieve; easily converts from right-
to left-hand.
Price: . . . .**$124.99–$139.99**

CABELA'S TLR
Model: 4, 5
Gear Ratio: 4.49
Weight: 7.76; 7.87
Spool Cap. (M): 30 lbs/200 yds WF10; 30 lbs/200 yds
WF12

Hand Retrieve: L or R
Line Weight: 9-10; 11-12
Features: Changeable weight system; durable anodized
finish; sealed Rulon disc drag.
Price: **$159.99**

CABELA'S WIND RIVER

Model: 1, 3, 5
Gear Ratio: 3; 3.38; 3.75;
Weight: 5.4 oz; 6.4 oz; 6.1 oz
Spool Cap. (M): 20 lbs/70 yds WF4; 20 lbs/100 yds WF6; 30 lbs/200 yds WF8

Hand Retrieve: L or R
Line Weight: 3-4; 5-6; 7-8
Features: Die-cast/machined-aluminum frame and spool; V-cut arbor spool; smooth Rulon drag.
Price:. **$29.99**

CABELA'S WLX

Model: 2.3, 4.5, 5.6, 7.8, 9.10, 11.12
Gear Ratio: 3; 3.15; 3.3; 3.63; 3.95; 4.25
Weight: 3.9 oz; 4.5 oz; 5 oz; 5.75 oz; 6.25 oz; 7.5 oz
Spool Cap. (M): 20 lbs/40 yds; 20 lbs/100 yds; 20 lbs/100 yds; 20 lbs/150 yds; 30 lbs/220 yds; 30 lbs/300 yds
Hand Retrieve: L or R

Line Weight: 2-3; 4-5; 5-6; 7-8; 9-10; 11-12
Features: Engineered exclusively for Cabela's by Waterworks-Lamson; lightweight 6061-T6 aircraft-grade aluminum; sealed drag with smooth-braking Rulon discs; rugged, non-glare anodized finish.
Price:. . . . . **$209.99–$219.99**

HARDY FORTUNA X
Model: 1, 2, 3, 4
Gear Ratio: 4.01; 4.25; 4.57; 5.24
Weight: 7.8 oz; 8.4 oz; 12 oz; 13.9 oz
Spool Cap. (M): 20 lbs/200 yds WF8; 30 lbs/200 yds WF10; 30 lbs/275 yds WF12; 30 lbs/550 yds WF14
Hand Retrieve: L or R

Features: Low start-up inertia; largest sizes generate up to 32 pounds of top-end drag; large backing capacities; multi carbon disk brake system; top grade 6061 anodized bar stock aluminium; simple left- to right-hand wind change with tool supplied; secure, quick release, interchangeable spools; seven-point sealed drag system; salt water safe; supplied with neoprene pouch.
Price: . . . .**$695–$845**

HATCH 1 PLUS FINATIC
Diameter: 2.9 in.
Weight: 2.8 oz
Hand Retrieve: L or R
Line Weight: 0W–2W

Features: We're talking small. You might even use one of these as a key chain. We had never considered a reel of this size since we very rarely fish with 0–2 weight rods. However, our minds changed when we had so many requests. How could we refuse?
Price: **$350**

REELS

REELS: **Freshwater Fly Fishing**

HATCH 3 PLUS FINATIC
Diameter: 3.25 in.
Weight: 4.8 oz
Hand Retrieve: L or R
Line Weight: 3W–5W

Features: The 3 Plus is capable of running 3–5 weight lines with ample backing capacity for the occasional whopper that might come along. At first glance you'll notice this ain't no dainty trout reel. This little wonder means business.
Price:.....................................**$400**

HATCH 4 PLUS FINATIC
Diameter: 3.425 in.
Weight: 5.2 oz
Hand Retrieve: L or R
Line Weight: 4W–6W

Features: The 4 Plus bridges the gap in size and weight between the 3 and 5 plus models. If you're looking for the perfect reel for your 9' 5-weight rod, then look no further.
Price:.....................................**$450**

HATCH 7 PLUS FINATIC
Diameter: 4 in.
Weight: 8.6 oz
Hand Retrieve: L or R
Line Weight: 7W–9W

Features: If I was stranded on a desert island and had only one reel to bring, it would be the 7 Plus. We have sold more of these bad boys than any other size in the Hatch lineup. From bonefish to permit, steelhead to carp, this reel has you covered.
Price: **$600**

HATCH 9 PLUS FINATIC
Diameter: 4.25 in.
Weight: 10.6 oz
Hand Retrieve: L or R
Line Weight: 9W–12W
Features: Where the rubber meets the road my friends! If you've been dreaming of a reel that has the look, feel, and

performance of a Ferrari, then look no further. Capable of running 9–12 weight lines, and your choice of mid or large arbor spools, this reel is one versatile hombre.
Price: **$750**

REELS: Freshwater Fly Fishing

L. L. BEAN DOUBLE L MID-ARBOR
Model: #1, #2, #3, #4
Spool Cap. (M): 20 lbs/95 yds WF-3; 20 lbs/115 yds WF-5; 30 lbs/160 yds WF-7; 30 lbs/230 yds WF-9
Hand Retrieve: L or R

Features: Heritage design with added benefits of a larger diameter arbor; retrieves line faster than traditional arbor reels; Aerospace-grade machined aluminum; quick change spool.
Price:.................................$119–$149

L. L. BEAN QUEST LARGE ARBOR
Model: #1, #2, #3
Weight: 6.1 oz; 7 oz; 8.6 oz
Spool Cap. (M): 20 lbs/130 yds WF-3; 20 lbs/140 yds WF-5; 30 lbs/240 yds WF-7
Hand Retrieve: L or R

Features: Our most popular reel for beginners; now even better; housing and spool are made from durable die-cast aluminum; smooth in-line disc-drag system protects finer tippets while stopping hard-fighting fish.
Price:.................................$45–$55

L. L. BEAN STREAMLIGHT ULTRA LARGE
Model: #1, #2, #3
Weight: 4.9 oz; 5.3 oz; 6.3 oz
Spool Cap. (M): 20 lbs/105 yds WF-3; 20 lbs/115 lbs WF-5; 30 lbs/170 yds WF-8
Hand Retrieve: L or R
Features: Packed with features you'd find on reels that cost twice as much; machined from bar-stock aluminum that's deeply anodized for corrosion resistance; in-line rulon disc drag is smooth and strong; please note: the flaw noted in customer reviews has been identified and corrected in all inventory.
Price: . . . . **$89–$109**

OKUMA CASCADE
Model: 4/6, 7/9
Gear Ratio: 2.9; 3.3
Weight: 4 oz; 6 oz
Spool Cap. (M): 20 lbs/125 yds WF4; 20 lbs/135 yds WF7
Hand Retrieve: L or R
Line Weight: 4-5-6; 7-8-9
Features: Fully adjustable multi-disc drag system; roller bearing allows the drag to engage in one direction only; precision machined brass bushing drive system; precision machined stainless steel spool shaft; super lightweight graphite frame construction; corrosion-resistant super large arbor spool design; easy to change left- to right-hand retrieval conversion.
Price: **$34.99**

REELS: Freshwater Fly Fishing

OKUMA HELIOS
Model: 34, 45, 56, 78a, 89a
Gear Ratio: 2.7; 3; 3.2; 3.5; 3.7
Weight: 4.5 oz; 5 oz; 5.3 oz; 5.9 oz; 6.2 oz
Spool Cap. (M): 12 lbs/105 yds WF3; 20 lbs/110 yds WF4; 20 lbs/130 yds WF5; 20 lbs/150 yds WF7; 20 lbs/250 yds WF8
Hand Retrieve: L or R
Line Weight: 3-4; 4-5; 5-6; 7-8; 8-9

Features: Maintenance-free waterproof drag system; multi-disc cork and stainless steel drag washers; roller bearing allows the drag to engage in one direction only; 2BB+1RB stainless steel drive system; precision machine stainless steel spool shaft; anodized aluminum machined rigid frame; machined aluminum large arbor spool design; non-slip positive grip rubberized handle knobs; easy to change left- to right-hand retrieval conversion.
Price:..........................$194.99–$209.99

OKUMA INTEGRITY
Model: 5/6b, 7/8b, 8/9b, 10/11b
Gear Ratio: 3; 3; 3.4; 3.9
Weight: 7 oz; 7.5 oz; 8 oz; 8.5 oz
Spool Cap. (M): 12 lbs/70 yds WF5; 20 lbs/50 yds WF7; 20 lbs/100 yds WF8; 30 lbs/170 yds WF10
Hand Retrieve: L or R
Line Weight: 5-6; 7-8; 8-9; 10-11

Features: 5/6 and 7/8 with multi-disc Rulidium drag washers; 8/9 and 10/11 with multi-disc cork drag washers; roller bearing engages drag system in one direction; precision machined stainless steel spool shaft; Alumilite die-cast aluminum frame design; rigid die-cast aluminum, large arbor spool design; precision machined, brass bushing drive; easy to change left- to right-hand retrieval conversion.
Price:..........................$69.99–$74.99

OKUMA SIERRA

Model: 4/5, 5/6, 7/8, 8/9, 10/11
Gear Ratio: 2.6; 2.9; 2.6; 2.9; 3.5
Weight: 5.3 oz; 5.3 oz; 5.3 oz; 5.7 oz; 6 oz
Spool Cap. (M): 12 lbs/105 yds WF4; 20 lbs/160 yds WF5; 20 lbs/75 yds WF7; 20 lbs/150 yds WF8; 30 lbs/285 yds WF10
Hand Retrieve: L or R

Line Weight: 4-5; 5-6; 7-8; 8-9; 10-11
Features: Fully adjustable Teflon and stainless drag system; roller bearing allows the drag to engage in one direction only; precision machined brass bushing drive system; precision machined stainless steel spool shaft; Alumilite die-cast aluminum frame; die-cast standard arbor spool design; easy to change left- to right-hand retrieval conversion.
Price: . . . .$44.99–$59.99

OKUMA SLV

Model: 2/3, 4/5, 5/6, 7/8, 8/9, 10/11
Gear Ratio: 2.6; 3; 3.2; 3.5; 3.7; 4.5
Weight: 4.5 oz; 4.8 oz; 5.3 oz; 5.5 oz; 6.1 oz; 9.7 oz
Spool Cap. (M): 12 lbs/50 yds WF2; 12 lbs/95 yds WF4; 20 lbs/140 yds WF5; 20 lbs/145 yds WF7; 30 lbs/150 yds WF8; 30 lbs/220 yds WF10
Hand Retrieve: L or R
Line Weight: 2-3; 4-5; 5-6; 7-8; 8-9; 10-11

Features: Multi-disc cork and stainless steel drag washers; roller bearing allows the drag to engage in one direction only; precision machined brass bushing drive system; precision machined stainless steel spool shaft; Alumilite die-cast; aluminum frame die-cast super large arbor spool design; non-slip positive grip rubberized handle knobs; easy to change left- to right-hand retrieval conversion.
Price: $64.99

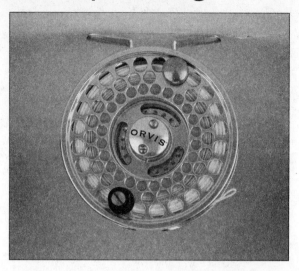

ORVIS ACCESS MID-ARBOR
Model: I, II, III, IV, V
Gear Ratio: 2.75; 3; 3.25; 3.5; 4
Weight: 4.29 oz; 4.45 oz; 4.62 oz; 5.28 oz; 5.88 oz
Spool Cap. (M): 12 lbs/150 yds WF1; 20 lbs/150 yds WF3; 20 lbs/150 yds WF5; 20 lbs/225 yds WF7; 30 lbs/250 yds WF9
Hand Retrieve: L or R
Line Weight: 1-3; 3-5; 5-7; 7-9; 9-11

Features: New Mirage gold anodizing; new larger Mirage-style handle; totally sealed drag surface; carbon fiber/stainless steel washer drag system; 6061 aircraft bar stock; available in sizes I-V; all models have a two carbon fiber, stainless steel washer drag system; positive drag click system; available in new gold, black, titanium.
Price: . . . .**$145–$185**

ORVIS BATTENKILL
Model: I, II, III
Gear Ratio: 2.75; 3; 3.25
Inches/Turn: 2.8 oz; 2.9 oz; 3.2 oz
Weight: 2.8 oz; 2.9 oz; 3.2 oz
Hand Retrieve: R or L
Features: Simple design and flawless construction make this the perfect click-and-pawl fly reel for nearly any freshwater fishing situation; features a classically styled, yet technically enhanced, four-position click-and-pawl drag system that is adjusted internally and is designed to work in tandem with the palm of your hand; constructed with a narrow spool for less line stacking on retrieve and a larger spool diameter for higher line retrieval rates; the ultra-lightweight fly reel design balances perfectly on shorter rods; machined from heavy-duty bar-stock aluminium for added durability; easily adjustable left- or right-hand retrieve; highlighted by laser-engraved logos; black nickel; imported.
Price: **$98**

ORVIS CFO DISC DRAG
Model: I, II, III
Gear Ratio: 2.75; 2.875; 3
Weight: 3.6 oz; 3.9 oz; 4 oz
Spool Cap. (M): 12 lbs/125 yds WF1; 20 lbs/75 yds WF3; 20 lbs/75 yds WF5
Hand Retrieve: L or R
Line Weight: 1-3; 3-5; 5-7
Features: The CFO fly-fishing reel has been the choice of technical fly fisherman since 1971. Reengineered to be lighter, smoother, and tougher. Although this fly fishing reel is machined using the most modern of materials and state-of-the-art machining technology, the CFO disc drag fly reel is a reverent nod to fly-fishing tradition. The reel's signature look and sound are synonymous for thousands of fly fisherman with great moments on the water. It matches as perfectly in spirit, looks, and performance with Orvis Superfine or bamboo fly rods as it does with our high-tech Helios fly rods.
Price:. . . . . **$325–$345**

ORVIS CLEARWATER LARGE ARBOR
Model: II, IV
Gear Ratio: 3.375; 3.875
Weight: 5.5 oz; 6.3 oz
Hand Retrieve: L or R
Line Weight: 4-6; 7-9
Features: Finally a cast aluminum large arbor fly-fishing reel that's lightweight enough to balance properly with your favorite fly rod and truly the best value fly reel around. Two years in design and development and with a powerful inline, Rulon to stainless, stacked disc drag that can hold its own with high-performance machined reels, the all new Clearwater Large Arbor costs significantly less than its machined cousins, but has not only the looks, but the guts of a higher-priced version. Easily converted to either left- or right-hand retrieve, the Clearwater fly reel has a positive click drag knob for consistent settings every time. Whether you're looking for your first large arbor, fishing on a budget, or want a spare or two in the bag, the new Clearwater Large Arbor can handle anything a machined reel can and completely changes the game in die-cast reels.
Price:. **$79**

ORVIS CLEARWATER LARGE ARBOR CASSETTE

Model: Clearwater Large Arbor Cassette
Gear Ratio: 3.875
Weight: 6.9 oz
Hand Retrieve: L or R
Line Weight: 6-8
Features: Finally a cast aluminium large arbor that's lightweight enough to balance properly with your favorite rod. Two years in design and development and with a powerful inline, Rulon to stainless, stacked disc drag that can hold its own with high-performance machined reels, the all new Clearwater Large Arbor cassette fly reel costs significantly less than its machined cousins, but has not only the looks, but the guts of a higher-priced version. Easily converted to either left- or right-hand retrieve, the Clearwater has a positive click drag knob for consistent settings every time. The innovative cassette offers extreme versatility and allows the angler to switch to the correct rig quickly and easily. Great performance, excellent versatility, and an incredibly low price. Cassette fly reel comes with two spare spools and a Cordura reel case.
Price:. **$125**

ORVIS MIRAGE

Model: I, II, III, IV, V, VI, VII Shallow, VII Deep
Gear Ratio: 3; 3.25; 3.5; 4; 4.25; 4.5; 5; 5
Weight: 3.8 oz; 4.3 oz; 4.8 oz; 7.2 oz; 7.7 oz; 10 oz; 11.7 oz; 11.5 oz
Spool Cap. (M): 12 lbs/150 yds WF1; 20 lbs/150 yds WF3; 20 lbs/150 yds WF5; 20 lbs/225 yds WF7; 30 lbs/250 yds WF9; 30 lbs/350 yds WF11; 30 lbs/350 yds WF11; 50 lbs/600 yds WF14
Hand Retrieve: L or R
Line Weight: 1–3, 3–5, 5–7, 7–9, 9–11, 11–13, 11–13, 13–15
Features: A completely sealed and maintenance-free drag surface, impervious to salt water, dirt, grit, and other corrosive elements to last longer and hold up to real world abuse. A positive-click drag knob for accurate and repeatable drag settings. True large arbor performance picks up line fast to give you the edge over all fresh and salt water fish: from trout and panfish to bonefish, stripers, tarpon, tuna, marlin, and sails. Crafted of strong yet lightweight anodized 6061 T6 aluminum with a heavily-ventilated spool to shed weight yet keep its strength. Special handle shape reduces line from catching. Aggressive diamond knurling on knob for easier grasp and adjustment mid-battle. Quick release spool and easy conversion from left- to right-hand retrieve.
Price:. . . . .**$425–$545**

PFLUEGER TRION
Model: 1934, 1956, 1978, 1990
Hand retrieve: L or R
Features: Ball bearings; instant anti-reverse bearing; forged, machined, and anodized aluminum frame and spool; central-disc drag system for total drag control; convertible left- and right-hand retrieve; large rosewood knob.
Price: **$130**

SCIENTIFIC ANGLERS CONCEPT 2
Model: Model 58
Gear Ratio: 3.31
Weight: 4.3 oz
Spool Cap. (M): 20 lbs/200 yds WF5
Hand retrieve: L or R
Features: Durable, lightweight composite polymer graphite; perforated for lighter, easier handling; counter-balanced spool for vibration-free runs; heavy-duty compression disc drag; palming rim for added drag pressure; durable, corrosion-resistant graphite composition; no tools needed easy-change from right to lefthand; easy-to-handle and built for bigger fish.
Price: **$33.95**

SCIENTIFIC ANGLERS SYSTEM 4
Model: 3/4, 5/6, 7/8
Gear Ratio: 3.125; 3.5; 3.75
Weight: 5.22 oz; 5.44 oz; 6.04 oz
Hand Retrieve: L or R
Line Weight: 3-8
Features: 6061-T6 proprietary aluminum alloy; Delrin 500AF with impregnated Teflon (space-age polymer that is durable, heat resistant, self-lubricating, and maintenance-free); Delrin 500AF to anodized aluminum interface (push

frame friction disc drag system with redundancy radial pawl engagement and seamless transition between line-in and drag engagement [no startup friction]); fully machined, one-piece frame, one-piece spool with a Delrin pressed hub (manufactured on automated CNC machining centers); Delrin hub rotating on a stainless steel spindle (Sizes 3/4, 5/6), oil impregnated bronze bushing rotating on a stainless steel spindle (Size 7/8), quick-release locking spool, easy left- hand to right-hand retrieve conversion.
Price: . . . .$200–$250

TEMPLE FORK BVK SUPER LARGE ARBOR REEL
Model: 0, I, II, III, IV
Gear Ratio: 2.75; 3.30; 3.75; 4.10; 4.75
Weight: 2.1 oz; 4.6 oz; 4.9 oz; 5.2 oz; 8.7 oz
Spool Cap. (M): 20 lbs/50 yds WF1; 20 lbs/75 yds WF4; 20 lbs/200 yds WF6; 20 lbs/205 yds WF8; 30 lbs/275 yds WF12
Hand Retrieve: L or R
Features: BVK reels are precision machined from bar stock aluminum. The moss green anodized frames and spools are

ported to eliminate excess weight. Equally at home in both fresh and salt water, the super large arbor design provides faster line pick up and helps the maintenance free drag system work at a more constant pressure than standard arbor reels. Delrin/Stainless stacked discs make the drag silky smooth and the one way clutch bearing makes engagement instant and left to right hand conversion simple. BVK reels are available in moss green only.
Price: . . . .$160–$325

TEMPLE FORK HSR

Model: I, II
Gear Ratio: 2.875; 3.25
Weight: 4 oz; 4.5 oz
Spool Cap. (M): 20 lbs/75 yds WF5; 20 lbs/150 yds WF8
Hand Retrieve: L or R

Features: The HSR family of reels is sure to make a big splash. These reels are machined aluminum and anodized for use in fresh or salt water. They feature a sealed stainless steel and Delrin drag system for maximum fish-stopping power without all the maintenance.
Price: . . . .**$160–$170**

TEMPLE FORK NXT

Model: I, II
Gear Ratio: 3.10; 3.40; 3.75; 4.25
Weight: 6.2 oz; 7.5 oz; 8 oz; 9.2 oz
Spool Cap. (M): 20 lbs/100 yds WF6; 20 lbs/150 yds WF8; 20 lbs/250 yds WF8; 30 lbs/275 yds WF10
Hand Retrieve: L or R

Features: TFO Large Arbor reels are machined from 6061 aluminum and offer a state-of-the-art draw bar/carbon fiber disc drag. Three bearings give our reel its smooth as silk spin, and a one-way roller bearing makes it easily convertible from left- to right-hand retrieve. TFO 375 reels are now available in Black, Red, Gold, and Pewter.
Price: **$50**

REELS

TEMPLE FORK PRISM CAST LARGE ARBOR

Model: 3/4, 5/6, 7/8, 9/11
Gear Ratio: 2.75; 3; 3.38; 4.25
Weight: 4.9 oz; 5.5 oz; 5.8 oz; 8.7 oz
Spool Cap. (M): 20 lbs/80 yds WF3; 20 lbs/100 yds WF5; 20 lbs/150 yds WF8; 30 lbs/265 yds WF10
Hand Retrieve: L or R

Features: Consistent with TFO's tradition of offering high-performance gear at an affordable price, the new Prism Cast Large Arbor Reels are made from cast aluminum with a cork disc drag and a one-way clutch bearing for instant drag engagement. They feature quick change spools and easy LH/RH conversion.
Price:................................ $90–$100

398 Hardy

398 Hatch

401 Okuma

401 Temple Fork

HARDY FORTUNA X
Model: 1, 2, 3, 4
Gear Ratio: 4.01; 4.25; 4.57; 5.24
Weight: 7.8 oz; 8.4 oz; 12 oz; 13.9 oz
Spool Cap. (M): 20 lbs/200 yds WF8; 30 lbs/200 yds WF10; 30 lbs/275 yds WF12; 30 lbs/550 yds WF14
Hand Retrieve: L or R

Features: Low start-up inertia; largest sizes generate up to 32 pounds of top-end drag; large backing capacities; multi carbon disk brake system; top grade 6061 anodized bar stock aluminium; simple left- to right-hand wind change with tool supplied; secure, quick release; interchangeable spools; seven-pint sealed drag system; salt water safe; supplied with neoprene pouch.
Price:...............................**$695–$845**

HATCH 5 PLUS FINATIC
Diameter: 3.625 in.
Weight: 6.5 oz
Hand Retrieve: L or R
Line Weight: 5W–7W

Features: We've used this workhorse surf fishing in So Cal, light steelheading in Oregon, chucking nasty streamers to ravenous browns in Montana, and stalking bones on the flats in Belize.
Price:......................................**$500**

HATCH 7 PLUS FINATIC
Diameter: 4 in.
Weight: 8.6 oz
Hand Retrieve: L or R
Line Weight: 7W–9W

Features: If I was stranded on a desert island and had only one reel to bring, it would be the 7 Plus. We have sold more of these bad boys than any other size in the Hatch lineup. From bonefish to permit, steelhead to carp, this reel has you covered.
Price: **$600**

HATCH 9 PLUS FINATIC
Diameter: 4.25 in.
Weight: 10.6 oz
Hand Retrieve: L or R
Line Weight: 9W–12W

Features: Where the rubber meets the road my friends! 'If you've been dreaming of a reel that has the look, feel and performance of a Ferrari, then look no further. Capable of running 9–12 weight lines, and your choice of mid or large arbor spools, this reel is one versatile hombre.
Price: **$750**

HATCH 11 PLUS FINATIC

Diameter: 4.625 in.
Weight: 11.1 oz
Hand Retrieve: L or R
Line Weight: 11W–12W

Features: The goal was to create a larger reel that bridged the gap between the 9 and 12 Plus models. We also wanted to make sure it had an oversized handle for greater grip control when fighting those big silver critters. The mid arbor option is also great for spey rods from 13.5–14.5 feet.
Price: **$825**

HATCH 12 PLUS FINATIC

Diameter: 5 in.
Weight: 15.6 oz
Hand Retrieve: L or R
Line Weight: 12W–16W
Features: Conventional wisdom says: Never take a knife to a gunfight. And when you're tackling big fish like the ones

this reel was designed for, then I think that's really sound advice. GTs or tuna, just to name a few, can undo your average gear in a fraction of a second. You will not find a better fish-fighting tool on the market for these situations. Oh yeah, it's also great for big spey applications.
Price: **$900**

OKUMA CEDROS
Model: 5/6, 7/8, 8/9
Gear Ratio: 3.2; 3.5; 3.7
Weight: 6 oz; 6.6 oz; 7.4 oz
Spool Cap. (M): 20 lbs/130 yds WF5; 20 lbs/150 yds WF7; 20 lbs/250 yds WF8
Hand Retrieve: L or R
Line Weight: 5-6; 7-8; 8-9

Features: Low start-up inertia; largest sizes generate up to 32 pounds of top-end drag; large backing capacities; multi carbon disk brake system; top grade 6061 anodized bar stock aluminium; simple left- to right-hand wind change with tool supplied; secure, quick release, interchangeable spools; seven-point sealed drag system; salt water safe; supplied with neoprene pouch.
Price: . . . . **$199.99–$219.99**

TEMPLE FORK HSR
Model: I, II
Gear Ratio: 2.875; 3.25
Weight: 4 oz; 4.5 oz
Spool Cap. (M): 20 lbs/75 yds WF5; 20 lbs/150 yds WF8
Hand Retrieve: L or R

Features: The HSR family of reels is sure to make a big splash. These reels are machined aluminum and anodized for use in fresh or salt water. They feature a sealed stainless steel and Delrin drag system for maximum fish-stopping power without all the maintenance.
Price: . . . .**$160–$170**

BANDIT LURES B-SHAD
Type: Crankbait
Color/Pattern: Chartreuse/Black Stripe, Red Chartreuse, Chrome/Black Back, Chrome/Blue Back, Popsicle, Khaki/Brown
Size: 3-1/2 in
Weight: 1/4 oz

Running Depth: 8 ft–10 ft
Features: Great for trolling the flats for walleye or working the shoreline to draw wary largemouths from the weeds; runs true right out of the package.
Price: **$6.49**

LURES

BASS PRO SHOPS CRAPPIE MAXX CRANK
Type: Crankbait
Color/Pattern: Pearl Shad, Chewing Gum, Lavender Shad, Midnight Fire, Chartreuse Shad, Watermelon Shad, Pinky Toe, Ole Miss, Albino Shad, Pearl Shad, Chewing Gum
Size: 1-5/8 in, 2 in

Weight: 3/16 oz, 1/3 oz, 5/16 oz, 1/4 oz
Running Depth: 4 ft, 6 ft, 10 ft
Features: Hottest bait to hit crappie fishing in a long time; serious slab enticing features; tight wobble; highly detailed design; 3D lazer eyes; quality components; fiving depths up to 10'.
Price: **$4.29**

LURES

BASS PRO SHOPS XPS BALSA BOOGIE CRANKBAIT

Type: Crankbait
Color/Pattern: Firetiger, Homer, Pearl Red Eye, Red Crawfish, Blue Silver Shad, Orange Brown Crawfish, Plum Crazy, Fried Green Tomato, Texas Shad, Chrome XXX Shad, Gold XXX Shad, Bone XXX Shad, Chartreuse Green Craw
Size: 2 3/4 in

Weight: 1/2 oz
Running Depth: 4 ft
Features: Balsa body with precisely angled diving lip; rolling, vibrating action bass can't refuse; 3D laser eyes; loud internal rattles; VMC premium hooks.
Price: **$5.99**

BASS PRO SHOPS XPS LAZER EYE

Type: Floating
Color/Pattern: Orange Pearl, Chrome Clown, Pink Lemonade, Orange Shad, Chartreuse Pearl, Perch, Purple Pearl, Natural Perch, Sultry Shad, Black Gold, Purple Tiger, Purple Dawn, Hollywood, XXX Shad, Psycho Perch, Spectrum, Blue Tiger, Purple Haze, Dyno-Mite, Copper Minnow, Blue Gill, Ghost Norman Flake, Blue Sparks,

Green Ghost, Lime Blue Pearl, Pumpkinseed, Natural Bream
Size: 2 1/4 in, 2 7/8 in, 3 in
Weight: 3/16 oz, 3/8 oz, 1/3 oz
Running Depth: 5 ft, 6 ft, 7 ft
Features: Naturally shaped body design; lifelike 3D laser eyes; extra-loud rattles; hot finishes; equipped with premium, extra-sharp hooks.
Price: **$4.49**

LURES: **Hardbait**

BASS PRO SHOPS XPS POP-N-TOP
Type: Popper
Color/Pattern: Bone Orange Belly, Bleeding Tennessee Shad, Chrome Black Back, Chartreuse Shad, XXX Shad
Size: 5 1/4 in
Weight: 7/8 oz

Running Depth: Topwater
Features: Weight transfer system for increased casting distance; weight balance system for "walk-the-dog" action; cupped mouth to "spit" water; dressed treble tail hook.
Price: **$5.99**

BASS PRO SHOPS XPS WHEEL N' DEAL
Type: Crankbait
Color/Pattern: Black/Orange, Black Shad, Pearl/White, Black Firetail, Black/Green, Black Frog, Dirty Duck
Size: 8 1/4 in
Weight: 2 1/4 oz
Running Depth: Topwater

Features: Twin chopper blade head section; single prop tail section; high-impact polystyrene body; 1.6 mm diameter through wire construction; 2–2/0 belly hooks; 1–3/0 tail hook.
Price: **$19.99**

BASS PRO SHOPS XPS Z9R PERCH

Type: Swimbait
Color/Pattern: Neon Bluegill, Shad, Green Perch, Bluegill
Size: 3 1/2 in
Weight: 3/4 oz

Features: High-quality construction and hardware; deeper-bodied perch profile; extreme realism, down to intricate gill, fin, and eye detail; precisely reproduced natural coloration.
Price:................................... **$11.99**

BERKLEY FLICKER SHAD

Type: Crankbait
Color/Pattern: Purple Cougar, Black Gold, Black Gold Sunset, Black Silver, Blue Tiger, Chartreuse Pearl, White Tiger, Red Tiger, Shad, Purple Tiger, Chrome Clown, Firetiger, Orange Tiger, Blue Scale Shad, Uncle Rico, Pearl White, Tennesse Shad, Dirty Craw, Chartreuse Growler, Blue Growler, Retro Shad, Perch
Size: 1 3/5 in; 2 in; 2 2/5 in; 2 3/4 in; 3 1/2 in;

Weight: 1/8 oz, 3/16 oz, 1/4 oz, 5/16 oz, 1/2 oz
Running Depth: 6 ft–8 ft, 9 ft–11 ft, 10 ft–12 ft, 11 ft–13 ft
Features: Designed by pros for optimal action, the Flicker Shad has a unique rattle and extra-sharp black-nickel hooks for solid hooksets. Ideal for trolling or cast and retrieve.
Price:............................... **$4.95–$5.95**

LURES: **Hardbait**

BERKLEY FLICKER SHAD PRO SERIES

Type: Crankbait
Color/Pattern: Slick Purple Candy, Slick Purple Bengal, Slick Sunset, Slick Chartreuse Purple, Slick Firetiger, Slick Mouse, Flashy Clown, Flashy Ghost, Flashy Perch, Flashy Purple Tiger
Size: 1 5/8 in, 2 in, 2 1/2 in, 2 3/4 in
Weight: 1/8 oz, 3/16 oz, 1/4 oz., 5/16 oz

Running Depth: 6 ft–8 ft, 9 ft–11 ft, 10 ft–12 ft, 11 ft–13 ft
Features: Wobbly action and unique rattle imitates a wounded baitfish to trigger strikes; flashy color patterns feature a translucent body with foil interior for a natural baitfish flash; slick colors sport an oil-slick pattern for maximum reflection; ideal for trolling or cast and retrieve.
Price: **$4.95**

BERKLEY FLICKER SHAD PRO SLICK

Type: Crankbait
Color/Pattern: Slick Chartreuse Pearl, Slick Firetiger, Slick Green Pearl, Slick Mouse, Slick Purple Bengal, Slick Purple Candy, Slick Purple Pearl, Slick Racy, Slick Sunset
Size: 1 1/2 in; 2 in; 2 1/4 in; 3 3/4 in
Weight: 1/8 oz, 3/16 oz, 1/4 oz, 5/16 oz

Running Depth: 6 ft–8 ft, 9 ft–11 ft, 10 ft–12 ft, 11 ft–13 ft
Features: Berkley has worked with the Pros to design multiple sizes of Flicker Shads to match the hatch. The unique action creates a "Flicker" that imitates a fleeing baitfish.
Price: **$4.95**

BOMBER DEEP LONG A

Type: Stick bait
Color/Pattern: Fire River Minnow, Chrome Orange Belly Black Back, Fire Tiger Bass, Silver Flash Red Head, Silver Prism Blue Black, Gold Chrome, Silver Flash, Silver Flash Orange Belly, Chartreuse Flash Orange Belly, Pearl Black Orange, Baby Striper, Silver Flash Blue Black, Rainbow Trout, Gold Prism Black Back Bars
Size: 2 1/2 in; 4 1/2 in
Weight: 3/8 oz, 3/4 oz

Running Depth: 10 ft–12 ft, 12 ft–15 ft
Features: Well-known as a big fish bait, the Bomber Deep Long A employs the original Long A's trademark action and adds a molded-in, deep-diving lip for extreme durability and out-of-the-package true-running performance. This deep-running version of the classic long A is especially effective when twitched for early season bass and can be trolled with precision for walleye, salmon, and striper.
Price: **$7.49**

BOMBER LONG A

Type: Stick bait
Color/Pattern: Fire River Minnow, Chrome Orange Belly Black Back, Fire Tiger Bass, Silver Flash Red Head, Silver Prism Blue Black, Gold Chrome, Silver Flash, Silver Flash Orange Belly, Chartreuse Flash Orange Belly, Pearl Black Orange, Baby Striper, Silver Flash Blue Black, Rainbow Trout, Gold Prism Black Back Bars
Size: 3 1/2 in; 4 1/2 in
Weight: 3/8 oz, 1/2 oz

Running Depth: 2 ft–3 ft, 3 ft–4 ft
Features: You won't catch many pros without a jerkbait rigged, no matter the season. That's because the minnow imitator is well known as one of the single most versatile baits. The Long A is the best of the best when it comes to replicating a lifelike swimming action. With a tight wiggle and castable design, the Long A is equally effective for largemouth, smallmouth, stripers, walleye, and pike.
Price: **$6.49**

LURES: **Hardbait**

BOMBER SWITCHBACK SHAD

Type: Crankbait
Color/Pattern: Hot Bream, Purple Darter, Red Crawfish, Sour Grape, Ghost Craw, Bama Shad, Foxy Phantom, Switchback Shad, Tennessee Special
Size: 2 1/2 in; 3 in
Weight: 1/2 oz, 3/4 oz
Running Depth: 4 ft–8 ft, 8 ft–14 ft, 10 ft–14 ft, 14 ft–18 ft
Features: It's easy to see why the Bomber Switchback Shad helped Tim win the 2007 Champion's Choice Elite event—it's action is so smooth! That day the fish were actively feeding on rock pile and Tim needed a subtle approach, not the reaction strike, and this bait proved to be the ticket. To further improve the design we incorporated a rattle you can turn on and off by locking the ball bearings in a chamber by simply rotating the crank until they're secure. It's very easy to do on the fly and adds a lot of versatility to your approach.
Price: **$7.99**

BOOYAH BOO FLEX RIG

Type: Umbrella rig
Color/Pattern: Alpine
Weight: 1/4 oz, 3/8 oz, 1/2 oz

Features: Fish any lure at any depth; attach spinnerbaits, crankbaits, or any other lure; add casting distance to ultralight lures.
Price: **$3.99**

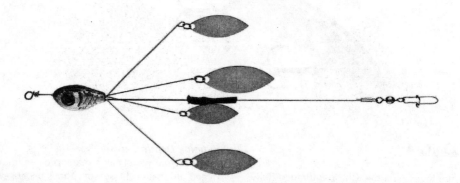

BOOYAH BOO RIG

Type: Umbrella rig
Color/Pattern: Alpine
Weight: 1/4 oz, 3/8 oz, 1/2 oz
Features: Four willow-leaf blades perfectly mimic a school of fish and a flexible arm lets you attach a crankbait, jig, or any other lure, making this setup deadly on any game fish; weight and design provide excellent castability, giving you the versatility to cast or troll; spinnerbait-style head is available in multiple sizes to match your quarry.
Price: **$6.99**

BOOYAH BOO SPIN RIG — WILLOW
Type: Umbrella rig
Color/Pattern: Alpine
Weight: 1/4 oz, 3/8 oz, 1/2 oz

Features: Irresistible bait-chase presentation; attach a crankbait, spinnerbait, or any other lure; easily snake through wood and other cover.
Price:. **$6.99**

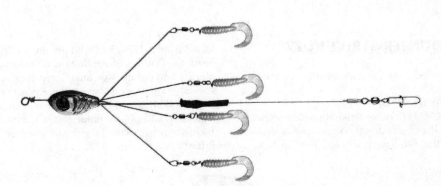

BOOYAH BOO TEASER RIG
Type: Umbrella rig
Color/Pattern: Alpine
Weight: 1/4 oz, 3/8 oz, 1/2 oz
Features: Add the highly effective bait-chase characteristic to any lure presentation; flexible arm lets crankbaits swim

naturally, enticing more fish to strike; four stiff outer arms come with curtail grub teasers that imitate a school of baitfish, a mouthwatering sight to large game fish; can be fished shallow or deep; spinnerbait-style head.
Price:. **$6.99**

BOOYAH BUZZ
Type: Buzzbait
Color/Pattern: Black, White/Chartreuse Shad, Chartreuse Shad, Citrus Shad, Limetreuse Shad, Snow White Shad
Weight: 1/4 oz, 3/8 oz, 1/2 oz
Features: The BOOYAH Buzz is made with premium hard coat paint, extra large 3D red eyes and flared red gills that

elicit vicious strikes; the BOOYAH Buzz Bait planes quickly and runs true out of the package. The BOOYAH Buzz Bait clacker really attacks the blade to provide additional fish attracting vibration and the 55-strand Bio-Flex silicone skirt and a 5/0 Mustad Ultra Point hook seal the deal.
Price:. **$4.69**

LURES

BOOYAH COUNTER STRIKE BUZZ

Type: Buzzbait
Color/Pattern: Alpine, Cortez Shad, Glowbee, Limesicle, Luna
Weight: 1/4 oz, 3/8 oz, 1/2 oz
Features: The BOOYAH Counter Strike Buzz's counter-rotating blades deliver exceptional stability and offer a distinctive sound that fish have not heard, even in heavily fished waters. Designed with the unique triangle-shaped head, the Counter Strike Buzz will plane to the surface quickly and cut through amazingly thick cover. A multi-step painting process that creates realistic scales and eyes, silicone skirt, plated blades that maximize flash, and an XCalibur Tx3 hook combine with Counter Strike Technology to create the ultimate buzzbait.
Price:. **$8.59**

BOOYAH DOUBLE WILLOW BLADE

Type: Spinnerbait
Color/Pattern: Chartreuse, Chartreuse Perch, Chartreuse White Shad, Citrus Shad, Gold Shiner, Perch, Satin Silver Glimmer, Silver Shad, Snow White, White Chartreuse, Wounded Shad
Weight: 3/8 oz, 1/2 oz, 3/4 oz, 1 oz
Features: The BOOYAH Double Willow Blade is a proven bass tournament winning spinnerbait. It's designed for maximum vibration, making it perfect for cool- or murky-water situations. The 55-strand Bio-Flex silicone skirt undulates like a baitfish and hides one of the toughest and sharpest hooks in the business.
Price:. **$5.99**

BOOYAH MICRO POND MAGIC

Type: Spinnerbait
Color/Pattern: Alpine, Fire Ant, Lightning Bug, Locust
Weight: 1/8 oz
Features: The Booyah Micro Pond Magic is a unique fish-catching bait in its own right. It's tough, durable, and catches fish in big lakes as well as ponds and streams. This 1/8 oz spinnerbait features a true-running "R" bend wire for incredible vibration and a single Colorado blade that provides the perfect amount of flash and water displacement. The 40 strand Bio-Flex silicone skirt features all of the baitfish and insect patterns available in the Pond Magic line. The head features realistic 3-D eye, a high-quality Mustad round-bend hook and a ball bearing swivel. Early season or any time fish are finicky, tie on a Micro Pond Magic.
Price: **$2.89**

LURES

BOOYAH MINI SHAD

Type: Spinnerbait
Color/Pattern: Chartreuse Gold Shiner, Golden Shiner, Pearl Shiner, Purple Glimmer Shad, Silver Chartreuse
Weight: 3/16 oz
Features: 3/16-ounce BOOYAH Mini Shad Spinnerbait A bait that was born in ultra clear water, the BOOYAH Mini Shad may be diminutive in stature but that doesn't mean it's not a big time, big fish bait. This spinnerbait has three willow blades, a 50-strand silicone skirt, amazing lifelike detail, and it is capable of running true at high retrieve speeds. This is the bait to call them up.
Price: **$5.99**

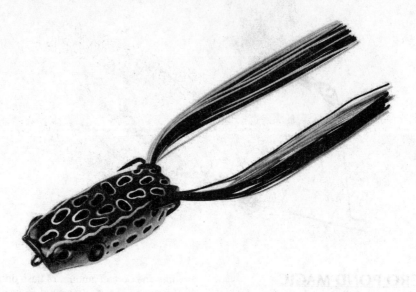

BOOYAH PAD CRASHER

Type: Frog
Color/Pattern: Aqua Frog, Albino Frog, Bull Frog, Kuro Frog, Leopard Frog, Swamp Frog, Cricket Frog, Shad Frog, Dart Frog
Size: 2 1/2 in
Weight: 1/2 oz
Running Depth: Topwater

Features: The BOOYAH Pad Crasher soft plastic is just the right consistency to ensure solid, consistent hook-ups while remaining weed and snag-free. The belly features "chines" that make "walking the frog" easy in open water, and it's just the right weight for pulling over slop or through the pads for big bass. Realistic decoration schemes and adjustable spinnerbait-style legs seal the deal for big bass.
Price: **$6.59**

BOOYAH POND MAGIC

Type: Spinnerbait
Color/Pattern: Craw, Firebug, Firefly, Grasshopper, Hornet, Junebug, Moss Back Craw, Nest Robber, Okie Craw, Shad, Sunrise Craw
Weight: 3/16 oz
Features: BOOYAH Pond Magic is specialized in color and blade combinations that have been hand selected to match the forage base of smaller waters. Small in size by spinnerbait standards but certainly not short on features. Premium components and 60-strand ultra fine silicone skirts make these every bit the quality of our BOOYAH Blades. Pick up a Pond Magic and you'll find out quickly that these are fish-catching machines.
Price: **$3.79**

www.skyhorsepublishing.com

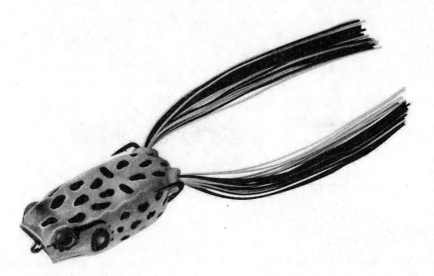

BOOYAH POPPIN' PAD CRASHER

Type: Frog
Color/Pattern: Aqua Frog, Bull Frog, Cricket Frog, Dart Frog, Leopard Frog, Shad Frog, Swamp Frog
Size: 2 1/2 in
Weight: 1/2 oz
Running Depth: Topwater
Features: The Booyah Poppin' Pad Crasher is perfect for those times when you need more surface disturbance to get the fish to commit. Windy days, thick slop, and finicky fish that have seen other frogs all day long still will take the different action of the Poppin' Pad Crasher. It's great for fishing the slop but, with the cupped mouth also doubles as a popper/chugger in open water. This BOOYAH fishing lure is a great topwater lure, ideal for bass fishing.
Price:. $6.59

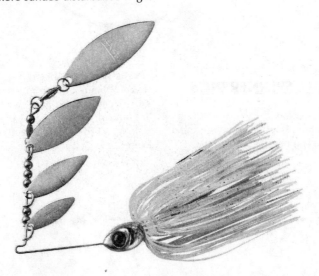

BOOYAH SUPER SHAD

Type: Spinnerbait
Color/Pattern: Golden Shiner, Purple Glimmer Shad, Silver Chartreuse
Weight: 3/8 oz
Features: The BOOYAH Super Shad Spinnerbait is a bit larger than other spinners, but most of those don't sport four blades! Put the Super Shad in motion, and you'll swear you're looking at a pod of baitfish fleeing through the water. So will the bass and muskie. Combine the Super Shad's quad blades with its seductively undulating skirt, and you've got a Booyah big fish spinner in a class all by itself.
Price:. $6.49

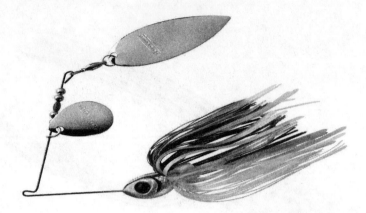

BOOYAH VIBRA-FLX

Type: Spinnerbait
Color/Pattern: AYU, Baby Bass, Blue Gill, Foxy Shad, Golden Shiner, Herring, Hitch, Kentucky Magic, Okie Shad, Shadtreuse
Weight: 3/8 oz, 1/2 oz
Features: BOOYAH Vibra-Flx spinnerbiat has added spinnerbait vibration, which means extra fish-attracting potency. The BOOYAH Vibra-Flx Spinnerbait apart of the BOOYAH Vibra-Flx fishing lures line. The BOOYAH Vibra-Flx Spinnerbait's frame is built from Vibra-Flx wire, which creates more vibration than standard stainless wire. In addition, Vibra-Flx wire offers flexible memory (meaning it stays tuned after several catches) and added toughness (twice as strong as standard stainless wire frames). Every BOOYAH Vibra-Flx Spinnerbait comes loaded with great features, including counter-rotating blades and a new Silo-Tek skirt, which undulates like flat rubber, but because it is silicone, it is much more durable.
Price: **$7.79**

CABELA'S DEATH ROLL SPINNER RIGS

Type: Bait rig
Color/Pattern: Glow, Chartreuse, Red
Features: A new twist on traditional walleye rigs with the introduction of the Death Roll spinner rigs. Thread the crawler on the hook and it spins as it's pulled through the water, enticing bites from lethargic walleye. Each comes fully rigged with a barrel swivel to prevent line twists, a 5mm bead, and one size 1 or one size 1/0 hook on a 36 in-long, 12-lb monofilament leader.
Price: **$3.99**

CABELA'S FISHERMAN SERIES BIG WATER WALLEYE RIG

Type: Bait rig
Color/Pattern: Watermelon, Emerald, Purple, Pink, Chartreuse, Firetiger, Clown
Blade size: 4, 5, 6
Features: Oversized, deep-cup blades come complete with larger hooks and heavier monofilament line than standard spinners and boast time-tested and proven big-water colors; rigged with 72 -in, 17-lb test monofilament and size 2 hooks.
Price: **$3.99**

LURES

CABELA'S FISHERMAN SERIES JOINTED SUSPENDING SHAD

Type: Crankbait
Color/Pattern: Glass Blue Shad, Firetiger, Glass Perch, Red Craw, Glass Black Shad, Glass Road Crew, Flasher, Glass Chartreuse Growler
Size: 2 1/8 in
Weight: 1/4 oz

Running Depth: 6 ft–10 ft
Features: The jointed design, rattling, and suspending action make this bait an optimum baitfish imitator that lures in walleye, bass, and oversized panfish; especially effective around submerged structures and can be cast or trolled; suspends at rest.
Price: **$3.99**

LURES

CABELA'S HDS ESOX MINNOW

Type: Stick bait
Color/Pattern: Northern Pike, Musky, Tiger Musky
Size: 4 3/4 in
Weight: 1/2 oz
Features: With Cabela's innovative High-Definition Series (HDS) technology for unsurpassed realism you have to see to believe, a special printing process transfers an actual

image of a live baitfish onto the lure, resulting in color and detail only a real fish can match. Modeled after the juvenile northern pike, one of the most sought-after forage fish in the lake; draws ferocious strikes from trophy bass, pike, musky, and walleye; rigged with quality Matzuo hooks.
Price: **$5.99**

Hardbait

CABELA'S HOT METAL SHAD

Type: Crankbait
Color/Pattern: Glass Purple Demon, Glass/Blue Back, Chrome Black Back, Flasher, Blue Racer, Perch, Purple Haze, Firetiger
Size: 2 3/8 in, 2 3/4 in

Weight: 1/4 oz, 3/8 oz
Features: Metallic, depth-control lip; mimics popular forage fish; rigged with quality Matzuo hooks; ideal for trolling for feeding walleye.
Price: **$4.99**

CREEK CHUB CHUG-A-LUG

Type: Topwater bait
Color/Pattern: Bunker, Squid, Mackerel, Funny Bone, Sweet Purple, Red Head, Blue Flyer
Size: 7 1/4 in
Weight: 4 oz
Features: Hydro-Ribs amplify vibration, which, combined with lifelike colors and large pupil eyes, draw aggresive fish

from a distance; stainless steel through-wire construction and hard wood body are built to withstand hard strikes from large fish; 300 lb test heavy belly hook swivel and triple split rings keep fish hooked; 3X saltwater-grade hooks withstand corrosion from harsh salt water, providing multiple seasons of use.
Price: **$24.99**

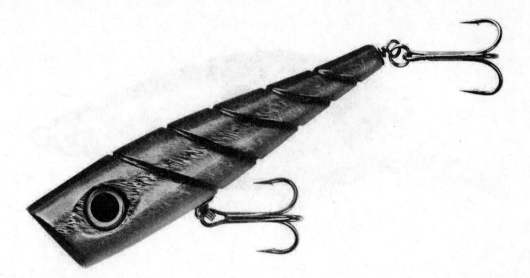

CREEK CHUB SURFSTER

Type: Crankbait
Color/Pattern: Bone, Yellow Croaker
Size: 4 1/2 in; 6 in; 7 in
Weight: 1 1/2 oz, 2 1/2 oz, 4 oz
Water Type: Saltwater

Features: Traditional stainless steel lip; super-tough stainless steel; ultra-realistic large pupil eyes; the perfect target for big predators; rugged heavy swivels; sturdy triple split rings; saltwater grade hooks.
Price: **$14.99**

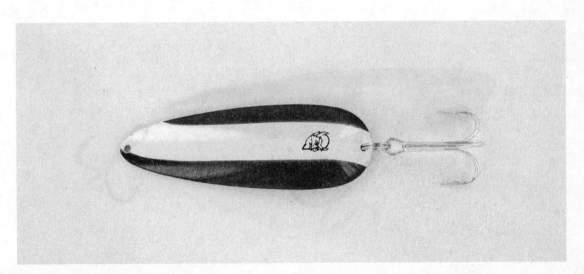

EPPINGER DARDEVLE SPOON

Type: Casting/trolling spoon
Color/Pattern: Nickel, Brass, Crackle Frog, Red/White, Black/White, Yellow/Black Diamond, Yellow/5 of Diamonds, Chartreuse/Orange Scale, Orange/Black Spots, Brown Trout, Pink Diamond, Glow Fluorescent Green Dot, Glow Fluorescent Orange Dot, Glow Green, Glow Blue, Glow Orange, Hot Firetiger/Black, Chartreuse/Lime, Grey Shad, Hot Shad, Rainbow Trout, Chartreuse/Red Spots, Orange/Green Perch Scale, Hammered Nickel/Blue, Hammered Nickel, Red/White Stripe, Fluorescent Orange/Black Spots, Yellow/Green Diamond
Size: 15/16 in–5 1/2 in
Weight: 3/16 oz, 1/4 oz, 2/5 oz, 3/4 oz, 1 oz, 1 3/4 oz, 2 oz, 3 1/4 oz
Features: Only high-quality metal, durable enamels and strong steel hooks are used on a genuine Dardevle spoon; for nearly a century, these perfectly balanced spoons and their wobble action have helped land fish; made in USA.
Price: . . . . **$3.99–$9.99**

GARY YAMAMOTO CHIKARA CRANKBAIT

Type: Crankbait
Color/Pattern: Black Red Flake, Pumpkin Black Flake, Silver Black Back, Silver Blue Back, Sexy Shad, Crawfish Green, Crawfish Red, Chartreuse Black Back, Olive Green Shad
Size: 2 in

Weight: 1/2 oz
Running Depth: 3 ft–4 ft, 6 ft–8 ft, 8 ft–10 ft
Features: The innovative design outperforms other lures when fishing in cover or open water; fish-enticing colors draw the wariest lunkers out of hiding.
Price: **$7.99**

GARY YAMAMOTO SHIBUKI POPPER

Type: Topwater bait
Color/Pattern: Silver Black Back, Silver Blue Back, White Bone, Black Bone, Green Frog
Size: 2 3/8in, 3 1/8 in
Weight: 1/4 oz, 7/16 oz

Features: A small concave-faced popper that can either move a lot of water or a little; premium color schemes drive fish crazy and sharp hooks catch them when they strike; ideal for imitating a fleeing baitfish of any species or drawing cautious fish out of cover.
Price: **$7.99**

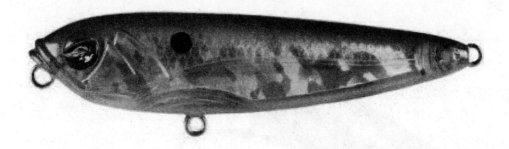

GARY YAMAMOTO TATE' PENCIL BAIT

Type: Crankbait
Color/Pattern: Silver Black Back, Silver Blue Back, Chartreuse Blue Back, White Bone, Black Bone, Green Frog
Size: 3 in, 4 in
Weight: 7/16 oz, 9/16 oz

Features: Tate', which means "dance" in Japanese, is a classic walk-the-dog topwater pencil bait with more character and zip than its counterparts. Even the most disinterested bass cannot help but take notice of this quivering lure. Whether it's mere inches from the surface or well into the depths, big fish will be suckered in.
Price: **$7.99**

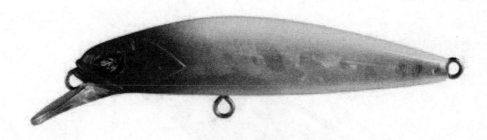

GARY YAMAMOTO TENKUU JERKBAIT

Type: Stick bait
Color/Pattern: Silver Black Back, Silver Blue Back, Crawfish Green, Crawfish Red, Chartreuse Black Back, Gold Fish, Olive Green Shad, Albino Shad
Size: 3 in, 4 in, 4 1/4 in

Weight: 1/3 oz, 1/2 oz, 3/4 oz
Running Depth: 4 ft, 8 ft, 10 ft
Features: Excellent for large, pre-spawn fish; can be fished successfully year-round; three sizes represent common baitfish.
Price: **$7.99**

LURES

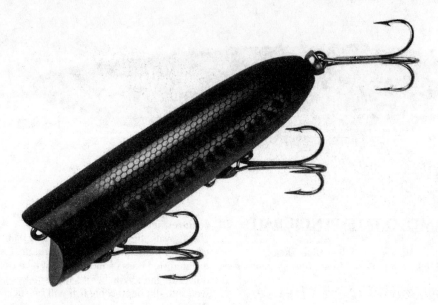

HEDDON LUCKY 13

Type: Topwater bait
Color/Pattern: Baby Bass Red Gill, Bullfrog, Fluorescent Green Crawdad, Black Shiner Glitter, Red Head
Size: 2 5/8 in; 3 3/4 in
Weight: 5/8 oz
Features: The Lucky 13 produces a deep, resonating sound that drives gamefish crazy when it's chugged. Long considered one of the best lures made for catching schooling fish, the Lucky 13's size and action make it a true fresh- and saltwater multispecies bait (bass, pike, stripers, white bass, speckled trout, redfish, and other inshore species).
Price: **$4.99**

HEDDON MOSS BOSS

Type: Crankbait
Color/Pattern: Black Scale, Bullfrog, Chartreuse/Black Scale, White/Scale
Size: 2 1/5 in; 3 in
Weight: 3/8 oz, 1/4 oz
Features: The Moss Boss is indeed the "boss" when it comes to tempting lunkers into striking from under the thickest moss, weed beds, and brush. The Moss Boss has been perfectly designed to glide easily over and through the heaviest of cover, the kind of cover that holds big muskie, bass, and northerns. When a lunker spies a Moss Boss sliding through the weeds overhead it makes for one of the most exciting strikes ever!
Price: **$3.99**

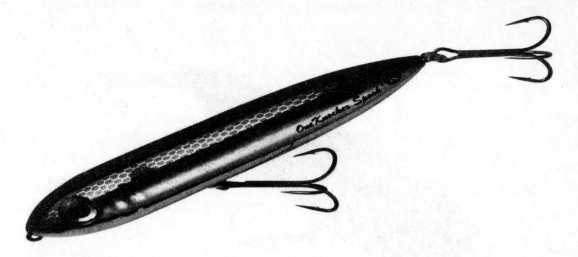

HEDDON ONE KNOCKER SPOOK

Type: Topwater bait
Color/Pattern: Blue Shad, Okie Shad, Baby Bass, G-Finish Shad, Ghost, G-Finish Bull Frog
Size: 4 1/2 in
Weight: 3/4 oz
Features: The One Knocker Spook thumps bass with a sound like no other topwater bait. The single tungsten rattle contained in a sound-intensifying chamber produces a loud thump that draws fish from long distances. Its positioning within the body of the lure makes walking-the-dog easier than ever. Fourteen color patterns and Mustad Triple Grip hooks take care of the rest.
Price: **$6.99**

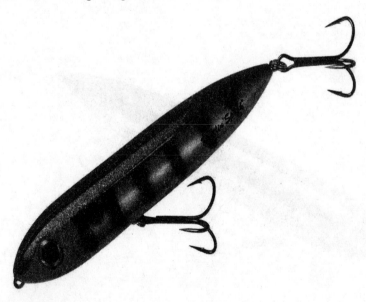

HEDDON RATTLIN' SPOOK

Type: Topwater bait
Color/Pattern: Bone, Foxy Momma, Foxy Shad, Ghost, Okie Shad, Pearl Melon, Pearl Shad
Size: 4 1/2 in
Weight: 3/4 oz
Features: The Rattlin' Spook adds tremendous sound to your dog walking. A new rattle chamber containing tungsten BB's amplifies and intensifies the sounds of panicked and fleeing baitfish. This unique sound chamber also makes it easier to produce smooth walk-the-dog retrieves. Fourteen realistic color patterns and Mustad Triple Grip Hooks seal the deal when big bass crash the surface.
Price: **$6.99**

HEDDON SPIT'N IMAGE

Type: Topwater bait
Color/Pattern: Gizzard Shad, Threadfin Shad.
Size: 3 in; 3 1/4 in
Weight: 5/16 oz, 7/16 oz

Features: The Heddon Spit'n Image perfectly mimics the frantic antics of a fleeing shad—in fact, it's the Spit'n Image of one! When retrieved, the Spit'n Image moves from side to side; at rest, the tail sits low in the water.
Price: **$4.99**

HEDDON SUPER SPOOK

Type: Topwater bait
Color/Pattern: Nickel, Chartreuse, Black/Chartreuse/Gold Insert, Spectrum, Florida Bass, Lake Fork Shad, Bleeding Shiner, Clear, Oakie Shad, Clown, Foxy Shad, Bone.
Size: 5 in
Weight: 7/8 oz

Features: Often imitated, impossible to duplicate, the Super Spook is just as deadly as the original Zara Spook introduced decades ago. Oversized eyes and the trademark walk-the-dog action make everything from bass to redfish attack with a vengeance. Fish don't simply bite a Super Spook, they attack it. Per each.
Price: **$5.99**

HEDDON SUPER SPOOK JR.

Type: Topwater bait
Color/Pattern: Bone/Silver, Chartreuse/Black Head, Black/
Chartreuse Gold, Spectrum, Golden Shiner, Red Head,
Silver Mullet, Speckled Trout.
Size: 3 1/2 in
Weight: 1/2 oz

Features: The Heddon Super Spook Jr. features the tough
construction and good looks of the full-sized Super Spook
in a smaller, but still explosive, fish-catching design.
Rugged line ties and hooks ensure the Super Spook Jr. will
hold up to opportunistic charges from schooling fish.
Realistic finishes provide the proper look for virtually any
topwater fishing situation.
Price: **$5.99**

LURES

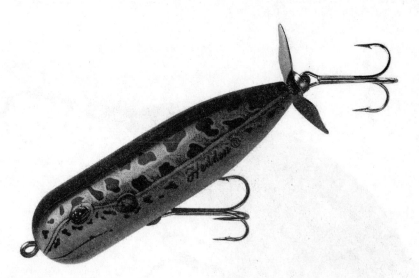

HEDDON TORPEDO

Type: Prop
Color/Pattern: Black Shiner, Natural Perch, Shad G-Finish,
Leopard Frog, Clear, Bullfrog, Black Shore Minnow, Brown
Crawdad, Baby Bass, Black Shiner, Natural Perch, Shad
G-Finish, Leopard Frog, Bullfrog, Black Shore Minnow,
Baby Bass, Black Shiner, Bullfrog, Baby Bass.
Size: 1 1/2 in; 1 7/8 in; 2 1/2 in; 3 5/16 in
Weight: 1/8 oz, 1/4 oz, 3/8 oz, 5/8 oz
Features: The Heddon Torpedos have been the world's top-
selling, top-producing spinner-equipped lures for

generations. Their shape and weight allow anglers to cast
these lures a little farther than many other prop-baits,
allowing them to reach those special fish-holding spots
quicker and easier. Torpedos create a wild splashing surface
disturbance, making them the perfect lures for schooling
fish. Use quick, short, and erratic twitches to make
Torpedos perform at their best . . . producing explosive,
heart-stopping surface strikes every time.
Price: **$4.99**

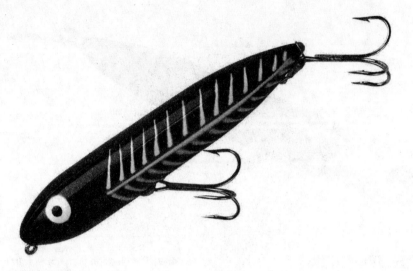

HEDDON ZARA SPOOK

Type: Topwater bait
Color/Pattern: Black Shiner, Red Head, Shad G-Finish, Leopard Frog, Blue Shad, Bullfrog, Flitter Shad, Baby Bass, Black Shiner, Red Head, Blue Shore Minnow, Shad G-finish, Leopard Frog, Blue Shad, Clear, Bullfrog, Fluorescent Green Crawdad, Flitter Shad, Baby Bass, Bone.

Size: 3 in; 4 1/2 in
Weight: 1/4 oz, 3/4 oz
Features: The Zara Spook and Zara Puppy are the original walk-the-dog lures. Heavy-duty construction holds up to vicious strikes and casts like a bullet.
Price: **$5.99**

LUCKY CRAFT LV RTO 150 LIPLESS CRANKBAIT

Type: Crankbait
Color/Pattern: Chrome Blue, TO Gill, FF Male Gill, Ghost Minnow, Chartreuse Shad, MS American Shad
Size: 5.2 in
Weight: 1/2 oz

Running Depth: 3 ft–4 ft
Features: Shimmy action irresistible to bass; flat head for a strong wobbling action; perfect in weedy areas and near structure.
Price: **$17.99**

LURES

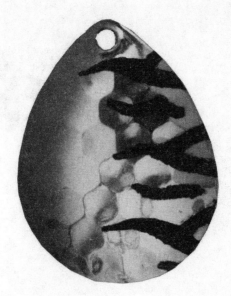

NORTHLAND CRAWLER HAULER SPEED SPINNER

Type: Bait rig
Color/Pattern: Silver Shiner, Gold Shiner, Gold Perch, Sunrise
Blade Size: 3, 4

Features: Life-like Holographic Baitfish-Image spinner blade rigged on a double stainless steel wire harness that is highly visible to fish; VMC Crawler Hauler Hook has a frantic action that induces strikes; molded Snap-Back-Barb bait keeper keeps bait firmly on your hook.
Price: **$3.99**

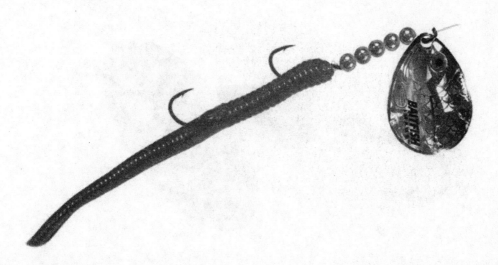

NORTHLAND IMPULSE RIGGED NIGHTCRAWLER

Type: Bait rig
Color/Pattern: Silver Shiner, Gold Shiner, Gold Perch, Sunrise

Size: 6 in
Blade Size: 3
Features: ActionCup tail; baitfish image spinner harness; mirrors swimming action of a live nightcrawler.
Price: **$4.59**

PANTHER MARTIN FISHSEEUV SALMON AND STEELHEAD SPINNERS

Type: InLine Spinner
Color/Pattern: UV Red Tiger, UV Pink Tiger, UV Chartreuse Lime Orange, UV Firetiger, UV Red White
Weight: 7/16 oz, 1/2 oz, 3/4 oz
Features: FishSeeUV paint on these Panther Martin Salmon and Steelhead Spinners adds to their already proven fish-catching ability and also increases their effectiveness on cloudy days or in murky waters; unique blades send an enticing vibration through the water that's irresistible to predatory fish; a great choice for salmon, steelhead, pike, and musky.
Price: . . . . **$4.79–$5.49**

PANTHER MARTIN HAMMERED SPINNERS

Type: InLine Spinner
Color/Pattern: Silver, Gold, UV Salmon Black, UV Lime Chartreuse, Yellow Red

Weight: 1/16 oz, 1/8 oz, 1/4 oz
Features: The awesome vibration of the original Panther Martin spinner with the added flash of a hammered blade; classic color options or fish-enticing FishSeeUV colors; effective on everything from panfish to pike.
Price: . . . . **$3.99–$4.19**

PANTHER MARTIN TAILWAGGER

Type: Tail-spinning
Color/Pattern: Super Shad, Albino, Chrome/Black, Chartreuse, Silver/Blue, UV Firetiger, UV Red/White
Weight: 3/8 oz, 1/2 oz
Features: New Super Shad color naturally attracts bass and trout; easiest and fastest spinning action in the world; sends out sonic vibrations that are irresistable to all gamefish; concave mouth to increase wobbling swimming action of the body; super sharp premium quality hooks keep fish caught!
Price: . . . . **$4.49–$4.99**

LURES

PANTHER MARTIN VIBRANT IMAGE SPINNER

Type: InLine Spinner
Color/Pattern: Firetiger, Bullfrog, Camo
Weight: 1/16 oz, 1/8 oz, 1/4 oz
Features: UV-enhanced iridescent pearl-base finish and colorful graphics for maximum underwater visibility; color graphics are digitally applied into the paint so they won't peel or fade; classic color options or fish-enticing FishSeeUV colors; effective on everything from panfish to pike.
Price: **$4.49**

LURES: **Hardbait**

PANTHER MUSKIE MARABUCK

Type: InLine Spinner
Color/Pattern: Electric Chicken, Gold/Black/Red, Gold/
Firetiger, Silver/Red/Black, Silver/White/Red, White/Purple/
Blue
Weight: 1 oz, 1 1/2 oz

Features: Genuine natural hand-tied marabou and bucktail;
the famous convex/concave blades in gold and silver; super
sharp and strong eagle claw treble hooks; oversized heavy
weighted brass bodies; can be used as a true countdown
lure.
Price: **$19.99; $21.99**

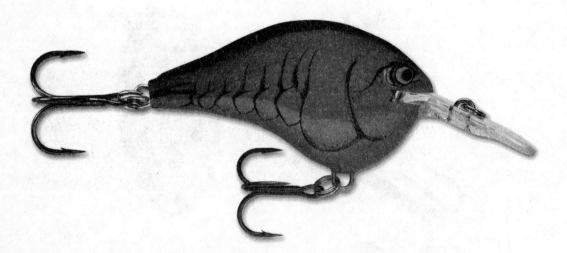

RAPALA DT (DIVES-TO) SERIES: 4, 6, 10, 14, 16

Type: Crankbait
Color/Pattern: Baby Bass, Bleeding Olive Shiner, Blue
Shad, Bluegill, Chartreuse Brown, Dark Brown Crawdad,
Firetiger, Helsinki Shad, Hot Mustard, Molting Blue Craw,
Olive Green Craw, Parrot, Pearl Grey Shiner, Perch, Purple
Olive Craw, Red Crawdad, Regal Shad, Shad, Silver, Yellow
Perch
Size: 2 in, 2 1/4 in, 2 3/4 in

Weight: 5/16 oz, 3/8 oz, 3/5 oz, 3/4 oz
Running Depth: 4 ft, 6 ft, 10 ft, 14 ft, 16 ft
Features: Quick-dive resting position; extra thin
polycarbonate lip; perfect balance; 3D holographic or
painted eyes; long-casting up to 150 ft; thin tail design;
internal rattle chamber; VMC SureSet tail hook; VMC black
nickel belly hook; balsa wood construction; hand-tuned
and tank-tested.
Price: **$7.99**

RAPALA ORIGINAL FLOATING MINNOW

Type: Stick bait
Color/Pattern: Silver, Gold, Hot Steel, Gold/Fluorescent Red, Blue, Perch, Firetiger, Silver Fluorescent/Chartreuse, Yellow Perch, Shiner, Brown Trout, Rainbow, Clown, Purpledescent, Bleeding Hot Olive, Bleeding Original Shad, Vampire
Size: 1 1/2 in, 2 in, 2 3/4 in, 3 1/2 in, 4 3/8 in, 5 1/4 in, 7 in
Weight: 1/16 oz, 1/8 oz, 3/16 oz, 1/4 oz, 11/16 oz
Running Depth: 2 ft–4 ft, 3 ft–5 ft, 4 ft–6 ft, 6 ft–11 ft

Features: The lure that started it all is still the number one "go-to" lure. Whether twitched on top as a surface bait, retrieved as a shallow runner, weighted with a split shot for medium depth, or bottom walked off a three-way swivel or bottom bouncer, the wounded minnow action continues to be irresistible to fish everywhere. Premium black nickel VMC hooks; hand-tuned and tank-tested to ensure that world-renowned action straight from the box.
Price: . . . .$8.99–$13.99

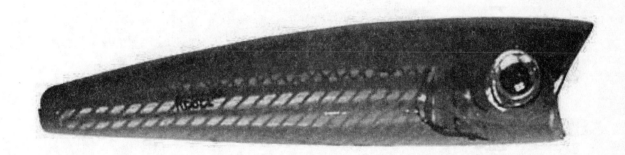

REBEL SALTWATER SUPER POP-R

Type: Topwater bait
Color/Pattern: Blue Stripe Mullet, Red Fish, Red Head, Speckled Trout, Barfish
Size: 3 1/8 in
Weight: 5/16 oz
Features: Produces an erratic, splashing action that induces bone-crushing topwater hits from large saltwater fish such

as red fish and ocean speckled trout; two #4 Permasteel treble hooks resist corrosion, even after 1,000 hours of saltwater exposure, maintaining a sharp point for deep hooksets; a variety of colors allow you to catch fish nearly anywhere, no matter what baitfish inhabit your target water.
Price: $6.99

LURES: **Hardbait**

LURES

SÉBILE ACTION FIRST BULL CRANK

Type: Crankbait
Color/Pattern: Black Chrome Gold Head, Smokin' Black Shad, Greenback Ghost, Smokin' Purple Pearl, Yellow Shad, Blue Red Craw
Size: 2 in, 2 1/2 in
Weight: 1/4 oz, 1/2 oz
Running Depth: 4 ft–7 ft, 8 ft–12 ft

Features: Engineered with intricate precision to be an exceptional swimmer, a square bill gives the bait a wider wobble and deflects off cover erratically; Xternal Weight System keeps the bait on a strike-inducing track and positions hooks for sure sets; near silent action prevents spooking and entices the most wary hogs in the school.
Price: **$6.99**

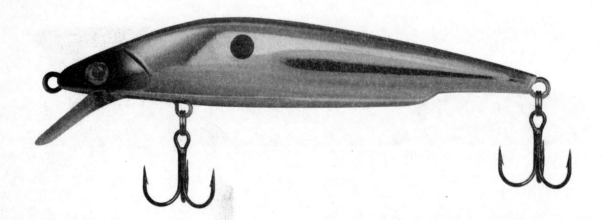

SÉBILE ACTION FIRST BULL MINNOW

Type: Jerkbait
Color/Pattern: Black Chrome, Black Gold, Bone Parrot, Chartreuse Tiger, Dark Blue Chrome, Eruption, Firetiger, Smokin' Black Shad', Smokin' Blue Chrome, Spotted Gray Shiner
Size: 4 in; 5 in
Weight: 1/2 oz, 3/4 oz

Running Depth: 2 ft–5 ft, 3 ft–6 ft
Features: Low, external weight allows for a lower center of gravity, higher buoyancy potential, and better tracking stability; shape design as a noisy traditional floating jerkbait; one mass transfer bead allows for better casting and knocking noise.
Price: . . . . **$5.59–$7.99**

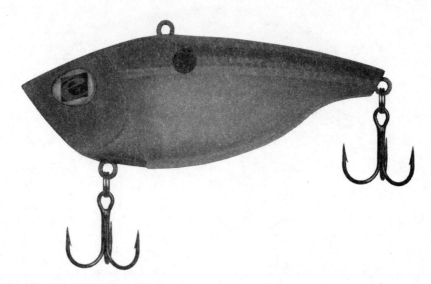

SÉBILE ACTION FIRST LIPLESS SEEKER

Type: Lipless bait
Color/Pattern: Greenback Ghost, Dark Blue Chrome, Lime Ghost, Black Gold, Black Chrome, Red Orange Craw, Firetiger
Size: 3 in

Weight: 1/2 oz
Features: Xternal Weight System creates optimal swim action; casts far and sinks fast; heavy bass beads cause a high-pitch rattle.
Price: **$5.99**

LURES

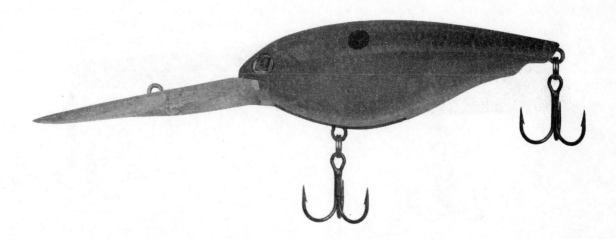

SÉBILE ACTION FIRST RACER

Type: Crankbait
Color/Pattern: Black Chrome Gold Head, Blue Red Craw, Eruption, Firetiger, Golden Ghost, Greenback Ghost, Lime Ghost, Red Gold, Smokin' Black Shad, Smokin' Purple Pearl, Spotted Blue Lime, Spotted Mess
Size: 2 in; 2 1/2 in; 3 in
Weight: 5/8 oz, 3/4 oz

Running Depth: 6 ft–8 ft, 8 ft–12 ft, 10 ft–15 ft
Features: Low, external weight allows for a lower center of gravity, higher buoyancy potential, and better tracking stability; shape designed as a tighter action diving crank; long bill designed to go deep but little resistance on the rod tip making it easy to work all day.
Price: . . . . **$4.89–$6.99**

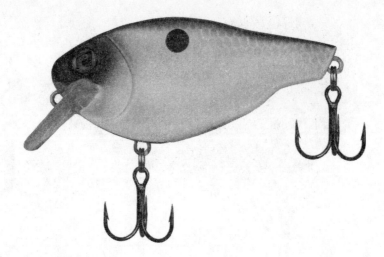

SÉBILE ACTION FIRST SQUAREBILL SUNFISH

Type: Crankbait
Color/Pattern: Greenback Ghost, Yellow Shad, Warmouth, Black Chrome Gold Head, Breeding Bluegill, Golden Ghost
Size: 2 1/2 in
Weight: 3/8 oz
Running Depth: 2 ft–6 ft

Features: A square bill gives the bait a wider wobble and deflects off cover erratically; the flat sides of the crank resemble a sunnie when viewed from above, below, or behind and give it a natural sunfish swimming action; Xternal Weight System keeps the bait on a strike-inducing track and positions hooks for sure sets; one internal free bead creates a knocking sound that could only be a sunfish encroaching on the bass's turf.
Price: **$6.99**

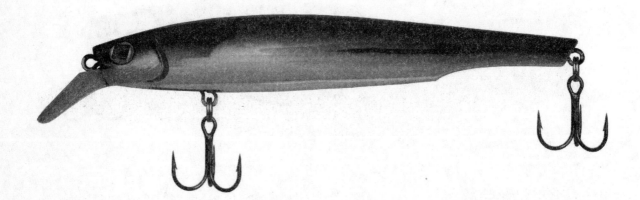

SÉBILE ACTION FIRST STAR SHINER

Type: Stick bait
Color/Pattern: Greenback Ghost, Smokin' Purple Pearl, Lime Perch, Spotted Mess, Black Chrome Gold Head, Golden Ghost, Red Gold, Ghost and Bones
Size: 3 1/2 in, 4 1/4 in
Weight: 1/4 oz, 1/2 oz
Running Depth: 2 ft–5 ft, 3 ft–6 ft

Features: One internal free bead makes a knocking sound, resembling an injured baitfish when jerked; Xternal Weight System works with the free bead to suspend the bait in perfect position when still; each minnow has two diving depths to cover the water column in the pivotal strike zones.
Price: **$7.99**

LURES

SÉBILE FLATT SHAD SNAGLESS

Type: Crankbait
Color/Pattern: Mat Brown/Red Crawdad, Holo Greenie, Gold Holo/Red/Chart, Hot Lime, Natural Blue Gill, Silver Liner
Size: 2 5/8 in
Weight: 1/2 oz, 3/4 oz
Running Depth: 3 ft–5 ft, 4 ft–6 ft
Features: Ultimate lipless vibrating bait at any speed and technique with the addition of making it snagless; all the features and benefits of the original Flatt Shad Unique Sébile double hook design allowing the bait to swim through snags with minimum risk of hanging up; feather tail adds another aspect of attraction; hooking and landing efficiency actually increases on big fish because hook is bigger; only hardbait that can be used for pitching and flipping; special designed hook with welded ring vs slip-on double hook.
Price: . . . .$10.82–$11.52

SÉBILE GHOST WALKER

Type: Floating
Color/Pattern: Amber Fashion, Yellow Pepper, Perchy, Hollow Mullet, White Lady, Natural Dark Blue Black, Natural Shiner, Natural Snook, Natural Seatrout, Natural Shiner
Size: 3 3/4 in; 4 1/4 in
Weight: 5/8 oz, 1 oz
Running Depth: Topwater
Features: The contour and airfoil of this lure give it incredible action. Different retrieves such as zigzags, darts and pauses, and rock and rolls are easily created with a twitch of the rod tip to dictate the retrieve, and under heavier jerks it's also possible to plunge the lure or violently impact the surface with its head. The Ghost Walker 110 is fully wire-reinforced for big game fish.
Price: . . . .$10.47–$14.95

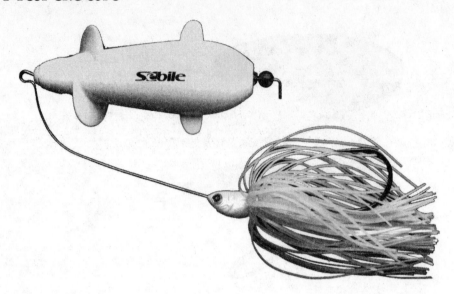

SÉBILE PROPPLER BUZZ

Type: Wire
Color/Pattern: Black Silver Eyes, Chartreuse Red Eyes, Gold, Natural White Perch, White Lady
Size: 3 in
Weight: 7/8 oz
Running Depth: Wake–3 in
Features: Designed to be fished in both finesse and everyday topwater conditions; lure combines the benefits of a top water frog and buzzbait; floating body filled with high pitch glass rattles for added noise; more than just a C&R buzzbait, the bait can be stopped and twitched in heavy cover due to buoyant hollow body, allowing the skirt to pulse and attract fish; hook is oversized as compared to other buzzbait hooks on the market for better hooking efficiency; great bait to employ the dressed trailer hook for short striking fish.
Price:. $17.45

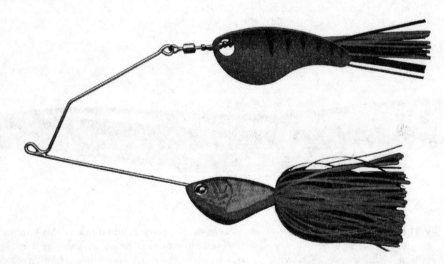

SÉBILE PRO SHAD TROPHY

Type: Wire
Color/Pattern: Orange Gold Black, Hot Lime, Craw Perch, Natural Shiner
Weight: 1 oz, 1 3/8 oz
Running Depth: 6 in–8 ft
Features: Collapsible in-line swivel arm allows for morehook ups and helicopter/fluttering action on the fall; welded line tie allows the use of a snap; blade shape (asymmetric) lowers the resistance allowing the angler to cover more of the water column; blade and body are shad-shaped; oversized wide gap hook more efficient at hooking and landing fish; added skirt behind blade spirals and emits a large profile during the retrieve or fall; great bait to employ the dressed trailer hook for short, striking fish.
Price:. $16.95

LURES

SÉBILE SPLASHER
Type: Floating
Color/Pattern: Holo Greenie, Natural White Perch, Natural Shiner, Sea Chrome, Holo Greenie, Natural Mullet, Natural Seatrout, Natural Shiner, Amber Fashion, Perchy, Hollow Mullet, White Lady, Natural Dark Blue Black
Size: 2 1/8 in; 3 in; 3 1/2 in; 4 3/4 in; 6 in
Weight: 1/8 oz, 3/8 oz, 5/8 oz, 1 1/2 oz, 2 3/4 oz
Running Depth: Topwater

Features: The specially designed concave face of the splasher make it superior to poppers and chuggers alike. Effortlessly the splasher will pop and throw water with the softest of twitches from the rod tip. A firm blow will cause the bait to chug and move water making its irritable presence noticeable in the roughest conditions. The special keel-on of the splasher causes the lure to lurch side to side in a zig-zag motion with rhythmic pops of the rod tip. The splasher is extremely versatile under all conditions.
Price: . . . .$10.82–$20.27

STORM ARASHI RATTLING DEEP
Type: Crankbait
Color/Pattern: Baby Bass, Black Silver Shad, Blue Back Herring, Bluegill, Crappie, Hot Blue Shad, Hot Chartreuse Shad, Mossy Chartreuse Craw, Parrot, Red Craw, Rusty Craw, Wakasagi
Size: 2 3/8 in
Weight: 9/16 oz

Running Depth: 10 ft
Features: Swims with a moderate rolling action for the right amount of search with loads of tail kick; multi-ball rattle for loud, variable pitch and a long-cast design for increased distance with accuracy; premium Black Nickel VMC hooks, size 4.
Price: **$8.99**

STORM ARASHI RATTLING FLAT

Type: Crankbait
Color/Pattern: Baby Bass, Black Silver Shad, Blue Back Herring, Bluegill, Crappie, Hot Blue Shad, Hot Chartreuse Shad, Mossy Chartreuse Craw, Parrot, Red Craw, Rusty Craw, Wakasagi
Size: 2 1/8 in

Weight: 7/16 oz
Running Depth: 7 ft
Features: Swims with a tight wiggling action creating maximum flash and vibration; multi-ball rattle for loud, variable pitch and a long-cast design for increased distance with accuracy; premium black Nickel VMC hooks, size 4.
Price: **$8.99**

STORM ARASHI SILENT SQUARE

Type: Crankbait
Color/Pattern: Baby Bass, Black Silver Shad, Blue Back Herring, Bluegill, Crappie, Hot Blue Shad, Hot Chartreuse Shad, Mossy Chartreuse Craw, Parrot, Red Craw, Rusty Craw, Wakasagi
Size: 2 1/8 in, 2 3/8 in
Weight: 1/2 oz, 5/8 oz
Running Depth: 3 ft, 5 ft

Features: Runs with a lively rolling action and a pronounced tail kick; buoyancy to back out of cover and square lip design for increased deflection are a perfect match for contacting structure; non-rattling for a silent approach to wary or pressured fish in shallow water; premium black Nickel VMC hooks, sizes 4 and 2.
Price: **$8.99**

LURES

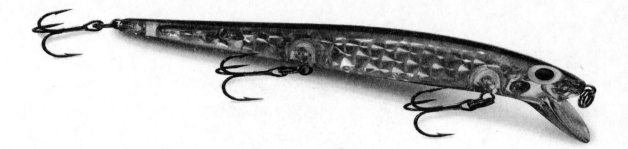

STORM ORIGINAL THUNDERSTICK

Type: Stick bait
Color/Pattern: Metalic Blue/Red Lip, Hot Tiger, Metallic Silver Black Back, Yellow Black Back, Chrome Yellow Perch, Black Chrome Orange, Blue Chrome Orange, Blue Steel Shad, Chartreuse Purple Shad, Chrome Clown, Metallic Gold/Chartreuse, Purple Fire UV, Blue Pink Fire UV, Green Fire UV, Orange Fire UV, Pink Fire UV
Size: 3 1/2 in, 4 3/8 in

Weight: 1/4 oz, 1/2 oz
Running Depth: 1 ft–5 ft, 2 ft–7 ft
Features: Original molds and components; original patterns and colors; original packaging style; rolling minnow action; premium VMC hooks, sizes 4 and 6; comes in Original, Deep, Deep Jr., and Jr. models.
Price: **$5.49**

STORM ORIGINAL WIGGLE WART

Type: Crankbait
Color/Pattern: Green Crawdad, Brown Scale Crawdad, Tennessee Shad, Phantom Brown Crayfish, Black/Glitter/Chartreuse, Naturistic Brown Crayfish, Naturistic Green Crayfish, Hot Tiger, Phantom Green Crayfish, Solid Fluorescent Pink, Metallic Blue/Black, Metallic Silver Fluorescent Red, Metallic/Silver/Chartreuse Lip, Metallic Blue Scale Red, Metallic Green Scale Red, Metallic Pink Black Lip, Metallic/Orange/Chartreuse, Black/Glitter/Fluorescent Red, Metallic Purple/Purple, Naturistic Red Crayfish, Watermelon, Tequila Glow, Black Chrome Orange, Blue Chrome Orange, Blue Steel Shad, Blazin'

Pink UV, Blazin Red UV, Blazin' Green UV, Blazin Blue UV, Bluegill, Blue Back Herring, Green Fire UV, Orange Fire UV, Pink Fire UV, Firetiger, Honey Mustard, Shad, Ghost Shad, Texas Crawdad
Size: 2 in
Weight: 3/8 oz
Running Depth: 7 ft–18 ft
Features: A smaller version of the Mag Wart; original molds, components, patterns, and colors; classic "wart" rattle; side-to-side crayfish action; multi-species; premium VMC super-sharp hooks, size 4.
Price: **$5.49**

LURES

LURES: Hardbait

TSUNAMI COCKTAIL SPINNERS

Type: InLine spinner
Color/Pattern: Black, White, Yellow, Firetiger, Chrome/White, Chartreuse
Weight: 1/16 oz, 1/8 oz, 1/6 oz, 1/4 oz

Features: Highly reflective blades spin with minimal movement; holographic bodies add flash for a larger bait profile; feather dressed, premium treble hook doesn't let them get off.
Price: $2.99

YO-ZURI 3DB JERKBAIT

Type: Stick bait
Color/Pattern: Prism Clown, Prism Gold Black, Prism Ghost Shad, Prism Silver Blue, Prism Silver Black, Prism Tennessee Shad
Size: 3 1/2 in
Weight: 7/16 oz
Running Depth: 2 ft

Features: Patent-pending 3D internal prism creates an unparalleled flash in the water, enticing fish to bite; patented wave-motion belly sends vibrations through the water that fish can detect with their lateral lines, bringing in lunkers from distances beyond what they can see; black-nickel hooks.
Price: $8.99

YO-ZURI 3DB MID CRANK

Type: Crankbait
Color/Pattern: Prism Shad, Prism Tennessee Shad, Prism Crawfish, Prism Firetiger, Prism Bluegill, Prism Parrot
Size: 2 3/4 in
Weight: 1/2 oz

Running Depth: 4 ft–6 ft
Features: 3D internal prism creates enticing flash; dives 4–6 ft on retrieve; floats when paused; patented wave-motion ribs send out irresistible vibrations.
Price: **$8.99**

YO-ZURI 3DB MINNOW

Type: Stick bait
Color/Pattern: Prism Gold Black, Prism Ghost Shad, Prism Silver Blue, Prism Silver Black, Prism Shad, Prism Tennessee Shad
Size: 3 1/2 in

Weight: 3/8 oz
Running Depth: 2 ft
Features: 3D internal prism creates enticing flash; patented wave-motion ribs send irresistible vibrations; mimics wobbly, wounded baitfish.
Price: **$8.99**

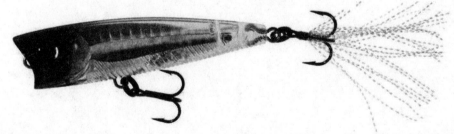

YO-ZURI 3DB POPPER

Type: Topwater bait
Color/Pattern: Prism Clown, Prism Frog, Prism Gold Black, Prism Ghost Shad, Prism Silver Blue, Prism Silver Black, Prism Shad
Size: 3 in
Weight: 3/8 oz
Running Depth: Floating

Features: The patented wave-motion belly sends vibrations through the water that fish can detect with their lateral lines, bringing in lunkers from distances beyond what they can see; a small, secondary popper cup throws water spray on the retrieve; lure rests in a horizontal position, perfectly mimicking a baitfish.
Price: **$8.99**

LURES: **Softbait**

BERKLEY GULP! ALIVE! LEECH HALF-PINT

Type: Leech
Color/Pattern: Black
Size: 3 in, 5 in
Quantity: 15, 10

Features: Artificial bait proven to outfish and outlast live bait; Alive! attractant is 20 percent more effective than the original; baits keep their natural shapes; recharge baits by placing them back into the attractant.
Price: **$9.95**

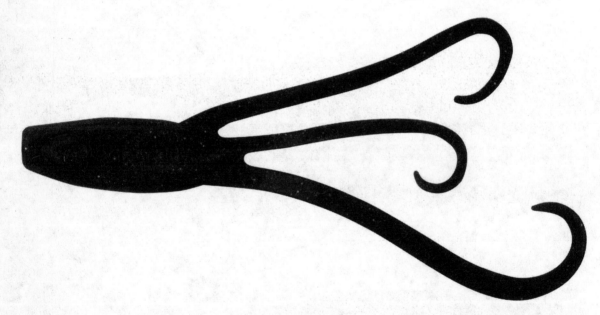

BERKLEY GULP! ALIVE! 6-IN SQUIDO

Type: Soft plastic
Color/Pattern: Glow, New Penny, Pink, Pearl White, Root Beer Fleck, Chartreuse, Camo, Watermelon Red Glitter
Size: 6 in
Quantity: 8

Features: Squido has a versatile body design for nearly unlimited rigging options; three legs kick and squirm in the water, delivering enticing looks that fish can't resist; absorbs 20 percent more Gulp! scent; durable and long-lasting, they look, smell, and feel like live squid; especially effective when used with heavy jigs to pull bottom dwellers out of structure.
Price: **$19.99**

BERKLEY GULP! ALIVE! MINNOW GRUB HALF-PINT

Type: Jerk bait
Color/Pattern: Chartreuse, Pearl White
Size: 3 in
Quantity: 13

Features: 100 percent biodegradeable; absorbs up to 20 percent more fish attractant by weight; great for jigs, drop-shot, and live-bait rigs; delivers natural action, scent, and taste.
Price: **$9.95**

BERKLEY GULP! ALIVE! MINNOW HALF-PINT

Type: Jerk bait
Color/Pattern: Black Shad, Emerald Shiner, Smelt

Size: 2 1/2 in, 3 in, 4 in
Quantity: 25, 15, 10
Features: Gulp! Minnow is ideal for drifting or jigging; it is 100 percent biodegradable.
Price: **$9.95**

BERKLEY GULP! ALIVE! NIGHTCRAWLER HALF-PINT

Type: Worm
Color/Pattern: Natural
Size: 6 in
Quantity: 12

Features: Looks, smells, and tastes like the real thing; 34 percent better swimming action than original Gulp!; made of water-soluble, natural ingredients; releases over 400 times more scent than other plastics.
Price: **$9.95**

Softbait

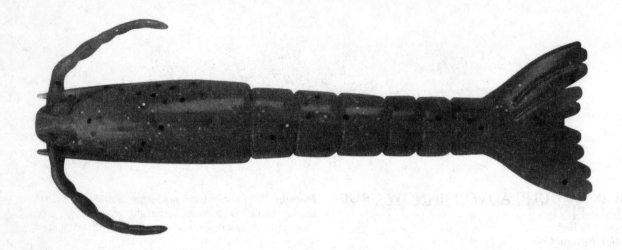

BERKLEY GULP! ALIVE! SHRIMP HALF-PINT

Type: Shrimp bait
Color/Pattern: Nuclear Chicken, Pearl White, Natural, New Penny
Size: 3 in, 4 in

Quantity: 7, 5
Features: Whether you're fishing expansive flats, a wreck, or oil rig, the fact that saltwater fish love shrimp remains the same; durable and long-lasting, they look, smell, and feel like live shrimp.
Price: **$9.95**

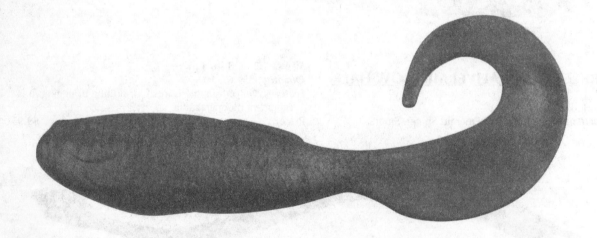

BERKLEY GULP! ALIVE! SWIMMING MULLET HALF-PINT

Type: Soft plastic
Color/Pattern: Pearl White, Glow Chartreuse, Chartreuse, Pink
Size: 4 in
Quantity: 14

Features: Baits come floating in "Magic Gravy," enabling you to recharge your baits by putting them back in the bucket; swimming tail action of the Mullet is irresistible to all saltwater species; environmentally safe 100 percent biodegradable plastic-free construction; highly durable and can stand up to multiple strikes.
Price: **$6.99**

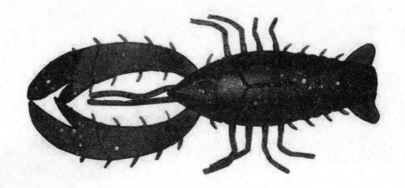

BIG BITE BAITS REAL DEAL CRAW

Type: Craw
Color/Pattern: Green Pumpkin, Watermelon Red Flake, Black Neon/Watermelon Red, HD Black/Red Craw, HD Crawdad, HD Blue Craw
Size: 4 in
Quantity: 7, 3 for HD

Features: Designed by Bassmaster Elite Series pro, Russ Lane; built with an extra-realistic craw profile; bursting with detail and covered in a texture that bass won't want to let go of; works great as a jig trailer or on a Texas-rig; can be fished with the claws together for a smooth, gliding movement, or with the claws cut for a lively swimming action.
Price: **$3.99**

LURES

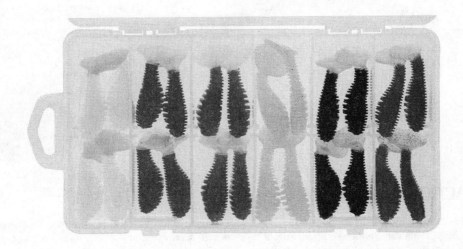

CABELA'S 25-PIECE SWIMMING SHAD KIT

Type: Kit
Color/Pattern: White/Chartreuse, Red/White, Blue/White, Chartreuse, Black/Chartreuse, Red/Chartreuse
Size: 1 3/4 in
Quantity: 24
Features: Filled with grubs known to be deadly on large crappies, bass, walleye, and a variety of other freshwater

fish, the 25-Piece Swimming Shad Kit is a must-have for any avid angler; includes a Plano 3500 utility box filled with 24 1 3/4 in swimming grubs in six attention-grabbing colors; each grub sports a fat-body design with an oversized boot tail that renders a pronounced thumping action.
Price: **$9.95**

CABELA'S ACTION TAIL 2-INCH FAT GRUB

Type: Grub
Color/Pattern: White, Chartreuse Sparkle, Black/Blue/Chartreuse, Lemon Meringue, Tennessee Shad, Bad Blood, Bubble Gum/Chartreuse, Firetiger, Pink/Yellow/Pearl, Orange/Chartreuse, Blue Shiner, Chartreuse/Shad, Junebug/Chartreuse, Red/Chartreuse, Purple Glitter/Opaque Chartreuse
Size: 2 in
Quantity: 25
Features: Fast-flitting tails; subtle, lifelike movements; ideal for large crappies and panfish.
Price: **$2.99**

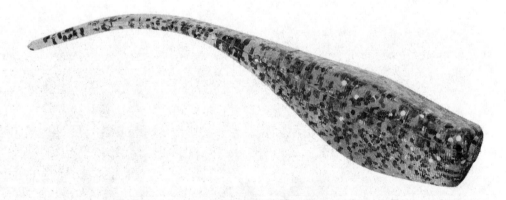

CABELA'S ACTION-TAIL MINNOW

Type: Jerk bait
Color/Pattern: Firecracker, Blue Pearl Pepper, Black/Chartreuse, Junebug/Chartreuse, Tennessee Shad, Purple Glitter/Opaque Chartreuse, Silver Glitter/Pearl, Black/Red/Chartreuse, Electric Chicken, Red/Chartreuse, Orange/Chartreuse, Black Neon/Pearl/Silver, Lemon Meringue, Alewife, Chartreuse Sparkle
Size: 1 3/4 in
Quantity: 15
Features: Darting action of a minnow in distress; thin-tail design seems to come to life; ideal for crappies and other panfish.
Price: **$2.49**

CABELA'S FISHERMAN SERIES 48-PIECE FINESSE TUBE KIT

Type: Kit
Color/Pattern: White Illusion Pepper, Smoke Pepper, Green Pumpkin Pepper, Chartreuse Pepper, Melon Pepper, Smoke Blue Green Flake
Size: 3 1/2 in

Quantity: 48
Features: Finesse tubes mimic a variety of prey including baitfish and crawfish; slender tube design has a small profile, perfect for lighter presentations; each tube is salted; kit comes in a reusable box; includes eight each of the colors.
Price: **$15.99**

LURES

CABELA'S FISHERMAN SERIES ASSORTED 44-PIECE BASS TUBE KIT

Type: Kit
Color/Pattern: Variable
Size: 2 ¾ in, 3 ½ in, 4 in

Quantity: 44
Features: Perfectly sized tube baits for bass; ideal for using in shallow or deep water; salted for a realistic sinking rate; two colors per size.
Price: **$10.99**

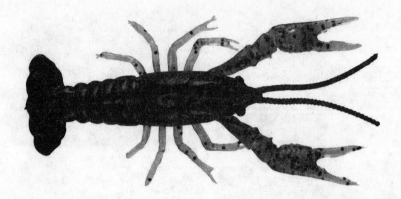

SAVAGE GEAR 3D CRAW

Type: Craw
Color/Pattern: Summer Craw, Spring Craw, Red, Black & Blue, PB&J
Size: 3 in, 4 3/4 in
Weight: 1/5 oz, 1/2 oz
Quantity: 4, 3
Features: Air-filled claws and head cavity on the 3D Craw deliver flotation and natural underwater movement, imitating crawfish, a favorite meal of many game fish; iodine makes crawfish a staple meal for a big female bass's egg development; lures come infused with iodine, salt, and crawfish scents; excellent for Carolina rigging, stand-up jigheads or fishing weedless on a weighted hook over heavy weed mats and then paused in openings for a slow, enticing fall; exaggerated antennae and legs add lifelike action on either a forward drag or tail-first retrieve.
Price: **$9.99**

SAVAGE GEAR 3D MANIC SHRIMP

Type: Shrimp bait
Color/Pattern: Brown, Red, Natural, Blue Pearl, Avocado, Gold
Size: 2 1/2 in, 4 in
Weight: 3/25 oz, 3/11 oz
Quantity: 1
Features: Molded using 3D scanning of a real shrimp, Savage Gear's Manic Shrimp wreaks havoc on a wide variety of saltwater sport fish; soft-plastic construction, lifelike paint scheme, and strike-inducing kicking action, make this realistic underwater bait one you'll never want to leave home without; exaggerated legs and antennae create attractive swimming movements on both the fall and the retrieve; pre-rigged with a weighted EWG hook; tail section is infused with nylon mesh to help prevent tearing on the hookset.
Price: **$5.99**

LURES

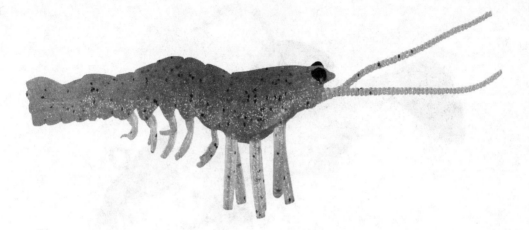

SAVAGE GEAR 3D SHRIMP

Type: Shrimp bait
Color/Pattern: Blue Pearl, Magic Brown, Krill Pink, Glow, Olive Brown, Golden
Size: 2 1/2 in, 4 in
Weight: 1/8 oz, 1/3 oz

Quantity: 6, 4
Features: Created using 3D scans of real shrimp; exaggerated legs and antenna create realistic underwater actions; use under a popping cork, on a jighead, or in thick weeds.
Price: **$5.99**

LURES

SÉBILE MAGIC SWIMMER—SOFT

Type: Soft plastic
Color/Pattern: Natural Shiner, Blue Black Herring, Ghostescent, Holo Greenie, Blue Gill, Electric Rainbow, Ayu, Golden Shiner, Brown/Red Craw, Perch, Fire Tiger
Size: 4 in, 5 in, 6-1/4 in, 8 in
Weight: 3/8 oz, 3/4 oz, 1 1/4 oz, 2 3/8 oz
Quantity: 1
Features: Can be rigged weedless due to large hollow slit that allows wide gap hook to fit nicely in body; longer lasting soft plastic due to hole in the nose and back allows the swimmer to slide on the leader once fish is hooked; soft body for fish to hold on longer; great for skipping under docks and trees; same quality of painting finish as the hard Magic Swimmer; very easy to rig: open the belly's cut, slide the wide gap hook point into it through the back hole, then pull on the head and place hook eye from inside the head to outside's mouth; perfect to be used with Soft Weight System; different position of the tungsten rubber weights on the hook provides different actions to fit fishes and situations.
Price: . . . .**$11.17–$15.95**

STORM WILDEYE LIVE BABY BASS
Type: Rigged plastic swimbait
Color/Pattern: Baby Bass
Size: 4 in
Weight: 1/2 oz

Quantity: 3
Features: Internally weighted bodies for lifelike action; 3D holographic WildEye eyes; holographic flash foil; durable soft outer body.
Price:....................................... **$6.49**

STORM WILDEYE LIVE BLUEGILL
Type: Rigged plastic swimbait
Color/Pattern: Bluegill
Size: 2 in, 3 in
Weight: 1/4 oz, 5/16 oz
Quantity: 3

Features: So realistic you will want to keep them in your livewell; internally weighted bodies give them a lifelike action that makes fish strike; 3D holographic WildEye eyes add to the successful imitation; holographic flash foil is highly visible to fish; soft outer body is durable for long-term use, hit after hit.
Price:............................... **$5.49–$5.99**

STORM WILDEYE LIVE RAINBOW TROUT

Type: Rigged plastic swimbait
Color/Pattern: Rainbow Trout
Size: 2 in, 3 in, 4 in
Weight: 1/8 oz, 1/4 oz, 5/16 oz
Quantity: 3
Features: Internally weighted body creates incredibly lifelike swimming; realistic color patterns and shape of the bait is backed up with 3D holographic WildEye, holographic swimmin' flash foil, and a tough yet soft outer body; swimbait has a rainbow trout body and color pattern and a back VMC needle point hook and a treble belly hook.
Price:............................ **$5.49–$6.49**

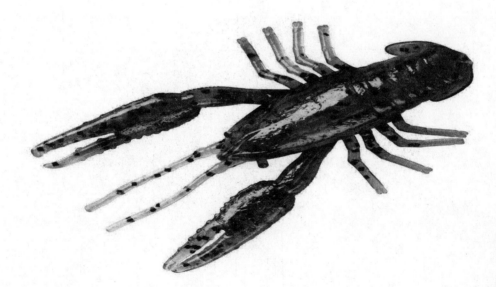

YUM F2 CRAWBUG

Type: Soft plastic
Color/Pattern: Watermelon Red Flake, Crawdad, Carolina Pumpkin, Green Pumpkin, Watermelon Seed, Black Blue
Size: 2 1/2 in, 3 1/4 in
Quantity: 10, 8
Features: With incredible 3D detail and a specially designed hollow body, this is the ultimate soft-plastic crawfish; designed to accurately imitate a fleeing crawfish, the super-soft CrawBug is scent-infused with exclusive F2 Crawfish Formula plus salt that won't dry out or lose its effectiveness; however you fish it—flip, rig, or jip—it's sure to become your go-to bass bait in any condition.
Price:.................................... **$2.99**

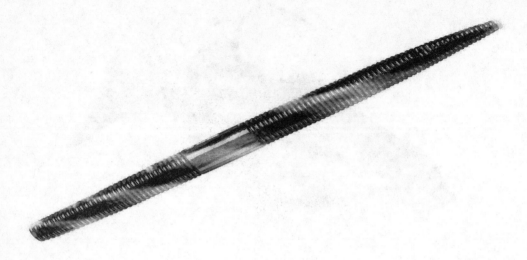

YUM F2 DINGER

Type: Soft plastic
Color/Pattern: Black Blue Flake, Watermelon Candy, June Bug, Green Pumpkin, Black Blue Laminate, Chartreuse Pepper, Red Shad, Ozark Smoke, Smoke Red Pepper, Green Pumpkin Chartreuse Tail, Bumble Bee Swirl, Bubble Gum Lemon Swirl, Mardi Gras, Green Pumpkin Neon, Cajun Neon, Bama Bug, Bama Magic, Bream, Watermelon/Red Flake, Watermelon Seed

Size: 4 in, 5 in, 6 in, 7 in
Quantity: 7, 12, 15
Features: Infused with Yum's F2 bass attractant; subtle, lifelike; won't dry and shrivel up when left out of the package; great for wacky worming and Texas rigging; attract, enrage, engage!
Price: **$3.49**

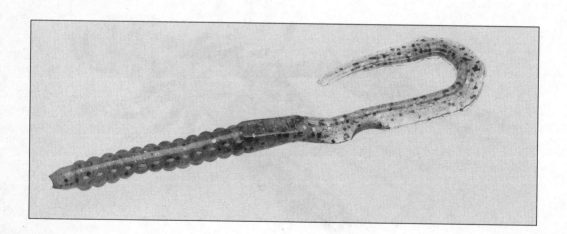

YUM F2 RIBBONTAIL

Type: Soft plastic
Color/Pattern: June Bug, Watermelon Seed, Red Shad, Tequila Sunrise, Red Bug, Green Pumpkin Purple Flake
Size: 7 1/2 in

Quantity: 15
Features: Slithering action of the sinuous tail; integral F2 scent; standard ploy for catching big bass.
Price: **$3.99**

YUM F2 LIZARD

Type: Soft plastic
Color/Pattern: Watermelon Red Lake, Junebug, Green Pumpkin, Watermelon Seed, White, Carolina Pumpkin Chartreuse, Green Pumpkin Purple Flake, Black Neon, Carolina Pumpkin, Black Blue, Black Neon Chartreuse
Size: 4 in, 6 in
Quantity: 15

Features: The ultimate finesse lizard, it has everything an angler needs to fool big, finicky bass—curly legs that create motion and a long curly tail that pushes a lot of water; tough, durable plastic holds up to multiple fish, yet remains soft and supple even when fished in cold water.
Price: **$2.99**

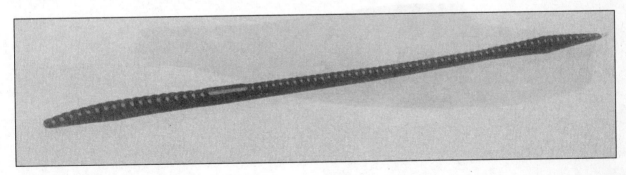

YUM F2 MIGHTEE WORM

Type: Soft plastic
Color/Pattern: Bama Bug, Blue Fleck, Grape Red Flake, Green Pumpkin, Junebug, Plum, Red Blood, Red Bug, Ultimate Craw, Virgo Blue, Watermelon Red Flake, Watermelon Seed
Size: 4 in, 6 in, 10 1/2 in
Quantity: 5

Features: Big bass look at the Yum F2 Mightee Worm like a hungry pilgrim looks at Thanksgiving dinner; it presents a massive profile in the water, and with F2 attractant infused during the molding process, it gives off a strong scent trail that bass can't resist; created for power shaking on Edwin Evers' Yum Pumkin Ed Standup Jig Head, it's also a great choice on a Texas-rig, Carolina-rig, or even a Wacky-rig.
Price: **$4.99**

YUM F2 WOOLY HAWGTAIL
Model: F2 Wooly Hawgtail
Type: Soft plastic
Color/Pattern: Watermelon/Red Flake, Green Pumpkin,
Red Shad, Green Flake, Black Blue, Dark Grasshopper,
Dark Watermelon

Size: 4 1/2 in
Quantity: 8
Features: Big-time big-fish soft plastic bait; works well on a
Carolina rig, pitched, flipped, or a Texas rig; produces
massive action, F2 scent-infused.
Price: **$2.99**

Z-MAN DIEZEL MINNOWZ
Type: Unrigged plastic swimbait
Color/Pattern: Smoky Shad, Pearl, Bad Shad, Opening
Night, Redbone, Houdini, Mulletron, Pinfish
Size: 4 in

Quantity: 5
Features: Best for fresh- or saltwater applications; ElaZtech
is 10 times stronger than traditional soft plastic; boasts one
of the highest fish-per-bait ratings.
Price: **$5.49**

Z-MAN HARD LEG FROGZ

Type: Frog bait
Color/Pattern: White, Watermelon/Chartreuse, Watermelon Red, Green Pumpkin, Redbone, Mud Minnow
Size: 4 in
Quantity: 3

Features: Get lively paddle-foot swimming action with the Z-Man Hard Leg FrogZ; made of ElaZtech, which is 10 times stronger than traditional soft plastic; resists nicks, cuts, and tears; boasts one of the highest fish-per-bait ratings in the industry at an affordable price; naturally buoyant; 100 percent nontoxic.
Price: **$5.49**

Z-MAN MINNOWZ

Type: Swimbait
Color/Pattern: Smoky Shad, Pearl, New Penny, Opening Night, Redbone, Houdini, Mood Ring, Pinfish
Size: 3 in
Quantity: 8
Features: Z-Man MinnowZ are an effective, universal baitfish imitation; popular inshore saltwater bait for redfish,

trout, snook, and flounder due to durability and action; superior smaller swimbait for rigging on a jighead, as a swim jig trailer, on a Fish Head Spin or on an umbrella rig; made of ElaZtech, which is ten times stronger than traditional soft plastic; resists nicks, cuts, and tears.
Price: **$5.49**

LURES: **Softbait**

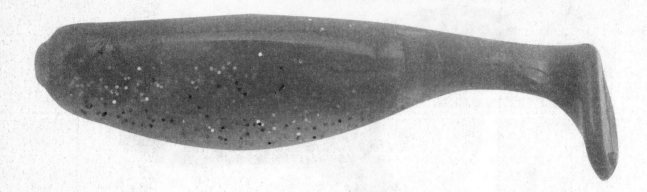

Z-MAN SCENTED POGYZ

Type: Unrigged plastic swimbait
Color/Pattern: Pearl, Root Beer/Chartreuse, New Penny, Pinfish
Size: 3 in

Quantity: 5
Features: Ultra-realistic profile, natural swimming action; irresistible to bass and game fish; mimics pinfish, threadfin, and pilchards.
Price: **$5.99**

Z-MAN TURBO CRAWZ

Type: Craw
Color/Pattern: Green Pumpkin, Green Pumpkin/Orange, Pearl, Watermelon Candy, Okeechobee Craw, Bluegill, Sprayed Grass, Silver Shadow
Size: 4 in
Quantity: 6

Features: The ultimate in durability, buoyancy, and action, this soft-bodied jig trailer is perfect for grabbing the attention of hungry bass; thick, eye-catching body, six legs, and flapping claws provide realistic movement on the retrieve that no largemouth will be able to resist.
Price: **$5.49**

New Lines

BERKLEY FIRELINE TRACER

Color: Smoke/flame green
Type: Superline
Length: 125 yd, 300 yd, 1500 yd
Lb. Test: 6, 8, 10, 14, 20, 30

Diameter: 0.006 in–0.015 in
Features: Unique alternating 5' hi-vis/5' low-vis Tracer coloration helps to easily measure, track, and detect line movement.
Price: . . . .**$17.95–$176.99**

BERKLEY IRONSILK MONOFILAMENT

Color: Green
Type: Monofilament
Length: 300 yd
Lb. Test: 6, 8, 10, 12, 14, 17, 20
Diameter: 0.010 in–0.016 in

Features: Super-polymer mono fishing line; features a built-in molecular reinforcing network that improves abrasion resistance, durability, and fighting power at a thinner diameter.

Price: **$9.95**

BERKLEY PROSPEC PREMIUM SALTWATER BRAID
Color: Cabo white
Type: Braid
Length: 500 yd, 2500 yd

Lb. Test: 30, 40, 50, 65, 80, 100, 130, 200,
Diameter:
Features: Premium saltwater braid; pro-tested performance; made with the World's Strongest Fiber, Dyneema.

Price: . . . . **$59.99–$649.99**

BERKLEY TRILENE 100% FLUOROCARBON
Color: Clear
Type: Fluorocarbon
Length: 25 yd
Lb. Test: 4, 6, 8, 10, 12, 15, 20, 25

Diameter: 0.008 in–0.019 in
Features: 100 percent fluorocarbon leader material; professional-grade formula; incredible knot strength; excellent abrasion resistance; high impact strength.

Price: . . . . **$8.99–$9.99**

New Lines

CABELA'S DEPTHMASTER LEAD-CORE FISHING LINE

Color: Blue
Type: Braid
Length: 100 yd, 200 yd
Lb. Test: 14, 18, 27, 36, 45

Diameter: N/A
Features: 99.9 percent pure lead core; new process creates virtually no color bleeding; smaller diameter than standard lead-core lines; color metering every 10 yds; great alternative to snapweights or divers.

Price: . . . . **$16.99–$29.99**

CORTLAND BLITZ

Color: Light Blue/Clear
Type: Fly
Length: 100 ft
Weight: 275 gr, 350 gr, 425 gr
Diameter: N/A

Features: Treated with heat-tempered HTx surface technology; compact head that delivers quick, accurate casts with minimal false casting; clear intermediate head is invisible to fish; stays near the surface; blue running line indicates time to recast; available in 275, 350 and 425 grain head weight configurations.

Price: **$80.00**

LINES

CORTLAND COMPETITION NYMPH MONO

Color: Light Blue
Type: Fly
Length: 72 ft, 90 ft
Weight: 0, 1
Diameter: N/A

Features: 0 wt. and 1 wt. mono core; built with proven taper; ultra-sensitive; thin, hard monofilament core that is round and stiff; core transfers energy better and reduces line sag between rod guides to improve feel, prevent drag and increase fishing range.

Price: **$59.95**

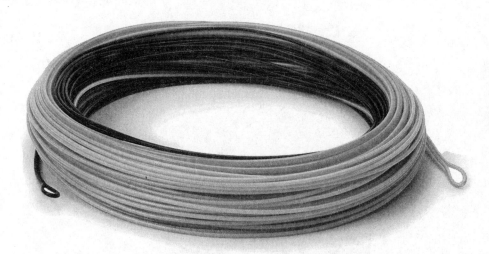

CORTLAND DEEP SALT

Color: Light Blue/Black
Type: Fly
Length: 98 ft
Weight: 275 gr, 350 gr, 425 gr
Diameter: N/A

Features: Treated with heat-tempered HTx surface technology; type VIII fast sinking 27' head; compact front taper; 12' transition area aids; available in 275, 350 and 425 grain head weight configurations.

Price: **$80.00**

New Lines

CORTLAND TROUT BOSS HTX
Color: Chartreuse/Ivory
Type: Fly WF
Length: 100 ft
Weight: 3, 4, 5, 6, 7, 8
Diameter: N/A

Features: Complex new taper; thinner core; treated with heat-tempered surface (HTx); 45 ft. 6 in. head management; thinner core gives smaller diameter-to-mass ratio without skewing its specific gravity or killing energy transfer; heat tempered coating seals out dirt and oils while maintaining an exceptionally low friction coefficient.
Price: **$80.00**

MR. CRAPPIE FISHING LINE
Color: Camo, clear, hi-vis yellow
Type: Monofilament
Length: 500 yd, 1000 yd, 1200 yd, 2000 yd
Lb. Test: 4, 6, 8
Diameter: .080mm–.010mm

Features: Field-tested and approved by Mr. Crappie—a.k.a. Wally Marshall; abrasion-resistant construction stands up to water and hard-fighting fish; low memory increases casting distance.
Price: . . . . **$4.99–$6.99**

ORVIS HYDROS HD BONEFISH

Color: Yellow/blue
Type: Fly WF
Length: N/A
Weight: 7, 8, 9, 10
Diameter: N/A
Features: Innovative microtexture "divots" similar to those on a golf ball offer better casting, enhanced distance, lower memory, easier pickup, and enhanced durability; stiff, braided monofilament core offers outstanding performance in hot, humid saltwater environments; color change shows optimum load length. HD texturing provides increased surface area, allowing the line to sit higher in the water, offering less drag, easier mending, less water spray, and easier pick-ups; micro-textured surface traps air to provide increases in both shootability and flotation while decreasing friction, and the microreplicated pattern increases line durability.
Price: **$98.00**

ORVIS HYDROS HD TROUT

Color: Willow/orange
Type: Fly WF
Length: N/A
Weight: 3, 4, 5, 6
Diameter: N/A
Features: Created with features to improve your cast and presentation, the Hydros HD Trout line gives you incredible frictionless casting for most trout fishing situations; HD texturing teamed with IS, our most versatile trout taper, a Hy-Flote Tip, and the new and improved welded loop; microreplicated pattern provides increased line durability, while allowing for easier pick-ups, less drag, easier mending, and greater shootability.
Price: **$98.00**

LINES

New Lines

P-LINE XTCB 8 BRAID

Color: Green, white
Type: Braid
Length: 150 yd, 300 yd, 2500 yd
Weight: 10, 15, 20, 30, 40, 50, 65, 80

Diameter: 0.23mm–0.50mm
Features: Ideal for both spinning and baitcasting reels; Teflon Surface Protector; more abrasion resistance; increased knot strength; longer casts; virtually zero stretch.
Price: . . . .**$14.99–$259.99**

RIO PERMIT

Color: Sand/aqua blue
Type: Fly WF
Length: 100 ft
Weight: 8, 9, 10
Diameter: N/A

Features: RIO's Permit line has been specifically designed for the Permit fly fisher; each line features an easy casting taper that loads at close range, and yet empowers the cast for quick distance; easy casting taper that presents typical crab patterns effortlessly; ideal for the wading or boat angler; hard, tropical coating will not wilt in the heat.

Price: **$89.95**

LINES

SEAGUAR SMACKDOWN BRAID

Color: Green
Type: Braid
Length: 150 yd
Weight: 10, 15, 20, 30, 50

Diameter: 0.005 in—0.015 in
Features: Incredible strength with smooth-casting performance; made of eight ultrathin, microweave strands; enhanced knot and tensile strength.

Price: **$29.99**

SPIDERWIRE STEALTH BRAID

Color: Green, yellow
Type: Braid
Length: 125 yd, 250 yd, 300 yd, 500 yd, 1500 yd, 3000 yd
Weight: 6, 8, 10, 15, 20, 30, 50, 65, 80, 100, 150, 250
Diameter: 0.005 in–0.032 in

Features: Smooth fluoropolymer coating silences line going through your guides; Colorlock Technology improves the line's color retention; wrapped around a thin, clear spool for convenient storage.

Price: . . . . **$13.99–$599.99**

LINES

New Lines

SPIDERWIRE STEALTH CAMO BRAID

Color: Camo
Type: Braid
Length: 125 yd, 300 yd
Weight: 6, 8, 10, 15, 20, 30, 50, 65, 80
Diameter: 0.005 in–0.016 in
Features: Varying color pattern to blend in with any water and vegetation condition; Color-Lock coating technology—casts farther, lasts longer; Dyneema PE Microfiber construction is strong, smooth and round; fluoropolymer treated microfibers—shoots through guides like a bullet; whisper quiet for "Stealth Attacks"; resists "diggin in" on reels.

Price:. . . . . **$14.99–$34.99**

SPIDERWIRE STEALTH GLO-VIS BRAID

Color: Glo-vis green
Type: Braid
Length: 125 yd, 175 yd, 250 yd, 300 yd, 1500 yd
Weight: 6, 8, 10, 15, 20, 30, 40, 50, 65, 80
Diameter: 0.005 in–0.016 in
Features: Fluorescent brighteners illuminate line above water, low vis green disappears below water; enhance ability to watch line and detect bites that may not be felt; Color-Lock coating technology; Dyneema PE Microfiber construction is strong, smooth, and round; fluoropolymer treated microfibers—shoots through guides like a bullet; whisper quiet for "Stealth Attacks"; resists "diggin in" on reels.
Price:. . . . . **$14.99–$164.99**

LINES

STREN BRAID SUPERLINE
Color: Lo-vis green
Type: Braid
Length: 150 yd
Weight: 10, 15, 20, 30, 40, 50, 65
Diameter: 0.007 in–0.016 in

Features: Made with Dyneema PE fibers for strength and durability; Glide Coat treatment provides smooth, fast line movement; round profile helps prevent line from digging in; excellent knot strength.

Price: $12.99

STREN CATFISH MONO
Color: Clear/blue fluorescent, fluorescent orange
Type: Monofilament
Length: 200 yd, 270 yd, 300 yd, 350 yd, 425 yd, 600 yd, 900 yd

Weight: 10, 15, 20, 30, 40
Diameter: 0.013 in—0.025 in
Features: Strong for lifting big catfish out of their holes; resists abrasion from rocks and other structure; glows in daylight and under black light.
Price: . . . . $6.99–$9.99

New Lines

SUFIX INVISILINE ICE FLUOROCARBON

Color: Clear
Type: Fluorocarbon
Length: 33 yd
Lb. Test: 2, 3, 4, 5, 6, 7, 8
Diameter: 0.005 in–0.009 in

Features: 100% fluorocarbon with stealth-like invisibility; hydrophobic/water repellent; superior strength, abrasion resistance and sensitivity; low-stretch index for optimal hook setting power; sinks 4 times faster than monofilament.
Price: **$6.99**

SUFIX PROMIX

Color: Clear, lo-vis green
Type: Monofilament
Length: 330 yd
Lb. Test: 2, 6, 8, 10, 12, 14, 17, 20

Diameter: 0.008 in–0.017 in
Features: Smooth, easy handling; high tensile and knot strength; low stretch and high shock absorption; low memory improves casting distance.
Price: **$5.99**

BASS PRO SHOPS CRAPPIE MAXX CAMO

Color: Camo
Length: 1420 yd, 1690 yd, 2040 yd, 3190 yd
Lb. Test: 4, 6, 8, 10
Diameter: 0.203mm–0.304mm

Features: Undetectable in any color water; fluorescent stripe easily seen above water; soft and supple; low memory for easy casting; high-abrasion resistance; excellent knot strength.
Price: **$8.29**

BASS PRO SHOPS CRAPPIE MAXX SUPER VIS

Color: Super hi-vis
Length: 1420 yd, 1690 yd, 2040 yd, 3190 yd
Lb. Test: 4, 6, 8, 10

Diameter: 0.203mm–0.304mm
Features: Great for dawn, dusk, or night fishing; glows in low light conditions; can see even the lightest twitch.
Price: **$8.29**

BASS PRO SHOPS EXCEL MONOFILAMENT—1 LB. SPOOL

Color: Clear, clear/blue fluorescent, green
Type: Monofilament
Length: 2250 yd, 2525 yd, 3240 yd, 4315 yd, 5065 yd, 6030 yd, 9000 yd

Lb. Test: 4, 6, 8, 10, 12, 14, 17
Diameter: 0.21mm–0.46mm
Features: Superior abrasion resistance; soft, smooth, and limp; limited stretch and high-impact shock strength.
Price:..................................... **$26.99**

BASS PRO SHOPS TOURNEY TOUGH MONOFILAMENT

Color: Clear, green
Type: Monofilament
Length: 275 yd
Lb. Test: 2, 4, 6, 8, 10, 12, 14, 17, 20, 25

Diameter: 0.18mm–0.52mm
Features: High-performance mono; copolymer construction; state-of-the-art extrusion; excellent knot strength and durability.
Price:..................................... **$3.99**

LINES

BASS PRO SHOPS XPS 8 ADVANCED BRAID

Color: Green
Type: Braid
Length: 150 yd
Lb. Test: 10, 20, 30, 50, 65, 80

Diameter: 0.18mm–0.44mm
Features: Bass Pro Shops's most advanced braided line yet; unparalleled strength and consistent roundness; woven from eight Dyneema fibers; enhanced color protection.
Price:. . . . . **$19.99–$23.99**

BASS PRO SHOPS XPS SIGNATURE SERIES FLUOROCARBON—FILLER SPOOL

Color: Clear
Type: Fluorocarbon
Length: 150 yd, 175 yd, 200 yd
Lb. Test: 6, 8, 10, 12, 14, 17, 20, 25

Diameter: 0.23mm–0.48mm
Features: Disappears in the water; twice as dense as monofilament; low stretch for increased sensitivity; low water absorption for superior knot strength.
Price:. . . . . **$19.99–$21.99**

BASS PRO SHOPS XPS SIGNATURE SERIES MONOFILAMENT

Color: Clear
Type: Monofilament
Length: 800 yd, 900 yd, 1000 yd
Lb. Test: 6, 8, 10, 12, 14, 17, 20

Diameter: 0.25mm–0.48mm
Features: Highest grade of monofilament; high abrasion resistance; superior tensile strength; locked-in knot-holding power; nearly frictionless surface for longer and smoother casts.
Price: . . . . **$11.99–$16.99**

BERKLEY BIG GAME BRAID

Color: Low-vis green
Type: Braid
Length: 300 yd
Lb. Test: 6, 8, 12, 15, 17
Diameter: 0.009 in–0.017 in

Features: Uses Dyneema, the world's strongest gel-spun polyethylene fiber; ultra-sensitive, with virtually no stretch; transmits lure action and strikes directly to the rod tip and reel for instant and positive hooksets.
Price: . . . . **$24.49–$31.49**

BERKLEY FIRELINE FUSED CRYSTAL
Color: Crystal
Type: Fused
Length: 125 yd, 300 yd, 1500 yd
Lb. Test: 2, 3, 4, 6, 8, 10, 14, 20, 30
Diameter: 0.005 in–0.015 in

Features: Combines the ultimate in low-visibility with all of the benefits of FireLine; incredibly thin diameter to work the tiniest micro bait; supple enough to handle the coldest weather; incredibly strong—three times stronger than mono; ultimate sensitivity to telegraph feel for structure and strikes.
Price: . . . . **$17.95–$37.49; 1500 yd: $176.99**

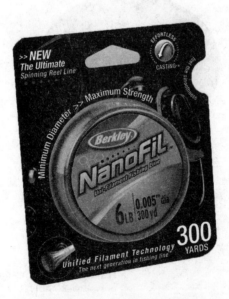

BERKLEY NANOFIL
Color: Clear mist, high-vis chartreuse, low-vis green,
Type: Uni-filament
Length: 150 yd, 300 yd
Lb. Test: 2, 3, 4, 6, 8, 10, 12, 14, 17
Diameter: 0.002 in–0.010 in

Features: Not a mono. Not a braid. The Next Generation in Fishing Line. Unified filament technology provides the ultimate advantage against a wide variety of species; cast farther and feel everything with the ultimate spinning reel line; minimum diameter, maximum strength; zero memory virtually eliminates line tangles.
Price: . . . . **$13.97–$179.95**

BERKLEY SOLUTIONS CASTING

Color: Green mist
Type: Monofilament
Length: 250 yd
Lb. Test: 10, 12, 14, 17
Diameter: 0.014 in–0.017 in

Features: Targeted for anglers who want to take the guesswork out of choosing line for their reel and spend more time fishing; specifically designed for low-profile or round baitcasting reels; strong, trouble free, and easy to use; stacks and handles well on baitcast reels.
Price: **$5.99**

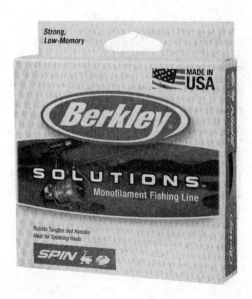

BERKLEY SOLUTIONS SPINNING

Color: Green mist
Type: Monofilament
Length: 250 yd
Lb. Test: 4, 6, 8, 10
Diameter: 0.008 in–0.011 in

Features: Targeted for anglers who want to take the guesswork out of choosing line for their reel and spend more time fishing; specifically designed for open face or closed face spinning reels; strong, trouble free, and easy to use; resists tangles and hassles.
Price: **$5.99**

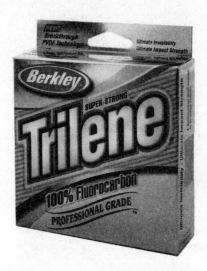

BERKLEY TRILENE 100% FLUOROCARBON - PROFESSIONAL GRADE

Color: Clear, green tint
Type: Fluorocarbon
Length: 110 yd, 200 yd
Lb. Test: 4, 6, 8, 10, 12, 15, 17, 20, 25

Diameter: 0.007 in–0.019 in
Features: Invisible fluorocarbon; proprietary 100 percent PVDF formula specially processed for the ultimate in impact strength; lower memory for superior casting; available in green tint for reduced sparkle and flash.
Price: . . . .**$10.99–$243.99**

BERKLEY TRILENE BIG CAT

Color: Solar green
Type: Monofilament
Length: 200 yd, 220 yd, 270 yd, 300 yd
Lb. Test: 15, 20, 30, 40
Diameter: 0.015 in–0.024 in

Features: High shock strength; controlled stretch adds fighting power for big cats; reflects sunlight or blacklight for high visibility; abrasion-resistant to stand tough against rough or sharp objects.
Price: **$7.29**

BERKLEY TRILENE COLD WEATHER

Color: Electric blue, fl. clear/blue
Type: Monofilament
Length: 110 yd
Lb. Test: 2, 3, 4, 6, 8, 10
Diameter: 0.005 in–0.011 in

Features: Improved formula is as flexible at 32°F as regular mono is at 70°F; extraordinary flexibility and low memory design to resist twists and tangles; available in electric blue color for maximum visibility against ice and snow.
Price: . . . . **$2.37–$4.19**

BERKLEY VANISH

Color: Clear
Type: Fluorocarbon
Length: 110 yd, 250 yd, 350 yd
Lb. Test: 2, 4, 6, 8, 10, 12, 14, 17, 20, 30, 40
Diameter: 0.006 in–0.022 in

Features: The most flexible, easiest casting fluorocarbon; best Vanish formula ever, with 20 percent better shock strength, improved knot strength and easier to handle; non-absorbing fluorocarbon maintains strength and abrasion resistance underwater.
Price: . . . . **$5.99–$199.99**

LINES

CABELA'S DACRON PLANER BOARD LINE

Color: Fluorescent orange
Type: Braid
Length: 150 feet
Lb. Test: 135

Diameter: 0.135 in
Features: High-visibility orange line; low-stretch braided Dacron; resists kinks and tangles.
Price: **9.99**

CABELA'S LEAD CORE

Color: 10 yd color changes
Type: Braid
Length: 100 yd, 200 yd
Lb. Test: 18, 27, 36, 45, 54
Diameter: 0.030 in–0.059 in

Features: Tightly braided, high-tenacity nylon multifilament yarn encapsulates a 99.9 percent pure lead core; smaller diameter than standard lead-core lines; color changes every 10 yards for accurate measurements of fishing depths without having to use a linecounter; great alternative to snapweights or divers; approximate sink rate is 1.25 feet with every 2 yards released, depending on speed.
Price: . . . . **$15.99–$29.99**

CABELA'S KING KAT

Color: Dirty green, hi-vis yellow
Type: Braid
Length: 200yd, 400 yd
Lb. Test: 20, 30, 50, 80
Diameter: 0.009 in–0.016 in
Features: A unique bi-component, small-diameter, braided superline with exceptional abrasion resistance and strength; made with Spectra fibers and a multifilament nylon tracer blended into the braid; nylon tracer increases the line's stretch by 5 percent so it's more forgiving when you set the hook; gives the line neutral buoyancy while hiding the line in the water with a mottled pattern; line is then permeated by a synthesized coating process that penetrates the braid.
Price: . . . .**$16.99–$39.99**

LINES

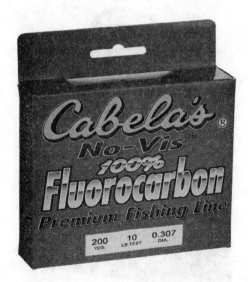

CABELA'S NO-VIS FLUOROCARBON LINE

Color: Clear
Type: Fluorocarbon
Length: 200 yd, 400 yd, 600 yd
Lb. Test: 4, 6, 8, 10, 12, 15, 20
Diameter: 0.007 in–0.016 in

Features: Virtually invisible under water (only 100 percent Fluorocarbon comes close to matching the light refraction index of water); abrasion resistance, knot strength, and tensile strength far exceeded expectations; extra-soft properties and minimal stretch.
Price: . **200 yd: $12.99–$16.99; 400 yd: $19.99–$26.99; 600 yd: $24.99–$39.99**

CABELA'S PROLINE

Color: Camo, clear, green, hi-vis yellow
Type: Monofilament
Length: 425 yds–3100 yds
Lb. Test: 4–30
Diameter: 0.008 in–0.022 in

Features: Controlled tensile strength enables ProLine to take the sudden shock and impact of bone-jarring hooksets with minimum stretch, while withstanding the runs and surges of any game fish; all of that in a small-diameter line with more than enough abrasion resistance to handle the toughest situations. Bulk spool also available.
Price: . . . . **$9.99–$29.99**

CORTLAND 444 CLASSIC FLY

Color: Brown, light brown, peach, peach/brown
Type: Fly DT, WF
Length: 90 feet
Weight: 3, 4, 5, 6

Features: The built-in buoyancy and slick surface of the 444 lines allows for smooth pickups and efficient casts; precision tapers turn over your leaders for perfect fly presentations.
Price: **$62**

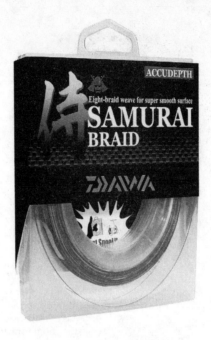

DAIWA SAMURAI BRAIDED

Color: Green
Type: Braid
Length: 150 yds, 300 yds, 1500 yds
Lb. Test: 15–150
Diameter: .18–.62
Features: Samurai line is unlike any other braided line on the market. Sure it's strong and sensitive, but it's also noticeably thinner, softer, smoother, and more flexible than ordinary braids. That means less friction for better casts; reduced line noise on the retrieve; and a faster sink rate due to less current resistance. Available in 150-yard, 300-yard, and 1500-yard spools.
Price: . . . . **$27.99–$279.99**

DAIWA STEEZ FLUOROCARBON

Color: Green
Type: Fluorocarbon
Length: 125 yds
Lb. Test: 5–20
Diameter: .007–.016
Features: Finally, a green-colored, super soft, super strong 100 percent Fluorocarbon line with the flexibility and castability of regular monofilament. Formulated exclusively for Steez spinning and casting reels, it is highly resistant to abrasion and offers a faster sink rate than monofilament. Parallel winding on the filler spool prevents dents and inconsistency in roundness that can reduce casting efficiency.
Price: . . . . **$19.99–$26.99**

LINES

ORVIS ACCESS WF TROUT

Color: Mist green
Type: Fly
Length: 90 feet
Weight: 3, 4, 5, 6, 7, 8
Features: Versatile freshwater floating trout fly line offering outstanding performance across a broad range of conditions; weight forward fly line with mid-length head for easy casting and mending; Orvis Line ID allows you to quickly and easily identify your line, with no more guessing; all of the lines are printed with the taper, weight, and functionality; Integrated Slickness additive is integrated throughout the PVC layer to provide lubrication for maximum distance, performance, and durability; new sleek and durable welded loop makes leader attachment quick and easy while holding up to repeated use—also helps to transfer energy more efficiently to the leader allowing better turnover; braided multifilament core provides excellent performance over a wide range of conditions; new paper pulp spool, made from recycled cardboard and kraft paper, is 100 percent compostable; mist green; line weights 3–8; length 90'; made in USA.
Price: **$59**

ORVIS CLEARWATER FLY

Color: Fluorescent yellow
Type: Fly
Length: 90 feet
Weight: 3, 4, 5, 6, 7, 8, 9
Features: An entry level fly line designed to aid the inexperienced caster; built a half-size heavy to help load the rod; Orvis Line ID allows you to quickly and easily identify your line, with no more guessing; all of the lines are printed with the taper, weight, and functionality; new sleek and durable welded loop makes leader attachment quick and easy while holding up to repeated use—also helps to transfer energy more efficiently to the leader allowing better turnover; Integrated Slickness additive produces high line slickness for longer casts and reduced friction, keeping lines cleaner longer to help with flotation and overall performance; braided multifilament core provides excellent performance over a wide range of conditions; new paper pulp spool, made from recycled cardboard and kraft paper, is 100 percent compostable; fluorescent yellow; line sizes 3–9; made in USA.
Price: **$39**

ORVIS HYDROS TROUT

Color: Olive dun
Type: Fly
Length: 90 feet
Weight: 4, 5, 6
Features: Textured fly line surface gives you incredible frictionless casting for most trout fishing situations; 3D Technology Microtexture surface reduces surface friction, improves flotation, and eliminates tangling; Hy-Flote Tip—highly specialized Micro-balloons concentrated in the front of the line to produce high floating tips; Integrated Slickness additive is integrated throughout the PVC layer to provide lubrication for maximum distance, performance, and durability; Orvis Line ID allows you to quickly and easily identify your line, with no more guessing; all of the lines are printed with the taper, weight, and functionality; new sleek and durable welded loop makes leader attachment quick and easy while holding up to repeated use—also helps to transfer energy more efficiently to the leader allowing better turnover; braided multifilament core provides excellent performance over a wide range of conditions; new paper pulp spool, made from recycled cardboard and kraft paper, is 100 percent compostable; in olive dun; 90'; line weights 4–6; made in USA.
Price: **$79**

ORVIS HYDROS BASS/WARMWATER

Color: Chartreuse
Type: Fly
Length: 90 feet
Weight: 5, 6, 7, 8, 9
Features: This bass fly line has a compact head and short front taper to turn over the big deer hair poppers and sliders with ease; drive flies into tight, heavy cover, under branches and back in holes where large bass lurk; latest generation of Wonderline coating is 20 percent slicker than the previous generation, resulting in the slickest fly lines on the market; casts farther with less effort, produces higher line speeds to cut through the wind and improve accuracy, repels dirt and grime, picks up off the water easier, improves flotation, and reduces tangles; Orvis Line ID allows you to quickly and easily identify your line, with no more guessing; all of the lines are printed with the taper, weight, and functionality; new sleek and durable welded loop makes leader attachment quick and easy while holding up to repeated use—also helps to transfer energy more efficiently to the leader allowing better turnover; braided multifilament core provides excellent performance over a wide range of conditions; new paper pulp spool, made from recycled cardboard and kraft paper is 100 percent compostable; in chartreuse; 90'; line weights 5–9.; made in USA.
Price: **$79**

LINES

ORVIS HYDROS SALMON/STEELHEAD

Color: Light olive
Type: Fly
Length: 105 feet
Weight: 7, 8, 9, 10
Features: Designed to handle the unique demands of salmon and steelhead fishing; super-long belly fly line body and rear taper (57' in an 8-wt.) provide a perfect platform for easy long-distance mending, roll casting, and singlehand Spey casting; latest generation of Wonderline coating is 20 percent slicker than the previous generation, resulting in the slickest fly lines on the market; casts farther with less effort, produces higher line speeds to cut through the wind and improve accuracy, repels dirt and grime, picks up off the water easier, improves flotation, and reduces tangles; Orvis Line ID allows you to quickly and easily identify your line, with no more guessing; all of the lines are printed with the taper, weight, and functionality; new sleek and durable welded loop makes leader attachment quick and easy while holding up to repeated use—also helps to transfer energy more efficiently to the leader allowing better turnover; braided multifilament core provides excellent performance over a wide range of conditions; new paper pulp spool, made from recycled cardboard and kraft paper, is 100 percent compostable; in light olive; made in USA.
Price: **$79**

ORVIS HYDROS SUPERFINE

Color: Willow
Type: Fly
Length: 90 feet
Weight: 1, 2, 3, 4, 5, 6
Features: An excellent fly line choice for spring creeks, slow moving, and clear water situations where stealth and technical expertise are at a premium; specially designed weightforward taper loads rods at short distances but still affords delicate presentations; latest generation of Wonderline coating is 20 percent slicker than the previous generation, resulting in the slickest fly lines on the market; casts farther with less effort, produces higher line speeds to cut through the wind and improve accuracy, repels dirt and grime, picks up off the water easier, improves flotation, and reduces tangles; Hy-Flote Tip—highly specialized Micro-balloons concentrated in the front of the line to produce high floating tips; Orvis Line ID allows you to quickly and easily identify your line, with no more guessing; all of the lines are printed with the taper, weight, and functionality; new sleek and durable welded loop makes leader attachment quick and easy while holding up to repeated use—also helps to transfer energy more efficiently to the leader allowing better turnover; braided multifilament core provides excellent performance over a wide range of conditions; new paper pulp spool, made from recycled cardboard and kraft paper, is 100 percent compostable; in willow; made in USA.
Price: **$79**

ORVIS HYDROS WF TROUT

Color: Olive dun, yellow
Type: Freshwater fly
Length: 90 ft
Weight: 3, 4, 5, 6, 7, 8
Features: Versatile weight-forward classic trout fly-line taper, now in the new Hydros configuration; fly line incorporates five new technological advances, including Hy-Flote Tip, Orvis Line ID, and Wonderline Coating; enhanced welded loop; innovative weight forward taper combined with slightly larger line diameters produce a line that is ideal at close to medium range, but still capable of delivering at distance; longer head than traditional weight-forward lines; braided multifilament core.
Price: **$59**

POWERPRO ZERO IMPACT MICROFILAMENT BRAIDED

Color: Aqua green, yellow hi-viz
Type: Braid
Length: 150 yd, 300 yd
Lb. Test: 20, 30, 50, 80
Diameter: 0.009 in–0.017 in
Features: 50 percent stronger Termination Zones; high-strength zones marked black; added strength without sacrificing line capacity.
Price: . . . .**$24.99–$42.99**

LINES

RIO AQUALUX MIDGETIP

Color: Clear, yellow
Type: Freshwater fly
Length: 90 ft, 100 ft
Features: The most effective fish-catching zone in the majority of lakes is within the top 6 feet of the water column. RIO's Sub-surface lake series fly lines are deadly effective on windy days and when fishing in shallow bays, close to lake shores and over the top of weed beds. Each line is built with a supple coldwater core and coating and features a welded loop in the front for fast rigging. One metre (39 inches) clear intermediate tip; perfect for fishing nymphs, emergers, and chironomids (buzzers) in the top twelve inches of the water column; great for shallow shorelines, sub-surface on windy days and over the top of weed beds.
Price: **$74.95**

RIO CONNECTCORE SHOOTING LINE

Color: Orange, teal
Type: Fly—Spey
Length: 100 ft
Features: RIO's new ConnectCore shooting line is the very best coated shooting line on the market with tremendous assets for the Spey fly fisher. Built on RIO's ConnectCore the shooting line has virtually no stretch, allowing anglers to stay perfectly in touch with their fly throughout the swing and feel every slight touch. A thicker diameter handling section prolongs the life of the line and ensures it is very easy to grip the line in cold conditions, while the highly visible front section makes it very easy to see when to stop stripping and make the cast; unique core also ensures the most perfect coils of line when stripping in, resulting in far fewer tangles and snarls; neat eight-inch welded loop at the front end allows for fast and efficient head changes, while the super slick XS Technology coating floats high and shoots far; ultra-low stretch ConnectCore allows anglers to feel every single touch; thick, highly visible handling section for durability and visibility.
Price: **$59.95**

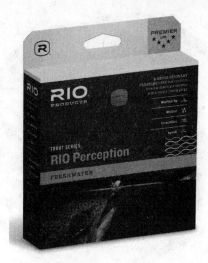

RIO PERCEPTION

Color: Camo, gray, green, tan
Type: Freshwater fly
Length: 80 ft, 90 ft, 100 ft
Features: Built with ultra-low stretch ConnectCore Technology, Perception lines provide groundbreaking levels of sensitivity for intuitively better cast timing, easier line lift, and sharp, precise mends; lack of stretch also means enhanced detection of subtle takes and faster reaction time when setting the hook; exclusive SureFire color system (RIO's unique tri-color distance measure) improves casting accuracy by making it easy to gauge exact distances with a quick glance; unique three-color SureFire system ensures deadly accurate distance control; ConnectCore improves casting timing, hook set, and mending; EasyID tag to quickly identify fly line; winner of best New Fly Line for 2014 at EFTTEX and IFTD shows.
Price: **$89.95**

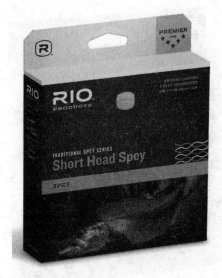

RIO SHORT HEAD SPEY

Color: Blue, straw
Type: Fly—Spey
Length: 100 ft
Features: Very easy casting, traditional style Spey line, which is ideal for Spey casters moving up from easier casting Scandi and Skagit heads; head length varies between forty feet and fifty feet, depending on line size, and it is a great choice of traditional Spey line for anglers using shorter rods and when fishing in tight quarters; longer head lengths (when compared to Skagit and Scandi heads) allow for less stripping in time at the end of each cast, which means more fishing time, and less loose line to handle and shoot with each cast; short head loads quickly and makes it simple to cast in tight quarters; rear-loaded weight distribution loads rods easily and ensures effortless, efficient Spey casts.
Price: **$89.95**

SHAKESPEARE MONOFILAMENT

Color: Clear
Type: Monofilament
Length: 700 yd
Lb. Test: 4–50

Features: 1/3 lb spool; excellent abrasion resistance; extremely affordable.
Price: $2.99

SPIDERWIRE EZ BRAID

Color: Moss green
Type: Braid
Length: 110 yds; 300 yds
Lb. Test: 10–50
Diameter: .007–.015

Features: Dyneema microfibers are 3X stronger than mono; diameters are 2 to 3X smaller than mono of the same weight test; super smooth for long, effortless casts; spider-sensitivity; near zero stretch to feel everything.
Price: . . . . $9.99–$18.95

SPIDERWIRE EZ FLUORO

Color: Clear
Type: Fluorocarbon
Length: 200 yds
Lb. Test: 2, 4, 6, 8, 10, 12, 15

Diameter: .006–.015
Features: 100 percent fluorocarbon for the key fluorocarbon benefits of virtual invisibility, sinking for less line between lure and reel and great wet strength; sensitive and abrasion resistant; good manageability, knot, and impact strength.
Price: . . . .**$7.99–$8.99**

SPIDERWIRE STEALTH GLOW-VIS

Color: Glow-Vis-Green Bulk
Type: Braid
Length: 125; 300 yds; 1500 yds
Lb. Test: 10–80
Diameter: .007–.016

Features: Fluorescent brighteners illuminate line above water; low-vis green disappears below water; enhances ability to watch line and detect bites that may not be felt.
Price: . . . . **$14.99–$164.99**

LINES

SPIDERWIRE ULTRACAST 100% FLUOROCARBON

Color: Clear
Type: Fluorocarbon
Length: 200 yds
Lb. Test: 6, 8, 10, 12, 15

Diameter: .009–.014
Features: Thinner diameters than most competitive fluorocarbons allows lures to perform better; awesome performance on spinning reels (4–10 lb. test); disappears to fish as it is virtually invisible; spider-sensitivity transmits strikes and structure.
Price: . . . . **$14.99–$16.99**

SPIDERWIRE ULTRACAST FLUORO-BRAID

Color: Moss green
Type: Braid
Length: 125; 300 yds; 1500 yds
Lb. Test: 10–80
Diameter: .008–.018

Features: Exceptionally high strength-per-diameter in a fluoro; thinner diameters than most competitive fluorocarbons allows lures to perform better; awesome performance on spinning reels (4–10 lb test); spider sensitivity transmits strikes and structure.
Price: . . . . **$20.99–$234.99**

SPIDERWIRE ULTRACAST INVISI-BRAID
Color: Clear
Type: Braid
Length: 125; 300 yds; 1500 yds; 3000 yds
Lb. Test: 10–80
Diameter: .007–.022

Features: Ultra smooth 8-carrier braid; innovative coldfusion process; translucency for near invisibility; extremely high strength-per-diameter; amazingly thin and sensitive; high pick count for roundness and durability.
Price:. . . . . $20.99–$449.99

SPIDERWIRE ULTRACAST ULTIMATE MONO
Color: Clear; Brown recluse
Type: Monofilament
Length: 330 yds
Lb. Test: 4–20
Diameter: .006–.016

Features: Breakthrough strength-to-diameter co-polymer is 33 percent stronger than the average mono; unprecedented 15 percent stretch for incredible sensitivity and hook setting power; thin diameter allows exceptional bait action and high line capacity; excellent knot and shock strength—even when wet; optimized for baitcast reels, but still castable and manageable on spinning reels.
Price:. $8.99

LINES

STREN 100% FLUORO
Color: Clear/Blue fluorescent
Type: Fluorocarbon
Length: 200 yds

Lb. Test: 6–20
Diameter: .01–.018
Features: Virtually invisible; maximum abrasion resistance.
Price:. . . . .**$16.99–$23.99**

STREN FLUOROCAST
Color: Clear
Type: Fluorocarbon
Length: 100 yds; 200 yds
Lb. Test: 4-17
Diameter: .007–.016

Features: Easy to cast and handle; excellent knot and shock strength; virtually invisible.
Price:. . . . .**$4.99–$9.99**

STREN MAGNATHIN
Color: Clear
Type: Monofilament
Length: 330 yds; 2600 yds
Lb. Test: 4–30

Diameter: .007–.018
Features: Extra strong; extra tough; castable and manageable.
Price:. . . . .**$9.49–$76.99**

STREN ORIGINAL
Color: Clear; Clear/Blue fluorescent; Hi-Vis Gold; Clear/Blue fluorescent; Lo-Vis Green
Type: Monofilament
Length: 100 yds; 330 yds; 1000 yds; 2400 yds
Lb. Test: 4–25

Diameter: .008–.02
Features: Superior knot strength; tough and abrasion resistant; low memory.
Price:. . . . .**$3.09–$62.49**

SUFIX 832 ADVANCED ICE BRAID

Color: Ghost, neon lime
Type: Braid
Length: 50 yd
Lb. Test: 4–30
Diameter: 0.004 in–0.011 in

Features: Most durable small diameter ice braid available; water-repellant protection to reduce freezing; GORE Performance Fiber adds incredible fray and abrasion resistance for durability.
Price:. **$11.49**

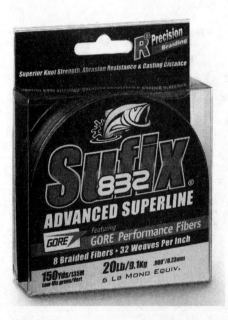

SUFIX 832 ADVANCED SUPERLINE

Color: Camo, ghost, hi-vis yellow, low-vis green, neon lime
Type: Braid
Length: 150 yd, 300 yd, 600 yd
Lb. Test: 6–80
Diameter: 0.006 in–0.018 in
Features: 8 fibers (Featuring one GORE Performance Fiber and 7 Dyneema Fibers); 32 pics (weaves) per inch; R8 precision braiding technology; patent-pending construction; ultimate abrasion resistance; unbeatable strength; proven castability improvements; TGP technology enhances color retention.
Price:. . . . . **$23.99–$449.99**

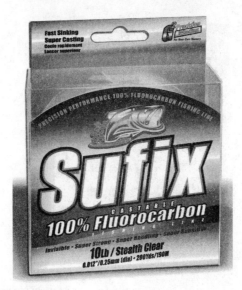

SUFIX CASTABLE INVISILINE 100% FLUOROCARBON

Color: Clear
Type: Fluorocarbon
Length: 100 yd, 200 yd
Lb. Test: 3–20
Diameter: 0.006 in–0.017 in

Features: Virtually disappears in the water for more natural presentation; low stretch; fast sinking; casts and handles like a premium monofilament; incredibly strong and abrasion resistant; resistant to ultra violet rays; performs great on casting and spinning reels; G² precision winding.
Price:.............................$14.49–$34.49

SUFIX ICE MAGIC

Color: Clear, neon orange
Type: Monofilament
Length: 100 yd
Lb. Test: 1, 2, 3, 4, 6, 8
Diameter: 0.004 in–0.010 in

Features: Designed to stay manageable even in frigid water; special additives deter water absorption that causes ice build-up; fast sinking for more natural presentation.
Price:.................................$3.99

LINES

SUFIX SIEGE

Color: Clear, camo, neon tangerine, smoke green
Length: 250 yd, 330 yd, 1000 yd, 3000 yd
Lb. Test: 4–35
Diameter: 0.008 in–0.022 in
Features: Superior casting distance with pinpoint accuracy due to its proprietary extrusion process; up to 15X greater abrasion resistance; exceptional knot strength and smooth handling; smooth, supple, handles beautifully—yet it is exceptionally strong; G² Precision Winding (330 yd spools) virtually eliminates line memory, even on spinning reels.
Price: . . . .**$9.49–$85.49**

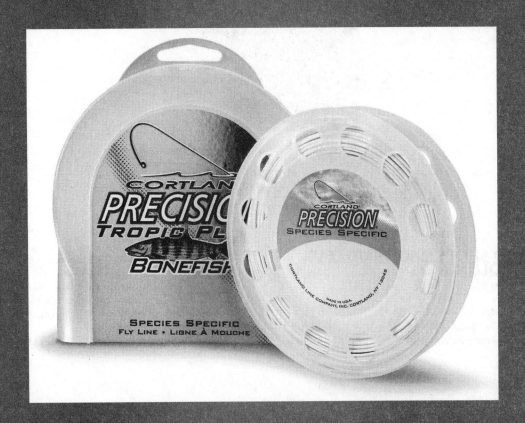

504 Bass Pro Shops	513 Daiwa	521 Spiderwire
504 Berkley	515 Orvis	524 Stren
508 Cabela's	518 Seaguar	526 Sufix
512 Cortland	520 Shakespeare	

BASS PRO SHOPS MAGIBRAID LEAD CORE TROLLING

Color: Metered
Type: Braid
Length: 100 yd
Lb. Test: 12, 15, 18, 27, 36, 45
Diameter: 0.61mm–0.89mm

Features: Manufactured with high tenacity, multifilament, Dupont nylon yarn tightly braided over a soft 99.9 percent-pure lead core; smaller-diameter line also allows more reel capacity than standard lead core lines; color metered every 10 yards with high visibility dye, this line enables the angler to determine depth at a glance.
Price:. . . . . **$13.99–$16.99**

BERKLEY BIG GAME BRAID

Color: Low-vis green
Type: Braid
Length: 300 yd
Lb. Test: 6, 8, 12, 15, 17
Diameter: 0.009 in–0.017 in

Features: Uses Dyneema, the world's strongest gel-spun polyethylene fiber; ultra-sensitive, with virtually no stretch; transmits lure action and strikes directly to the rod tip and reel for instant and positive hooksets.
Price:. . . . . **$24.49–$31.49**

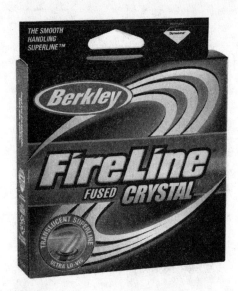

BERKLEY FIRELINE FUSED CRYSTAL

Color: Crystal
Type: Fused
Length: 125 yd, 300 yd, 1500 yd
Lb. Test: 2–30
Diameter: 0.005 in–0.015 in
Features: Combines the ultimate in low-visibility with all of the benefits of FireLine; incredibly thin diameter to work the tiniest micro bait; supple enough to handle the coldest weather; incredibly strong—three times stronger than mono; ultimate sensitivity to telegraph feel for structure and strikes.
Price: . . . . **$17.95–$37.49; 1500 yd: $176.99**

BERKLEY NANOFIL

Color: Clear mist, high-vis chartreuse, low-vis green,
Type: Uni-filament
Length: 150 yd, 300 yd
Lb. Test: 2–17
Diameter: 0.002 in–0.010 in
Features: Not a mono. Not a Braid. The Next Generation in Fishing Line. Unified filament technology provides the ultimate advantage against a wide variety of species; cast farther and feel everything with the ultimate spinning reel line; minimum diameter, maximum strength; zero memory virtually eliminates line tangles.
Price: . . . . **$13.97–$179.95**

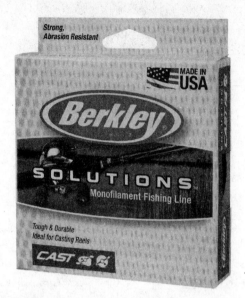

BERKLEY SOLUTIONS CASTING

Color: Green mist
Type: Monofilament
Length: 250 yd
Lb. Test: 10, 12, 14, 17
Diameter: 0.014 in–0.017 in

Features: Targeted for anglers who want to take the guesswork out of choosing line for their reel and spend more time fishing; specifically designed for low-profile or round baitcasting reels; strong, trouble free, and easy to use; stacks and handles well on baitcast reels.
Price: **$5.99**

BERKLEY SOLUTIONS SPINNING

Color: Green mist
Type: Monofilament
Length: 250 yd
Lb. Test: 4, 6, 8, 10
Diameter: 0.008 in–0.011 in

Features: Targeted for anglers who want to take the guesswork out of choosing line for their reel and spend more time fishing; specifically designed for open face or closed face spinning reels; strong, trouble free, and easy to use; resists tangles and hassles.
Price: **$5.99**

LINES

BERKLEY TRILENE BIG CAT
Color: Solar green
Type: Monofilament
Length: 200 yd, 220 yd, 270 yd, 300 yd
Lb. Test: 15, 20, 30, 40
Diameter: 0.015 in–0.024 in

Features: High shock strength; controlled stretch adds fighting power for big casts; reflects sunlight or blacklight for high visibility; abrasion-resistant to stand tough against rough or sharp objects.
Price: **$7.29**

BERKLEY TRILENE COLD WEATHER
Color: Electric blue, fl. clear/blue
Type: Monofilament
Length: 110 yd
Lb. Test: 2, 3, 4, 6, 8, 10
Diameter: 0.005 in–0.011 in

Features: Improved formula is as flexible at 32°F as regular mono is at 70°F; extraordinary flexibility and low memory design to resist twists and tangles; available in electric blue color for maximum visibility against ice and snow.
Price: .... **$2.37–$4.19**

BERKLEY VANISH

Color: Clear
Type: Fluorocarbon
Length: 110 yd, 250 yd, 350 yd
Lb. Test: 2-40
Diameter: 0.006 in–0.022 in

Features: The most flexible, easiest casting fluorocarbon; best Vanish formula ever, with 20 percent better shock strength, improved knot strength and easier to handle; non-absorbing fluorocarbon maintains strength and abrasion resistance underwater.
Price:.............................$5.99–$199.99

LINES

CABELA'S PRESTIGE BRAIDED DACRON LINE

Color: Clear
Type: Braid
Length: 200 yd, 500 yd, 1200 yd
Lb. Test: 20, 30, 50, 80, 130

Features: Proven to be excellent for casting and trolling; perfect for muskie and saltwater bill fish; abrasion- and deterioration-resistant; mold and mildew resistant.
Price:.............................$29.99–$62.99

CABELA'S DACRON PLANER BOARD LINE

Color: Fluorescent orange
Type: Braid
Length: 150 feet
Lb. Test: 135
Diameter: 0.135 in

Features: High-visibility orange line; low-stretch braided Dacron; resists kinks and tangles.
Price: **$9.99**

CABELA'S KING KAT

Color: Dirty green, hi-vis yellow
Type: Braid
Length: 200 yd, 400 yd
Lb. Test: 20, 30, 50, 80
Diameter: 0.009 in–0.016 in
Features: A unique bi-component, small-diameter, braided superline with exceptional abrasion resistance and strength; made with Spectra fibers and a multifilament nylon tracer blended into the braid; nylon tracer increases the line's stretch by 5 percent so it's more forgiving when you set the hook; gives the line neutral buoyancy while hiding the line in the water with a mottled pattern; line is then permeated by a synthesized coating process that penetrates the braid.
Price: . . . .**$16.99–$39.99**

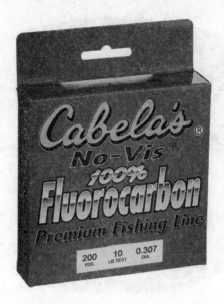

CABELA'S NO-VIS FLUOROCARBON LINE

Photo: IK-115174
Color: Clear
Type: Fluorocarbon
Length: 200 yd, 400 yd, 600 yd
Lb. Test: 4–20
Diameter: 0.007 in–0.016 in

Features: Virtually invisible under water, (only 100 percent Fluorocarbon comes close to matching the light refraction index of water); abrasion resistance, knot strength, and tensile strength far exceeded expectations; extra-soft properties and minimal stretch.
Price: . . . .**$12.99–$39.99**

CABELA'S PROLINE

Color: Camo, clear, green, hi-vis yellow
Type: Monofilament
Length: 425 yds–3100 yds
Lb. Test: 4–30
Diameter: 0.008 in–0.022 in
Features: Controlled tensile strength enables ProLine to take the sudden shock and impact of bone-jarring hooksets

with minimum stretch, while withstanding the runs and surges of any game fish; all of that in a small-diameter line with more than enough abrasion resistance to handle the toughest situations. Bulk spool also available.
Price: . . . .**$9.99–$29.99**

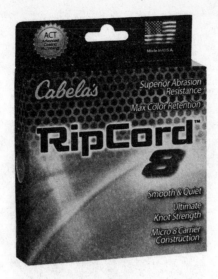

CABELA'S RIPCORD 8 BRAIDED

Color: Green, yellow
Type: Braid
Length: 150 yd, 300 yd
Lb. Test: 6, 8, 10, 15, 20, 30, 40, 50, 65, 80, 100, 130
Features: Unique bi-axial braid construction that realigns fibers to provide a smooth exterior; quieter through the rod guides and creates less friction for longer casts; realignment of the fibers also gives greater knot strength than traditional braided lines; Advanced Coating Technology adds superior abrasion resistance and increased color.
Price:.............................$19.99–$39.99

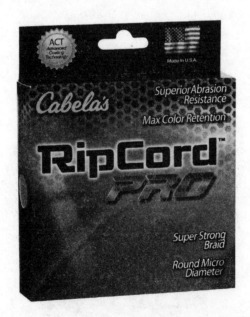

CABELA'S RIPCORD PRO

Color: Frost, green, yellow
Type: Braid
Length: 150 yd, 300 yd, 600 yd, 1200 yd
Lb. Test: 6, 8, 10, 15, 20, 30, 40, 50, 65, 80, 100, 130
Features: Advanced Coating Technology penetrates on the molecular level; increased abrasion resistance and color retention; unparalleled knot strength and virtually no-stretch feel; superior strength equated to a rounded, smaller diameter.
Price:............................$16.99–$189.99

CABELA'S SALT STRIKER LINE – 1/4-LB. SPOOL

Color: Blue, chartreuse, clear
Type: Monofilament
Length: 400 yds–1350 yds

Lb. Test: 10, 15, 20, 25, 30
Features: Special UV additives; abrasion-resistant finish; low-stretch high-tensile strength; thinner-diameter copolymer line; also available in 1 lb. and 2 lb. spools.
Price: **$7.99**

CORTLAND LIQUID CRYSTAL FLY

Color: Crystal
Type: Fly Fused
Weight: 8, 9, 10, 12

Features: Advanced composition of super-strong polyethylene and copolymers creates a line with twice the strength of PVC lines PE+ jacket is naturally lighter than water, eliminating the need for microspheres or other agents for flotation; ultrasmooth, abrasion-resistant finish.
Price: **$80**

LINES

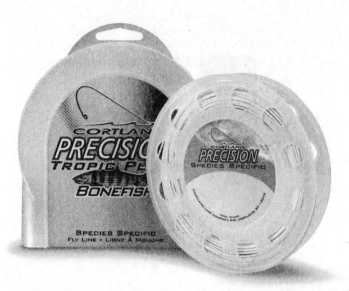

CORTLAND PRECISION TROPIC PLUS FL

Color: Light yellow
Type: Saltwater braid
Length: 90 ft
Lb. Test: 6, 7, 8, 9, 10, 12

Features: This all-purpose tropical line features a slick, abrasion-resistant coating to withstand harsh saltwater elements in warm-weather climates; braided mono core reduces line memory, and its long body taper provides quick loading and smooth, accurate casts.
Price:.......................................**$72**

DAIWA SALTIGA BOAT BRAIDED

Color: Multi
Type: Braid
Length: 1800 meters
Lb. Test: 40–150
Features: Designed for deep drop fishing with Dendoh Style power assist reels, eight woven braids make it super-strong, yet one of the finest diameter braids available; less affected by currents for a straighter, more accurate drop. Its smooth surface means less friction and noise from guides on the retrieve. Color changes every ten meters, with five and one meter indicators, shows depth and line movement. Coded for quick programming into Dendoh reel memory for maximum readout accuracy.
Price:..........................**$249.95–$379.95**

LINES

DAIWA SAMURAI BRAIDED

Color: Green
Type: Braid
Length: 150 yds, 300 yds, 1500 yds
Lb. Test: 15–150
Diameter: .18 in–.62 in
Features: Samurai line is unlike any other braided line on the market. Sure, it's strong and sensitive, but it's also noticeably thinner, softer, smoother, and more flexible than ordinary braids. That means less friction for better casts, reduced line noise on the retrieve, and a faster sink rate due to less current resistance. Available in 150-yard, 300-yard, and 1500-yard spools.
Price: . . . .**$27.99–$279.99**

DAIWA STEEZ FLUOROCARBON

Color: Green
Type: Fluorocarbon
Length: 125 yds
Lb. Test: 5–20
Diameter: .007 in–016 in
Features: Finally, a green colored, super soft, super strong 100 percent Fluorocarbon line with the flexibility and castability of regular monofilament. Formulated exclusively for Steez spinning and casting reels, it is highly resistant to abrasion and offers a faster sink rate than monofilament. Parallel winding on the filler spool prevents dents and inconsistency in roundness that can reduce casting efficiency.
Price: . . . .**$19.99–$26.99**

ORVIS ACCESS SALTWATER

Color: Mist green
Type: Fly
Length: 90 feet
Weight: 6–10
Features: Orvis Line ID allows you to quickly and easily identify your line, with no more guessing; all of the lines are printed with the taper, weight, and functionality; Integrated Slickness additive is integrated throughout the PVC layer to provide lubrication for maximum distance, performance, and durability; new sleek and durable welded loop makes leader attachment quick and easy while holding up to repeated use—also helps to transfer energy more efficiently to the leader allowing better turnover; braided multifilament core provides excellent performance over a wide range of conditions; new paper pulp spool, made from recycled cardboard and kraft paper, is 100 percent compostable; made in USA.
Price: $59

ORVIS HYDROS 3D BONEFISH

Color: Sand; yellow
Type: Fly
Length: 105 feet
Weight: 7, 8, 9, 10
Features: Orvis Line ID allows you to quickly and easily identify your line, with no more guessing; all of the lines are printed with the taper, weight, and functionality; Integrated Slickness additive is integrated throughout the PVC layer to provide lubrication for maximum distance, performance, and durability; new sleek and durable welded loop makes leader attachment quick and easy while holding up to repeated use—also helps to transfer energy more efficiently to the leader allowing better turnover; braided multifilament core provides excellent performance over a wide range of conditions; new paper pulp spool, made from recycled cardboard and kraft paper, is 100 percent compostable; made in USA.
Price: $95

ORVIS HYDROS ALL ROUNDER SALTWATER

Color: Horizon blue
Type: Fly
Length: 100 feet
Weight: 6–12
Features: The best-selling all-purpose floating line for saltwater or freshwater big game; works well for stripers and blues as well as bass and pike; allows for close-in or long-distance presentations, and turns over heavy flies in the wind; latest generation of Wonderline coating is 20 percent slicker than the previous generation, resulting in the slickest fly lines on the market; casts farther with less effort, produces higher line speeds to cut through the wind and improve accuracy, repels dirt and grime, picks up off the water easier, improves flotation, and reduces tangles; Orvis Line ID allows you to quickly and easily identify your line, with no more guessing; all of the lines are printed with the taper, weight, and functionality; new sleek and durable welded loops make leader attachment quick and easy while holding up to repeated use—also helps to transfer energy more efficiently to the leader allowing better turnover; saltwater lines have an enhanced rear loop as well for attaching to backing; braided multifilament core provides excellent performance over a wide range of conditions; new paper pulp spool, made from recycled cardboard and kraft paper, is 100 percent compostable; in horizon blue; 100'.
Price: **$79**

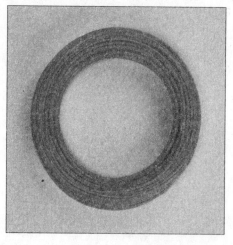

ORVIS HYDROS BLUEWATER

Color: Bright orange
Type: Fly
Length: 80 feet
Weight: 14, 15
Features: Full-sinking specialty line designed to throw monster flies to sailfish, marlin, and sharks; sinks 4 ½"-5" per second to cut through the waves and keep your fly in the strike zone; has a 25' head to turn over big flies with ease; small diameter running line cuts through the water, helping to minimize break-offs; Integrated Slickness additive is integrated throughout the PVC layer to provide lubrication for maximum distance, performance and durability; Orvis Line ID allows you to quickly and easily identify your line, with no more guessing; all of the lines are printed with the taper, weight, and functionality; braided monofilament core offers outstanding performance in hot, humid saltwater environments; new paper pulp spool, made from recycled cardboard and kraft paper, is 100 percent compostable.
Price: **$85**

LINES

ORVIS HYDROS BONEFISH

Color: Blue; sand
Type: Fly
Length: 105 feet
Weight: 7–9
Features: Special weight-forward taper for quick, accurate presentations to fast-moving bonefish; trigger color change at 30' load point increases accuracy and eliminates unnecessary false casting; latest generation of Wonderline coating is 20 percent slicker than the previous generation, resulting in the slickest fly lines on the market; casts farther with less effort, produces higher line speeds to cut through the wind and improve accuracy, repels dirt and grime, picks up off the water easier, improves flotation, and reduces tangles; Orvis Line ID allows you to quickly and easily identify your line, with no more guessing; all of the lines are printed with the taper, weight, and functionality; new sleek and durable welded loops make leader attachment quick and easy while holding up to repeated use—also helps to transfer energy more efficiently to the leader allowing better turnover; saltwater lines have an enhanced rear loop as well for attaching to backing; an innovative weight forward taper combined with slightly larger line diameters produce a line that is ideal at close to medium range, but still capable of delivering at distance; braided monofilament core offers outstanding performance in hot, humid saltwater environments; new paper pulp spool, made from recycled cardboard and kraft paper, is 100 percent compostable.
Price: **$79**

ORVIS HYDROS REDFISH

Color: Sand
Type: Fly
Length: 105 feet
Weight: 7–9
Features: A floating redfish fly line designed to work from a boat or while wading for redfish; short, heavy compact head aids in making quick, accurate deliveries while moderate front taper turns over the leader and fly easily; latest generation of Wonderline coating is 20 percent slicker than the previous generation, resulting in the slickest fly lines on the market; casts farther with less effort, produces higher line speeds to cut through the wind and improve accuracy, repels dirt and grime, picks up off the water easier, improves flotation, and reduces tangles; Orvis Line ID allows you to quickly and easily identify your line, with no more guessing; all of the lines are printed with the taper, weight, and functionality; new sleek and durable welded loops make leader attachment quick and easy while holding up to repeated use—also helps to transfer energy more efficiently to the leader allowing better turnover; saltwater lines have an enhanced rear loop as well for attaching to backing; braided monofilament core offers outstanding performance in hot, humid saltwater environments; new paper pulp spool, made from recycled cardboard and kraft paper, is 100 percent compostable.
Price: **$79**

ORVIS HYDROS STRIPER INTERMEDIATE

Color: Blue; stealth tip
Type: Fly
Length: 105 feet
Weight: 8–10
Features: Gets your fly down just below the surface chop, helping you keep tight to the fly to detect subtle takes; great line for stripers, bluefish, false albacore, and other cool-water fish species; won't tangle when fishing from a stripping basket; Integrated Slickness additive is integrated throughout the PVC layer to provide lubrication for maximum distance, performance, and durability; Orvis Line ID allows you to quickly and easily identify your line, with no more guessing; all of the lines are printed with the taper, weight, and functionality; new sleek and durable welded loops make leader attachment quick and easy while holding up to repeated use—also helps to transfer energy more efficiently to the leader allowing better turnover; saltwater lines have an enhanced rear loop as well for attaching to backing; braided multifilament core provides excellent performance over a wide range of conditions; new paper pulp spool, made from recycled cardboard and kraft paper, is 100 percent compostable.
Price: **$85**

SEAGUAR FLUOROCARBON SALMON STS LEADER

Type: Fluorocarbon
Length: 100 yd
Lb. Test: 20, 25, 30, 40, 50
Diameter: 0.016 in–0.026 in

Features: Genuine 100 percent fluorocarbon leader material delivers incredible abrasion resistance and maximum impact and knot strength, all with a smaller line diameter than monofilament.
Price: . . . .**$15.99–$24.99**

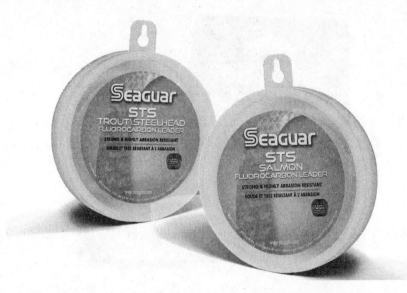

SEAGUAR FLUOROCARBON STEELHEAD/ TROUT STS LEADER

Type: Fluorocarbon
Length: 100 yd
Lb. Test: 4, 6, 8, 10, 12, 15, 17
Diameter: 0.007 in–0.015 in

Features: Incredible abrasion resistance and 30 percent better knot strength at a smaller diameter than monofilament; fast-sinking line gets you in the strike zone quicker; with a lower refractive index than monofilament, it is significantly less visible to fish underwater.
Price: . . . .**$11.99–$13.99**

SEAGUAR SMACKDOWN SLEEK, ULTRA-STRONG 8-STRAND BRAID

Color: Green, yellow
Type: Braid
Length: 150 yd
Lb. Test: 10, 15, 20, 30, 40, 50, 65
Diameter: 0.005 in–0.016 in

Features: This next generation Seaguar braid is so thin that 20 lb test has the diameter of 6 lb monofilament; Smackdown Braid is made with 8 ultra-thin, micro-weave strands in a round, smooth-casting profile with extra sensitivity; it provides exceptional knot and tensile strength with unparalleled abrasion resistance.
Price: **$32**

LINES

SEAGUAR THREADLOCK ULTRA-STRONG 16-STRAND HOLLOW-CORE BRAID

Color: Blue, green, white, yellow
Type: Braid
Length: 600 yd, 2500 yd
Lb. Test: 50, 60, 80, 100, 130, 200
Diameter: 0.015 in–0.030 in

Features: Designed for offshore saltwater anglers who are targeting pelagic species and looking for solid connections in structure and kelp; in smaller pound test sizes, Threadlock is also a perfect line choice for certain heavy cover freshwater applications like Flippin' and Punchin'.
Price: . . . . **$18–$499**

SHAKESPEARE MONOFILAMENT

Color: Clear
Type: Monofilament
Length: 700 yd
Lb. Test: 4, 6, 8,10, 12, 15, 20, 25, 30, 50

Features: 1/3 pound spool; excellent abrasion resistance; extremely affordable.
Price: **$2.99**

SPIDERWIRE EZ BRAID

Color: Moss green
Type: Braid
Length: 110 yds; 300 yds
Lb. Test: 10–50
Diameter: .007–.015

Features: Dyneema microfibers are 3X stronger than mono; diameters are 2 to 3X smaller than mono of the same weight test; super smooth for long, effortless casts; spider-sensitivity; near zero stretch to feel everything.
Price: . . . .**$9.99–$18.99**

SPIDERWIRE EZ FLUORO

Color: Clear
Type: Fluorocarbon
Length: 200 yds
Lb. Test: 2–15
Diameter: .006–.015

Features: 100 percent fluorocarbon for the key fluorocarbon benefits of virtual invisibility, sinking for less line between lure and reel and great wet strength; sensitive and abrasion resistant; good manageability, knot, and impact strength.
Price: . . . .**$7.99–$8.99**

SPIDERWIRE STEALTH GLOW-VIS
Color: Glow-Vis-Green Bulk
Type: Braid
Length: 125 yds; 300 yds; 1500 yds
Lb. Test: 8–80
Diameter: .007–.016

Features: Fluorescent brighteners illuminate line above water; low-vis green disappears below water enhance ability to watch line and detect bites that may not be felt.
Price:..............................**$14.99–$164.99**

SPIDERWIRE ULTRACAST 100% FLUOROCARBON
Color: Clear
Type: Fluorocarbon
Length: 200 yds
Lb. Test: 6, 8, 10, 12, 15
Diameter: .009–.014

Features: Thinner diameters than most competitive fluorocarbons allows lures to perform better; awesome performance on spinning reels (4–10 lb. test); disappears to fish as it is virtually invisible; spider-sensitivity transmits strikes and structure.
Price:..............................**$14.99–$16.99**

SPIDERWIRE ULTRACAST FLUORO-BRAID

Color: Moss green
Type: Braid
Length: 125 yds; 300 yds; 1500 yds
Lb. Test: 10–80
Diameter: .008–.018

Features: Exceptionally high strength-per-diameter in a fluoro; thinner diameters than most competitive fluorocarbons allow lures to perform better; awesome performance on spinning reels (4–10 lb test); spider sensitivity; transmits strikes and structure.
Price: . . . .**$20.99–$234.99**

SPIDERWIRE ULTRACAST INVISI-BRAID

Color: Clear
Type: Braid
Length: 125 yds; 300 yds; 1500 yds; 3000 yds
Lb. Test: 6–80
Diameter: .007–.022

Features: Ultra smooth 8-carrier braid; innovative cold-fusion process; translucency for near invisibility; extremely high strength-per-diameter; amazingly thin and sensitive; high pick count for roundness and durability.
Price: . . . .**$20.99–$449.99**

LINES

SPIDERWIRE ULTRACAST ULTIMATE MONO

Color: Clear; Brown recluse
Type: Monofilament
Length: 330 yds
Lb. Test: 4–20
Diameter: .006–.016

Features: Breakthrough strength-to-diameter co-polymer is 33 percent stronger than the average mono; unprecedented 15 percent stretch for incredible sensitivity and hook setting power; thin diameter allows exceptional bait action and high line capacity; excellent knot and shock strength even when wet; optimized for baitcast reels, but still castable and manageable on spinning reels.
Price: **$8.99**

STREN 100% FLUORO

Color: Clear/Blue fluorescent
Type: Fluorocarbon
Length: 200 yds

Lb. Test: 6–20
Diameter: .01–.018
Features: Virtually invisible; maximim abrasion resistance.
Price: . . . . **$16.99–$23.99**

STREN FLUOROCAST
Color: Clear
Type: Fluorocarbon
Length: 100 yds; 200 yds
Lb. Test: 4–17

Diameter: .007–.016
Features: Easy to cast and handle; excellent knot and shock strength; virtually invisible.
Price: . . . . **$4.99–$9.99**

LINES

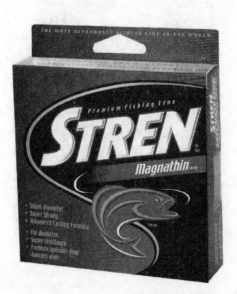

STREN MAGNATHIN
Color: Clear
Type: Monofilament
Length: 330 yds; 2600 yds

Lb. Test: 4–16
Diameter: .007–.018
Features: Small diameter; super strong; advanced casting formula.
Price: . . . . **$9.49–$76.99**

STREN ORIGINAL

Color: Clear; Clear/Blue fluorescent; Hi-Vis Gold; Clear/Blue fluorescent; Lo-Vis Green;
Type: Monofilament
Length: 100 yds; 330 yds; 1000 yds; 2400 yds
Lb. Test: 4–20

Diameter: .008–.02
Features: Superior knot strength; tough and abrasion resistant; low memory.
Price: . . . .$3.09–$62.49

SUFIX 832 ADVANCED ICE BRAID

Color: Ghost, neon lime
Type: Braid
Length: 50 yd
Lb. Test: 4–30

Diameter: 0.004 in–0.011 in
Features: Most durable small diameter ice braid available; water-repellant protection to reduce freezing; GORE Performance Fiber adds incredible fray and abrasion resistance for durability.
Price: $11.49

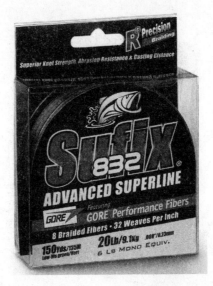

SUFIX 832 ADVANCED SUPERLINE

Color: Camo, ghost, hi-vis yellow, low-vis green, neon lime
Type: Braid
Length: 150 yd, 300 yd, 600 yd
Lb. Test: 6–80
Diameter: 0.006 in–0.018 in

Features: 8 fibers (Featuring one GORE Performance Fiber and 7 Dyneema Fibers); 32 pics (weaves) per inch; R8 precision braiding technology; patent-pending construction; ultimate abrasion resistance; unbeatable strength; proven castability improvements; TGP technology enhances color retention.
Price:..........................**$23.99–$449.99**

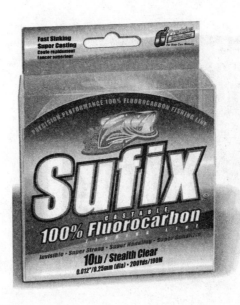

SUFIX CASTABLE INVISILINE 100% FLUOROCARBON

Color: Clear
Type: Fluorocarbon
Length: 100 yd, 200 yd
Lb. Test: 3–20
Diameter: 0.006 in–0.017 in

Features: Virtually disappears in the water for more natural presentation; low stretch; fast sinking; casts and handles like a premium monofilament; incredibly strong and abrasion-resistant; resistant to ultra violet rays; performs great on casting and spinning reels; G² precision winding.
Price:..........................**$14.49–$34.49**

LINES

SUFIX ICE MAGIC

Color: Clear, neon orange
Type: Monofilament
Length: 100 yd
Lb. Test: 1–8

Diameter: 0.004 in–0.010 in
Features: Designed to stay manageable even in frigid water; special additives deter water absorption that causes ice build-up; fast sinking for more natural presentation.
Price: **$3.99**

SUFIX SIEGE

Color: Clear, camo, neon tangerine, smoke green
Length: 250 yd, 330 yd, 1000 yd, 3000 yd
Lb. Test: 4–35
Diameter: 0.008 in–0.022 in
Features: Superior casting distance with pinpoint accuracy due to its proprietary extrusion process; up to 15X greater abrasion resistance; exceptional knot strength and smooth handling; smooth, supple, handles beautifully—yet it is exceptionally strong; G² Precision Winding (330 yd spools) virtually eliminates line memory, even on spinning reels.
Price: . . . .**$9.49–$84.49**

Directory of Manufacturers & Suppliers

13 FISHING
13323 W. Hillsborough Avenue, Unit 103
Tampa, FL 33635
(800) 508-6013
13fishing.com

ABU GARCIA
1900 18th Street
Spirit Lake, IA 51360
(800) 228-4272
abugarcia.com

BAGLEY BAIT CO
10205 Avenue North, Suite A1
Plymouth, MN 55441
(855) 246-9600
bagleybait.com

BANDIT LURES INC.
444 Cold Springs Road
Sardis, MS 38666
(662) 563-8450
banditlures.com
customerservice@banditlures.com

BASS PRO SHOPS
2500 East Kearney
Springfield, MO 65898
(417) 873-5000
basspro.com

BEAVERKILL ROD CO.
32 Andrea Lane
Scarsdale, NY 10583
(914) 490-3052
bkrod.com

BERKLEY CUSTOMER SERVICE
1900 18th Street
Spirit Lake, IA 51360
(800) 237-5539
berkley-fishing.com

TTI BLAKEMORE
P.O. Box 1177
Wetumpka, AL 36092
(800) 421-5768
ttiblakemore.com

BIG BITE BAITS, INC
PO Box 1375
Eufaula, AL 36072
(877) 222-7429
bigbitebaits.com
bbbaits@bellsouth.net

BOMBER, PRADCO-FISHING
3601 Jenny Lind Road
Fort Smith, AR 72901
(479) 782-8971
lurenet.com

BOOYAH, PRADCO-FISHING
3601 Jenny Lind Road
Fort Smith, AR 72901
(479) 782-8971
lurenet.com

BUCKEYE LURES INC.
310 Commerce Drive
Martinez, GA 30907
(706) 863-5468
buckeyelures.com

Directory of Manufacturers & Suppliers

CABELA'S
One Cabela Drive
Sidney, NE 69160
(800) 2430-6626
cabelas.com

CASTAWAY RODS
118 Cape Conroe Drive
Montgomery, TX 77356
(936) 582-1677
castawayrods.com

CORTLAND LINE CO.
3736 Kellogg Road
Cortland, NY 13045
(607) 756-2851
cortlandline.com
info@cortlandline.com

CREEK CHUB, PRADCO-FISHING
3601 Jenny Lind Road
Fort Smith, AR 72901
(479) 782-8971
lurenet.com

DAIWA CORPORATION
11137 Warland Drive
Cypress, CA 90630
(562) 375-6800
daiwa.com
admail@daiwa.com

DAMIKI FISHING TACKLE
26017 Huntington Lane Unit D
Valencia, CA 91355
(661) 702-0506
damiki.com
daniel@damiki.com

DOCKSIDE BAIT & TACKLE
Slidell, LA 70458
(985) 707-9049
docksidela.com

EAGLE CLAW FISHING TACKLE CO.
4245 East 46th Avenue
Denver, CO 80216
(303) 321-1481
eagleclaw.com
Info@eagleclaw.com

ECO PRO TUNGSTEN, INC.
311 Mechanics Street
Boonton, NJ 07005
(973) 396-2959
ecoprotungsten.com

FALCON RODS
1823 West Reno
Broken Arrow, OK 74012
(918) 251-0020
falconrods.com

FENWICK CUSTOMER SERVICE
1900 18th Street
Spirit Lake, IA 51360
(877) 336-7637
fenwickfishing.com
fenwick@purefishing.com

GARY YAMAMOTO CUSTOM BAITS
849 Coppermine Road
Page, AZ 86040
(928) 645-9699
baits.com

MANUFACTURERS

Directory of Manufacturers & Suppliers

GENE LAREW LURES, LLC
10702 East 11th Street
Tulsa, OK 74128
(918) 949-6291
genelarew.com

HARDY & GREYS LIMITED
Willowburn
Alnwick, Northumberland, UK
NE66 2PF
01665-602-771 + OPTION 2
hardyfishing.com

HATCH OUTDOORS, INC.
1001 Park Center Drive
Vista, CA 92081
(760) 734-4343
hatchoutdoors.com

HEDDON LURES, PRADCO-FISHING
3601 Jenny Lind Road
Fort Smith, AR 72901
(479) 782-8971
lurenet.com

JACKALL, SHIMANO AMERICAN CORP.
1 Holland Drive
Irvine, CA 92618
(949) 470-4199
jackall-lures.com

JOHNSON, PURE FISHING
7 Science Court
Columbia, SC 29203
(800) 237-5539
johnsonfishing.com

KALIN'S, UNCLE JOSH FISHING BAIT COMPANY
525 Jefferson Street
Fort Atkinson, WI 53538
(866) 244-2277
unclejosh.com

KEITECH USA
6 Bonaparte Point Road
Hopatcong, NJ 07843
(973) 398-7608
keitechusa.com

KOKABOW FISHING TACKLE, LLC
2496 N Marburg Avenue
Meridian, ID 83646
(208) 859-5870

LAMIGLAS, INC.
1400 Atlantic Avenue
Woodland, WA 98674
(800) 325-9436
lamiglas.com12
info@lamiglas.com

LEW'S
2253 E. Bennett
Springfield, MO 65804
(877) 470-5397
lews.com
info@lews.com

LINDY, PRADCO-FISHING
3601 Jenny Lind Road
Fort Smith, AR 72901
(479) 782-8971
lurenet.com

MANUFACTURERS

Directory of Manufacturers & Suppliers

LIVETARGET, KOPPERS FISHING & TACKLE CORP.
342 Townline Road, S.S. #4, Unit 2
Niagara-on-the-Lake ON L0S 1J0
Canada
(888) 231-4448
livetargetlures.com

L. L. BEAN INC
15 Casco Street
Freeport, ME 04033-0001
(800) 441-5713
llbean.com

G.LOOMIS
1 Holland Drive
Irvine, CA 92618
(877) 577-0600
gloomis.com

LUNKERHUNT LP
160 Tycos Drive, Unit #8
Toronto ON M6B 1W8
Canada
(416) 792-0385
lunkerhunt.com

MACK'S LURE
2514 Easy Street
Wenatchee, WA 98801
(509) 667-9202
mackslure.com

MISTER TWISTER
PO Box 996
Minden, LA 71058-0996
(318) 377-8818
mistertwister.com

MR. CRAPPIE, TTI BLAKEMORE
P.O. Box 1177
Wetumpka, AL 36092
(800) 421-5768
mrcrappie.com

NAUTILUS REELS
1549 NW 165th Street
Miami, FL 33169
(305) 625-3437
nautilusreels.com

NORTHLAND FISHING TACKLE
1001 Naylor Drive SE
Bemidji, MN 56601
(218) 751-6723
northlandtackle.com
Sales@NorthlandTackle.com

OKUMA FISHING
2310 E Locust Street
Ontario, CA 91761
(909) 923-2828
okumafishing.com

THE ORVIS COMPANY
1711 Blue Hills Drive
Roanoke, VA 24012-8613
(888) 235-9763
orvis.com
customerservice@orvis.com

PANTHER MARTIN
19 N. Columbia Street
Port Jefferson, NY 11777
(800) 524-4742
panthermartincom
staff@panthermartincom

MANUFACTURERS

Directory of Manufacturers & Suppliers

PRADCO-FISHING
3601 Jenny Lind Road
Fort Smith, AR 72901
(479) 782-8971
lurenet.com

PENN FISHING TACKLE COMPANY
1900 18th Street
Spirit Lake, IA 51360
(800) 228-4272
pennreels.com

PFLUEGER CUSTOMER SERVICE
7 Science Court
Columbia, SC 29203
(800) 554-4653
pfluegerfishing.com

P-LINE FISHING
460 Valley Drive
Brisbane, CA 94005
(415) 468-0452
p-line.com

POWER PRO
1 Holland Drive
Irvine, CA 92618
(877) 577-0600
powerpro.com

QUANTUM FISHING
6105 E. Apache
Tulsa, OK 74115
(800) 588-9030
quantumfishing.com
email.quantum@zebco.com

RAT-L-TRAP
3240 Baldwin Avenue
Alexandria, LA 71301
(800) 633-4861
rat-l-trap.com

REBEL, PRADCO-FISHING
3601 Jenny Lind Road
Fort Smith, AR 72901
(479) 782-8971
lurenet.com

RIO PRODUCTS
5050 S. Yellowstone Hwy
Idaho Falls, ID 83402
(800) 553-0838
rioproducts.com

RISE FISHING CO.
PO BOX 3282
East Hampton, NY 11937
(800) 399-0712
risefishing.com
info@risefishing.com

SAGE MANUFACTURING
8500 Northeast Day Road
Bainbridge Island, WA 98110
(800) 533-3004
sageflyfish.com
sagecs@sageflyfish.com

SAVAGE GEAR, SVENDSEN SPORTS UK
Mariner House
Tamworth
UK
+44 (0) 182-759-659
savage-gear.com
uk@Svendsen-Sport.com

SCOTT FLY ROD COMPANY
2355 Air Park Way
Montrose, CO 81401
(970) 249-3180
scottflyrod.com
info@scottflyrod.com

MANUFACTURERS

Directory of Manufacturers & Suppliers

SEAGUAR DIVISION, KUREHA AMERICA
420 Lexington Avenue - Suite 2510
New York, NY 10170
(212) 867-7040
seaguar.com

SÉBILE US
1900 18th Street
Spirit Lake, IA 51360
(855) 792-3234
sebile.com
sebile@purefishing.com

SHAKESPEARE CUSTOMER SERVICE
7 Science Court
Columbia, SC 29203
(800) 466-5643
shakespeare-fishing.com

SHIMANO AMERICAN CORP.
1 Holland Drive
Irvine, CA 92618
(949) 951-5003
shimano.com

SOUTHERN PRO TACKLE
PO Box 425
Brookland, AR 72417
(870) 931-4501
southernpro.com

SPRO CORPORATION
3900 Kennesaw 75 Parkway, Suite 140
Kennesaw, GA 30144
(770) 919-1722
spro.com

ST. CROIX OF PARK FALLS, LTD
856 4th Avenue North, PO Box 279
Park Falls, WI 54552
(715) 762-3226
stcroixrods.com

STORM, RAPALA VMC CORPORATION
Tehtaantie 2
17200 Vääksy
Finland
358-9-7562-540
stormlures.com
info@rapala.fi

STREN
7 Science Court
Columbia, SC 29203
(866) 447-8736
stren.com
stren@purefishing.com

STRIKE KING LURE COMPANY
466 Washington Street
Collierville, TN 38017
(901) 853-1455
strikeking.com

SUFIX, RAPALA VMC CORPORATION
Tehtaantie 2
17200 Vääksy
Finland
358-9-7562-540
sufix.com
info@rapala.fi

SUICK LURE COMPANY
630 Industrial Park Road
Antigo, WI 54409
(715) 623-7883
suick.com

Directory of Manufacturers & Suppliers

TEMPLE FORK OUTFITTERS
8105 Sovereign Row
Dallas, TX 75247
(214) 638-9052
tforods.com

TIGHTLINES UV
112 E. 4th Street
Maryville, MO 64468
(660) 853-9290
uv-tackle.com

TSUNAMI LURES, TOMBSTONE CO., LTD
2-12 Nishihitotsuya Settsu-shi
Osaka, Japan 566-0044
06-6340-9556
tsunami-lures.com

UNCLE JOSH FISHING BAIT COMPANY
525 Jefferson Street
Fort Atkinson, WI 53538
(866) 244-2277
unclejosh.com

R.L. WINSTON ROD CO.
205 S Main Street
Twin Bridges, MT 59754
(406) 684-5674
winstonrods.com
info@winstonrods.com

WRIGHT & MCGILL CO.
4245 E. 46th Avenue
Denver, CO 80216
(720) 941-8700
wright-mcgill.com
info@wright-mcgill.com

YO-ZURI
668 N W Enterprise Drive
Port St. Lucie, FL 34986
(888) 336-9775
yo-zuri.com
info@yo-zuri.com

YUM, PRADCO-FISHING
3601 Jenny Lind Road
Fort Smith, AR 72901
(479) 782-8971
lurenet.com

ZEBCO
6105 E. Apache
Tulsa, OK 74115
(800) 588-9030
zebco.com
email.zebco@zebco.com

Z-MAN FISHING PRODUCTS, INC.
4100 Palmetto Commerce Pkwy
Ladson, SC 29456
(843) 747-4366
zmanfishing.com

MANUFACTURERS

IGFA FRESHWATER & SALTWATER ALL-TACKLE RECORDS

Reprinted Courtesy of the International Game Fish Association

IGFA Freshwater & Saltwater All-Tackle Records

All-Tackle records are kept for the heaviest of each species caught by an angler in any line class up to 60 kg (130 lb). The following are records granted as of October 15, 2014.

SPECIES	SCIENTIFIC NAME	WEIGHT	PLACE	DATE	ANGLER
Acara paragaio	Hoplarchus psittacus	.71 kg 1 lb 9 oz	Rio Negro Brazil	07-Nov-99	James Wise, M.D.
Acara paragaio (TIE)	Hoplarchus psittacus	.71 kg 1 lb 9 oz	Rio Negro Brazil	09-Feb-07	Capt. Jay Wright Jr.
Acara roi roi	Geophagus proximus	.48 kg 1 lb 0 oz	Igarape do Capitari Amazonas, Brazil	20-Dec-09	Gilberto Fernandes
Acara Tucanare	Satonoperca lillith	.7 kg 1 lb 8 oz	Igarape do Capitari Brazil	05-Dec-09	Gilberto Fernandes
Acara, silver	Chaetobranchus flavescens	.78 kg 1 lb 11 oz	Igarape do Capitari Amazonas, Brazil	03-Jun-10	Gilberto Fernandes
Aimara (jeju)	Hoplerythrinus unitaeniatus	.68 kg 1 lb 8 oz	Rio Tapera, Amazon Brazil	01-Feb-03	Martin Arostegui
Akahata	Epinephelus fasciatus	1.62 kg 3 lb 9 oz	Izu-Oshima Tokyo, Japan	26-May-13	Kyoko Yamada
Akodai	Sebastes matsubarae	3.04 kg 6 lb 11 oz	Shimoda Shizuoka, Japan	21-Mar-05	Jun Yamada
Albacore	Thunnus alalunga	39.97 kg 88 lb 2 oz	Gran Canaria Canary Islands, Spain	19-Nov-77	Siegfried Dickemann
Alfonsino	Beryx decadactylus	3.77 kg 8 lb 5 oz	Norfolk Canyon Virginia Beach, Virginia, USA	10-Oct-10	Kevin Wong
Altai Osman	Oreoleuciscus potanini	5.82 kg 12 lb 13 oz	Hoton Lake Mongolia	14-Jun-09	Iurii Diachenko
Amberjack, greater	Seriola dumerili	71.15 kg 156 lb 13 oz	Iki Island Nagasaki, Japan	19-Nov-10	Hideyuki Nemoto
Angelfish, grey	Pomacanthus arcuatus	1.83 kg 4 lb 0 oz	South Beach Jetty Miami, Florida, USA	12-Jul-99	Rene de Dios
Angelshark, Japanese	Squatina japonica	9.25 kg 20 lb 6 oz	Hiratsuka Kanagawa, Japan	17-Feb-13	Yusaku Nagai
Angler	Lophius piscatorius	57.5 kg 126 lb 12 oz	Sagnefiorden Hoyanger, Norway	04-Jul-96	Gunnar Thorsteinsen
Ara	Niphon spinosus	11 kg 24 lb 4 oz	Kashima Ibaraki, Japan	15-Dec-02	Masato Ishizuka
Aracu	Leporinus agassizi	.82 kg 1 lb 12 oz	Puraquequara Lake Amazonas, Brazil	27-Jul-09	Gilberto Fernandes
Araçu comum	Schizodon vittatus	.96 kg 2 lb 2 oz	Thaimaçu Lodge Brazil	18-Jul-07	Tacito De Almeida
Aracu, fat head	Leporinus trifasciatus	1.15 kg 2 lb 8 oz	Lago Puraquequara Brazil	24-Jul-09	Gilberto Fernandes
Aracu, pau-de-nego	Rhytiodus microlepis	.54 kg 1 lb 3 oz	Puraquequara Lake Amazonas, Brazil	03-Jul-10	Gilberto Fernandes

SPECIES	SCIENTIFIC NAME	WEIGHT	PLACE	DATE	ANGLER
Arawana	*Osteoglossum bicirrhosum*	6.58 kg 14 lb 8 oz	Miriti, Rio Preta da Eva Amazonas, Brazil	22-Oct-09	Jorge Masullo de Aguiar
Arawana, black	*Osteoglossum ferreirai*	2.27 kg 5 lb 0 oz	Bita River Colombia	14-Mar-87	Capt. Dan Kipnis
Argentine, greater	*Argentina silus*	.7 kg 1 lb 8 oz	Hardangerfjord Norway	06-Aug-01	Ms. Sandra Marquard
Asp	*Aspius aspius*	5.66 kg 12 lb 7 oz	Lake Vanern Sweden	25-Sep-93	Jan-Erik Skoglund
Ayamekasago	*Sebastiscus albofasciatus*	2.5 kg 5 lb 8 oz	Irozaki Shizuoka, Japan	13-Aug-98	Mikio Suzuki
Barb, eye-spot	*Hampala dispar*	.69 kg 1 lb 8 oz	Khon Kaen Thailand	11-Jan-13	Ali Abdul Kadir
Barb, giant	*Catlocarpio siamensis*	61 kg 134 lb 7 oz	Gillhams Fishing Resorts Krabi, Thailand	09-Oct-13	Keith Williams
Barb, golden belly	*Hypsibarbus wetmorei*	1.85 kg 4 lb 1 oz	River Kwai Ratchaburi, Thailand	01-May-13	Benchawan Thiansungnoen
Barb, golden tinfoil	*Hypsibarbus malcomi*	.46 kg 1 lb 0 oz	Kong Lai Thailand	29-Dec-10	Jean-Francois Helias
Barb, hampala	*Hampala macrolepidota*	6.5 kg 14 lb 5 oz	Temenggor Lake State of Perak, Malaysia	22-Sep-02	Teh Teck
Barb, Java	*Barbonymus gonionotus*	2.6 kg 5 lb 11 oz	Khao Laem Dam Kancuanaburi, Thailand	22-Dec-13	Per Gunnar Jansen
Barb, lagleri	*Hypsibarbus lagleri*	1.13 kg 2 lb 7 oz	Luang Prabang Laos	28-Nov-11	Dale C. Fischer
Barb, Laos	*Poropuntius laoensis*	.53 kg 1 lb 2 oz	Nam Song River Laos	06-Feb-10	Jean-Francois Helias
Barb, mad	*Leptobarbus hoevenii*	6 kg 13 lb 3 oz	Bung Sam Lan Lake Thailand	31-Aug-02	Loke Wong
Barb, Smith's	*Puntioplites proctozysron*	.8 kg 1 lb 12 oz	Srinakarin Dam Thailand	02-May-02	Jean-Francois Helias
Barb, soldier river	*Cyclocheilichthys enoplus*	3.84 kg 8 lb 7 oz	Ratchaburi Thailand	18-Nov-10	Gavin Clarke
Barb, tinfoil	*Barbonymus schwanenfeldii*	1.3 kg 2 lb 13 oz	Temmenggor Dam Perak, Malaysia	06-Apr-03	Ngu Sen
Barbel	*Barbus barbus*	6.12 kg 13 lb 8 oz	St. Patrick's Stream Bershire, United Kingdom	29-Dec-04	Eric Charles Roberts
Barbel, comizo hybrid	*Barbus steindachner*	6.95 kg 15 lb 5 oz	Guadiana River Spain	26-Oct-09	Stan Nabozny
Barenose, bigeye	*Monotaxis grandoculis*	5.89 kg 13 lb 0 oz	Otec Beach, Kailua Kona, Hawaii, USA	12-Jul-92	Rex Bigg
Barracuda, bigeye	*Sphyraena forsteri*	7.9 kg 17 lb 6 oz	Chagos Diego Garcia	07-Nov-10	Phillip W. Richmond, Jr.
Barracuda, blackfin	*Sphyraena qenie*	13.38 kg 29 lb 8 oz	Indian Ocean Diego Garcia	18-Jan-13	Matthew Olson

SPECIES	SCIENTIFIC NAME	WEIGHT	PLACE	DATE	ANGLER
Barracuda, great	*Sphyraena barracuda*	39.55 kg 87 lb 3 oz	Christmas Island Kiribati	23-Sep-12	Christian Loranger
Barracuda, Guinean	*Sphyraena afra*	46.4 kg 102 lb 4 oz	Barra du Kwanza Angola	14-Feb-13	Thomas Gibson
Barracuda, Hellers	*Sphyraena helleri*	2.04 kg 4 lb 8 oz	Molokai Hawaii, USA	18-Jan-05	Dan Stockdon Jr.
Barracuda, Mexican	*Sphyraena ensis*	12.87 kg 28 lb 6 oz	Isla Secas Panama	08-Mar-10	Jilberto Cansari
Barracuda, Pacific	*Sphyraena argentea*	4.31 kg 9 lb 8 oz	Ensenada Mexico	27-May-13	Peter F. Binaski
Barracuda, pickhandle	*Sphyraena jello*	15 kg 33 lb 1 oz	Malindi Kenya	19-Nov-08	Thomas Knill
Barracuda, yellowmouth	*Sphyraena viridensis*	10.2 kg 22 lb 8 oz	Lanzarote Island Canaries, Spain	06-Feb-07	Steven Carr
Barramundi	*Lates calcarifer*	44.64 kg 98 lb 6 oz	Lake Monduran Queensland, Australia	12-Dec-10	Denis Harrold
Barrelfish	*Hyperoglyphe perciformis*	13.15 kg 29 lb 0 oz	Big Pine Key Florida, USA	27-Nov-10	Walter McManus
Baru	*Uara amphiacanthoides*	.48 kg 1 lb 0 oz	Igarape do Capitari Amazonas, Brazil	03-Jan-10	Gilberto Fernandes
Bass, Australian	*Macquaria novemaculata*	3.75 kg 8 lb 4 oz	Lake Wivenhoe Queensland, Australia	24-Jul-05	Neil Schultz
Bass, barred sand	*Paralabrax nebulifer*	5.98 kg 13 lb 3 oz	Huntington Beach California, USA	29-Aug-88	Robert Halal
Bass, black sea	*Centropristis striata*	4.65 kg 10 lb 4 oz	Virginia Beach Virginia, USA	01-Jan-00	Allan Paschall
Bass, damsel	*Hemanthias signifer*	.68 kg 1 lb 8 oz	Playa Zancudo Costa Rica	10-Jun-95	Craig Whitehead, MD
Bass, European	*Dicentrarchus labrax*	10.12 kg 22 lb 5 oz	Pirou France	28-May-99	Philippe Boulet
Bass, giant sea	*Stereolepis gigas*	255.6 kg 563 lb 8 oz	Anacapa Island California, USA	20-Aug-68	James McAdam, Jr.
Bass, goldspotted sand	*Paralabrax auroguttatus*	4.64 kg 10 lb 4 oz	Thetis Bank, Baja California, USA	01-Nov-06	Dan Cash
Bass, Guadalupe	*Micropterus treculi*	1.67 kg 3 lb 11 oz	Lake Travis, Austin Texas, USA	25-Sep-83	Allen Christenson, Jr.
Bass, Guadalupe x smallmouth	*Micropterus treculi x M. dolomieu*	1.9 kg 4 lb 3 oz	Blanco River Texas, USA	18-Jun-95	John Weaver
Bass, kelp (calico)	*Paralabrax clathratus*	6.54 kg 14 lb 7 oz	Newport Beach California, USA	02-Oct-93	Thomas Murphy
Bass, largemouth	*Micropterus salmoides*	10.09 kg 22 lb 4 oz	Montgomery Lake Georgia, USA	02-Jun-32	George W. Perry
Bass, largemouth (TIE)	*Micropterus salmoides*	10.12 kg 22 lb 4 oz	Lake Biwa Shiga, Japan	02-Jul-09	Manabu Kurita

RECORDS

SPECIES	SCIENTIFIC NAME	WEIGHT	PLACE	DATE	ANGLER
Bass, leather	*Dermatolepis dermatolepis*	12.47 kg 27 lb 8 oz	Isla Clarion Revillagigedo Islands, Mexico	26-Jan-88	Allan Ristori
Bass, longtail	*Hemanthias leptus*	2.94 kg 6 lb 8 oz	Islamorada Florida, USA	12-Feb-00	Ms. Bonnie Murphy
Bass, meanmouth	*Micropterus dolomieu x M. punctulatus*	3.88 kg 8 lb 8 oz	Vetrans Lake, Sulphur Oklahoma, USA	27-Mar-06	Dru Clayton Kinslow
Bass, Ozark	*Ambloplites constellatus*	.45 kg 1 lb 0 oz	Bull Shoals Lake Arkansas, USA	13-May-97	Gary Nelson
Bass, Ozark (TIE)	*Ambloplites constellatus*	.45 kg 1 lb 0 oz	James River Missouri, USA	18-Apr-14	William Brent Evans
Bass, Ozark (TIE)	*Ambloplites constellatus*	.45 kg 1 lb 0 oz	James River Missouri, USA	04-Jun-14	William Brent Evans
Bass, Roanoke	*Ambloplites cavifrons*	.62 kg 1 lb 5 oz	Nottoway River Virginia, USA	11-Nov-91	Thomas Elkins
Bass, rock	*Ambloplites rupestris*	1.36 kg 3 lb 0 oz	York River Ontario, Canada	01-Aug-74	Peter Gulgin
Bass, rock (TIE)	*Ambloplites rupestris*	1.36 kg 3 lb 0 oz	Lake Erie Pennsylvania, USA	18-Jun-98	Herbert Ratner, Jr.
Bass, shadow	*Ambloplites ariommus*	.82 kg 1 lb 13 oz	Spring River Arkansas, USA	05-Jul-99	James Baker
Bass, shoal	*Micropterus cataractae*	3.99 kg 8 lb 12 oz	Apalachicola River Florida, USA	28-Jan-95	Carl Davis
Bass, smallmouth	*Micropterus dolomieu*	5.41 kg 11 lb 15 oz	Dale Hollow Lake Tennessee, USA	09-Jul-55	David Hayes
Bass, spotted	*Micropterus punctulatus*	4.73 kg 10 lb 7 oz	New Melonies Reservoir Angels Camp, California, USA	22-Feb-14	Keith Bryan
Bass, spotted sand	*Paralabrax maculatofasciatus*	2.24 kg 4 lb 15 oz	San Diego California, USA	12-Jul-03	Paul Weintraub
Bass, striped	*Morone saxatilis*	37.14 kg 81 lb 14 oz	Long Island Sound Westbrook, Connecticut, USA	04-Aug-11	Gregory Myerson
Bass, striped (landlocked)	*Morone saxatilis*	31.55 kg 69 lb 9 oz	Black Warrior River Alabama, USA	28-Feb-13	James R. Bramlett
Bass, Suwannee	*Micropterus notius*	1.75 kg 3 lb 14 oz	Suwannee River Florida, USA	02-Mar-85	Ronnie Everett
Bass, white	*Morone chrysops*	3.09 kg 6 lb 13 oz	Lake Orange Orange, Virginia, USA	31-Jul-89	Ronald Sprouse
Bass, white (TIE)	*Morone chrysops*	3.09 kg 6 lb 13 oz	Amite River Louisiana, USA	27-Aug-10	Corey Crochet
Bass, whiterock	*Morone saxatilis x M. chrysops*	12.38 kg 27 lb 5 oz	Greers Ferry Lake Arkansas, USA	24-May-97	Jerald Shaum
Bass, yellow	*Morone mississippiensis*	1.16 kg 2 lb 9 oz	Duck River Waverly, Tennessee, USA	27-Feb-98	John Chappell
Bass, yellow (hybrid)	*Morone mississippiensis x M. chrysops*	1.81 kg 4 lb 0 oz	Lake Fork Texas, USA	26-Mar-03	C. Runyan

SPECIES	SCIENTIFIC NAME	WEIGHT	PLACE	DATE	ANGLER
Batfish, orbicular	Platax orbicularis	2.01 kg 4 lb 7 oz	Racha Noi Island Phucket, Thailand	21-Feb-04	Tony Stuart
Batfish, tiera	Platax teira	1.92 kg 4 lb 3 oz	Kut Island Thailand	17-Jan-06	Steven M. Wozniak
Biara	Rhaphiodon vulpinus	2.1 kg 4 lb 10 oz	Xingu River Brazil	21-Apr-00	Marcio Borges de Oliveira
Bicuda	Boulengerella cuvieri	6.8 kg 15 lb 0 oz	Teles Pires River, Mato Grosso Brazil	13-Dec-02	Sandro Francio
Bigeye	Priacanthus arenatus	2.85 kg 6 lb 4 oz	Baja da Guanabara Rio de Janeiro, Brazil	30-Aug-97	Jayme Garcia
Bigeye, short	Pristigenys alta	.56 kg 1 lb 4 oz	Hatteras North Carolina, USA	24-Apr-04	John D. Overton, Jr.
Binga	Dimidiochromis kiwinge	.51 kg 1 lb 2 oz	Maleri Island Lake Malawi, Malawi	30-Nov-96	Garry Whitcher
Blackfish, smallscale	Girella melanichthys	3.4 kg 7 lb 7 oz	Hachijokojima Hachijo Island, Japan	08-Jan-98	Papa Otsuru
Bludger	Carangoides gymnostethus	9.7 kg 21 lb 6 oz	Bartholmeu Dias Mozambique	17-Jun-97	Joh Haasbroek
Bluefish	Pomatomus saltatrix	14.4 kg 31 lb 12 oz	Hatteras North Carolina, USA	30-Jan-72	James Hussey
Bluegill	Lepomis macrochirus	2.15 kg 4 lb 12 oz	Ketona Lake Alabama, USA	09-Apr-50	T. Hudson
Bocaccio	Sebastes paucispinis	12.64 kg 27 lb 14 oz	Elfin Cove Alaska, USA	24-Aug-11	George Bogen
Boga	Leporinus obstusidens	7.26 kg 16 lb 0 oz	Uruguay River Concordia River, Argentina	22-Apr-13	Ray Snyder
Bonefish	Albula vulpes	7.26 kg 16 lb 0 oz	Bimini Bahamas	25-Feb-71	Jerry Lavenstein
Bonefish, roundjaw	Albula glossodonta	4.65 kg 10 lb 4 oz	Kahuku Oahu, Hawaii, USA	16-Jul-13	Jamie Hamamoto
Bonefish, sharpjaw	Albula virgata	2.49 kg 5 lb 8 oz	North Shore Oahu, Hawaii, USA	11-Oct-13	Jamie Hamamoto
Bonefish, smallscale	Albula oligolepis	8.61 kg 19 lb 0 oz	Zululand South Africa	26-May-62	Brian Batchelor
Boneytongue, Australian	Scleropages jardinii	5.72 kg 12 lb 9 oz	Central Queensland Australia	20-Aug-11	Grant Zietsman
Bonito, Atlantic	Sarda sarda	8.3 kg 18 lb 4 oz	Faial Island Azores, Portugal	08-Jul-53	D. Higgs
Bonito, Australian	Sarda australis	9.4 kg 20 lb 11 oz	Montague Island N.S.W., Australia	01-Apr-78	Bruce Conley
Bonito, leaping	Cybiosarda elegans	.96 kg 2 lb 2 oz	Macleay River Australia	07-May-95	Wayne Colling
Bonito, Pacific	Sarda chiliensis lineolata	9.67 kg 21 lb 5 oz	181 Spot California, USA	19-Oct-03	Kim Larson

RECORDS

SPECIES	SCIENTIFIC NAME	WEIGHT	PLACE	DATE	ANGLER
Bonito, striped	*Sarda orientalis*	10.65 kg 23 lb 8 oz	Victoria, Mahe Seychelles	19-Feb-75	Anne Cochain
Bowfin	*Amia calva*	9.75 kg 21 lb 8 oz	Forest Lake, Florence South Carolina, USA	29-Jan-80	Robert Harmon
Boxfish, bluespotted	*Ostracion immaculatus*	.54 kg 1 lb 3 oz	Akazawa Ito, Shizuoka, Japan	30-Sep-12	Yuuma Nishino
Bracanjuva	*Brycon orbignyanus*	.62 kg 1 lb 6 oz	Mato Grosso Piguiri River, Brazil	16-Apr-98	Helder Coutinho
Bream	*Abramis brama*	6.01 kg 13 lb 3 oz	Hagbyan Creek Sweden	11-May-84	Luis Rasmussen
Bream, African red	*Pagrus africanus*	5.55 kg 12 lb 3 oz	Nouadhibou Mauritania	13-Mar-86	Bernard Defago
Bream, black	*Hephaestus fuliginosus*	6.17 kg 13 lb 9 oz	Lake Tinaroo Queensland, Australia	16-Jan-97	Brian Seawright
Bream, blue-lined large-eye	*Gymnocranius grandoculis*	5.5 kg 12 lb 2 oz	Amami-oshima Kagoshima, Japan	28-May-00	Hitoshi Suzuki
Bream, collared large-eye	*Gymnocranius audleyi*	2.72 kg 6 lb 0 oz	Great Barrier Reef Cairns, Australia	30-Oct-01	Dennis Triana
Bream, Japanese large-eye	*Gymnocranius euanus*	1.95 kg 4 lb 4 oz	Anejima, Ogasawara Tokyo, Japan	16-Jul-14	Masakazu Naohara
Bream, King soldier	*Argyrops spinifer*	1.25 kg 2 lb 12 oz	Dubai United Arab Emirates	20-Feb-11	Steven M. Wozniak
Bream, twoband	*Diplodus vulgaris*	1.3 kg 2 lb 13 oz	Europa Point Gibraltar	03-Sep-95	Ernest Borrell
Bream, white	*Abramis bjoerkna*	.76 kg 1 lb 10 oz	Holandselva Akershus, Norway	25-May-04	Jan Bredo Nerdrum
Brotula, bearded	*Brotula barbata*	8.52 kg 18 lb 12 oz	Destin Florida, USA	10-Apr-99	Joe Dollar
Buffalo, bigmouth	*Ictiobus cyprinellus*	31.89 kg 70 lb 5 oz	Bastrop Louisiana, USA	21-Apr-80	Delbert Sisk
Buffalo, black	*Ictiobus niger*	28.74 kg 63 lb 6 oz	Mississippi River Iowa, USA	14-Aug-99	Jim Winters
Buffalo, smallmouth	*Ictiobus bubalus*	37.29 kg 82 lb 3 oz	Athens Lake Texas, USA	06-May-93	Randy Collins
Bullhead, black	*Ameiurus melas*	3.37 kg 7 lb 7 oz	Mill Pond, Wantagh Long Island, New York, USA	25-Aug-93	Kevin Kelly
Bullhead, brown	*Ameiurus nebulosus*	3.35 kg 7 lb 6 oz	Mahopac Lake New York, USA	01-Aug-09	Glenn Collacuro
Bullhead, yellow	*Ameiurus natalis*	2.89 kg 6 lb 6 oz	Drevel Missouri, USA	27-May-06	John R. Irvin
Bullseye, longfinned	*Cookeolus japonicus*	3.02 kg 6 lb 10 oz	Chichijima, Ogasawara Tokyo, Japan	12-Mar-14	Toshihiro Yokoshima
Bullseye, moontail	*Priacanthus hamrur*	.55 kg 1 lb 3 oz	Hachijo Is. Tokyo, Japan	15-Aug-05	Yuuma Nishino

SPECIES	SCIENTIFIC NAME	WEIGHT	PLACE	DATE	ANGLER
Burbot	*Lota lota*	11.4 kg 25 lb 2 oz	Lake Diefenbaker Saskatchewan, Canada	27-Mar-10	Sean Konrad
Buri (Japanese amberjack)	*Seriola quinqueradiata*	22.1 kg 48 lb 11 oz	Ijika, Mie Japan	11-Dec-05	Kyoichi Kitamura
Burrfish, spotfin	*Chilomycterus reticulatus*	4.1 kg 9 lb 0 oz	Kozushima Tokyo, Japan	13-Jul-04	Junzo Okada
Burrfish, spotted	*Chilomycterus atringa*	6.25 kg 13 lb 12 oz	Haulover Florida, USA	28-Apr-03	Tim O'Quinn
Burrfish, striped	*Chilomycterus schoepfi*	.63 kg 1 lb 6 oz	Delaware Bay New Jersey, USA	13-Aug-89	Donna Ludlam
Butterfish, Brazilian	*Hyperoglyphe macrophthalma*	10.12 kg 22 lb 4 oz	Rio de Janeiro Brazil	19-Mar-04	Eduardo Baumeier
Butterflyfish, lined	*Chaetodon lineolatus*	.45 kg 1 lb 0 oz	Kona Hawaii, USA	15-Jul-12	Steven M. Wozniak
Cabezon	*Scorpaenichthys marmoratus*	10.43 kg 23 lb 0 oz	Juan De Fuca Strait Washington, USA	04-Aug-90	Wesley Hunter
Cachorro, peixe	*Acestrorhynchus falcirostris*	.91 kg 2 lb 0 oz	Wiuni River Brazil	29-Jan-07	Ian-Arthur de Sulocki
Cachorro, peixe (TIE)	*Acestrorhynchus falcirostris*	.94 kg 2 lb 1 oz	Rio Negro Brazil	09-Feb-07	Rebecca Wright
Captainfish	*Pseudotolithus senegalensis*	12 kg 26 lb 7 oz	Archipelago dos Bijagos Guinea-Bissau	17-May-98	Eric Legris
Carp, bighead	*Aristichthys nobilis*	40.82 kg 90 lb 0 oz	Guntersville Lake Tennessee, USA	02-Jun-05	Jeffrey J. Rorex
Carp, black	*Mylopharyngodon piceus*	18.5 kg 40 lb 12 oz	Edo River Chiba, Japan	01-Apr-00	Kenichi Hosoi
Carp, common	*Cyprinus carpio*	34.35 kg 75 lb 11 oz	Lac de St. Cassien France	21-May-87	Leo van der Gugten
Carp, crucian	*Carassius carassius*	2.01 kg 4 lb 7 oz	Ostanforsan Falun, Sweden	12-Jun-88	Lars Jonsson
Carp, grass	*Ctenopharyngodon idella*	39.75 kg 87 lb 10 oz	Piasuchnik Dam Bulgaria	22-Jul-09	Stoian Iliev
Carp, mrigal	*Cirrhinus cirrihinus*	8 kg 17 lb 10 oz	Gillhams Fishing Resorts Krabi, Thailand	03-Jan-12	Eddie Grey
Carp, predatory	*Chanodichthys erythropterus*	4.75 kg 10 lb 7 oz	Chengwen Reservoir Chiayi County, Taiwan	18-May-14	Duane Jeffrey Christie
Carp, silver	*Hypophthalmichthys molitrix*	32 kg 70 lb 8 oz	Andong-s, Kyungsangbok-Do Korea	04-Jun-06	Chongdae Lim
Carpsucker, river	*Carpiodes carpio*	3.48 kg 7 lb 11 oz	Canadian Co. Oklahoma, USA	18-Apr-90	W. Kenyon
Catfish, Amazon Sailfin	*Pterygoplichthys pardalis*	1.02 kg 2 lb 4 oz	Miami Canal Miami, Florida, USA	06-Mar-10	Dennis Triana
Catfish, amur	*Silurus asotus*	3.75 kg 8 lb 4 oz	Tama River Tokyo, Japan	15-Nov-13	Fumiya Okuyama

RECORDS

SPECIES	SCIENTIFIC NAME	WEIGHT	PLACE	DATE	ANGLER
Catfish, Asian redtail	*Hemibagrus nemurus*	3.2 kg 7 lb 0 oz	Khao Laem Dam Kanchanaburi, Thailand	06-Jan-12	Benchawan Thiansungnoen
Catfish, black	*Hemibagrus wyckii*	4.05 kg 8 lb 14 oz	Palm Tree Lagoon Thailand	25-Nov-12	Benchawan Thiansungnoen
Catfish, blue	*Ictalurus furcatus*	64.86 kg 143 lb 0 oz	Kerr Lake Buggs Island, Virginia, USA	18-Jun-11	Richard Nicholas Anderson
Catfish, channel	*Ictalurus punctatus*	26.3 kg 58 lb 0 oz	Santee-Cooper Reservoir South Carolina, USA	07-Jul-64	W. Whaley
Catfish, duckbill	*Sorubim lima*	1.5 kg 3 lb 4 oz	Xingu River Brazil	02-Jun-03	Ms. Roberta Mathias
Catfish, Eurasian	*Silurus biwaensis*	17.2 kg 37 lb 14 oz	Imazuhama Lake Biwa, Shiga, Japan	04-Jul-97	Shoji Matsuura
Catfish, firewood	*Surubimichthys planiceps*	16 kg 35 lb 4 oz	Rio Amazonas Amazonas, Brazil	12-Mar-11	Gilberto Fernandes
Catfish, flathead	*Pylodictis olivaris*	55.79 kg 123 lb 0 oz	Elk City Reservoir Independence, Kansas, USA	19-May-98	Ken Paulie
Catfish, flatwhiskered	*Pinirampus pirinampu*	7.68 kg 16 lb 15 oz	Xingu River Brazil	07-Aug-01	Ian-Arthur de Sulocki
Catfish, forked tail	*Hemibagrus wyckii*	2.3 kg 5 lb 1 oz	Temenggor Dam Malaysia	14-Jun-01	Jean-Francois Helias
Catfish, gafftopsail	*Bagre marinus*	4.54 kg 10 lb 0 oz	Boca Raton Florida, USA	10-Feb-07	Nicholas F. Grecco
Catfish, giant (Mekong)	*Pangasianodon gigas*	117.93 kg 260 lb 0 oz	Gillhams Fishing Resorts Krabi, Thailand	29-Nov-10	Martin David Kent
Catfish, gilded	*Brachyplatystoma rousseauxii*	38.8 kg 85 lb 8 oz	Rio Amazonas Amazonas, Brazil	15-Nov-86	Gilberto Fernandes
Catfish, granulated	*Pterodoras granulosus*	7.03 kg 15 lb 8 oz	Xingu River Brazil	13-Aug-11	Martini Arostegui
Catfish, grey eel	*Plotosus canius*	8.5 kg 18 lb 11 oz	Nakorn Nayok River Thailand	04-Apr-02	Ms. Anongnart Sungwichien
Catfish, hardhead	*Arius felis*	2.13 kg 4 lb 11 oz	Dania Florida, USA	11-Apr-14	Angelo Dorry
Catfish, mandi	*Pimelodon ornatus*	1.02 kg 2 lb 4 oz	Japato Amazonas, Brazil	10-Feb-09	Russell Jensen
Catfish, redtail (pirarara)	*Phractocephalus hemioliopterus*	56 kg 123 lb 7 oz	Rio Amazonas Amazonas, Brazil	03-Apr-10	Gilberto Fernandes
Catfish, ripsaw	*Oxydoras niger*	21.5 kg 47 lb 6 oz	Amazonas Furo do Curari, Brazil	13-Mar-10	Gilberto Fernandes
Catfish, shark	*Pangasianodon hypophthalmus*	3.3 kg 7 lb 4 oz	Kong Mae Lai Thailand	18-Jan-13	Philippe Adam
Catfish, sharptooth	*Clarias gariepinus*	42.18 kg 93 lb 0 oz	Orange River Kakamas, South Africa	23-Apr-03	Hennie Moller
Catfish, slobbering	*Brachyplatystoma platynemum*	10.34 kg 22 lb 12 oz	Rio Amazonas Amazonas, Brazil	16-Jun-12	Gilberto Fernandes

SPECIES	SCIENTIFIC NAME	WEIGHT	PLACE	DATE	ANGLER
Catfish, smoothmouth sea	*Arius heudelotii*	10 kg 22 lb 0 oz	Archipelago des Bijagos Guinea-Bissau	03-Apr-02	Jacques Sibieude
Catfish, smooth-mouth sea (TIE)	*Arius heudelotii*	10 kg 22 lb 0 oz	Rubane Guinea-Bissau	02-Apr-03	Michel Garcia
Catfish, suckermouth	*Hypostomus plecostomus*	1.2 kg 2 lb 10 oz	Bung Sam Lan Lake Thailand	25-Nov-02	Dirk Mueller
Catfish, swai	*Pangasianodon hypophthalmus*	21.3 kg 46 lb 15 oz	Bung Sam Lan Lake Thailand	09-May-09	Jakub Vagner
Catfish, Thai shark	*Helicophagus leptorhynshuc*	11.05 kg 24 lb 5 oz	Palm Tree Lagoon Ratchaburi, Thailand	18-Dec-13	Michael Antony Bailey
Catfish, thickspined	*Arius nenga*	.7 kg 1 lb 8 oz	Bang Pakong River Thailand	26-Mar-04	Wayne Chung Wei Lau
Catfish, tigerstriped	*Merodontotus tigrinum*	4.21 kg 9 lb 4 oz	Amazon River Amazonas, Brazil	12-Feb-13	Gilberto Fernandes
Catfish, walking	*Clarias batrachus*	1.19 kg 2 lb 10 oz	Delray Beach Florida, USA	15-Jul-01	Patrick Keough
Catfish, white	*Ameiurus catus*	8.78 kg 19 lb 5 oz	Oakdale California, USA	07-May-05	Russell D. Price
Catfish, white sea	*Genidens barbus*	1.36 kg 3 lb 0 oz	Sepitiba Bay Brazil	04-May-10	Steven M. Wozniak
Catfish, zebra	*Brachyplatystoma juruense*	4.76 kg 10 lb 7 oz	Rio Amazonas Amazonas, Brazil	23-Mar-13	Gilberto Fernandes
Catla	*Catla catla*	18.9 kg 41 lb 10 oz	Palm Tree Lagoon Ratchaburi, Thailand	23-Dec-11	Gerhard Posch
Catshark, brown-banded bamboo	*Chiloscyllium punctatum*	*3.18 kg* 7 lb 0 oz	Kut Island Thailand	07-Apr-12	Steven M. Wozniak
Catshark, small-spotted	*Scyliorhinus canicula*	5.28 kg 11 lb 10 oz	Guerande France	08-May-02	Jacques Andre
Chalceus, pinktail	*Chalceus macrolepidotus*	.45 kg 1 lb 0 oz	Unini River Brazil	15-Nov-05	Martin Arostegui
Char, Arctic	*Salvelinus alpinus*	14.77 kg 32 lb 9 oz	Tree River Northwest Territories, Canada	31-Jul-81	Jeffery Ward
Char, whitespotted	*Salvelinus leucomaenis*	7.96 kg 17 lb 8 oz	Urbyeyah River, Okhotsk Russia	06-Jun-06	Hajime Murata
Chilipepper	*Sebastes goodei*	1.54 kg 3 lb 6 oz	San Clemente Island California, USA	11-Mar-00	George Bogen
Chilipepper (TIE)	*Sebastes goodei*	1.54 kg 3 lb 6 oz	San Clemente Island California, USA	11-Mar-00	Stephen D. Grossberg
Chinamanfish	*Symphorus nematophorus*	13.2 kg 29 lb 1 oz	Dampier Australia	08-Mar-96	Mark Cottrell
Chub, Bermuda	*Kyphosus sectatrix*	6.01 kg 13 lb 4 oz	Ft. Pierce Inlet Florida, USA	05-Mar-97	Sam Baum
Chub, brassy (Isuzumi)	*Kyphosus vaigiensis*	2.83 kg 6 lb 4 oz	Kahuku Hawaii, USA	03-Nov-13	Jamie Hamamoto

RECORDS

SPECIES	SCIENTIFIC NAME	WEIGHT	PLACE	DATE	ANGLER
Chub, Cortez sea	*Kyphosus elegans*	2.44 kg 5 lb 6 oz	Alijos Rocks Mexico	19-Sep-08	Bob Blum
Chub, European	*Leuciscus cephalus*	3.05 kg 6 lb 11 oz	Rhein bei Weil am Rhein, Germany	14-Dec-09	Dieter Lindenmann
Chub, grey sea	*Kyphosus bigibbus*	2.85 kg 6 lb 4 oz	Izu-Oshima Tokyo, Japan	15-Aug-10	Takashi Nishino
Chub, Utah	*Gila Atraria*	.57 kg 1 lb 4 oz	Snake River Idaho, USA	18-Mar-07	Deborah S. Krick
Chub, yellow	*Kyphosus incisor*	3.85 kg 8 lb 8 oz	Sabine Pass Texas, USA	29-May-94	Stephen McDonald
Cichlid, banded	*Heros severus*	.45 kg 1 lb 0 oz	Miami Florida, USA	30-Jul-14	Jan Forszpaniak, MD
Cichlid, giant tanganyika	*Boulengerochromis microlepis*	2.94 kg 6 lb 7 oz	Lake Tanzania Tanzania	02-May-09	Jakub Vagner
Cichlid, Mayan	*Cichlasoma urophthalmus*	1.13 kg 2 lb 8 oz	Holiday Park Florida, USA	20-Feb-99	Capt. Jay Wright Jr.
Cichlid, melanura	*Paraneetroplus melanura*	.91 kg 2 lb 0 oz	North Miami Canals Florida, USA	02-Apr-11	Martin Arostegui
Cichlid, midas	*Amphilophus citrinellus*	1.25 kg 2 lb 12 oz	Miami Canals Miami, Florida, USA	05-Sep-11	Martini Arostegui
Cichlid, Rio Grande	*Herichyhys cyanoguttatus*	.91 kg 2 lb 0 oz	Lake Dunlap Texas, USA	02-Sep-11	Chuck Dewey
Cichlid, turquoise	*Caquetaia umbrifera*	4.76 kg 10 lb 8 oz	Quebrada Yanacue Colombia	31-Dec-10	Alejandro Linares
Cisco	*Coregonus artedi*	3.35 kg 7 lb 6 oz	North Cross Bay Cedar Lake, Manitoba, Canada	11-Apr-86	Randy Huff
Cobia	*Rachycentron canadum*	61.5 kg 135 lb 9 oz	Shark Bay W.A., Australia	09-Jul-85	Peter Goulding
Cod, Atlantic	*Gadus morhua*	47.02 kg 103 lb 10 oz	Sørøya Norway	28-Apr-13	Michael Eisele
Cod, cow	*Sebastes levis*	11.79 kg 26 lb 0 oz	San Clemente Island California, USA	09-Jan-99	Stephen D. Grossberg
Cod, New Zealand blue	*Parapercis colias*	1.72 kg 3 lb 12 oz	Bench Island Stewart Island, New Zealand	25-Mar-12	Scott Tindale
Cod, Pacific	*Gadus macrocephalus*	17.5 kg 38 lb 9 oz	Kawashiro, Kamoenai Hokkaido, Japan	16-Jan-05	Atsunori Takahira
Cod, red rock	*Scorpaena cardinalis*	2.88 kg 6 lb 5 oz	Stevenson Island New Zealand	05-Feb-14	Scott Tindale
Codling, southern bastard	*Pseudophycis barbata*	3.04 kg 6 lb 11 oz	Cape Brett Bay of Islands, New Zealand	09-Feb-13	Scott Tindale
Coney	*Cephalopholis fulva*	.56 kg 1 lb 4 oz	Key West Florida, USA	01-Feb-03	Dennis Triana
Coney, Gulf	*Hyporthodus acanthistius*	14.66 kg 32 lb 5 oz	Huatulco Oaxaca, Mexico	19-Oct-12	George Hurchalla

SPECIES	SCIENTIFIC NAME	WEIGHT	PLACE	DATE	ANGLER
Conger	Conger conger	60.44 kg 133 lb 4 oz	Berry Head South Devon, United Kingdom	05-Jun-95	Vic Evans
Conger, cape	Conger wilsoni	3.4 kg 7 lb 7 oz	Kaipara Flats New Zealand	05-Oct-13	Scott Tindale
Conger, Hawaiian mustache	Conger marginatus	1.81 kg 4 lb 0 oz	Kona Coast Hawaii, USA	30-May-14	Steven M. Wozniak
Conger, Japanese	Conger japonicus	5.77 kg 12 lb 11 oz	Tokyo Bay Japan	03-Dec-02	Phillip W. Richmond Jr.
Conger, mulatto	Enchelycore nigricans	1.32 kg 2 lb 14 oz	Fowey Light Florida, USA	25-May-98	Rene de Dios
Conger, red pike	Cynoponticus coniceps	2.04 kg 4 lb 8 oz	Puerto Vallarta Mexico	24-May-13	Steven M. Wozniak
Coralgrouper, blacksaddled	Plectropomus laevis	24.2 kg 53 lb 5 oz	Hahajima, Ogasawara Island Tokyo, Japan	27-Sep-97	Hideo Morishita
Coralgrouper, highfin	Plectropomus oligacanthus	1.2 kg 2 lb 10 oz	Buso Point Huon Gulf, Papua New Guinea	01-May-94	Justin Mallett
Coralgrouper, leopard	Plectropomus leopardus	9.2 kg 20 lb 4 oz	Susami Wakayama, Japan	06-Jul-11	Tomoki Nakatani
Corb (shi drum)	Umbrina cirrosa	3.1 kg 6 lb 13 oz	Corse France	07-Jun-01	Patrick Sebile
Corbina, California	Menticirrhus undulatus	3.6 kg 7 lb 15 oz	Mission Bay California, USA	09-May-04	Scott Matthews
Coris, yellowstripe	Coris flavovittata	4.62 kg 10 lb 3 oz	Keahole Point Kailua Kona, Hawaii, USA	01-Jan-96	Rex Bigg
Cornetfish	Fistularia tabacaria	1.47 kg 3 lb 4 oz	Miami Florida, USA	06-Jun-14	Austin Porter
Cornetfish, red	Fistularia petimba	4.87 kg 10 lb 11 oz	Goto Nagasaki, Japan	07-Jun-14	Hiroaki Okano
Coroata	Platynematichthys notatus	7.25 kg 15 lb 15 oz	Lago dos Reis Amazonas, Brazil	26-Jun-09	Gilberto Fernandes
Corvina, hybrid	Cynoscion xanthulus x C. nebulosus	4.76 kg 10 lb 8 oz	Calaveras Lake San Antonio, Texas, USA	27-Jan-87	Norma Cleary
Corvina, orangemouth	Cynoscion xanthulus	24.6 kg 54 lb 3 oz	Sabana Grande Guayaquil, Ecuador	29-Jul-92	Felipe Estrada E.
Corvina, shortfin	Cynoscion parvipinnis	4.71 kg 10 lb 6 oz	San Diego Bay California, USA	20-Jun-08	Carmen C. Rose
Cowfish, roundbelly	Lactoria diaphana	.55 kg 1 lb 3 oz	Jogasaki Shizuoka, Japan	02-Oct-11	Takashi Nishino
Crappie, black	Pomoxis nigromaculatus	2.26 kg 5 lb 0 oz	Private Lake Missouri, USA	21-Apr-06	John R. Horstman
Crappie, white	Pomoxis annularis	2.35 kg 5 lb 3 oz	Enid Dam Mississippi, USA	31-Jul-57	Fred Bright
Creole-fish	Paranthias furcifer	.68 kg 1 lb 8 oz	Apalachicola Florida, USA	08-May-06	Scott Rider

RECORDS

SPECIES	SCIENTIFIC NAME	WEIGHT	PLACE	DATE	ANGLER
Croaker, Atlantic	*Micropogonias undulatus*	3.94 kg 8 lb 11 oz	Chesapeake Bay Virgina, USA	17-Aug-07	Norman T. Jenkins
Croaker, black	*Chielotrema saturnum*	.45 kg 1 lb 0 oz	Long Beach California, USA	18-Jun-13	Steven M. Wozniak
Croaker, Boeseman	*Boesemania microlepis*	7 kg 15 lb 6 oz	Chaopraya River Pakkred, Thailand	18-Nov-98	Jean-Francois Helias
Croaker, camaroon	*Pseudotolithos moorii*	.91 kg 2 lb 0 oz	Banjul Gambia	02-Feb-10	Stan Nabozny
Croaker, Cassava	*Pseudotolithus senegalensis*	14.2 kg 31 lb 4 oz	Bubaque Island Guinea-Bissau	04-Aug-09	Michel Delaunay
Croaker, law	*Pseudotolithus senegallus*	15.5 kg 34 lb 2 oz	Luanda Angola	13-Jul-13	Ary Sousa
Croaker, longneck	*Pseudotolithus typus*	15.02 kg 33 lb 2 oz	Banjul Gambia	25-Mar-98	Alberto Hernandez
Croaker, S. A. silver	*Plagioscion squamosissimus*	5.1 kg 11 lb 4 oz	Jatapo Amazonas, Brazil	05-Feb-09	Russell Jensen
Croaker, spotfin	*Roncador stearnsii*	4.48 kg 9 lb 14 oz	Jesus Maria Baja, California, USA	20-Jul-12	Dick Tomlinson
Croaker, whitemouth	*Micropogonias furnieri*	3.75 kg 8 lb 4 oz	Guanabara Bay Brazil	03-Aug-02	Lula Bulhoes
Croaker, yellowfin	*Umbrina roncador*	2.49 kg 5 lb 8 oz	East Cape Mexico	22-May-01	Capt. Jay Wright Jr.
Cui-ui	*Chasmistes cujus*	2.72 kg 6 lb 0 oz	Pyramid Lake Nevada, USA	30-Jun-97	Mike Berg
Cunner	*Tautogolabrus adspersus*	1.59 kg 3 lb 8 oz	Revere Beach Revere, Massachusetts, USA	24-May-09	Sam Mac Allister
Curbinata, black	*Plagioscion auratus*	3.45 kg 7 lb 9 oz	Rio Cuieiras Amazonas, Brazil	15-Jun-13	Gilberto Fernandes
Cutlassfish, Atlantic	*Trichiurus lepturus*	3.68 kg 8 lb 1 oz	Rio de Janeiro Brazil	06-Sep-97	Felipe Soares
Dab (Kliesche)	*Limanda limanda*	1 kg 2 lb 3 oz	Hauganes Iceland	28-Jun-07	Skarphendinn Asbjornsson
Dab, long rough	*Hippoglossoides platessoides*	.99 kg 2 lb 2 oz	Straumbotn Andorja, Norway	23-Jun-03	Dan Lundblom
Dab, long rough (TIE)	*Hippoglossoides platessoides*	1.01 kg 2 lb 3 oz	Straumbotn, Andorja Norway	03-Jul-05	Patrik Tjornmark
Dainan-anago	*Conger erebennus*	5.45 kg 12 lb 0 oz	Oiso Kanagawa, Japan	10-Mar-12	Yusaku Nagai
Dainanumihebi	*Ophisurus macrorhynchus*	2.05 kg 4 lb 8 oz	Shimoda Shizuoka, Japan	16-Apr-08	Takashi Nishino
Dart, largespotted	*Trachinotus botla*	1.36 kg 3 lb 0 oz	Benguerra Island Mozambique	19-Mar-08	Jodie L. Johnson

RECORDS

SPECIES	SCIENTIFIC NAME	WEIGHT	PLACE	DATE	ANGLER
Dentex	*Dentex dentex*	14.25 kg 31 lb 6 oz	Los Cristianos Tenerife Canary Islands, Spain	29-Jan-99	Torsten Wetzel
Dentex, canary	*Dentex canariensis*	9.1 kg 20 lb 0 oz	Lanzarote Spain	20-Jun-09	Juan Carlos Puerto Ortega
Dentex, pink	*Dentex gibbosus*	15.94 kg 35 lb 2 oz	Algarve Portugal	03-Jul-11	Hugo Silva
Doctorfish	*Acanthurus chirurgus*	.57 kg 1 lb 4 oz	Stetson Rock Texas, USA	14-Apr-97	Jerry McCullin
Doctorfish (TIE)	*Acanthurus chirurgus*	.57 kg 1 lb 4 oz	Marathon Florida, USA	01-Dec-07	Dennis Triana
Dogfish, Cuban	*Squalus cubensis*	1.13 kg 2 lb 8 oz	Praia Forte Brazil	23-Feb-14	Steven M. Wozniak
Dogfish, northern spiny	*Squalus griffini*	2.32 kg 5 lb 1 oz	The Trench Tutukaka, New Zealand	10-Dec-13	Scott Tindale
Dogfish, smooth	*Mustelus canis*	17.01 kg 37 lb 8 oz	Cape May New Jersey, USA	16-Jun-07	David E. Spletzer
Dogfish, spiny	*Squalus acanthias*	7.14 kg 15 lb 12 oz	Kenmare Bay Co. Kerry, Ireland	26-May-89	Horst Muller
Dolly Varden	*Salvelinus malma*	9.46 kg 20 lb 14 oz	Wulik River Alaska, USA	07-Jul-01	Raz Reid
Dolphinfish	*Coryphaena hippurus*	39.46 kg 87 lb 0 oz	Papagayo Gulf Costa Rica	25-Sep-76	Manuel Salazar
Dorada	*Brycon moorei*	3.63 kg 8 lb 0 oz	Rio Corcorna Colombia	04-Jul-09	Juan Marcos Tamayo
Dorado	*Salminus maxillosus*	25.28 kg 55 lb 11 oz	Uruguay River, Concordia Argentina	11-Jan-06	Andre L. S. de Botton
Dourado	*Salminus hilarii*	2.04 kg 4 lb 8 oz	Rio Guatiquia Colombia	16-Jan-04	Alejandro Linares
Drum, black	*Pogonias cromis*	51.28 kg 113 lb 1 oz	Lewes Delaware, USA	15-Sep-75	Gerald Townsend
Drum, Canary	*Umbrina canariensis*	.73 kg 1 lb 9 oz	Vila Real Santo Antonio Portugal	12-Nov-06	Luis Ceia
Drum, freshwater	*Aplodinotus grunniens*	24.72 kg 54 lb 8 oz	Nickajack Lake Tennessee, USA	20-Apr-72	Benny Hull
Drum, red	*Sciaenops ocellatus*	42.69 kg 94 lb 2 oz	Avon North Carolina, USA	07-Nov-84	David Deuel
Drum, yellow	*Nibea albiflora*	1.25 kg 2 lb 12 oz	Tamano Okayama, Japan	03-Mar-12	Yukio Takata
Durgon, black	*Melichthys niger*	.68 kg 1 lb 8 oz	Port Lucaya Bahamas	02-Feb-02	Dennis Triana
Durgon, black (TIE)	*Melichthys niger*	.68 kg 1 lb 8 oz	Bimini Bahamas	04-Aug-12	Martini Arostegui

RECORDS

SPECIES	SCIENTIFIC NAME	WEIGHT	PLACE	DATE	ANGLER
Durgon, black (TIE)	Melichthys niger	.68 kg 1 lb 8 oz	Bimini Bahamas	10-Sep-13	Roberta G. Arostegui
Durgon, black (TIE)	Melichthys niger	.68 kg 1 lb 8 oz	Bimini Bahamas	10-Sep-13	Martin Arostegui
Durgon, black (TIE)	Melichthys niger	.68 kg 1 lb 8 oz	Bimini Bahamas	09-Sep-13	Steven M. Wozniak
Eel, American	Anguilla rostrata	4.21 kg 9 lb 4 oz	Cape May New Jersey, USA	09-Nov-95	Jeff Pennick
Eel, conger	Conger oceanicus	6.8 kg 15 lb 0 oz	Cape May Harbor New Jersey, USA	02-Nov-02	Ryan Dougherty
Eel, European	Anguilla anguilla	3.59 kg 7 lb 14 oz	River Lyckeby Sweden	08-Aug-88	Luis Rasmussen
Eel, European (TIE)	Anguilla anguilla	3.6 kg 7 lb 14 oz	River Aare Buren, Switzerland	10-Jul-92	Christoph Lave
Eel, fire	Mastacembelus erythrotaenia	1.4 kg 3 lb 1 oz	River Kwai Ratchaburi, Thailand	26-Apr-13	Benchawan Thiansungnoen
Eel, Japanese	Anguilla japonica	.95 kg 2 lb 1 oz	Yokohama, Kanagawa Japan	04-Jul-10	Yuuma Nishino
Eel, king snake	Ophichthus rex	23.58 kg 52 lb 0 oz	Gulf of Mexico Texas, USA	11-Feb-97	Patrick Lemire
Eel, leopard moray	Enchelycore pardalis	2 kg 4 lb 6 oz	Akazawa, Ito Shizuoka, Japan	25-May-13	Yuuma Nishino
Eel, marbled	Anguilla marmorata	16.36 kg 36 lb 1 oz	Hazelmere Dam Durban, South Africa	10-Jun-84	Ferdie Van Nooten
Eel, shortfin	Anguilla australis	7.48 kg 16 lb 8 oz	Lake Bolac Victoria, Australia	17-Nov-98	Bernard Murphy
Eel, stippled spoon-nose	Echiophis punctifer	7.48 kg 16 lb 8 oz	Port Mansfield Texas, USA	28-Aug-04	Taylor Ashley Walker
Emperor, longface	Lethrinus olivaceus	10.35 kg 22 lb 13 oz	Amami-Oshima Kagoshima, Japan	08-Mar-09	Satoshi Touchi
Emperor, Pacific yellowtail	Lethrinus atkinsoni	.85 kg 1 lb 13 oz	Higashison Okinawa, Japan	02-Sep-12	Tomohisa Nakasone
Emperor, pink ear	Lethrinus lentjan	1.4 kg 3 lb 1 oz	Gulf of Siam Thailand	13-Mar-13	Jean-Francois Helias
Emperor, spangled	Lethrinus nebulosus	9.45 kg 20 lb 13 oz	Muroto Kochi, Japan	19-Sep-02	Takuya Kano
Emperor, yellowlip	Lethrinus xanthochilus	5.44 kg 12 lb 0 oz	Lifuka Island Tonga	25-Nov-91	Peter Dunn-Rankin
Escolar	Lepidocybium flavobrunneum	78.81 kg 173 lb 12 oz	Grand Cayman Cayman Islands	28-Sep-11	Emil Terry
Escolar, Roudi	Promethichthys prometheus	2.44 kg 5 lb 6 oz	Colt 45 Gulf of Mexico Texas, USA	22-Jul-07	Eric Ozolins
Fallfish	Semotilus corporalis	1.62 kg 3 lb 9 oz	Susquehanna River Owego, New York, USA	15-Apr-09	Jonathan McNamara

RECORDS

SPECIES	SCIENTIFIC NAME	WEIGHT	PLACE	DATE	ANGLER
Fanray	*Platyrhina sinensis*	2.1 kg 4 lb 10 oz	Akazawa, Ito Shizuoka, Japan	06-May-08	Takashi Nishino
Fanray (TIE)	*Platyrhina sinensis*	2.1 kg 4 lb 10 oz	Akazawa Ito, Japan	03-May-10	Yuuma Nishino
Featherback, clown	*Chitala ornata*	6 kg 13 lb 3 oz	Sri Nakharin Dam Thailand	26-Feb-03	Terry Mather
Featherback, clown (TIE)	*Chitala ornata*	6 kg 13 lb 3 oz	Bung Sam Lan Lake Thailand	16-Mar-04	Bruce Dale
Featherback, giant	*Chitala lopis*	9.08 kg 13 lb 6 oz	Srinakarin Dam Thailand	21-Apr-06	Anongnat Sungwichien-Helias
Featherback, Indochina	*Chitala blanci*	2.74 kg 6 lb 0 oz	Rathcaburi Thailand	29-Dec-08	Syringa Eade
Filefish, scrawled	*Aluterus scriptus*	2.15 kg 4 lb 11 oz	Pompano Beach Florida, USA	20-Jan-98	Jonathan Angel
Filefish, thread-sail	*Stephanolepis cirrhifer*	1.05 kg 2 lb 5 oz	Kenzaki Kanagawa, Japan	07-Apr-07	Takashi Kumaki
Filefish, unicorn	*Aluterus monoceros*	3.65 kg 8 lb 1 oz	St. Augustine Florida, USA	27-Mar-03	Nathan Zimmer
Flagfin, royal	*Aulopus filamentosus*	.68 kg 1 lb 8 oz	Key West Florida, USA	23-Nov-10	Martini Arostegui
Flathead, bar-tailed	*Platycephalus indicus*	3.7 kg 8 lb 3 oz	Amami-Oshima Kagoshima, Japan	24-Feb-07	Tatsuki Matsumoto
Flathead, crocodile	*Cociella crocodila*	1.05 kg 2 lb 5 oz	Hiratsuka Kanagawa, Japan	30-Jul-08	Rintaro Shinohara
Flathead, dusky	*Platycephalus fuscus*	6.33 kg 13 lb 15 oz	Wallis Lake, Forster N.S.W., Australia	07-Jun-97	Glen Edwards
Flier	*Centrarchus macropterus*	.56 kg 1 lb 4 oz	Little River, Spring Lake North Carolina, USA	24-Aug-88	R. Snipes
Flier (TIE)	*Centrarchus macropterus*	.56 kg 1 lb 4 oz	Lowndes Co. Georgia, USA	26-Feb-96	Curt Brooks
Flounder, arrow tooth	*Atheresthes stomias*	3.86 kg 8 lb 8 oz	Gulf of Alaska Alaska, USA	07-Aug-10	Capt. Jay Wright, Jr.
Flounder, Brazilian	*Paralichthys brasiliensis*	6.25 kg 13 lb 12 oz	Guanbam Bay Brazil	17-Jul-04	Mr. Roberto Silva
Flounder, European	*Platichthys flesus*	2.93 kg 6 lb 7 oz	Maurangerfjorden Norway	10-Jan-04	Anne Karin Lothe
Flounder, gulf	*Paralichthys albigutta*	3.23 kg 7 lb 2 oz	Bogue Sound North Carolina, USA	04-Oct-11	Charlie I. Aman
Flounder, marbled	*Pleuronectes yokohamae*	1.9 kg 4 lb 3 oz	Kashima Ibaraki, Japan	15-May-04	Michiaki Takahashi
Flounder, marbled (TIE)	*Pleuronectes yokohamae*	1.95 kg 4 lb 4 oz	Kashima Ibaraki, Japan	13-Feb-05	Masakazu Naohara
Flounder, olive	*Paralichthys olivaceus*	14.5 kg 31 lb 15 oz	Okinoshima Shimane, Japan	16-Mar-08	Noboru Shinagawa

RECORDS

SPECIES	SCIENTIFIC NAME	WEIGHT	PLACE	DATE	ANGLER
Flounder, slime (babagarei)	*Microstomus achne*	2.5 kg 5 lb 8 oz	Shikabe Hokkaido, Japan	25-Sep-11	Kiyoshi Iwata
Flounder, small-eyed	*Paralichthys microps*	3.22 kg 7 lb 1 oz	Renaca Vina del Mar, Chile	09-Feb-11	Jon Wood
Flounder, southern	*Paralichthys lethostigma*	9.33 kg 20 lb 9 oz	Nassau Sound Florida, USA	23-Dec-83	Larenza Mungin
Flounder, starry	*Platichthys stellatus*	4.79 kg 10 lb 9 oz	Bolinas California, USA	09-Aug-07	Andrew Kleinberg
Flounder, stone	*Kareius bicoloratus*	3.48 kg 7 lb 10 oz	Kamezaki Port Aichi, Japan	02-Oct-09	Taiki Aoyama
Flounder, summer	*Paralichthys dentatus*	10.17 kg 22 lb 7 oz	Montauk New York, USA	15-Sep-75	Capt. Charles Nappi
Flounder, toothed	*Cyclopsetta querna*	.91 kg 2 lb 0 oz	Puerto Vallarta Mexico	24-May-13	Steven M. Wozniak
Flounder, winter	*Pleuronectes americanus*	3.17 kg 7 lb 0 oz	Fire Island New York, USA	08-May-86	Dr. Einar Grell
Flounder, yellowbelly	*Rhombosolea leporina*	.68 kg 1 lb 8 oz	Kaipara Lagoon West Auckland, New Zealand	04-Aug-13	Scott Tindale
Forkbeard	*Phycis phycis*	3.91 kg 8 lb 10 oz	Mahon-Menorca Island Spain	12-Dec-00	Ciceron Pascual
Forkbeard, greater	*Phycis blennoides*	3.54 kg 7 lb 12 oz	Straits of Gibraltar Gibraltar	12-Jul-97	Ms. Susan Holgado
Fusilier, redbelly yellowtail	*Caesio cuning*	.45 kg 1 lb 0 oz	Southern Islands Thailand	17-Apr-10	Steven M. Wozniak
Fusilier, redbelly yellowtail (TIE)	*Caesio cuning*	*.47 kg* 1 lb 0 oz	Kut Island Gulf of Siam, Thailand	07-Apr-12	Anongnart Sungwichien-Helias
Gar, alligator	*Atractosteus spatula*	126.55 kg 279 lb 0 oz	Rio Grande Texas, USA	02-Dec-51	Bill Valverde
Gar, Florida	*Lepisosteus platyrhincus*	4.53 kg 10 lb 0 oz	Florida Everglades Florida, USA	28-Jan-02	Herbert Ratner, Jr.
Gar, longnose	*Lepisosteus osseus*	22.68 kg 50 lb 0 oz	Trinity River Texas, USA	30-Jul-54	Townsend Miller
Gar, shortnose	*Lepisosteus platostomus*	3.71 kg 8 lb 3 oz	Lake Contrary St. Joseph, Missouri, USA	12-Oct-10	George F. Pittman, Sr.
Gar, spotted	*Lepisosteus oculatus*	4.44 kg 9 lb 12 oz	Lake Mexia Mexia, Texas, USA	07-Apr-94	Rick Rivard
Gar, tropical	*Atractosteus tropicus*	14.76 kg 32 lb 8 oz	Rio Frio Costa Rica	23-Feb-14	Dr. Jose Pereira-Perez
Garpike	*Belone belone*	1.18 kg 2 lb 9 oz	La Teste France	14-May-02	David Mesure
Geelbek	*Atractoscion aequidens*	14.91 kg 32 lb 14 oz	Algoa Bay, Port Elizabeth South Africa	16-Jun-94	Carel Sanders
Gemfish, silver	*Rexea solandri*	7.95 kg 17 lb 8 oz	Sue's Rock New Zealand	28-Feb-12	Scott Tindale

SPECIES	SCIENTIFIC NAME	WEIGHT	PLACE	DATE	ANGLER
Gengoro-Buna	Carassius cuvieri	1.88 kg 4 lb 2 oz	Chigusa River Hyogo, Japan	04-Apr-06	Masahiro Oomori
Gnomefish (mutsu)	Scombrops boops	16.1 kg 35 lb 7 oz	Nanbu Wakayama, Japan	05-May-00	Takayuki Nishioka
Goatfish, blackspot	Parupeneus spilurus	1.26 kg 2 lb 12 oz	Kubotsu Kochi, Japan	09-Jul-05	Kenji Tamura
Goatfish, doublebar	Parupeneus trifasciatus	.57 kg 1 lb 4 oz	Fanning Island Kiribati	29-May-13	Martini Arostegui
Goatfish, gold-saddle	Parupeneus cyclostomus	1.36 kg 3 lb 0 oz	Kona Hawaii, USA	28-Jun-13	Steven M. Wozniak
Goatfish, Indian	Parupeneus indicus	.92 kg 2 lb 0 oz	Amami-Oshima Kagoshima, Japan	31-Aug-03	Hironobu Hayashi
Goatfish, Pfleuger's	Mulloidichthys pfluegeri	.91 kg 2 lb 0 oz	Kona Coast Hawaii, USA	02-Jun-14	Steven M. Wozniak
Goatfish, whitesaddle	Parupeneus ciliatus	1.81 kg 4 lb 0 oz	Mokuleia Beach Oahu, Hawaii, USA	08-Sep-13	Jamie Hamamoto
Goatfish, yellow	Mulloidichthys vanicolensis	.55 kg 1 lb 3 oz	Hachijo Island Tokyo, Japan	15-Aug-05	Takashi Nishino
Goatfish, yellowfin	Mulloidichthys vanicolensis	.6 kg 1 lb 5 oz	Paiko Beach Oahu, Hawaii, USA	20-Oct-13	Jamie Hamamoto
Goatfish, yellowstripe	Mulloidichthys flavolineatus	.45 kg 1 lb 0 oz	Oahu Hawaii, USA	13-Nov-12	Steven M. Wozniak
Goby, marble	Oxyeleotris marmorata	2.37 kg 5 lb 3 oz	Chiang Mai Thailand	01-Oct-08	John Merritt
Goldeye	Hiodon alosoides	1.72 kg 3 lb 13 oz	Pierre South Dakota, USA	09-Aug-87	Gary Heuer
Goldfish, Asian	Carassius auratus langsdorfii	1.74 kg 3 lb 13 oz	Myotokuji River Aichi, Japan	25-Apr-12	Takumi Kojima
Goldfish-Carp hybrid	Carassius auratus x Cyprinus carpio	1.58 kg 3 lb 8 oz	Cermak Quarry Lyons, Illinois, USA	22-Aug-90	Donald Czyzewski
Goonch	Bagarius bagarius	75 kg 165 lb 5 oz	River Ramganga India	06-Mar-09	Jakub Vagner
Goosefish	Lophius americanus	23.25 kg 51 lb 4 oz	Stellwagen Bank Massachusetts, USA	12-Apr-08	Robert Solberg
Gourami, giant	Osphronemus goramy	9.05 kg 19 lb 15 oz	Palm Tree Lagoon Thailand	25-Nov-12	Benchawan Thiansungnoen
Grayling	Thymallus thymallus	2.18 kg 4 lb 12 oz	Steinfeld River Drava, Austria	25-Nov-09	Adriano Garhantini
Grayling, Arctic	Thymallus arcticus	2.69 kg 5 lb 15 oz	Katseyedie River Northwest Territories, Canada	16-Aug-67	Ms. Jeanne Branson
Grayling, Mongolian	Thymallus brevirostris	3.12 kg 6 lb 14 oz	Lake Khurgan Mongolia	04-Jun-10	Iurii Diachenko

RECORDS

SPECIES	SCIENTIFIC NAME	WEIGHT	PLACE	DATE	ANGLER
Graysby	*Cephalopholis cruentata*	1.13 kg 2 lb 8 oz	Stetson Rock Texas, USA	02-Mar-98	George Flores
Graysby, Panama	*Cephalopholis panamensis*	.9 kg 2 lb 0 oz	Golfo Dulce Costa Rica	28-Apr-06	Karrie A. Ables
Greenling, fat (ainame)	*Hexagrammos otakii*	3.2 kg 7 lb 1 oz	Omoe, Miyako Iwate, Japan	15-Aug-07	Kazuya Sugawara
Greenling, fat (ainame) (TIE)	*Hexagrammos otakii*	3.25 kg 7 lb 2 oz	Saware, Mori-cho Hokkaido, Japan	29-Jul-09	Takanori Sasaki
Greenling, kelp	*Hexagrammos decagrammus*	1.81 kg 4 lb 0 oz	Gulf of Alaska Alaska, USA	08-Jul-07	Capt. Jay Wright Jr.
Greenling, masked	*Hexagrammos octogrammus*	1.5 kg 3 lb 4 oz	Rausu Hokkaido, Japan	08-Sep-03	Ms. Kazumi Takizawa
Greenling, rock	*Hexagrammos lagocephalus*	2.37 kg 5 lb 3 oz	Kushiro Hokkaido, Japan	23-Jul-11	Masaru Fukuoka
Grenadier, roundnose	*Coryphaenoides rupestris*	1.69 kg 3 lb 11 oz	Trondheimsfjorden Norway	26-Nov-93	Knut Nilsen
Grouper, areolate	*Epinephelus areolatus*	1.46 kg 3 lb 3 oz	Jogashima Kanagawa, Japan	14-Aug-11	Yuuki Kosuge
Grouper, black	*Mycteroperca bonaci*	56.24 kg 124 lb 0 oz	Gulf of Mexico Texas, USA	11-Jan-03	Tim Oestreich, II
Grouper, blue & yellow	*Epinephelus flavocaeruleus*	3.6 kg 7 lb 14 oz	Sardunia Bay Port Elizabeth, South Africa	22-Mar-95	Mario Bruno
Grouper, broomtail	*Mycteroperca xenarcha*	45.35 kg 100 lb 0 oz	El Muerto Island Ecuador	29-Dec-98	Ernesto Jouvin
Grouper, brown-marbled	*Epinephelus fuscoguttatus*	17 kg 37 lb 7 oz	North Nilandoo Atoll Maldives	14-Dec-03	Klaus Bars
Grouper, cloudy	*Epinephelus erythrurus*	.63 kg 1 lb 6 oz	Kut Island, Gulf of Siam Thailand	22-Feb-06	Supachai "Noi" Boongayson
Grouper, comb	*Mycteroperca acutirostris*	5.25 kg 11 lb 9 oz	Cagarras Islands Brazil	05-Jun-04	Flavio Campos Reis
Grouper, comet	*Epinephelus morrhua*	7.65 kg 16 lb 13 oz	Zenisu Tokyo, Japan	06-Apr-06	Masaki Tsuchiya
Grouper, convict (mahata)	*Epinephelus septemfasciatus*	120 kg 264 lb 8 oz	Yonaguni Island Okinawa, Japan	25-Apr-11	Koji Yoshida
Grouper, dot-dash	*Epinephelus poecilonotus*	4.6 kg 10 lb 2 oz	Chagos Archipelago Diego Garcia	31-Dec-10	Phillip W. Richmond, Jr.
Grouper, dusky	*Epinephelus marginatus*	21.25 kg 46 lb 13 oz	Porto Cervo Sardinia, Italy	05-Nov-90	Luca Bonfanti
Grouper, duskytail	*Epinephelus bleekeri*	.94 kg 2 lb 1 oz	Kut Island Thailand	21-Feb-07	Anongnart Sungwichien-Helias
Grouper, duskytail (TIE)	*Epinephelus bleekeri*	.95 kg 2 lb 1 oz	Kut Island Thailand	11-Feb-08	Bruno Binet

RECORDS

SPECIES	SCIENTIFIC NAME	WEIGHT	PLACE	DATE	ANGLER
Grouper, gag	*Mycteroperca microlepis*	36.46 kg 80 lb 6 oz	Destin Florida, USA	14-Oct-93	Bill Smith
Grouper, giant	*Epinephelus lanceolatus*	179.5 kg 395 lb 11 oz	Latham Island Tanzania	10-Mar-04	Shayne Keith Nelson
Grouper, goldblotch	*Epinephelus costae*	1.35 kg 2 lb 15 oz	Detached Mole Gibraltar	09-Apr-95	Joseph Triay
Grouper, goliath	*Epinephelus itajara*	308.44 kg 680 lb 0 oz	Fernandina Beach Florida, USA	20-May-61	Lynn Joyner
Grouper, gulf	*Mycteroperca jordani*	51.25 kg 113 lb 0 oz	Loreto Baja California Sur, Mexico	25-Apr-00	William Klaser
Grouper, Hawaiian	*Epinephelus quernus*	14.42 kg 31 lb 12 oz	Pacific Ocean Midway Atoll	03-Jul-01	Gary Giglio
Grouper, Hong Kong	*Epinephelus akaara*	2.83 kg 6 lb 3 oz	Tsushima Nagasaki, Japan	14-Jun-08	Masahiko Wakana
Grouper, Island	*Mycteroperca fusca*	6.9 kg 15 lb 3 oz	Lanzarote Spain	15-Jun-09	Miguel Cardoso Lopez
Grouper, leopard	*Mycteroperca rosacea*	9.98 kg 22 lb 0 oz	Playa Hermosa Mexico	19-May-02	William Favor
Grouper, longfin	*Epinephelus quoyanus*	.53 kg 1 lb 2 oz	Koh Kut Gulf of Siam, Thailand	12-Mar-13	Bernard Marcand
Grouper, longtooth	*Epinephelus bruneus*	38 kg 83 lb 12 oz	Mikurajima Tokyo, Japan	13-Jul-02	Ms. Naomi Moritani
Grouper, Malabar	*Epinephelus malabaricus*	38 kg 83 lb 12 oz	Bourake New Caledonia	27-Jan-02	Patrick Sebile
Grouper, marbled	*Dermatolepis inermis*	13.78 kg 30 lb 6 oz	Garden Banks Block Gulf of Mexico, Louisiana, USA	09-Oct-10	Jeff Kudla
Grouper, mottled	*Mycteroperca rubra*	49.7 kg 109 lb 9 oz	East Side Gibraltar	13-Aug-96	Albert Peralta
Grouper, moustache	*Epinephelus chabaudi*	55 kg 121 lb 4 oz	Desroches Island Seychelles	01-Jan-98	Charles-Antoine Roucayrol
Grouper, Nassau	*Epinephelus striatus*	17.46 kg 38 lb 8 oz	Bimini Bahamas	14-Feb-94	Lewis Goodman
Grouper, netfin	*Epinephelus miliaris*	.85 kg 1 lb 13 oz	Los Chagos Diego Garcia	18-Dec-10	Phillip W. Richmond, Jr.
Grouper, olive	*Epinephelus cifuentesi*	23.85 kg 52 lb 9 oz	Alijos Rocks Mexico	15-Jun-02	Anthony Crawford
Grouper, orange-spotted	*Epinephelus coioides*	22.5 kg 49 lb 9 oz	Amami-oshima Kagoshima, Japan	13-Jul-03	Kouji Nobori
Grouper, potato	*Epinephelus tukula*	77.85 kg 171 lb 10 oz	Miyako Island Okinawa, Japan	04-Jun-11	Takayuki Shibayama
Grouper, red	*Epinephelus morio*	19.16 kg 42 lb 4 oz	St. Augustine Florida, USA	09-Mar-97	Del Wiseman, Jr.

RECORDS

SPECIES	SCIENTIFIC NAME	WEIGHT	PLACE	DATE	ANGLER
Grouper, redmouth	Aethaloperca rogaa	1.5 kg 3 lb 4 oz	Chagos Archipelago Diego Garcia	31-Mar-10	Phillip W. Richmond, Jr.
Grouper, sawtail	Mycteroperca prionura	14.06 kg 31 lb 0 oz	Palmas Secas Mexico	01-Apr-01	William Favor
Grouper, small scaled	Epinephelus polylepis	1.45 kg 3 lb 3 oz	Charna Island Karachi, Pakistan	30-Oct-10	Hamza Ali Khan
Grouper, snowy	Epinephelus niveatus	31.95 kg 70 lb 7 oz	Norfolk Canyon Virginia, USA	22-May-11	Roger C. Burnley
Grouper, snubnose	Epinephelus macrospilos	1.13 kg 2 lb 8 oz	Kiritimati Island Kiribati	01-Jun-13	Martini Arostegui
Grouper, speckled blue	Epinephelus cyanopodus	19.05 kg 41 lb 15 oz	Chichijima, Ogasawara Tokyo, Japan	09-Mar-06	Mitsuo Takahashi
Grouper, spotted (cabrilla)	Epinephelus analogus	22.31 kg 49 lb 3 oz	Cedros/Natividad Islands Baja California, Mexico	18-Nov-90	Barry Morita
Grouper, star studded	Epinephelus niphobles	11.34 kg 25 lb 0 oz	Zancudo Costa Rica	08-Mar-08	Karrie A. Ables
Grouper, starry	Epinephelus labriformis	.95 kg 2 lb 1 oz	Zancudo Costa Rica	08-Feb-05	Betsi Chatham
Grouper, tiger	Mycteroperca tigris	6.57 kg 14 lb 8 oz	Bimini Bahamas	30-May-93	Michael Meeker
Grouper, Warsaw	Epinephelus nigritus	198.1 kg 436 lb 12 oz	Gulf of Mexico Florida, USA	22-Dec-85	Steve Haeusler
Grouper, white	Epinephelus aeneus	10.5 kg 23 lb 2 oz	Grand Bereby Ivory Coast	21-Apr-99	Patrick Sebile
Grouper, white-blotched	Epinephelus multinotatus	8.65 kg 19 lb 1 oz	Chagos Archipelago Diego Garcia	08-Jan-11	Phillip W. Richmond, Jr.
Grouper, yellow	Epinephelus awoara	.55 kg 1 lb 3 oz	Shimane Peninsula Shimane, Japan	11-Sep-07	Yukio Takata
Grouper, yellowedge	Epinephelus flavolimbatus	22.03 kg 48 lb 9 oz	Dauphin Island Alabama, USA	30-Jun-12	Tyler M. Kennedy
Grouper, yellowfin	Mycteroperca venenosa	19.05 kg 42 lb 0 oz	Cypremort Point Louisiana, USA	26-Jul-02	Jim Becquet
Grouper, yellowmouth	Mycteroperca interstitialis	10.2 kg 22 lb 8 oz	Murrell's Inlet South Carolina, USA	02-Sep-01	Brian Ford
Grunt, African striped	Parapristipoma octolineatum	1.03 kg 2 lb 4 oz	Vila Real Santo Antonio Algar, Portugal	19-Feb-07	Luis Ceia
Grunt, bastard	Pomadasys incisus	.5 kg 1 lb 1 oz	Vila Real de Santo, Antonio Portugal	20-Jan-06	Luis Ceia
Grunt, biglip	Plectorhinchos macrolepus	4.82 kg 10 lb 10 oz	Banjul Gambia	02-Feb-10	Stan Nabozny
Grunt, bluestriped	Haemulon sciurus	.57 kg 1 lb 4 oz	Cap Cana Dominican Republic	25-Apr-13	Steven M. Wozniak

SPECIES	SCIENTIFIC NAME	WEIGHT	PLACE	DATE	ANGLER
Grunt, bluestriped	*Haemulon sciurus*	.68 kg 1 lb 8 oz	Punta Cana Dominican Republic	13-Sep-13	Steven M. Wozniak
Grunt, burrito	*Anisotremus interruptus*	4.53 kg 10 lb 0 oz	Morro, Santo Domingo Mexcio	27-Apr-06	Harold Lance Rigg
Grunt, burro	*Pomadasys crocro*	1.85 kg 4 lb 1 oz	Los Chiles, Rio Fio Costa Rica	04-Dec-95	John Corry
Grunt, longspine	*Pomadasys macracanthus*	.62 kg 1 lb 5 oz	Sierpe Estuary South Pacific, Costa Rica	08-May-05	Carlos Luis Campos Palma
Grunt, Pacific roncador	*Pomadasys bayanus*	3.4 kg 7 lb 7 oz	Savegre River, Quepos Costa Rica	06-Mar-05	Damian Gallardo
Grunt, rubberlip	*Plectorhinchus mediterraneus*	7.92 kg 17 lb 7 oz	Europa Point Gibraltar	10-Sep-96	Michael Berllaque
Grunt, silver	*Pomadasys argenteus*	.8 kg 1 lb 12 oz	Nishida River, Iriomote Is. Okinawa, Japan	24-Aug-06	Horo Izawa
Grunt, sompant	*Pomadasys jubelini*	3.09 kg 6 lb 13 oz	Gambia River Banjul, Gambia	30-Apr-09	Stan Nabozny
Grunt, Spanish	*Haemulon macrostomum*	.57 kg 1 lb 4 oz	Miami Florida, USA	16-Aug-12	Martini Arostegui
Grunt, tomtate	*Haemulon aurolineatum*	.56 kg 1 lb 4 oz	Hatteras North Carolina, USA	13-May-06	John D. Overton Jr.
Grunt, white	*Haemulon plumieri*	2.94 kg 6 lb 8 oz	North Brunswick Georgia, USA	06-May-89	J.D. Barnes, Jr.
Grunt, white (Pacific)	*Pomadasys leuciscus*	.59 kg 1 lb 5 oz	Mazatlan Mexico	20-Jun-99	David Boswell, III
Grunter, javelin	*Pomadasys kaakan*	1.93 kg 4 lb 4 oz	Nomenade River Weipa, QLD, Australia	22-Apr-09	Steven M. Wozniak
Grunter, saddle	*Pomadasys maculatus*	3.2 kg 7 lb 0 oz	St. Lucia South Africa	11-Dec-91	J.J. van Rensburg
Guapote	*Parachromis dovii*	6.8 kg 15 lb 0 oz	Lago Apanas Jinotega, Nicaragua	14-Feb-99	Hubert Gordillo
Guapote, jaguar	*Cichlasoma managuense*	1.67 kg 3 lb 11 oz	Kendale Lakes Florida, USA	10-Sep-06	William T. Porter
Gudgeon, northern mud	*Ophiocara porocephala*	.7 kg 1 lb 8 oz	Tabaru River Yonaguni Island, Okinawa, Japan	23-Jul-13	Yukio Takata
Guitarfish, blackchin	*Rhinobatos cemiculus*	49.9 kg 110 lb 0 oz	Batanga Gabon	11-Jun-98	Philippe Le Danff
Guitarfish, giant	*Rhynchobatus djeddensis*	54 kg 119 lb 0 oz	Bird Island Seychelles	09-Oct-95	Peter Lee
Guitarfish, lesser	*Zapteryx brevirostris*	.68 kg 1 lb 8 oz	Isla Grande Brazil	17-Mar-11	Steven M. Wozniak
Guitarfish, shovelnose	*Rhinobatos productus*	9.75 kg 21 lb 8 oz	Manhattan Beach California, USA	22-Sep-96	Robert Young
Guitarfish, yellow	*Rhinobatus schlegelii*	3 kg 6 lb 9 oz	Akazawa Ito, Shizuoka, Japan	13-Apr-13	Yuuma Nishino

RECORDS

SPECIES	SCIENTIFIC NAME	WEIGHT	PLACE	DATE	ANGLER
Gurnard, bluefin	Chelidonichthys kumu	1.35 kg 2 lb 15 oz	Kaipara Flats New Zealand	02-Sep-13	Scott Tindale
Gurnard, flying	Dactylopterus volitans	1.81 kg 4 lb 0 oz	Gulf of Mexico Panama City, Florida, USA	07-Jun-86	Vernon Allen
Gurnard, grey	Eutrigla gurnardus	.62 kg 1 lb 5 oz	La Middleground Kattegatt, Sweden	20-Apr-98	Lars Kraemer
Gurnard, red	Chelidonichthys cuculus	1.42 kg 3 lb 2 oz	Falmouth Bay Cornwall, United Kingdom	20-Oct-11	Emma Hodge
Gurnard, red (hobo)	Chelidonichthys spinosus	1.35 kg 2 lb 15 oz	Ohara Chiba, Japan	06-Feb-04	Norikazu Fukunaga
Gurnard, spotted	Pterygotrigla antertoni	1.83 kg 4 lb 0 oz	Kumara Patch Tutukaka Coast, New Zealand	12-Jan-13	Scott Tindale
Gurnard, tub	Chelidonichthys lucerna	3.06 kg 6 lb 11 oz	Dieppe France	22-Nov-11	Guillaume Fourrier
Haddock	Melanogrammus aeglefinus	6.8 kg 14 lb 15 oz	Saltraumen Norway	15-Aug-97	Ms. Heike Neblinger
Hake, Argentine	Merluccius hubbsi	1.15 kg 2 lb 8 oz	Rio de Janeiro Brazil	12-Oct-02	Eduardo Baumeier
Hake, European	Merluccius merluccius	13.24 kg 29 lb 2 oz	Sotra Bergen, Norway	09-Jun-14	Judith Saetre Brommeland
Hake, gulf	Urophycis cirrata	2.54 kg 5 lb 9 oz	Gulf of Mexico Texas, USA	16-Apr-96	Patrick Lemire
Hake, Pacific	Merluccius productus	.98 kg 2 lb 2 oz	Tatoosh Island Washington, USA	26-Jun-88	Steven Garnett
Hake, red	Urophycis chuss	5.81 kg 12 lb 13 oz	Mudhole Wreck New Jersey, USA	20-Feb-10	Billy Watson
Hake, silver	Merluccius bilinearis	2.04 kg 4 lb 8 oz	Perkins Cove Ogunquit, Maine, USA	08-Aug-95	Erik Callahan
Hake, white	Urophycis tenuis	20.97 kg 46 lb 4 oz	Perkins Cove Ogunquit, Maine, USA	26-Oct-86	John Audet
Halfmoon	Medialuna californiensis	.82 kg 1 lb 13 oz	Catalina Island California, USA	04-Jul-13	Andrew Chang
Halibut, Atlantic	Hippoglossus hippoglossus	190 kg 418 lb 13 oz	Vannaya Troms Norway	28-Jul-04	Thomas Nielsen
Halibut, California	Paralichthys californicus	30.53 kg 67 lb 5 oz	Santa Rosa Island California, USA	01-Jul-11	Francisco J. Rivera
Halibut, Greenland	Reinhardtius hippoglossoides	4.5 kg 9 lb 14 oz	Kummiut Greenland	28-Aug-08	Kai Witt
Halibut, Pacific	Hippoglossus stenolepis	208.2 kg 459 lb 0 oz	Dutch Harbor Alaska, USA	11-Jun-96	Jack Tragis
Halibut, shotted	Eopsetta grigorjewi	1.15 kg 2 lb 8 oz	Hedate Aomori, Japan	27-May-12	Shu Sasaki

SPECIES	SCIENTIFIC NAME	WEIGHT	PLACE	DATE	ANGLER
Happy, pink	*Sargochromis giardi*	2.45 kg 5 lb 6 oz	Upper Zambezi Zambia	14-Aug-98	Graham Glasspool
Hawkfish, giant	*Cirrhitus rivulatus*	4.3 kg 9 lb 7 oz	Cuajiniquil Guanacaste, Costa Rica	24-Mar-12	Esteban de Jesus Blanco Morales
Herring, Atlantic	*Clupea harengus*	1.03 kg 2 lb 4 oz	Dieppe France	22-Nov-11	Guillaume Fourrier
Herring, skipjack	*Alosa chrysochloris*	1.7 kg 3 lb 12 oz	Watts Bar Lake Kingston, Tennessee, USA	14-Feb-82	Paul Goddard
Hind, peacock	*Cephalopholis argus*	1.58 kg 3 lb 8 oz	Honokohau-Kona Hawaii, USA	24-Mar-05	Lauren Miller
Hind, peacock (TIE)	*Cephalopholis argus*	1.59 kg 3 lb 8 oz	Kona Hawaii, USA	15-Jul-12	Steven M. Wozniak
Hind, red	*Epinephelus guttatus*	3.84 kg 8 lb 7 oz	East Flower Bank Gulf of Mexico, Florida, USA	21-Oct-04	Marcus Trapp
Hind, rock	*Epinephelus adscensionis*	4.08 kg 9 lb 0 oz	Ascension Island United Kingdom	25-Apr-94	William Kleinfelder
Hind, speckled	*Epinephelus drummondhayi*	23.81 kg 52 lb 8 oz	Destin Florida, USA	21-Oct-94	Russell George Perry
Hind, tomato (azahata)	*Cephalopholis sonnerati*	2.35 kg 5 lb 2 oz	Amami-Oshima Kagoshima, Japan	05-Nov-02	Koji Kai
Hogfish	*Lachnolaimus maximus*	9.95 kg 21 lb 15 oz	Georgetown Hole Charleston, South Carolina, USA	11-Sep-11	Wesley Adair Covington
Hogfish, Hawaiian	*Bodianus albotaeniatus*	2.49 kg 5 lb 8 oz	Kanuku Oahu, Hawaii, USA	03-Nov-13	Jamie Hamamoto
Hogfish, Spanish	*Bodianus rufus*	.69 kg 1 lb 8 oz	Stetson Bank Gulf of Mexico, USA	19-Feb-05	Ronnie Vaughn
Hokke	*Pleurogrammus azonus*	2.2 kg 4 lb 13 oz	Shiretoko Hokkaido, Japan	17-Jul-05	Takayuki Kuroe
Horsehead, white	*Branchiostegus albus*	1.15 kg 2 lb 8 oz	Nobeoka Miyazaki, Japan	09-Mar-14	Yukinobu Akimoto
Hottentot	*Pachymetopon blochii*	1.7 kg 3 lb 12 oz	Cape Point South Africa	28-May-89	Byron Ashington
Houndfish	*Tylosurus crocodilus*	4.88 kg 10 lb 12 oz	Goulding Cay Nassau, Bahamas	14-Apr-13	Daniel John Leonard
Houndfish, Mexican	*Tylosurus crocodilus fodiator*	9.86 kg 21 lb 12 oz	Cabo San Lucas Mexico	10-Aug-93	John Kovacevich
Huchen	*Hucho hucho*	34.8 kg 76 lb 11 oz	Gemeinde Spittal/Drau Austria	19-Feb-85	Hans Offermanns
Huchen, Japanese	*Hucho perryi*	10.45 kg 23 lb 0 oz	Sarufutsu River Hokkaido, Japan	11-May-10	Masaki Konishi
Ide	*Leuciscus idus*	3.36 kg 7 lb 6 oz	Grangshammaran Borlange, Sweden	24-Jun-01	Sonny Pettersson
Inconnu	*Stenodus leucichthys*	24.04 kg 53 lb 0 oz	Pah River Alaska, USA	20-Aug-86	Lawrence Hudnall

RECORDS

SPECIES	SCIENTIFIC NAME	WEIGHT	PLACE	DATE	ANGLER
Isaki	*Parapristipoma trilineatum*	1.4 kg 3 lb 1 oz	Nigishima Owase, Mie, Japan	02-Aug-09	Kosuke Hori
Itoyoridai	*Nemipterus virgatus*	1.2 kg 2 lb 10 oz	Hiratsuka Kanagawa, Japan	05-Jan-14	Yuji Hayashi
Iwatoko-namazu	*Silurus lithophilus*	1.5 kg 3 lb 4 oz	Kozuhama, Lake Biwa Shiga, Japan	26-Jun-01	Yoshitaka Sakurai
Izuhime-ei	*Dasyatis izuensis*	1.7 kg 3 lb 11 oz	Izuo'shima Tokyo, Japan	04-Aug-13	Takashi Nishino
Izukasago	*Scorpaena izensis*	1.5 kg 3 lb 4 oz	Numazu Shizuoka, Japan	28-Oct-00	Kouji Kimura
Jack, almaco	*Seriola rivoliana*	59.87 kg 132 lb 0 oz	La Paz Baja California, Mexico	21-Jul-64	Howard Hahn
Jack, bar	*Caranx ruber*	3.32 kg 7 lb 5 oz	Martim Vaz Island Brazil	04-May-12	Fernando de Almeida
Jack, black	*Caranx lugubris*	18.8 kg 41 lb 7 oz	Hurricane Bank Mexico	16-May-13	Robert J. Seidler
Jack, cornish	*Mormyrops anguilloides*	11.25 kg 24 lb 12 oz	Zambezi River Zambia	24-Aug-96	Pieter Jacobsz
Jack, cottonmouth	*Uraspis secunda*	2.27 kg 5 lb 0 oz	Argus Bank Bermuda	28-Jun-14	Cindy Mitchell
Jack, crevalle	*Caranx hippos*	30 kg 66 lb 2 oz	Barra Do Dande Angola	01-Jun-10	Carlos Alberto Leal Simoes
Jack, fortune	*Seriola peruana*	6.12 kg 13 lb 8 oz	Loreto BCS, Mexico	15-Jun-13	Chris Wheaton
Jack, green	*Caranx caballus*	2.81 kg 6 lb 3 oz	Cabo San Lucas Mexico	28-May-00	Jamey Damon
Jack, horse-eye	*Caranx latus*	14.51 kg 32 lb 0 oz	Gulf of Mexico Texas, USA	08-Sep-12	Terry Lee Ramsey
Jack, island	*Caranx orthogrammus*	6.61 kg 14 lb 9 oz	Oahu Hawaii, USA	02-Jan-95	Alex Ancheta
Jack, Pacific crevalle	*Caranx caninus*	17.69 kg 39 lb 0 oz	Playa Zancudo Costa Rica	03-Mar-97	Ms. Ingrid Callaghan
Jack, senegal	*Caranx senegallus*	9.5 kg 20 lb 15 oz	Archipelago des Bijagos Guinea-Bissau	31-Oct-95	Patrick Sebile
Jack, yellow	*Carangoides bartholomaei*	10.77 kg 23 lb 12 oz	Duck Key Florida, USA	19-Nov-13	Douglas J. Pfeffer
Jacopever, false	*Sebastes capensis*	.94 kg 2 lb 1 oz	Hout Bay South Africa	24-Mar-07	George Bogen
Jacunda	*Crenicichla lugubris*	.79 kg 1 lb 12 oz	Tapera River Brazil	10-Jan-04	Martin Arostegui
Jacunda, johans	*Crenicichla johanna*	.45 kg 1 lb 0 oz	Solimoes River Brazil	27-Oct-08	Martin Arostegui
Jacunda, lenticulated	*Crenicichla lenticulata*	.91 kg 2 lb 0 oz	Tapera River Brazil	13-Jan-08	Gonzalo Arostegui

RECORDS

SPECIES	SCIENTIFIC NAME	WEIGHT	PLACE	DATE	ANGLER
Jacunda, lenticulated (TIE)	*Crenicichla lenticulata*	.9 kg 2 lb 0 oz	Agua Boa River Brazil	16-Dec-05	Dan. E. Stockton Jr.
Jacunda, marbled	*Crenicichla marmorata*	.68 kg 1 lb 8 oz	Sucunduri River Brazil	13-Jul-10	Martini Arostegui
Jacunda, marbled (TIE)	*Crenicichla marmorata*	.68 kg 1 lb 8 oz	Sucunduri River Brazil	13-Jul-10	Martin Arostegui
Jacunda, striped	*Crenicichla cincta*	.97 kg 2 lb 2 oz	Rio Preto da Eva, Amazonas, Brazil	22-May-10	Gilberto Fernandes
Jandia	*Rhamdia sebae*	4.3 kg 9 lb 8 oz	Urariquera River Amazonas, Brazil	21-Jan-03	Russell Jensen
Jau	*Zungaro zungaro*	49.44 kg 109 lb 0 oz	Urariquera River Amazonas, Brazil	31-Jan-04	Russell Jensen
Jawfish, finespotted	*Opistognathus punctatus*	1.13 kg 2 lb 8 oz	Turner Island Sonora, Mexico	11-Jun-88	Ms. Lorna Garrod
Jobfish, crimson	*Pristipomoides filamentosus*	4.08 kg 9 lb 0 oz	Kona Hawaii, USA	30-Dec-08	Steve Kwiat
Jobfish, green	*Aprion virescens*	20.2 kg 44 lb 8 oz	Iriomote Island Tokyo, Japan	16-Jul-03	Hiroyuki Manatsu
Jobfish, lavender	*Pristipomoides sieboldii*	8.4 kg 18 lb 8 oz	Chichijima, Ogasawara Tokyo, Japan	05-Apr-98	Yusuke Nakamura
Jobfish, rusty	*Aphareus rutilans*	6.6 kg 14 lb 8 oz	Tokara Kagoshima, Japan	19-May-02	Ms. Yuuko Hirashima
Jumprock, greater	*Moxostoma lachneri*	.57 kg 1 lb 4 oz	Flint River Georgia, USA	13-Sep-12	Martini Arostegui
Jumprock, greater	*Moxostoma lachneri*	.57 kg 1 lb 4 oz	Flint River Georgia, USA	13-Sep-12	Steven M. Wozniak
Jundia	*Leiarius marmoratus*	13.01 kg 28 lb 11 oz	Jatapo Amazonas, Brazil	02-Feb-09	Russell Jensen
Jurupoca	*Hemisorubim platyrhynchos*	1.54 kg 3 lb 6 oz	Miranda River Brazil	08-Sep-11	Fernando de Almeida
Kahawai (Australian salmon)	*Arripis spp.*	8.74 kg 19 lb 4 oz	Currarong Australia	09-Apr-94	Stephen Muller
Kasago	*Sebastiscus marmoratus*	2.8 kg 6 lb 2 oz	Niijima Tokyo, Japan	23-Jun-96	Osamu Hida
Kawakawa	*Euthynnus affinis*	13.15 kg 29 lb 0 oz	Isla Clarion Revillagigedo Islands, Mexico	17-Dec-86	Ronald Nakamura
Kingfish, butterfly	*Gasterochisma melampus*	41.35 kg 91 lb 2 oz	Portland Victoria, Australia	31-May-12	Simon Falkiner
Kingfish, gulf	*Menticirrhus littoralis*	1.38 kg 3 lb 0 oz	Salvo North Carolina, USA	09-Oct-99	Ms. Betty Duke
Kingfish, northern	*Menticirrhus saxatilis*	1.11 kg 2 lb 7 oz	Salvo North Carolina, USA	12-Jul-00	William Graham

RECORDS

SPECIES	SCIENTIFIC NAME	WEIGHT	PLACE	DATE	ANGLER
Kingfish, southern	Menticirrhus americanus	1.27 kg 2 lb 13 oz	Virginia Beach Virginia, USA	29-Sep-02	Chip Watters
Kitsune-mebaru	Sebastes vulpes	2.8 kg 6 lb 2 oz	Shiribetsu Hokkaido, Japan	22-May-10	Masamitsu Okayama
Knifefish, clown	Chitala chitala	6.12 kg 13 lb 8 oz	Lake Clarke Shores Florida, USA	16-Dec-08	Nick Fusco
Kob	Argyrosomus hololepidotus	66.75 kg 147 lb 2 oz	Sunday's River Port Elizabeth, South Africa	22-Nov-98	Ronnie Botha
Kobudai	Semicossyphus reticulatus	14.66 kg 32 lb 5 oz	Shiroura Mie, Japan	04-Jul-99	Shunzo Takada
Koheru	Decapterus koheru	.93 kg 2 lb 0 oz	Flax Island New Zealand	10-Apr-14	Scott Tindale
Kokanee	Oncorhynchus nerka	4.37 kg 9 lb 10 oz	Wallowa Lake Oregon, USA	13-Jun-10	Ronald A. Campbell
Kokuni	Chrysichthys cranchii	30 kg 66 lb 2 oz	River Congo Congo	08-Jan-09	Jakub Vagner
Korai-kitsunemebaru	Sebastes ijimae	1.94 kg 4 lb 4 oz	Shizugawa Miyagi, Japan	06-Jan-04	Tetsuya Abe
Korai-Nigoi	Hemibarbus labeo	3.32 kg 7 lb 5 oz	Ibo River Hyogo, Japan	05-Jan-14	Masahiro Oomori
Kuromenuke	Sebastes glaucus	2.75 kg 6 lb 1 oz	Kushiro Hokkaido, Japan	17-Jun-04	Tetsuya Kataoka
Kurosoi	Sebastes schlegeli	5.1 kg 11 lb 3 oz	Ishikari Hokkaido, Japan	01-Jun-08	Tomohiro Matsui
Labeo barbatulus	Labeo barbatulus	4.1 kg 9 lb 0 oz	Theerasart Thailand	16-Jun-12	Tung Beng Lee
Labeo, orangefin	Labeo calbasu	2.7 kg 5 lb 15 oz	Cauvery River India	17-Dec-12	Jean-Francois Helias
Ladyfish	Elops saurus	3.62 kg 8 lb 0 oz	Sepatiba Bay Brazil	21-Feb-06	Ian-Arthur de Sulocki
Ladyfish, Hawaiian	Elops hawaiensis	6.6 kg 14 lb 8 oz	Southwest Reef, Dampier W.A., Australia	16-Dec-01	Anthony La Tosa
Ladyfish, Senegalese	Elops senegalensis	5.9 kg 13 lb 0 oz	Archepeligo des Bijagos Guinea-Bissau	12-Apr-94	Gerard Cittadini
Ladyfish, springer	Elops machnata	10.8 kg 23 lb 12 oz	Ilha do Bazaruio Mozambique	28-Oct-93	Zaqueu Paulo
Largemouth, humpback	Serranochromis altus	3.85 kg 8 lb 7 oz	Upper Zambezi River Zambia	15-Aug-98	Richie Peters
Largemouth, purple-faced	Serranochromis macrocephalus	.58 kg 1 lb 4 oz	Kariba Zimbabwe	04-Oct-99	Graham Mitchell
Largemouth, thinface	Serranochromis angusticeps	1.66 kg 3 lb 10 oz	Upper Zambezi River Zambia	13-Sep-99	Howard Voss

SPECIES	SCIENTIFIC NAME	WEIGHT	PLACE	DATE	ANGLER
Lates, forktail	*Lates microlepis*	8.3 kg 18 lb 4 oz	Lake Tanganyika Zambia	01-Dec-87	Steve Robinson
Lates, Japanese (akame)	*Lates japonicus*	33 kg 72 lb 12 oz	Shimanto River Kochi, Japan	31-May-96	Yoshio Murasaki
Lau-lau (piraiba)	*Brachyplatystoma filamentosum*	155 kg 341 lb 11 oz	Rio Solimoes Amazonas, Brazil	29-May-09	Jorge Masullo de Aguiar
Leaffish, Malayan	*Pristolepis fasciata*	.9 kg 1 lb 15 oz	Khao Lam Dam Kanchanaburi, Thailand	23-Dec-13	John Duffy
Leatherjack, longjaw	*Oligoplites altus*	1.58 kg 3 lb 8 oz	Rio Coto Puntarenas, Costa Rica	06-Feb-90	Craig Whitehead, MD
Leatherjack, longjaw (TIE)	*Oligoplites altus*	1.58 kg 3 lb 8 oz	Playa Zancudo Costa Rica	27-May-95	Craig Whitehead, MD
Leatherjacket, six-spined	*Meuschenia freycineti*	.68 kg 1 lb 8 oz	Port Hacking Australia	26-Aug-09	Steven M. Wozniak
Leerfish (Garrick)	*Lichia amia*	27.8 kg 61 lb 4 oz	L'Ampolla Spain	30-Apr-00	Oriol Ribalta
Lenok	*Brachymystax lenok*	4.08 kg 9 lb 0 oz	Anui River Russia	02-Jun-00	Thomas Cappiello
Ling, blue	*Molva dypterygia*	16.05 kg 35 lb 6 oz	Trondheimsfjorden Norway	23-Nov-93	Oyvind Braa
Ling, European	*Molva molva*	40.1 kg 88 lb 6 oz	Shetland Islands United Kingdom	05-Apr-02	Gareth Laurenson
Lingcod	*Ophiodon elongatus*	37.45 kg 82 lb 9 oz	Gulf of Alaska Homer, Alaska, USA	27-Jul-07	Robert Hammond
Lionfish, red	*Pterois volitans*	.74 kg 1 lb 10 oz	Miami Florida, USA	07-Sep-13	Capt. Mike Murias
Lizardfish, Atlantic	*Synodus saurus*	.76 kg 1 lb 10 oz	San Eugenio, Tenerife Spain	22-Mar-06	Rob Rennie
Lizardfish, inshore	*Synodus foetens*	1.13 kg 2 lb 8 oz	Miami Beach Florida, USA	12-Aug-03	Joshua Otis
Lizardfish, wanieso	*Saurida wanieso*	3.6 kg 7 lb 14 oz	Tateyama Chiba, Japan	18-May-06	Harunori Kinjo
Lookdown	*Selene vomer*	2.15 kg 4 lb 12 oz	Flamingo Florida, USA	21-Mar-04	Rebecca Wright
Lord, Red Irish	*Hemilepidotus hemilepidotus*	1.11 kg 2 lb 7 oz	Depoe Bay Oregon, USA	26-Apr-92	Ronald Chatham
Lord, yellow Irish	*Hemilepidotus jordani*	1.19 kg 2 lb 10 oz	Kachemak Bay Alaska, USA	02-Aug-08	David Witherell
Lyretail, yellow-edged	*Variola louti*	6.3 kg 13 lb 14 oz	Chichijima, Ogasawara Tokyo, Japan	22-Jun-13	Masako Hariya
Ma-Anago	*Conger myriaster*	1.05 kg 2 lb 5 oz	Hiratsuka Kanagawa, Japan	10-Mar-12	Yuji Hayashi
Machaca	*Brycon guatemalensis*	4.32 kg 9 lb 8 oz	Barra del Colorado Costa Rica	24-Nov-91	Ms. Barbara Fields

RECORDS

SPECIES	SCIENTIFIC NAME	WEIGHT	PLACE	DATE	ANGLER
Machaca (Sabalo pipon)	*Brycon behreae*	2.28 kg 5 lb 0 oz	Rio Savegre Costa Rica	02-May-09	Luis Diego Montero Sanchez
Mackerel, atka	*Pleurogrammus monopterygius*	1.35 kg 2 lb 15 oz	Notoromisaki Hokkaido, Japan	28-Jul-08	Rintaro Shinohara
Mackerel, Atlantic	*Scomber scombrus*	1.2 kg 2 lb 10 oz	Kraakvaag Fjord Norway	29-Jun-92	Jorg Marquard
Mackerel, Australian spotted	*Scomberomorus munroi*	9.25 kg 20 lb 6 oz	South West Rocks N.S.W., Australia	05-Jul-87	Greg Laarkamp
Mackerel, blue	*Scomber australasicus*	2.14 kg 4 lb 11 oz	Hibiscus Coast New Zealand	15-Nov-11	Scott Tindale
Mackerel, broadbarred	*Scomberomorus semifasciatus*	9.3 kg 20 lb 8 oz	The Patch, Dampier Australia	12-Jun-97	Ms. Tammy Yates
Mackerel, bullet	*Auxis rochei*	1.84 kg 4 lb 1 oz	L'ampolla Spain	24-Jul-04	Raul Roca
Mackerel, cero	*Scomberomorus regalis*	8.16 kg 18 lb 0 oz	Bimini Bahamas	08-Jun-13	Jimmy Wickett
Mackerel, chub	*Scomber japonicus*	2.17 kg 4 lb 12 oz	Guadalupe Island Mexico	05-Jun-86	Roy Ludt
Mackerel, double-lined	*Grammatorcynus bilineatus*	3 kg 6 lb 10 oz	Willis Island, Queensland Australia	28-Nov-06	George B. Sowers Jr.
Mackerel, frigate	*Auxis thazard*	1.85 kg 4 lb 1 oz	Portofino Genoa, Italy	24-Oct-12	Capt. Fabio Storelli
Mackerel, greenback horse	*Trachurus declivis*	.59 kg 1 lb 4 oz	Army Bay New Zealand	12-Nov-11	Scott Tindale
Mackerel, Japanese jack	*Trachurus japonicus*	1.19 kg 2 lb 9 oz	Kowaura Mie, Japan	25-Apr-10	Katsuyuki Akita
Mackerel, Japanese Spanish	*Scomberomorus niphonius*	9.35 kg 20 lb 10 oz	Shirasaki Wakayama, Japan	29-Apr-07	Tomoki Nakatani
Mackerel, king	*Scomberomorus cavalla*	42.18 kg 93 lb 0 oz	San Juan Puerto Rico	18-Apr-99	Steve Graulau
Mackerel, narrowbarred	*Scomberomorus commerson*	44.91 kg 99 lb 0 oz	Scottburgh, Natal South Africa	14-Mar-82	Michael Wilkinson
Mackerel, Pacific sierra	*Scomberomorus sierra*	8.16 kg 18 lb 0 oz	Isla de la Plata Ecuador	24-Mar-90	Jorge Begue W.
Mackerel, Pacific sierra (TIE)	*Scomberomorus sierra*	8.16 kg 18 lb 0 oz	Salinas Ecuador	15-Sep-90	Luis Flores A.
Mackerel, queen	*Scomberomorus plurilineatus*	5.56 kg 12 lb 4 oz	Benguerra Island Mozambique	06-May-08	Stan Nabozny
Mackerel, shark	*Grammatorcynus bicarinatus*	12.3 kg 27 lb 1 oz	Bribie Island, Brisbane Queensland, Australia	24-Mar-89	Kathy Maguire
Mackerel, snake	*Gempylus serpens*	4.5 kg 9 lb 14 oz	Yinaguni Iz. Okinawa, Japan	02-Nov-08	Takashi Odagiri

SPECIES	SCIENTIFIC NAME	WEIGHT	PLACE	DATE	ANGLER
Mackerel, Spanish	*Scomberomorus maculatus*	5.89 kg 13 lb 0 oz	Ocracoke Inlet North Carolina, USA	04-Nov-87	Robert Cranton
Mackerel, West African Spanish	*Scomberomorus tritor*	6 kg 13 lb 3 oz	Grand Bereby Ivory Coast	27-Dec-98	Dorchies Jacques
Madai	*Pagrus major*	11.3 kg 24 lb 14 oz	Awashima Is. Nigata, Japan	09-May-05	Katsuhito Takeuchi
Madai (TIE)	*Pagrus major*	11.3 kg 24 lb 14 oz	Kawana, Ito Shizuoka, Japan	16-May-11	Tooru Okada
Ma-Fugo	*Takifugu porphyreus*	.65 kg 1 lb 6 oz	Kurihama Kanagawa, Japan	18-May-08	Junko Kato
Mahseer	*Tor tor*	43.09 kg 95 lb 0 oz	Cauvery River India	26-Mar-84	Robert Howitt
Mahseer, deccan	*Tor khudree*	5.96 kg 13 lb 2 oz	Cauvery River India	14-Dec-12	Jean-Francois Helias
Mahseer, golden	*Tor putitora*	12.25 kg 27 lb 0 oz	Ramganga River India	29-May-08	Jeff Currier
Mahseer, stracheyi	*Neolissochilus stracheyi*	4.5 kg 9 lb 14 oz	Nam Song River Laos	29-Nov-11	Gavin Clarke
Mahseer, Thai	*Tor tambroides*	12 kg 26 lb 7 oz	Jeram Besu, Benta Pahang, Malaysia	24-Jul-01	Mohamed bin Ibrahim
Mandarin fish, leopard	*Siniperca scherzeri*	.7 kg 1 lb 8 oz	Nakdong River South Korea	14-Jun-14	Phillip W. Richmond, Jr.
Manduba	*Ageneiosus inermis*	3.62 kg 8 lb 0 oz	Xingu River Altamira, Brazil	04-Sep-05	Ian-Arthur De Sulocki
Maomao, blue	*Scorpis violaceus*	.74 kg 1 lb 10 oz	The Twins Bay of Islands, New Zealand	04-May-12	Sue Tindale
Maomao, pink	*Caprodon longimanus*	1.01 kg 2 lb 3 oz	Burgese Island New Zealand	23-Sep-11	Sue Tindale
Margate, black	*Anisotremus surinamensis*	6.92 kg 15 lb 4 oz	Fort Pierce Florida, USA	27-Feb-11	Joe Bahto
Margate, white	*Haemulon album*	8.85 kg 19 lb 8 oz	Dry Tortugas Florida, USA	06-Feb-11	Hector Vasallo
Marimba	*Diplodus argenteus argenteus*	1.5 kg 3 lb 4 oz	Guanabara Bay Brazil	31-Aug-02	Flavio Reis
Marlin, black	*Istiompax indica*	707.61 kg 1560 lb 0 oz	Cabo Blanco Peru	04-Aug-53	Alfred Glassell, Jr.
Marlin, blue (Atlantic)	*Makaira nigricans*	636 kg 1402 lb 2 oz	Vitoria Brazil	29-Feb-92	Paulo Amorim
Marlin, blue (Pacific)	*Makaira nigricans*	624.14 kg 1376 lb 0 oz	Kaaiwi Point Kona, Hawaii, USA	31-May-82	Jay de Beaubien
Marlin, striped	*Kajikia audax*	224.1 kg 494 lb 0 oz	Tutukaka New Zealand	16-Jan-86	Bill Boniface

RECORDS

SPECIES	SCIENTIFIC NAME	WEIGHT	PLACE	DATE	ANGLER
Marlin, white	*Kajikia albida*	82.5 kg 181 lb 14 oz	Vitoria Brazil	08-Dec-79	Evandro Coser
Matrincha	*Brycon falcatus*	3.03 kg 6 lb 10 oz	Rio Azul Para, Brazil	27-Jul-11	Guilherme Drigo De Almeida
Meagre	*Argyrosomus regius*	48 kg 105 lb 13 oz	Nouadhibou Mauritania	30-Mar-86	Laurent Morat
Meagre, Japanese	*Argyrosomus japonicus*	66.75 kg 147 lb 2 oz	Sunday's River Port Elizabeth, South Africa	22-Nov-98	Ronnie Botha
Mebaru	*Sebastes inermis*	1.12 kg 2 lb 7 oz	Shirahama Chiba, Japan	19-Jan-10	Shuhei Okada
Medai (Japanese butterfish)	*Hyperoglyphe japonica*	13.8 kg 30 lb 6 oz	Mikura Is. Tokyo, Japan	04-Apr-06	Toru Yamaguchi
Megrim	*Lepidorhombus whiffiagonis*	.95 kg 2 lb 1 oz	Hardangerfjord Norway	05-Aug-01	Ms. Sandra Marquard
Mejina	*Girella punctata*	2.15 kg 4 lb 11 oz	Yokohama Kanagawa, Japan	15-Dec-10	Mari Kitagawa
Mekong pangasius	*Pangasius mekongensis*	8.94 kg 19 lb 11 oz	Luang Prabang Laos	01-Dec-10	Dale C. Fischer
Menada	*Liza haematocheila*	6 kg 13 lb 3 oz	Hamada River Chiba, Japan	30-Apr-08	Toshihiko Shoji
Mihara-hanadai	*Giganthias immaculatus*	1 kg 2 lb 3 oz	Irozaki Shizuoka, Japan	13-Aug-98	Mikio Suzuki
Milkfish	*Chanos chanos*	19.73 kg 43 lb 7 oz	Bocana el Cordonsillo Costa del Sol, El Salvador	01-Feb-12	Javier Vairo Puig
Mojarra, striped	*Diapterus plumieri*	1.02 kg 2 lb 4 oz	West Palm Beach Florida, USA	21-Aug-87	James Black, Jr.
Mojarra, yellow	*Caquetaia kraussii*	.45 kg 1 lb 0 oz	Cienaga la Rica Colombia	07-Jun-11	Alejandro Linares
Mojarra, yellowfin	*Gerres cinereus*	.99 kg 2 lb 3 oz	Jupiter Florida, USA	12-May-13	Tim Oxenford
Moncholo	*Pimelodus albicans*	3.18 kg 7 lb 0 oz	Uruguay River El Salto Dam, Uruguay	23-Jan-12	Roberta G. Arostegui
Moncholo, amarillo	*Megalonema platanum*	.45 kg 1 lb 0 oz	Carmello Uruguay	17-Feb-14	Steven M. Wozniak
Monkfish, European	*Squatina squatina*	25.96 kg 57 lb 4 oz	Fenit, Tralee Bay County Kerry, Ireland	20-May-89	Jim Dooley
Mooneye	*Hiodon tergisus*	.7 kg 1 lb 8 oz	Lake of the Woods Minnesota, USA	13-Jun-01	Dan McGuire
Moray, Australian mottled	*Gymnothorax prionodon*	1.16 kg 2 lb 9 oz	Burgens Northland, New Zealand	11-Jan-14	Scott Tindale
Moray, banded	*Gymnothorax rueppellii*	.45 kg 1 lb 0 oz	Waimanalo Oahu, Hawaii, USA	17-Mar-13	Jamie Hamamoto

SPECIES	SCIENTIFIC NAME	WEIGHT	PLACE	DATE	ANGLER
Moray, blackedge	*Gymnothorax nigromarginatus*	1.4 kg 3 lb 1 oz	Gulf of Mexico Texas, USA	30-May-99	Ronnie Vaughn
Moray, blacktail	*Gymnothorax kolpos*	1.09 kg 2 lb 6 oz	Gulf of Mexico Texas, USA	24-Mar-98	George Flores
Moray, chestnut	*Gymnothorax castaneus*	4.76 kg 10 lb 8 oz	Golfito Costa Rica	19-Dec-13	Martini Arostegui
Moray, green	*Gymnothorax funebris*	15.19 kg 33 lb 8 oz	Marathon Key Florida, USA	15-Mar-97	Rene de Dios
Moray, grey	*Gymnothorax nubilus*	1.06 kg 2 lb 5 oz	Bergen's Point Northland, New Zealand	14-Jan-14	Scott Tindale
Moray, grey (TIE)	*Gymnothorax nubilus*	1.08 kg 2 lb 6 oz	Stevenson Island Whangaroa, New Zealand	05-Feb-14	Scott Tindale
Moray, highfin (Amime-utsubo)	*Gymnothorax pseudothyrsoideus*	1.76 kg 3 lb 14 oz	Kozujima Tokyo, Japan	02-May-04	Takashi Nishino
Moray, honeycomb	*Muraena melanotis*	6 kg 13 lb 3 oz	Grand Bereby Ivory Coast	26-Apr-99	Patrick Sebile
Moray, hourglass	*Muraena clepsydra*	1.59 kg 3 lb 8 oz	Golfito Costa Rica	19-Dec-13	Martini Arostegui
Moray, jewel	*Muraena lentiginosa*	.45 kg 1 lb 0 oz	Puerto Vallarta Mexico	25-May-13	Steven M. Wozniak
Moray, Mediterranean	*Muraena helena*	6.2 kg 13 lb 11 oz	Vila Real Santo Antonio Algarve, Portugal	24-Jan-07	Eduardo Soares
Moray, peppered	*Gymnothorax pictus*	4.99 kg 11 lb 0 oz	Kona Hawaii, USA	09-Jul-12	Steven M. Wozniak
Moray, purplemouth	*Gymnothorax vicinus*	.75 kg 1 lb 10 oz	Port Everglades Reef Florida, USA	19-Jun-98	Rene de Dios
Moray, reticulate hookjaw	*Enchelycore lichenosa*	1.3 kg 2 lb 13 oz	Akazawa, Ito Shizuoka, Japan	02-Jun-14	Yuuma Nishino
Moray, slender giant	*Thyrsoidea macrura*	5.35 kg 11 lb 12 oz	St. Lucia South Africa	29-Aug-87	Graham Vollmer
Moray, snowflake	*Echidna nebulosa*	.57 kg 1 lb 4 oz	Hawaii Kai Oahu, Hawaii, USA	10-Mar-13	Jamie Hamamoto
Moray, spotted	*Gymnothorax moringa*	2.51 kg 5 lb 8 oz	Marathon Key Florida, USA	01-Apr-00	Rene de Dios
Moray, turkey	*Gymnothorax meleagris*	.57 kg 1 lb 4 oz	Kona Town Hawaii, USA	22-Jun-13	Steven M. Wozniak
Moray, undulated	*Gymnothorax undulatus*	1.81 kg 4 lb 0 oz	Hawaii Kai Oahu, Hawaii, USA	02-Jun-13	Jamie Hamamoto
Moray, viper	*Enchelynassa canina*	1.36 kg 3 lb 0 oz	Keauhou Kona, Hawaii, USA	21-Jun-13	Steven M. Wozniak
Moray, yellow	*Gymnothorax prasinus*	2.19 kg 4 lb 13 oz	Flat Island Wangaroa, New Zealand	12-Jul-13	Sue Tindale

RECORDS

SPECIES	SCIENTIFIC NAME	WEIGHT	PLACE	DATE	ANGLER
Moray, yellow-edged	Gymnothorax flavimarginatus	3.18 kg 7 lb 0 oz	Keauhou Kona, Hawaii, USA	23-Jun-13	Steven M. Wozniak
Moray, zebra	Gymnomuraena zebra	.57 kg 1 lb 4 oz	Waimea Bay Point Oahu, Hawaii, USA	19-Jun-10	Steven M. Wozniak
Morwong, blackbarred	Goniistius quadricornis	.5 kg 1 lb 1 oz	Suou-Oshima Yamaguchi, Japan	10-Mar-09	Yukio Takata
Morwong, Peruvian	Cheildoactylus variegatus	.45 kg 1 lb 0 oz	Bujama Mala Peru	28-Feb-14	Steven M. Wozniak
Morwong, spottedtail	Goniistius zonatus	.9 kg 1 lb 15 oz	Nomashi, Oshima Tokyo, Japan	15-Aug-07	Takashi Nishino
Mrigal	Cirrhinus cirrhosus	8.65 kg 19 lb 1 oz	Palm Tree Lagoon Ratchiburi, Thailand	19-May-13	Sasiprapsa Thiansungnoen
Mullet, hog	Joturus pichardi	3.25 kg 7 lb 2 oz	Rio Sarapiqui Costa Rica	09-Aug-95	Carlos Barrantes R.
Mullet, liza	Mugil liza	1.45 kg 3 lb 3 oz	Rio de Janeiro Brazil	20-Sep-99	Erich Filho
Mullet, striped	Mugil cephalus	4.71 kg 10 lb 6 oz	Upper Laguna Madre Texas, USA	13-Mar-09	Scott Lindner
Mullet, thicklip	Chelon labrosus	3.48 kg 7 lb 11 oz	Barseback Sweden	16-Mar-91	Bengt Olsson
Mullet, thicklip (TIE)	Chelon labrosus	3.52 kg 7 lb 12 oz	Ymuiden Zuid Pier, Holland	20-Aug-96	Frits Kromhout vander Meer
Mullet, thinlip	Liza ramada	3.18 kg 7 lb 0 oz	Malpas Cornwall, United Kingdom	07-May-12	Steven Maliska
Mullet, white	Mugil curema	.68 kg 1 lb 7 oz	Rio de Janeiro Brazil	13-Apr-01	Erich Filho
Murasoi	Sebastes pachycephalus	2.11 kg 4 lb 10 oz	Ogatsu Miyagi, Japan	11-Dec-03	Fuminori Sato
Muroranginpo	Pholidapus dybouskii	.5 kg 1 lb 1 oz	Shibetsu Hokkaido, Japan	09-Sep-13	Yukihiro Sakamoto
Muskellunge	Esox masquinongy	30.61 kg 67 lb 8 oz	Lake Court Oreilles Hayward, Wisconsin, USA	24-Jul-49	Cal Johnson
Muskellunge, tiger	Esox masquinongy x Esox lucius	23.21 kg 51 lb 3 oz	Lac Vieux-Desert Michigan, USA	16-Jul-1919	John Knobla
Musselcracker, black	Cymatoceps nasutus	32.2 kg 70 lb 15 oz	Richards Bay South Africa	25-Aug-96	John Harvey
Myleus, redhook	Mylopus rubripinnis	1.5 kg 3 lb 4 oz	Xingu River, Mato Grosso Brazil	18-Oct-99	Capt. Kdu Magalhaes
Nase	Chondrostoma nasus	2.49 kg 5 lb 7 oz	Rhein bei Weil am Rhein, Germany	05-Jan-10	Dieter Lindenmann
Needlefish, Atlantic	Strongylura marina	1.84 kg 4 lb 1 oz	Cape May Reef New Jersey, USA	24-Aug-04	Nicholas Reiner

RECORDS

SPECIES	SCIENTIFIC NAME	WEIGHT	PLACE	DATE	ANGLER
Needlefish, flat	Ablennes hians	4.8 kg 10 lb 9 oz	Zavora Mozambique	25-Dec-97	Leon deBeer
Needlefish, Pacific agujon	Tylosurus pacificus	7.26 kg 16 lb 0 oz	Islas Secas Panama	08-Dec-12	Olivier Charpentier
Nembwe	Serranochromis robustus	3.6 kg 7 lb 15 oz	Zambezi River Zambia	20-Sep-07	Donald John Bousfield
Nigoi	Hemibarbus barbus	3.2 kg 7 lb 0 oz	Tama River Tokyo, Japan	10-Apr-11	Shumpei Yokozuka
Nkupe	Distichodus mossambicus	5.5 kg 12 lb 2 oz	Chete Gorge Lake Kariba, Zimbabwe	12-Dec-00	Malcolm Pheasant
Oilfish	Ruvettus pretiosus	63.5 kg 139 lb 15 oz	White Island New Zealand	12-Apr-86	Tim Wallace
Okina-mejina	Girella mezina	.75 kg 1 lb 10 oz	Miyake Island Tokyo, Japan	05-Jun-11	Fumiya Okuyama
Okin-buna	Carassius auratus buergeri	1.1 kg 2 lb 6 oz	Ichikawa Hyogo, Japan	06-Oct-03	Masahiro Oomori
Okuchi-ishinagi	Stereolepis doederleini	84.8 kg 186 lb 15 oz	Gentatsuse Fukui, Japan	21-Jun-00	Takehiro Isaka
Oniokoze	Inimicus japonicus	.48 kg 1 lb 0 oz	Ikitsukijima Nagasaki, Japan	08-Nov-99	Masaki Takano
Opah	Lampris guttatus	73.93 kg 163 lb 0 oz	Port San Luis Obispo California, USA	08-Oct-98	Thomas Foran
Opaleye	Girella nigricans	.74 kg 1 lb 10 oz	Long Beach California, USA	02-Aug-13	Andrew Chang
Oscar	Astronotus ocellatus	1.58 kg 3 lb 8 oz	Pasadena Lakes Florida, USA	30-Jul-99	Capt. Jay Wright Jr.
Oshitabirame	Arelia bilineata	.95 kg 2 lb 1 oz	Odawara Kanagawa, Japan	03-Jun-04	Harukazu Tsuchida
Ougon-murasoi	Sebastes pachycephalus nudus	1.35 kg 2 lb 15 oz	Motoyoshi Miyagi, Japan	25-Oct-04	Masato Onodera
Pacu, black (pirapatinga)	Piaractus brachypomus	24.95 kg 55 lb 0 oz	Tamarac Florida, USA	05-Oct-10	Gary Roberts
Pacu, caranha	Piaractus mesopotamicus	10.21 kg 22 lb 8 oz	Rio Tarija Bolivia	28-Sep-08	Alejandro Linares
Pacu, Seringa	Prosomyleus rhomboidalis	1.5 kg 3 lb 4 oz	Rio Iriri Brazil	28-Aug-10	Dr. Justin Grubich
Paloma	Brycon rubricauda	.72 kg 1 lb 9 oz	Rio Calderas Colombia	25-Jun-02	Alejandro Linares
Palometa	Trachinotus goodei	.81 kg 1 lb 12 oz	Port Aransas Texas, USA	12-Jun-06	Henry B. Flores Jr.
Pandora	Pagellus erythrinus	3.24 kg 7 lb 2 oz	Dontie Gordo Portugal	16-May-96	Geoff Flores

RECORDS

SPECIES	SCIENTIFIC NAME	WEIGHT	PLACE	DATE	ANGLER
Pangasius, giant	*Pangasius sanitwongsei*	62 kg 136 lb 10 oz	Snom Egg Fishery Kampang, Thailand	05-Feb-13	Bruce Dale
Pangasius, shortbarbel	*Pangasius micronemus*	22 kg 48 lb 8 oz	Seletar Reservoir Singapore	27-Sep-01	Khoo Lee
Pangasius, spot	*Pangasius larnaudii*	11.2 kg 24 lb 11 oz	Ratchaburi Thailand	11-Mar-12	Jean-Francois Helias
Parrotfish, blue	*Scarus coeruleus*	3.63 kg 8 lb 0 oz	Islamorada Florida, USA	10-Jul-14	Austin Porter
Parrotfish, Japanese	*Calotomus japonicus*	1.8 kg 3 lb 15 oz	Jogasaki, Ito Shizuoka, Japan	31-Dec-07	Takashi Nishino
Parrotfish, midnight	*Scarus coelestinus*	4.19 kg 9 lb 4 oz	Key Largo Florida, USA	25-Mar-05	Stephen H. Helvin
Parrotfish, rainbow	*Scarus guacamaia*	4.88 kg 10 lb 12 oz	Key Largo Florida, USA	06-Jun-10	William T. Porter
Parrotfish, redtail	*Sparisoma chrysopterum*	.91 kg 2 lb 0 oz	Islamorada Florida, USA	10-Jul-14	Austin Porter
Parrotperch, Japanese	*Oplegnathus fasciatus*	7.3 kg 16 lb 1 oz	Ushine, Iruma Shizuoka, Japan	09-Jul-03	Toshiro Kawawaki
Parrotperch, spotted	*Oplegnathus punctatus*	12.08 kg 26 lb 10 oz	Hachijo Island Tokyo, Japan	05-May-96	Tsunehisa Kanayama
Pati	*Luciopimelodus pati*	1.36 kg 3 lb 0 oz	Carmello Uruguay	17-Feb-14	Steven M. Wozniak
Payara	*Hydrolycus spp.*	17.8 kg 39 lb 4 oz	Uraima Falls Venezuela	10-Feb-96	Bill Keeley
Peacock, blackstriped	*Cichla intermedia*	3.86 kg 8 lb 8 oz	Villacoa River Valencia, Venezuela	04-Jan-08	William F. Craig
Peacock, blue	*Cichla piquiti*	4.54 kg 10 lb 0 oz	Serra da Mesa Lake Brazil	12-Nov-11	Fabricio Bigua
Peacock, butterfly	*Cichla ocellaris*	5.71 kg 12 lb 9 oz	Chiguao River Bolivar State, Venezuela	06-Jan-00	Antonio Campa G.
Peacock, Melaniae	*Cichla melaniae*	3.3 kg 7 lb 4 oz	Xingu River Brazil	23-Aug-10	Dr. Justin Grubich
Peacock, mirianae	*Cichla mirianae*	4.08 kg 9 lb 0 oz	Ronuro River Mato Grosso, Brazil	10-Aug-11	Martini Arostegui
Peacock, Orinoco	*Cichla orinocensis*	7.31 kg 16 lb 1 oz	Urubaxi River Amazonas, Brazil	12-Feb-10	George Wiltse Walters
Peacock, pinima	*Cichla pinima*	11.09 kg 24 lb 7 oz	Barragem Do Castanhão Brazil	10-Mar-12	Patrick Romulo
Peacock, pleiozona	*Cichla pleiozona*	4.58 kg 10 lb 1 oz	Gatun Lake Panama	03-Mar-02	Horacio A. Clare, III
Peacock, popoca	*Cichla monoculus*	3.18 kg 7 lb 0 oz	South Dade Canals Miami, Florida, USA	22-Aug-12	Martin Arostegui

SPECIES	SCIENTIFIC NAME	WEIGHT	PLACE	DATE	ANGLER
Peacock, popocha (TIE)	Cichla monoculus	3.18 kg 7 lb 0 oz	Cutler Bay Florida, USA	19-Dec-13	Ryan Montesino
Peacock, speckled	Cichla temensis	13.19 kg 29 lb 1 oz	Santa Isabel Do Rio Negro Amazonas, Brazil	03-Nov-10	Andrea Zaccherini
Peacock, vazzoleri	Cichla vazzoleri	4.76 kg 10 lb 8 oz	Sucunduri River Brazil	13-Jul-10	Robert W. Simmons
Peacock, yellow	Cichla kelberi	1.83 kg 4 lb 0 oz	Nova Avanhandava Dam Brazil	03-Jul-13	Gedson Junqueira Bersante
Pejerrey	Odontesthes bonariensis	1.13 kg 2 lb 8 oz	Rio de la Plata Buenos Aires, Argentina	25-Aug-09	Tomas Felipe Restano
Pellona, Amazon	Pellona castelnaeana	7.1 kg 15 lb 10 oz	Caurama Lodge Caura River, Venezuela	15-Jan-99	Stephen Ray
Pellona, yellowfin river	Pellona flavipinnis	3 kg 6 lb 9 oz	Rio Preto da Eva Amazonas, Brazil	18-Sep-11	Gilberto Fernandes
Perch, Chinese	Siniperca chuatsi	4.76 kg 10 lb 8 oz	Seibo Dam Reservoir China	26-Jul-09	Salvino A. J. Bernardes
Perch, creole	Percichthys trucha	.89 kg 1 lb 15 oz	Maullin River Chile	21-Mar-02	Capt. Kdu Magalhaes
Perch, European	Perca fluviatilis	2.9 kg 6 lb 6 oz	Kokar Aland Islands, Finland	04-Sep-10	Kalle Vaaranen
Perch, Nile	Lates niloticus	104.32 kg 230 lb 0 oz	Lake Nasser Egypt	20-Dec-00	William Toth
Perch, pile	Rhacochilus vacca	1.02 kg 2 lb 4 oz	Monterey California, USA	30-Jul-13	Matthew Michie
Perch, red gurnard	Helicolenus percoides	.9 kg 1 lb 15 oz	Sue's Rock Tutukaka Coast, New Zealand	11-Jan-13	Scott Tindale
Perch, Sacramento	Archoplites interruptus	1.44 kg 3 lb 3 oz	Crowley Lake California, USA	22-Sep-95	Richard J. Fischer
Perch, white	Morone americana	1.38 kg 3 lb 1 oz	Forest Hill Park New Jersey, USA	06-May-89	Edward Tango
Perch, yellow	Perca flavescens	1.91 kg 4 lb 3 oz	Bordentown New Jersey, USA	01-May-1865	Dr. C. Abbot
Permit	Trachinotus falcatus	27.21 kg 60 lb 0 oz	Ilha do Mel, Paranagua Brazil	14-Dec-02	Renato Fiedler
Piabanha	Brycon insignis	1.81 kg 4 lb 0 oz	Paraiba do Sul River Brazil	03-Sep-02	Capt. Kdu Magalhaes
Piau	Leporinus piau	2 kg 4 lb 6 oz	Cel. Vanick River Brazil	13-Sep-00	Capt. Kdu Magalhaes
Piau, red	Leporinus brunneus	.45 kg 1 lb 0 oz	Rio Negro Brazil	09-Nov-05	Capt. Kdu Magalhaes
Piavucu	Leoporinus macrocephalus	.45 kg 1 lb 0 oz	Pesqueiro Matsumura Ponds Sao Paolo, Brazil	08-May-10	Steven M. Wozniak

RECORDS

SPECIES	SCIENTIFIC NAME	WEIGHT	PLACE	DATE	ANGLER
Pickerel, chain	*Esox niger*	4.25 kg 9 lb 6 oz	Homerville Georgia, USA	17-Feb-61	Baxley McQuaig, Jr.
Pickerel, grass	*Esox americanus vermiculatus*	.45 kg 1 lb 0 oz	Dewart Lake Indiana, USA	09-Jun-90	Mike Berg
Pickerel, redfin	*Esox americanus americanus*	1.02 kg 2 lb 4 oz	Gall Berry Swamp North Carolina, USA	27-Jun-97	Edward Davis
Picuda	*Salminus affinis*	4.99 kg 11 lb 0 oz	Rio Nare Colombia	28-Jun-09	Alejandro Linares
Pigfish, red	*Bodianus unimaculatus*	1.65 kg 3 lb 10 oz	Motutapere Island Cavalli Islands, New Zealand	01-May-12	Sue Tindale
Pigfish, western	*Bodianus vulpinus*	1.52 kg 3 lb 5 oz	Little Barrier Island New Zealand	26-Aug-11	Sue Tindale
Pigfish, western (TIE)	*Bodianus vulpinus*	1.52 kg 3 lb 5 oz	East Cape Little Barrier Island, New Zealand	28-Sep-11	Scott Tindale
Pigfish, yellowfin	*Bodianus flavipinnis*	1.2 kg 2 lb 10 oz	Kumera Patch Tutukaka Coast, New Zealand	17-Feb-12	Sue Tindale
Pigfish, yellowfin (TIE)	*Bodianus flavipinnis*	1.2 kg 2 lb 10 oz	Kumara Patch Tutukaka Coast, New Zealand	12-Jan-13	Scott Tindale
Pike, northern	*Esox lucius*	25 kg 55 lb 1 oz	Lake of Grefeern Germany	16-Oct-86	Lothar Louis
Pike-characin, golden	*Boulengerella lucius*	.45 kg 1 lb 0 oz	Cano Cuica Colombia	28-Jan-10	Alejandro Linares
Pike-conger, common	*Muraenesox bagio*	7.1 kg 15 lb 10 oz	Markham River, Lae Huon Gulf, Papua New Guinea	07-Mar-93	Barry Mallett
Pikeminnow, northern	*Ptychocheilus oregonensis*	3.57 kg 7 lb 14 oz	Snake River Almota, Washington, USA	15-May-08	Pamela Ramsden
Pikeminnow, Sacramento	*Ptychocheilus grandis*	3.15 kg 6 lb 15 oz	Kaweah River California, USA	31-Aug-02	Hayden Marlow
Pinfish	*Lagodon rhomboides*	1.51 kg 3 lb 5 oz	Horn Island Mississippi, USA	04-Sep-92	William Fountain
Pinook	*Oncorhynchus gorbuscha x O. tshawytscha*	7.25 kg 16 lb 0 oz	Sault Ste. Marie Ontario, Canada	20-Sep-99	David Conlin
Piracatinga	*Calophysus macropterus*	1.34 kg 2 lb 15 oz	Puraquequara Lake Amazonas, Brazil	19-Jan-14	Gilberto Fernandes
Pirambeba	*Serrasalmus humeralis*	2.26 kg 5 lb 0 oz	Iriri River Brazil	25-Jul-03	Doug Olander
Piramutaba	*Brachyplatystoma vaillantii*	5.04 kg 11 lb 1 oz	Rio Amazonas Amazonas, Brazil	16-May-09	Gilberto Fernandes
Piranha, black	*Serrasalmus rhombeus*	3.83 kg 8 lb 7 oz	Jatapo Amazonas, Brazil	10-Feb-09	Russell Jensen
Piranha, black spot	*Pygocentrus cariba*	.68 kg 1 lb 8 oz	Cano La Pica Edo Apure, Venezuela	18-Dec-03	Juan Carlos Campagnolo Trentin

SPECIES	SCIENTIFIC NAME	WEIGHT	PLACE	DATE	ANGLER
Piranha, Manueli's	Serrasalmus manueli	3.85 kg 8 lb 8 oz	Xingu River Para, Brazil	09-Jul-97	Jedediah Colston
Piranha, red	Pygocentrus nattereri	1.55 kg 3 lb 7 oz	Cuiaba River Brazil	07-Jul-94	Dr. H. Siegel
Piranha, serrulatus	Serrasalmus serrulatus	.58 kg 1 lb 4 oz	Rio Urubu Amazonas, Brazil	21-Aug-08	Gilberto Fernandes
Piranha, white	Serrasalmus spilopleura	.91 kg 2 lb 0 oz	Sucunduri River Brazil	12-Jul-10	Martini Arostegui
Piraputanga	Brycon hilarii	3.31 kg 7 lb 5 oz	Sao Benedicto River Para, Brazil	26-Apr-97	Luiz Nolasco
Piraputanga (TIE)	Brycon hilarii	3.36 kg 7 lb 6 oz	Rio Arinos Brazil	03-Sep-97	Marcio Borges de Oliveira
Pirarucu	Arapaima gigas	154 kg 339 lb 8 oz	Amazonia Ecuador	18-Feb-10	Jakub Vagner
Pollack, European	Pollachius pollachius	12.41 kg 27 lb 6 oz	Salcombe Devon, United Kingdom	16-Jan-86	Robert Milkins
Pollock	Pollachius virens	22.7 kg 50 lb 0 oz	Salstraumen Norway	30-Nov-95	Thor-Magnus Lekang
Pollock, Alaska	Theragra chalcogramma	3.23 kg 7 lb 2 oz	Kachemak Bay Alaska, USA	04-Jul-11	Nancy L. Witherell
Pomfret	Taractes rubescens	8.66 kg 19 lb 1 oz	Gulf of Mexico Mexico	04-May-04	Matt McLeod
Pomfret, bigscale	Taractichthys longipinnis	9.35 kg 20 lb 10 oz	St. Augustine Florida, USA	17-Oct-04	W. Gordon Davis
Pomfret, Brevort's	Eumegistus brevorti	3.06 kg 6 lb 12 oz	Bimini Bahamas	16-Nov-98	Horst Schneider
Pomfret, lustrous	Eumegistus illustris	7.71 kg 17 lb 0 oz	Kona Hawaii, USA	06-Jul-05	George Bogen
Pomfret, Pacific	Brama japonica	2 kg 4 lb 6 oz	Jogashima Kanagawa, Japan	05-May-13	Yukihiro Sakamoto
Pompano, African	Alectis ciliaris	22.9 kg 50 lb 8 oz	Daytona Beach Florida, USA	21-Apr-90	Tom Sargent
Pompano, blackblotch	Trachinotus kennedyi	11.06 kg 24 lb 6 oz	Puerto Vallarta Mexico	18-Sep-07	Larry R. Walker
Pompano, dolphin	Coryphaena equiselis	3.86 kg 8 lb 8 oz	Baltimore Canyon Maryland, USA	07-Aug-08	Charles Champon
Pompano, Florida	Trachinotus carolinus	3.76 kg 8 lb 4 oz	Port St. Joe Bay Florida, USA	16-Oct-99	Barry Huston
Pompano, gafftopsail	Trachinotus rhodopus	1.7 kg 3 lb 12 oz	Rancho Leonero, Baja California Sur, Mexico	24-Apr-06	Brett Philip
Pompano, Irish	Diapterus auratus	.68 kg 1 lb 8 oz	St. Lucie River Florida, USA	17-Dec-00	Richard Morgan, Sr.

RECORDS

SPECIES	SCIENTIFIC NAME	WEIGHT	PLACE	DATE	ANGLER
Pompano, snubnose	Trachinotus blochi	3.4 kg 7 lb 7 oz	Port Hedland W.A., Australia	29-Apr-01	Anthony Boekhorst
Pompano, southern	Trachinotus africanus	6.23 kg 13 lb 12 oz	Karachi Pakistan	28-Feb-04	Asif Khan
Porae	Nemadactylus douglasi	2 kg 4 lb 6 oz	Tokerau Beach New Zealand	10-Jan-14	Anna Cameron
Porcupinefish	Diodon hystrix	3.74 kg 8 lb 4 oz	Haleiwa Harbor Oahu, Hawaii, USA	19-Jun-10	Steven M. Wozniak
Porcupinefish, black-blotched	Diodon liturosus	1.05 kg 2 lb 5 oz	Koh Kut Island, Gulf of Siam Thailand	10-Feb-06	Lootjirot Panphrapat
Porcupinefish, longspine	Diodon holocanthus	.95 kg 2 lb 1 oz	Kataura Kagoshima, Japan	02-Jul-05	Katsuhiko Ohana
Porgy, black	Acanthopagrus schlegeli	4.25 kg 9 lb 5 oz	Nanko, Osaka Bay Japan	17-Jul-10	Mikio Watanabe
Porgy, Canary	Dentex canariensis	8.06 kg 17 lb 12 oz	Monte Gordo Portugal	14-Jul-97	Joseph Triay
Porgy, jolthead	Calamus bajonado	10.54 kg 23 lb 4 oz	Madeira Beach Florida, USA	14-Mar-90	Harm Wilder
Porgy, knobbed	Calamus nodosus	2.63 kg 5 lb 12 oz	Gulf of Mexico Texas, USA	21-Feb-00	Stanley Sweet
Porgy, littlehead	Calamus proridens	.56 kg 1 lb 4 oz	Elliot Key Florida, USA	08-Feb-03	Dennis Triana
Porgy, littlehead (TIE)	Calamus proridens	.56 kg 1 lb 4 oz	Key Largo Florida, USA	06-Dec-03	Dennis Triana
Porgy, pluma	Calamus pennatula	.45 kg 1 lb 0 oz	Key Largo Florida, USA	19-Jan-04	Dennis Triana
Porgy, red	Pagrus pagrus	7.72 kg 17 lb 0 oz	Gibraltar	12-Jul-97	Richard Gomila
Porgy, saucereye	Calamus calamus	4.08 kg 9 lb 0 oz	Longboat Key Mexico	02-Oct-04	Bucky Wolden
Porgy, sheepshead	Calamus penna	3.95 kg 8 lb 11 oz	Tijucas Island, Rio de Janeiro Brazil	19-Jan-07	Flavio Campos Reis
Porgy, whitebone	Calamus leucosteus	1.7 kg 3 lb 12 oz	Hatteras North Carolina, USA	24-Jul-14	Michael E. Hayes
Porkfish	Anisotremus virginicus	.99 kg 2 lb 3 oz	Key Largo Florida, USA	30-Apr-06	Austin Porter
Pouting	Trisopterus luscus	.92 kg 2 lb 0 oz	Boulogne Sur Mer France	16-Oct-11	Guillaume Fourrier
Powan	Coregonus lavaretus	5.39 kg 11 lb 14 oz	Skrabean Nymolla, Sweden	15-Dec-94	Allan Englund
Prickleback, monkeyface	Cebidichthys violaceus	1.47 kg 3 lb 4 oz	Yaquina Bay Newport, Oregan, USA	29-Jun-08	Todd Pietsch

SPECIES	SCIENTIFIC NAME	WEIGHT	PLACE	DATE	ANGLER
Puddingwife	*Halichoeres radiatus*	1.58 kg 3 lb 8 oz	Key West Florida, USA	26-Apr-03	David Pesi
Puffer, oceanic	*Lagocephalus lagocephalus*	3.17 kg 7 lb 0 oz	Sandy Hook New Jersey, USA	28-Aug-91	Ms. Jane Jagen
Puffer, panther (higan-fugu)	*Takifugu pardalis*	1.2 kg 2 lb 10 oz	Nojima Kanagawa, Japan	30-Mar-09	Takashi Nishino
Puffer, prickly	*Ephippion guttifer*	5 kg 11 lb 0 oz	Grand Bereby Ivory Coast	27-Nov-98	Patrick Sebile
Puffer, smooth	*Lagocephalus laevigatus*	5.21 kg 11 lb 7 oz	Cape May Inlet New Jersey, USA	24-Aug-01	Shawn Clark
Puffer, whitespotted	*Arothron hispidus*	2.01 kg 4 lb 7 oz	Iroquois Point Hawaii, USA	31-Oct-92	George Cornish
Pufferfish, Japanese	*Takifugu rubripes*	1.35 kg 2 lb 15 oz	Enoshima Kanagawa, Japan	26-May-13	Tetsuo Oshima
Pumpkinseed	*Lepomis gibbosus*	.63 kg 1 lb 6 oz	Mexico New York, USA	27-Apr-85	Ms. Heather Finch
Queenfish, doublespotted	*Scomberoides lysan*	3.29 kg 7 lb 4 oz	Benguerra Island Mozambique	04-Jun-08	Stan Nabozny
Queenfish, needlescaled	*Scomberoides tol*	1.02 kg 2 lb 4 oz	Bazaruto Archipelago Mozambique	22-Mar-08	Jodie L. Johnson
Queenfish, talang	*Scomberoides commersonianus*	17.89 kg 39 lb 7 oz	Umkomaas South Africa	23-May-10	Craig Oliver
Quillback	*Carpiodes cyprinus*	2.94 kg 6 lb 8 oz	Lake Michigan Indiana, USA	15-Jan-93	Mike Berg
Ratfish, spotted	*Hydrolagus colliei*	1.29 kg 2 lb 13 oz	Tacoma Washington, USA	23-Apr-97	Kenneth Dunn
Raven, sea	*Hemitripterus villosus*	2.4 kg 5 lb 4 oz	Muroran Hokkaido, Japan	09-Nov-13	Satoshi Yamaguchi
Ray, backwater butterfly	*Gymnura natalensis*	82.6 kg 182 lb 1 oz	Knysna Lagoon South Africa	11-Jul-92	Hilton Gervais
Ray, bat	*Myliobatis californica*	82.1 kg 181 lb 0 oz	Huntington Beach Pier California, USA	30-Jun-78	Bradley Dew
Ray, blonde	*Raja brachyura*	14.28 kg 31 lb 8 oz	Jersey Channel Islands United Kingdom	03-Apr-89	John Thompson
Ray, bluespotted ribbontail	*Taeniura lymma*	1.43 kg 3 lb 2 oz	Kut Island Thailand	18-Jan-06	Steven M. Wozniak
Ray, bull	*Pteromylaeus bovinus*	46.6 kg 102 lb 11 oz	Cape Skirring Senegal	18-Feb-99	Daniel Bidel
Ray, bull (Australian)	*Myliobatis australis*	66 kg 145 lb 8 oz	Port River Australia	02-Sep-07	Steven Evangelou
Ray, common eagle	*Myliobatis aquila*	27.5 kg 60 lb 10 oz	Pyla France	09-Sep-96	Patrick Sebile

RECORDS

SPECIES	SCIENTIFIC NAME	WEIGHT	PLACE	DATE	ANGLER
Ray, discus	*Paratrygon aiereba*	53 kg 116 lb 13 oz	Rio Negro and Branco Brazil	20-Dec-00	Keith Sutton
Ray, eagle	*Myliobatis tenuicaudatus*	32.85 kg 72 lb 6 oz	Omokoiti Flats Kaipara Harbour, New Zealand	21-Jun-12	Sue Tindale
Ray, Japanese eagle	*Myliobatis tobijei*	45.5 kg 100 lb 4 oz	Tsushima Nagasaki, Japan	04-Nov-05	Kei Hiramatsu
Ray, longheaded eagle	*Aetobatus flagellum*	32.48 kg 71 lb 9 oz	Himeji Port Hyogo, Japan	11-Jul-02	Masahiro Oomori
Ray, painted	*Raja microocellata*	4.5 kg 9 lb 15 oz	Jersey Channel Islands, United Kingdom	02-Aug-88	Andrew Mitchell
Ray, pale	*Raja lintea*	11.15 kg 24 lb 9 oz	Langesund Stavern, Norway	13-Jun-99	Bjorn Persson
Ray, southern fiddler	*Trygonorrhina fasciata*	6.7 kg 14 lb 12 oz	Marion Bay South Australia, Australia	11-Aug-90	Marcel Vandergoot
Ray, spiny butterfly	*Gymnura altavela*	60 kg 132 lb 4 oz	Nouadhibou Mauritania	05-May-84	Robin Michel
Ray, spotted eagle	*Aetobatus narinari*	124.06 kg 273 lb 8 oz	Galveston Bay Texas, USA	02-Jun-12	Jimmy L. Anderson
Ray, starry	*Raja asterias*	1.4 kg 3 lb 1 oz	Vila Real Santo Antonio Algarve, Portugal	23-Mar-07	Luis Ceia
Ray, thornback	*Raja clavata*	7.59 kg 16 lb 12 oz	Jersey, Channel Islands United Kingdom	11-Jul-88	John Thompson
Ray, undulate	*Raja undulata*	4.2 kg 9 lb 4 oz	Arcachon France	18-May-01	Patrick Sebile
Rebeca	*Megalodoras uranoscopus*	3 kg 6 lb 9 oz	Xingu River Brazil	30-May-03	Capt. Kdu Magalhaes
Red devil	*Amphilophus labiatus*	.45 kg 1 lb 0 oz	Wahiawa Reservoir Oahu, Hawaii, USA	03-Oct-12	Dennis Triana
Red devil (TIE)	*Amphilophus labiatus*	.45 kg 1 lb 0 oz	Lake Wilson Wahiawa, Hawaii, USA	08-May-13	Martini Arostegui
Redfin, Pacific	*Tribolodon brandti*	2.5 kg 5 lb 8 oz	Tama River Kanagawa, Japan	16-Mar-12	Phillip W. Richmond, Jr.
Redfish	*Centroberyx affinis*	2.85 kg 6 lb 4 oz	Kumera Patch New Zealand	17-Feb-12	Sue Tindale
Redfish, Acadian	*Sebastes faciatus*	1.13 kg 2 lb 8 oz	Grindavik Iceland	13-Jun-10	George Bogen
Redfish, golden	*Sebastes norvegieus*	12.14 kg 26 lb 12 oz	Heidrun Statoil Oil Rig, Norway	21-Nov-12	Alexander R. Thomassen
Redhorse, black	*Moxostoma duquesnei*	1.02 kg 2 lb 4 oz	French Creek, Franklin Pennsylvania, USA	22-Feb-98	Richard Faler, Jr.
Redhorse, blacktail	*Moxostoma poecilurum*	.68 kg 1 lb 8 oz	Tallapoosa River Alabama, USA	24-Apr-05	Max W. Beebe

SPECIES	SCIENTIFIC NAME	WEIGHT	PLACE	DATE	ANGLER
Redhorse, golden	Moxostoma erythrurum	1.85 kg 4 lb 1 oz	French Creek Franklin, Pennsylvania, USA	09-Feb-97	Richard Faler, Jr.
Redhorse, greater	Moxostoma valenciennesi	4.16 kg 9 lb 3 oz	Salmon River, Pulaski New York, USA	11-May-85	Jason Wilson
Redhorse, river	Moxostoma carinatum	4.08 kg 9 lb 0 oz	Muskegon River Michigan, USA	09-Jun-01	Andy Tulgetske
Redhorse, shorthead	Moxostoma macrolepidotum	5.75 kg 12 lb 11 oz	Sauk River, Melrose Minnesota, USA	20-May-05	Robin Schmitz
Redhorse, silver	Moxostoma anisurum	5.18 kg 11 lb 7 oz	Plum Creek Wisconsin, USA	29-May-85	Neal Long
Remora, common	Remora remora	2.49 kg 5 lb 8 oz	Cat Cay Bahamas	12-Jun-02	Michael Orleans
Roach	Rutilus rutilus	1.84 kg 4 lb 1 oz	Colwick Nottingham, United Kingdom	16-Jun-75	R. Jones
Roach-Bream	Rutillus rutilus x Abramis brama	3.52 kg 7 lb 12 oz	Norfolk Estate Lakes United Kingdom	25-Jun-08	John Bailey
Rock-bacu	Lithodoras dorsalis	21 kg 46 lb 4 oz	Parana do Cambixe Amazonas, Brazil	21-Dec-13	Gilberto Fernandes
Rockcod, bluelined	Cephalopholis formosa	.7 kg 1 lb 8 oz	Kut Island Thailand	08-Feb-06	Jean-Francois Helias
Rockfish, bank	Sebastes rufus	1.98 kg 4 lb 6 oz	San Clemente Island California, USA	14-Feb-98	Stephen D. Grossberg
Rockfish, black	Sebastes melanops	6.03 kg 13 lb 5 oz	Gulf of Alaska Alaska, USA	12-Aug-05	Ashley Eslick
Rockfish, blackgill	Sebastes melanostomus	3.53 kg 7 lb 12 oz	San Clemente Island California, USA	27-Dec-00	Stephen D. Grossberg
Rockfish, blue	Sebastes mystinus	3.79 kg 8 lb 6 oz	Whaler's Cove Alaska, USA	27-Jul-94	Dr. John Whitaker
Rockfish, bronzespotted	Sebastes gilli	4.96 kg 10 lb 15 oz	San Clemente Island California, USA	25-Mar-00	George Bogen
Rockfish, brown	Sebastes auriculatus	1.81 kg 4 lb 0 oz	San Gregorio California, USA	13-Jul-08	Hin Fan Tsang
Rockfish, canary	Sebastes pinniger	4.53 kg 10 lb 0 oz	Westport Washington, USA	17-May-86	Terry Rudnick
Rockfish, chameleon	Sebastes phillipsi	1.22 kg 2 lb 11 oz	San Clemente Island California, USA	14-Mar-01	Stephen D. Grossberg
Rockfish, China	Sebastes nebulosus	1.84 kg 4 lb 1 oz	Gulf of Alaska Alaska, USA	15-Jun-11	Howard B. Rudnick
Rockfish, copper	Sebastes caurinus	3.6 kg 7 lb 15 oz	Shelter Cove Humboldt County, California, USA	11-Aug-14	Daniel K. Stamos
Rockfish, dusky	Sebastes ciliatus	2.81 kg 6 lb 3 oz	Knight Island Alaska, USA	29-Jul-13	Wayne Dobbs
Rockfish, flag	Sebastes rubrivinctus	1.45 kg 3 lb 3 oz	San Clemente Island California, USA	14-Feb-99	Stephen D. Grossberg

RECORDS

SPECIES	SCIENTIFIC NAME	WEIGHT	PLACE	DATE	ANGLER
Rockfish, goldeye	Sebastes thompsoni	1.1 kg 2 lb 6 oz	Oshika Miyagi, Japan	03-Mar-05	Fuminori Sato
Rockfish, gopher	Sebastes carnatus	2.83 kg 6 lb 4 oz	Pillar Point California, USA	17-Aug-08	Hin Fan Tsang
Rockfish, grass	Sebastes rastrelliger	2.89 kg 6 lb 6 oz	Yaquina Bay Newport, Oregon, USA	18-Mar-07	Darryoush E. Pishvai
Rockfish, grass (TIE)	Sebastes rastrelliger	2.89 kg 6 lb 6 oz	Newport Oregon, USA	30-Mar-07	Todd Pietsch
Rockfish, greenspotted	Sebastes chlorostictus	1.01 kg 2 lb 3 oz	San Clemente Island California, USA	04-Nov-00	Stephen D. Grossberg
Rockfish, greenstriped	Sebastes elongatus	.63 kg 1 lb 6 oz	San Clemente Island California, USA	18-Mar-00	Stephen D. Grossberg
Rockfish, honeycomb	Sebastes umbrosus	.57 kg 1 lb 4 oz	San Martin Island Baja California Sur, Mexico	27-Oct-00	Stephen D. Grossberg
Rockfish, kelp	Sebastes atrovirens	.91 kg 2 lb 0 oz	Pacific Grove California, USA	14-Aug-13	Martini Arostegui
Rockfish, Mexican	Sebastes macdonaldi	2.72 kg 6 lb 0 oz	San Clemente Island California, USA	09-Dec-00	Stephen D. Grossberg
Rockfish, olive	Sebastes serranoides	1.8 kg 3 lb 15 oz	Carmel Bay California, USA	28-Sep-06	David J. Babineau
Rockfish, pink	Sebastes eos	2.9 kg 6 lb 9 oz	San Clemente Island California, USA	03-Mar-02	Stephen D. Grossberg
Rockfish, quillback	Sebastes maliger	3.28 kg 7 lb 4 oz	Depoe Bay Oregon, USA	18-Mar-90	Kelly Canaday
Rockfish, redbanded	Sebastes babcocki	4.44 kg 9 lb 12 oz	Whaler's Cove Alaska, USA	11-Jul-99	Thomas Stroud
Rockfish, Rosethorn	Sebastes helvomaculatus	1.49 kg 3 lb 4 oz	Elrington Island Alaska, USA	20-Jul-04	Bob Martin
Rockfish, rougheye	Sebastes aleutianus	6.69 kg 14 lb 12 oz	Langara Island British Columbia, Canada	18-Aug-07	George Bogen
Rockfish, shortraker	Sebastes borealis	18.46 kg 40 lb 11 oz	Cross Sound Alaska, USA	22-Jun-13	Eric Christopher Otte
Rockfish, silvergray	Sebastes brevispinis	7.37 kg 16 lb 4 oz	Elfin Cove Alaska, USA	02-Jul-12	Jessica DeVeies
Rockfish, speckled	Sebastes ovalis	.95 kg 2 lb 1 oz	Santa Barbara Island California, USA	04-Dec-99	Bill Grossberg
Rockfish, splitnose	Sebastes diploproa	.81 kg 1 lb 12 oz	San Clemente Island California, USA	17-Mar-01	Stephen D. Grossberg
Rockfish, starry	Sebastes constellatus	1.25 kg 2 lb 12 oz	Point Loma California, USA	27-Oct-13	Justin Domaguin
Rockfish, tiger	Sebastes nigrocinctus	3.14 kg 6 lb 15 oz	Elfin Cove Alaska, USA	05-Aug-05	David A. Browne
Rockfish, tiger (TIE)	Sebastes nigrocinctus	3.17 kg 7 lb 0 oz	Chugach Island Alaska, USA	07-Aug-05	Nicole Loffredo

SPECIES	SCIENTIFIC NAME	WEIGHT	PLACE	DATE	ANGLER
Rockfish, vermillion	*Sebastes miniatus*	5.45 kg 12 lb 0 oz	Depoe Bay Oregon, USA	02-Jun-90	Joseph Lowe
Rockfish, widow	*Sebastes entomelas*	2.43 kg 5 lb 6 oz	Elfin Cove Alaska, USA	24-Aug-03	Keith Sturm
Rockfish, yelloweye	*Sebastes ruberrimus*	17.82 kg 39 lb 4 oz	Whalers Cove Alaska, USA	18-Jul-00	David Mundhenke
Rockfish, yellowtail	*Sebastes flavidus*	3.32 kg 7 lb 5 oz	Mayne Island British Columbia, Canada	06-May-12	Jason Ritter
Rohu	*Labeo rohita*	12.5 kg 27 lb 8 oz	Dan Tchang Dam Thailand	08-Jul-03	Pakron Suwannaat
Roosterfish	*Nematistius pectoralis*	51.71 kg 114 lb 0 oz	La Paz Baja California, Mexico	01-Jun-60	Abe Sackheim
Rosefish, blackbelly	*Helicolenus dactylopterus*	2.35 kg 5 lb 3 oz	Norfolk Canyon Virginia, USA	14-Feb-09	Jess Bradford Cadwallender
Rubyfish	*Plagiogeneion rubiginosum*	1.94 kg 4 lb 4 oz	Sue's Rock Tutukaka Coast, New Zealand	11-Jan-13	Scott Tindale
Rubyfish, Japanese	*Erythrocles schlegelii*	4 kg 8 lb 13 oz	Yonaguni Island Okinawa, Japan	05-Nov-10	Takashi Odagiri
Rudd	*Scardinius erythrophthalmus*	1.58 kg 3 lb 7 oz	Ljungan River Sweden	31-Jul-88	Luis Rasmussen
Runner, blue	*Caranx crysos*	5.05 kg 11 lb 2 oz	Dauphin Island Alabama, USA	28-Jun-97	Ms. Stacey Moiren
Runner, rainbow	*Elagatis bipinnulata*	17.05 kg 37 lb 9 oz	Isla Clarion Revillagigedo Islands, Mexico	21-Nov-91	Tom Pfleger
Sabaleta	*Brycon henni*	1.12 kg 2 lb 7 oz	Quebrada la Compania Colombia	12-Jul-02	Alejandro Linares
Sabalo	*Brycon melanopterus*	4.35 kg 9 lb 9 oz	Rio Tambopata Peru	10-Oct-92	James Wise, M.D.
Sablefish	*Anoplopoma fimbria*	15.96 kg 35 lb 3 oz	Cross Sound Elfin Cove, Alaska, USA	23-Aug-13	Capt. Joe Calandra
Sailfin, vermiculated	*Pterygoplichthys disjunctivus*	1.36 kg 3 lb 0 oz	Broward County Canal Florida, USA	03-Jun-06	Capt. Jay Wright Jr.
Sailfish, Atlantic	*Istiophorus platypterus*	64.6 kg 142 lb 6 oz	Lobito Angola	12-Mar-14	Marco Couto
Sailfish, Pacific	*Istiophorus platypterus*	100.24 kg 221 lb 0 oz	Santa Cruz Island Ecuador	12-Feb-47	Carl Stewart
Sailors choice	*Haemulon parra*	.45 kg 1 lb 0 oz	Key West Florida, USA	15-Mar-03	Ms. Maria Ortega
Sailors choice (TIE)	*Haemulon parra*	.45 kg 1 lb 0 oz	Cat Cay Bahamas	03-Jul-04	Dennis Triana
Sailors choice (TIE)	*Haemulon parra*	.45 kg 1 lb 0 oz	John Pennekamp Park Florida, USA	16-Aug-07	Jonathan Legaz

RECORDS

SPECIES	SCIENTIFIC NAME	WEIGHT	PLACE	DATE	ANGLER
Sailors choice (TIE)	Haemulon parra	.45 kg 1 lb 0 oz	John Pennekamp Park Florida, USA	13-Aug-07	Dennis Triana
Salema	Sarpa salpa	1.18 kg 2 lb 9 oz	Faro-Ria Forhosa Portugal	24-Sep-06	Luis Ceia
Salmon, Atlantic	Salmo salar	35.89 kg 79 lb 2 oz	Tana River Norway	01-Jan-1928	Henrik Henriksen
Salmon, Atlantic (landlocked)	Salmo salar	12.13 kg 26 lb 12 oz	Torch Lake Michigan, USA	22-Oct-10	Thomas Aufiero
Salmon, Chinook	Oncorhynchus tshawytscha	44.11 kg 97 lb 4 oz	Kenai River Alaska, USA	17-May-85	Les Anderson
Salmon, Chinook-coho	Oncorhynchus x O. kisutch	16.1 kg 35 lb 8 oz	Salmon River, Pulaski New York, USA	21-Oct-01	Brooks Gerli
Salmon, chum	Oncorhynchus keta	15.87 kg 35 lb 0 oz	Edye Pass British Columbia, Canada	11-Jul-95	Todd Johansson
Salmon, coho	Oncorhynchus kisutch	15.08 kg 33 lb 4 oz	Salmon River Pulaski, New York, USA	27-Sep-89	Jerry Lifton
Salmon, pink	Oncorhynchus gorbuscha	6.74 kg 14 lb 13 oz	Monroe Washington, USA	30-Sep-01	Alexander Minerich
Salmon, sockeye	Oncorhynchus nerka	6.88 kg 15 lb 3 oz	Kenai River Alaska, USA	09-Aug-87	Stan Roach
Samson Fish	Seriola hippos	36.5 kg 80 lb 7 oz	Cape Naturaliste W.A., Australia	31-Jan-93	Terry Coote
Sand diver	Synodus intermedius	1.07 kg 2 lb 6 oz	Pompano Beach Florida, USA	05-Mar-05	Kenneth A. Myers
Sandbass, parrot	Paralabrax loro	1.02 kg 2 lb 4 oz	Tamarindo Costa Rica	14-Feb-07	George Bogen
Sandperch, Brazilian	Pinguipes brasilianus	1 kg 2 lb 3.2 oz	Mar del Plata Argentina	26-Apr-10	Tomas Felipe Restano
Sandperch, namorado	Pseudopercis numida	20.2 kg 44 lb 8 oz	Rio de Janeiro Brazil	07-Mar-98	Eduardo Baumeier
Sardinata	Brycon whitei	4.08 kg 9 lb 0 oz	Rio Negro Colombia	02-Mar-08	Alejandro Linares
Sargo	Anisotremus davidsonii	1.81 kg 4 lb 0 oz	Newport Beach Harbor California, USA	09-May-12	Gregory Taite
Sauger	Stizostedion canadense	3.96 kg 8 lb 12 oz	Lake Sakakawea North Dakota, USA	06-Oct-71	Mike Fischer
Saugeye	Stizostedion vitreum x S. canadense	5.81 kg 12 lb 13 oz	Clendening Reservoir Ohio, USA	19-Nov-01	Fred Sulek
Sawtail, scalpel	Prionurus scalprum	2.5 kg 5 lb 8 oz	Miyake Island Tokyo, Japan	28-May-12	Fumiya Okuyama
Scabbardfish, channel	Evoxymetopon taeniatus	3.89 kg 8 lb 9 oz	Rio de Janeiro Brazil	06-Apr-02	Eduardo Baumeier
Scabbardfish, silver	Lepidopus caudatus	6.4 kg 14 lb 1 oz	Europa Point Gibraltar	16-Jul-95	Ernest Borrell
Scad, amberstripe	Decapterus muroadsi	1.13 kg 2 lb 8 oz	Kona Hawaii, USA	30-Dec-08	George Bogen
Scad, false	Caranx rhonchus	.56 kg 1 lb 3 oz	Vila Real Santo Antonio Algarve, Portugal	28-Oct-07	Luis Ceia

SPECIES	SCIENTIFIC NAME	WEIGHT	PLACE	DATE	ANGLER
Scad, mackerel	*Decapterus macarellus*	.55 kg 1 lb 3 oz	Hachijo Island Tokyo, Japan	16-Aug-05	Chieko Nishino
Scad, oxeye	*Selar boops*	.45 kg 1 lb 0 oz	Kiritimati Island Kiribati	31-May-13	Martini Arostegui
Scad, shortfin	*Decapterus macrosoma*	1 kg 2 lb 3 oz	Niijima Tokyo, Japan	15-Jun-14	Yuumi Fukunaga
Scamp	*Mycteroperca phenax*	13.44 kg 29 lb 10 oz	Dauphin Island Alabama, USA	22-Jul-00	Robert Conklin
Scombrops, Atlantic	*Scombrops oculatus*	9.88 kg 21 lb 12 oz	Bimini Bahamas	15-Jul-97	Doug Olander
Scorpionfish, black	*Scorpaena porcus*	1.05 kg 2 lb 5 oz	South Moue Gibraltar	04-May-14	Michael J. Hernandez
Scorpionfish, California	*Scorpaena guttata*	1.98 kg 4 lb 6 oz	Cedros Island Mexico	30-Aug-06	Dennis Toussieng
Scorpionfish, darkblotch	*Scorpaena histrio*	.53 kg 1 lb 3 oz	Zancudo Costa Rica	08-Feb-05	Phillip Mark Bauer
Scorpionfish, large-headed	*Pontinus macrocephalus*	1.36 kg 3 lb 0 oz	Kona Hawaii, USA	12-Jul-12	Steven M. Wozniak
Scorpionfish, red	*Scorpaena scrofa*	2.96 kg 6 lb 8 oz	Gibraltar Gibraltar	30-May-96	Stuart Brown-Giraldi
Scorpionfish, spinycheek	*Neomerinthe hemingwayi*	1.5 kg 3 lb 5 oz	Fort Morgan Alabama, USA	11-Jun-11	Capt. Mark Sagerholm
Scorpionfish, spotback	*Pontinus vaughani*	1.07 kg 2 lb 6 oz	San Jose Del Cabo Baja California Sur, Mexico	26-Feb-06	George Bogen
Scorpionfish, spotted	*Scorpaena plumieri*	1.55 kg 3 lb 7 oz	Angra Dor Reis Bay Rio de Janeiro, Brazil	25-May-97	Pedro Cabral de Menezes
Sculpin, great	*Myoxocephalus polyacanthocephalus*	5.24 kg 11 lb 8 oz	Osatube Hokkaido, Japan	08-Nov-10	Yoshitatsu Honda
Sculpin, shorthorn	*Myoxocephalus scorpius*	.58 kg 1 lb 4 oz	Lodmundarfjordur Iceland	30-May-03	Skarphedinn Asbjornsson
Sculpin, spinyhead	*Dasycottus setiger*	.85 kg 1 lb 13 oz	Uljin South Korea	01-Feb-14	Phillip W. Richmond, Jr.
Sculpin, stellar's (gisukajika)	*Myoxocephalus stelleri*	3.73 kg 8 lb 3 oz	Kushiro Hokkaido, Japan	05-May-11	Masaru Kukuoka
Scup	*Stenotomus chrysops*	2.06 kg 4 lb 9 oz	Nantucket Sound Massachusetts, USA	03-Jun-92	Sonny Richards
Seabass, blackfin	*Lateolabrax latus*	10.91 kg 24 lb 0 oz	Katsuura Chiba, Japan	10-Feb-11	Yuki Inoue
Seabass, Japanese (Suzuki)	*Lateolabrax japonicus*	13.14 kg 28 lb 15 oz	Katada River Oita, Japan	08-Oct-06	Yoshiaki Kubo
Seabass, Peruvian rock	*Paralabrax humeralis*	1.36 kg 3 lb 0 oz	Bujama Mala Peru	28-Feb-14	Steven M. Wozniak

RECORDS

SPECIES	SCIENTIFIC NAME	WEIGHT	PLACE	DATE	ANGLER
Seabass, rosy	*Doederleinia berycoides*	.85 kg 1 lb 13 oz	Hasaki Ibaraki, Japan	13-Sep-13	Yuji Hayashi
Seabass, spotted	*Dicentrarchus punctatus*	1.77 kg 3 lb 14 oz	Sesimbra Portugal	19-Mar-14	Hugo Silva
Seabass, white	*Atractoscion nobilis*	37.98 kg 83 lb 12 oz	San Felipe Mexico	31-Mar-53	Lyal Baumgardner
Seabream, axillary	*Pagellus acarne*	.6 kg 1 lb 5 oz	Anglet France	08-Jun-01	Jean Baibarac
Seabream, black	*Spondyliosoma cantharus*	1.9 kg 4 lb 3 oz	Bonifacio Corsica, France	16-Sep-02	Patrick Sebile
Seabream, bluespotted	*Pagrus caeruleostictus*	11.62 kg 25 lb 9 oz	Detached Mole Gibraltar	04-Jun-00	Charles Bear
Seabream, crimson (chidai)	*Evynnis japonica*	1.2 kg 2 lb 10 oz	Kurihama Kanagawa, Japan	17-May-03	Tsumishi Koide
Seabream, daggerhead	*Chrysoblephus cristiceps*	7.3 kg 16 lb 1 oz	Algoa Bay, Port Elizabeth South Africa	10-Oct-93	Eddie De Reuck
Seabream, gilthead	*Sparus aurata*	7.36 kg 16 lb 3 oz	Florn Estuary Brest, France	13-Oct-00	Jean Serra
Seabream, Moroccan white	*Diplodus sargus cadenati*	1.6 kg 3 lb 8 oz	Dakhla Morocco	26-May-03	Patrick Sebile
Seabream, Okinawa	*Acanthopagrus sivicolus*	3.05 kg 6 lb 11 oz	Naoto, Amami-oshima Kagoshima, Japan	23-Feb-03	Shusaku Hayashi
Seabream, red stumpnose	*Chrysoblephus gibbiceps*	7.5 kg 16 lb 8 oz	Kie Mouth Deep Eastern Cape, South Africa	09-Sep-12	John Richard Luef
Seabream, redbanded (murudai)	*Pagrus auriga*	*3 kg* 6 lb 9 oz	Nouadhibou Mauritania	09-Mar-86	Serge Bensa
Seabream, saddle	*Oblada melanura*	.6 kg 1 lb 5 oz	Frejus France	25-Sep-02	Bruno Ansquer
Seabream, Scotsman	*Polysteganus praeorbitalis*	7.8 kg 17 lb 3 oz	St. Lucia Estuary South Africa	25-Nov-94	G.J. Van Der Westhuizen
Seabream, sharpsnout	*Diplodus puntazzo*	1.68 kg 3 lb 11 oz	La Sela Gibraltar Bay, Gibraltar	23-Nov-96	Brian Soiza
Seabream, striped	*Lithognathus mormyrus*	.8 kg 1 lb 12 oz	Dakhla Morocco	17-Sep-93	Patrick Sebile
Seabream, white	*Diplodus sargus*	1.87 kg 4 lb 1 oz	Gibraltar Bay Gibraltar	28-Apr-96	Anthony Loddo
Seabream, yellowback (Kidia)	*Dentex tumifrons*	1.15 kg 2 lb 8 oz	Mikura Island Tokyo, Japan	19-Jun-04	Takeshi Date
Seabream, yellowfin	*Acanthopagrus latus*	2.7 kg 5 lb 15 oz	Keihin-unga Kanagawa, Japan	05-Jul-05	Shotaro Ono
Seabream, zebra	*Diplodus cervinus cervinus*	3.94 kg 8 lb 11 oz	Vila Real Santo Antonio Algarve, Portugal	02-Apr-07	Joao Pardal
Seachub, blue	*Kyphosus cinerascens*	.59 kg 1 lb 5 oz	Raiatea Lagoon Tahiti	16-Jun-06	Dennis Triana

SPECIES	SCIENTIFIC NAME	WEIGHT	PLACE	DATE	ANGLER
Seaperch, spotted scale	*Lutjanus johni*	10.5 kg 23 lb 2 oz	Cairns Queensland, Australia	02-Mar-86	Mac Mankowski
Seaperch, striped	*Embiotoca lateralis*	.68 kg 1 lb 8 oz	Pacific Grove California, USA	21-Apr-12	Martini Arostegui
Searobin, striped	*Prionotus evolans*	2.04 kg 4 lb 8 oz	Shinnecock Inlet New York, USA	01-Jun-13	Charlie Plym
Seatrout, sand	*Cynoscion arenarius*	2.78 kg 6 lb 2 oz	Dauphin Island Alabama, USA	24-May-97	Steve Scoggin
Seatrout, silver	*Cynoscion nothus*	.56 kg 1 lb 4 oz	Aransas Pass Texas, USA	24-Nov-06	Brandi Huff
Seatrout, spotted	*Cynoscion nebulosus*	7.92 kg 17 lb 7 oz	Ft. Pierce Florida, USA	11-May-95	Craig F. Carson
Seerfish, Chinese	*Scomberomorus sinensis*	131 kg 288 lb 12 oz	Kwan-Tall Island Cheju-Do, Korea	06-Oct-82	Boo-Il Oh
Seerfish, kanadi	*Scomberomorus plurilineatus*	12.5 kg 27 lb 8 oz	Mapelane, Zululand Natal, South Africa	11-Jul-97	Daniel Van Tonder
Sennet, southern	*Sphyraena picudilla*	1.14 kg 2 lb 8 oz	Indian River Florida, USA	29-Jan-99	Chris Kirkhart
Serrana, blacktail	*Serranus atricauda*	.88 kg 1 lb 15 oz	El Lomo Gibraltar	23-Jun-02	Paul Henwood
Seventy-four	*Polysteganus undulosus*	16 kg 35 lb 4 oz	Mapuzi, Transkei South Africa	17-Aug-85	Nolan Sparg
Shad, allis	*Alosa alosa*	2.32 kg 5 lb 2 oz	Aulne River, Chateaulin France	06-May-05	Dr. Samuel P. Davis
Shad, American	*Alosa sapidissima*	5.1 kg 11 lb 4 oz	Connecticut River Massachusetts, USA	19-May-86	Bob Thibodo
Shad, gizzard	*Dorosoma cepedianum*	1.98 kg 4 lb 6 oz	Lake Michigan Indiana, USA	02-Mar-96	Mike Berg
Shad, hickory	*Alosa mediocris*	1.3 kg 2 lb 14 oz	Econlockhatchee River Florida, USA	15-Jan-08	Dave Chermanski
Shad, Mediterranean	*Alosa fallax nilotica*	.88 kg 1 lb 15 oz	Taro River S. Secondo Italy	29-Apr-06	Mauro Mazzo
Shad, Mediterranean (TIE)	*Alosa fallax nilotica*	.91 kg 2 lb 0 oz	Po River Italy	09-Jul-13	Martin Arostegui
Shad, twaite	*Alosa fallax*	.7 kg 1 lb 8 oz	North Sea Netherlands	21-Aug-98	P.C. Ouwendijk
Shark, Atlantic sharpnose	*Rhizoprionodon terraenovae*	7.25 kg 16 lb 0 oz	Port Mansfield Texas, USA	12-Oct-94	R. Shields
Shark, banded (hound)	*Triakis scyllium*	15.25 kg 33 lb 9 oz	Akazawa, Ito-Shi Shizuoka, Japan	10-Jun-06	Takashi Nishino
Shark, bigeye thresher	*Alopias superciliosus*	363.8 kg 802 lb 0 oz	Tutukaka New Zealand	08-Feb-81	Ms. Dianne North

RECORDS

SPECIES	SCIENTIFIC NAME	WEIGHT	PLACE	DATE	ANGLER
Shark, bignose	*Carcharhinus altimus*	167.8 kg 369 lb 14 oz	Markham River Lae, Papua New Guinea	23-Oct-93	Lester Rohrlach
Shark, blackmouth cat	*Galeus melastomus*	1.37 kg 3 lb 0 oz	Mausundvar Trondheim, Norway	17-Sep-94	Per Hagen
Shark, blacknose	*Carcharhinus acronotus*	18.86 kg 41 lb 9 oz	Little River South Carolina, USA	30-Jul-92	Jon-Paul Hoffman
Shark, blacktail	*Carcharhinus wheeleri*	33.7 kg 74 lb 4 oz	Kosi Bay, Zululand South Africa	25-May-87	Trevor Ashington
Shark, blacktip	*Carcharhinus limbatus*	122.75 kg 270 lb 9 oz	Malindi Bay Kenya	21-Sep-84	Jurgen Oeder
Shark, blacktip reef	*Carcharhinus melanopterus*	13.55 kg 29 lb 13 oz	CargadosCarajos Shoals Saint Brandon, Mauritius	22-Oct-95	Dr. Joachim Kleidon
Shark, blotchy swell	*Cephaloscyllium umbratile*	7.5 kg 16 lb 8 oz	Akazawa, Ito Shizuoka, Japan	10-Mar-13	Yuuma Nishino
Shark, blue	*Prionace glauca*	239.49 kg 528 lb 0 oz	Montauk Point New York, USA	09-Aug-01	Joe Seidel
Shark, bonnethead	*Sphyrna tiburo*	14.51 kg 32 lb 0 oz	St. Vincent Sound Apalachicola Bay, Florida, USA	01-Jul-13	Kelli Jo Stephenson
Shark, brown smooth-hound	*Mustelus henlei*	2.95 kg 6 lb 8 oz	Long Beach California, USA	29-Jun-12	Steven M. Wozniak
Shark, bull	*Carcharhinus leucas*	316.5 kg 697 lb 12 oz	Malindi Kenya	24-Mar-01	Ronald de Jager
Shark, Caribbean reef	*Carcharhinus perezi*	69.85 kg 154 lb 0 oz	Molasses Reef Florida, USA	09-Dec-96	Rene de Dios
Shark, dusky	*Carcharhinus obscurus*	346.54 kg 764 lb 0 oz	Longboat Key Florida, USA	28-May-82	Warren Girle
Shark, finetooth	*Carcharhinus isodon*	4.08 kg 9 lb 0 oz	Hilton Head South Carolina, USA	24-Jul-12	Martini Arostegui
Shark, Galapagos	*Carcharhinus galapagensis*	140 kg 308 lb 10 oz	Ascension Island United Kingdom	02-Jul-04	Denis J. Froud
Shark, great hammerhead	*Sphyrna mokarran*	580.59 kg 1280 lb 0 oz	Boca Grande Florida, USA	23-May-06	Bucky Dennis
Shark, Greenland	*Somniosus microcephalus*	775 kg 1708 lb 9 oz	Trondheimsfjord Norway	18-Oct-87	Terje Nordtvedt
Shark, gulper	*Centrophorus uyato*	7.34 kg 16 lb 3 oz	Bimini Bahamas	15-Jul-97	Doug Olander
Shark, gummy	*Mustelus antarcticus*	30.8 kg 67 lb 14 oz	Mcloughins Beach Victoria, Australia	15-Nov-92	Neale Blunden
Shark, Japanese bullhead	*Heterodontus japonicus*	12.25 kg 27 lb 0 oz	Akazawa Ito, Shizuoka, Japan	14-Apr-13	Yuuma Nishino
Shark, lemon	*Negaprion brevirostris*	183.7 kg 405 lb 0 oz	Buxton North Carolina, USA	23-Nov-88	Ms. Colleen Harlow
Shark, leopard	*Triakis semifasciata*	20.16 kg 44 lb 7 oz	San Diego Bay California, USA	31-Dec-11	Maria de la Luz Johnson

RECORDS

SPECIES	SCIENTIFIC NAME	WEIGHT	PLACE	DATE	ANGLER
Shark, mako	*Isurus spp.*	553.84 kg 1221 lb 0 oz	Chatham Massachusetts, USA	21-Jul-01	Luke Sweeney
Shark, milk	*Rhizoprionodon acutus*	5 kg 11 lb 0 oz	Archipelago dos Bijagos Guinea-Bissau	01-Apr-01	Adrien Bernard
Shark, narrowtooth	*Carcharhinus brachyurus*	242 kg 533 lb 8 oz	Cape Karikari New Zealand	09-Jan-93	Ms. Gaye Harrison-Armstrong
Shark, night	*Carcharhinus signatus*	76.65 kg 169 lb 0 oz	Bimini Bahamas	13-Jul-97	Capt. Ron Schatman
Shark, nurse	*Ginglymostoma cirratum*	119.63 kg 263 lb 12 oz	Port St. Joe Florida, USA	21-Jul-07	Nic Jeter
Shark, oceanic whitetip	*Carcharhinus longimanus*	167.37 kg 369 lb 0 oz	San Salvador Bahamas	24-Jan-98	Reid Hodges
Shark, pig-eye	*Carcharhinus amboinensis*	45.5 kg 100 lb 4 oz	Moreton Bay Australia	29-Mar-03	Gordon Macdonald
Shark, porbeagle	*Lamna nasus*	230 kg 507 lb 0 oz	Pentland Firth Caithness, Scotland	09-Mar-93	Christopher Bennett
Shark, salmon	*Lamna ditropis*	209.36 kg 461 lb 9 oz	Valdez Alaska, USA	15-Jul-09	Thomas E. Farmer
Shark, sand tiger	*Odontaspis taurus*	158.81 kg 350 lb 2 oz	Charleston Jetty South Carolina, USA	29-Apr-93	Mark Thawley
Shark, sandbar	*Carcharhinus plumbeus*	240 kg 529 lb 1 oz	Archipelago des Bijagos Guinea-Bissau	05-Apr-02	Patrick Sebile
Shark, scalloped hammerhead	*Sphyrna lewini*	160.11 kg 353 lb 0 oz	Key West Florida, USA	19-Apr-04	Rick Gunion
Shark, sevengill	*Notorynchus cepedianus*	94.8 kg 208 lb 15 oz	Ngunguru Beach Northland, New Zealand	07-Jun-11	Sue Tindale
Shark, sicklefin lemon	*Negaprion acutidens*	10.6 kg 23 lb 5 oz	Darwin Harbour Australia	07-Dec-98	Craig Johnston
Shark, silky	*Carcharhinus falciformis*	346 kg 762 lb 12 oz	Port Stephen's N.S.W., Australia	26-Feb-94	Bryce Henderson
Shark, silvertip	*Carcharhinus albimarginatus*	186.2 kg 410 lb 7 oz	Latham Island Tanzania	14-Nov-11	Andrea Pellegrini
Shark, sixgilled	*Hexanchus griseus*	588.76 kg 1298 lb 0 oz	Atlantic Ocean United Kingdom	21-Nov-02	Clemens Rump
Shark, smallfin gulper	*Centrophorus moluccensis*	2.4 kg 5 lb 4 oz	Lae, Huon Gulf Papua New Guinea	13-Feb-93	Justin Mallett
Shark, smooth hammerhead	*Sphyrna zygaena*	167.6 kg 369 lb 7 oz	Bay of Plenty New Zealand	26-Jan-02	Scott Tindale
Shark, spinner	*Carcharhinus brevipinna*	94.6 kg 208 lb 9 oz	Port Aransas Texas, USA	13-Dec-09	Raymond F. Ireton
Shark, thresher	*Alopias spp.*	348 kg 767 lb 3 oz	Bay of Islands New Zealand	26-Feb-83	D.L. Hannah

RECORDS

www.skyhorsepublishing.com

SPECIES	SCIENTIFIC NAME	WEIGHT	PLACE	DATE	ANGLER
Shark, tiger	*Galeocerdo cuvier*	807.4 kg 1780 lb 0 oz	Cherry Grove South Carolina, USA	14-Jun-64	Walter Maxwell
Shark, tiger (TIE)	*Galeocerdo cuvier*	810 kg 1785 lb 11 oz	Ulladulla Australia	28-Mar-04	Kevin James Clapson
Shark, tope	*Galeorhinus galeus*	33 kg 72 lb 12 oz	Parengarenga Harbor New Zealand	19-Dec-86	Ms. Melanie Feldman
Shark, velvet belly lantern	*Etmopterus spinax*	.85 kg 1 lb 13 oz	Langesundbukta Norway	07-Oct-00	Arild Borresen
Shark, white	*Carcharodon carcharias*	1208.38 kg 2664 lb 0 oz	Ceduna Australia	21-Apr-59	Alfred Dean
Shark, whitetip reef	*Triaenodon obesus*	18.25 kg 40 lb 4 oz	Isla Coiba Panama	08-Aug-79	Dr. Jack Kamerman
Sharkminnow, black	*Labeo chrysophekadion*	6.45 kg 14 lb 3 oz	Khao Lagm Dam Kanchanaburi, Thailand	22-Jul-13	Benchawan Thiansungnoen
Sharkminnow, tricolor	*Balantiocheilos melanopterus*	.99 kg 2 lb 2 oz	Salapee Thailand	13-Aug-09	Jean-Francois Helias
Sharksucker	*Echeneis naucrates*	5.38 kg 11 lb 14 oz	Molasses Reef Florida, USA	09-Aug-01	Ms. Yolanda Morejon
Sharksucker, whitefin	*Echeneis neucratoides*	.68 kg 1 lb 8 oz	Marathon Florida, USA	08-Feb-14	Dennis Triana
Sheephead, California	*Semicossyphus pulcher*	12.88 kg 28 lb 6 oz	Isla Roca Partida Revillagigedo Islands, Mexico	04-Nov-99	Marshall Madruga
Sheepshead	*Archosargus probatocephalus*	9.63 kg 21 lb 4 oz	New Orleans Louisiana, USA	16-Apr-82	Wayne Desselle
Shimazoi	*Sebastes trivittatus*	3.35 kg 7 lb 6 oz	Shiribetsu Hokkaido, Japan	20-Apr-08	Chiharu Okayama
Shiro-Guchi	*Pennahia argentata*	.57 kg 1 lb 4 oz	Handa Port Aichi, Japan	20-Sep-08	Taiki Aoyama
Shosai-fugu	*Takifugu snyderi*	.54 kg 1 lb 3 oz	Kozu Is. Tokyo, Japan	05-May-05	Takashi Nishino
Sicklefish	*Drepane punctuata*	.68 kg 1 lb 8 oz	Ponggol Marina Singapore	18-Apr-10	Steven M. Wozniak
Sierra, Atlantic	*Scomberomorus brasiliensis*	6.71 kg 14 lb 13 oz	Mangaratiba Brazil	20-Jun-99	Ms. Paula Boghossian
Silver eye	*Polymixia japonica*	1.3 kg 2 lb 13 oz	Oshima Tokyo, Japan	18-May-08	Kenji Kaneshin
Skate	*Raja batis*	97.07 kg 214 lb 0 oz	Scapa Flow Orkney, United Kingdom	16-Jun-68	Jan Olsson
Skate, big	*Raja binoculata*	41.27 kg 91 lb 0 oz	Humbolt Bay Eureka, California, USA	06-Mar-93	Scotty Krick
Skate, California	*Raja inornata*	1.25 kg 2 lb 12 oz	Long Beach California, USA	22-Mar-14	Steven M. Wozniak

RECORDS

SPECIES	SCIENTIFIC NAME	WEIGHT	PLACE	DATE	ANGLER
Skate, starry	Raja radiata	4.25 kg 9 lb 5 oz	Hvasser Norway	10-Oct-82	Knut Hedlund
Skipjack, black	Euthynnus lineatus	11.79 kg 26 lb 0 oz	Thetis Bank Baja California, Mexico	23-Oct-91	Clifford Hamaishi
Sleeper, bigmouth	Gobiomorus dormitor	2.03 kg 4 lb 7 oz	Rio Sarapiqui Costa Rica	17-Mar-01	Alexander Arias A.
Slimehead, Darwin's	Gephyroberyx Darwinii	3.4 kg 7 lb 8 oz	Norfolk Canyon Virginia Beach, Virginia, USA	19-Aug-08	Ron Van Kirk
Smoothhound, Florida	Mustelus norrisi	13.78 kg 30 lb 6 oz	Gulf of Mexico Destin, Florida, USA	01-Apr-92	Stephen Wilson
Smoothhound, spotted estuary	Mustelus lenticulatus	2.8 kg 6 lb 2 oz	Kaipara Harbour New Zealand	12-Nov-13	Scott Tindale
Smoothhound, starry	Mustelus asterias	4.76 kg 10 lb 8 oz	Nab Rocks Isle of Wight, United Kingdom	18-Jul-84	Ms. Sylvia Steed
Smoothhound, star-spotted	Mustelus manazo	5.72 kg 12 lb 9 oz	Lae, Huon Gulf Papua New Guinea	13-Feb-93	Justin Mallett
Snakehead, blotched	Channa maculata	3.02 kg 6 lb 10 oz	Ryonan-cho Kagawa, Japan	16-Aug-03	Yoshikazu Kawada
Snakehead, chevron	Channa striata	3.6 kg 7 lb 14 oz	Tseng Wen Reservoir Chiayi County, Taiwan	08-Oct-11	Gerhard Terblanche
Snakehead, emperor	Channa marulioides	3.95 kg 8 lb 11 oz	Sungai Pejing, Maran Pahang, Malaysia	20-Sep-09	Yap Choo
Snakehead, giant	Channa micropeltes	11.79 kg 26 lb 0 oz	Nakohon Ratchasima Korat Province, Thailand	19-Apr-13	Bkkguy John Ang Woon Heng
Snakehead, great	Channa marulius	6.35 kg 14 lb 0 oz	Margate Canal Florida, USA	16-Feb-13	Corey E. Nowakowski
Snakehead, great (TIE)	Channa marulius	6.35 kg 14 lb 0 oz	Margate Canal Florida, USA	06-Oct-13	Corey E. Nowakowski
Snakehead, northern	Channa argus	8.05 kg 17 lb 12 oz	Quantico Creek Triangle, Virginia, USA	20-May-14	Luis Aragon
Snakehead, splendid	Channa lucius	2.05 kg 4 lb 8 oz	Kenyir Trenggarm, Malaysia	19-Jun-10	Christopher S.G. Tan
Snapper (squirefish)	Pagrus auratus	17.2 kg 37 lb 14 oz	Mottiti Island New Zealand	02-Nov-92	Mark Hemingway
Snapper, African brown	Lutjanus dentatus	22 kg 48 lb 8 oz	Monogaga Ivory Coast	03-Feb-95	Patrick Sebile
Snapper, African red	Lutjanus agennes	60 kg 132 lb 4 oz	Keur Saloum Senegal	18-Feb-01	Stephane Talavet
Snapper, black	Apsilus dentatus	4.08 kg 9 lb 0 oz	Cape Eleuthera Bahamas	16-Feb-12	Ben Mahler
Snapper, blackfin	Lutjanus buccanella	3.86 kg 8 lb 8 oz	Key West Florida, USA	14-Jun-11	Martini Arostegui

RECORDS

SPECIES	SCIENTIFIC NAME	WEIGHT	PLACE	DATE	ANGLER
Snapper, blacktail	*Lutjanus fulvus*	.57 kg 1 lb 4 oz	Oahu Hawaii, USA	12-Nov-12	Jamie Hamamoto
Snapper, Brigham's	*Pristipomoides zonatus*	1.22 kg 2 lb 11 oz	Kokohead, Oahu Hawaii, USA	01-Jan-07	George Bogen
Snapper, brown-striped red	*Lutjanus vitta*	.45 kg 1 lb 0 oz	Kut Island Thailand	07-Apr-12	Steven M. Wozniak
Snapper, Colorado	*Lutjanus colorado*	10.92 kg 24 lb 1 oz	Golfo Dulce Costa Rica	09-Sep-04	Wilbur D. Forbes
Snapper, common blueline	*Lutjanus kasmira*	.57 kg 1 lb 4 oz	Keauhou Kona, Hawaii, USA	29-Jun-13	Steven M. Wozniak
Snapper, cubera	*Lutjanus cyanopterus*	56.59 kg 124 lb 12 oz	Garden Bank Louisiana, USA	23-Jun-07	Marion Rose
Snapper, dog (Atlantic)	*Lutjanus jocu*	10.9 kg 24 lb 0 oz	Hole in the Wall Abaco, Bahamas	28-May-94	Capt. Wayne Barder
Snapper, emperor	*Lutjanus sebae*	17.9 kg 39 lb 7 oz	Chichijima, Ogasawara Tokyo, Japan	09-Nov-99	Tadashi Kawabata
Snapper, flame (Hamadai)	*Etelis coruscans*	7.6 kg 16 lb 12 oz	Yonaguni Is. Okinawa, Japan	16-Nov-07	Takashi Odagiri
Snapper, Gorean	*Lutjanus goreensis*	5.5 kg 12 lb 2 oz	Archipelago dos Bijagos Guinea-Bissau	23-Mar-01	Patrick Sebile
Snapper, greenbar	*Hoplopagrus guentheri*	13.49 kg 29 lb 12 oz	Puerto Penasco Mexico	19-Jun-10	Douglas Patrick McLaughlin
Snapper, grey	*Lutjanus griseus*	7.71 kg 17 lb 0 oz	Port Canaveral Florida, USA	14-Jun-92	Steve Maddox
Snapper, humpback red	*Lutjanus gibbus*	1.55 kg 3 lb 6 oz	Yonaguni Island Okinawa, Japan	05-Nov-10	Takashi Odagiri
Snapper, lane	*Lutjanus synagris*	3.72 kg 8 lb 3 oz	Horseshoe Rigs Mississippi, USA	25-Aug-01	Stephen Wilson
Snapper, mahogany	*Lutjanus mahogoni*	.82 kg 1 lb 13 oz	Pacific Reef Miami, Florida, USA	10-Jan-12	Eddie N. Ortiz
Snapper, Malabar	*Lutjanus malabaricus*	7.91 kg 17 lb 7 oz	Cairns Queensland, Australia	03-Aug-89	Gregory Albert
Snapper, mangrove red	*Lutjanus argentimaculatus*	11.62 kg 25 lb 9 oz	Ashizuri Misaki Kochi, Japan	03-May-06	Takuya Kano
Snapper, mullet	*Lutjanus aratus*	20.75 kg 45 lb 12 oz	Cerralvo Island La Paz, Mexico	06-Jun-07	Rolla Cornell
Snapper, mutton	*Lutjanus analis*	13.72 kg 30 lb 4 oz	Dry Tortugas Florida, USA	29-Nov-98	Richard Casey
Snapper, Pacific cubera	*Lutjanus novemfasciatus*	35.72 kg 78 lb 12 oz	Bahia Pez Vela Costa Rica	23-Mar-88	Steven Paull
Snapper, Pacific red	*Lutjanus peru*	7.9 kg 17 lb 7 oz	Uncle Sam Banks Mexico	20-Oct-01	Lon Mikkelsen

RECORDS

SPECIES	SCIENTIFIC NAME	WEIGHT	PLACE	DATE	ANGLER
Snapper, Papuan black	*Lutjanus goldiei*	20.87 kg 46 lb 0 oz	Kumimaipa River Gulf Province, Papua New Guinea	30-Jul-12	Jason N. Yip
Snapper, queen	*Etelis oculatus*	12.36 kg 27 lb 4 oz	Islamorada Florida, USA	09-Oct-08	Bill Ismer
Snapper, red	*Lutjanus campechanus*	22.79 kg 50 lb 4 oz	Gulf of Mexico Louisiana, USA	23-Jun-96	Capt. Doc Kennedy
Snapper, ruby	*Etelis carbunculus*	30.4 kg 67 lb 0 oz	Los Chagos Diego Garcia	24-Dec-10	Phillip W. Richmond, Jr.
Snapper, Russell's	*Lutjanus russellii*	1.85 kg 4 lb 1 oz	Kamikoshiki-jima Kagoshima, Japan	17-Jun-02	Ms. Tomoko Iwakari
Snapper, scarlet	*Etelis radiosus*	11.8 kg 26 lb 0 oz	Yonaguni Iz. Okinawa, Japan	03-Nov-08	Takashi Odagiri
Snapper, schoolmaster	*Lutjanus apodus*	6.02 kg 13 lb 4 oz	North Key Largo Florida, USA	03-Sep-99	Gustavo Pla
Snapper, silk	*Lutjanus vivanus*	8.32 kg 18 lb 5 oz	Gulf of Mexico Venice, Florida, USA	12-Jul-86	James Taylor
Snapper, Spanish flag	*Lutjanus carponotatus*	.68 kg 1 lb 8 oz	Southern Islands Singapore	21-Apr-10	Steven M. Wozniak
Snapper, spotted rose	*Lutjanus guttatus*	1.31 kg 2 lb 14 oz	Playa Hermosa Mexico	04-Jul-99	William Favor
Snapper, two-spot red	*Lutjanus bohar*	14.5 kg 31 lb 15 oz	Rodriguez Island Mauritius	25-Nov-12	Anne-Laure Bruneau
Snapper, vermillion	*Rhomboplites aurorubens*	3.26 kg 7 lb 3 oz	Gulf of Mexico Mobile, Alabama, USA	31-May-87	John Doss
Snapper, yellow (amarillo)	*Lutjanus argentiventris*	5.44 kg 12 lb 0 oz	Golfito Costa Rica	11-Aug-98	John Olson
Snapper, yellowstreaked	*Lutjanus lemniscatus*	1.42 kg 3 lb 2 oz	Kut Island, Gulf of Siam Thailand	11-Feb-08	Jean-Francois Helias
Snapper, yellowtail	*Ocyurus chrysurus*	4.98 kg 11 lb 0 oz	Challenger Bank Bermuda	16-Jun-04	Mr. William B. DuVal
Snoek	*Thyrsites atun*	5.42 kg 11 lb 15 oz	Hauraki Gulf Auckland, New Zealand	14-Mar-13	Scott Tindale
Snook, common	*Centropomus undecimalis*	24.32 kg 53 lb 10 oz	Parismina Ranch Costa Rica	18-Oct-78	Gilbert Ponzi
Snook, fat	*Centropomus parallelus*	4.96 kg 10 lb 14 oz	Mampituba River, Torres RS, Brazil	12-Aug-05	Gilney Braido
Snook, Mexican	*Centropomus poeyi*	10.69 kg 23 lb 9 oz	Rio Palizada Campeche, Mexico	19-Apr-09	Alejandro Lagunes Cabrera
Snook, Pacific black	*Centropomus nigrescens*	27 kg 59 lb 8 oz	Puerto Quepos Costa Rica	3-Mar-14	Capt. Ward Michaels
Snook, Pacific blackfin	*Centropomus medius*	3.2 kg 7 lb 0 oz	Esquinas River Costa Rica	29-Jan-02	Rodolfo Dodero

RECORDS

SPECIES	SCIENTIFIC NAME	WEIGHT	PLACE	DATE	ANGLER
Snook, Pacific white	Centropomus viridis	21.54 kg 47 lb 8 oz	Cabo San Lucas Mexico	04-Jul-01	Vito Allessandro
Snook, swordspine	Centropomus ensiferus	.7 kg 1 lb 9 oz	Port St. Lucie Florida, USA	11-Jun-04	DJ Cook
Snook, tarpon	Centropomus pectinatus	1.42 kg 3 lb 2 oz	Dona Bay Nokomis, Florida, USA	19-Sep-96	Capt. David Coudal
Soldierfish, bigscale	Myripristis berndti	.45 kg 1 lb 0 oz	North Shore Oahu, Hawaii, USA	07-Jul-13	Jamie Hamamoto
Sole	Solea solea	.8 kg 1 lb 12 oz	North Sea Netherlands	12-Jul-97	P.C. Ouwendijk
Sole, fantail	Xystreurys liolepis	3.99 kg 8 lb 12 oz	San Clemente Island California, USA	03-Jun-01	Allan Sheridan
Sole, lemon	Microstomus kitt	1.8 kg 3 lb 15 oz	Andorja Norway	08-Jun-04	Robert Stalcrona
Sole, Northern	Lepidopsetta polyxystra	1.22 kg 2 lb 11 oz	Cape Duget Alaska, USA	10-Aug-04	Richard M. Koster
Sole, Pacific sand	Psettichthys melanostictus	.68 kg 1 lb 8 oz	Santa Cruz California, USA	21-Aug-13	Jim Tolonen
Sole, southern rock	Lepidopsetta bilineata	1.02 kg 2 lb 4 oz	Farralon Islands California, USA	21-Aug-10	Steven M. Wozniak
Sole, yellowfin	Limanda aspera	.91 kg 2 lb 0 oz	Kachemak Bay Alaska, USA	04-Jul-07	Peter W. Witherell
Sorubim, barred	Pseudoplatystoma fasciatum	16.17 kg 35 lb 10 oz	Rio Amazonas Amazonas, Brazil	26-Apr-08	Gilberto Fernandes
Sorubim, spotted	Pseudoplatystoma coruscans	53.5 kg 117 lb 15 oz	Rio Parana Corrientes, Argentina	16-Feb-00	Joao Neto
Sorubim, tiger	Pseudoplatystoma tigrinum	22 kg 48 lb 8 oz	Rio Amazonas Amazonas, Brazil	13-Feb-11	Gilberto Fernandes
Spadefish, Atlantic	Chaetodipterus faber	6.75 kg 14 lb 14 oz	Chesapeake Bay Virginia, USA	13-Jun-09	Roland E. Murphy
Spearfish, longbill	Tetrapturus pfluegeri	58 kg 127 lb 13 oz	Puerto Rico Gran Canaria, Canary Islands, Spain	20 -May-99	Paul Cashmore
Spearfish, Mediterranean	Tetrapturus belone	41.2 kg 90 lb 13 oz	Madeira Island Portugal	02-Jun-80	Joseph Larkin
Spearfish, roundscale	Tetrapturus georgii	31.75 kg 70 lb 0 oz	Baltimore Canyon Maryland, USA	20-Aug-10	Andres Fanjul
Spearfish, shortbill	Tetrapturus angustirostris	50 kg 110 lb 3 oz	Botany Bay Sydney, Australia	03-May-08	Edward Tolfree
Spinefoot, mottled	Siganus fuscescens	.86 kg 1 lb 14 oz	Nomashi, Oshima Tokyo, Japan	17-Aug-07	Takashi Nishino
Spinefoot, mottled	Siganus fuscescens	.9 kg 1 lb 15 oz	Kamisakiura Mie, Japan	23-Sep-07	Kazuhiko Mizutani

SPECIES	SCIENTIFIC NAME	WEIGHT	PLACE	DATE	ANGLER
Spinefoot, orange-spotted	*Siganus guttatus*	2.2 kg 4 lb 14 oz	Iejima Okinawa, Japan	01-Jun-07	Hiroaki Higa
Spinefoot, streaked	*Siganus javus*	.68 kg 1 lb 8 oz	Kut Island Thailand	07-Apr-12	Steven M. Wozniak
Splake	*Salvelinus namaycush x S. fontinalis*	9.39 kg 20 lb 11 oz	Georgian Bay Ontario, Canada	17-May-87	Paul Thompson
Splendid, alfonsino	*Beryx splendens*	2.6 kg 5 lb 11 oz	Mikomoto, Shimoda Shizuoka, Japan	04-May-08	Takashi Odagiri
Spot	*Leiostomus xanthurus*	.65 kg 1 lb 7 oz	Hampton Roads Bridge Tunnel Virginia, USA	02-Oct-04	Lorraine H. Gousse
Squirrelfish, blue lined	*Sargocentron tiere*	.45 kg 1 lb 0 oz	Keauhou Kona, Hawaii, USA	22-Jun-13	Steven M. Wozniak
Squirrelfish, sabre	*Sargocentron spiniferum*	2.55 kg 5 lb 10 oz	Keahole Point Kailua Kona, Hawaii, USA	26-Mar-95	Rex Bigg
Stargazer	*Uranoscopus scaber*	.94 kg 2 lb 1 oz	Gibraltar United Kingdom	04-Dec-94	Albert Ward
Stargazer, northern	*Astroscopus guttatus*	4.87 kg 10 lb 12 oz	Cape May New Jersey, USA	20-Jun-98	John Jacobsen
Stargazer, spotted Australian	*Ichthyscopus sannio*	5.82 kg 12 lb 13 oz	Gold Coast Seaway Australia	10-Jul-02	Gordon Macdonald
Steenbras, red	*Petrus rupestris*	56.6 kg 124 lb 12 oz	Aston Bay, Eastern Cape South Africa	08-May-94	Terry Goldstone
Stingray, Atlantic	*Dasyatis sabina*	4.87 kg 10 lb 12 oz	Galveston Bay Texas, USA	03-Jul-94	David Anderson
Stingray, black	*Dasyatis thetidis*	57.5 kg 126 lb 12 oz	Laurieton N.S.W., Australia	03-Jul-94	David Shearing
Stingray, bluespotted	*Dasyatis kuhlii*	1.55 kg 3 lb 6 oz	Kaminato Hachijo Island, Japan	04-May-03	Takashi Nishino
Stingray, bluntnose	*Dasyatis say*	16.62 kg 36 lb 10 oz	Galveston Texas, USA	26-May-03	Richard Olszak, Jr.
Stingray, common	*Dasyatis pastinaca*	201.39 kg 444 lb 0 oz	Faial, Azores Horta, Spain	01-Sep-99	Bob de Boeck
Stingray, cowtail	*Hypolophus sephen*	18 kg 39 lb 10 oz	Bang Pakong River Thailand	19-Mar-04	Jean-Francois Helias
Stingray, daisy	*Dasyatis margarita*	19.5 kg 42 lb 15 oz	Etintite Guinea-Bissau	27-Oct-96	Jean Lafage
Stingray, diamond	*Dasyatis dipterura*	46.26 kg 102 lb 0 oz	Mission Bay San Diego, California, USA	07-Aug-93	Roger Ehlers
Stingray, Haller's round	*Urobatis halleri*	1.36 kg 3 lb 0 oz	Santa Clara River Ventura, California, USA	03-Sep-89	Paul Bodtke
Stingray, pelagic	*Dasyatis violacea*	6.2 kg 13 lb 10 oz	Bonifacio Corsica, France	08-Jun-01	Patrick Sebile

RECORDS

SPECIES	SCIENTIFIC NAME	WEIGHT	PLACE	DATE	ANGLER
Stingray, pitted	*Dasyatis matsubarai*	3.7 kg 8 lb 2 oz	Izuoshima Tokyo, Japan	22-Aug-12	Takashi Nishino
Stingray, red (akaei)	*Dasyatis akajei*	26.55 kg 58 lb 8 oz	Ogusu, Sajima Kanagawa, Japan	18-Jun-08	Takashi Nishino
Stingray, roughtail	*Dasyatis centroura*	183.7 kg 405 lb 0 oz	Islamorada Florida, USA	01-Feb-72	Geoff Flores
Stingray, round	*Taeniura grabata*	95.5 kg 210 lb 8 oz	Canary Islands Gran Canarias, Spain	11-Oct-09	Michael Bartels
Stingray, S.A. freshwater	*Potamotrygon motoro*	12.59 kg 27 lb 12 oz	Rio Agua Boa, Roraima Brazil	09-Jan-00	Ben Wise
Stingray, sepia	*Urolophus aurantiacus*	.65 kg 1 lb 6 oz	Akazawa, Ito Shizuoka, Japan	09-Mar-13	Yuuma Nishino
Stingray, short-tail	*Dasyatis brevicaudata*	84.6 kg 186 lb 8 oz	Akitio, Northern Waiararapa New Zealand	24-Feb-06	Neil McDonald
Stingray, southern	*Dasyatis americana*	111.58 kg 246 lb 0 oz	Galveston Bay Texas, USA	30-Jun-98	Carissa Egger
Stingray, whip	*Dasyatis hastata*	75.98 kg 167 lb 8 oz	Banjul Gambia	31-Jan-10	Stan Nabozny
Stingray, w-mouth	*Dasyatis hypostigma*	6.35 kg 14 lb 0 oz	Sepitiba Bay Brazil	03-May-10	Steven M. Wozniak
Stumpnose, red	*Chrysoblephus gibbiceps*	5.8 kg 12 lb 12 oz	St. Croix Island Port Elizabeth, South Africa	20-Dec-93	Craig Saunders
Sturgeon, beluga	*Huso huso*	102 kg 224 lb 13 oz	Guryev Kazakhstan	03-May-93	Ms. Merete Lehne
Sturgeon, lake	*Acipenser fulvescens*	76.2 kg 168 lb 0 oz	Georgian Bay Ontario, Canada	29-May-82	Edward Paszkowski
Sturgeon, shortnose	*Acipenser brevirostrum*	5.04 kg 11 lb 2 oz	Kennebacis River New Brunswick, Canada	31-Jul-88	Lawrence Guimond
Sturgeon, shovelnose	*Scaphirhynchus platorynchus*	4.88 kg 10 lb 12 oz	Missouri River, Loma Montana, USA	14-Jun-85	Arthur Seal
Sturgeon, white	*Acipenser transmontanus*	212.28 kg 468 lb 0 oz	Benicia California, USA	09-Jul-83	Joey Pallotta, III
Sucker, desert	*Catostomus clarkii*	.79 kg 1 lb 12 oz	Lower Salt River Arizona, USA	25-Oct-13	Martin Arostegui
Sucker, desert (TIE)	*Catostomus clarkii*	.79 kg 1 lb 12 oz	Salt River Arizona, USA	10-Mar-14	Steven M. Wozniak
Sucker, flannelmouth	*Catostomus latipinnis*	1.09 kg 2 lb 6 oz	Colorado River Colorado, USA	07-Jul-90	Ms. Karen DeVine
Sucker, Klamath smallscale	*Catostomus rimiculus*	1.13 kg 2 lb 8 oz	Trinity River Del Loma, California, USA	29-Jan-11	Steven M. Wozniak
Sucker, largescale	*Catostomus macrocheilus*	1.67 kg 3 lb 11 oz	Woodland Park Pond Kalispell, Montana, USA	29-May-12	Kevin Marshall Fraley

RECORDS

SPECIES	SCIENTIFIC NAME	WEIGHT	PLACE	DATE	ANGLER
Sucker, longnose	*Catostomus catostomus*	2.97 kg 6 lb 9 oz	St. Joseph River Michigan, USA	02-Dec-89	Ben Knoll
Sucker, northern hog	*Hypentelium nigricans*	.79 kg 1 lb 12 oz	Sigel Pennsylvania, USA	12-Apr-08	Richard E. Faler Jr.
Sucker, Owens	*Catostomus fumeiventris*	.68 kg 1 lb 8 oz	Owens River California, USA	19-Jun-14	Martini Arostegui
Sucker, Sacramento	*Catostomus occidentalis*	.68 kg 1 lb 8 oz	Putah Creek California, USA	7-Jun-14	Martini Arostegui
Sucker, Sonora	*Catostomus insignis*	1.47 kg 3 lb 4 oz	Salt River Arizona, USA	10-Mar-14	Steven M. Wozniak
Sucker, spotted	*Minytrema melanops*	1.5 kg 3 lb 5 oz	Chickamauga Reservoir Tennessee, USA	09-Mar-08	Greg Henry
Sucker, Utah	*Catostomus ardens*	1.13 kg 2 lb 8 oz	Sevenmile Creek Utah, USA	21-Jun-14	Kyle Kurzner
Sucker, white	*Catostomus commersoni*	2.94 kg 6 lb 8 oz	Rainy River, Loman Minnesota, USA	20-Apr-84	Joel Anderson
Sunfish, green	*Lepomis cyanellus*	.96 kg 2 lb 2 oz	Stockton Lake Missouri, USA	18-Jun-71	Paul Dilley
Sunfish, hybrid	*Lepomis macrochirus x L. microphilus*	.48 kg 1 lb 1 oz	Shakey Slough Indiana, USA	02-May-98	Mike Berg
Sunfish, hybrid (TIE)	*Lepomis macrochirus x L. microphilus*	.48 kg 1 lb 1 oz	Shakey Slough Indiana, USA	02-May-98	Steven Berg
Sunfish, longear	*Lepomis megalotis*	.79 kg 1 lb 12 oz	Elephant Butte Lake New Mexico, USA	09-May-85	Ms. Patricia Stout
Sunfish, redbreast	*Lepomis auritus*	.79 kg 1 lb 12 oz	Suwannee River Florida, USA	29-May-84	Alvin Buchanan
Sunfish, redear	*Lepomis microlophus*	2.61 kg 5 lb 12 oz	Lake Havasu Arizona, USA	16-Feb-14	Hector Brito
Surfperch, barred	*Amphistichus argenteus*	2.01 kg 4 lb 7 oz	Oxnard California, USA	15-Mar-14	Bert Uyemura
Surfperch, black	*Embiotoca jacksoni*	.57 kg 1 lb 4 oz	Tiburon California, USA	04-Feb-12	Steven M. Wozniak
Surfperch, calico	*Amphistichus koelzi*	.91 kg 2 lb 0 oz	Morro Bay California, USA	16-Feb-06	Marvin L. Green
Surfperch, redtail	*Amphistichus rhodoterus*	.57 kg 1 lb 4 oz	Orick California, USA	03-Aug-13	Steven M. Wozniak
Surfperch, rubberlip	*Rhacochilus toxotes*	1.25 kg 2 lb 12 oz	Tiburon California, USA	28-Apr-12	Steven M. Wozniak
Surgeonfish, eyestripe	*Acanthurus dussumieri*	1.13 kg 2 lb 8 oz	Ke Iki Beach Oahu, Hawaii, USA	10-Aug-13	Jamie Hamamoto
Surgeonfish, yellowfin	*Acanthurus xanthopterus*	2.38 kg 5 lb 4 oz	Golfito Costa Rica	13-Mar-13	Martin Arostegui

RECORDS

SPECIES	SCIENTIFIC NAME	WEIGHT	PLACE	DATE	ANGLER
Sweep	*Scorpis lineolata*	.73 kg 1 lb 9 oz	Kewa Rocks New Zealand	10-Mar-14	Sue Tindale
Sweetlips, painted	*Diagramma pictum*	3.29 kg 7 lb 4 oz	Prachuap Kiri Kaian Thailand	11-Apr-14	Steven M. Wozniak
Sweetlips, trout	*Plectorhinchus pictus*	6.9 kg 15 lb 3 oz	Moreton Island Queensland, Australia	24-Jul-93	Ms. Kathy McGuire
Swordfish	*Xiphias gladius*	536.15 kg 1182 lb 0 oz	Iquique Chile	07-May-53	Louis Marron
Taimen	*Hucho taimen*	41.95 kg 92 lb 8 oz	Keta River Siberia, Russia	11-Aug-93	Yuri Orlov
Takenokomebaru	*Sebastes oblongus*	3 kg 6 lb 9 oz	Oshika Miyagi, Japan	28-Dec-04	Fuminori Sato
Takenokomebaru (TIE)	*Sebastes oblongus*	3 kg 6 lb 9 oz	Motoyoshi Miyagi, Japan	15-Dec-05	Yoshihiko Onodero
Tambaqui	*Colossoma macropomum*	32.4 kg 71 lb 7 oz	Lago Grande Amazonas, Brazil	25-Aug-07	Jorge Masullo de Aguiar
Tanuki-Mebaru	*Sebastes zonatus*	2.99 kg 6 lb 9 oz	Kuji Iwate, Japan	16-May-10	Satoshi Yamaguchi
Tarakihi	*Nemadactylus macropterus*	2.23 kg 4 lb 14 oz	Kumera Patch Tutukaka Coast, New Zealand	17-Feb-12	Sue Tindale
Tararira	*Hoplias lacerdae*	3.06 kg 6 lb 12 oz	Daiman River Uruguay	22-Jan-12	Martin Arostegui
Tarpon	*Megalops atlanticus*	129.98 kg 286 lb 9 oz	Rubane Guinea-Bissau	20-Mar-03	Max Domecq
Tarpon, oxeye	*Megalops cyprinoides*	2.99 kg 6 lb 9 oz	Tide Island Queensland, Australia	14-May-00	Neil Schultz
Tautog	*Tautoga onitis*	11.33 kg 25 lb 0 oz	Ocean City New Jersey, USA	20-Jan-98	Anthony Monica
Tench	*Tinca tinca*	4.64 kg 10 lb 3 oz	Ljungbyan Sweden	02-Jul-85	Dan Dellerfjord
Tetra, disk	*Myleus schomburgkii*	.88 kg 1 lb 15 oz	Lago Acarituba Amazonas, Brazil	29-May-09	Jorge Masullo de Aguiar
Tetra, true big-scale	*Brycinus macrolepidotus*	2.95 kg 6 lb 8 oz	Volta Lake Ghana	05-Oct-13	Marc Towers
Thornyhead, shortspine	*Sebastolobus alascanus*	2.31 kg 5 lb 1 oz	Los Coranados Islands Baja California Sur, Mexico	03-Feb-01	Stephen D. Grossberg
Threadfin, East Asian	*Eleutheronema rhadinum*	7.48 kg 16 lb 8 oz	Lantau Island Hong Kong, China	20-Feb-09	Kelvin Ng
Threadfin, giant African	*Polydactylus quadrifilis*	49.6 kg 109 lb 5 oz	Barra do Kwanza Angola	17-Jan-99	Marco da Silva Couto
Threadfin, Indian	*Alectis indicus*	16 kg 35 lb 4 oz	Gazaruto Island Mozambique	22-Aug-07	Gary Bluett
Threadfin, king	*Polydactylus macrochir*	12.5 kg 27 lb 8 oz	Dampier Creek Broome, Australia	24-Apr-96	Brian Albert

SPECIES	SCIENTIFIC NAME	WEIGHT	PLACE	DATE	ANGLER
Threadfin, moi	Polydactylus sexfilis	3.17 kg 7 lb 0 oz	Hanalei Hawaii, USA	03-Sep-88	Harry Paik
Threadfin, smallscale	Polydactylus oligodon	.62 kg 1 lb 6 oz	Jensen Beach Florida, USA	09-Oct-98	Ralph Bailey, III
Threadfin, striped	Polydactylus plebeius	1.65 kg 3 lb 10 oz	Ukenmura, Amami-oshima Kagoshima, Japan	24-Oct-99	Masaaki Sudo
Threadfish, African	Alectis alexandrinus	8.1 kg 17 lb 13 oz	Dakhla Morocco	18-Sep-93	Patrick Sebile
Tigerfish	Hydrocynus vittatus	16.1 kg 35 lb 7 oz	Kariba Zimbabwe	12-Sep-01	Ms. Jennifer Daynes
Tigerfish, Campbells	Datnioides campbelli	1.45 kg 3 lb 3 oz	Fly River, W. Province Papua New Guinea	18-Mar-06	Noritaka Takeishi
Tigerfish, four-barred Siamese	Coius quadrifasciatus	.6 kg 1 lb 5 oz	Bang Pakong River Thailand	31-May-05	Anongnart Sungwichien-Helias
Tigerfish, giant	Hydrocynus goliath	44 kg 97 lb 0 oz	Zaire River Kinshasa, Zaire	09-Jul-88	Raymond Houtmans
Tigerfish, North African	Hydrocynus brevis	12.93 kg 28 lb 8 oz	Lake Volta Ghana	29-Mar-12	Marc Towers
Tilapia, blue	Oreochromis aureus	4.34 kg 9 lb 9 oz	South Fork River Stuart, Florida, USA	31-Aug-10	Pamela J. Henry
Tilapia, hornet	Tilapia buttikoferi	1.36 kg 3 lb 0 oz	Airport Lakes Miami, Florida, USA	23-Apr-13	Steven M. Wozniak
Tilapia, Mozambique	Oreochromis mossambicus	3.11 kg 6 lb 13 oz	Loskop Dam South Africa	04-Apr-03	Eugene Kruger
Tilapia, Nile	Oreochromis niloticus	6.01 kg 13 lb 3 oz	Antelope Island Kariba, Zimbabwe	05-Jul-02	Sarel van Rooyen
Tilapia, redbreast	Tilapia rendalli	1.62 kg 3 lb 9 oz	Zambezi River Namibia	14-Nov-94	Bill Staveley
Tilapia, spotted	Tilapia mariae	1.81 kg 4 lb 0 oz	Plantation Florida, USA	06-Jun-05	Reed McLane
Tilapia, threespot	Oreochromis andersonii	4.71 kg 10 lb 6 oz	Upper Zambezi Zambia	03-Nov-98	Ben Van Wyk
Tilefish, Atlantic goldeye	Caulolatilus chrysops	2.27 kg 5 lb 0 oz	Gulf of Mexico Orange Beach, Alabama, USA	16-May-12	Mikel R. Hott
Tilefish, Bahama	Caulolatilus williamsi	1.31 kg 2 lb 14 oz	Grand Bahama Island Bahamas	22-Aug-00	Capt. Jay Cohen
Tilefish, blackline	Caulolatilus cyanops	.45 kg 1 lb 0 oz	Key West Florida, USA	10-Apr-04	Dennis Triana
Tilefish, blueline	Caulolatilus microps	9.3 kg 20 lb 8 oz	Norfolk Canyon Virginia, USA	14-Jul-13	David Cohn
Tilefish, golden-eyed	Caulolatilus affinis	2.27 kg 5 lb 0 oz	Golfito Costa Rica	17-Dec-13	Martini Arostegui
Tilefish, great northern	Lopholatilus chamaeleonticeps	29.57 kg 65 lb 3 oz	Poorman's Canyon New Jersey, USA	08-Aug-12	Angelo Ruvio

RECORDS

SPECIES	SCIENTIFIC NAME	WEIGHT	PLACE	DATE	ANGLER
Tilefish, red	Branchiostegus japonicus	1.75 kg 3 lb 13 oz	Hiratsuka Kanagawa, Japan	23-Jan-11	Yuumi Fukunaga
Tilefish, red (TIE)	Branchiostegus japonicus	1.75 kg 3 lb 13 oz	Hiratsuka Kanagawa, Japan	20-Jan-13	Shungo Asano
Tilefish, sand	Malacanthus plumieri	1.95 kg 4 lb 4 oz	Oak Island North Carolina, USA	16-Apr-04	Frank L. Ballas
Tilefish, southern	Lopholatilus villarii	8.5 kg 18 lb 11 oz	Rio de Janeiro Brazil	31-Aug-02	Eduardo Baumeier
Toadfish, Gulf	Opsanus beta	.54 kg 1 lb 3 oz	Corpus Christi Channel Port Aransas, Texas, USA	08-Oct-13	Barry Osborn
Toadfish, leopard	Opsanus pardus	1.27 kg 2 lb 13 oz	Orange Beach Alabama, USA	22-Apr-03	Chuck Andre
Toadfish, Lusitanian	Halobatrachus didactylus	2.5 kg 5 lb 8 oz	Dakhla Morocco	05-Jun-03	Patrick Sebile
Toadfish, oyster	Opsanus tau	2.23 kg 4 lb 15 oz	Ocracoke North Carolina, USA	04-Jun-94	David Tinsley
Torpedo, Atlantic	Torpedo nobiliana	40.6 kg 89 lb 8 oz	Misquamicut Beach Rhode Island, USA	21-Jun-08	Chuck Adams
Torpedo, spotted	Torpedo marmorata	5.5 kg 12 lb 2 oz	Arcachon France	01-Aug-02	Patrick Sebile
Trahira	Hoplias malabaricus	4.04 kg 8 lb 14 oz	Timbo River Santa Catarina, Brazil	31-Oct-13	Luis Octavio Mendes de Oliveira
Trahira, giant	Hoplias aimara	14.95 kg 32 lb 15 oz	Sinamary River Takari-Kante, French Guiana	21-Mar-07	Cittadini Gerard
Trevally, bigeye	Caranx sexfasciatus	14.3 kg 31 lb 8 oz	Poivre Island Seychelles	23-Apr-97	Les Sampson
Trevally, blacktip	Caranx heberi	8.2 kg 18 lb 1 oz	Bazaruto Island Mozambique	22-May-08	Garett Charles Hume
Trevally, blue	Carangoides ferdau	2.26 kg 5 lb 0 oz	Pacific Ocean Midway Atoll	30-May-01	Matthew Stewart
Trevally, bluefin	Caranx melampygus	13.24 kg 29 lb 3 oz	Clipperton Atoll Mexico	13-Apr-12	Kathleen J. Rounds
Trevally, brassy	Caranx papuensis	7.9 kg 17 lb 6 oz	Bazaruto Island Mozambique	17-May-08	Kim Frank McDonald
Trevally, coastal	Carangoides coeruleopinnatus	1.05 kg 2 lb 5 oz	Ginanzaki Okinawa, Japan	05-Mar-08	Ayaka Kosuge
Trevally, giant	Caranx ignobilis	72.8 kg 160 lb 7 oz	Tokara Kagoshima, Japan	22-May-06	Keiki Hamasaki
Trevally, golden	Gnathanodon speciosus	14.75 kg 32 lb 8 oz	Point Samson W.A., Australia	09-Nov-02	Jason Hornhardt
Trevally, island	Carangoides orthogrammus	4.08 kg 9 lb 0 oz	Farquar Seychelles	24-Mar-13	Meredith McCord
Trevally, orange spotted	Carangoides bajad	.45 kg 1 lb 0 oz	Torres Straits Australia	25-Dec-06	Theda C. Little

RECORDS

SPECIES	SCIENTIFIC NAME	WEIGHT	PLACE	DATE	ANGLER
Trevally, white	*Caranx dentex*	15.25 kg 33 lb 9 oz	Hahajima, Ogasawara Tokyo, Japan	06-Jul-98	Kazuhiko Adachi
Trevally, yellowspotted	*Caranx fulvoguttatus*	13.75 kg 30 lb 5 oz	Sudwana Bay North Coast Natal, South Africa	11-May-10	Rory Francis Eidelman
Triggerfish, blueline	*Xanthichthys caeruleolineatus*	.79 kg 1 lb 12 oz	Kona Coast Hawaii, USA	23-May-11	Steven M. Wozniak
Triggerfish, blueline (TIE)	*Xanthichthys caeruleolineatus*	.79 kg 1 lb 12 oz	Kona Hawaii, USA	14-Jul-12	Steven M. Wozniak
Triggerfish, blunthead	*Pseudobalistes naufragium*	6.6 kg 14 lb 9 oz	La Paz Mexico	23-Aug-05	Kenny Duong
Triggerfish, bridled	*Sufflamen fraenatus*	1.02 kg 2 lb 4 oz	Kona Hawaii, USA	12-Jul-12	Steven M. Wozniak
Triggerfish, finescale	*Balistes polylepis*	7.37 kg 16 lb 4 oz	Kaena Point Oahu, Hawaii, USA	02-Feb-13	Hoala Greevy
Triggerfish, grey	*Balistes capriscus*	6.15 kg 13 lb 9 oz	Murrells Inlet South Carolina, USA	03-May-89	Jim Hilton
Triggerfish, ocean	*Canthidermis sufflamen*	6.12 kg 13 lb 8 oz	Pompano Beach Florida, USA	07-Mar-95	Frederick Lauriello
Triggerfish, orangeside	*Sufflamen verres*	1.02 kg 2 lb 4 oz	Golfito Costa Rica	19-Dec-13	Martin Arostegui
Triggerfish, pinktail	*Melichthys vidua*	.68 kg 1 lb 8 oz	Kona Coast Hawaii, USA	02-Jun-14	Steven M. Wozniak
Triggerfish, queen	*Balistes vetula*	6.44 kg 14 lb 3 oz	Cancun Mexico	26-Jan-09	Martin T. Gnad
Triggerfish, red-toothed	*Odonus niger*	.45 kg 1 lb 0 oz	Dibba Oman	21-Feb-11	Steven M. Wozniak
Triggerfish, spotted Oceanic	*Canthidermis maculata*	1.02 kg 2 lb 4 oz	Kona Coast Hawaii, USA	23-May-11	Steven M. Wozniak
Triggerfish, titan	*Balistoides viridescens*	2.05 kg 4 lb 8 oz	Amagi Tokunoshma, Kagosima, Japan	06-Nov-11	Masaaki Sudoh
Triggerfish, yellowmargin	*Pseudobalistes flavimarginatus*	2.75 kg 6 lb 1 oz	Chagos Archipelago Diego Garcia	03-Nov-10	Phillip W. Richmond Jr.
Triggerfish, yellowspotted	*Pseudobalistes fuscus*	3.29 kg 7 lb 4 oz	Aqaba Jordan	31-Dec-09	Steven M. Wozniak
Tripletail	*Lobotes surinamensis*	19.2 kg 42 lb 5 oz	Zululand South Africa	07-Jun-89	Steve Hand
Trout, Apache	*Oncorhynchus apache*	2.36 kg 5 lb 3 oz	White Mtn. Apache Reservoir, Arizona, USA	29-May-91	John Baldwin
Trout, aurora	*Salvelinus fontinalis*	2.22 kg 4 lb 14 oz	Carol Lake Ontario, Canada	08-Oct-96	Robert Bernardo
Trout, biwamasu	*Oncorhynchus masou rhodurus*	3.58 kg 7 lb 14 oz	Lake Biwa Shiga, Japan	27-Sep-09	Takao Saiki
Trout, brook	*Salvelinus fontinalis*	6.57 kg 14 lb 8 oz	Nipigon River Ontario, Canada	01-Jul-1916	Dr. W. Cook

RECORDS

SPECIES	SCIENTIFIC NAME	WEIGHT	PLACE	DATE	ANGLER
Trout, brown	*Salmo trutta*	19.1 kg 42 lb 1 oz	Ohau Canal New Zealand	08-Mar-13	Otwin Kandolf
Trout, bull	*Salvelinus confluentus*	14.51 kg 32 lb 0 oz	Lake Pend Oreille Idaho, USA	27-Oct-49	N. Higgins
Trout, cutbow	*Oncorhynchus mykiss x O. clarki*	15.73 kg 34 lb 11 oz	American Falls Reservoir Idaho, USA	25-Jul-11	Mark J. Adams
Trout, cutthroat	*Oncorhynchus clarki*	18.59 kg 41 lb 0 oz	Pyramid Lake Nevada, USA	01-Dec-25	John Skimmerhorn
Trout, gila	*Oncorhynchus gilae gilae*	1.56 kg 3 lb 7 oz	Frye Mesa Resevoir Arizona, USA	19-Mar-11	Bo Nelson
Trout, golden	*Oncorhynchus aguabonita*	4.98 kg 11 lb 0 oz	Cooks Lake Wyoming, USA	05-Aug-48	Chas Reed
Trout, lake	*Salvelinus namaycush*	32.65 kg 72 lb 0 oz	Great Bear Lake Northwest Territories, Canada	19-Aug-95	Lloyd Bull
Trout, masu	*Oncorhynchus masou masou*	5.25 kg 11 lb 9 oz	Kuzuryu River Fukui, Japan	06-May-95	Takeshi Matsuura
Trout, ohrid	*Salmo letnica*	6.46 kg 14 lb 4 oz	Platte River Wyoming, USA	26-Jan-86	Ms. Kim Durfee
Trout, ohrid (TIE)	*Salmo letnica*	6.49 kg 14 lb 4 oz	Watauga Lake Tennessee, USA	28-Mar-86	Richard Carter
Trout, rainbow	*Oncorhynchus mykiss*	21.77 kg 48 lb 0 oz	Lake Diefenbaker Canada	05-Sep-09	Sean Konrad
Trout, red spotted masu	*Oncorhynchus masou macrostomus*	1.69 kg 3 lb 11 oz	Yoshino River Tokushima, Japan	27-May-10	Akira Wada
Trout, tiger	*Salmo trutta x Salvelinus fontinalis*	9.44 kg 20 lb 13 oz	Lake Michigan Wisconsin, USA	12-Aug-78	Pete Friedland
Trunkfish	*Lactophrys trigonus*	3.31 kg 7 lb 4 oz	Palm Beach Florida, USA	01-Apr-00	Charlie Colon
Tuna, bigeye (Atlantic)	*Thunnus obesus*	178 kg 392 lb 6 oz	Puerto Rico Gran Canaria, Spain	25-Jul-96	Dieter Vogel
Tuna, bigeye (Pacific)	*Thunnus obesus*	197.31 kg 435 lb 0 oz	Cabo Blanco Peru	17-Apr-57	Dr. Russel Lee
Tuna, blackfin	*Thunnus atlanticus*	22.39 kg 49 lb 6 oz	Marathon Florida, USA	06-Apr-06	Capt. Matthew E. Pullen
Tuna, bluefin	*Thunnus thynnus*	678.58 kg 1496 lb 0 oz	Aulds Cove Nova Scotia, Canada	26-Oct-79	Ken Fraser
Tuna, dogtooth	*Gymnosarda unicolor*	104.32 kg 230 lb 0 oz	LeMorne Mauritius	18-Jan-93	Roger Amand
Tuna, dogtooth (TIE)	*Gymnosarda unicolor*	104.5 kg 230 lb 6 oz	Rodrigues Island Mauritius	25-Oct-07	Mercier Christian
Tuna, longtail	*Thunnus tonggol*	35.9 kg 79 lb 2 oz	Montague Island N.S.W., Australia	12-Apr-82	Tim Simpson
Tuna, Pacific bluefin	*Thunnus orientalis*	411.6 kg 907 lb 6 oz	Three Kings New Zealand	19-Feb-14	Donna Pascoe

SPECIES	SCIENTIFIC NAME	WEIGHT	PLACE	DATE	ANGLER
Tuna, skipjack	*Katsuwonus pelamis*	20.54 kg 45 lb 4 oz	Flathead Bank Baja California, Mexico	16-Nov-96	Brian Evans
Tuna, slender	*Allothunnus fallai*	11.85 kg 26 lb 1 oz	Taiaroa Heads Otago, New Zealand	01-May-01	Gary Wilson
Tuna, southern bluefin	*Thunnus maccoyii*	167.5 kg 369 lb 4 oz	Tathra Australia	09-Jul-09	Phil Body
Tuna, yellowfin	*Thunnus albacares*	193.68 kg 427 lb 0 oz	Cabo San Lucas Mexico	18-Sep-12	Guy Yocom
Tunny, little	*Euthynnus alletteratus*	16.32 kg 36 lb 0 oz	Washington Canyon New Jersey, USA	05-Nov-06	Jess Lubert
Turbot, spottail spiny	*Psettodes belcheri*	2 kg 4 lb 6 oz	Rubane Guinea-Bissau	10-Jan-03	Johan de Vlieger
Tusk	*Brosme brosme*	17.2 kg 37 lb 14 oz	Soroya Norway	18-Jul-08	Anders Jonasson
Tuskfish, blackspot	*Choerodon schoenleinii*	9.5 kg 20 lb 15 oz	Bribie Island Queensland, Australia	19-Jun-88	Ms. Olga Mack
Tuskfish, scarbreast	*Choerodon azurio*	.65 kg 1 lb 6 oz	Sagami Bay Japan	23-Dec-12	Phillip W. Richmond, Jr.
Ugui	*Tribolodon hakonensis*	1.15 kg 2 lb 8 oz	Tama River Tokyo, Japan	30-Apr-09	Yukiyo Okuyama
Ukkarikasago	*Sebastiscus tertius*	3.15 kg 6 lb 15 oz	Onjuku Chiba, Japan	24-Jul-08	Shigeshi Tanaka
Umazura Hagi	*Thamnaconus modestus*	.61 kg 1 lb 5 oz	Kinuura Port Aichi, Japan	15-Feb-09	Taiki Aoyama
Umeiro	*Paracaesio xanthura*	.7 kg 1 lb 8 oz	Mikurajima Tokyo, Japan	09-May-04	Junzo Okada
Unicornfish, bluespine	*Naso unicornis*	1.47 kg 3 lb 4 oz	Ke Iki Beach Oahu, Hawaii, USA	10-Aug-13	Jamie Hamamoto
Unicornfish, orangespine	*Naso lituratus*	.68 kg 1 lb 8 oz	He'eia Kea Pier Oahu, Hawaii, USA	03-Aug-13	Jamie Hamamoto
Utsubo	*Gymnothorax kidako*	4.3 kg 9 lb 7 oz	Akazawa, Ito. Shizuoka, Japan	23-Nov-08	Takashi Nishino
Velvetchin, short barbeled	*Hapalogenys nigripinnis*	1.08 kg 2 lb 6 oz	Akazawa, Ito Shizuoka, Japan	14-Aug-13	Yuuma Nishino
Vimba (Zahrte)	*Vimba vimba*	1.11 kg 2 lb 7 oz	Hossmoan Kalmar, Sweden	09-Jun-87	Luis Rasmussen
Vimba (Zahrte) (TIE)	*Vimba vimba*	1.14 kg 2 lb 8 oz	Olandsan Sweden	01-May-90	Sonny Pettersson
Vundu	*Heterobranchus longifilis*	32.5 kg 71 lb 10 oz	Lake Kariba Zimbabwe	26-Dec-00	Rob Konschel
Wahoo	*Acanthocybium solandri*	83.46 kg 184 lb 0 oz	Cabo San Lucas Mexico	29-Jul-05	Sara Hayward
Wallago	*Wallago attu*	18.6 kg 41 lb 0 oz	Khaolam Dam Sangklaburi, Thailand	04-Dec-03	Kasem Lamaikul (Na Noo)

RECORDS

SPECIES	SCIENTIFIC NAME	WEIGHT	PLACE	DATE	ANGLER
Walleye	*Sander vitreus*	11.34 kg 25 lb 0 oz	Old Hickory Lake Tennessee, USA	02-Aug-60	Mabry Harper
Warmouth	*Lepomis gulosus*	1.1 kg 2 lb 7 oz	Guess Lake, Yellow River Holt, Florida, USA	19-Oct-85	Tony Dempsey
Weakfish	*Cynoscion regalis*	8.96 kg 19 lb 12 oz	Staten Island New York, USA	07-May-08	Dave Alu
Weakfish, acoupa	*Cynoscion acoupa*	18.14 kg 40 lb 0 oz	Cayenne French Guiana	06-Oct-12	Eric Ribas
Weakfish, boccone	*Cynoscion praedatorius*	4.46 kg 14 lb 4 oz	Golfito Costa Rica	20-Apr-06	Betsy Bullard
Weakfish, green	*Cynoscion virescens*	13.6 kg 29 lb 15 oz	Ilha de Comandatuba Hotel Transamerica, Brazil	03-Nov-98	Martin Holzmann
Weakfish, gulf (corvina)	*Cynoscion othonopterum*	2.43 kg 5 lb 5 oz	Vista del Oro Mexico	16-Sep-00	William Favor
Weakfish, Stolzmann's	*Cynoscion stolzmanni*	9.52 kg 21 lb 0 oz	Mazatlan Sinaloa, Mexico	20-Dec-00	Sergio Escutia
Weakfish, striped (corvina)	*Cynoscion reticulatus*	1.13 kg 2 lb 8 oz	Mazatlan Sinaloa, Mexico	22-Feb-01	Sergio Escutia
Wedgefish, African	*Rhynchobatus luebberti*	57 kg 125 lb 10 oz	Rubane, Archipelago Dos Bijagos, Guinea-Bissau	26-Mar-06	Michel Rumin
Weever, greater	*Trachinus draco*	1.74 kg 3 lb 13 oz	La Gomera Canary Islands, Spain	11-Jun-05	John H. Williams
Wels	*Silurus glanis*	134.97 kg 297 lb 9 oz	River Po Italy	11-Mar-10	Attila Zsedely
Wenchman	*Pristipomoides aquilonaris*	1.99 kg 4 lb 6 oz	Bimini Bahamas	13-Jul-97	Dan Upton
Whipray, pink	*Himantura fai*	18.5 kg 40 lb 12 oz	Bali Beach Bali	20-Jul-95	Bo Johansson
Whitefish, broad	*Coregonus nasus*	4.08 kg 9 lb 0 oz	Tozitna River Alaska, USA	17-Jul-89	Al Mathews
Whitefish, lake	*Coregonus clupeaformis*	6.52 kg 14 lb 6 oz	Meaford Ontario, Canada	21-May-84	Dennis Laycock
Whitefish, mountain	*Prosopium williamsoni*	2.49 kg 5 lb 8 oz	Elbow River, Calgary Alberta, Canada	01-Aug-95	Randy Woo
Whitefish, ocean	*Caulolatilus princeps*	7.74 kg 17 lb 1 oz	Hurricane Bank California, USA	11-Jan-11	Craig T. Ito
Whitefish, round	*Prosopium cylindraceum*	2.72 kg 6 lb 0 oz	Putahow River Manitoba, Canada	14-Jun-84	Allan Ristori
Whiting, blue	*Micromesistius poutassou*	.83 kg 1 lb 13 oz	Drobak Norway	19-Sep-98	Trond Raade
Whiting, European	*Merlangius merlangus*	3.11 kg 6 lb 13 oz	Dypdalen Norway	10-Jun-97	John Kofoed
Wolffish, Atlantic	*Anarhichas lupus*	23.58 kg 52 lb 0 oz	Georges Bank Massachusetts, USA	11-Jun-86	Frederick Gardiner

RECORDS

SPECIES	SCIENTIFIC NAME	WEIGHT	PLACE	DATE	ANGLER
Wolffish, Bering	*Anarhichas orientalis*	12.3 kg 27 lb 1 oz	Uotoro, Hokkaiso Japan	04-Jul-06	Hideki Nakai
Wolffish, northern	*Anarhichas denticulatus*	17 kg 37 lb 7 oz	Holsteinsborg Greenland	19-Aug-82	Jens Hansen
Wolffish, spotted	*Anarhichas minor*	27.9 kg 61 lb 8 oz	Vannoy Trohs Fylke, Norway	29-May-00	Kolbjorn Melien
Wrasse, ballan	*Labrus bergylta*	4.35 kg 9 lb 9 oz	Clogher Head Co. Kerry, Ireland	20-Aug-83	Bertrand Kron
Wrasse, Brazilian	*Halichoeres brasiliensis*	.45 kg 1 lb 0 oz	Isla Grande Brazil	17-Mar-11	Steven M. Wozniak
Wrasse, crimson-banded	*Notolabrus gymnogenis*	.57 kg 1 lb 4 oz	Port Hacking Australia	26-Aug-09	Steven M. Wozniak
Wrasse, girdled	*Notolabrus cinctus*	.67 kg 1 lb 7 oz	Edward's Island Stewart's Island, New Zealand	25-Mar-12	Scott Tindale
Wrasse, humphead Maori	*Cheilinus undulatus*	19.8 kg 43 lb 10 oz	Platt Island Seychelles	04-Apr-97	Vincent Hock Boon
Wrasse, peacock	*Iniistius pavo*	.91 kg 2 lb 0 oz	Yokohama Bay Oahu, Hawaii, USA	29-Jun-13	Jamie Hamamoto
Wrasse, purple (hou)	*Thalassoma purpureum*	1.16 kg 2 lb 9 oz	Kalapana Hawaii, USA	08-Feb-92	Chris Hara
Wrasse, ringtail Maori	*Oxycheilinus unifasciatus*	.68 kg 1 lb 8 oz	Kona Coast Hawaii, USA	23-May-11	Steven M. Wozniak
Wrasse, rock	*Halichoeres semicinctus*	.45 kg 1 lb 0 oz	Long Beach California, USA	22-Mar-14	Martini Arostegui
Wrasse, scarlet	*Pseudolabrus miles*	.58 kg 1 lb 4 oz	Panaki Island Cavalli Islands, New Zealand	01-May-12	Sue Tindale
Wrasse, scarlet (TIE)	*Pseudolabrus miles*	.6 kg 1 lb 5 oz	Motueka Island New Zealand	02-May-12	Sue Tindale
Wrasse, yellow-saddled	*Notolabrus fucicola*	1 kg 2 lb 3 oz	Edward's Island Stewart Island, New Zealand	25-Mar-12	Scott Tindale
Wreckfish	*Polyprion americanus*	86.2 kg 190 lb 0 oz	Ranfurny Bank New Zealand	02-Mar-10	Terence Price
Yellowfish, largemouth	*Labeobarbus kimberleyensis*	9.52 kg 21 lb 0 oz	Vaal River South Africa	08-Mar-05	Ian Couryer
Yellowtail, California	*Seriola lalandi*	49.5 kg 109 lb 2 oz	Ohara Chiba, Japan	24-Oct-09	Masakazu Taniwaki
Yellowtail, southern	*Seriola lalandi*	52 kg 114 lb 10 oz	Tauranga New Zealand	05-Feb-84	Mike Godfrey
Yellowtail, southern (TIE)	*Seriola lalandi*	52 kg 114 lb 10 oz	White Island New Zealand	09-Jan-87	David Lugton
Zander	*Sander lucioperca*	11.42 kg 25 lb 2 oz	Trosa Sweden	12-Jun-86	Harry Tennison
Zander, volga	*Sander volgensis*	.45 kg 1 lb 0 oz	Tisza River Tiszafured, Hungary	18-Oct-10	Steven M. Wozniak

RECORDS